Elsie Clews Parsons

Elsie Clews Parsons

Elsie Clews Parsons

INVENTING MODERN LIFE

Desley Deacon

Women in Culture and Society
A series edited by Catharine R. Stimpson

THE UNIVERSITY OF CHICAGO PRESS
CHICAGO AND LONDON

Desley Deacon is associate professor of American studies and sociology at the University of Texas at Austin. She is the author of *Managing Gender: The State, the New Middle Class and Women Workers 1830–1930* (Oxford University Press, 1989) and co-author of *Elites in Australia* (Routledge and Kegan Paul, 1979).

The University of Chicago Press, Chicago 60637
The University of Chicago Press, Ltd., London
© 1997 by The University of Chicago
All rights reserved. Published 1997
Printed in the United States of America

06 05 04 03 02 01 00 99 98 97   1 2 3 4 5

ISBN 0–226–13907–7 (cloth)

Frontispiece: Elsie Clews Parsons Papers, American Philosophical Society Library.

Library of Congress Cataloging-in-Publication Data

Deacon, Desley.
    Elsie Clews Parsons: inventing modern life / Desley Deacon.
        p.   cm. — (Women in culture and society)
    "Bibliography of Elsie Clews Parsons, 1896–1962": p. 485.
    Includes bibliographical references and index.
    ISBN 0–226–13907–7 (alk. paper)
    1. Parsons, Elsie Worthington Clews, 1874–1941.   2. Women anthropologists—United States—Biography.   3. Women social scientists—United States—Biography.   4. Feminists—United States—Biography.   5. Feminism—United States—History.   6. Sex role—United States—History.   7. United States—Intellectual life—20th century.   8. United States—Race relations.   9. United States—Social conditions.   I. Title.   II. Series.
GN21.P37D43   1997
301'.092
[B]—dc20   96-36257
                                        CIP

To my parents
Frank and Molly Straker
and my aunt
Irene Straker

CONTENTS

LIST OF ILLUSTRATIONS AND MAPS

Maps

> If you want biographies, do not desire those which bear the legend,
> "Herr So-and-so and his age," but those upon whose title page
> there would stand "a fighter against his age."

—Nietzsche, *Untimely Meditations*

ELSIE Clews Parsons was "a carrier of culture rather than its
freight." Born in 1874 in the wake of the American Civil War, she
helped create modernism—a new way of thinking about the world
that has given the twentieth century its distinctive character—and
she applied it, not to art or literature, but to life itself. Eric Hobs-
bawm, in his magisterial overview, concludes that the major revolution of the twentieth century—the one that has, in his words,
brought millions of people out of the Middle Ages—is the revolution in social relations. Elsie Clews Parsons—feminist, anthropologist, public intellectual—was a leader in this revolution, using the
new cultural anthropology to "kill" nineteenth-century ideas of
classification and hierarchy, and to establish new twentieth-century
standards of sexual plasticity and cultural tolerance. In a new world
that stressed secularism, empiricism, honesty, pluralism in thought
and social relationships, and a fluid and constantly evolving self,
the "new woman" was, in Parsons's words, "the woman not yet
classified, perhaps not classifiable." And a vital culture was one that
could, like the Southwestern Pueblos she studied, "keep definite
cultural patterns in mobile combination."

The assertion of sexual plasticity and cultural mobility was part
of the modernist project to repudiate history, to deconstruct established theoretical systems and their related concepts and classifications, and to demolish existing systems of values. Central to this
"transvaluation of values" was the feminist destruction of the
nineteenth-century concepts of "woman" and "family," and the
creation of new, pragmatic relationships and moralities based on
experience and experiment. Closely associated with this feminist

project was a dismantling of hierarchical racial classifications and the assertion of the value and interrelatedness of all cultures.

The life of Elsie Clews Parsons exemplifies this movement from nineteenth-century to modernist thought and practice. Born into the New York elite in 1874, she gained a doctorate from Columbia University in 1899 in the face of considerable family opposition. She married Republican politician Herbert Parsons in 1900 in what she considered an "experimental" relationship, and over the next few years, she helped establish Greenwich House settlement and taught sociology at Barnard College through two pregnancies.

Between 1905 and 1917, as she painfully worked out a modernist combination of family and work, Parsons wrote extensively in a distinctive, spare, witty style on sex roles, sexual morality, and the family. Using ethnographic data to devastating effect, she detonated the concepts of "woman," "progress," "civilized," and "moral" that were basic to nineteenth-century systems of thought. But she was more interested in inventing the future than in destroying the past. If the modern condition was to be orphaned, widowed, and deracinated, as her mother's family were by the Civil War, Parsons's modernist project was to reconstitute social relationships in a manner that was appropriate to the twentieth century—to make each precious relationship count; to ensure that no person or group was excluded by virtue of race, sex, age, or national boundaries from the circle of possible social contacts; and to assure all groups entry to new forms of social organization, such as the invisible college of professional work. She argued persuasively, therefore, for a new, flexible morality based on sincerity and privacy that included trial marriage, divorce by mutual consent, access to reliable contraception, independence and elasticity within relationships, and an increased emphasis on obligations to children rather than to sexual partners.

In 1906, Parsons was denounced from the pulpits for her endorsement of trial marriage. But from 1912 she found a receptive audience among young intellectuals, especially the women and men who were beginning to call themselves "feminists," and the mainly immigrant students of anthropologist Franz Boas, who were energetically reconstructing anthropology along modernist scientific lines. Modern cultural anthropology, with its skepticism of nineteenth-century systems of thought, its emphasis on the flexibility and relativity of all cultures, and the importance it placed on careful, and often arduous, fieldwork, provided Parsons with the perfect vehicle for becoming the archetypal modern professional woman—physically and intellectually adventurous, independent, many-sided, mobile, adaptable. From 1915, when the youngest of her four children entered school, anthropology became the center of her intellectual and collegial life, and in the process, she undertook extended periods of fieldwork in the American Southwest, the Caribbean, and Mexico.

Elsie Clews Parsons brought to anthropology a determination to use its methods to educate the public to accept and welcome sexual and cultural diversity. She used her wealth to support cultural anthropology when its association with "queer foreigners" during the Americanization mania of the First World War threatened its collapse; and she encouraged innovation and diversity in the discipline by attracting and supporting radical young graduate students— many of them women. She used her social position and her hard-won self-assurance to break the sexual taboos against unmarried men and women working together in the field. And she used her notoriety as a clever and outspoken member of the intellectual avant-garde to combat "Nordic nonsense" about racial purity, and to illustrate from her own work on the Pueblos of the American Southwest and the townspeople of Mitla, Mexico, the vigor created by a "tangle and fusion" of cultures. Her contributions to the discipline were recognized in 1941 when she became president of the American Anthropological Association—the first woman to be elected to that position.

Elsie Clews Parsons was a true "modern" in that she put her ideas into practice in her own life, testing the new relationships and moralities she advocated. Her "experimental life," which included marriage, children, lovers, and friends, adventurous and arduous travel, and professional commitment and distinction, demonstrated to an interested public the practical working out of modernism by one of its pioneering theorists. Appropriately for someone born the same year as the first Impressionist exhibition, Parsons's life can be compared to a modernist work of art, composed of a number of separate elements that merge in different ways and frustrate any attempt by the viewer to impose an order or a category. We could say also that her life followed the canons of modernist science, the object of continual inquiry and experimentation.

Parsons's life is richly documented in her extensive personal and professional papers and in the memoirs, fiction, and private papers of her friends and colleagues. In particular, her difficult and enigmatic relationship with her husband, Herbert Parsons, is documented in almost daily letters during their frequent separations; many of her field trips with the artist, photographer, and architect Grant LaFarge are detailed in his unpublished writing; and her modernist approach to work and love is unsparingly dissected by Robert Herrick in a series of best-selling stories and novels based on their relationship. In addition, Parsons herself, like any good modernist, used her own experience as data for her intellectual work, sometimes incorporating illustrations from life, sometimes reworking situations and events in fictional form. Again, as a modernist, she was keenly aware of the difference the teller makes to the story, and she developed from childhood a spare, precise style in which every word was carefully chosen and placed. Parsons and her modernist friends and associates were, by definition, deliberately and articulately self-conscious. I have tried to present their distinctive voices and perspectives as much as possible, presenting multiple narratives where they are available, not presenting any one of them as truth. But the story in this book is, in the end, my own, very personal selection and reconstruction, and in that telling, perhaps reveals as much about me, a late-twentieth-century woman, as it does about Elsie Clews Parsons.

Parsons fought to assure women entry into the unseen but crucial networks of professional scholarship. Working on this book has demonstrated how important that virtual fellowship is in the essentially lonely life of the writer-scholar. I began the research for the book in 1988, three years after I moved to the United States in midlife and midcareer. The generous welcome and support I received from Joan Scott, Theda Skocpol, Kathryn Kish Sklar, Mary Jo Deegan, Shulamit Reinharz, Barbara Laslett, Dorothy Ross, Barrie Thorne, George Wolf, Christine Williams, and Emily Cutrer sustained me through my difficult years as a "stranger." Joan, Kathryn, Shulamit, George, Christine, and Emily all read the manuscript, Emily bringing her sharp sense of style and her encyclopedic knowledge of American culture to a long early version as well as a slimmed-down (but still lengthy) second draft. Since then I have been extraordinarily lucky in having the manuscript assessed by an ideal readership—Richard Adams, Robert Crunden, Ellen Fitzpatrick, William Goetzmann, Terence Halliday, Helen Horowitz, Louise Lamphere, Rosalind Rosenberg, Mark Smith, Catharine

Stimpson, Pauline Strong, and Kamala Visweswaran. Apen Ruiz and Mauricio Tenorio Trillo also saved me from embarrassment by correcting my Spanish (and, incidentally, Elsie's). John Higley drew on his formidable editing skills and a great deal of his time to help me cut the original long manuscript to something close to publishable. And Jean Gottlieb used her adroit scalpel to bring it to its current length without sacrificing anything essential.

Biographies are expensive to research, and I could not have made the numerous long visits to distant archives without the support of the National Endowment for the Humanities, the American Council of Learned Societies, and the University of Texas Research Institute. They are also expensive of time. I am grateful to the National Endowment for the Humanities for a year-long Fellowship for University Teachers just at the moment when I really needed it; to the history department of the University of Melbourne, the sociology departments in the Research School of the Social Sciences and the Faculties, Australian National University, and the Humanities Research Centre, Australian National University, for their hospitality; and to Ann Curthoys, John Docker, Patricia Grimshaw, Rosanne Kennedy, Stuart McIntyre, and Jill Matthews for warm welcomes and stimulating discussions. At the University of Texas at Austin, several cohorts of graduate students, particularly Cheryl Malone, have shared my enthusiasm for feminism and modernism; Jane Bowers has been my (unpaid) design consultant and guide; and Janice Bradley's cool competence has provided a calm center from which to work.

Biographies depend on family members conserving papers, archives preserving them, and archivists revealing their mysteries. I am grateful to Elsie Clews Parsons's nephew, Peter Hare, and her late son, John Parsons, for collecting her personal and professional papers and depositing them in the American Philosophical Society Library, where Beth Carroll-Horrocks quietly and competently aids researchers to exploit their riches. I am also grateful to Susan Morison, who was director of the Rye Historical Society when they owned Lounsberry, the beautiful and historic Parsons home in Harrison, New York, which Elsie's grandson David Parsons has recently brought back into the family. When I first visited Lounsberry in 1989, Susan and her staff had discovered steamer trunks full of papers and photographs that had escaped the earlier collection. During that visit, I sorted through this new material as it sat in a great pile in one room of the house. As I visited the collection over the next couple of years, I saw it gradually turned into the orderly archive, housed in the Rye Historical Society, that it is today.

One of the pleasures of writing about Elsie Clews Parsons was meeting two of her children, Herbert and Mac Parsons; two of her grandchildren, David and Marnie; and Mac's wife, Marjorie. One of the first questions people ask me about Parsons is, "What did her children feel about having such an unusual mother?" I am happy to report, from Herbert's and Mac's testimony, that they greatly loved and admired her. Herbert Parsons unfortunately died last year, so did not have the opportunity to read the manuscript. But Mac and Marjorie Parsons read it with enthusiasm and interest— gratifying praise from an eminent social scientist and a former script editor at MGM.

The modern family, though diverse in character and scattered geographically, is more than ever the bulwark against isolation and alienation. My sons, Nick and Ben Deacon, are always in my heart and mind, no matter how many miles separate us, and how absorbed I am in my work. And to my parents, Molly and Frank Straker, I am always grateful that they let me take my own path, even though they no doubt often questioned the wisdom of doing so.

Elsie Clews Parsons

Strength to *Forget* the Past

Henry Clews (third from left) and Lucy Worthington (second from left) with friends around the time of their marriage in 1874. Elsie Clews Parsons Papers, American Philosophical Society Library.

I break for the weak the chains of memory which hold them to
the past; but stronger souls are independent of me. They can
unloose the iron links and free themselves. Would that more
had the needful wisdom and strength thus serenely to put
their past behind them, leaving the dead to bury their dead,
and go blithely forward, taking each new day as a life by itself,
and reckoning themselves daily reborn,
even as they verily are!

—Edward Bellamy, *Dr. Heidenhoff's Process,* 1887

LIKE many of her generation, Elsie Clews Parsons had little use for
the past. She ignored birthdays on principle, and until her husband,
Herbert Parsons, consulted her mother's family bible in 1924 she
was not sure exactly when and where she was born. "You were born
on Friday November 27, 1874 at 7.30 P.M. at Grosvenor House on
Fifth Avenue at 10th," Herbert wrote on her fiftieth birthday. Born
in the same year as Gertrude Stein, Elsie Clews Parsons was part of
that American generation who were irrevocably cut off from the
past by the trauma of the Civil War, the massive forces of industrial-
ization, urbanization, and immigration it unleashed, and the Dar-
winian intellectual revolution. Impatient for change, she wished, as
a young woman, that she could emulate Bellamy's hero and "see
'our times' in retrospect." But she also wanted to play an active
role in the radical transformations she expected to take place. Like
Stein, she knew from childhood that she was "there to kill what
was not dead, the 19th century which was so sure of evolution and
prayers."[1]

Elsie's family history fortified her "strength to *forget* the past."
Her father, the wealthy New York banker Henry Clews, was a
self-made man who migrated from England as a youth and made a
fortune during the Civil War. Her socialite mother, Lucy Madison
Worthington Clews, came from a distinguished Southern family

who were ruined by the Civil War and by a major corruption scandal during the second Grant administration that cut her off from her Southern roots. Henry Clews's forgetting of the past was the careless disregard of the immigrant made good. But her mother's forgetting was a deliberate and bitter shutting of the door that gave a decisive edge to Elsie's childhood.[2]

The years surrounding Elsie Clews's birth were a watershed in American history, and in the history of her family. It is not surprising that her mother banished them from the family memory. Between 1872 and 1876, American public life reached its nadir with a series of financial scandals that involved senior members of the Grant administration. The scandal that more than any other defined this low point in public life involved a prominent member of young Elsie's family, Secretary of War William Belknap. But more important for Elsie, this scandal also implicated his wife, Amanda—Elsie's glamorous Aunt "Puss." This exemplary case of "official and domestic dishonor" revealed with sudden clarity that an era had ended. Engrossing the public for months when Elsie Clews was two years old, the Belknap scandal showed clearly that in the world of gender relations, as in politics, "nine-tenths of . . . education was useless, and the other tenth harmful."[3]

Puss Belknap was the much younger sister of Elsie's grandmother Anna. Puss and Anna were two of six strikingly beautiful sisters born into a prominent Kentucky family descended from the Connecticut and Virginia elites. The Civil War brought tragedy and financial ruin to the sisters. Widowed and orphaned, they had to recoup the family fortunes as best they could through advantageous marriages. The most consequential was made by Puss, who married William Belknap in December 1873.[4]

Family ties had been the principal means for securing political influence and financial security before the war—particularly in the South—and women played an important role in maintaining and extending these ties. For Puss, her sister Anna, and Anna's daughter Lucy, Secretary Belknap was the linchpin in their attempts to revive their family's influence and fortune. Puss quickly became the center of Washington social life, presiding over one of the capital's most luxurious and fashionable houses. By all accounts "gorgeous," with a "marvellous figure" set off by splendid jewels and Worth dresses, she was smart and witty, and everyone liked her, including President and Mrs. Grant.[5]

But Puss Belknap's reign as political hostess was short-lived. On 2 March 1876—a bare two years after her marriage—the chairman of the Committee on Expenditures in the War Department reported to the House of Representatives that he had found "Unquestioned evidence of the malfeasance in office by General William W. Belknap." Charged with selling traderships in the Oklahoma Territory, Belknap escaped conviction in a long-running trial before the Senate. But he was effectively disgraced, and spent much of the rest of his life abroad, dying alone, possibly by suicide, in 1890.[6]

The Belknap scandal marked the end of a political era. "Since the death of Mr. Lincoln, I have never seen more sadness in the House," James Garfield noted on the day of Belknap's impeachment, conveying his sense that new and frightening forces were sweeping away a golden age when politics (and business) were the province of a few upright and trusted families. To many political commentators, the Belknap scandal epitomized "Grantism"—the degeneration of family-based politics into government by the president's family and "a cabal of cronies"—in "an era of ostentation and ruin" that contrasted with the elegance, simplicity, and rigor of the "Republican court" of Washington, Jefferson, Madison, Monroe, and Adams.[7]

Although William Belknap was the principal culprit in this affair, the spotlight of censure fell on Puss, who attempted to save her husband (and the family fortunes) by deflecting the blame onto herself. The Republican party, desperate to save Grant's administration, gladly made her a scapegoat. The press followed suit, and a tirade of misogyny, which covered the front pages of the newspapers for weeks, was directed against the hapless Puss. Every detail of her life, appearance, and character was analyzed minutely. Her "handsome face and figure," her "witty conversational powers," her clear, fair complexion, her bright black eyes were avidly discussed. Newspapers gave long descriptions of her Paris gowns, and made much of her size 1½ shoe.[8]

From its beginning, the scandal of the Belknap affair was that it involved family, as well as official, corruption. Under the headline "Shameful Revelations of Official and Domestic Dishonor," the *New York World*'s front page on 3 March 1876 turned the scandal into a gothic family romance, in which "a scene of extravagance, temptation, official corruption and moral ruin, stands revealed in the place of what was supposed to be a happy, prosperous and virtuous American household." General Belknap, the newspapers decided, was "a high-toned soldier of scrupulous honor," who owed "this dreadful and unmerited disgrace to a vain, extravagant and wicked wife."[9]

The glare of publicity on Puss Belknap came at a time when the American political system was reorganizing decisively around parties and masculinity. In the earlier family-based politics, women had a legitimate part to play as behind-the-scenes partners of men, cementing social contacts and arranging useful alliances. In the new politics of parties women had no place. In fact, much of the organization and symbolism designed to build party loyalty was based on an aggressive masculinity that quite specifically excluded women. To the new political organizers, Puss Belknap represented an illegitimate interloper, a prominent example of the new and dangerous woman lobbyist, the worm in the apple of American politics. Women "lack the perception necessary for the distinction between good and evil," the *New York Times* declared. Women had turned Washington into "a public mart where 'influence' and 'information' have been daily bought and sold"—merely to gratify "their vulgar passion for diamonds and display."[10]

Puss Belknap's vilification by the press marked clearly and publicly the end of family-based politics. It also marked a major change in the nature of the nineteenth-century women's movement. Excluded from the masculinized world of party-dominated politics, women formed their own institutions outside the formal political structure. Making a virtue of difference, women politicized their "sisterhood," and claimed superior morality and concern for the "common wealth," in contrast to the male political world's corruption and preoccupation with personal aggrandizement. In the rhetoric of the new female politics, exemplified by the Woman's Christian Temperance Union, women's differences from men, and their essential purity and domesticity, were emphasized in an appeal to this new, separate constituency.[11]

Elsie Clews was born in November 1874 into a world rapidly being reshaped by the changes the Belknap scandal starkly revealed. Her mother, Lucy Worthington, grew up amid the family upheavals and deprivations of the 1860s. Lucy's father, William, had been killed early in the Civil War, and her mother, Anna, had remarried in 1864, when Lucy was twelve. Close in age to her glamorous aunt, Lucy met Henry Clews at a White House ball and married him in February 1874, two months after Puss married William Belknap.

Nine months later, Puss and Lucy gave birth on successive days to daughters Alice Belknap and Elsie Worthington Clews.[12]

The Belknap scandal cast a pall over Lucy's young married life. Although the two families remained close, Lucy never referred to the scandal, and she closed the book on her early life. The Washington years were never discussed in the family, even though Henry Clews made no secret, in his 1888 history of the New York Stock Exchange, of the fact that he made his fortune through his association with the administrations of Lincoln and Grant. When Henry died in 1923, Lucy destroyed his correspondence from that period, and she was indignant when her grandson dredged up the affair for his Yale senior thesis. In her New York life, Lucy remade herself as a romantic Southern belle, identifying with the Old South rather than the border states where she had spent her childhood among Northern sympathizers.[13]

In marrying Henry Clews, Lucy tied her fortunes to the new economic forces that were destroying Puss and William Belknap's world. Henry Clews was one of the new men enriched by the Civil War. Leaving England in 1850 at the age of sixteen, he never looked back, taking advantage of every opportunity his new country offered. By the early 1870s, when he was ready to marry, he had a flourishing New York banking and brokerage firm and a ground-floor seat in the Gilded Age's new aristocracy of money.[14]

But Lucy Clews never made a new role for herself as the wife of a "new man." Instead she clung with even greater tenacity to the role of hostess and beauty that Puss Belknap exemplified. According to family lore, the marriage was a business proposition—at least on Lucy's part. Three children were born in quick succession—Elsie in 1874, Henry in 1876, and Robert in 1877. But the marriage quickly disintegrated into a formality, as Henry's preoccupation with making money and Lucy's with spending it became the only things—apart from the children—that they had in common.

This hollow marriage hid Lucy's other, more personal secret. Before she married Henry Clews, she had been in love with Edward Wolcott, an attractive young man from a prominent Connecticut family. According to her granddaughter, Lissa, to whom she was very close, Lucy knew Wolcott "when they were both very young, in their teens. They were very much in love and neither of them had a penny. Something had to be done about that, and he went off to Colorado to seek his fortune." By the time Wolcott's illustrious political and business career got under way, she had married Henry Clews.[15]

Sometime around 1889, Lucy Clews and Edward Wolcott renewed their relationship—probably when he was elected to the United States Senate. The affair was well-known but never openly acknowledged. Elsie knew him as a close family friend when she was growing up. When he died in 1905 she wrote in her journal: "Ex-Senator Wolcott has died in Monte Carlo. A very genial man. He was one of my mother's first loves & probably her last."[16]

Lucy's servants and friends took pride in the way she kept her "secret." "He was abroad when he died and the word got to this country," her granddaughter recounts. "My grandmother was giving a big dinner party that night, and there was a good deal of talk about how she carried that off." Her hairdresser and confidante was despatched to Europe to collect Wolcott's legacy, which gave Lucy financial independence for the first time in her life. The affair had also given her the romance her marriage never had. "My grandmother had extraordinarily small feet, and they were beautifully shaped," Lissa recalls. "There was a famous bootmaker in Paris who was really an artist . . . [and] only took clients who he thought had pretty feet. . . . She was his prize customer. And Wolcott had a little white satin slipper of hers and he hung it by the heel over his bed at night, and he used to keep his watch in it."[17]

Elsie Clews was aware from an early age that her parents were not "harmonious." She characterized her father in 1906 as "jealous, suspicious, ungenerous, intensely vain and egotistical." "There had been jealousies," Elsie's fictional counterpart confides in a 1932 picture of her family, "an attachment crudely resented . . . by the possessive husband, although he himself had not hesitated to become vagrant." Covering up these resentments was a facade of politeness. "He was always helping her in and out of the carriage," his granddaughter recalled, " 'Would you like your robe?' or 'Would you like your shawl?' " But his solicitude was not reciprocated: "She just took all this, and I never saw her give anything." Henry Clews channeled his considerable energy into his business. A formal man, always fastidiously dressed, he was never an acute observer of people, content to skate on the surface of social life. At fifty, ten years after his marriage, he seemed to one acquaintance the model of an English clergyman, with "a bald dome-like forehead; large, speaking eyes; formal, mutton-chop whiskers, [and] a pleasant but quick and resolute address." His daughter Elsie twenty years later found him "prosy."[18]

This unfortunate marriage formed the empty shell in which Elsie Clews grew up. Although her parents had abandoned, for their different reasons, the authority of the past, they clung to the forms of a traditional marriage and a social life which seemed to their daughter to be without substance. This sense of the past's weakness and inutility gave the young Elsie the motivation to question her parents' sexual and social world, and the confidence to set about building her own moral universe. With Henry Adams—that quintessential product of the nineteenth century—she agreed that "All that had gone before was useless, and some of it was worse."[19]

PART ONE

Looking Forward

Ralph sometimes called his mother and grandfather the Aborigines, and likened them to those vanishing denizens of the American continent doomed to rapid extinction with the advance of the invading race. He was fond of describing Washington Square as the "Reservation," and of prophesying that before long its inhabitants would be exhibited at ethnological shows, pathetically engaged in the exercise of their primitive industries.

—Edith Wharton, *The Custom of the Country*, 1913

Elsie at the Rocks around the time of her graduation, 1896.
Parsons Family Papers, Rye Historical Society.

CHAPTER ONE

The Young Adventuress

"**IN** quick apprehension of personal relations, no one excelled her," anthropologist Leslie Spier noted of Elsie Clews Parsons in 1943. Surrounded by family secrets and silences, and by a wall of conventionalities, the young Elsie Clews developed a heightened sensitivity to the subtleties of relationships, and a determination to conduct her own life openly and honestly. From an early age, she demonstrated what she later saw in herself as an extraordinary—and unfeminine—facility "for detaching herself from her experience, for viewing it and even acting upon it impersonally." It was this facility, she pointed out in 1913, "which made her appear to the simpleminded so disquieting, to others so inhuman, and to still others so witty."[1]

When the Belknap family returned from their self-imposed exile in 1888, her cousin Alice found the fourteen-year-old Elsie quite different from any girl she knew. Elsie wrote about "the queerest things" in a manner that was distinctly her own. "Your letter was written exactly in your style," Alice wrote in 1889. "I could have told it was from you even if it had not been signed." She had no time for sentimentality or flattery; she liked athletic games; and she laughed when Alice complained of a sunburned face. Alice sometimes ventured to send "a kiss on your dear little neck," in fashionable sentimental style, but for Elsie, "Your sincere friend" was the highest expression of regard.[2]

Elsie's originality and forthrightness did not find such an admiring audience in her mother. Although she conceded that Elsie had been both "good" and "interesting" as a baby, Lucy Clews generally found her daughter very trying. She told her granddaughter Lissa that "she never could understand [her] from the time she was a little girl." As an adult, Elsie recalled that she had played with boys in Bryant Park although her mother said it was unladylike; she took off her veil or gloves when her mother's back was turned; she stayed in her room two days rather than put on stays; she got out of paying calls to go riding or sailing; and she kept to regular hours of study in spite of protests that she was selfish. To her mother's despair, she was unwilling to conform to conventional canons of behavior. "I hope you will enjoy yourself and *adapt* yourself to Mrs Adams wishes, and do not force any of your own ideas no matter how convinced you are of being right," Lucy wrote in 1888. "Remember *not* to insist, and control the *voice*. . . . you know how to be agreeable and can make yourself most charming in a home circle," she reiterated the following year. "Pray be careful with the toilette."[3]

The Gynocracy

The Clews family had a fashionable "cottage" on the oceanfront in Newport and a town house in New York, where they mingled with the Vanderbilts, the Astors, the Goulds, and the Goelets at the Horse Show, the Patriarchs Ball, and other assemblies of the Four Hundred. When Edith Wharton described the stifling conventionality and emotional shallowness of this milieu in *The House of Mirth* (1905), Elsie recognized it as "an extraordinarily close picture of some people we know or rather I knew or rather I have known." Like Edith Wharton, Elsie rebelled against the constricted roles of women in this milieu, who did nothing but "bathe, curl, anoint, powder, manicure etc, and think about dress all day long"; and she never lost her dismay at their wasted lives, empty relationships, pervasive amorality, and social rigidity.[4]

The world in which Elsie Clews grew up was, like Edith Wharton's, bounded by Washington Square and Central Park in the winter and Newport in the summer, and by a seemingly impenetrable hedge of good form. The low brownstone houses of the New York bourgeoisie, with their "desperate uniformity of style," mirrored the uneventful and apparently decorous life within. "A little world so well-ordered and well-to-do does not often produce either eagles or fanatics," Wharton notes, and conformity—that "bane of middle-class communities"—ruled. The "little-girl life" in this stable world was ruled by "copy-book axioms" so taken-for-granted that they seemed natural.[5]

Henry Clews was part of the "detachment of big money-makers" who ultimately destroyed this "safe, guarded, monotonous" world. But Lucy—like most wives of the newcomers to New York society—ensured that the life of "amiable hospitality" continued, with fishing, boating, and shooting for the men, "calling" and dress for the women, and the Season, "coming out," and well-chaperoned house parties for the young. There was one major difference, however, between the old and the new society. In old New York, the men as well as the women were leisured, while the men of the new rich devoted most of their time and energy to making and keeping their fortunes. As money-making came to depend more and more on male networks maintained in the new city clubs and links with powerful political figures who were unacceptable socially, the men became reluctant participants in what was essentially a female ritual that had outlived its function. As Elsie pointed out years later in an obituary for her mother's way of life, "there are no kings in American 'Society'—there are only queens."[6]

Left behind by the tide of history, the women Elsie grew up with maintained the conventions of a disappearing world with a fervor that equaled the new male work ethic. Describing the "gynocratic caste" to which her mother belonged, Elsie pointed out that society life often provided the only means by which these women could gratify ambition. Getting into society and staying in it were arduous; the art of conspicuous waste it relied on was exacting; and the social duties involved, such as the ceremonial of calling—an "onerous and endless business"—were time-consuming and exhausting. "They require a kind of self-devotion which verges on asceticism," Elsie noted, and this appeals to "the energetic and self-denying spirit of the American woman."[7]

In this exclusive, inward looking, and segregated social world, relations between men and women were regulated by a web of etiquette and propriety that ensured that interaction was formal and impersonal. Women's sexual behavior was severely policed by other women. Young women were expected to preserve the innocence, "manufactured by a conspiracy of mothers and aunts and grandmothers," that terrifies Wharton's hero in his bride-to-be in *The Age of Innocence*. Girls were introduced to society when they "came out" at eighteen, and they were encouraged to marry as soon as possible. In the meantime, any indiscretion, such as Lily Bart committed in *The House of Mirth* by drinking tea in a man's apartment, banished her forever from the ranks of eligible young women. Society women averted their eyes from youthful "wild oats" and extramarital activity in men; but divorce was unheard of until Alva Vanderbilt began her career as a social rebel by divorcing her philandering husband in 1895 and marrying Oliver Belmont.[8]

Elsie never forgave her "Elders"—as she always called those who policed "good form" and morality—for their concealment and formalization of sexual expression, and for their segregation of young men and women. The young are bullied into conventionalizing and repressing their passion, she wrote in 1915, no doubt remembering her own upbringing. They are made to feel that sexual feeling must be guarded against and held in check. Girls are taught that virginity is a jewel whose loss is irreparable; young men are warned that intimacy with women is effeminizing; and both are made to feel that passion is objectionable, making men brutal, vicious, and selfish, and women weak and immoral. If it cannot be repressed, it must be concealed. Its public expression is the height of ill-breeding, and its manifestations—pregnancy, childbearing, and lactation—are so embarrassing that they require seclusion.[9]

The Rebellion of the Daughters

Elsie's revolt against this constricted world was shared by a number of her contemporaries, who later thought of themselves as modernists. Modernism was a rebellion against the parents— literally and figuratively—against the father whose law was no longer enforceable or useful and against the mother who was contemptuous of but still complicitous in the father's rule. Gertrude Stein could serenely remake her world in the wake of her parents' deaths when she was in her teens. Djuna Barnes had to savagely repudiate her demanding, imperious father and the mother who failed to protect her. And Christina Stead's young alter ego, Louie, had to help her stepmother commit suicide and abandon her father in order to be free to "take a walk around the world." Elsie's rebellion against her parents merely took the form of putting them aside, as if they were of no consequence.[10]

"The rebellion of the daughters"—as Elsie later called it—was not as difficult as it seemed to the young women themselves. This was "a civilization that had played itself out." An inward-looking, self-satisfied group, ready with a "hoard of petty maxims with which its elders preached down every sort of initiative," society was being undermined by men who built railroads or found oil or manufactured farm machinery, and by women who found other ways of using their energies, in pressure groups such as the Woman's Christian Temperance Union and in settlement houses among the new immigrants of an industrializing, urbanizing, diversifying

America. "Given such opportunities for acquiring wealth as we possess," Elsie observed in 1916, "and no sumptuary laws on expending it, caste exclusiveness through consumption is but a flimsy principle." And given American habits of imitation, noneconomic distinctions are short-lived. "Imitation and economic elasticity— these are the enemies of our gynocratic caste from without," while "increasing outlets for feminine energy and ambition" weaken it from within. "Without boundaries, without leaders," she asked, "what hope of a future existence is there . . . for the gynocratic caste?"[11]

New York in the last two decades of the century was less hospitable to the gynocratic caste than the other great center of nineteenth-century culture, Boston. "Milder manners, a great love of ease . . . distinguished the colonial New Yorkers from the conscience-searching children of the 'Mayflower,'" Wharton noted. The Episcopal Church allowed a "greater suavity and tolerance" to New Yorkers, who seemed "from the outset to have been more interested in making money and acquiring property than in predestination and witch-burning." In addition, New York was always, as Van Wyck Brooks put it in 1920, "the 'least American' of cities, the most exposed, that is, to the perpetual contagion of Europe."[12]

Despite the hold of society standards over the Four Hundred and those who aspired to join that exclusive group, the cosmopolitan milieu of New York fostered the more radical, egalitarian branches of the nineteenth-century woman's movement. The acceptance in wealthy New York circles of its most outrageous forms is caricatured by Henry James in *The Bostonians,* where Mrs. Burrage encourages her son's marriage to Verena, the feminist orator considered beyond the pale by Boston matrons. In contrast to woman-focused organizations based on the evangelical religious tradition, such as the Woman's Christian Temperance Union, New York preserved the earlier tradition of the Seneca Falls Convention, with its emphasis on natural rights, equality, and the tyranny of custom and law. Elizabeth Cady Stanton lived in New York from 1862 until her death in 1902, and it was the headquarters of the National Woman's Suffrage Association she and Susan B. Anthony established in 1869. The name of their short-lived journal, the *Revolution,* and its motto, "Men, their rights and nothing more; women, their rights and nothing less," epitomize the uncompromising stand toward women's rights that characterized New York.[13]

The closed, protected world of New York society was, indeed, disappearing rapidly during Elsie's childhood. The tragedy of Wharton's heroine Lily Bart was that she could not adapt to these rapid changes. The perfect product of that world and its "excessive sex-distinction," the links of her bracelet were "manacles chaining her to her fate." Elsie was luckier, or at least better equipped, to find that state of personal freedom Wharton's hero called "the republic of the spirit." "It's a country one has to find the way to one's self," he tells Lily. "There are sign-posts—but one has to know how to read them."[14]

Elsie found the first signpost to her personal republic of the spirit in her father's library. She learned at an early age that she could escape from the tensions and restrictions of family life through books. An older friend remembered her at the age of five engrossed in *The Tinted Venus*. She was always an avid reader. As she grew older, she found the persona of scholar sympathetic, as well as useful, for setting herself apart from her family and establishing her originality and independence.[15]

Like most girls of her class, Elsie was taught at home by French and German governesses until she was about ten years old. This home instruction continued after she went to school, with a succession of frauleins and mademoiselles polishing her fluency in French and German. By 1887, when she was thirteen years old, she could speak and write both languages well. These educated, self-supporting women probably had more influence on the serious Elsie than her mother, who was busy with her exacting social duties, and possibly with her lover.[16]

From about 1884, Elsie attended Mme Ruel's School. A small school with high scholarly standards, Mme Ruel's prepared its students for Vassar, the women's college just outside New York. Although social demands began to intrude on her New York life from about the age of fourteen, Elsie had a remarkable capacity for hard work. "Do you still get up at six o'clock to study?" Alice Belknap asked, fascinated, in 1889. In the summer of 1890, Elsie was reading Emerson and Bryce, reporting to a friend, "the library is my only refuge." A letter to her art teacher that September reveals her as an earnest young woman carefully planning her future. When another friend reported a teacher's comment two years later that Elsie had "such clear, well-balanced brain power," it was only the first of many such accolades she received during her school and college career.[17]

The intellectual hero for Elsie's group of ambitious and original young women was Ralph Waldo Emerson. "I wonder if I told you that I had the same little volumes of Emerson's Essays as you have," her school friend Aimée Lawrence wrote her in 1890, when they were sixteen years old. "I owe you a friend in Emerson—he always expresses my thoughts for me and constantly gives me new ones." Emerson articulated perfectly the young women's rebellion against their parents' values, urging them to "be original and not conventional," and not to "capitulate to badges and names, to large societies and dead institutions." "Emerson really had passion," Gertrude Stein told an interviewer later in her life; and it was this passion that appealed to the young women of her generation, who were constantly being told "*not* to insist, and control the *voice*." With Emerson at their backs, they were ready to "enter into the state of war, and wake Thor and Woden, courage and constancy." And the weapon with which they set out to "affront and reprimand the smooth mediocrity and squalid contentment of the times" was readily available, even to sixteen-year-old girls—it merely required "speaking the truth."[18]

Barnard College

Elsie recalled in 1913 that she was brought up "in a circle of society opposed to college-going for girls." There was a long American tradition of education for women based on the argument that women played the primary role in socializing future citizens. But as the leading exponent of this argument was the sister of the "common" Harriet Beecher Stowe, it no doubt generally fell on deaf ears among people in society. Furthermore, the women's colleges that were established in the decades after the Civil War—Vassar, Wellesley, Smith, and Byrn Mawr—were often seen, somewhat erroneously, as training institutions for middle-class women who were unfortunate enough to have to earn their own living as teachers or governesses. Probably more important, they were residential schools where young women were removed from home influence and were not available to accompany their mothers on calls or to Europe.[19]

Elsie was saved from a major battle with her family by the opening of Barnard in the fall of 1889 as a college for women affiliated with Columbia University. Barnard allowed a compromise whereby Elsie could continue her studies and at the same time live at home and participate in the form, if not the spirit, of her set's social obligations. Early in 1890, when she was fifteen years old, she began to make inquiries about the college's entrance requirements. Because students could enter Barnard at sixteen, she probably hoped to qualify during the 1890–91 academic year and begin college in the fall of 1891. However, the tragic death of her youngest brother, Bobby, in February 1890 pulled the ties of family obligation around her and put the whole project in jeopardy.[20]

Elsie's younger brothers Henry and Bobby, aged fourteen and thirteen, boarded during the week at the Westminster School. During a weekend at home, Bobby died suddenly of a cerebral hemorrhage. This devastating loss gave Lucy Clews a binding moral claim on her daughter's time. As Jane Addams pointed out in discussing "the family claim," daughters were expected to provide company for their mothers, especially if they were widowed or bereaved. Elsie had to postpone her preparation for college and accompany her mother on an extended European tour.[21]

On her return, Elsie set to work to catch up on lost studies, cramming Greek and mathematics, which she had never studied, during the 1891 summer and a final school year, this time at the intellectual Brearley School. Again obliged to accompany her mother to Europe for the 1892 summer, she sat for the Columbia entrance examinations just before sailing. She had written "a very excellent examination," Barnard principal Ella Weed wrote her in June. As Alice Belknap wrote that November, "What a girl you are! Still working away, *excelcioring*—progressing—upwards onwards—I am so abominably lazy—I never do or say anything worth either living for or recording."[22]

When Elsie entered Barnard College in the fall of 1892, she had succeeded in plotting her own course in the face of considerable opposition. "I should stay home, I was told, and be companionable," she later recalled. "I had never noticed that my mother found me companionable. In those years we were not congenial." "Of course it is half fun, when I say you try to *discipline* me," Lucy wrote her strong-minded daughter in a typical letter during her college years, but "you do, more than I fancy you are conscious of." "Henry and I have been inseparable companions all summer— and no *scraps!*" she added in a common comparison of her son and daughter.[23]

As Elsie pointed out, her mother's main complaint was that a scholarly daughter was not companionable. When Elsie refused to accompany her to Europe for the 1897 summer, Lucy Clews's letters were an eloquent mixture of moral outrage and blackmail: "I can not tell you how strange it seems to be in Europe without you!" she wrote from Paris. "I have stood being *alone* quite well until I arrived here last night, and the minute I entered the Langham I got in a *panic*, so before I took off my gloves I sent a frantic note to Dolly [Elsie's friend Dolly Potter], which brought her to me in a few minutes, and she stopped until I went to bed, and has been with me all day, took lunch with me, and this afternoon we drove, and this evening I dined with them." In contrast to Elsie, the Potter sisters were everything daughters should be: "I find Louise and Dolly looking very well, *lovely clothes!* . . . Dolly's attitude in the family is one of the finest things I know, in fact she is a *splendid all round girl!* I do hope some nice man will fall in love with her this summer."[24]

As well as being sociable and finding a husband, young women were expected to occupy themselves in Paris with the excitement of shopping. Lucy Clews was noted for her beauty and elegance and had the reputation, probably apocryphal, of putting aside $10,000 a year for mistakes in her wardrobe. Something of the excitement of the clothes hunt is conveyed in a letter from Alice Belknap: "We are certainly in possession of a quantity of the most marvellous creations of Worth & Paquin parentage—In fact early in the game we lost all track of what we wanted or what they were trying to do—Betsey says she has kept on purely from a *collectors instinct,* but I have *never wavered* in my convictions!!! . . . Not even when I was obliged to move out of my room, because it was no longer possible for me to get into it—!!" But shopping, as Elsie put it some years later, "always gives me a headache," and Lucy Clews usually had to make do with admonishing her recalcitrant daughter from afar: "You will be coming home now in a few days," she wrote in 1897, "and I hope you will find all your things *right,* and like the new *maid,* you must *train* her to suit you, do take the *time* for your hair, and pay some attention to that *important* matter this summer. . . . Be sure and tell me *truly* if your are gaining in *weight.*"[25]

The Outdoor Life

Her parents' related concern, as the characteristic ending of this letter suggests, was that all Elsie's study would ruin her health. This was a genuine concern during the years following Dr. Edward Clarke's 1873 warning that women's intellectual work, especially during adolescence, would undermine their health and permanently damage their reproductive capacity. Fears for Elsie's health run through letters from her parents and older friends. Henry Clews's letter of July 1892, when she was in Europe after sitting for the college entrance examinations, was typical: "I am glad . . . the Baths at Schwalbach have done you so much good," he wrote, "and that your weight has increased to 132 lbs—don't study too hard hereafter so as to break you down again, what you did in that way the three months before you left here came very near breaking you up permanently." "You must remember," he counseled, "you can't over tax yourself without producing ill effects and undermining your vital powers, you must learn to take life easier and then the enjoyment of it will increase."[26]

Characteristically, Elsie and other young women of her generation who sought alternatives to the social world of their mothers turned this concern with their health to their advantage—and in ways that only increased their parents' anxiety. Women's colleges answered these fears by instituting demanding health and fitness training as part of the college curriculum. Young women's enthusiasm for exercise and outdoor sporting activities was encouraged by the fashion for "strenuous" living popularized by Teddy Roosevelt and magazines such as *Outing,* which pictured women canoeing, cycling, fishing, and hunting.[27]

The most influential hero of the strenuous life for Elsie and her friends was not Roosevelt but the British writer and traveler Robert Louis Stevenson. If Emerson was the text for these young women, Stevenson was the practice. In 1883 he wrote about his trip across the United States to marry his American lover and their subsequent open-air honeymoon in a popular series in the *Century.* When he returned in 1887, the acclaimed author of *Treasure Island, Kidnapped,* and *Doctor Jekyll and Mr. Hyde,* his search for a cure for his tuberculosis in the Adirondacks, then in the South Seas, and finally on the Pacific island of Samoa was followed with intense interest, and his death in 1894 was greeted with great sorrow.[28]

Stevenson's cheerful asceticism provided a new ethics for the young, combining happiness, simplicity, adventure, and a love of the outdoors. His *Travels with a Donkey* set the tone that thrilled Elsie's generation. In an account of a walking trip he made in the 1870s, Stevenson described a kind of epiphany: "The outer world, from which we cower into our houses, seemed after all a gentle habitable place; and night after night a man's bed, it seemed, was laid and waiting for him in the fields, where God keeps an open house. I thought I had rediscovered one of those truths which are revealed to savages and hid from political economists; at the least, I had discovered a new pleasure for myself." Not only did he help waken a generation to the pleasures of the outdoor life, but he also linked these pleasures to a new, simpler companionship with the other sex. "To live out of doors with the woman a man loves is of all lives the most complete and free," Stevenson wrote, in words that resonated to a generation who had grown up surrounded by a wall of sexual conventions.[29]

The Clews's "cottage" in Newport was the perfect setting for Elsie to practice Stevenson's prescriptions to be happy and healthy. The Rocks, of fashionable shingle design, stood on the island's choice position, a rocky promontory looking south toward the Atlantic Ocean, overlooking the famous Spouter Rock and next to the exclusive Bailey's Beach. The house was close enough to the ocean to be wrecked in the 1938 hurricane, when the sea reached within three feet of the crest of the hill on which it was built. For Elsie this ocean was "a part of my sub-consciousness which I can always bring up over the threshold of consciousness for minutes of comfort and pleasure." A swim and a run on the beach at Newport always exhilarated her and helped her to tolerate the "grotesqueries" of her family's fashionable life.[30]

The Clews family spent every summer at Newport. These summers provided a world of "inexhaustible delights" for Elsie. There she and her friends could swim and ride, clamber over the rocks, fish for "scupers" and "porgies," and sail over the waters of Narragansett Bay in the graceful wide-sailed catboats that flecked the bay like seagulls. From at least 1887, when she was thirteen years old, Elsie played tennis, fenced, and rode regularly, throwing herself into these activities with an enthusiasm and recklessness that alarmed her mother, and later her husband. When she was fourteen, her mother deprived her of riding for the summer because of a "wild ride" which, in her mother's opinion, risked her life.[31]

A Sister to Them All

These outdoor activities enabled Elsie to rebel against restrictive social expectations about young women's roles and their relationships with men. The mingling of unmarried men and women indoors was covered by an elaborate system of conventions based on the

Elsie, age about twelve, exploring the Newport beach behind the family's newly built "cottage," the Rocks (second house from right), with her brothers Henry and Bobby. Parsons Family Papers, Rye Historical Society.

assumption that any mixing of the sexes had one major aim—that of a suitable marriage. The outdoors provided an arena where new rules could be negotiated between youth and the Elders, and between young men and women themselves. There Elsie found that she could cultivate friendships that were free of artifice or sentimentality—free, in other words, from an artificial emphasis on sex. Numerous letters from her male and female friends testify to the fact that her liveliness and originality made her a popular companion. Her flock of male admirers cheerfully called her "sister," in line with Emerson's ideas on the superiority of friendship over more conventionalized relationships. As Dolly Potter wrote her in 1892, "Payne [Whitney] told me to give you his love, 'to sister'—he is forever talking about the lecture you gave, on being a sister to them all."[32]

In the summer of 1893, when Elsie had finished her freshman year at Barnard, she met Sam Dexter, a Harvard graduate who was spending the summer at Newport with his mother and sister. Known at Harvard as "Big Sam," Dexter graduated in 1890 after a college career in which he had been class president every year and manager

Elsie, age nineteen, enjoying the beach with Sam Dexter (center). Elsie Clews Parsons Papers, American Philosophical Society Library.

of the boat club. Photos of Sam show a large handsome young man, who probably resembled his father, who was described by a biographer as tall, with an athletic frame, genial and affable, luxurious in his habits, and artistic in his tastes.[33]

In Sam Dexter, Elsie found an ideal companion who also seemed to stir her sexually. Sam delighted in her difference from other women. "I have never been able to talk to a young woman as you and I can talk," he wrote in December 1893. "I miss our talks so, for the people with whom I feel tempted to go beyond the commonplace are few." "Absence of manner is the best manner," he commented appreciatively on her direct, honest approach to social life. She for her part enjoyed his "very straight way of seeing things."[34]

During the 1893 summer, Elsie and Sam shared all the things she loved about Newport—swimming, walking, riding, sailing, clam chowder on the beach, reading in the Redwood Library. When Sam returned to Chicago, where he was establishing himself in the law, Elsie wrote, "I ride with Mr. Stewart [her New York Senate friend] and I sail with Dolly [Potter], but I walk a great deal by myself."

Sam Dexter, early 1890s. Katharine Dexter McCormick Papers, negative KDM68, The MIT Museum.

He in turn assured her that he was swimming every day, "with swinging rings, a trapeze, and spring board thrown in" though "there is no salt of the sea nor of the earth to compare with the tank at Newport" and "I find it a great disadvantage to be so far away from my trainer." They read Pierre Loti, du Maurier, and Stevenson, and after Sam's departure Elsie joked about the lure of "the Latin chaps" (Euripides, Tacitus, and Seneca) who were calling her back to New York. Sam was reading James's "The Real Thing"; and Elsie shared her delight in Frederic Harrison's essays on the eighteenth and nineteenth centuries. She was pleased with the copy of *Don Quixote* Sam sent her for Christmas. It was, the future sociologist reported, "on the list of books Harrison reports from Auguste Comte."[35]

Lucy Clews was probably relieved to see her serious and recalcitrant daughter falling in love like any other young woman. Until Elsie married in 1900 and proved otherwise, her mother was convinced that falling madly in love would cure her of her strange opinions and ambitions. Despite having to reprimand Sam for swimming with Elsie "without a suitable audience" in a " 'tonic' swim memorable in the annals of Newport as having furnished a topic of conversation for lunch table," Lucy encouraged the relationship, even lifting her censorship of Elsie's mail.[36]

Elsie for her part was happy and relaxed with Sam. She was pleased to be able to demonstrate that "college and 'society' are such a good fit." During the 1893 winter she threw herself into the Season, fulfilling Stevenson's "duty of being happy." "Can you make a 'mental photograph' of me in front of a box talking exceedingly cheap talk to the smilingly polite?" she wrote Sam in November. "I have been indulging in a great deal of cheap talk for the past week—the brilliant week of the Horse Show." "The season and my gay butterfly career have begun. So don't be surprised to find a 'frivolous society girl' on the 12th or 13th of December," she warned, looking forward to his arrival. "It was fun last night and tonight too—I am becoming a social creature," she wrote him after his visit. "This week is gay: a dance every night." In March 1894, after a week in Vermont "tobogganing, bob-sledding, ice-boating— all new," she resolved that she was going to get up next morning at six—"rarer than before." But with Sam she could be serious as well. In April 1894 she wrote, "I have been rubbing Papa's head, reading Browning and thinking of you." She was also ruminating on women's suffrage and the position of women, a topic that was especially current following the State Woman Suffrage Association convention and circulation of a petition to the Constitutional Convention the following month. "According to my idea of the family there are two heads and then the woman should have a part in the representing too," she wrote to Sam, perhaps thinking of the possibility of such a family with him.[37]

Unexpectedly—unbelievably—Sam Dexter was dead a month later, carried off by an unidentified sudden illness in a manner that is almost incredible to the late-twentieth-century mind. "Am at the hospital with a slight fever," he wrote Elsie in his last note. "Don't know when I shall be out." "He loved your directness, genuineness and simplicity," wrote his devastated mother, returning Elsie's letters with a lock of Sam's baby hair—which can still be found today among her correspondence, in a handkerchief case in Sam's letter file.[38]

CHAPTER TWO

Travels of the Mind

THE Clews and Dexter families had planned to travel together in Europe in the summer of 1894. Sam's death cast a pall over what they had all expected to be a golden summer. Elsie followed her mother dutifully around Fontainbleu, Barbizon, London, and Paris and could hardly endure what a friend referred to ironically as her "new double role—student and shopper." After this dreary summer she refused to play the role of social companion her mother wanted of her: the following summer, preceding her final year at college, she did not go to Europe on the excuse that she had to study; in 1896, after her graduation, she went on her own terms, spending the entire Paris visit in the Bibliotèque Nationale; in 1897 her mother traveled complainingly alone; and except for a European trip in 1902 and a trip to the Philippines, Japan, and China in 1905 with her husband, Elsie's travels were for many years defiantly work-oriented and North American.[1]

The one bright spot of the dreadful 1894 summer was her growing friendship with Sam's mother and sister, Josephine and Katharine Dexter. Josephine Dexter became Elsie's "summer mother" when the Dexters returned to the United States at the end of 1895. Mrs. Dexter was an intelligent and sophisticated woman whose friends included the actress Ellen Terry and the writers Sarah Orne Jewett and Annie Fields; but she was also sentimental and moralistic in the late-nineteenth-century feminine mode, and her influence waned as Elsie became more assured in her critique of American women's lives. In fact, she became an exemplar of the repressive morality of the Elders in Elsie's later writing.

Elsie's friendship with Katharine Dexter was more important and longer-lasting. A year younger than Elsie, Katharine shared her rebellion against women's restricted roles and was anxious to begin work toward a science degree at the Massachusetts Institute of Technology. Sam's death, like that of Robert Clews for Elsie, post-

Katharine Dexter, early 1900s. Katharine Dexter McCormick Papers, negative KDM85, The MIT Museum.

poned that plan. More compliant than Elsie, she traveled around Europe for eighteen months as her bereaved mother sought consolation in constant movement. But the two young women supported each other by letter, commiserating over Robert Louis Stevenson's death, discussing Katharine's driving and riding exploits, Russian novels, their plans for a walking tour, and the mathematician Sonia Kovalesky. "Your description of your college work makes me as ever envious," Katharine wrote from Rome in response to Elsie's complaint about her economics and psychology courses. "I do not believe that the so-called 'dismal science' can be dismal—and I am sure that when I am able I shall take a much needed dose of physics and psychology." By January 1896, thoroughly sick of her enforced dilettantism, Katharine was grateful to be settled back in Boston, where she immediately plunged into intense study for entrance into MIT's three-year preparatory course in science. In the fall of 1896, she formally began the eight-year course of study that led to her degree in biology in 1904.[2]

The New World of Sociology

On the first anniversary of Sam's death, Josephine Dexter wrote to Elsie with style, rhetoric, and sentiments typical of the late-nineteenth-century woman: "Last year at Easter! The day has been full of memories—I have lived it over and over—You remember my calling at your house in the afternoon—and finding Sam there—then in the evening—cousin Gordon was giving a dinner—and Sam came to me just before we went down—and asked me to help him get off early—as he wished to go and see you—and he was so sweet about it—said I was such a 'good mumsey.' . . . Ah! my child—you must not ponder on the materialistic side—there is only one way—keep close to Heaven—'God's child in God's world.' "[3]

Elsie had no intention of turning to heaven or the past for consolation. Sam's loss was a blow, but she faced it in her own way, through an intensification of her drive for serious work and strenuous pleasure. His death was in effect a watershed that confirmed her earnestness of purpose and saved her from an early marriage that might have reduced her opportunities to pursue her vision of self-development.

When Elsie returned to Barnard in the fall of 1894, she found the vehicle she needed to translate that vision into practice in the new discipline of sociology. Introduced to Columbia and Barnard by Franklin Giddings, sociology opened up a new world for Elsie. Although she eventually differed with him sharply, Giddings's influence was decisive in establishing her identity as a social scientist. When she first encountered Giddings in 1894, he was thirty-nine years old and at the height of his powers. With several careers already behind him in journalism and political science, he had transformed himself into Columbia's first professor of sociology between 1891 and 1894, despite the fact that he did not have the fashionable new Ph.D. In his 1948 *History of Sociology,* Harry Elmer Barnes praised Giddings as the ablest sociologist the United States had produced and named his *Principles of Sociology* (1896) the most important volume published in the field. Giddings was working on this book when Elsie began studying sociology. The courses she took with him and the discussions they had over the next eleven years of close association were no doubt a distillation of this and the four other books he published during that prolific period. Giddings was an impressive man, original, widely read, and energetic, with a gift for verbal and written exposition. His students loved the vigor and enthusiasm of his classes, and they probably also enjoyed their informality, if not their unsystematic character.[4]

Giddings, who came to Columbia from the highly intellectual women's college, Bryn Mawr, had always been supportive of his best female students, including the new Barnard dean, Emily James Smith. He and the eager, hard-working Elsie Clews were delighted with each other from the first. "Just after you must have left the tea on Class Day, I saw Prof. Giddings for a moment or so," wrote one of her classmates at the end of their first year of sociology. "He asked after you and I endeavored to please each of you by hunting for you, but you had disappeared. . . . So you lost the chance of a good-bye chat with our dear Professor."[5]

Elsie was just the sort of student Giddings appreciated. Political scientist Charles Merriam, who studied with Giddings during the 1890s, reports that Giddings liked to shock his students "by drawing them up either to the edge of atheism or immorality or what not, and pressing them hard." Elsie had been moving along an iconoclastic path since early childhood and was quite ready to follow Giddings's lead in pursuing intellectual and moral issues that shocked his large contingent of theology students. Giddings's active pursuit of a rational, secular society based on the cooperation of free individuals was extremely attractive to her, especially when he linked this pursuit to health and pleasure. "The ethical motive," Giddings argued, echoing Stevenson, "is derived from vitality. To neglect bodily development, therefore, is not merely to do wrong in a sense which all intelligent persons now recognize . . . but in the much deeper sense of impairing the very springs of moral conduct." In the same way, "morality without pleasure of some kind . . . is unthinkable." Giddings's active, healthy individuals were sociable creatures involved in voluntary associations and passionately concerned with the advancement of their fellows. Basing his sociology on the idea of "consciousness of kind," his ideal society was one in which like-mindedness developed out of rigorous discussion and debate and an awareness of the world beyond one's immediate circle.[6]

Attracted by the combination of activity, cooperation, and change in Giddings's work, Elsie plunged into the study of sociology, and at the same time into the world of philanthropy and social settlements that was closely associated with it. Reform-minded Columbia president Seth Low had explicitly linked the introduction of sociology to an attack on New York's urban problems. His aim was to fuse the ideal of the German research-oriented university with the Columbia tradition of civic responsibility—a vision of a practical, democratic, and socially responsible social science he shared with the founders of the social settlement movement and the new

European-trained social scientists. Pursuing this vision, Low helped found the University Settlement on the Lower East Side in 1892 and, as university president and then as mayor of New York, he supported its efforts to improve resources for the city's underprivileged. In accordance with Low's ideas of dialogue and mutual service between university and community, Giddings's courses focused initially on social problems and included fieldwork with such established philanthropies as the Charity Organization Society, of which Low was vice-president, and the social settlements that were replacing them.[7]

Caught up in her enthusiasm for sociology and its teacher, Elsie soon became familiar with New York's charities and settlements. She was particularly impressed by the opportunities the new settlement houses provided for women such as herself to develop their abilities in socially useful ways. In February 1895, in her junior year, she began a ten-year association with the settlement movement by establishing a chapter of the College Settlements Association at Barnard.[8]

A Common Meeting Ground for All Classes

When Elsie was introduced to the settlement movement in 1894, it was just beginning to gain momentum among young educated men and women. Driven by what Jane Addams identified as a subjective need for action and an objective need for greater social and economic democracy, young women such as Addams at Hull House in Chicago, and young men such as James Reynolds at University Settlement in New York, had gone to live in the crowded ghettos of American cities in an effort to bridge the social and economic gaps between native born and immigrant, affluent middle class and working class. As Jane Robbins—one of the women who established College Settlement on New York's Lower East Side—put it, they wanted a home "in a neighborhood of working people in which educated women might live, in order to furnish a common meeting ground for all classes for their mutual benefit and education."[9]

Young women's involvement in settlements began in 1887 when Wellesley College teacher Vida Scudder interested Katharine Coman, Katharine Lee Bates, and Cornelia Warren in working for the establishment of a women's settlement on the model of the British men's settlement Toynbee Hall. The four women formed the College Settlements Association, which bought a house at 95

Rivington Street in New York in 1889. The College Settlement, as it was called, preceded the establishment of Chicago's Hull House by only a few months. Head resident Jean Fine inspired Giddings's former Bryn Mawr students Emily Balch and Helena Dudley to found Boston's Denison House in 1892. By 1894 there were at least seven other settlements in Chicago, New York, Boston, and Philadelphia, including Lillian Wald's Nurses Settlement in New York, which became the well-known House on Henry Street in 1895.[10]

College Settlement was a beautiful old house with a spacious backyard on a crowded, noisy street on the Lower East Side, close to the red-light district. The neighboring streets "sweated humanity"—filled mostly by newly arrived immigrants fleeing from persecution in small Jewish towns in eastern Europe. The district had a distinctive flavor, a mixture of poverty and vitality. "The somber streets, the thoughtful abstracted eyes, the tramping feet making even a silent night noise-conscious, the hanging, waving things from windows and pushcarts, those raucous shoutings advertising wares, that queer smell of hot bread, pickled apples, fish, and damp clothing" cast a lasting spell over its native-born American visitors. Yiddish newspapers, theater, and literary clubs thrived among the tenements and sweatshops, and cafes provided gathering places for discussions of anarchism and socialism. As Mary Kingsbury Simkhovitch, a College Settlement resident in 1897, put it years later, the area provided a "marvellous revelation" to the college graduates who visited and made their homes there: "It was a new kind of university with the lessons hot from the griddle." "Its impact upon a young New England woman was terrific," Simkhovitch recalled. "The East Side raised a thousand questions. It demanded study, understanding, friendship, action. It meant a rapid plunge—first, to learn to read and speak Yiddish, to go to the theaters and restaurants, to participate in the social and political life of the community. In the long period of my education, this was the most exciting chapter, for here everything was tested."[11]

College Settlement, University Settlement, and the Nurses Settlement, all within a few blocks of each other, worked closely together on neighborhood projects, particularly those concerned with education. Settlement workers saw that the children and young adults among their immigrant neighbors needed new forms of education tailored to their specific requirements and space in which to study and play. They agreed that public schools were logical centers for the development of community facilities for child care, play and physical education, after-school study, adult education, social gatherings, meetings, and forums. As Lillian Wald put it, "The stronghold of our democracy is the public school. This conviction lies deep in the hearts of the social enthusiasts who would keep the school free from the demoralization of cant and impure politics, and restore it to the people, a shrine for education, a center for public uses." To Wald and her fellow workers the role of the settlement, with its flexibility of purpose, was to experiment with extensions of the school's role, to inform public opinion, and to lobby for educational innovation. So closely did the settlements work with the public schools during their early years that "teacher" became a generic term for settlement resident.[12]

In spring 1896, during her senior year, Elsie took a pioneering course in the history and philosophy of education with Nicholas Murray Butler that determined the direction her settlement work would take. Butler, then an ambitious young professor of philosophy, ethics, and psychology, and principal of Columbia's newly established Teachers College, was the leader of a movement to reform the New York public school system. With the help of the "Goo Goos"—the Good Government Club—he had fought for several years for the divorce of schools from politics, the centralization of authority in an expert superintendent of schools, and the control of business matters by a small lay board of education. Rank-and-file teachers suspected that "Professor Nicholas Miraculous" was mounting an elitist attack on local (and teacher) control of schools. But he presented his program for the professionalization of education as a revolution that would bring relevance back into schools.[13]

Out of the ferment surrounding the fight for control of schools developed the Public Education Association, an alliance of influential women, innovative teachers, and settlement workers who fought for evening schools, playgrounds, vocational studies, free lunches, home-school liaison, and special classes for mentally and physically handicapped children. When Elsie Clews first became involved in settlement work in 1895, association members were organizing clubs and play centers in the settlements, and by 1898 they had persuaded the new Board of Education to make schools available for such purposes.[14]

During 1896–97, Elsie wrote her master's thesis, under Franklin Giddings's supervision, on poor-relief in New York City. This research, along with a brief, unpleasant taste of "friendly visiting" in the Charity Organization Society district east of the Bowery, convinced her that the settlement method was far superior to these older approaches to social problems. Throughout 1896 and 1897, she struggled to find a way to combine her interests in settlement work and new approaches to education. From 1896, she worked with the City History Club, teaching children about their city through outings that gave them firsthand experience of its diversity—the first example of her lifelong application of the principles of experimental education inspired by Harvard psychology professor William James and John Dewey, then a young professor at the University of Chicago. In 1896, Nicholas Murray Butler introduced Elsie to Julia Richman, an innovative teacher who became the first female superintendent of schools and the founder, in 1906, of Teachers House, a settlement based on the idea of the teacher as a district's natural social worker. Sometime in 1897, when she took a graduate seminar with Butler, Elsie formulated a plan similar to Richman's for an "Experimental College Settlement" to promote "intelligent study of all forms of public education and social service" in association with the Teachers College. Although she was then twenty-three years old, her parents apparently vetoed the idea of her leaving home to head such an institution. Frustrated in her attempts to move into a leadership role in one of these experimental institutions, as her friend and fellow graduate student Mary Kingsbury did in 1898, Elsie agreed to stay at home for at least two more years, as long as she was allowed to continue on to a Ph.D. and to spend her summers as she wished. In fall 1897, she enrolled in the School of Philosophy to begin a doctorate in education supervised by Nicholas Murray Butler, with minors in sociology, philosophy, and statistics.[15]

Inventors of the Future

Elsie's metamorphosis into "the busiest young woman in New York," taken up with what one admirer called her "multifarious tasks among the submerged," was viewed with dismay and incomprehension by her mother. Lucy Clews had not been brought up to the evangelical devotion to good works that characterized many wealthy Northern women. But she probably shared the suspicion of settlement workers' newfangled, secular ideas expressed by one of Elsie's older friends. "I should be very glad to go with you & Miss Potter to see the College Settlement," Bessie Davis wrote in

December 1894, but "I won't subscribe until you have explained why dancing & music does poor children more good than more solid help. I have always feared that it dissatisfies them with their condition." In contrast to the previous season, when Elsie reveled in dancing until the early hours, in 1894 she attended only one public ball. From Rome Mrs. Dexter wrote, "Yr mother says you are overdoing," reflecting the fact that study and visits to settlement houses were considered far more debilitating than dancing till dawn. When Elsie announced that she was staying in Newport for the 1895 summer to prepare for her senior year, she was warned that "your brain can only do just so much." "Your summer . . . must be lonely," Mrs. Dexter wrote anxiously.[16]

Elsie's decision to go on to graduate school in 1896 was the final straw for her mother, especially when she demonstrated what this meant for family sociability by spending her entire Paris summer in the library working on a translation of Gabriel Tarde's *Laws of Imitation*. Lucy Clews's aggrieved letters the following summer, when she had to travel to Europe without Elsie, reveal the conflict the graduate school decision caused—particularly the recent, more perplexing, determination to continue on to a doctorate. "Bear in mind," Lucy Clews wrote in September 1897, "that *you* have been allowed to direct your own life as against what *we* thought best—and we can not see *what* it will lead to."[17]

Her mother's moral blackmail, and, no doubt, her lack of independent financial means, prevented Elsie from leaving home. But Lucy Clews's disapproval was countered by the support Elsie found in her new life. Her college friends were full of "awe and veneration" for her "brilliant example," her "strong will," and her "energy which accomplishes all." Barnard registrar Mrs. Liggett was probably typical of Elsie's college mentors in considering her a perfect example of the "plucky" American girl molded by higher education.[18]

With a strong support network to help counter "the family claim," Elsie found that her sociological studies provided her with the sturdy intellectual rationale she needed to insist on living life her own way. In 1919, she recalled in her presidential address to the American Folklore Society that "the first theory in science to make an effectual demand . . . on my imagination, was Gabriel Tarde's theory of social imitation." Elsie encountered the work of this influential French sociologist in Giddings's introductory class in 1894. Tarde quickly replaced Giddings as Elsie's intellectual model.

Although she was attracted by Giddings's general theoretical perspective, she was impatient with his cautious approach to social change, his emphasis on social consensus at any cost, and his condescending attitude toward underprivileged groups and foreigners. Her later contempt for America's colonial pretensions and the coercive homogenizing of "Americanization" implicitly condemned the "legislator" notion of social control that was basic to Giddings's sociology. Tarde, in her view, had a respect for individual difference and autonomy that Giddings ultimately lacked.[19]

Considered the world's leading sociologist in the 1890s, Gabriel Tarde stimulated the development of social psychology with a highly individualized challenge to the organic determinism of influential nineteenth-century thinkers such as Herbert Spencer. Despite the title of his best-known book, *The Laws of Imitation,* Tarde was concerned neither with the promulgation of laws nor with ideas of mass society. Instead his work was a rallying cry to the "wild and undisciplined spirit[s]" who were "the inventors of the future." Emphasizing individual freedom and creativity, Tarde saw social change as a series of explosions ignited by "the accidental, the irrational . . . the accident of genius" rather than a gradual, linear transformation brought about by rational, collective means. In his much-publicized debate with the up-and-coming Emile Durkheim, Tarde articulated an anti-institutional perspective allied politically to anarchism and the less doctrinaire forms of socialism, while Durkheim defended order and authority. As the French sociologist Bouglé put it, "In his eyes, everything stemmed from the individual, and everything came back to him." Tarde's extraordinarily popular and influential successor at the Collège de France, Henri Bergson, was the apotheosis of the emphasis on spontaneity and innovation initiated by Tarde.[20]

Tarde's focus on the phenomena of imitation and—more important to him—nonimitation, invention, and the "logical duel" was the result of his interest in the psychological processes that brought about change. He argued that voluntary and persistent nonimitation between generations and the logical duel in which rival ideas are thrashed out have purgative roles that open the way for invention and imaginative borrowing. For Tarde, invention, selective borrowing, and the logical duel increased diversity and promoted tolerance. When we borrow from "a hundred, a thousand, or ten thousand," he argued, the nature and choice of the elements of thought or action that we combine "expresses and accentuates our original personality." At the same time, the process encouraged awareness and appreciation of others, and a fellow-feeling that no longer tolerated injustice. The eventual outcome of the prolonged action of imitation was, Tarde believed, both "the purest and most potent individualism" and a "consummate sociability."[21]

Beginning the Conversation

In Gabriel Tarde, Elsie found a vision of a new and better world where respect for individual difference was the basis of social harmony. He also gave her a program of action through the promotion of what he called "conversation." For Tarde, mass communications, new, extended patterns of loyalty, and overlapping group memberships enabled people to shift ideological perspectives and form coalitions with greater flexibility. These processes in turn facilitated the development of rationality, tolerance, and peace. Through more democratic and spontaneous personal relationships, in other words, the effects of broader structural forces could be mitigated. The important basis for all this "conversation" is face-to-face interaction. "Never, except in a duel, does one observe an individual with all the force of one's attention unless one is talking with him, and that is the most constant, the most important, and the least observed effect of conversation," Tarde pointed out. "If people did not talk, it would be futile to publish newspapers. . . . they would exercise no durable or profound influence on people, they would be like a vibrating string without a sounding board." Conversation is therefore "the strongest agent of imitation, of the propagation of sentiments, ideas, and modes of action."[22]

Tarde's notions of imitation, invention, and conversation gave Elsie the basis for her life's work. In her early settlement work, the idea of conversation was the dominant motif. As she encountered in her personal life the deadening hand of custom, she focused on the processes of imitation and invention, becoming the deliberate and public inventor of the future and promoter of scandalous conversation whom Alfred Kroeber fondly called "Dear Propagandist." Later, devastated by the First World War's blow to civilized conversation, Elsie devoted herself to an exacting study of the historical processes of imitation and invention in the making of the Pueblo communities of America's Southwest, a study that fulfilled all Tarde's methodological tenets in its attention to detail, personality, and wide-ranging comparison.[23]

Mary Kingsbury, mid-1890s. Mary Kingsbury Simkhovitch, *Neighborhood: My Story of Greenwich House* (New York: Norton, 1938).

Tarde gave Elsie a theoretical perspective and a program of action. But it was her fellow graduate student Mary Kingsbury who demonstrated the practical working out of this program. Mary entered the Columbia graduate program with Elsie in 1896 with an enviable amount of experience behind her. She had just returned from studying in Berlin and attending the Socialist International in London. In her native Boston she had been involved in settlement work with Helena Dudley and Emily Balch. After a year at graduate school, she became head worker at College Settlement. In 1898 she moved to Friendly Aid House, the Unitarian settlement on East Thirty-fourth Street.[24]

Mary Kingsbury saw the settlement's main role as empowering the community by encouraging cohesion and local leadership. "If social improvements are to be undertaken by one class on behalf of another, no permanent changes are likely to be effected," she argued. Basic to her work was Tarde's idea of face-to-face conversation. "Before any help can be given the situation must be felt, realized and understood at first hand," she wrote. "Only that which is lived can be understood and translated to others." The campaign for local schools to be used as neighborhood centers was central to her ideas on fostering community. She also supported neighborhood theater and helped establish a music school, and in her major effort to improve public housing, she tried where possible to encourage restoration of old buildings and reconstruction of small-scale traditional neighborhoods.[25]

An Experimental Relationship

Elsie's life was not all high seriousness, although it often seemed so to her mother. After Sam's death, her social life took two conflicting directions, reflecting the restricted alternatives available for young women of her class. On the one hand, she led a carefree outdoors life with New York's fast set. The central figure in this set was the frenetic Stanford White, architect and decorator extraordinaire to the wealthy of New York and Newport. White is as well known now for the manner of his death as for his architecture. Shot in 1906 by the jealous husband of a former lover, White was portrayed in the long-drawn-out trials that followed his murder as a sensual beast who seduced young women in his tower apartment at Madison Square Garden. He apparently had many extramarital affairs, but in his friendship with Elsie he appeared pleasure-loving and gregarious rather than evil. Certainly Elsie asserted at the time of his death: "Stanford was one of the noblest, most chivalrous & magnanimous men I have ever known, and I would like to say so on the witness stand. . . . I could also testify that *I* never was drugged in the tower room!"[26]

Elsie met White early in 1894, probably through Helen Benedict, the daredevil daughter of a wealthy shipping magnate. She found White more agreeable than the usual "dancers and diners-out." They soon fell into an easy friendship in which they skated, sailed, and cycled, sometimes together and sometimes with Helen Benedict or White's wife, Bessie. A typical note from White, often signed with a caricature of his hair *en brosse*, read "Dear Miss Elsie The last boat leaves end of 34th St at 4.20 P.M. tomorrow—bring your old clothes—Bicycle suit & waterproof & rubbers. Yours SW."[27]

Elsie enjoyed being carried off from her books on bicycling expeditions or "yachting sprees," especially during the 1895 summer when she was supposedly sacrificing her pleasure and health by not going to Europe. Benedict suspected, in fact, that Elsie was not quite as devoted to her books as she found it useful to appear. After Elsie graduated, Benedict invariably called her "Dear Honorable," which White elaborated into "Dear & Honorable Miss Else" and teased

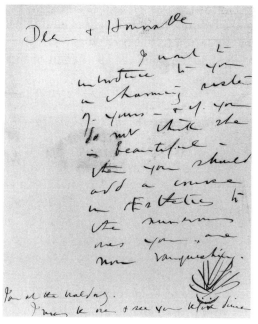

Stanford White to Elsie, ca. June 1896. Parsons Family Papers, Rye Historical Society.

her about always being "up to some learned or athletic mischief." White was a great favorite of Lucy Clews: both women allowed him to call at hours Elsie usually reserved for work; and Elsie was allowed to accompany the Whites on a memorable camping and fishing trip to Quebec with Helen Benedict and her future husband, architect Tommy Hastings, during her first "free" summer in 1897.[28]

At the same time as she enjoyed the unpredictable, imaginative, and somewhat dangerous company of Stanford White and Helen Benedict, Elsie was being courted by Herbert Parsons, an entirely different young man she was to marry in 1900. She met Herbert at a weekend party at Lenox, where his family had a magnificent country house, in the December after Sam Dexter died. She had just turned twenty and he was twenty-five. Herbert was a politically active young lawyer who had graduated from Yale in 1890 and Harvard Law School in 1893. He was born in New York City in 1869 to Mary Dumesnil McIlvaine Parsons and John Edward Parsons, a prominent lawyer who made his name (and apparently his fortune) designing and defending the monopoly of the American Sugar Refining Company.[29]

Brought up within walking distance of Elsie's home, with the enormously wealthy Phelps Stokes and Morgans as neighbors, Herbert's and Elsie's circles never overlapped. His family were strict Presbyterians who summered, along with the Phelps Stokes, at Lenox, where the luxuriousness of the houses was just as great as at Newport, but the sterner virtues were enforced. They also owned Lounsberry, a beautiful Greek revival house in Harrison, just outside New York, built on an acre of land overlooking Long Island Sound by Herbert's grandfather. Herbert's parents took the family abroad for a year when he was ten years old; they sent him to Berlin for a year's study after his graduation from Yale; and his sisters religiously traveled in Europe in search of aesthetic education. But none of these travels was tinged by the sense of adventure that Robert Louis Stevenson advocated.

When Elsie met Herbert at the end of 1894, he was working in the law offices of Strong and Cadwalader. The following year he was admitted to the New York bar and joined his father's firm, Parsons, Shepard, and Ogden. In 1902 he went into partnership with his father, Tompkins McIlvaine, and William Carnochan. An earnest young man who took his Presbyterian faith seriously, Herbert had plunged into political and social reform activities by joining the Good Government movement, in which he helped activists such as James Reynolds, head resident of University Settlement, establish the Citizens Union in 1894 to challenge the domination of Tammany Hall. He was elected alderman for the Twenty-fifth Assembly District in 1899, and again in 1901, on the Republican and Citizens Union ticket. Seth Low, Columbia's president, stood for mayor in 1897 on the same ticket, and was elected in 1901, with Reynolds becoming his private secretary. When Herbert met Elsie in 1894, he belonged, therefore, to a circle that included Theodore Roosevelt, Seth Low, and residents of University Settlement such as Reynolds, J. G. Phelps Stokes, and Hamilton Holt, student of sociology and editor of the liberal journal, the *Independent*.

Throughout his life, Herbert devoted himself to social reform as well as to politics. Indeed, as a true Progressive, the two were inextricably linked for him. He was for many years the superintendent of a large mission Sunday School on New York's West Side; with his sisters he maintained St. Helen's Home for Children, founded by his father in memory of a dead sister. In addition, he was president of Memorial Hospital for the Treatment of Cancer, the board of trustees of Canton Christian College in China, and the Greenwich House settlement, and a manager of the Society for the

Reformation of Juvenile Delinquents, the Manhattan Eye, Ear, Nose, and Throat Hospital, and the New York Association for Improving the Conditions of the Poor.[30]

Herbert's seriousness was tempered by a strong sense of fun, and Elsie's intelligence and enthusiasm caught his attention. He described their meeting in a letter to their children written on Mothers Day 1918 while on military duty in France. "It was 23 years ago in December that I first met mother," he wrote. "It was on the way to Lenox in a private railroad car in a party that the Stokeses were giving over New Year's in the present Carnegie house. Mother was then regarded as a wonderful person because she was in college and enjoyed herself also. . . . There was a lot of snow & all Stockbridge Bowl was frozen over. I on skates pulled her on a sled to the outlet & back & walking up we talked & were late for lunch and that was the beginning of it all." Herbert was immediately smitten by the unusual and attractive young woman, who dominated his thoughts as he lay convalescing from pneumonia a few weeks later. Elsie obviously found the house party stimulating too. By May 1895, Herbert was competing with Stanford White, Helen Benedict, and a host of admirers for Elsie's company on rides and walks, and during the summer when she stayed in Newport ostensibly to study, Elsie managed to see quite a bit of him. By the end of the 1895 summer, he was her acknowledged favorite.[31]

Elsie was just beginning to take an active interest in New York's social problems when she met Herbert. From the start, they shared the conviction that they had a duty to use their wealth and privilege for the benefit of the wider society. Elsie no doubt found Herbert's greater experience in civic politics interesting and useful, and he was glad to find a potential partner who was sympathetic to his reform interests. When the summer was over, however, and Elsie returned to her strict regime of study and organizational activity, Herbert found there were disadvantages to falling in love with such a "new" woman. He discovered she disliked unscheduled calls, and he soon found himself cycling at dawn in order to fit into her busy schedule. When Elsie decided to go on to graduate work in 1896, Herbert was probably as dismayed as her parents. It is clear that he tried to discuss his feelings for her during that spring and summer and that she resisted this step: writing to her in Europe in July he sent "a most fervent, though of course impersonal, sentiment," using the irony he often used to deflect his disappointment or disapproval of her more implacable stances. But as was often the case, Elsie was implacable only through great control of her emotional inclinations. During that same summer, she made it clear to her other admirer, Holken Abbott, that her deep affections lay elsewhere; and when she returned to New York she and Herbert were so absorbed in one another that Lucy Clews was alarmed at what people would think, when no marriage was planned.[32]

By the end of 1896, after two years of courtship, Herbert hoped that he could persuade Elsie to marry him. "I am deeply interested in what you write of Miss Clews," his cousin Edward wrote. "If you get nearer 'the cliff where reason ends' I hope you will let me know." But Elsie had other ideas. She was suspicious of marriage, both because of her parents' example and because it seemed incompatible with women's development; and she was convinced of the superiority of friendship as a relationship that combined intimacy with independence. She apparently persuaded Herbert to at least try such a relationship. As Edward Parsons replied skeptically to Herbert in April 1897, "I never had an intimate woman friend—I fell over the 'verge' too soon—but I think it is much more satisfactory to be over." There is no evidence of what degree of physical intimacy was involved in this "intimate friendship"; but given the vigilance of her parents, her own ambitions, and Herbert's moral scruples, it was probably more chaste than otherwise. Robert Herrick, Elsie's lover thirty years later, wrote unkindly in a novel based on her life that "Edgar [the Herbert character who is 'efficient Y.M.C.A.'] had recognized from the start that the only way to hold the intellectual woman whom he had wooed and won was to make a display of his liberality, his modernity (as he had in his courtship when they were both interested in social 'movements,' settlements and the like)." Certainly during the spring of 1897 Herbert made every effort to support Elsie in her busy schedule of work. She in turn devoted whatever free time she had to him. "I should not have believed it possible," Stanford White wrote in March 1897, "with you in town & myself there also all this time should have passed without my seeing the light of your eyes."[33]

In 1897 Elsie felt confident about the independent direction of her life. She had come to an understanding with Herbert about their relationship. Her friendships with Helen Benedict, Katharine Dexter, and Mary Kingsbury gave her the support of three like-minded women. She had successfully completed her master's degree, and her first scholarly article had been accepted—a survey of pedagogy courses at colleges and universities based on a paper from

Butler's seminar. As Lucy Clews wrote from Amsterdam, Elsie had made a "bold flight" that summer with her policy of independence and should have felt "quite securely entrenched" in her rights.[34]

But there were definite limits to these rights as long as she was a single woman living at home. Instead of accompanying her mother to Europe during the 1897 summer, Elsie had gone with the Whites and Helen Benedict to Canada, and she was intent on some similar adventure with Herbert. "How soon can you be ready to start with me for Alaska? The Klondikes are exerting an over-powering attraction upon me and I am eager to go at all sacrifices," she wrote jokingly on her return from Quebec. "I have just been presented with a light but deadly rifle by Stanford White, the most welcome gift I have ever received not excepting skates," she wrote two weeks later. She was enthusiastic when Herbert proposed that she join him, with his married sister as chaperone, on a camping trip in the Adirondacks with his friend Walton Martin: "I have never been in our mountains and the camping out plan appeals to me greatly. . . . I have just written a most diplomatic letter to my father about the plan. Unless he takes to it at once it might not be amiss for you to pay him a visit and present details with your accustomed skill. The more I think of the details the more keen I become. You know I am only too easy in matters of expedition."[35]

Lucy Clews reacted with horror from Paris, Amsterdam, and Berlin. Vacations away from the family could be endured; but any hint of sexual scandal was outside the bounds of what was permitted for an unmarried woman, even if she was twenty-three years old and a master of arts. When she heard of Elsie's plan, Lucy telegraphed peremptorily, "Absolutely opposed Adirondacks." Henry Clews agreed. "I am sorry to deny you your desire in this matter," he wrote, "but it is best it should be done—there are some things you can do you know and there are things it is not well to do, and this is one of them because the 'World' so decides."[36]

Herbert's family apparently agreed that the relationship should not be encouraged if it was not going to lead to engagement and marriage. Earlier in the summer, he had been mortified to have to retract an invitation for Elsie to visit them. "I confess that I too am disappointed about Lenox," Elsie had written. "I have been thinking of some long rides over the hills with you, getting home very late for dinner"; but, she ended, referring to his apologetic letter, I believe 'it is not personal.'" But when her parents later vetoed the Adirondacks expedition, she could not resist a barb: "There is nothing 'personal' to use your expression," she wrote Herbert.[37]

Despite family disapproval, Elsie and Herbert continued their ambiguous friendship as she plunged into her doctoral studies in the fall of 1897. Her carefully constructed defenses against "falling desperately in love" were breached, however, early in 1898, when it seemed that Herbert would join up to fight in the Spanish-American War. "And will you believe it—when the Spanish war came in 1898 & I was trying to go to it I found that she was fond of me," he wrote to their children in 1918. Early in May, Elsie wrote to Herbert, who was in army camp after a brief leave, with something of the war-bride mentality she deplored in later life: "I am very happy . . . to have these painful barriers down. If you only knew how much you are to me. . . . But you can't know yet: some things about me you have never seen . . . and probably with Henry you think I am so hard as to be a bit inhuman. At any rate, before, I always tried to make you and the rest of the world think that." Aware of the pent-up emotions her confession of love released, Elsie warned Herbert of the more unattractive side of her feelings: "Would it surprise you very much to learn that I have a jealous disposition? I am beginning to surprise myself with that piece of information. It threatens to be a very great bore to myself."[38]

Although she admitted her love in 1898, Elsie still refused to marry Herbert. A year later, when she completed her dissertation, he reacted with despair when she accepted the Hartley House Fellowship to direct student fieldwork for Giddings the following year. Urging him to break off their relationship if it was unacceptable to him, she wrote uncompromisingly: "A year ago I thought I had done you a great wrong in telling you that I loved you but, at the same time, I should never be willing to marry you. I still think I am doing you wrong. I think that our relation is not doing you harm now,—and I have been watching carefully,—but it will in the future. And so, if you are reasonable, you will break it off. I have not changed in my aversion to matrimony; indeed it is stronger than ever, or rather I am more convinced than ever that I shall never marry. For, although I love you better than I love or can conceive of loving anybody else,—moreover if I had to choose between you on one side and all my family and friends on the other I would choose you,—yet I should let you go entirely out of my life rather than marry you."[39]

As was to happen many times in her life, the strain of keeping to her principles in the face of strong feelings to the contrary led to a physical collapse just before her doctoral examination. She passed, however, with flying colors, and a month later she and Herbert were reconciled. In July 1899 they were discussing marriage. Gradually this step seemed more possible. Mary Kingsbury had married Vladimir Simkhovitch in January that year, and Barnard dean Emily James Smith had married publisher George Haven Putnam in April, and both had continued in their jobs, Mary and Vladimir living on the upper floor of Friendly Aid House.[40]

Ethnographer of the Family

But Elsie was determined to establish her professional identity before she married. Over the past two years, she had divided her energies between practical settlement work and library research for an exhaustive, but dry, survey of colonial educational legislation for her dissertation. As director of sociological fieldwork for Giddings, she found a congenial way to combine her interests in innovative education, scholarly research, and practical social reform. She had always been a keen observer of social mores, especially in her own family. Now, as she supervised her students' observations of tenement house families on New York's West Side, she quickly developed the technique and point of view that she refined over a lifetime of ethnographic observation. Abandoning the standard schedules based on the family monograph method of French sociologist Le Play, she decided that "the real life of the tenements" was revealed by the "neglected psychological social fact" rather than the economic data that was Le Play's focus. The new guidelines she drew up for her students followed recent anthropology in focusing on the observation of beliefs, ideals, interests, amusements, and superstitions. As a reviewer in *L'Année Sociologique* observed several years later of the original method of studying family life that Elsie developed, "This consists in insisting on the psychology of groups rather than their economic character, and proposes not to provide family budgets, but to reproduce in all its complexity and detail the history and life of the households studied." The social group is studied as if it is a tribe, characterized above all by their beliefs and superstitious customs, and regular visits to the families are used "to truly penetrate their intimate life." The method, the reviewer concluded, is extraordinarily like that of an explorer who gathers as many details as possible and strives above all to present them literally.[41]

By the following spring, Elsie was launched in a modest but decisive way on her career as an socially committed ethnographer. She felt confident that she had found work that was useful and that engrossed her. She was assured of at least another two years in her Columbia position. She was deeply involved in the work of the College Settlements Association and with Mary Simkhovitch at Friendly Aid House, and she had recently been appointed a public schools inspector. Her friend, the brilliant mathematician Alice Duer, had recently married in what she and Elsie agreed was an "experimental" step. In April 1900, after six years of courtship and three years of "intimate friendship," Elsie decided that she too could make the experiment and marry Herbert. She was no longer going to be a mere reporter on the family—she was going to be a participant observer.[42]

CHAPTER THREE

The Experimental Life

WHEN Elsie Clews married Herbert Parsons in September 1900, she was consciously embarking on an experimental life. Just as young white women of M. Carey Thomas's day, haunted by "the clanging chains of that gloomy specter, Dr. Edward Clarke's *Sex in Education*," did not know whether their health could stand the strain of education, those of Elsie's day did not know if they could successfully combine work, marriage, and childbearing.[1]

The prejudices against the experiment were strong. Most career women of Carey Thomas's generation deliberately eschewed marriage in favor of households of women or a loving relationship with another woman. Often separating the spirituality of love from the physical character of sexuality, they found satisfaction in female friendships, relationships with kin, or in devotion to needy groups. Unmarried women, either as couples or alone, sometimes adopted children or took responsibility for orphaned nephews or nieces; but husbands and pregnancies were seen to be incompatible with regular work outside the home. Many female friendships provided sexual as well as spiritual companionship, but the erotic element was rarely acknowledged publicly and the apparent celibacy of many professional women was not regarded as a problem.

New York did offer some prominent role models of professional women who were also wives and mothers, such as journalist Jane Croly and physician Mary Putnam Jacobi. Among Elsie's own generation, she had the example of Mary Kingsbury Simkhovitch and Emily James Putnam. But just as Elsie and Herbert were announcing their engagement in April 1900, the pregnant Emily Putnam reluctantly resigned from Barnard owing to "ill health" after a bitter struggle to keep her position; and her friend Alice Duer Miller had forfeited a promising career in mathematics to write "amid the ven-

Elsie and Herbert on camping trip in Adirondacks with family and friends just before their marriage, August 1900. Elsie Clews Parsons Papers, American Philosophical Society Library.

omous hardships of bungalow life" in Costa Rica, where Harry Miller, never a businessman, expected to make a fortune in land speculation.[2]

The older generation of women who worked with Elsie were skeptical of the younger women's experiments. Charity Organization Society founder Carlotta Russell Lowell wrote, "I am ashamed to say that at first I felt rather badly for I had hoped we were going to work together & feared this might interfere with it. However I hope you are right in thinking it won't." A former Barnard professor wrote, "I am not going to congratulate you at all. You and Alice Duer were the two girls I had made up my mind would make great names for yourselves, and show women what they can do, and now you just come down to the level of us ordinary mortals." Annie Nathan Meyer, the Barnard founder who had insisted on Emily Putnam's resignation, was more definite: "I heartily congratulate you that marriage may mean a going on without a giving up—but in time it seems wisest to change one's activities you will find there are many to fill one's life. Your work, however, need not—I should think—present any problems, certainly not for a while. A Fellow or an Instructor or even a *Professor* is different from a Dean."[3]

Elsie's students were "very glad and surprised" to hear that she intended to continue her work with their class. "We had all the time been making up our mind for such a day as this when we would have to finally say goodbye." Her University Settlement co-worker James Reynolds wrote supportively, "you have done too much good work yourself to abandon it for a mere man and I hope you will continue your interest along the lines where you have been so useful in the past." Her College Settlement colleague Jane Robbins was more doubtful: "One of my frivolous friends says that devotion to one person is the vanishing point of altruism." But to a younger colleague, Susan Walker, who was contemplating marriage herself, she was a welcome role model. "I am mightily glad you don't think matrimony incompatible with other things," she wrote. "I have similar views & so far have only Mary Simkhovitch to fall back upon for proof. May I long be able to quote you among the noble minority."[4]

New Marriage: The Theory

During the period Elsie was considering marriage to Herbert, considerable changes were taking place in attitudes to marriage, women's capabilities, and women's sexuality. In 1891 Edward Westermarck's enormously detailed comparative study of sexual practices, kinship, and moral ideas, *The History of Human Marriage,* dealt a body blow to the idea that current institutions and moral codes represented the peak of civilized progress. Instead he demonstrated a chaotic variety of practices and beliefs. Submerging the divine-origin view of morals in "a lethal bath of facts," as C. Wright Mills colorfully put it, Westermarck argued that moral systems were not universal and given but were created by acts of individual choice in particular historical situations.[5]

The generally held belief that celibacy was not injurious to women also began to crumble in the 1890s. Edward Carpenter, one of the most influential proselytizers for a new approach to women's sexuality, argued in 1896 that "passion is a matter of universal experience; and . . . for the understanding of life—of one's own life, of that of others, and of human nature in general—as well as for the proper development of one's own capacities, such experience as a rule is needed. In the social life of the future, this need will surely be recognised, and . . . the state of enforced celibacy in which vast numbers of women live today will be looked upon as a national wrong, almost as grievous as that of prostitution."[6]

Carpenter's ideas enjoyed great popularity among young intellectuals of the 1890s and the early years of the twentieth century. His advocacy of the naturalness and importance of sexuality was part of a complete philosophy of the simple life that included open-air life and labor, minimal housekeeping and expenditure, and comfortable, practical clothing. His rejection of the straitjacket of bourgeois life had much in common with Stevenson's: like Stevenson he argued that pleasure should come as a natural accompaniment of life, and like Stevenson he was an advocate of alfresco sex, deploring the fact that "sexual embraces themselves seldom receive the benison of Dame Nature, in whose presence alone, under the burning sun or the high canopy of the stars and surrounded by the fragrant atmosphere, their meaning can be fully understood; but take place in stuffy dens of dirty upholstery and are associated with all unbeautiful things." Elsie had already embraced the open-air life, the necessity of productive activity, the simple dress and restrained expenditure, and the ethical nature of pleasure. It is likely therefore that she also agreed with Carpenter that the highest form of sexual experience—that between people in a long-term, intimate relationship—was necessary to her full development.[7]

Carpenter's ideas on the beneficial and, indeed, indispensable character of sexual expression were given scientific weight during the 1890s and early twentieth century by the enormous compilations of the British physician Havelock Ellis. Always a harbinger of what he called in 1890 "the New Spirit," Ellis considered sex "the chief and central function of life . . . ever wonderful, ever lovely." His enthusiasm was manifested in massive studies of every aspect of sexual expression, published in a series of six volumes between 1896 and 1910.[8]

Ellis's relentless empiricism and his reluctance to form judgments appealed to a generation tired of nineteenth-century system-building and hungry for information with which to form their own ethical and behavioral codes. But beneath his appearance of dispassionate inquiry was a program which was extremely appealing to searching minds such as Elsie's. The clear message of his first highly controversial volume, *Sexual Inversion* (1896), was the plasticity and variety of sexual expression, and the idea that sexual differentiation was a matter of degree. *Auto-Eroticism* (1899) underlined the spontaneous nature of sexuality and, by emphasizing the prevalence of masturbation among women, undermined the idea of women's sexual passivity. Ellis's positive approach to sexuality was part of an affirmation of all forms of desire as expressions of a questing spirit. Elsie's ideas on sexuality fitted closely with Ellis's throughout her life, and although there is no direct evidence that she read his work before her marriage, it is very likely that his new positive approach to sexuality influenced her decision to marry.[9]

Another strong impetus toward marriage for Elsie was her desire for children, not only for the emotional satisfaction of a family, but also as a means of shaping the future. The sense of her generation that they needed to start anew, to kill the nineteenth century, was manifested in their intense interest in new forms of child-rearing and education. For them, the child was the hope of a new world, free of the hypocrisies and delusions of the old. Children were seen as "spontaneous as spring . . . pure and uninfluenced by calculation and duplicity and adult reserve," their emotions undistorted by convention and self-consciousness. In a series of studies they regarded as the result of a uniquely American impulse to take a "fresh, independent look at the primal facts of human nature and at growth itself," psychologists closely observed the development of their own children and enlisted schoolteachers to observe and report on their pupils. The most important of these studies was carried out by James Mark Baldwin, who traced in his own infant daughter the growth of functions such as will and conscience that were previously believed to be innate. Baldwin described the processes of socialization by imitation and the approval and disapproval of primary caregivers. But, like Tarde, he emphasized the active role of the individual in fashioning the personality rather than the more social "looking-glass self" popularized by Charles Cooley and George Herbert Mead. In particular, Baldwin demonstrated the roles of language, play, and art as aids to invention. The parent, as well as being an important source of imitation, was also responsible for providing an environment in which inventive self-fashioning could take place.[10]

Baldwin's research promoted an enthusiasm for motherhood among "inventors of the future" such as Elsie Clews Parsons, Alice Duer Miller, and Mary Simkhovitch that was quite separate from the conservative eugenics of the "race suicide" howlers Edward A. Ross and Teddy Roosevelt. As Elsie pointed out in 1906 in a new justification of education for women, mothers have previously been conservers of social traditions, but in rapidly changing times they must also become the initiators of social progress. "Does not the latter role require a very high order of intelligence and conscience," she asked, "and will it not be the final argument for the 'higher education' of women both in the college and in life?" Novelist Robert Herrick, in notes made in 1924 for Jessica Stowe, a fictional character closely based on Elsie, says flatly, "She marries for children, professedly, and has them in fairly rapid succession." This may be a simplification, but it was true that she wanted a large family, and she brought her children up carefully in ways designed to encourage independence and innovation.[11]

Elsie and her friends had another, related, sense of mission in their experimental marriages. Thorstein Veblen had pointed out in *The Theory of the Leisure Class* (1899), a little book almost entirely ignored in its day, that many married women were merely ornaments used to display their husbands' wealth. If people had noticed that most illuminating book, Elsie wrote in 1906, they would not be so quick to claim that the United States was "unhampered by caste." On the contrary, she noted, "wherever there is an unproductive American woman there we find soil for the spirit of caste." In a heartfelt cry for useful activity, plain housekeeping, and simple dress, she argued that unoccupied women were vulnerable to the tyranny of things and fashion. Having nothing else to do, women eat, dress, and amuse themselves in the most time- and energy-consuming ways. Their social positions depend on their possessions, and they rank themselves and other women by what they have and how they dress rather than by what they are or do. Women's slavery to possessions and fashion affects not only their immediate circle, Elsie argued, but it also exacerbates class distinctions and promotes envy and lack of sympathy among women. And it determines patterns of consumption, not only among the wealthy, but also in the rest of the population. "Suffrageless as women are," Elsie observed, "the fate of democracy depends more on them than on men. The simple life is indispensable to true democracy and it is women who either complicate or simplify the material sides of living. It is a pity that men do not fully realize this—that it only comes home to them when they grumble over mounting bills." Big bills are merely the symbol of unproductive activities, she argued: working wives have neither time nor energy to eat and dress in elaborate ways.[12]

New Marriage: The Practice

"I think that I would like to be married for a while just to show people how," Elsie had written Herbert in 1898. Now she had the opportunity to do so. In embarking on their experimental life, Elsie and Herbert agreed on a plan that Herbert felt would lead to "a truer, fuller life, not only in its pleasures but also in its responsibilities, than that you once contemplated." "I love you, Elsie, & hope I can make you happy & in that way if no other help you to accomplish real purposes," he wrote. This promise of partnership in a wider field of accomplishment was an important factor in Elsie's decision to marry. Marriage to Herbert would, she hoped and expected, provide the freedom for socially useful self-development that was impossible while she lived with her parents. Some sense of their shared plan for social service is given in a letter Elsie wrote to her father-in-law supporting Herbert's desire to run for Congress. Outlining their financial situation, she pointed out that she held "certain views which would make it extremely distasteful . . . ever to increase our present scale of living whatever our income might be." In fact, she said, they currently gave away between one-third and one-quarter of their income. "If Herbert becomes a politician his public service would be an equivalent for his philanthropic gifts and activities."[13]

Elsie claimed nine years later—when her marriage was actually in a state of crisis—that she had no real anticipation of the happiness she would find in marriage. Writing to her son John in 1926, when he was contemplating marriage, she advised him that "one of the best criteria of the quality of love, it has seemed to me, is whether the experience is capacitating or not in other relations." Much of the happiness Elsie did experience in the early years of marriage came from the sense of accomplishment she felt in demonstrating the possibility of a new sort of marriage that widened women's capacities rather than narrowed them.[14]

Elsie's wedding, which took place at the Rocks, at noon on 1 September 1900, was as simple as Lucy Clews would allow it to be. Elsie would have only one fitting for her wedding dress, so a sewing girl of her height and figure modeled it. "Holken Abbott, Henry and I were the critics," Mrs. Clews wrote Herbert. "We all approved except it is not train enough to suit Henry, but Elsie gave orders!" The *New York Herald*'s account noted, "The bride of to-day was graduated from Barnard College, where she has been an instructress for some time. She has always been averse to social display and much more interested in the more serious affairs of life."[15]

Elsie wanted to go to Mexico or Colorado for their honeymoon, but Herbert was embroiled in his first congressional campaign. He was successful in the party primary the day before the wedding, and he and Elsie enjoyed only a brief trip through New England before he returned to the campaign. When he lost, exhausted, in November, Elsie saw him sleep in the daytime for the first and only time in his busy life. But Herbert was not the only one who was busy. September saw not only her marriage, but also the publication in Nicholas Murray Butler's *Educational Review* of her first sociological article, an account of the fieldwork methods she devised for her Barnard class.[16]

Elsie and Herbert set up house in a row of plain brownstones at 112 East Thirty-fifth Street, just off Park Avenue, close to Mary and Vladimir Simkhovitch at Friendly Aid House and only a few blocks from her parents. One important freedom that marriage brought her was that she could at last walk alone at night. Discussing in 1914 the restrictions placed on single women by a "protective" sexual code, Elsie recalled, "Brought up in one of [the most conservative circles] myself I was going on thirty before I went walking alone at night in New York." "How exciting and delightful that first night walk was—to an evening meeting of my Local School Board. Since then I have been alone at night in various strange parts of the world, but that first thrill of adventure I have never quite recovered."[17]

When she became pregnant within six weeks of the wedding, Elsie was glad of the opportunity to put her theories fully to the test. Herbert, as he admitted, "the pettifogger who cannot see the big side," hoped that she would discontinue her work. "My long head (hem!) could see the possibility of considerable danger to the good name of your course & of Barnard if great care was not exercised," he cautioned. "The risks to be taken in such experimental work should be lessened, for fear of unpleasant even if prejudiced & illogical questions." But she continued her work with confidence and optimism, despite Herbert's apprehension, and even took on new duties. Giddings affected not to notice her condition and wrote at the end of June 1901, when she was eight months pregnant, that he and his wife were "greatly interested in the news of yourself. . . .

I am very glad that you did not think it necessary to cut short the work at Barnard, and I congratulate you on your good sense."[18]

When New York suffered a heat wave during Elsie's last month of pregnancy, Lucy Clews wrote anxiously from Carlsbad, where she was taking the cure. She was not reassured when Herbert told her that Elsie was not complaining: "The fact that Elsie did not complain, meant nothing to me as Elsie is not of the complaining kind, that is part of her plot of life!" Miss Carmody, the nurse who cared for all six Parsons babies and became a lifelong friend, arrived early in July to prepare for the birth. Labor did not begin until four weeks later, on 4 August. Lissa was born at 10:26 A.M. on the sixth, weighing 6 lb. 10 oz. Always the careful scientist, Elsie recorded the details in a special diary with a feminist flourish: "The twentieth century is high time that women should shout and shout I did," she wrote in Lissa's persona. "I don't believe mother knew how much she wanted me. I will teach her to be glad I came and I'll be to her the best companion she could have, barring, of course, father." Poking gentle fun at Elsie, Herbert sent her brother Henry a telegram from Lissa announcing, "I am a scientific fact."[19]

Alice Duer Miller, whose son Denning was born the same year, wrote welcoming Lissa: "Although I suppose every woman who admires her husband pays him the compliment of wanting a son, I'm not sure but what the age is not more in need of intelligently brought-up daughters." Mary Simkhovitch, who was pregnant with her first child, exclaimed, "what a modern young lady she will be." "I am also collecting information about babies," she warned, "& expect you to give me some scientific first hand information." Even Lucy Clews forgot her resentments and hoped Lissa would prove "as interesting and as good a baby as her mother was."[20]

Two weeks later Elsie was up and about, and at the end of August the family moved to Lenox, where they had taken over the farmhouse on Herbert's father's grand estate, Stonover. Her father was surprised she was able to travel so soon. "It shows your great recuperative powers, you are certainly a marvelous young woman." If she was not feeling as energetic as she appeared, she was not going to admit it, as Lucy pointed out perceptively. In 1922, when Lissa's first baby was born, Elsie wrote to Mabel Dodge Luhan, whose son John was born in 1901, "Lissa's baby arrived, & with much less agony than was our lot, gas in the second stage of the pains. I put it down a little to feminism as well as to science. A development in

Elsie and Lissa, early 1902.
Elsie Clews Parsons Papers,
American Philosophical Society
Library.

technique has at last seemed worth while to the doctors." And in
1907, when she was recovering from her fourth confinement, she
confessed that "my mind, when it comes to anything practical, goes
back on me. It is always so at these times, and the weakness lasts
for at least two months." But in 1901, however she felt, Elsie was
back at Barnard by early November, and was immediately involved
in an unsuccessful campaign to persuade Mayor Low to appoint
women, and herself in particular, to the new Greater New York
Board of Education.[21]

The birth of Mary Simkhovitch's son Stephen in January 1902
put the young women's experiment to the test for the first time. The
board of Friendly Aid House objected to Mary bringing up a baby
in the settlement and, with much acrimony, forced her to resign.
Within a few months she and Elsie had the backing of an influential
group of churchmen, reformers, academics, and bankers for a new
settlement. By early summer, Mary was again pregnant. The baby
was due in February, but she was resolute that it would not change
her plans. During the summer she found a suitable house at 26
Jones Street, which eventually became Greenwich House, and Elsie

set to work to raise the money necessary for its repair. A crowded list of meetings, books, and baby necessities that survives in Elsie's papers provides a glimpse of the busy and complex lives she and Mary had made for themselves.[22]

The following July, with Stephen eighteen months old and Helena six months, Mary wrote to Elsie with a sigh of relief from her summer home in Maine: "Here as usual all is peace. The babies flourish. V. takes to fishing and I enjoy the domesticity of the entire situation. Down here I'm just plain wife, mother, and no tinge of anything else. It's a bad thing, too much of that! But a little is all right and spiritually refreshing."[23]

Elsie was also glad of the summer break. She had become pregnant again in October 1902, just as the academic year and her work as chair of the Greenwich House finance committee was beginning. That year she had been appointed lecturer in sociology at Barnard and had taken over Giddings's popular course on the family. Her son John was born at 10:09 P.M. on 15 August 1903 after a day's labor. A month later her translation of Tarde, with an introduction by Franklin Giddings, was published. By the beginning of November, she was back at work at Barnard, organizing finance for a social hall at Greenwich House, helping Mary with her children, and continuing with her work as treasurer of the College Settlements Association and chair of its fellowship committee. "You and Mrs Simkhovitch should be written up in vindication of the essential womanhood of the intellectual woman," Katharine Coman wrote when Elsie missed the College Settlement's October meeting, due to what Coman called the "superior claims of your son."[24]

As Elsie points out in "Little Essays in Lifting Taboo," which she began sketching out in 1904, women like herself and Mary had to overcome a number of sexual taboos in order to carry on their work while pregnant and nursing. "Pregnancy is still thought of among us as a matter to be ignored. The pregnant woman at any rate in the latter half of pregnancy is more or less expected to live in retirement. She is particularly bound 'for the sake of decency' to avoid gatherings of young people. This pregnancy taboo is both hurtful to the pride and a serious handicap to the productive activity of child-bearing women. It may lengthen the period of her incapacity to work from a natural period of one or two months to a conventional period of six or eight months." "There is a like although much slighter taboo upon lactation," she adds. "Moderate work is not injurious to suckling; but the nursing mother cannot perform this function well if she is under the strain of accommodating her nursing to her work. Her work must be accommodated to her nursing, and this means that provision must be made for nursing at convenient times and places in connection with her work. This provision will never be made as long as a lactation taboo persists."[25]

Recreating Elsie's early married life in his 1926 novel *Chimes,* Robert Herrick pictures her as a determined and self-assured young woman, untouched by public opinion. Stylishly dressed, she was tall and delicately molded, with small firm features, a very definite chin, a slightly ironical droop to the upper lip, and tiny, exquisite hands. One of the new social scientists with a brilliant and controversial Ph.D. (which Elsie's was not), everything about her was experimental. Self-contained and coolly observant, she went quietly and determinedly her own way, much to the interest of the university community. As her children were born, she "fulfilled the orthodox roles of wife and mother acceptably." "Exquisitely dainty, feminine in person," she never paraded her maternity, but never forgot the obligation.

"She refused to be classified, identified, submerged in any function, maternal, matrimonial, or professional," Herrick's hero notes with fascination of this "experimental" young scholar and mother. "Her cool aloofness of attitude seemed to say, 'Yes, I happen to be a woman, and I hope an attractive one. I am married and a mother—but what of it? I am more than all that—I am myself, free in spirit to undertake any engagement that I may happen to choose.' No formula, rule, prescription made by others should hem in her life."[26]

Talking about Sex

But Elsie's new life as a wife and mother did not go as smoothly as her fictional counterpart's. During those busy years of work and childbearing, Herbert became increasingly involved in New York's political life. He served as alderman from the Twenty-fifth Assembly District from 1899 to 1903, and from 1901 until April 1903, when he was ousted by Tammany supporters, he was chairman of the Board of Aldermen's finance committee. From 1902 he was Republican leader of his district. In October 1904, after much heartsearching, he accepted nomination as candidate for the Thirteenth Congressional District and the following month was elected to Congress as the representative of a heterogeneous constituency forming a narrow strip on either side of Fifth Avenue from Ninety-third Street to Greenwich Village. Although Elsie supported Herbert's political aspirations wholeheartedly, she became seriously ill during the last weeks of the campaign, indicating, perhaps, her apprehension at the major changes his election would make in her life. Mary Simkhovitch understood what Herbert's success meant to their work and friendship. "The fact that Herbert got elected (I prayed for his defeat!) and that means I suppose Washington for you has made me unhappy," she wrote Elsie in November 1904, inarticulate in her distress. "I don't want you to go to Washington. I don't want you to be ill. The fact is I love you."[27]

The move to Washington, which did not finally take place until late 1905, was not wholly unwelcome to Elsie. She saw Herbert's election as an opportunity to break her links with the settlement movement, to widen her experience and audience, and to take up controversial issues that did not fit well with the institutional constraints of the settlement and the university. Tarde considered mass communications and face-to-face talk the most important ways of encouraging and spreading innovation. Without giving up her scholarly work, Elsie now envisaged a much more outspoken role for herself as a "public" intellectual, using journals of social comment and Washington conversation as forums for new ideas. From late 1904 she began to ask more searchingly and publicly the question Edith Wharton posed in the *House of Mirth* the following year— how can women find a "republic of the spirit"?[28]

Robert Herrick claims starkly in *Chimes* that the "vague emotional basis" of applied sociology lost validity for his heroine as she became more absorbed in her scientific work. But Elsie's move from social reformer to professional ethnographer and public intellectual was more complicated than that. Since 1904 she had been working on a college textbook on the family, based on the Barnard course she taught from 1902 to 1905. *The Family,* published in 1906, reveals the degree to which this course immersed her in the burgeoning comparative ethnographic and psychological literature on the family and sexuality. It is clear that she eagerly embraced this scholarship's new message of cultural relativity, recognizing that it gave scientific validity to her own rebellions against conventional ideas of the family. In the book's carefully prepared lecture guides, Elsie suggests the sort of comparison between so-called primitive peoples and New York society that became the trademark of her popular writing: the "coming out party" as an initiation ceremony;

the conditions and authority under which infanticide and feticide are permitted; animistic notions in modern society concerning pregnancy, birth, and child-rearing; wife "guarding" in modern society; actions by married women that are considered "improper" or "indiscreet."[29]

In an extension of the systematic observation of tenement house families she initiated in 1899, Elsie required her students to study a community from a list that included the people of the United States, modern French, and Anglo-Saxons alongside the natives of Australia, Slave and Gold Coast Africa, and ancient Babylonians. And in her final chapter, she posed the questions that would preoccupy her over the next ten years: "Is the religious sanction (1) necessary, (2) desirable in social education?" "Outline a program for the instruction of adolescents in sex hygiene and morality." "Make a study of prevailing public opinion and of practice in regard to the preclusion of the unfit from parentage." "Analyse in different industries and professions present inadequacies of conditions imposed on women workers, and recommend readjustments making labour conditions compatible with healthy child-bearing and rearing."[30]

Sometime in 1904, as she started to prepare her textbook and Herbert campaigned for Congress, Elsie began to consider these and other related questions systematically in the sort of ethnography of everyday modern life she suggested to her students. When she made preparatory visits to Washington early in 1905 and accompanied Herbert on an official visit to the Philippines, China, and Japan that summer, she made careful notes of her observations, which she planned to publish as "Memoirs of Washington & Outlying Provinces: By a Political Wife." Systematically observing and critiquing the sexual conventions of her family and class, and the institutions in which they were embedded, Elsie decided that the area of women's lives most urgently in need of change was the "tabooed" area of sexuality. As she looked back at her family's hostility to her flouting of conventional sex roles, her students' fieldwork in New York's tenements, and Mary's experiences with Friendly Aid House, and observed her own social set in New York and Washington, she was convinced that sexual mores were more impervious to innovation than any other area of social life. Without major changes in sexual beliefs and practices, she concluded, little change in women's economic situation was possible.[31]

In a series of hard-hitting articles in the settlement journal, *Charities and the Commons,* and the sociologically oriented *Independent* during 1905 and 1906, Elsie argued that the well-to-do family and the women's college left young women unprepared for the actual conditions of modern life—the family because it remained enmeshed in outmoded conventions, the women's college because it failed to develop appropriate curricula to prepare its privileged students for useful lives. The settlement house—one of the few places where these young women could find employment—suffered from their blinkered education and restricted alternatives. Consequently, she argued, settlement workers tended in practice to replace local institutions and to legislate for community members, destroying in the process the personal, family, and local initiatives settlements were designed to foster.[32]

The basic problem for all of these institutions, in Elsie's opinion, was that they refused to come to grips with the problem that was central to women's lack of autonomy and individuality—sex relations. Elsie never lost sight of class inequality and the importance of women's access to work, for both personal development and economic independence; but from 1905 she focused on the conventions surrounding sex relations, particularly among middle-class women and men, as the crucial arena in which the battle for equality had to be fought. With the establishment of the Socialist Party in 1900, its support among some of the younger members of the privileged classes, and the organization of the Women's Trade Union League in 1903, women could talk about work and economic exploitation; but the topics of sex and sexual oppression, especially among those women who appeared to be materially well-off, were unacceptable. "Long after the problem of economic monopoly will have been solved the question of human monopoly will continue to harry us," she argued.[33]

Elsie castigated both home and college for their failure to challenge sex taboos in economic life and to prepare women for what she called democratic sexual relations and childbearing. Attacking the New York Board of Education's attempt to outlaw married women teachers as "mere Rip Van Winkleism," she argued that the community should instead be studying the conditions under which women can work best. This involved facing up to questions of sexuality and childbearing from both a practical and an ideological point of view. As a student of Tarde, Elsie was most interested in the question of ideology. What changes in popular sentiment are necessary, she asked, to make sexual life, including childbearing and breastfeeding, socially compatible with a public, productive life for women? Elsie's answer was quite unequivocal: a lifting of the taboo on sexuality. Without frank discussion and acceptance of the moral and physical aspects of sex relations, she argued, girls develop a general hostility toward marriage and sexuality as personally confining and physically unaesthetic. The retirement of the pregnant woman from social life, the taboo on the nursing mother, and the ban on discussion of contraception were all, in her opinion, serious handicaps to the useful activity of childbearing women and to the development of more democratic relations between men and women.[34]

Current discussion of sexual morality, in Elsie's opinion, was insincere, fallacious, and unenlightening. Taking up three widely discussed aspects of sexuality, she asked: Why characterize prostitution as a "necessary evil" without discussing frankly the reasons it is "necessary" or the consequences if it is "evil"? Why condemn divorce without discussing the social and economic causes of marital incompatibility? Why express horror of "race-suicide" without acknowledging that girls' ignorance of sex and maternity, the widespread resort to prostitution, and the overcultivation of the leisure-class wife are factors that need to be discussed?[35]

The Family, published in November 1906, was conceived by Elsie as her contribution to sex education and to thinking through these questions of sex morality. As her subtitle announced, the book was *An Ethnographical and Historical Outline, with Descriptive Notes, planned as a Text-book for the use of College Lecturers and Directors of Home-Reading Clubs*. Although relentlessly scholarly and empirical, Elsie pulled no punches in the information she provided for her college students and women's clubs. As a reviewer in the British *Athenaeum* put it disapprovingly, "Girls and boys of this age are to be 'enlightened' in all the matters of marriage and parenthood [ranging from] the function of *atna-ariltha-kuma* or the *piraungaru* relation (we take refuge behind the decent obscurity of the Australian terms) to the effects of the 'continental system' of State-regulated prostitution"; and the list of references Elsie provided included "strong" and "highly-flavored" material that British authorities labeled as "not suitable for the general lay reader."[36]

Although this reviewer begged that "the *jeune fille* be spared," Elsie was deliberately countering what she considered dangerous misinformation about alternative sexual and gender practices currently being disseminated through religious-based college courses and women's reading groups. Religion was, in Elsie's opinion, one of the main enemies of open discussion, because it "fosters the state of mind which is intolerant of innovation and respectful of whatever is traditional or authoritative." *The Family* was intended as an alternative to the study guides—so popular among women's groups—based on accounts by female missionaries that contrasted the privileged and protected position of American women and the superiority of the American family with the benighted situation of women in the Philippines, China, or Turkey. Indeed, *The Family* constituted a strong rebuttal of such religious views of family and sexual matters. But, more important, Elsie set out clearly and courageously, in the book's final chapter, her own recipe for an ethically responsible family.[37]

The ethically responsible family—a family capable of preparing a child for a changing world and fostering its capacity for individual choice—is one that encourages women's full development, she argued. Christianity's condemnation of sexual desire, in her opinion, was "a grave obstacle" to this development. Formulating a new ethics for the family that took into account women's needs and the value of sexual expression, Elsie contended that monogamy and conjugal equality were desirable, not because they are morally right, but because they allowed the development of complex, independent personalities fit to educate children. The importance of monogamy and reciprocal rights and duties in this pragmatic family ethics gave a new significance to sexual choice, which should be made, she argued, only by the relatively mature. The necessity for late marriage led in turn to the question of premarital sex. Given that the age-old solution of prostitution was as incompatible with modern democracy as slavery, there were only two alternatives: absolute chastity of both sexes until marriage or toleration of sexual intercourse on the part of the unmarried of both sexes. In the new family ethics, sexual intercourse would be disapproved of only if it was detrimental to the health or emotional or intellectual activities of either partner. As monogamous relations were most conducive, in Elsie's opinion, to emotional and intellectual development and health, it would be sensible, she concluded, to encourage what she called early trial marriage. Such a relationship should be entered into with a view to permanency, she suggested, but with the possibility of divorce without public condemnation if it proved unsuccessful and if there were no children. The development of such a new morality depended, she pointed out, on "the outcome of present experiments in economic independence for women," on "revelations of physiological science

. . . through the discovery of certain and innocuous methods of preventing conception," and on "a more enlightened and purposive approach to parenthood." With the need for sexual restraint largely gone, the possibility of quite different relations between the sexes should emerge, she concluded.[38]

A Revolutionary and Indecent Performance

By late 1906, when *The Family* was published, Elsie had good reason to focus her attention on the problem of sexuality for women. In the summer of 1905, she conceived just as she and Herbert were leaving with the congressional delegation to the Philippines, Japan, and China. She was never well during that pregnancy, and the baby died two weeks after it was born in April 1906. Although she considered herself knowledgeable about birth control and had access to the "best" medical advice, she was pregnant again within six weeks. Then, just as she was recovering from the loss of her baby and reconciling herself to the new pregnancy, her beloved Stanford White was shot dead by the husband of a former lover, and ugly stories of his extramarital sexual activities were revealed to a salacious public. Before this terrible summer was over, her friend Katharine Dexter became involved in a tragedy of major proportions which illustrated starkly the consequences of sexual repression and reticence.[39]

In 1903 Katharine met Stanley McCormick, the youngest of the brothers who controlled the International Harvester Corporation in Chicago. After a troubled courtship, they married in 1904. When Katharine was preparing to enter graduate school during the summer of 1906, Stanley began to display acute signs of mental instability. In October he had to be hospitalized. He never recovered, and his care became a source of contention between Katharine and his sister, Anita McCormick Blaine, until his death in 1947.

The source of Stanley's problems was not clear. He was a sensitive and artistic young man who suffered more than usual guilt about his family's wealth and battled to introduce his socialist ideas into the family business. But an important component of his breakdown was sexual. He was the youngest child of aging business magnate Cyrus McCormick, who died when Stanley was ten years old, and his much younger wife. Nettie Fowler McCormick was rigid, devout, and puritanical, bringing Stanley up never to touch his body or to allow anyone to see him naked. At the same time, she left much of his upbringing to nurses and to his older sister, Anita. When he returned from Princeton, he was the only child living at home with his mother, who supervised his social life and morals with a vigilant eye. In the numerous analyses of Stanley's condition after his breakdown, it emerged that he was so troubled by his practice of masturbation that he had rigged up a harness to prevent his hands from touching his genitals while sleeping; that he had been seduced by his nurse as a child; that he was strongly sexually attracted to his sister; and that, burdened by this load of Victorian guilt and self-loathing, he had been unable to consummate his marriage with Katharine.[40]

The most influential discussion of sexuality in 1906 was the phenomenally successful *Adolescence* by psychologist G. Stanley Hall. As the sprawling length of his book suggests, Hall thought that sex education was essential. But he saw sexuality as a dangerous force that was not justified as an end in itself. Hall's rhetoric in extolling the virtues of (marital) sexual intercourse needs to be quoted at length to appreciate the obfuscatory language used by this ardent advocate of sex education:

> Every gemmule is mobilized and the sacred hour of heredity normally comes when adolescence is complete in wedlock and the cerebro-spinal rings up the sympathetic system, and this hands over the reins to the biophores and germ cells, which now assert their dominance over those of the soma. In the most unitary of all acts, which is the epitome and pleroma of life, we have the most intense of all affirmations of the will to live and realize that the only true God is love, and the center of life is worship. Every part of mind and body participates in a true pangenesis. This sacrament is the annunciation hour, with hosannas which the whole world reflects. Communion is fusion and beatitude. It is the supreme hedonic narcosis, a holy intoxication, the chief ecstacy, because the most intense of experiences; it is the very heart of psychology, and because it is the supreme pleasure of life it is the eternal basis and guarantee of optimism. It is this experience more than any other that opens to man the ideal world. Now the race is incarnated in the individual and remembers its lost paradise.[41]

Given this tortured mixture of "science" and morality, it is clear that, in speaking out with even guarded frankness and clarity on sexuality, Parsons was treading on dangerous ground. This was the province of anarchists and freethinkers, not of wives of congressmen. As recently as 1900, sex reformer Ida Craddock had committed suicide rather than face another prison sentence for the publication of her pamphlet *Wedding Night,* and Moses Harman, editor of the long-running anarchist newspaper *Lucifer, the Light-Bearer,* had been jailed in 1905 for his pamphlet *The Right to Be Born Well.* In 1905 Anthony Comstock, the reformer who had fervently guarded the purity of the nation since 1873, had attempted to prevent the staging of Shaw's *Mrs. Warren's Profession* in New York and had arrested *Physical Culture* editor Bernarr Macfadden for promoting a "mammoth physical exhibition" with "obscene" photographs of young men and women. In the summer of 1906, there was an uproar over the arrest of a nineteen-year-old bookkeeper at the offices of the Art Students League, who was held responsible for the mailing of a pamphlet advertising the study of nudes.[42]

By 1906, however, the tide was turning on "comstockery," as George Bernard Shaw called it. As middle-class liberals rallied in defense of civil liberties in the wake of federal laws banning the entry of anarchists to the United States and a drive to ban radical newspapers and magazines from the mails, issues of free speech, political freedom, and sexual freedom became inextricably linked. Emma Goldman, notorious for her connection with Alexander Berkman's assassination attempt on business magnate Henry Clay Frick, began to lecture publicly on sexuality, and her journal *Mother Earth* became a forum for discussion of sexual emancipation from its first edition in March 1906.[43]

Given the heated nature of the discussions of free speech and sexuality at the time and their association with the most radical elements in the society, it is not surprising that Elsie found it difficult to publish many of her articles, even in censored form, and that *The Family* was greeted in many quarters with horror. On the day of its publication in November 1906, the *New York Herald* declared that "no more radical declaration from the pen of an author relating to matrimony has been published," and the *Evening Sun* descended immediately to personal attack: "The spread of divorce is turning many marriages into something of the sort our New York philosopher advocates," a reporter wrote. "Especially is this true among the author's circle of friends." (Elsie's brother Henry had married a divorcée in 1902 to the accompaniment of much newspaper comment.) The *New York Herald* returned to the attack next day, condemning the book's ethics as "the morality of the barnyard" and expressing alarm that "a woman of education and social position should have taken it upon herself to assist in knocking down the bars that are falling down enough as it is." The *Sun* agreed: "This is the most revolutionary and indecent performance of anything I have ever heard. I cannot understand why a woman in her position expressed such ideas." The *New York Daily Tribune* protested that "The idea of men and women living like animals, separating at will and contracting new alliances . . . is barbarism and nothing else." The *New York Herald* attacked again, referring to the book as "Absurd, pretentious, diabolical. I cannot see how a woman of her prominence could give utterance to such strange and impossible theories. They strike at home and hence the State." Meanwhile, a steady stream of newspapermen besieged Herbert outside their Washington home. "If my wife were to advocate such principles as does Congressman Parsons' wife, she would have to choose another place to live pretty quickly," the *World*'s reporter declared. Within three days, the book was the subject of discussion in the City Court, where it was pleaded as defense in a seduction case. "Miserable and impracticable as the book is," the judge pronounced, "its scheme of moral laxity does not cover a criminal of your stripe. There is no book that has ever been written which excused a man from ruining the life of a young girl." After two prominent clergymen condemned the book from their pulpits at Thanksgiving, the *New York Daily Tribune* again lambasted its "disgusting theory," wondering if the author would advocate trial marriage to her own daughter.[44]

By writing about sexuality, Elsie was quite deliberately linking the issue of women's emancipation with the dangerous cause of free speech. In the preface to her projected, but never published, "Little Essays in Lifting Taboo," written sometime in 1906, she emphasized the importance of new concepts for opening up new ways of thinking. The Polynesian word *tapu* was particularly useful for naming, and therefore recognizing and lifting, the modern taboos of sex and women's work, she noted. The rapid social transitions taking place in these areas were not, in her opinion, being dealt with rationally and purposefully. But women must think clearly about these changes if they are to take control of their lives. "How much longer can misinterpretations of social facts lurk in the medieval corners of our minds?" she asked. "Sociology, the youngest of the sciences, is also the last to have its truths become commonplaces."

Defending herself against the accusation that no "decent" woman would publicly discuss sex, she argued that no one else could successfully carry out the task of improving attitudes to sexuality. "Men merely because they are men, live or are reputed to live too firmly encased in glass houses to lead in the stone-throwing." The unmarried, the divorced, the unhappily married, and the childless woman was also handicapped in such a discussion. To disarm criticism *ad feminam,* Elsie pointed out in a dictum she followed throughout her life, women who were particularly well off in life should be the first to come forward, especially if, like herself, they were familiar with very different cultures or had directly observed different economic or cultural classes in their own society.[45]

Other champions of free speech immediately recognized an influential ally. Theodore Schroeder, a lawyer involved in the Free Speech Leagues and one of New York's leading opponents of the Comstock laws, contacted Elsie soon after the publication of her article "Penalizing Marriage and Child-Bearing" in January 1906. "From your writings and translations I know you to be of that earnest and unsuperficial class, of which I meet so few," he wrote, inviting her to speak to the Brooklyn Philosophical Association. Then eight months pregnant, Parsons did not accept Schroeder's invitation, but he remained an important associate over the next ten years. He immediately came to her defense after what he called the "hysterical uproar" over *The Family.* In a long review in *Arena,* he mocked "the unconscious humor of the morals snobs" responsible for the outcry against her, by quoting some of the clergy and women's leaders who found her book blasphemous, destructive, disgraceful, "an instrument of evil," "perfectly beastly," idiotic, impracticable, indelicate, and "an advocacy of the most unbridled licence." "After reading a few columns of such righteous vituperation," he wrote, "I began to suspect that a good book had been written."

Mrs. Parsons, Schroeder said approvingly, is a woman who thinks. She has pursued the scientific and not the theologic method, and therein lies her sole offense. "I cannot better recommend the book to the serious student of sociology, than to quote a few of the offending passages which will exhibit her rigid adherence to the scientific method and viewpoint and at the same time exhibit the utter absence of these in her clerical critics." After summarizing Elsie's discussions of sex taboos, polygamy, sexual choice, divorce, prostitution, and trial marriage, Schroeder concluded, "It must be apparent to all thinkers that instead of being an argument for 'unbridled licence' or an 'instrument of evil' or 'beastly' or 'indelicate' or 'idiotic,' it is a very sane, healthy-minded, frank and scientific advocacy of a monogamy far more constant and wholesome than we now have."[46]

Schroeder's support and the highly favorable reviews Elsie received from the liberal scientific community were not enough to rescue her from depression, however. She was shocked by the virulence of her critics and deeply worried by the possible effect of her notoriety on Herbert's career. The loss of her much-desired baby early in February 1907, less than a year after her previous baby had died, was a bitter blow. As if this was not enough, two months after her February confinement she was again pregnant. "Somewhat farcical, isn't it?" she wrote Herbert, "Of course it wouldn't have happened had I not depended on Swift's [her obstetrician's] assurances." "Don't consider yourself at all responsible, for you were not in the least," she scrawled in a postscript. Although she faced the prospect of the pregnancy bravely, she was in no state to carry the baby successfully to term, and the pregnancy appears to have been terminated. By mid-June 1907 she was again menstruating, but she felt "pretty seedy" and found it "hard to get back to thoroughgoing work habits": "I have so many 'fear-thoughts,' first one & then another," she wrote Herbert.[47]

PART TWO

We Secessionists . . .

> East were the
> Dead kings and the remembered sepulchres:
> West was the grass.

—Archibald MacLeish, "America Was Promises," 1939

Elsie setting out from Pajarito Ranch, New Mexico, September 1912.
Parsons Family Papers, Rye Historical Society.

CHAPTER FOUR

The Voyage Out

WEAKENED physically and mentally by continuing reproductive problems, and silenced by concern for Herbert's congressional career and the social obligations it imposed on her, Elsie wrote almost nothing between 1907 and 1912. But throughout this difficult period, as she began to question the success of her "experimental" marriage, she strenuously resisted her decline in physical, mental, and moral strength. Attempting to combat her obsessive "fear-thoughts," she found particularly helpful William James's 1906 presidential address to the American Philosophical Association, which she read soon after her baby died in February 1907. Drawing on the doctrine of action formulated by the young Italian pragmatist and later Futurist Giovanni Papini, James asked the question that haunted Elsie over the next few years: How can we break down "the barriers which life's routine [has] concreted round the deeper strata of the will?" We are all victims of habit-neurosis, he argued, and the line between the "normal" and the "morbid" is thin: "The human individual lives usually far within his limits; he possesses powers of various sorts which he habitually fails to use. He energizes below his maximum, and he behaves below his optimum. In elementary faculty, in coordination, in power of inhibition and control, in every conceivable way, his life is contracted like the field of vision of an hysteric subject—but with less excuse, for the poor hysteric is diseased, while in the rest of us it is only an inveterate *habit*—the habit of inferiority to our full self—that is bad." James's recipe for breaking out of this "psychasthenia" and bringing "unused energies into action" was thoroughly modernist: through deliberate exposure to excitements, to new ideas, and to mental and physical challenges.[1]

Arduous Travel and Challenging Work

During the stressful Washington years, which ended in 1911 after Herbert's electoral defeat in November 1910, Elsie took James's advice to heart. She had always found outdoor activity liberating mentally and socially. Over the next few years, she increasingly undertook arduous and exciting trips as a means of combating depression, lethargy, and despair about her marriage. At first she tried to interest Herbert in the out-of-the-way travel she craved. Within two weeks of the baby's death in 1907, she and Herbert were discussing ideas for a trip, to be taken in conjunction with his work, either to Puerto Rico and Cuba or to the western United States. "A trip now would help me out quite a little as I shall have to get in a stock of cheerfulness and serenity for what is ahead again," she wrote in April when she realized she was once more pregnant. "My chief foe under these circumstances is the middle age state of mind and a jaunt militates against that."[2]

When that pregnancy was terminated, leaving her low in mind and body, a retreat to the outdoor life of Newport brought back her old sense of exhilaration. During the 1907 summer, Elsie accompanied Herbert on part of an official trip to Chicago, Minneapolis, and Banff, eagerly reading up on the native populations of the area in the newly published *Handbook of the North American Indians*. Back in Lenox, she found she could return to regular work and exercise. She appears to have missed a period again during the trip, as she often did when she was traveling; but a few weeks later she reported to Herbert, "Menstruation set in without any pain yesterday."[3]

The tonic effect of the trip with Herbert was only temporary, however, and by the middle of 1908 Elsie was suffering under Washington's "sacrificial" and conservative social life and the threat of another pregnancy. Herbert was too busy to accompany her to the Adirondacks, but she found six weeks there invigorating and instructive. Alone at first, she made a new and admiring friend in the young Reginald Fitz, who galvanized her into doing "all sorts of young things." Katharine Dexter McCormick joined her later, having finally accepted that Stanley would be permanently confined under care at his Santa Barbara estate. Katharine was a vigorous athlete who rode astride and knew how to get the most out of life, despite the tragedy of her marriage. Together they swam "au naturel," tramped "undiscovered country" with enthusiasm, and they both looked to the future with optimism. "I have been inviting my soul, taking stock of spiritualities," Elsie wrote Herbert. This Adirondacks adventure set a pattern for the future, in which Elsie enjoyed demanding trips alone or with a variety of male and female friends.[4]

While she was in the Adirondacks, Elsie declined an invitation to discuss the current controversy over birth control with Teddy Roosevelt, whose conservatism on family issues she had come to despise. "I have almost forgotten up here that I have views," she wrote Herbert, "which of course is an excellent thing." She had been a public advocate since 1906 of a new type of family life based on the availability of birth control, and her own experience of the results of inadequate and faulty knowledge gave her very definite ideas on the issues surrounding the diminishing birthrate that were "too drastic for the President." At the end of 1908, fortified by the spiritual and physical stocktaking of the Adirondacks trip, Elsie attempted to pick up the threads of her sociological work and present her considered views in the new, professional forum provided by the American Sociological Society.[5]

Organized in 1905, the American Sociological Society was an eclectic mixture of college and university teachers, applied sociologists such as Jane Addams, Edward Devine, and Charlotte Perkins Gilman, and propagandists such as Gaylord Wilshire, the millionaire editor of the socialist *Wilshire's Magazine,* and Edwin C. Walker, editor of the free-thought journal the *Truth Seeker* and president of the Manhattan Liberal Club. Elsie does not appear to have been involved in the society during its formative years—no doubt because of her continual pregnancies.[6]

Elsie attended the sociology meetings in Atlantic City in December 1908 at the invitation of Washington sociologist George Veditz, who asked her to reply to two papers on the impact on the family of women's higher education and nondomestic work. She used the occasion to make a carefully argued, witty, and devastating attack on the panic-mongers, like Roosevelt, who accused educated women of neglecting their duty to produce children. She also took the opportunity to turn the question around and comment informally on the psychological importance of regular nonfamily work for mothers. Among Elsie's papers is a set of remarks made during this discussion: "At the risk of incurring the very criticism I am making, I hazard a personal experience; for, after all, personal testimony is at times more telling than any other argument. Last year my two days old baby died. I am convinced that had I not been able during convalescence under these trying circumstances to think & write at

Lissa (second from left) and John (third from right) dressed for a children's party at the Rocks, Newport, 1908. The only concession to Elsie's taste is their sandals. Elsie Clews Parsons Papers, American Philosophical Society Library.

first for a few minutes each day & then for a few hours about a scientific subject in which I had been much interested, return to a happy & normal life would have been slower. My interest & habit of thought dated from college days. If people but realize it, there are more circumstances in the average woman's life, even in the life of the happiest & most protected women, that need the solace of an impersonal point of view than there are in men's lives."[7]

"My Atlantic City trip was a success," she wrote Herbert. "I enjoyed meeting with my kind, my little paper took well and didn't get into the papers." She talked with William Sumner, the society's president, and sat with his wife through his "tiresome and fairly unscholarly address." She attended the Economic Society's dinner as Franklin Giddings's guest, where he and up-and-coming sociologist Edward Ross told "strong" jokes and Charlotte Perkins Gilman juggled place cards to sit next to her. She walked on the beach with reformer Robert Hunter and dined with Ross, who had just published a book on social psychology, and she listened to papers by Prince Morrow on venereal disease and by Edward Devine on "a remarkable Pittsburgh social survey they have been making."[8]

Jealousy

Elsie's return to health and intellectual productivity was short-lived. In January 1909 she was pregnant once more; and during this pregnancy, whose outcome she awaited anxiously, a major crisis developed which eventually forced her to confront basic problems in her marriage. During the 1908 summer, Elsie and Herbert had become friendly with Huntington Wilson, a State Department official, and his wife, Lucy. The following spring the two couples saw a lot of each other. In a fictionalized account, "The Imaginary Mistress," written in 1913, Elsie described the pleasures they enjoyed together that season. "Washingtonians alone of North Americans know how to celebrate the spring," she wrote. "We breakfasted at the Old Mill in Rock Creek Park; we canoed on the Canal; we motored to the Dower House and to the Great Falls, and we were all the time in the best of company." Lucy was a quiet, self-effacing woman, charmingly dressed and pretty, with a delightful caressing voice. Elsie began to realize that Herbert enjoyed Lucy's company more than her own.[9]

The Wilson marriage was not happy. Huntington was, in Elsie's opinion, "an insignificant little squirt," and Herbert spoke of the couple's "little spats." All was not well in the Parsons marriage either. On the infrequent weekends they spent together as Elsie's pregnancy advanced, Herbert was easily irritated by her faults. "I was very much ashamed of my behavior both on the way over & at Stockbridge. . . . Do forgive me. . . . It grieves me to have been so ungracious after so much happiness," he wrote typically after a weekend at Lenox that summer. Elsie, for her part, felt uncharacteristically dependent on Herbert's approval as she became more and more nervous about her pregnancy's outcome. "When you get put out or mad justifiably or unjustifiably (which merely means for things which I would or wouldn't be disturbed by) I feel utterly helpless, resourceless and 'low in my mind,'" she wrote him unhappily.[10]

Elsie spent the summer as usual in Lenox, Boston, and Newport. During the last two months of her pregnancy, she was at Newport, which Herbert detested, and he found few opportunities to join her. Alone in Washington, he saw the Wilsons nearly every day. Years later, after they had met again in London during the war, Lucy Wilson reminded Herbert in a long rambling letter of her happiness "the spring & summer of 1909 up to Lent 1910. I think that was the happiest time I had in the years 1904–1915." Meanwhile, Elsie read and reread Herbert's letters describing his Washington activities and brooded over their implications. "I would sit at times for three hours at a stretch making a show of reading or writing but really intent on a train of emotional speculation aroused by some phrase of the letter, some incident it related," she wrote in her later account. She found it particularly galling that Herbert shared activities with Lucy with a pleasure he did not enjoy with her. "Often I had found him passing on my suggestions to her, suggestions about places to walk in, pictures to see, sometimes a book I had given him, or even a newspaper cutting," her fictional counterpart wrote. Even more hurtful to Elsie, they discussed ideas in a way she and Herbert never had—their enjoyment, for instance, of a novel in which a wife sacrifices her lover for the sake of an empty marriage. "It was a vindication of the conventional ideas held by both Alice [Lucy] and Anson [Herbert] about marriage," the fictional Elsie wrote. "When I remarked to Anson that I thought it a stupid waste of two lives, he said he would have expected me to say that, that was just one of my peculiar ideas, an idea too immoral to discuss."[11]

Elsie, who had always prided herself on being independent and in control of her life, found herself in the grip of an obsessive jealousy which submerged her identity in that of her husband. The lively companionship of Katharine Dexter McCormick and Alice Duer Miller, both of whom were busy with the revitalized suffrage movement, helped her to get through that difficult summer. Alice and Harry Miller had returned penniless to New York in 1903 after their adventure in Central America, and Harry tried his luck on Wall Street while Alice taught mathematics at Barnard until she began to write full-time. In 1909, her novel *Less than Kin* was the first success in a sparkling career as a lightly satirical novelist, playwright, poet, newspaper columnist, and screenwriter. Elsie found Alice's combination of perceptiveness and detachment calming. "Alice and I had a most illuminating talk last night in the moonlight over jealousy and remorse, my speciality and yours," she wrote Herbert. "We agreed that in spite of the possibility of there being thin ice, interest in the other sex at large shakes you up out of any settled, sodden conjugality and was therefore desirable, a much weightier conclusion for me than for her, for like you, as a superior

Lissa and John swimming "au naturel," as Elsie preferred, with Herbert at Lenox, 1909. Elsie Clews Parsons Papers, American Philosophical Society Library.

type, she doesn't really know what jealousy is like, and can only see with her reason the advantages to the woman of a man's interest in other women. I see them just as clearly as she does—with my reason. The capacity for remorse [Herbert's speciality] she analyses as lack of foresight. One doesn't see at the time the position one is putting the other in. If one did realize it, one wouldn't have the face to go ahead & do it and be sorry for it afterwards."[12]

After the birth of Herbert Jr.—at last a healthy baby—in October 1909 and her return to Washington, Elsie could not escape the conviction that Herbert would be happier if he were married to someone like Lucy. Herbert, however, refused to discuss the question or to acknowledge his feelings for Lucy. Over the next two years, the issue simmered under the surface of their lives.[13]

Detachment

True to the example of Robert Louis Stevenson and the exhortations of William James, Elsie refused to allow her emotional and physical problems to overwhelm her. During the unhappy spring of 1909, when she was pregnant with Herbert Jr. and Herbert's admiration for Lucy Wilson was deepening, she sought alternative companions among her Washington and Newport friends. The adoration of the young Reginald Fitz in the Adirondacks in 1908 had reminded her that many people found her fascinating and stimulating precisely because of her "views" and not in spite of them. In Washington, Herbert's congressional colleague Andrew Peters became Elsie's admiring companion until he married in 1910. In the early months of her pregnancy, they enjoyed numerous excursions, "full of adventures, just as I like," she wrote Herbert. In June, when she and Peters met up again in Boston, Elsie enjoyed educating him to ignore her now obvious pregnant state. "I had written to him from Lenox that I was expecting. In Washington we had joked about a test that was ahead of him," Elsie wrote Herbert. "I really think that he will stand it & that he will be able to emancipate himself from the American prejudice & not believe with Gillett [another male friend] in compulsory isolation."[14]

In the spring of 1910, Elsie began to take walks, horseback rides, and canoe trips with George Young, a secretary at the British Embassy. She and Herbert had known and liked Young and his wife since 1908, and this attractive couple were part of the group who enjoyed the Washington spring together in 1909. The eldest son of a British baronet, and an authority on Ottoman law, George Young was in many ways Elsie's perfect counterpart—aristocratic, intelligent, and adventurous mentally and physically.[15]

George Young was in the early years of a brilliant but controversial career when he and Elsie met. His younger brother, the mountaineer Geoffrey Winthrop Young, described him as "independent of commonplace opinion or of convention in his every idea and action." With a "romantic individualism" aided by a "fanciful humour," he preserved to the end of his long life "an unusual mental and physical agility, an eager pursuit of the unknown through the realms of history and of thought, and a never-failing generosity of purpose and motive."[16]

This singular young diplomat-scholar found Elsie the most interesting woman in Washington. We can catch a glimpse of the woman he admired through the conservative Southern eyes of one of Taft's gossipy military aides, at a lunch in May 1909 also attended by Young. "Mrs. Parsons, who is the daughter of Henry Clews, is a Southerner by birth, I think," he wrote inaccurately, "but holds the most extraordinary views, even were she a New Englander." George Young was more appreciative of the unusual Mrs. Parsons, whom he teasingly called "Missessie" in reference to her attenuated Southern roots; and during her unhappy 1909 spring they became firm friends. Like her he believed that "life isn't or oughtn't to be sliding along one groove and climbing one ladder." Young came from a family who made an art of conversation and debate, and he found Elsie a fascinating conversational partner. With Young she began to explore some of the ideas she could not share with Herbert. As he wrote when he read the fruit of these discussions in her witty and controversial 1912 book, *The Old-Fashioned Woman*, "The book is good reading—but nothing like so good as you talking about the same things would be."[17]

The combination of adventure and intellect that George Young represented was fascinating to Elsie, and they embarked on a friendship which he remembered for "the breath of pine woods" and "the Shenandoah and those wild rivers." In Young, Parsons found the perfect companion for the sort of adventures she loved. Like Alice Miller, he had a great capacity for both enjoyment and silence, though he loved to talk too when the time was right.[18]

"George Young met us & we trolleyed out to Great Falls," Elsie wrote Herbert in May 1911, when she was five months into her final pregnancy. "From there canoed in a large canoe . . . across the river to the canal boat waiting for us. The three hours on it were entrancing. The quiet slipping thro' the water,—no noise, vibration, dirt,—the loveliness of the vegetation—judas & dogwood perfect, violets, azaleas, wild flax etc. the curves of the canal & glimpses of the river, the lights, were a combination of sheer joy & loveliness. . . . We walked in today to Cabin John, I getting a long haul on a canal boat." From the Potomac, Elsie and Young moved on to the marshlands of the Atlantic coast and the delights of canoe camping, where she learned skills that stood her in good stead for the rest of her life. According to Robert Herrick's fictionalized account twenty years later, "She was at her best in a canoe and knew it. It was amazing what strength her slim arms possessed and what slow tenacity she had when the canoe was caught in an eddy or a swift rapid."[19]

When George Young returned to England in 1912, he wrote nostalgically of their relationship, "I sometimes feel as though youth and I had finally parted company somewhere in the Blue Mountains or on the green Shenandoah." But his companionship between 1910 and 1912 rejuvenated Elsie and helped her to take positive steps to redirect her life. "Conjugal detachment is really necessary to conjugal attachment," she concluded in a letter to Herbert in June 1910, following one of her periodic outbursts of jealousy. During that summer in Newport, she established a disciplined system for herself and the children, now aged nine, seven, and nine months, by "bullying the whole household most painfully," and by swimming, sailing, and cycling regularly. Feeling robust in character and body, she embarked on a trip to the American Southwest that would prove to be a turning point in her life.[20]

The Southwest

Elsie's introduction to the Southwest in the summer of 1910 was due, as she put it in a later account, to "the accident of the forester." Herbert, as a member of the Committee on Public Lands, was taking a trip to the Southwest with a forestry official. Elsie wanted to accompany them, but the official resisted this mixing of business and pleasure. Armed with a new sense of self-sufficiency and adventure, she decided to visit the cliff houses of New Mexico alone before meeting up with Herbert at the Grand Canyon. She arrived in Santa Fe early in August, intending to see the country from horseback, in the George Young style. Infuriated by the conventional reception she received from Department of Interior officials from whom she sought guidance ("the country was very rough indeed," "you couldn't ride in the West as you did in the East," "the sun was too hot"), she took the train to nearby Española.

On the train, she met a woman who knew and loved the area. This was Clara True, rancher, horse-trader, former schoolteacher for the Indian Bureau, and deputy excise commissioner. True invited Elsie to spend the night at her ranch, and within a few minutes the two women alighted at Clara True's railroad siding. Miss True lived with her mother and a friend—"a New Englander tempered by California"—on an apple orchard they had restored on the Rio Grande in the shadow of the Pajarito plateau north of Santa Fe. She was, according to Elsie, the first woman to be elected to the irrigation committee of the valley, and the first to run a ranch with

Indian employees only. She felt ill at ease with white men, and she liked women to whom she could play the man. "She was in short a feminist of the militant type," Elsie concluded in the terms that were just becoming current, "although she did not know it. She was rather against woman suffrage than for it; of my habits of smoking and of wearing breeches she much disapproved."[21]

With Clara True's cool adobe ranch as a base, Elsie explored the area on horseback, testing her new skill of riding astride, with Pedro Baca, a Pueblo from nearby Santa Clara, as a guide. They rode across the valley, scrambled up the canyon, and made their way across the plateau to the ruins at Puyé. They camped in one of the many cliff dwellings carved out of the soft tufa cliffs below the great stretches of mesa. Elsie was immediately captivated by the area's wild beauty, which had something of the quality she loved in Newport, and later in Maine. That night she "looked out . . . on the moonlit talus below and the pines beyond and thought that whether Indian or White one was fortunate indeed to live for a time in a world of such beauty."

The country also engaged her intellectually. Digging in the ruins, she was intrigued by signs of recent ceremonial use, which Pedro Baca was reluctant to explain. "One thing at least I have learned on this trip," she thought as they rode back to the ranch, "what interests me most. Not the artifacts we've dug up or the construction of that chamber or the contents of that wall niche or even the impressions of a woman's hand on the plaster of that northern wall, none of these, but the comment of Santiago [Pedro Baca], more particularly his unspoken comment. I am more curious about what he would not tell me and why he would not tell than about any particular of the excavation. If ever I come to work seriously in this country, I suspect it will not be as archeologist, but as a student of the culture of today. It is interesting to reconstruct the culture of the ancient town builders, but it is still more interesting to study the minds and ways of their descendants."

Elsie's interest in the culture and social organization of Pedro Baca's people was further piqued when he called on her with his wife, who presented her with a bowl she had made of the striking polished black ware which is characteristic of the Santa Clara potters. And she was just as intrigued by the evidence of cultural adaptation to the tourist market she saw in the fake rain gods manufactured in the pueblos of San Ildefonso and Tesuque during another ride over the vivid red soil of hillocks and arroyo into Santa Fe.[22]

Ten days later she rode in the Grand Canyon "on a trail half way between rim and river, thirty miles to a cross canyon, to a waterfall and a bed of grass for the night." "What a night!" she wrote. "A full moon gave outline to those black masses of towering cliffs and pinnacles, and played on the ripples in the pool under the waterfall. It was hot, and between dozes I would leave my bed of grass to stand breast-high in the pool, where I could reach out & touch maiden hair fern and cardinal flower. After the aridity of what the stable boy from Idaho called the Devil's Half Acre, after the immensities of the incredible canyon, the freshness and intimacy of grass and pool were delicious beyond compare." After another night by the pool, she met Herbert at the rim. A week later in Yosemite, as if to mark the beginnings of her emotional separation from Herbert, she lost her wedding ring.[23]

After the freedom and exhilaration of her expeditions with George Young and her foray into the Southwest, Elsie's vacation with the more cautious Herbert demonstrated that they could not successfully travel together. Two years later, during a frank exchange of letters about their different ideas of companionship, Elsie spoke bitterly about this trip as being "painful for us both"; and Herbert acknowledged the truth of this, confessing that her "unconventional & to my mind insufficiently cautious proceedings prey on my mind in a way that I cannot disguise." The lesson of Yosemite was hammered home a few months later when Elsie joined Herbert at Lake Mohonk for a meeting with Roosevelt. Back in Lenox after a frustrating few days, Elsie wrote to Herbert angrily, though trying to keep a light tone: "I love your company always, except in motors and carriages perhaps, and everywhere, except in dressing rooms, certainly. I regret that two of the pleasantest things of the trip were done without you—the walks this morning and yesterday afternoon. Yesterday I struck down thro the woods, northwards. For half an hour I dozed on a ledge of rocks in the setting sun. Returning it was a most lovely prospect."[24]

Back in Washington, armed with a new sense of purpose and independence, Elsie began to prepare herself for fieldwork in anthropology. In a notebook labeled "American Ethnology SW," the page marked "Plans" included a list of things she needed to learn. Along with Spanish, cooking (which she tried but never managed), riding astride, and masonry, she noted: "Practice with pistol, with compass." Like cooking, she later found she could do without the pistol.

Throughout 1911 she read voraciously about the Southwest, established contact with the National Museum in Washington and the American Museum of Natural History in New York, and returned to an exhaustive survey she began in 1906 of anthropological accounts of the relationship between religion and sexual psychology. With Herbert in New York much of the time reestablishing his law practice after his November 1910 defeat, Elsie rode, canoed, walked, and camped with George Young, despite her new pregnancy.[25]

Setting Out

Following the birth of her third son, McIlvaine (Mac), in August 1911—a confinement during which she nearly died—Elsie moved back to New York and to Herbert. Having lived virtually apart for a year, their renewed proximity brought the question of their marriage to a head. Early in 1912 Elsie began to write and travel again in earnest. In February she made a strenuous trip through the Bahamas and Haiti, and in her first popular article since 1906, she hit out at religious control of women in the *Independent*. By July 1912 she had delivered the scholarly *Religious Chastity* to the publisher; and finding her iconoclastic line of thought suddenly fashionable, she was working on a popular book to be called *The Old-Fashioned Woman*.[26]

The summer dragged, however, with George Young returned permanently to England and no substitute partner in adventure available. At Herbert's suggestion, the Wilsons rented a cottage at Newport. Their intrusion on Elsie's beloved territory, and Herbert's enjoyment with Lucy of a place he had always avoided, precipitated a major confrontation. During a desultory weekend in August, Herbert was upset when Elsie displayed her boredom with the afternoon drives he enjoyed by going sailing instead with Alice Miller. Following an inconclusive discussion of their grievances, Elsie wrote frankly to Herbert after he left for New York on Sunday evening:

> My theory is of course that you have been in love with Lucy
> Wilson these three years—on & off. Just how much you have
> yourself realized it, I dont know; but about the fact itself I have
> never been uncertain. I believe it has made no difference in your
> feeling for me, that you care for me now as much as you ever did.
> In fact, as you once told me, that you enjoy my company even

more after having been with her. As far as I can see too she does you good.

So in my better moments I have honestly wanted you to see as much of her and as intimately, as possible. But try as I will, and during the last three years I have resorted to many devices, I still have despicable moments, moments which I dont understand in the least.

Now the only possible way for you to help me thro' them is not to pay any attention to them. It is much better for me to be unsocial for an hour or two as I was this afternoon than to pretend for an hour or two like yesterday afternoon & the day before & then become hysterical. But I dont want you to be hurt by my unsociability as you seemed to be tonight.[27]

In the discussion that ensued, it became clear that the basic problem was not Lucy Wilson but their directly conflicting ideas about the role of habit in marriage. Herbert found pleasure and contentment in the routines of married life. "The happiest times I used to have in Lenox were our afternoon drives together," he wrote. "I took them as an institution which I knew contributed pleasure to me. The same is true in Newport. . . . when you don't go I feel lost & when you do go I feel pleasantly. It seems to me that your objection to institutionalism goes to the extent of blinding you to the very satisfactory opportunity that institutions are for regular recurrent companionship":

> I confess I don't understand you in some of your new ways. Apparently travel, things new & unconventional are necessary to your enjoyment. Whatever you really wish to do I wish you to do, even tho I may not express or feel happiness over it. And I hope that in the future you will so act. That does not mean however that specific things that you do give me selfish satisfaction. I did not selfishly enjoy it this past year when you went off for Saturdays & Sundays, my freest time, even if you returned for Sunday dinner (generally tired out & fit only to go to bed). . . . I did not selfishly enjoy the news that you & Alice were going sailing Sunday afternoon. My selfish pleasure is in feeling you nearby & my preference would be that your trips & sailings take place at times when I am away at work. I mention these things—not to complain, but to indicate that when I am thus separated from you I miss you darling even if I don't say so & that while you should do these things if they are necessary for your happiness, you are not doing them with immediate selfish pleasure to me, though I theoretically will not gainsay them. The imprisonment of child-bearing naturally makes

a person of spirit wish to be free at other times but don't let it be on the theory that I like to be left alone for I don't.[28]

Elsie agreed that they had always had different concepts of companionship, although this had only become clear since he met Lucy Wilson. In a long cry of disappointment, she confessed the lack she had always felt in their marriage:

> It is my new experiences, my new ideas, and feelings, my fresh impressions of persons and places that I have wanted to share with you. The more interesting or exciting or delightful a thing was the more I wanted you in connection with it. From the very beginning of life together it was a great distress to find you indifferent to so much that most mattered to me. It hurt awfully when you didn't want me to hear you make a speech or when you wouldn't read a paper that I had written. Do you realize that apart from the family and the routine of life all my energy and a very large part of my interest have gone into writing which you have never shown the slightest interest in? That my first book you didn't read, my second, published anonymously, (you being still in public office when it went to print) you didn't even know about and the one I am writing now and talking to every one but you about (for, as it is popular, I get help from all sides) you also ignore? Your indifference or even antagonism once certainly hurt my vanity, but now I have no vanity about writing. But now as always to have you absolutely out of so large a part of my life is cutting. It isn't that I want your agreement. Any kind of criticism or ridicule of the ideas themselves would be welcome. Then there is so much in talk that I have constantly to repress because I know it would put you out with me. Religions and many philosophic ideas we can never touch upon. Companionship in new places . . . you dont seem to care for at all with me. In fact the last one we had together, in the Yosemite, was painful for us both. And yet until about three years ago although I had short times of much unhappiness I was very happy in your companionship and made the most of your theory of companionship—a kind of emotional easy chair. Then Lucy Wilson stepped in and I saw you acting and reacting with her as *from the time we were married* I had wanted you to do with me. It was awful for me and I *had* to do something about it. Trips with others was one of my most successful devices. But always I had rather have gone with you. The only alternative was staying home with you depressed and so repressed that I knew that at any moment I might be very disagreeable in all sorts of unreasonable ways.
>
> Not that I haven't been happy during this time in our *institutional* companionship. I like easy chairs very often myself. More-

over our relation is still the chief thing in the world to me and it seems grotesque to even have to tell you so.

My trips and my occasional flirtations (unfortunately the latter are rare, as so few men are able to work up an interest in me or I in them) keep me from making uninstitutional demands on you which you won't or can't meet.

This time I did not get away in time—thanks to Mac. Hence the break in your serenity and my upset digestion (headaches, obsessions etc.) I am sorry. On the other hand perhaps the resultant frankness will keep us happier in the future.[29]

Herbert replied full of contrition at Elsie's revelations of her unhappiness and dissatisfaction:

Your letter of yesterday morning came to-day. I am glad you wrote so frankly tho it has given me an unhappy day.

I think I have read all your articles, at least all that I have known about. The Family I did not read except in part. I suppose cowardice is my reason. I feared that there would be so many points on which we would not agree that life would run more smoothly if I did not cross them. I have tried to be tolerant in other ways & thought I had been, though I could not always smile at it. I should have read the book and now will.

I never knew a second book had been published. I supposed that that event was still to happen & that the manuscripts you mysteriously gave me to take to Alice were of it.

I think you would find it hard to take criticism or ridicule of the ideas themselves from *me*. Long have I held the theory that you only learn from experience or from suggestion of those not very close to. you. . . .

As to trips together—I have little keenness for trips in winter after travel each week for six months in the year. They frequently mean cutting in on a week-day, something that I have thought unwise when I was just resuming practice of the law. They always mean being away from the children & the time will come in a few years when John & perhaps Lissa will be away from home most of the time that I am there, so that now is the time to enjoy them. Apart from these points, however, the matter of cowardice again comes in. I have been afraid to try it since our Yosemite experience. . . . I was probably very disagreeable & my fear is that I would be again. . . . Under the circumstances I have felt that there was more happiness for both of us in not attempting it, yet that is an absurd position, the future considered. Write me *anything*. Hereafter talk *anything* to me. Don't repress. I love you sweetheart & I wish to make you happy.[30]

"Alice [Lucy] he didn't mention," Elsie wrote of this confrontation in her fictionalized account the following year. "I wish he had written how he felt about her, taken me in, so to speak, as he might have a friend. I doubt though if he would have talked to anyone about her. She was his closed garden. He cherished her loyalty, as he certainly called it, to her husband. All her little conjugal ways pleased him. So did her conventionalities with him. He wouldn't for the sake of any immediate pleasure for himself have had her do anything amiss. Her conventionalities made it easy for him too of course to see her without trepidation or sense of danger. He had wanted me too to protect him—in the eyes of the world—and of the Smiths [Lucy and Huntington Wilson] and in his own eyes. . . . He was so afraid of scandal in everything."[31]

This marital crisis precipitated Elsie's decision to make her first professionally oriented trip to the Southwest. Clara True had notified her that she would be riding to the Apache dances outside Dulce in northern New Mexico early in September. Armed with a commission from the young anthropologists she had recently met at the American Museum of Natural History to collect ethnographic material, Elsie set off for the Southwest. Herbert, meanwhile, took the boys to the Adirondacks, where they were joined, unknown to Elsie, by Lucy and Huntington Wilson.

Clara True met Elsie at Santa Fe, and they rode with Pedro Baca north along the Rio Grande to Pajarito Ranch, which True had just acquired. "I had forgotten the glory of this place," Elsie wrote to Herbert. "I do wish you could see and feel it." Back at the ranch a week later after their ride to Dulce, she was exultant:

> I hope your week was as enjoyable, but not as hard as mine. I could not have stood it outside of New Mexico. We rode about 230 miles, including 36 the afternoon I arrived here from Santa Fe. The same horses and a pack animal's gait. Too cold at night for me ever to sleep sound, & never any time to rest at the midday's stop. At the end of our 30 miles yesterday morning under an unmitigated sun & with weary horses, I was all in; but today I have rested up and the sunburn pains in my face have gone.
>
> We had about 1½ days (all told) stretch of monotonous sage brush desert country; but the rest was very beautiful, varying mountain outlooks, cliffs, tablelands, river courses. Plenty of water, but only one swim in the Chama. North of Abiquii the country was pretty wild. Clara True saw a mountain lion, I, a coyote, & one night the coyotes barked & laughed around us. The lake where the Apaches camped was covered with duck. Our guide, a Santa Clara Indian, shot a badger & I got him to skin it for John. Via

C.T. I made some interesting ethnological pursuits of evenings around the camp fire. So far my collecting for the Museum consists of the washed up drum cast after last year's feast into the lake. The Apache encampment was most interesting. Scattered tepees over a rolling pasture land. We picked a knoll overlooking the race track. It was a sort of a stage box to which all day long all kinds of visitors came—Santa Clara Indian friends, Indians from other pueblos with pottery or fruit to peddle, Apaches to sell horses . . . ranching white men, & strange-looking white women from Dulce, the Apache settlement. But what brought us most visitors were our 4 beaver skins. The Indians braid their hair with beaver fur, and word going abroad that we had it, they came to look at it, hankering like a Fifth Ave shopper. I bought two blankets of a Navaho who had begun to make a deal for the beaver. The foot races were rather interesting, but the dancing didn't amount to much. We saw nothing ceremonial. They said they were too poor this year to pay for ceremonies. They may also have been too drunk the night the ceremony was due. And so we brought back the beaver skins wh. C.T. had taken as an admission bribe.

"At times I have missed you awfully," she concluded, "but sometimes in the ride when I lagged behind I was glad you were not there to feel responsible and become annoyed. If only you could get over *feeling* responsible for me, I could make you happier, and we would not have to forego 'trips' together." Before she left for New York, Elsie collected data from Clara True's Indian employees and rode up Black Mesa, "where the Rio Grande Indians made their last stand against the Spaniards," she reported to Herbert. "I picked up arrowheads and potsherds, and had glorious views, enjoyed fording the river and did not enjoy nearly stepping on a great yellow & red snake. It is a beautiful moonlight, and if you were here I would go out to enjoy it instead of going to bed."[32]

Elsie's hardiness during this trip won her Clara True's endorsement as a bona fide Southwesterner. "I'm a poor stick at saying things," she wrote Elsie, "but I think you are *all right,* which expression means much when we say it in a certain way out here." George Young also understood and approved her initiative. Writing enviously of "the clear air and wide spaces you live in," he placed her in his own category of adventurer. "I think we have both of us the stuff of princes and have blazed a trail or two and built some outposts," he replied to her description of the trip. "I feel jealous of P. Baca—I'm sure he has a more attractive taciturnity than I."[33]

The End of Love

In "The Imaginary Mistress," written over the next twelve months, Elsie related a disturbing end to her New Mexico trip and to Herbert's vacation in the Adirondacks. Her account was transposed to the winter, but if it actually occurred it took place in September 1912, when she returned from the Southwest. "I met the returned travelers at the railroad station—Anson was just as glad to see me as I to see him. We had a delightful evening together and the following days and nights were very happy. Anson had had his camera with him in the Woods and one afternoon his pictures arrived from the printer. Bobbie [her son John] saw the envelope containing them on his father's desk and with my consent eagerly opened it to show me the pictures. Among the photographs were several of the Smiths taken on snowshoes in a group with Bobbie, skating together, and a pretty one of her standing alone against a background of lake and mountain. . . . I had at first a sense of amazement and then, I suppose that's what it was, a sense of rage. I wished her out of the way, dead. Anson I could have struck at that moment. Luckily he came home late after my paroxysm was over and that night we dined out."[34]

The account depicts Elsie being pushed by Herbert's need for Lucy's friendship into the divided life she gradually constructed. "In February I went to Yucatán. For years I had wanted to see the Maya ruins there, and New York had become intolerably dreary to me. Besides I felt that if I were out of the way Anson would be freer to see Alice. In spite of the photograph incident I had kept to my decision to suggest to Anson my taking the Smiths naturally again. Within a week or so I did open the subject with him. As usual he said little; but he was also clearly evasive and on later occasions he rebuffed me in my effort to express a friendly interest in the affairs of the Smiths. He would never be frank in the old way about them again. Did he distrust my equanimity or was he perhaps loath to forego the detached relation he had lately been enjoying with her? At any rate I wasn't needed any more as far as she was concerned. In fact I felt I was a barrier. If I went away he would see more of her. On the steamer I wrote suggesting a visit for him to Washington on the chance that he might still care about my endorsement. I wanted ever so much to be 'nice' to him, and I had a real pity for him in his self-suppression and a kind of maternal desire for him to get what he craved. The idea of his being with Alice didn't disturb me in the least. It rarely had disturbed me. . . . It was the idea that I was in the way, that he was with me because he felt—to himself—he ought to be."[35]

Elsie did go to the Yucatán in January 1913, armed with letters of introduction from Franz Boas, the professor of anthropology at Columbia University whose acquaintance she had resumed through her contacts at the American Museum of Natural History. From the ship she wrote to Herbert: "I wish there were not so many unreal things between us. I said things today to that Virginian fruit grower & even to that vicious Connecticut man that I wouldn't feel free to say to you. Why, I wonder? There is something wrong, & it lessens by just so much the joy of our companionship. I dont want to love you merely as I do a child, & if I can't talk freely to you & *be myself* to you that is what it will come to." "Do encourage yourself with Lucy Wilson," she added as if in an afterthought. "I promise never never again to be as foolish as I was last summer. I hated the attitude you took about not seeing her those two times in Washington but of course I realized I was to blame for it." Herbert answered, ignoring her postscript: "Do feel free to say anything you wish to me. On some things we disagree so absolutely & I feel my side against yours so strongly that I can only control my rude emotions when the talk is on such things, by keeping quiet, which is better than being actively disagreeable. It is because I am so fond of you that differences on such things take such strong hold of me. I too can talk to others on anything & endure any point of view. I realize, however, that it is unwise to let the area of differences increase or even continue. So talk away when you return & keep at it no matter how green I look."[36]

Convinced by their experiences of the past year that she and Herbert could only stay together if each found companionship and intellectual stimulation elsewhere, Elsie set out with a copy of Stephens's *Yucatán,* intent on furthering her anthropological education. During this trip she also began to consider the possibility—and desirability—of sexual as well as psychical freedom. She was, of course, a keen follower of Havelock Ellis's ideas, and probably agreed with him on the importance of sexual fulfillment. George Young had stimulated Elsie to strike out alone in a new and difficult field of activity; but she was still committed to her marriage during that relationship, and she sought from him only the intellectual and adventurous companionship she did not find with Herbert. "I have never been in the least in love with him," she wrote Herbert early in 1911, "altho he charms me in some ways more than anyone I have ever met." Young, for his part, teased her about the intellectual nature of their relationship. "I am amusing myself by writing a love-story," he wrote her at the end of 1911. "My heroine never says a word from the beginning to end—I'm taking no chances." But he had no intention of jeopardizing his own marriage. His wife, Helen, was wary of his friendship with Elsie and vetoed any plans she felt would trespass on her marriage; and Young himself resisted any plan that interfered too seriously with his family life. He did, however, treat Elsie as an attractive, sexual woman—and one whose attractiveness came from her unusual, complex character—and he was aware that Herbert's response was quite different. "Are you going to be painted in your character of Tindal the atheist or Polynesian hostess," he asked when she was having her portrait done. "You would prefer the first. I the second—but Herbert who I suppose is most concerned would certainly object to either."[37]

In February 1913, Elsie was feeling much more alone and needy than she was during her relationship with George Young. She had lost the assurance that came from her unexamined love for Herbert, and partly for the sake of the children and partly because of her residual feelings for him, she was battling to construct a new, but still viable, marital relationship. When her ship arrived in the Yucatán port, Progresso, she met an English journalist, Ernesto Balch. They traveled together for the next two weeks. According to Elsie's fictional account, they visited Uxmal, Labná, Kabah, and Chichén Itzá, mostly by horseback, sometimes in "the antique wagons of the country," sometimes by train. At Chichén they slung their hammocks in a high vaulted room in one of the ruined palaces and enjoyed a "glamorous night," talking for hours seated on the top step of the palace stairway. Later, "as Don [Balch] . . . was fastening the mosquito net around me in my hammock, without a word, being an Englishman—he kneeled and kissed my neck." But she was unable to respond, then or later when he kissed her again. "I couldn't. It was the idea of Anson, I suppose, that kept me from it. It would have seemed so 'bad' to him. And yet I didn't care much about that, for it didn't seem wrong to me, it was all so natural. But it would have hurt Anson, not in a jealous way, he hadn't any taint of jealousy in him, but in some way I couldn't define it would have wounded him to the quick. From the realization of that I couldn't get away. The feeling was like a ball and chain."[38]

In his 1924 notes for Jessica, the character based on Elsie, Robert

Herrick told the story differently and more brutally. "She is not sexually cold, has never been satisfied, and it is her 'views' less than her subnormal sex craving that leads her, quite deliberately to take her first lover, as an experiment in her theories. She has this man while abroad on study and drops him or rather he drops her on landing in New York." Balch's letters, which peter out in June 1913, suggest that Elsie's account was closer to the truth, and that it was she who did not continue the relationship.[39]

Whatever actually happened in the Yucatán, Elsie's fictionalized rendition suggests an almost desperate search for a new way of life during that "year of misery." In the rest of her account, she finds on her return that she cannot win back Anson's love, that he will not consider the divorce she suggests, and she experiences a series of dreams that underline her failure as a woman. A play Elsie wrote around this time portrays a discussion of divorce between a couple very much like Herbert and herself. And their letters suggest that Elsie at least contemplated that they "might quite soon begin to dislike each other and so of course part for good." "He was no longer the centre of my life," Elsie wrote in her fictional persona later that year. "The old sense of oneness with him which I had ridiculed as a conjugal tradition but which had been a profound and joyful reality for me had disappeared. He became alien and at moments I had the pain of feeling that our physical intimacy might become not merely indifferent but repugnant. This change in me did not affect the surface of our life at all—at least in his eyes. He did not notice. He was quite content."[40]

CHAPTER FIVE

New Science

ELSIE Clews Parsons observed accurately in 1909 that she required a time-consuming occupation to preserve her peace of mind—or "serenity," as she termed her ideal state of being. And her heartfelt cry to Herbert, during their 1912 confrontation, for companionship in new places, was as much a plea for adventurous intellectual companionship as it was for a partner in physical adventures. Her forays into the American Southwest in 1910 and 1912 brought her into contact with an extraordinary group of young New York anthropologists who quickly became challenging intellectual partners. In these young men (later joined by a number of young women), Parsons found a sympathetic and admiring collegial circle. And through them she found the vital thread that, along with her children, kept the diffuse parts of her life together. With stimulating work to pull from her ever-present book bag, she was always able to telegraph from New Mexico, or Barbados, or Haiti, "All serene."

A New American School

When Parsons first made contact with the American Museum of Natural History in New York, during 1911 or early in 1912, a group of Young Turks were in the process of revolutionizing American anthropology. All except Pliny Goddard, the museum's associate curator of ethnology, were former students of Franz Boas at Columbia University. The central figures were three Jewish-Americans, Alexander Goldenweiser, Robert Lowie, and Paul Radin. Closely linked to them, though distant geographically, were Alfred Kroeber at Berkeley and Edward Sapir in Ottawa. Through the unlikely pages of the *Journal of American Folklore*, this maverick group had become, by 1912, the voice of a new anthropology, which they called, with the arrogance of youth, "the American School."

In 1912, Franz Boas was fifty-four years old and was just beginning to take his dominant place in American anthropology with the publication the previous year of *The Mind of Primitive Man*. He had moved to the United States from Germany in 1887 after visiting his uncle and aunt, the eminent physicians Abraham and Mary Putnam Jacobi, in New York during field trips to the Arctic and the Pacific Northwest. Trained in physics and geography, he was by 1887 more interested in culture and language. The following year, he accepted a position at Clark University, the experimental graduate university the psychologist G. Stanley Hall was setting up in Worcester, Massachusetts. Boas left Clark four years later in a rebellion against Hall's administration that brought a number of talented young faculty from Clark to the new University of Chicago. But anthropology was essentially a museum-based profession at that time, and Chicago's fledgling sociology department already had its one anthropologist, Frederick Starr. After a brief, unhappy period at the Chicago Natural History Museum, Boas was unemployed for a year before he joined the American Museum of Natural History as assistant curator of ethnology and somatology in 1896. At the same time, he was appointed lecturer in physical anthropology at Columbia. He was promoted to professorial rank in 1899, and the position was made permanent in 1901, when Boas was forty-three. He was also elevated to curator at the museum that same year. But he broke with them two years later over his refusal to publish his findings quickly, and Columbia remained the base for his battle to transform anthropology.[1]

This transformation was carried out by Boas's graduate students rather than by Boas himself. Boas had little talent or temperament for public controversy, although he was uncompromising in his opposition to the way most anthropology was then practiced. But he encouraged independence and pugnacity in his students. Melville Herskovits put it kindly when he said that the quality of Boas's graduate teaching was "subtle." "Of individual direction, there was almost none," Herskovits recalled of his 1920s experience. In accordance with the German university tradition in which Boas was trained, there were no examinations, and students were expected to acquire the necessary languages and other prerequisites for the courses they took. As Herskovits pointed out wryly, "Boas' indifference to such matters was Olympian. In the famous anthropometry course which, it was held, could not be understood unless taken at least twice, Boas simply assumed the mathematical competence needed to grasp the development of the intricate statistical formulae he employed; in his courses on linguistics, he took an adequate knowledge of technical phonetics similarly for granted."[2]

Given Boas's "Olympian" detachment from the everyday intellectual dilemmas of his students, it is not surprising that they developed a strong and independent student culture. His linguistics students, Alfred Kroeber and Edward Sapir, had clear problems on which to work, and in Sapir's case, had previous linguistics training, so they tended to depend less on this culture; and Kroeber, as Boas's first Columbia student, had already completed his Ph.D. and was in California by the time there were sufficient numbers to form a group. But from about 1904, Boas's reputation as an innovative and austere "scientist" began to attract young intellectuals such as Robert Lowie and Paul Radin who were excited by the changes they sensed were taking place in the scientific project.[3]

Boas remained the distant inspiration for the intellectual inquiries of these young scholars. The central figure in their day-to-day education was their fellow student Alexander Goldenweiser. Always known affectionately as "Shura" or "Goldy," even when his friends were most exasperated with him, Goldenweiser came from a prominent intellectual Russian-Jewish family. His father brought him to the United States in 1900 to escape the student riots and police repression that were tearing apart the universities of his native Kiev. The brilliant and thoroughly unreliable Shura entered the Columbia anthropology graduate program in 1902 after studying philosophy at Harvard. He dominated it until 1910, when he finally finished his Ph.D. after studying in Berlin and returning to Russia for obligatory army service.[4]

Goldenweiser was Boas's favorite among his early graduate students, and the younger and less sophisticated students hero-worshiped him. As Robert Lowie confessed in an unpublished memoir, "I fell under the sway of his charm; and until about the beginning of 1914 we were united by what I conceived as an ideal friendship." In Goldenweiser, Lowie and his friends found a model of the "intellectual," a new social category described by William James in 1907, but previously identified in Russia and familiar on New York's Lower East Side as these young men were growing up. Goldenweiser was one of the generation of Jewish intellectuals who were radicalized by their savage exclusion from the Russian bourgeoisie. In the more peaceful streets of New York, intellectuals gathered in Lower East Side cafes, "at once neither orthodox Jews nor Americans . . . habitually intoxicated with the excitement of ideas."

Alexander Goldenweiser, 1930s.
Reproduced by permission of the
American Anthropological Associ-
ation from *American Anthropolo-
gist* 43:2, pt. 1 (April–June 1941).
Not for further reproduction.

While Lowie and his fellow students struggled to make sense of
Boas's difficult teaching, Goldenweiser taught them how to be scholars. He loaned them books on psychology and philosophy, and
organized discussion groups on the model of those formed by Russian gymnasium students where these "serious youthful fellow-
thinkers" mulled over the philosophical problems that preoccupied
them.[5]

In 1906, Goldenweiser organized the most influential of his discussion groups, the Pearson Circle. The group included anthropology students Lowie and Radin and philosopher Morris Cohen, all
friends from the College of the City of New York, where the city's
less affluent obtained a free college education. From middle-class
Jewish families who came to New York from middle or eastern
Europe when their sons were in their teens, these young men readily
soaked up what both the settlement houses and cafe society offered
them, reading the *Arbeiter Zeitung,* discussing socialism, and studying American literature, culture, and history at classes such as those
given by the young Elsie Clews. They shared a cultured, European
background; they could read fluently in several languages; and they
were familiar with the latest intellectual and artistic trends.[6]

A mutual interest in the philosophy of science drew these young
intellectuals together. Lowie and Radin found Boas's general ap-

proach to anthropology more compatible with their intellectual interests than the conventional science courses that initially attracted them, although the specifics of anthropology were of little interest to Lowie when he joined Boas's program. Instead, he recalled, "I devoted my real energies to straightening out my world-view." Visiting lectures by the renowned physicist-philosopher Wilhelm Ostwald excited Lowie much more than his anthropology classes. When Morris Cohen returned from Harvard, where he studied with William James, and Goldenweiser returned from Berlin, the group began a systematic examination of the implications for anthropology of the current reaction against theory.[7]

"We were not wholly concerned with finding out whether the Plains Indians put up tipis on foundations of three or four poles," the rigorously empirical Lowie wrote fifty years later. "In philosophical terms, the ethnologists of that era had passed from the naively metaphysical to an epistemological stage and in this were reflecting the spirit of the times." That spirit was embodied in the second edition of Karl Pearson's *Grammar of Science*—the first work studied by the Pearson Circle—and by William James's *Pragmatism* (1907) and *Pluralistic Universe* (1909), the work of Henri Poincaré and Wilhelm Ostwald, and (less important to the group) of John Dewey, who joined the Columbia faculty in 1904.

But more important than any of these for the Pearson Circle was the work of the Austrian physicist and philosopher of science Ernst Mach. Lowie recalled that he found the worldview he had been groping for in Mach's work, and that by understanding Mach he was able to understand Boas: "What impressed me in those days was that . . . Boas and Mach were doing much the same thing . . . scrutinizing such blanket terms as 'schizophrenia,' 'totemism,' 'matter' and trying to discover their factual basis." In sum, the members of the Pearson Circle learned from Mach and Boas "to view catchwords with suspicion."[8]

Critical Positivism

Ernst Mach was an Austrian physicist, mathematician, and historian of science, born in 1838, whose work had an enormous impact on turn-of-the-century scientific and artistic worlds. "Physics is not a church," Mach argued, and even the most useful theoretical system, such as Newtonian mechanics, must be continually challenged and understood in its historical context. Mach used his historical investigations and his experimental studies of perception to question the bases of knowledge claims and to critique basic scientific concepts. His "positivistic chastity," as Robert Lowie called it, rejected all metaphysical speculation and based all knowledge claims in experience. In effect, Mach embraced what postmodernists call an "incredulity toward metanarratives." For Mach all knowledge was a provisional processing of sensory data for the purposes of survival. All we can know is given through our sensations, he argued, to which the mind gives shape according to need. Ideas of space, time, body, and ego are all personal cuts into the chaos of sensations according to current necessity, to be discarded in the face of new experiences and new requirements. For Mach, theories were "like withered leaves, which drop off after having enabled the organism of science to breathe for a time." The metanarratives implicit in words, concepts, classifications, and theories were, therefore, temporarily useful fictions to be discarded before they impeded adaptation to new conditions.[9]

Mach's insistence on tearing down current systems of thought gave his positivism a radical edge that made it attractive to the modernist avant-garde, to revolutionary political groups, to innovative intellectuals, and to the women and men who were beginning to call themselves "feminists." In emphasizing experience as the only legitimate source of knowledge, Mach's critical positivism eliminated the authority of history and validated the idea of starting over—the idea of the "new" which was the basis of modernism. It also legitimated the search for experience itself, as a means of seeking a wider basis for formulating useful knowledge, thereby underpinning the restlessness and continuing search for novelty that characterized the modernist. Its emphasis on the provisional character of all knowledge initiated a wholesale critique of language and of conceptual, classificatory, and theoretical systems. It brought the body and its senses back in as an important factor in the constitution of knowledge. And perhaps most interesting, it treated the ego as but one of many useful fictions subject to reconceptualization. "The Ego cannot be saved," Mach wrote in 1886, in what must be one of the first announcements of the "death of the subject." This relativistic characterization of the self opened the way to a new conception of the "personality," whose complex character made each person more open to sincere interaction with others and more tolerant of difference. One could be a "personality" without being consistent or self-contained.[10]

Mach's views, which were set out in lucid and engagingly modest prose, electrified the generation of intellectuals who came to adulthood in the 1890s and the first decade of the twentieth century, and they strongly influenced a number of important contemporaries. William James met Mach in 1882, when they had four hours of "unforgettable conversation." Nietzsche's formulations in "The Will to Power in Science," written between 1883 and 1889, display remarkable parallels with Mach's writings. The young Einstein read Mach in a discussion group very similar to the Pearson Circle, and was profoundly influenced by Mach's critique of Newtonian concepts, which opened the way for his Special Theory of Relativity. Mach's experiments on perception and his theory of knowledge strongly influenced the European avant-garde in literature and the arts. At Jagellonian University, the young Polish scholar Bronislaw Malinowski wrote his doctoral dissertation on Mach; while the promising novelist Robert Musil did the same at the University of Berlin. Meanwhile, most interestingly, Mach's Russian admirers constituted Machism as a serious rival to Marxism. Indeed, Lenin's *Materialism and Empirio-Criticism* (1909) was a direct response to the Machian challenge.[11]

Washing Metaphysics out of Anthropology

The young intellectuals who made up the Pearson Circle were drawn to the mixture of scientific rigor and critique in Mach's work. As immigrants with backgrounds in the European professional class, they were secure outsiders, a status that allowed them to be critical of established intellectual thought and able to tolerate the uncertainties implicit in Mach's approach to knowledge. When Elsie Clews Parsons met Lowie and Goldenweiser in 1912 they were embarked, under Mach's inspiration, on a wholesale critique and reconstruction of the central concepts and theoretical systems of nineteenth-century ethnology on the basis of careful empirical research and fieldwork. As Lowie put it in a call to arms in 1914: "Like the generation of thinkers that preceded ours, we are living in an age of revolt, but the object of our revolt is different from theirs. Our predecessors fought tradition as arrayed against reason. We have the task of exorcising the ghosts of tradition raised in the name of reason herself. There is not only a folklore of popular belief, but also a folklore of philosophical and scientific system-mongers. Our present duty is to separate scientific fact from its envelope of scientific folklore."[12]

The "envelope of scientific folklore" at which Lowie and his associates took aim was evolutionary theory. Looking back on their project in 1922, Lowie was able to say with satisfaction that "the anthropological school headed by Professor Boas" had supplanted "with a sounder historical insight the cruder evolutionary speculation of the past." The weapon in this "transvaluation of theoretical values" was that formulated by the Pearson Circle—"a stout faith in the virtues of reasoned nonconformism." "In the insidious influence of group opinions," he warned, "whether countenanced by Church, State or scientific hierarchy, lies the basic peril."[13]

Lowie's letters to his sister Risa convey something of the excitement of these young revolutionaries. In August 1908, he had just finished his Ph.D. and was plotting with Boas and Radin to take over the American Folklore Society and its journal, to "preach methodological nihilism, take a tilt at William James, write [a] novel." Two years later, he and his fellow conspirators were rocking the American Anthropological Association. "I read my paper," he wrote Risa, "which aroused (with Shura's and Paul's aid) more discussion than any paper within the memory of the oldest living anthropologist." "I was appointed to the nominating committee," he concluded confidently. "We shall probably win Friday."[14]

This sense of winning in a revolutionary struggle had a strong basis in reality in 1910. Lowie was established as assistant curator at the American Museum of Natural History, where he and linguist Pliny Goddard formed a bridge between the museum and the Columbia department, countering the effect of curator Clark Wissler, who disliked Boas, his former teacher and colleague, and considered most of their crowd, according to Kroeber, "queer foreigners or half foreigners." Boas had installed the youthful Edward Sapir as chief of the Canadian Geological Survey's new division of anthropology in 1910, and Sapir in turn contracted with Goldenweiser and Radin to do fieldwork among Canada's native peoples. With Goldenweiser also lecturing at Columbia, and Kroeber gradually building a department at Berkeley, Boas's "school" was becoming an important new center of gravity in American anthropology. The Boas circle had indeed taken over the *Journal of American Folklore* in 1908, and until they gained control of the *American Anthropologist,* with Goddard as editor, in 1915, the journal's formerly staid pages echoed with the challenges and controversies of the new anthropology, whose "American" label brashly ignored anthropology's long history in the United States.[15]

The leader of the attack was Alexander Goldenweiser, and its expositor, popularizer, and historian was Robert Lowie. Its centerpiece was Goldenweiser's brilliant dissertation, published in the *Journal of American Folklore* in 1910, which took apart the time-honored concept of totemism. His fellow student Paul Radin characterized the dissertation in 1929 as the best example and, at the same time, the reductio ad absurdum of Boas's rigorous analytic approach to culture. In 1910, it was a rousing call to arms. In an article discussing the significance of Goldenweiser's pathbreaking work the following year, Lowie identified an "American view" based on "methodological principles that are becoming the common property of all the active younger American students of ethnology." Painstakingly analyzing how Goldenweiser deconstructed the concept of totemism by demonstrating important differences between its various manifestations, Lowie concluded his exegesis with a Machian flourish: "Popular philosophy has always had the tendency to assume a necessary bond between the constituents of a relatively stable complex of observed elements—to assume that there is a 'thing' which has properties, an ego which has sensations, feelings, and other manifestations of consciousness." But, he argued, "a 'thing' is nothing distinct from its properties." Once thought is no longer arrested by the expectation of a "mystic unity," the scientist is able to proceed. Then "the nature and interrelations of these elements themselves becomes the highest, nay only possible, goal of investigation."[16]

Goldenweiser's deconstruction of the totemism concept was only the forerunner of a wave of critiques of premature classification and faulty observation by Lowie, Radin, and himself. Too much ethnology is based on loose generalizations supported by an incoherent mass of ethnographical material, Goldenweiser wrote in 1911, calling for a systematic account of actual distribution of cultural elements in concrete cultural areas. "Ethnology is a relatively young science, and it is natural that the mode of classification in vogue . . . should have a pre-scientific tang," the thirty-year-old Lowie wrote in 1912. "But the time has come to recognize that an ethnologist who identifies a two-class system in Australia with a two-class system in America . . . sinks to the level of a zoologist who should class whales with fishes, and bats with birds."[17]

By 1914, when Elsie Clews Parsons began to know him well, Robert Lowie had become the intellectual spokesman for the Machian (and Boasian) project of critical positivism in cultural anthropol-

Robert Lowie, 1920s. Elsie Clews Parsons Papers, American Philosophical Society Library.

ogy. In a series of major programmatic statements beginning in January 1914, he placed the new cultural anthropologists alongside similar revolutionaries in philosophy, physics, and biology. "We secessionists," he announced in the language of the young modernists, revolt against the "naively synthetic constructions" of the evolutionists, which hide a much more diverse—even chaotic—range of facts. "Instead of the dull uniformity of the theorists," he concluded in a typical statement of the "secessionist" position, "we may have all the motley variety of real life with its profusion of individual differences." Responding to a 1917 lecture series where Lowie further defined the direction of the discipline, Boas's friend Berthold Laufer agreed: "The more theories will be smashed, the more new facts will be established, the better for the progress of our science. . . . As nature has no laws, so culture has none. It is as vast and as free as the ocean, throwing its waves and currents in all directions. It is absurd to seek the origin of civilization in any particular region or to trace it to a single nation."[18]

Lowie's classic statement of modern ethnology's project was *Primitive Society,* published in 1920. Putting nineteenth-century evolutionary theory to rest, Lowie asserted that "that thing . . . called civilization" was a "planless hodge-podge," made up of "shreds and patches." Cultures develop mainly through borrowings due to chance contact, he claimed baldly: there was no evidence of either necessity or design. This did not mean for Lowie that design could not be infused into the "amorphous product": it meant instead that this task was much more difficult than the "evolutionary optimism of the seventies" had ever imagined; and it meant that each individual was responsible for helping to create a "rational scheme" to replace the "chaotic jumble."[19]

Her Gang

Claude Lévi-Strauss attests in *Tristes Tropiques* to the liberating quality of Lowie's doctrine when he stumbled across it in 1933: "Instead of notions borrowed from books and at once metamorphosed into philosophical concepts, I was confronted with an account of first-hand experience," he wrote. "My mind escaped from the closed circuit which was what the practice of academic philosophy amounted to. . . . Like a townsman let loose in the mountains, I made myself drunk with the open spaces and my astonished eye could hardly take in the wealth and variety of the scene."[20]

As Lévi-Strauss did a generation later, Elsie Clews Parsons found these young men and their deconstructive project sympathetic and liberating. Like them, she was a secure outsider—secure by virtue of her wealth and social position, an outsider by virtue of her gender and subversive ideas. Their critical positivism fitted well with her own skepticism of received wisdom and her training in careful observation and sifting of evidence. For the first time since she began to speak openly about her "views" in 1905, she found a group of people who did not consider her particularly unusual, embarrassingly unconventional, or amusingly outrageous. Instead they took her seriously as a courageous and innovative thinker and welcomed her as a kindred spirit into the discipline they were transforming. Although they teased her about her stances as a public intellectual openly committed to using ethnology to effect social change, they shared her beliefs and goals; and they appreciated her social perceptiveness, her vision, and the breadth of her scholarship. Through them she found a supportive group of colleagues and friends who soon included Franz Boas and Alfred Kroeber. In the early 1920s, "her gang" was joined by Gladys Reichard and the two women she helped move from secretarial positions in Boas's office into fieldwork and professional anthropology, Esther Schiff Goldfrank and Ruth Bunzel—significantly a Quaker, a Jewish-American, and a German-American—all outsiders in their way.

It is not clear exactly when Parsons first met these deceptively respectable young revolutionaries. Boas, Kroeber, and Lowie all agreed in 1942 that Pliny Goddard was her first point of contact with the group, sometime after her 1910 Southwestern trip. She probably met Goddard at the American Museum of Natural History early in 1912 soon after she returned to New York following Mac's birth. The oldest of the group at forty-three, Goddard was a Quaker lay missionary among the Californian Hupa before completing a Ph.D. in linguistics at Berkeley in 1904. Between 1901 and 1909, he helped Kroeber set up Berkeley's anthropology department. Through Kroeber he was introduced into Boas's circle, first in California to fellow linguist Edward Sapir, and then, when his extensive knowledge of Californian and Southwestern Indian languages brought him to the museum in 1909, to his assistant curator, Robert Lowie, and to Franz Boas, to whom he quickly became devoted. When Parsons met Goddard in 1912, he was redesigning the museum's Southwestern exhibits and preparing his handbook *Indians of the Southwest.*[21]

Parsons could not have found a better person to draw her into the new anthropology. Pliny Goddard was a talented scholar, with "ethnological discrimination of the rarest," according to Kroeber. His intellect was keen and quick, his critical faculty incisive, and his wit was pungent—attributes that Parsons always found attractive. An apostate, he shared the group's enthusiasm for "the recent victory over God." But he retained much of the Quaker reformist spirit—"idealist, devotee of the simple in humanity and the direct in relations, martyr if necessary," as Kroeber put it. Like Parsons, Goddard loved a cause: "his eye lit up, the steel in him flashed, and he rejoiced in the cleanness of combat." His frankness, wit, and charm were combined with a passionate loyalty to those he loved and absolute devotion to those he saw as heroes in the causes he cared about. Later, when everyone was doing Jungian analysis, Edward Sapir classified him, with Goldenweiser, as a feeling extrovert, that is, someone who is highly subjective and rigid in his passions.[22]

Goddard's approach to anthropology, with its combination of an almost sensual feeling for data with an intense interest in the possibilities revealed by cultural diversity, helped Parsons clarify her ideas and methods. A true Boasian in spirit, Goddard had little

Pliny Goddard, 1920s. Esther Goldfrank Papers, Smithsonian Institution
Photo No. 86-1309.

interest in analysis, and even less in synthesis. Language, his speciality, interested him primarily as a reflection of experience and personality. He took an intense satisfaction in securing his data and presenting them, as far as possible, in the native speech. "All his work
was highly charged with feeling," Kroeber wrote. "A culture as such
meant much less to him than that part of a culture lived and felt by
a particular Indian."[23]

Like Boas and his young colleagues, Goddard was just as interested in his own culture as in those of the Native Americans he
studied. He recognized immediately that Parsons, a wealthy woman
from a society family, had an extraordinary talent for perceiving
the minutiae of behavior and thought which formed the building
blocks of that culture. Too hot-headed to battle effectively against
the cultural restraints that fettered him, he admired the way she
could combine the zeal of a propagandist with a cool detachment.
She may have reflected Goddard's assessment in her 1913 account
of her struggle with jealousy, "The Imaginary Mistress," when she
assigned her fictional counterpart "an extraordinary facility . . . for
detaching herself from her experience, for viewing it and even acting
upon it impersonally, so to speak."[24]

Although there is little direct evidence for it, Goddard's encouragement was clearly crucial to Parsons's increasing involvement in
anthropology during 1912 and 1913. When she told Herbert during
their traumatic confrontation in August 1912 that she was writing
a new, popular book and getting enthusiastic advice from everyone,

Goddard was probably one of those encouraging her to turn "native informant" by noting down the folkways and folklore of her set and applying her wide knowledge of ethnography to the problems of her own society. When she went to the Southwest in September 1912, she had a commission to collect material for the museum, undoubtedly from Goddard. By the end of 1912, she was the expert on the psychology and anthropology of religion for *Current Anthropological Literature,* the review journal launched the previous year by Lowie and his fellow secessionists. And it was no doubt Goddard who encouraged her, when she planned her Yucatán trip early in 1913, to seek a letter of introduction from Boas, who had just spent a year in Mexico.[25]

During 1913, Goddard's support helped her redirect her energies from the frustrations of her marriage to the beginnings of a disciplined career as public intellectual and professional anthropologist. He ensured that her scholarly anthropological study *Religious Chastity,* published anonymously early that year, was well-reviewed; he put her in touch with other fieldworkers when she returned to New Mexico in October 1913—this time for brief visits to Laguna and Acoma, then Cochiti, Santo Domingo, San Felipe, Santa Ana, Zia, and Jemez—and he encouraged her to attend the meetings of the American Anthropological Association in New York that December.[26]

By the fall of 1913, Pliny Goddard was an admiring friend and colleague. "I should like to form a partnership with you for senior partner, for ethnological work," he wrote in November 1913. Always a little in love with her, he was eagerly seeking Elsie's company and her good talk by the beginning of 1914. "The cigarettes are waiting, so am I," he wrote after she had spoken at the Cosmopolitan Club on "the future of the family." "You promised to tell me how you have settled the family. Lowie told me a little. He admires your courage. Really I would like to talk over my lectures with you. Do come in."[27]

CHAPTER SIX

New Woman

ELSIE Clews Parsons and her new anthropological colleagues were not alone in seeking to free themselves from the "closed circuit" of late-nineteenth-century certainties. Her return to New York at the end of 1911 plunged her into a vibrant intellectual world. She found to her delight that the conversation between diverse groups that she tried to stimulate in 1906 had become a reality—at least in the part of New York that was becoming known as Greenwich Village. In this tiny area surrounding Washington Square had assembled a close-knit community of intellectuals who melded American traditions of dissent with the newer pragmatism and the imported creeds of socialism and anarchism. Young women and men of Quaker, Unitarian, and freethinking backgrounds, wealthy young men uneasy about their privileges, equally wealthy young women full of rebellion, and sons and daughters of Jewish middle-class immigrants embraced a range of revolutionary ideas from the conversation of Tarde to the dynamite of Bukharin. They often called it "socialism" or "anarchism," but they all shared one basic aim—to jettison conventional ideas and practices and to rebuild the world on a more tolerant, egalitarian, and flexible basis.

This intellectual community grew out of the work of the settlement houses and the "ethical bohemia" that developed around them. The concentration of settlements in Greenwich Village and the Lower East Side, and a fascination with the area's ethnic diversity, brought an array of social workers, socially concerned clergy, journalists, writers, educators, actors, political activists, and social investigators to live in the settlements or in houses, apartments, and rooms nearby. Drawn by the charismatic personality of Lillian Wald at Henry Street or the gentler, more intellectual Mary Simkhovitch at Greenwich House, and by the promise of purpose in their lives, wealthy uptown women flocked to the boards, classrooms, and projects of the settlements—and some came to stay. The College Settlements Association fellowship, for instance, with which Parsons was associated for many years, brought a steady stream of young college graduates to the area, many of whom were by 1912 central figures in the New York reform world and the life of the Village.[1]

New York's geography gave it an advantage over spread-out cities like Chicago in fostering such a community. As novelist Edna Ferber observed, Chicago never developed a lasting bohemia because it took so long to travel from one part of the city to another. Greenwich Village, by contrast, provided cheap accommodations and eateries close to the settlements, publishing houses, and ethnic communities that provided work, subject matter, and the stimulus of imported ideas and cultural practices. The old and the new America collided palpably at Washington Square. To the north, as resident George Middleton observed, lingered the remains of aristocratic New York, with the city's most gracious row of houses; to the south "the new America with its foreign strains"; to the east the New York University building looked down on a mélange in which "frilled nurses pushed well-groomed baby carriages amid the ragamuffin groups."[2]

Feminism

The radicals of Greenwich Village had an exuberant feeling that the past could be swept away and the future was theirs to build. This sensitivity to future possibilities was nurtured by scientists such as Ernst Mach, philosophers such as William James and Henri Bergson, and novelists such as H. G. Wells, while a wholesale rejection of past moral systems was stimulated by the sexology of Havelock Ellis and a surge of interest in Nietzsche's work. The strong sense of breaking with the past was manifested dramatically in 1909 when the Italian Futurists denounced everything that was "pastist" and energetically set about constructing the future in a flood of strident manifestos.[3]

For Parsons, one of the most important movements to emerge from this modernist revolution in science, art, and morals was feminism. In 1917, when the newspaper-reading public had caught up, at least partially, with the avant-garde, the *New York Evening Sun* reported that "some people think that women are the cause of modernism, whatever that is." Whether women invented it or not, the new and exciting feminist movement was an integral part of the rejection of the past, the improvisation of the present, and invention of the future that constituted modernism.[4]

The words "feminism" and "feminist" were just becoming current when Parsons returned to New York in 1911. By 1913, they referred quite explicitly to a movement for women's emancipation that distinguished itself sharply from the nineteenth-century "woman movement." The new movement went much further than suffragism in demanding independence and freedom for women. As Nancy Cott points out, "feminism" and "feminist" were semantic claims to female modernism. For Edna Kenton, a writer who was a central figure in the definition of feminism in the United States, the new movement stood for a "troop of departures from the established order of women's lives."[5]

Elsie Clews Parsons immediately recognized her own priorities in the new term "feminism." When her mother asked her, during a flurry of publicity in 1914, to explain it, she replied that she had always been a feminist:

> When I would play with the little boys in Bryant Park although you said it was rough and unladylike, that was feminism. When I took off my veil or gloves whenever your back was turned or when I stayed in my room two days rather than put on stays, that was feminism. When I got out of paying calls to go riding or sailing, that was feminism. When I kept to regular hours of work in spite of protests that I was selfish, that was feminism. When I had a baby when I wanted one, in spite of protests that I was not selfish enough, that was feminism.

Her mother's dismissive reply that these were just the acts of a rebellious daughter was quite accurate, of course: rebellion against the past was exactly what feminism was about.[6]

Elsie had in fact been following the development of feminism since her graduate student days. The French word *féministes* was barely known in the United States in 1899 when her friend Margaret Chanler sent a brochure from Geneva in which the author talked of the *Société d'Etudes féminines* and the *Féministes*. "I dont know exactly who she means by the Feministes," Margaret wrote. Elsie was probably already familiar with the term, which was just gaining international use. She was in Paris translating Tarde's *Laws of Imitation* in 1896 when the word arrived in the United States from France, and she used the word "feminist" in her Tarde translation when it was published in 1903. She probably also noted two articles on *feminisme* and *le mouvement feministe* listed in the *American Journal of Sociology*'s bibliography in 1898. Elsie was certainly considered knowledgeable on the subject later in 1899 when Margaret Chanler urged her to read Charlotte Perkins Stetson's recently published *Women and Economics* so that she and other friends could discuss it "under your Doctorat." It is very radical, Margaret added by way of encouraging Elsie, "but none too much so for me."[7]

The set of attitudes that came to be called "feminism" first manifested themselves in popular form on the more radical edges of the suffrage movement from about 1909. The suffrage movement had been diversifying for several years, as the College Equal Suffrage Association and the Equality League of Self-Supporting Women attracted college women, working-class women, trade union leaders, socialist intellectuals, and Village radicals to the cause, and added streetcorner meetings to the staid repertoire of suffragist strategies.[8]

In 1909, the Massachusetts chapter of the National American Woman Suffrage Association put the new tactics to work. Under the leadership of Parsons's settlement friend Susan Fitzgerald and the formidable Mary Ware Dennett, enthusiastically supported by Katharine Dexter McCormick, the chapter held a number of outdoor meetings throughout the state. Parsons had been an active member of the New York College Equal Suffrage Association from its founding in 1906, and had fruitlessly tried to "take the idea out for an airing" in Washington in the days when "it lived in the most unventilated and darkest of quarters." Not the least of her frustrations during the 1909 summer, when she was pregnant with Herbert Jr., was her exclusion from the more exacting aspects of the revitalized campaign. While visiting Boston, she had to stand by and watch Katharine and Susan motor to surrounding villages to speak on suffrage. "Not I, unfortunately," she wrote Herbert. The newspapers were full of the tactics of the British suffragists, who had escalated their militance to include physical violence, and the always up-to-date *Independent* reported on "the unrest of modern women." But the American experience was a pale reflection of its British counterpart. Elsie reported to Herbert that on Susan's motor campaign crowds of two to six hundred gathered but were unresponsive and sometimes shamefaced. "No heckling whatsoever—more like a prayer meeting," she commented. "The police most polite every where. It would be impossible to be martyrized."[9]

Back in Newport during the trying period when she first struggled with her obsessive jealousy of Lucy Wilson, Parsons diverted herself by watching as Katharine persuaded the wealthy Alva Belmont to have "a $5 pay meeting" for the suffrage cause at her ostentatious Newport "cottage" ("isn't that a ludicrous concatenation?"). She teased Alice Duer Miller into trying her arguments on Newport's more recalcitrant antisuffragists, and laughed at her father for arguing "if women vote, who will have the babies?—Seeing to whom and in whose presence he unhumorously said it." She did her part in making the Belmont meetings a success by trying to persuade her friend President Taft to attend. The day after the first meeting, she reported to Herbert that there were about six hundred people there. "Mrs. Howe was the belle of the occasion," she wrote, referring to her neighbor, the woman's movement veteran Julia Ward Howe. "Her remarks were simple and graceful, and she was very decorative." Katharine and Susan Fitzgerald sat on the platform with "that old timer, Mrs. Ida Husted Harper. Do you remember she dined with us in Washington? Katharine looked very pretty & was a good foil. The Rev. Anna Shaw did well—an elegant mixture of logic and emotion. She was much more modern and potentially socialistic than I supposed such an old girl could be. She exaggerated the vote as a panacea of course. . . . Newport cottagers were scarce."[10]

By the end of 1909, women's suffrage had become popular and respectable. As feminist editor Mabel Potter Daggett put it in the *Delineator,* suffrage had entered the drawing room. With the British Women's Social and Political Union holding 4,000 peaceful demonstrations that year, Elizabeth Cady Stanton's daughter, Harriott Blatch, organized New York's first major suffrage parade in May 1910. In 1911, when the parade included men, Elsie was pregnant and living quietly in Lenox, but Herbert reported that his sister Edith marched and that "the crowd was orderly except towards the men in it." In 1914, when Elsie attended a dinner for the secretary of state, her neighbor turned to the topic of suffrage "just as in by-gone days he would have turned to the play running its week in town."[11]

Despite her enjoyment of the thrust and parry of the suffrage fight, Parsons never saw it as the major issue for women. It was Herbert rather than Elsie who became central to the suffrage cause. A supporter of women's suffrage from his first political campaign, Herbert was invited to join the Men's Suffrage League organized by Max Eastman in 1909. In 1914, he agreed to carry the suffrage question to the floor of the Republican state convention. At the convention he met Vira Whitehouse, a capable Southerner with a beguiling accent who chaired one of the district committees of the Women's Political Union. This began a long friendship which eventually replaced that with Lucy Wilson. Although they often quarreled over tactics, the two made a good partnership in the successful campaign for a state suffrage referendum which ended in November 1917.[12]

Elsie contributed articles on suffrage when requested, enjoyed Katharine's and Alice's suffrage gossip, and in 1915, when the first state referendum was coming up, she stated her position with her usual wit in the *Herald,* tackled her crusty Lenox neighbor Joseph Choate, and even decided "I oughtter march" in the spectacular yellow, blue, and white parade. But she found the arguments of the "old time half baked suffragists" such as Ida Husted Harper "very glib and illogical," and she became increasingly critical of the suffrage campaign for its emphasis on women's special moral sensibilities. With her longtime supporter, free-speech advocate Theodore Schroeder, she agreed that the best argument for women's suffrage was not their "present stupid moral sentimentalism," but the hope that the vote would widen women's experience and, as a result, broaden their moral vision.[13]

Internal Tyrants

Parsons found a more comfortable place in the new "feminism," which gradually differentiated itself from the suffrage movement between 1909 and 1913. The more militant tactics of the suffrage movement were early stirrings of feminism in the United States. By undermining nineteenth-century stereotypes of women as passive, gentle, and nurturing, they opened the way for more radical women to form alliances with anarchists, free-speech advocates, and modernists, who were attacking institutions, challenging taboos, and gleefully consigning the past to the rubbish heap. The dialogue among these groups was carried on most forcefully in Emma Goldman's *Mother Earth.* As Alice Wexler points out, Goldman and Alexander Berkman, who edited *Mother Earth* after his release from prison late in 1906, used the journal to reconcile their European education and radical values with their commitment to America, and to teach Americans about their own traditions of dissent. The journal thus formed a bridge between nineteenth-century libertarianism and the rebellions of the 1910s. Some of *Mother Earth*'s supporters worried that anarchism was becoming too middle class, fighting Comstock rather than capitalists. But Goldman, with a modernist insistence on erasing boundaries, argued that a mainstream movement was more valuable than the timid radicalism of immigrants who never associated with native-born Americans.[14]

The ideas disseminated in *Mother Earth* were popularized by Goldman's sensational lecture tours, which began in 1907. Constantly pushing the limits of the respectable, she asserted, as Parsons had tried to do in 1906, the right and the need to discuss questions of sex. In "The Tragedy of Woman's Emancipation," she addressed the middle-class, professional woman who had economic independence but little satisfaction in her personal life. Speaking of the "emptiness in woman's soul that will not let her drink from the fountain of life," she argued that the "internal tyrants"—ethical and social conventions—were far more harmful than the "external tyrannies" of politics and economics. Changing women's external conditions was comparatively easy, she asserted in the *New York Sun* in 1909. More difficult were inner changes of thought and desire. Goldman urged women to take responsibility for their own lives, by asserting themselves as "personalities," by "trying to learn the meaning and substance of life in all its complexities," and by freeing themselves from fear of public opinion. An important element in this assertion of personality for Goldman was control over reproduction, and from 1910 she defied the law openly by lecturing on birth control and distributing pamphlets describing available forms of contraception. Inspired by Goldman, Margaret Sanger began her long career in the birth control movement the following year with a series of articles in the socialist *New York Call*. When Goldman published her lectures in *Anarchism and Other Essays* early in 1911, her friend Hutchins Hapgood reviewed it glowingly in the *Bookman,* conferring the young intelligentsia's seal of approval.[15]

Freewomen

Goldman's message appealed to a strong sense of the possibilities inherent in the human condition that was encouraged among young American intellectuals by the vitalist philosophy of Henri Bergson, Tarde's successor at the Collège de France. Bergson was "a herald in whom the unrest of modern times has found a voice," Walter

Lippmann, recently out of Harvard, wrote in 1912. Bergson's enormously successful *L'Evolution créatrice* (1907) was hailed by William James as "a marvel, a real wonder," and he lectured to large and admiring audiences when he visited the United States in 1913. Lippmann's *Preface to Politics,* written under Bergson's influence in 1912, was a showcase for Bergson's injunctions to young modernists: the questioning of established principles, the importance of resourcefulness, the need for constructive effort, and a willingness to act on conclusions based on observations of everyday life.[16]

Bergson's message of optimistic struggle was attractive to women who were in the process of reconstituting their lives on feminist principles. James's former student Gertrude Stein was one of the many Parisians and American visitors who flocked to Bergson's lectures at the Collège de France during the 1910–11 winter. Stein passed on her enthusiasm to the small British and American community, including Mabel Dodge, who gathered in Florence during the 1911 summer. Stein had just brought to a conclusion a long struggle with her own family history in *The Making of Americans* (which she subtitled *Being a History of a Family's Progress,* referring ironically to the evolutionist's favorite concept). "Dead is dead," she wrote in a climactic episode. "Old ones come to be dead," she repeated again and again in her final chapter. With the nineteenth century "dead dead dead," women like Stein felt they were free to create a different future through a more intense engagement with the present. As Marion Cox put it in the *Forum* in 1913, Bergson's message to feminism was "his insistent demand that we turn away from the intellectualism of life to life itself"—"and this," she added, "also is the aim of feminism."[17]

By the end of 1911, the word "feminism" was widely used among New York intellectuals. Its essence was captured by the British magazine the *Freewoman,* which published its first issue that November. This "feminist review" was the brainchild of an extraordinary woman, Dora Marsden. Marsden is one of the casualties of history, her significance obliterated by the benevolent cacophony of Ezra Pound, who took over the journal in his inimitable way and turned it into the *Egoist* and a forum for the early James Joyce. Marsden was a decisive woman of her times, determined to break with everything the nineteenth-century woman movement stood for. She was a brilliant philosopher who had studied with one of the major British students of Bergson's work. A tiny woman with "a face like a Florentine angel," Marsden become an organizer for the Women's Social and Political Union in 1909 and founded the *Freewoman* two years later out of disgust at the organization's "unthought out and nebulous feminism," which used up women's energies on the "overvalued" issue of suffrage. Harriet Weaver, the wealthy woman who became a lifelong supporter of Marsden's projects (her other protégé was James Joyce), wrote that the *Freewoman* "must have been edited on a mountain-top, it breathed so deeply of the spirit of freedom." "The genuine sort," she added, "which is prepared to count the costs, and, finding them heavy, agrees to pay."[18]

The *Freewoman* was concerned with psychology and philosophy rather than with politics and economics, and it was directed toward "Freewomen" rather than "Bondwomen." Bondwomen, Marsden explained, are women who are the complements of others rather than individuals in their own right: "By habit of thought, by form of activity, and largely by preference, they round off the personality of some other individual, rather than create or cultivate their own." Freewomen, by contrast, are those who abandon their "servant" attributes and seek a place among the "masters." Feminism, for Marsden as for Goldman, was a movement to free women from "the great soporifics—comfort and protection," to instill in them "the sense of quality, the sense that a woman has gifts, the sense that she is a superior," and to give them the strength to "be content to seize the 'love' in passing, to suffer the long strain of effort, and to bear the agony of producing creative work." Women will learn, she insisted, "that their own freedom will consist in appraising their own worth, in setting up their own standards and living up to them."[19]

The *Freewoman* and its editor attracted an admiring audience in the United States, especially among the growing number of Bergson enthusiasts. Frances Maule Bjorkman, a member of the new feminist group Heterodoxy, told *Forum* readers at the end of 1912 that the *Freewoman* was a "significant and compelling sign of new developments taking place within the woman movement." Edna Kenton, one of Chicago's "wilful modernists" who began that group's chain migration to Greenwich Village, was secretary of the *Freewoman*'s New York committee late in 1912, and her friend Marjorie Jones was its Evanston representative. In January 1913, Jones's lover Floyd Dell hurriedly added Marsden to his series "Modern Women" in the *Friday Literary Review*. When the series was published as

Women as World Builders, its subtitle, *Studies in Modern Feminism,* was aimed at those women and men who saw themselves on the cutting edge of this new phase of the women's movement.[20]

Heterodoxy

There is no evidence whether or not Parsons read the *Freewoman,* although her own feminist writing over the next few years gave the same importance to freedom and courage. She was, however, closely involved with Heterodoxy, which was formed late in 1912, probably on the model of the London Discussion Circle organized by the *Freewoman* a few months earlier. A feminist discussion group that met for lunch every other Saturday, except in the summer, from 1912 until the early 1940s, Heterodoxy provided "a wonderful freemasonry of women" for "women who did things and did them openly," according to two of its members, Elizabeth Gurley Flynn and Mabel Dodge Luhan. Elsie Clews Parsons, Alice Duer Miller, and Vira Whitehouse were early members of the group, to which they remained faithful till the end of their lives.[21]

Heterodoxy was the idea of Marie Jenny Howe, a former Unitarian minister married to progressive reformer Fred Howe, whose work and marriage had placed her at the center of a group of women and men who were passionately concerned with individual freedoms. Moving to New York in 1910, Marie and Fred settled on the edge of Greenwich Village where their home became the center for "brilliant young people, full of vitality, ardent about saving the world." Marie Howe wanted Heterodoxy to provide a setting for conversation "where social constraints and conventional politeness were outweighed by the sheer delight in honest disagreement and differences which opened the mind to new possibilities, new ways of thinking, living, being." "On summoning the charter members of Heterodoxy / She bade us think—but nothing USUAL!" Paula Jakobi wrote in tribute in 1920, echoing a Marsden editorial of 1911.[22]

Early in 1913, Columbia student Randolph Bourne, always a bellwether of things modern, wrote to a friend about a "most delightful group of young women" he met in Greenwich Village. They were mostly social workers and magazine writers who constituted what he called "a real 'Salon.' " "They have an amazing combination of wisdom and youthfulness, of humor and ability, and innocence and self-reliance. . . . They are of course all self-supporting and independent, and they enjoy the adventure of life; the full, reliant, audacious way in which they go about makes you wonder if the new woman isn't to be a very splendid sort of person."[23]

This new "new woman" was publicized dramatically by Howe and her coterie in a number of well-orchestrated public forums at Cooper Union. In February 1914, she gained front-page headlines for the new movement when she chaired the First Feminist Mass Meeting, with Floyd Dell, George Middleton, Max Eastman, Frances Perkins, Crystal Eastman, Henrietta Rodman, and others testifying to the influence of feminism in their lives. At a second meeting three days later, Rheta Dorr, Fola La Follette, Rose Schneiderman, and Charlotte Perkins Gilman were among those who provided personal testimony in a discussion entitled "Breaking into the Human Race." Feminism is "woman's struggle for freedom," Marie Howe wrote in the *New Review* a few months later, summarizing Dora Marsden's ideas in simpler and more dramatic language. "Its political phase is woman's will to vote. Its economic phase is woman's effort to pay her own way. Its social phase is woman's revaluation of outgrown customs and standards. . . . Feminism means more than a changed world. It means a changed psychology, the creation of a new consciousness in women."[24]

"Salvage Ethnology"

Parsons reveled in the talk that accompanied and stimulated the creation of this new feminist consciousness. "I am going to a talky-talky dinner tonight on mothers' pensions," she wrote in "The Journal of a Feminist," which she began to compile in August 1913, noting down all this talk. She joined in the lively discussions at Heterodoxy. She attended the salon organized by Mabel Dodge—who had returned from Florence full of Bergson and Gertrude Stein. She discussed marriage at the Cosmopolitan Club with economists, historians, and scientists from Columbia University. She attended "problem plays" at the Stage Society. She reported on the First Feminist Mass Meeting in the "Journal," noting there was little sex antagonism in the audience, and that the most decided applause was for condemnations of the idle, parasitical woman. She tried to explain feminism to her mother, who immediately sent the thirteen-year-old Lissa the white kid gloves and gauze veil Elsie would not buy for her. And she talked provokingly about sex and marriage in the discussions organized by her own set—Betty Sage, Charlotte

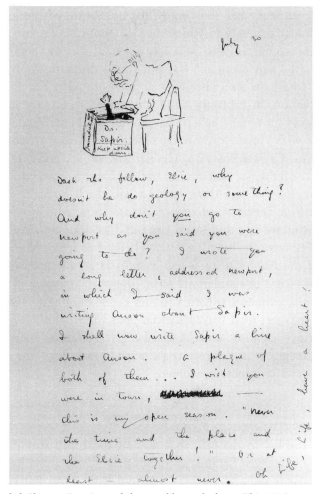

The crippled Clarence Day Jr. used the post like a telephone. This 1918 note, with its typical self-portrait, refers to Elsie's attempt to place Edward Sapir's famous article "Culture, Genuine and Spurious." Elsie Clews Parsons Papers, American Philosophical Society Library.

Sorchan, Walton Martin, Alice and Harry Miller, Grant LaFarge, Vira and Norman Whitehouse, Frances and Learned Hand, Norman Hapgood, and Clarence Day.[25]

For Parsons, feminism and anthropology were inextricably linked; and at the same time as she was a passionate participant in all this talk, she was also the cool observer. The young anthropologists she made contact with early in 1912, and their mentor Franz Boas, all had "their" people, whom they studied intensively in what has often been called "salvage ethnology." Parsons had been systematically observing "her" people—those of her own social milieu—at least since 1904. Back in New York, with Herbert no longer in political office, she turned more seriously to this ethnography of everyday life as a means of dealing with current social problems, especially those of sex and marriage.

In 1906, when she published *The Family,* Parsons had made an indirect, scholarly attack on the evolutionary paradigm—bolstered by reports from female missionaries—that represented the white, "Nordic" family as the peak of civilization. Now she had an explicitly modernist scientific program to draw on, as well as a new, receptive audience of young feminists and modernists who wanted to hear this message. But this audience wanted to have fun as well. With *The Old-Fashioned Woman* (1913), the book that "everyone" but Herbert was talking to her about in August 1912, Parsons developed the slyly witty, terse, ironic style that became her trademark, mingling ethnographic accounts from Polynesia, Turkey, or aboriginal Australia with observations from her own New York life.[26]

The Old-Fashioned Woman: Primitive Fancies about the Sex represented a direct attack on evolutionary ideas of sex and race. Posing as a piece of salvage ethnology, it was an extended feminist joke that tore down the distinction between primitive and civilized and, popularizing Goldenweiser's deconstructive methodology, mercilessly questioned the reality that lay behind the concept "woman." It was a delightfully modernist piece of work, turning expectations upside-down, exploding categories, indiscriminately mixing times and places, and swamping the reader with a "lethal bath of facts" reminiscent of Westermarck, drawn from sources ranging from *The Sacred Books of the East* to the *Reports of the Cambridge Anthropological Expedition to Torres Straits* and *A Girl's Life Eighty Years Ago.*[27]

The message of *The Old-Fashioned Woman* was that "woman" was an outmoded category kept alive only by the bizarre rituals of the Elders. The author apologized for adding to "the already disproportionate bibliography on Woman," acknowledging that books about women were archaic. Indeed, she expected "to be gathered up some day with the others as an exhibit in a Woman's Museum, a museum for collections of female poetry and biography and romance, of models of women's apartments, women's hotels, and women's buildings at fairs, of specimens of women's industries and arts and clothes; for collections of the first book read by Woman or the first newspaper, the first law brief or the first novel written by her, the first joke made by her, the first medical prescription signed or the first bone set by her, the first degree conferred upon her, the first ballot cast by her." Like pieces of archeological evidence, these exhibits "alone will be able to prove to a doubting posterity that once women were a distinct social class, the very special object of society's interest."[28]

Native Informant

Having disposed of the concept of "woman," Parsons began to draw on her own experience even more deliberately. In "The Imaginary Mistress," written after her traumatic return from Yucatán in spring 1913, and "The Journal of a Feminist, 1913–1914" and its successor, "The Journal of a Pacifist" (1914–15), she turned native informant, reporting on New York upper-class and intellectual culture as an insider might to a visiting ethnographer.

In adopting the persona of native informant, Parsons was again playing—half seriously, half in fun—with the latest anthropological methodology. Boas established the guidelines for the method in 1900 when he observed that one of the chief aims of anthropology was to study the "infinite" variety exhibited by the mind of man under varying conditions of race and environment. "In order to understand these clearly," he pointed out, "the student must endeavor to divest himself entirely of opinions and emotions based upon the peculiar social environment into which he is born. He must adapt his own mind, so far as feasible, to that of the people whom he is studying. . . . He must follow lines of thought that are new to him. He must participate in new emotions, and understand how, under unwonted conditions, both lead to actions."[29]

In trying to conform to this prescription, Boas and his students relied heavily on native informants. The evidence they gathered from an informant was usually in the form of folktales and detailed accounts of ceremonials, which were used as windows into the native mind. In their attempts to keep this material as uncontaminated as possible by their own cultural assumptions, the Boasians collected "native texts" in the informant's own language, involved the informant in the translation process, and published those texts with the original transcription interlined with the translation. Paul Radin extended this approach most radically by using native autobiography in an attempt to elicit an account of the informant's belief system that was even less weighted by the anthropologist's assumptions, and less skewed toward the ceremonial and the traditional.[30]

In experimenting with native autobiography, Radin was applying to anthropology what had become during the previous decade a popular literary and sociological form among young modernists. William James's students were among the pioneers of this new genre, but James was only the most influential of the exponents of a view of the world that was common to Mach, Tarde, Bergson, Boas, and other definers of modernism. Drawing his inspiration from Robert Louis Stevenson's "The Lantern-bearer," James articulated during the 1890s the philosophy that was basic to the settlement house movement and to the new education: an insistence that each person must attempt an imaginative understanding of the experience and feelings of others. Only then, he argued, would the aggregate life of man, otherwise monstrous, repetitive, and trivial, take on dignity and richness. "The obstinate insisting that tweedledum is not tweedledee is the bone and marrow of life," he observed.[31]

James's student Hutchins Hapgood took this idea into popular journalism between 1897 and 1910 when he experimented with participant observation, biography, and autobiography as methods of conveying the direct experience of immigrant, working-class, and underworld life. A more diverse, "ordinary," and authentic collection of autobiographies was published in 1906 by Parsons's fellow sociology student, *Independent* editor Hamilton Holt. One of the enthusiastic reviewers of Holt's *Life Stories of (Undistinguished) Americans As Told by Themselves* was University of Chicago sociologist W. I. Thomas, who made the "human document"—primarily autobiographies and letters—the central methodological tool in the monumental study, *The Polish Peasant in Europe and America* (1918–20), he carried out with Bergson scholar Florian Znaniecki.[32]

Feminists and immigrants were quick to claim the human document as their own. The autobiography, the journal, the life story allowed them to speak with their own voices, unmediated by patriarchal or nativist interpretations; and the cool, flat, unembellished style of the human document gave their words the flavor of the "real world" favored by the new "chaste" scientists. The period 1905 to 1913 was crucial in the lives and work of a number of feminist writers, as it was for Parsons. Like Parsons, Gertrude Stein, Edith Wharton, Mary Heaton Vorse, and Neith Boyce struggled to free themselves from traditional expectations about relationships and work. All experimented, during this period, with new ways of describing the world from their point of view as women. Stein did this most dramatically, writing her family's story compulsively through the night in her Paris studio, gradually eliminating punctuation, sentences, paragraphs, and narrative until she disposed finally of the weight of her family history and of patriarchal forms of language. Then, between 1911 and 1913, she placed herself confidently among the new geniuses, such as Matisse and Picasso, who had the gift of perceiving the world in an almost unmediated fashion; and she set about redescribing her world, piece by piece, person by person.[33]

"How can you read a book how can you read a book and look. / I have no book. / I look," Stein wrote in 1922. This is exactly what Parsons and her feminist friends were attempting to do in those years—to see and describe the world through their own eyes and voices rather than those of traditional authorities whose perceptions were enshrined in books, religious teaching, and laws. Turning themselves into native informants, they described their own lives in dispassionate prose and, with the enhanced perception of the "insider/outsider" or the Stranger—to use Georg Simmel's 1909 term—reported on the customs of the people around them.[34]

William James contended in 1890 that "what is called our 'experience' is almost entirely determined by our habits of attention." Our selective attention is strengthened by words and concepts to which we "grow more and more enslaved" with the years, and objects that fail to conform to our semantic "pigeonholes" are "simply not taken account of at all." Not only do such words and concepts determine what objects are noticed, they also distort perceptions of those objects. For "whilst part of what we perceive comes through our senses from the objects before us, another part (*and it may be the larger part*) always comes out of our own mind." We rarely perceive a datum in its "sensational nudity."[35]

Parsons's popular writing between 1912 and 1917 was a concerted attempt to make people perceive the data of sex, age, race, and culture in their "sensational nudity." As native informant, she focused on the most "exoteric" manifestations of New York and Washington culture—those aspects of everyday thought that were so taken-for-granted that they were almost impossible to perceive. H. L. Mencken described Parsons's subject matter in an admiring review as "thinking that is only half intellectual, the other half being as automatic and unintelligent as swallowing, blinking the eye or falling in love." Of these exoteric beliefs Parsons took as her speciality "the conventionalities." "Conventionalities are those beliefs and customs which modern society has begun to question," Parsons explained in the preface to *Fear and Conventionality* in 1914. They are therefore "in decomposition, more or less conscious of their own decay." In her view, the tenacity with which conventionalities were adhered to in the face of their obvious obsolescence provided valuable evidence about contemporary psychoses. "A dying out type of psychosis may be in even more need of description than a dying out people," she noted in 1915.[36]

The first contemporary psychosis Parsons examined was her own obsessive jealousy. In "The Imaginary Mistress"—which parallels closely the story of her own marriage between 1908 and 1913—she posed as an ethnographer reporting an informant's autobiographical account of that most perplexing of modern dilemmas, "human monopoly." As the title indicates, Parsons was interested in exploring in this account that part of her relationship with Herbert and Lucy Wilson that "came out of her own mind"—to put it in James's terms. In the two "Journals," which record in thinly disguised form her conversations with Herbert, her children, her mother, and her friends, she is a native informant making daily field notes on the sexual mores and nationalistic passions of her "tribe" for the social psychologist Elsie Clews Parsons, who adds an introduction and interpretive footnotes. The advantage of the native informant, she has "Elsie Clews Parsons" tell us in the introduction to the "Journal of a Feminist," is that she can capture "the differences in mentality met in the same society"—"a picture that the sojourner among savages rarely if ever undertakes at all and that the drawing room portraitist, the novelist, usually colors up to match tradition."[37]

"The Imaginary Mistress" and the two "Journals" were never published. But they provided the empirical basis for the popular books and articles on the conventionalities of sex, race, age, and nation that Parsons published between 1914 and 1917; and they constituted the stepping-off point for much of her specialist anthropological work as well. In *Fear and Conventionality* (1914), Parsons exposed and poked fun at the ceremonials that hedged interactions between strangers, between different social and age groups, and between the sexes; and in *Social Freedom* (1915) and *Social Rule* (1916), she extended her analysis to the "primitive" thinking surrounding ethnicity, nationality, and patriotism. In these books she diagnosed two major contemporary psychoses—fear and what she called, in Nietzsche's term, the will to power.

Social Freedom

Robert Lowie told Paul Radin in 1920 that anthropology, under Mach's inspiration, had performed the function of psychoanalysis for him. Once rescued from bondage by Mach, he wrote, he resolved that there would be "no more systems or faiths, religious or non-religious for me. I'd rather gambol on the green under the blue dome of the sky than go back to the Black Hole, however camouflaged."[38]

Anthropology performed the same function for Parsons. Just as Mach tried to free modern physics from superfluous concepts and categories, Parsons used anthropology to free herself from the "black hole" of outmoded and unnecessary age, sex, marital, and cultural classifications, and the "psychoses" they brought with them. As she struggled to refashion her personal and professional life between 1912 and 1916, she found that an eclectic mix of Mach, ethnology, and feminism helped her to abandon certitudes and develop a more original, complex, and flexible approach to life, work, and social problems.

Human beings have a passion for classification and a fear of anomalies, Parsons argued in *Social Freedom* in 1915, summing up the set of ideas she had been developing since 1912. In other words, they fear those who are unclassified or unclassifiable. What is more, the established social categories take on a life of their own, spreading over all aspects of life, no matter how remote. "The modern Chinaman, however feminist he may be, cannot avoid referring to darkness or cold or the evil side of the world by the same word he uses for woman," she observed ironically. "Nor can he write the ideograph for wrangling or intrigue without using the character for woman." Classifications also arrest innovative thought: "The classification once made is still binding, more binding than the bandages [the feminist Chinaman] is now removing from the feet of his daughters." The urge to classify, fear of social change, and structures of social control are closely related, Parsons contended in *Social Rule* in 1916. "Social categories are an unparalled means of gratifying the will to power. The classified individual may be held in subjection in ways the unclassified escapes."[39]

Given the power of classification, the main objective of feminism for Parsons was "the declassification of women as women, the recognition of women as human beings or personalities." "The more thoroughly a woman is classified the more easily is she controlled," Parsons wrote in *Social Rule*. "The *new woman*," therefore, "means the woman not yet classified, perhaps not classifiable." The most important outcome of declassification would be the substitution of "personality" for some more rigidly defined and consistent identity. For Mach, the ego was only a makeshift, designed for provisional orientation and for definite practical ends; and he was adamant that this delimitation of identity was often "insufficient, obstructive, and untenable." "The primary fact is not the ego, but the elements [of sensation]," he emphasized. "The ego must be given up."[40]

This view of the ego as a theoretical construction, like the category "woman," opened the way for Parsons's view of the "personality." A personality did not have any preconceived characteristics or consistency. Instead, it reacted spontaneously to its environment. In Parsons's conception of social freedom, men and women would have wider scope for different expressions of self, and these would be more frankly represented in their relationships. "The day will come," she wrote in the "Journal of a Feminist," "when the individual . . . [will not] have to pretend to be possessed of a given quota of femaleness or maleness. . . . This morning perhaps I feel like a male; let me act like one. This afternoon I may feel like a female; let me act like one. At midday or at midnight I may feel sexless; let me therefore act sexlessly. . . . It is such a confounded bore to have to act one part endlessly."

"Men too may rebel some time against the attribute of maleness," Parsons emphasized, bringing out the point that feminism was a movement for men as well as for women. "The taboo on a man acting like a woman has ever been stronger than the taboo on a woman acting like a man. Men who question it are ridiculed as effeminate or damned as perverts. But I know men who are neither 'effeminate' nor perverts who feel the woman nature in them and are more or less tried by having to suppress it." Someday, she concluded, "there may be a 'masculinism' movement to allow men to act 'like women.'"[41]

For Parsons, the new cultural anthropology had the potential to assist the development of what she called an "unconventional society" by clarifying concepts and questioning classifications. "A maturing culture struggles against its categories," she wrote in 1915. "At first it aims for mobility within them and then, as in these latter days, for freedom away from them." In a world where categories are only temporary expedients for practical purposes, "willingness to change [will be] a recognized virtue, a criterion in fact of morality," she wrote in *Fear and Conventionality* in 1914, in the first major statement of her ideas on social freedom. "Differences in others will no longer be recognized as troublesome or fearful. . . . Nor will presumptions of superiority or inferiority attach to differences *per se*." Unconstrained by fixed categories, people would become more curious, more daring, more open, and more sincere, Parsons argued, and at the same time they would enjoy a degree of privacy previously impossible to achieve.[42]

Unclassified, Unclassifiable

Parsons's project in her life and work from 1912 was to free the self from the prison house of categorization. Judith Ryan has demonstrated in *The Vanishing Subject* that the fragmentation of the self was a major preoccupation of modernist writers under the influence of Mach and William James. Interestingly, it is the women she studies—Gertrude Stein and Virginia Woolf—who are the most accepting of the world without a self, as one of Woolf's characters put it. For Woolf, release from the "damned egotistical self" (which she attributes to Joyce in her diary) is a liberation that allows a fluid subjectivity which is better able to challenge the categorizing and controlling tendencies of patriarchy that Parsons also exposes.[43]

Parsons's own life from this time was a deliberate attempt to create a life without a rigidly defined self, to reconstruct herself as a truly new woman who was, as she put it, unclassified, unclassifiable. Mach had said that physics was only experience, arranged in economical order. Basic to Parsons's feminist project was the notion, reminiscent of Tarde and James, of experience as the source of knowledge, adaptability, and power. If women were to resist classification and help create a more flexible approach to knowledge and life, they had to deliberately seek out a wider experience. Feminism for Parsons was therefore both a mental and a physical "adventure" involving the crossing of boundaries and the challenging of classifications. The female traveler and the female stranger epitomized for her the modern, independent woman. As she observed in 1914: "In no culture have women shown desire to do anything which requires running the risks of being alone. Women hermits are extremely scarce, there are few women explorers, there are no women vagabonds. . . . Rarely indeed do women go off by themselves—into the corner of a ballroom, into the wilderness, to the play, to the sacred high places of the earth, or to the Islands of the Blessed. Penelope stays at home."[44]

Parsons considered sex one of the most difficult barriers to cross. According to her observations, classification by sex maintained the segregation of the sexes, preventing women from encroaching on men's territory. In fact, men and women were like strangers from another country, their separation emphasized by all sorts of taboos. "The streets of Seoul were once taboo to women by day," she noted, remembering her own sheltered upbringing. "There are streets of New York once taboo to them at night." One of the most important means of breaking down the barriers of sex, and the greatest opportunity for the expression of personality, as she had realized from childhood, was friendship, because it was "so regardless of conventions, so heedless of status." Marriage, with its obstinate claim to conjugal identity, tended, as she had found out to her sorrow, to obliterate all expression of personality.[45]

In her attempt to develop personality and reject categorization, Parsons deliberately cultivated an adventurous life, physically, intellectually, and emotionally, and exposed herself to a variety of situations that forced her to interact in personal rather than conventional ways. Anthropological fieldwork provided her with the ideal vehicle for the sort of multifaceted self she wanted to create. After 1911, when Mac, the last of her four children, was born, she spent at least part of each year in the field. At first these field trips were short, because of her young family; but as the children grew older and she and Herbert worked out a more egalitarian approach to family and work, they became longer. These trips were almost always both physically and mentally challenging—and deliberately so. They also combined work and pleasure. Her fieldwork and her wealth allowed her to spend her life in a variety of places—winters in New York and summers in Newport, Lenox, or Maine, or, depending on the children's ages and needs, somewhere in the field. And she cultivated a wide variety of relationships—as wife, mother, lover, colleague, and friend—allowing none of them to dominate or exclude the others.[46]

Parsons's living experiment in destroying the concept of "woman," and with it the idea of the unified self, was a difficult one that often met with considerable opposition and incomprehension. Herbert eventually came to terms with it. Her children were chagrined or delighted by it according to their different personalities. The friends she made over these years, such as writers and critics Clarence Day, Francis Hackett, and Randolph Bourne, relished her immediacy, freshness, and originality; while Robert Herrick, her lover during the 1920s, alternately adored and condemned her refusal to subsume her personality in their relationship. She is "a good deal talked about for advanced ideas and peculiar conduct . . . [and] is generally considered a cold, queer woman," Herrick wrote in one of his more negative moments.[47]

In her anthropological colleagues, however, Parsons found an understanding and supportive group. Although they teased her about her "dual nature"—the cultural "propagandist" and public intellectual in the winter and detached anthropological researcher in the summer—they found in her "propaganda" an expression of their own vision of a culturally diverse and tolerant world. In 1916, Robert Lowie drew an explicit parallel between "[her] individualism, [her] insistence that persons should be regarded as 'individuals, as elusive, many-sided personalities'" and "the pluralism of the historical ethnologist, who insists on grasping any particular fact as a *unique* phenomenon and refuses to pigeon-hole it in some such rubric as an historical law." And Franz Boas acknowledged the similarities of their projects when he inscribed his photograph to her in 1936: "To Elsie Clews Parsons, fellow in the struggle for freedom from prejudice."[48]

Perry Anderson has suggested that modernism flowered in the space between the still useable past, an indeterminate technical present, and a profoundly ambiguous future. Mach's critical positivism captured the uncertainties and possibilities of this space; and it was there that feminism emerged, grasping the fragility of the self and turning it into a source of emancipation, in a sort of politics of the self. For Parsons, Mach's dissolving self was an important resource through which she could reconstruct her life as a form of permanent revolution, forever escaping definition and imprisonment by the expectations of others. Her anthropological reference group, who understood her project, provided the supportive environment that helped her sustain it.[49]

CHAPTER SEVEN

New Marriage

AFTER five years of anguish, Parsons's life began to take a more satisfying shape in 1914. Not only did she have supportive anthropological friends and colleagues in Pliny Goddard and Robert Lowie, but she had found an audience eager for her "views." Everyone wanted to talk about sex, and following the publication of *The Old-Fashioned Woman* in April 1913, Parsons was sought after for her sparkling and incisive analyses of sexual mores. "I haven't forgotten my ethnological quest of finding out what you think about human mating," Goddard wrote in November 1913, "and why you came to think it when most people do not dare to cross."[1]

Separating Sex and Parenthood

In August 1913, as she was finishing "The Imaginary Mistress"—an exercise that seemed to exorcise, at least temporarily, her marital problems—Parsons had began noting down the sexual folkways of her social set in her "Journal of a Feminist." *Current Opinion* had just announced that it was "sex o'clock in America," and her friend Norman Hapgood, who had taken over the editorship of *Harper's Weekly*, announced, rather rashly, "We intend, if possible, to make ourselves the official organ for the Feminist Movement." Hapgood proved too timid to publish anything as radical as Parsons's ideas. But he included enough feminist (or suffragist) material to annoy more conservative readers. In a cutting review of Parsons's *Social Freedom* three years later, when the *Weekly* was about to go under, James L. Ford attributed its "present prosperity" to its "wise selection of editorials of incredible stupidity" and its "many pages of what is known as 'sex matter' or 'advanced feminism.'" Ford suggested sarcastically that the owners of this "great instrument for the moulding of modern thought" should employ Mrs. Parsons. "Constant brooding over the great problems of the day has caused *Harper's Weekly* to shrink like a flannel undershirt, until it is now about the size of an ivory paper cutter, but thought has broadened Mrs. Parsons' horizon, so that it sheds its gleams over the entire world." Especially good, Ford thought, "is the chapter on sex, a theme that has driven bonnets from the minds of thousands of advanced women. . . . That the volume will be thoroughly enjoyed by those who compose New York's eminent thinking classes I cannot for a moment doubt."[2]

Ford's advice might actually have saved the *Weekly,* because the "eminent thinking classes" were very keen to hear what Mrs. Parsons had to say. "They do consult me as a sort of mother confessor," she wrote in "Journal of a Feminist" in August 1913. "I'm supposed to have 'views,' you see, on almost any question between the sexes, having written a book on some of them." Noting down and reflecting on the sexual conventions among her friends that kept even "illicit" relations from maintaining their freshness, Parsons drew up the code of behavior in family and sexual relationships that she advocated in print and lived by in private for the rest of her life.[3]

Parsons had "settled the family," as Goddard put it, in February 1914 in a talk to the Cosmopolitan Club, one of the many New York discussion groups that fed on the new, open conversation about previously forbidden topics. In "The Future of the Family," Parsons employed the methodology she had used the previous year in *The Old-Fashioned Woman*—this time to question the very concept of "the family." Sexual relations and parenthood are distinct and separable facts, she argued, and until people are conscious of that distinction, their ethics and conduct will be uncertain, confused, and unnecessarily tragic. Echoing Goldenweiser and Lowie, Parsons contended that habitual associations tend to be seen as necessary. In this way, the Christian idea that passion was only justified by the production of children hardened into a belief that mating was necessarily linked with parenting. But we can no longer allow ourselves to be bullied by tradition, she maintained. "Are the elders . . . they who feel least the impulses of sex, the fittest to regulate them?"

Taking hope from the current willingness to question traditional ideas and behavior, Parsons looked forward to a time "when in social theory, but mind you not necessarily in actuality, marriage and parenthood will be divorced." Then, she went on, stating the central tenet of her approach, sexual relations will be a purely private matter. Parenthood, on the other hand, will take on much more public significance. A parents' registry and court will replace the marriage registry and divorce court; a parents' certificate will replace the marriage certificate; and parent contract law, with provision for the support of the mother during pregnancy and for a given period after childbirth—by the mother, the father, or the state—will replace matrimonial property laws.

Under the existing system, Parsons observed, the state interferes only when affairs have become a mess. With a system that distinguished between mating and parenthood, she envisaged "the same provisions made amicably and with foresight before the birth of the child that are now made in many cases in the divorce court—with friction and pain." She acknowledged that acceptance of "the momentous and comparatively new knowledge of how to regulate conception" was basic to her plan, but she emphasized that it was much less radical than it appeared: "It leaves a man and a woman free to co-operate in a family life. It also leaves either man or woman free not to co-operate. Both systems are worked now. All it does is to help the individual to open his or her eyes to all his or her acts, and to help the public to place responsibilities where they belong." "But this," she added, "is—something."[4]

A Feminist Sexual Ethics

In a series of articles published in the *International Journal of Ethics* between 1915 and 1917, but worked out during this period of soul-searching from 1913 to 1914, Parsons spelled out the ethical consequences of her feminist analysis of the family. Disentangling private sex relations and public parental relations would allow sexual issues to be decided on their own merits, she argued. Once the antiquated issue of legitimate heirs was disposed of, the idea of marriage as ownership dissolved and marital rape was conceivable. Age of consent and of marriage would be based on the interests of the young rather than their elders. Seduction (or, as Parsons redefined it, deception in love) would become a private matter. The concept of adultery would disappear, and important for Parsons herself, the problem of jealousy would be mitigated. "With the conditions for privacy more or less formalized and their observance a conventionality, with the advertisement of a sex relationship discountenanced," she reasoned, "the spirit of monopoly towards another will be condemned, even getting the habit of being always with another will be discouraged."

With "the flotsam of a traditional and inept morality" removed, Parsons was hopeful that new standards of sincerity, honor, and responsibility would emerge for parenthood as well as for sexual relations. The concept of illegitimacy would disappear, and in its place parents who reproduced under circumstances injurious to the child would be stigmatized as irresponsible. Parsons also welcomed the opportunity for women to take more responsibility, economic and otherwise, for childbearing and rearing: this might prompt young women and their families to insure for maternity as they would for any possible economic disadvantage, and to insist on a parents' contract before the possibility of conception arises, just as they now insisted on a marriage contract. As parenthood became more voluntary, Parsons hoped, it would become a more significant enterprise for both men and women.[5]

Discussing the importance of sexual ethics for feminism, Parsons noted that sex was rarely theorized for itself: generally it was considered for "the good of society" (in other words, for the good of the Elders) or, more recently, for the good of the unborn. But Parsons felt strongly that consideration of sex for its own sake opened up major opportunities for improved relations between the sexes. Late-nineteenth-century feminists, caught up in the rhetoric of female purity, had worried too much about public opinion and had allowed themselves to be driven back into "one corner of the proprietary fold" by the charge of "free love"—"a little anti-feminist strategy far from novel," she observed. Accumulating there "a good deal of sex resistance and sex bitterness," they wasted their energies and closed off an important area of common interest with men. Increasing acceptance of birth control—due, she noted, to medical advances and economic pressure on men more than to feminism—meant that the distinction between sexual relations and parenthood could be extended to women as it always had been to men. This in turn allowed reciprocity as a new standard for sex relations; questions of mutual satisfaction became paramount; and candor about what each party asks or offers—desire for children, social position, property or support, or the momentary satisfaction of passion—became a priority. "The relationship . . . should be frank," she urged, "as frank in marriage . . . as it is now in prostitution."

With reciprocity and candor the basis of sex relations "permanence will cease to be the final criterion of virtue," Parsons predicted. "It is of course the criterion society is fondest of because of the guaranty it affords every one against readjustment. . . . Impermanence in mating is too upsetting to society to be accounted anything but unworthy, base, to be precluded at any price . . . even at the price sometimes of all that makes the relationship worthy." Lasting love was a blessing, like lasting health or energy or happiness, but change "should be met, not lied about or shirked." The loss of love may be a tragedy, she argued, but it should not be seen as an offense.

Parsons suggested that sincerity and wholeheartedness should replace permanence as the measure of passionate love. "We subscribe now to that standard," she observed, obviously referring to her own experience, "but in words merely. For . . . we welcome conditions which make for a meagre, partial, and impoverished relationship. The daily familiarity we so insist upon in marriage would of itself take the edge off any spiritual intimacy. . . . A degree of loneliness is essential to fervor. And, for many of us, other personal relationships. It is only when monogamy is an observance, not a spiritual relationship, that it is dependent upon a continuous and exclusive intercourse."[6]

Privacy and Sincerity in Love Affairs

In a talk to the Heretics, one of the many discussion groups she participated in between 1913 and 1915, Parsons elaborated her ideas on privacy in love affairs. One of her clever, pithy articles in the *Masses* reports a conversation stimulated by a Respectable Married Woman—no doubt herself at the Heretics dinner—who remarked that if she began over again, she would "keep any intimacy an entirely private concern, a concern of the man she loved and herself." She resented the intrusions of others as "a gross impertinence, a very amazing condition to which we subjected ourselves." In a surprising alliance in favor of publicity, one man, defending the proprietary theory, argued that such lack of advertisement would be unfair to other men, and a "professional feminist" (probably the radical schoolteacher Henrietta Rodman) argued that advertisement had the virtue of eliminating the possibility of sex, thus allowing women to have intellectual and human relations with men.

The Respectable Married Woman disagreed with both: "Between a relationship all sex as in the ante-feminist past and the entirely sexless relationship you say appeals to you I don't see much to choose from," she countered in an argument that was central to Parsons's ideas and practice on the role of sex in the workplace. Why keep sex so tagged and docketed? So shunted off from human relations? Sex is a part of every personality, and into any personal relations between a man and a woman it naturally enters—more or less. Whether more or less is to be decided for itself in each case,

[handwritten margin notes: privacy is context + personal, not social status; which helps + personal]

otherwise a relationship isn't personal at all, it's impersonal, a status relationship, a relationship of the old order."[7]

Continuing the discussion in an unpublished article, the Respectable Married Woman emphasized the importance of sincerity in love affairs. Free lovers and marriage advocates alike place a high priority on publicity and permanence, she observed. "When the people around you know just what your relationship is they help you to keep it fixed. . . . I'm for permanence too in a sense. . . . But when it ceases to be a good thing I don't want it. . . . It may be all right to accept the second best or the third best in insignificant things, but love-making isn't a trifling business."

"Publicity is harmful to sincerity in the relation of marriage and furtiveness to integrity in illicit relations," the Respectable Married Woman continued. "Furtiveness makes any relationship onesided, limited; publicity makes it insincere . . . because a public relation is subject to the group will. . . . And what the group wants in personal relations is the static, the permanent." But "to be sincere a personal relation must be changing. . . . As soon as it is static it becomes dead, impersonal, insincere."[8]

One major contributor to insincerity in personal relations, according to Parsons, was the "tagger-on spouse problem." In a much-discussed article in the *New Republic* in June 1916, she observed mordantly that "A husband or a wife is a personal taste, a private taste." "To force your predilections on others is generally accounted in bad taste, so why draw the line at the conjugal relation?" The identification of husband and wife may be all right for ceremonial occasions, she conceded. "But when we ask people to dine with us or to join a discussion group or a tennis game or a yachting party are we motivated by a desire to support the sanctity of institutions, of the family or even of marriage?" A slight change in polite usage—the sending of separate invitations—would facilitate a new, less institutional, more personal form of social intercourse that would be welcomed by all concerned. "Although in itself a small matter, the separate invitation would contribute . . . somewhat like the separate dressing room or the separate bank account, to the establishment of personal decency and dignity."[9]

A Modern Relationship

As Parsons worked out these principles for modern sex relations, she forged an important new relationship with an old friend, the

Grant LaFarge, 1913. Elsie Clews Parsons Papers, American Philosophical Society Library.

architect Grant LaFarge. She and Herbert had known LaFarge for many years. The son of the well-known artist John LaFarge and Margaret Perry, he was brought up in Newport, and his cousin Aimée Lawrence was one of Parsons's childhood friends. He lived in New York and had a summer cottage at Saunderstown opposite Newport, where the family owned two miles of the rugged coastline. LaFarge was a skilled outdoorsman who shared Parsons's delight in sailing, canoeing, and camping. He had gone west as a young man and explored the Rocky Mountains with Teddy Roosevelt, with whom he was a founder of the Boone and Crockett Club. His camping trips along Canadian lakes and rivers brought him into contact with the native population of that region. He was also fluent in Spanish. His son Oliver, born in 1901, became an anthropologist, advocate for Native Americans, and writer, whose fictionalized account of Navajo life, *Laughing Boy,* won the Pulitzer Prize in 1929.[10]

Parsons seems to have deliberately sought out Grant LaFarge as an agreeable canoeing companion soon after her unhappy return from the Yucatán in the spring of 1913. He quickly divined in her "a wonderful place that is compounded of directness . . . and a very generous sweetness." Throughout that summer he was part of the group at Newport whose sexual perplexities and behaviors Parsons noted in the "Journal." By the fall, as she developed her ideas on sex and marriage, and began to ponder the larger concept of social freedom, their relationship had developed into the "uninstitutional" sexual companionship that she was seeking.[11]

The essence of a good relationship for Parsons was its unpublicized nature. We therefore know little about LaFarge or the relationship. As the son and brother of famous artists, the brother of a Catholic educator of note, and the father of two well-known writers, we can glean something of his character from various accounts of the family. John LaFarge, the father, was six feet tall, with dark brown hair and grey-green eyes set in deep sockets, and a long, straight, aristocratic nose. Grant LaFarge apparently shared his father's long, lean, dark looks and his temper, which was, by all accounts, "frightful." He also appears to have shared his father's unsentimental curiosity. John LaFarge "was concerned in somewhat eighteenth-century fashion with all varieties of human beings, near and far," his youngest son recollected, "different races and types of men, their ways, their habits, their songs, their dances, their customs, and their wars, their psychology, the peculiarities of old and young, men and women." According to Grant LaFarge's son Oliver, his father's voice was always quiet. "He used wild country as Indians do, in co-operation and communion with it, finding any form of noise a baneful disharmony." "Learning from him," Oliver LaFarge wrote, "we were always conscious of his reserves of experience. Canadian Indians accepted him as an equal canoeman. He was utterly at home in Arizona. He had sailed with our own Rhode Island fishermen long before a power-driven smack was dreamed of. The wild goose, the mountain goat, the elk, salmon, moose and caribou, snowshoes, pack-horses, tump-line and fishing smack were his familiars." "He was a very easy man to talk to," the younger LaFarge recalled, "radiating his great personal charm and warmth."[12]

Grant LaFarge had been married since 1895 to Florence Bayard Lockwood, a confidante of Roosevelt and member of a prominent political family. If a conversation with her canoeing partner that Parsons reports in "Journal of a Feminist" for August 1913 is accurate, he "had already experimented [with an extramarital affair], and disastrously." He was fond of his wife, but no longer in love with her, and his wife was not in love with him either. But she still thought it was an indignity for him to fall in love with someone else.[13]

A discussion with her friend Charlotte Sorchan a few months later, again lightly fictionalized in the "Journal," gives us some insight into Parsons's own marriage at that time. Ethel (Charlotte), a "half rebel in sex" who had children, a husband, and a lover, had been shocked by H. G. Wells's recent novel, *The Passionate Friends.* "But could you live with one man if you were in love with another," she asked Parsons, meaning, of course, "have sex with." "Could you even conceive of living with two men at the same time?" "Perhaps, given our society," the journal writer replies. "Its typical husband wants so very little that it might be easy to gratify him from mere affection. Besides living with a man, as you put it, may be such an indifferent, mechanical kind of a performance—a few minutes of unfeeling passivity twice a week now and then. If a man wants no more, he gets no more." "But is not physical intimacy a base thing unless it means more than that? . . . Shouldn't it always be an expression of one's highest feelings?" "I don't know. Actually of course we know it isn't. In the same relationship too it differs from time to time enormously. Why should we have such fixed preconceptions about one of our senses? . . . I wonder sometimes if we don't greatly exaggerate the meaning of physical intimacy. . . . why should one part of the body be more taboo, more 'sacred,' more inviolable than another?"

"To this tirade I got no answer," the journal writer observed. "Ethel has institutionalized her lover quite as thoroughly as once she did her husband. . . . Most women do that—and most men. The lover is still quite as conventional a figure as the husband. . . . A woman may be taken out to dinner by her lover, but not by her husband. She may be kissed by her husband in a railroad station, but not by her lover. In either situation has the physical contact or the lack of it any personal meaning?"[14]

Talking to Clarence Day the following evening, Parsons mulled over the whole question of monogamy. As she put it in the "Journal," Earnest (Day) "has the art of that talk that can be so intimate because it is so impersonal." Divining, as he often did, what she was thinking, he asked, "Isn't permanent monogamy the best of all relationships after all?" "Perhaps it is," she answered, "if . . . you mean an enduring relationship, many-sided and intimate and in so far as it is passionate, exclusive. . . . That is . . . the best that can come to one. . . . But . . . that kind of relationship has never been tried out. . . . The institution of marriage imposes conditions fatal to passion. Because a man knows he can get what he wants at any time he stops taking trouble to get it. His uncourted wife has become a passive, passionless woman, at best only a friend, at worst a jealous proprietress. The institution of adultery . . . kills passion too . . . by fear and furtiveness and endless restrictions. . . . In marriage conditions are too easy; in adultery they are too difficult. Marriage includes everything but passion, adultery excludes everything except passion. So there you are. Love at its best between a man and a woman is really not recognized at all by society. It never has been. So that it has no standards or norm or code."[15]

Meditating later on her conversation with Clarence, Parsons continued her "monologue" on marriage. "The problem of sex feminists have now to face is primarily a psychological problem," she decided. "How are women to live *with* men, not *without* men like the ruthless fighters for institutional freedom, and not in the old way *through* men. The old way is the easy, self-indulgent way. For there seems to be a marked impulse to subjection in the normal woman. Self-surrender is one of the dominant characters of her passion . . . but . . . it tends to spread over the whole of a woman's life and to become both a conventionality and a curse . . . to both man and woman. Her continuous self-surrender persuades him that she is his for the asking or for less. He takes her for granted. Then of course her moment of tragedy begins—to end, like as not, inarticulately and in resignation. As for him, he finally appreciates that she has come to humor him and that her self-surrender is no longer the expression of desire but of mere habit. Thereafter passion is impossible for either, whatever the outward relationship they see fit to maintain. Married or unmarried they have ceased to be lovers."

How can a relationship be kept fresh and passionate, Parsons asked herself, articulating the question she had been anguishing over since her frank exchange of views with Herbert the previous year. "What is compelling, or . . . disciplinary for love?" Her answer was that of the twentieth-century woman: "Work . . . any work that is interesting and exacting." Rather than viewing work as a means of making women economically independent of men, Parsons emphasized its importance as a means of keeping them together. "It is only through work one can be quite sure one is taking life at first hand, and it is only by taking life at first hand, by being the spiritual equal of her lover that a woman may preserve a free and passionate life with him," she argued. "Let us turn away from the antiquated advocacy of work in lieu of love, as an alternative to love, and let us look to work for the sake of love, as a means of salvation for love."

Parsons's final suggestion for the salvation of love was one that she tested for herself over the next few years: what Crystal Eastman called in 1923 "Marriage under Two Roofs." "Godwin realized that continually living under the same roof together might spoil marriage and so he denied himself the unbroken familiarity of bed and board with Mary Wollstonecraft," Parsons mused, referring to the famous late-eighteenth-century feminist and her lover. "But Godwin would be considered as much of a crank today," she decided ruefully, "as he was a hundred years ago."[16]

You with Your Work, and I with Mine

With privacy, reciprocity, candor, and sincerity its guiding criteria, the relationship between Grant LaFarge and Elsie Clews Parsons lasted from 1913 to 1922. By privacy, Parsons did not mean secrecy. She never hid the fact that she was going camping with Grant, just as she went tramping with Walton Martin, or invited Pliny Goddard to Lenox for the weekend, or called to see the crippled Clarence Day. What she did keep private was the nature of each of these relationships. We know from a few letters that survive from 1913 and 1914 and some poems written in 1918 that LaFarge was very much in love with Parsons; and he mentions nostalgically toward the end of their relationship that she had written him from New Mexico in 1913 "something that you have since—is it forgotten or repudiated?" But the quality of their relationship is best conveyed by an extraordinary love letter he wrote her sometime around 1920, as he felt their relationship slipping away. Titled "Rivers and Recollections," it is a loving and detailed remembrance of all their canoeing trips, from the first hasty bivouac in a rough field by the Delaware River, where they "discussed falling in love," to a windy November evening on a little New Jersey river.[17]

"Moonlight, firelight, memories, hopes of days with you," La-Farge ends this poem to rapids, portages, tents, fern beds, cranberry bogs, and swamps: "Hither, at timely seasons, must I go with you, for long days of dear delight. You with the spoils of arduous gatherings to be set in order; ready, eager for the change, for days of peaceful work and wholesome play, for nights of restoring sleep. You with your work and I with mine; mine to make, in one way or another, pictures—that, yes, but more than that, in the province of paddle and portage, of tent and axe and fire, of gun and rod, to do that work which more than any other brings to me reward: to surround your work with pleasure, ease, with happiness, perhaps even with romance?"[18]

The steady figure of Grant LaFarge stands behind Elsie Clews Parsons's transition to professional anthropology. We know from his "Rivers and Recollections" and from Parsons's own and other accounts that he often accompanied her on folklore collecting trips and that he acted as "court photographer" and artist for many of her field trips to the Southwest. This long-lasting relationship provided, along with her children, the stable personal base Parsons needed during those transitional years. As she and Herbert slowly and shakily worked out a new modus vivendi that gave him greater responsibility for the older children, and her privacy and time for her work, she also began, from the end of 1913, to put into practice the "pragmatic experiment" she contemplated in the "Journal" that November, of marriage under two roofs. Abandoning New York life as much as was possible with the children's schooling to consider, she established herself more permanently at Stonover Farm, the family's modest home in Lenox in the Berkshire hills. There she confirmed her identity as a writer and scholar by building a writing cabin in the woods, designed for her by LaFarge, from which she could enjoy what he jokingly called "the high advantages of psychical distance." With a companion for her sorties into unfamiliar and rough territory, a retreat from the conventional demands of family and society, and a place to work, she was beginning to create her own "republic of the spirit."[19]

CHAPTER EIGHT

Dear Propagandist

ELSIE Clews Parsons's absorption into the world of Boasian cultural anthropology was gradual. Her children were still young: Lissa was thirteen in 1914, John eleven, and the two "little boys," Herbert and Mac, five and three respectively. Between 1913 and 1915, as she passed her fortieth birthday, Parsons's life was centered in New York, Newport, and Lenox, her thirst for adventure satisfied by an exciting intellectual life varied by camping and canoeing expeditions with Grant LaFarge. Her only trip to the Southwest during this period was the week's ride through the Rio Grande pueblos in the fall of 1913. During the following summer, she tried once more to travel with Herbert and the children, but their five-week western trip was disastrous. "American cities have nothing to give you and the National Parks, if not 'sentimental,' are 'unreal,'" she wrote Herbert. "Although I wasn't cranky enough to spoil things (as I had feared I might be) you must see now that there wasn't the slightest point in my being of the party. At times I may have been of some advantage to Lissa, but in ways that she will have me to call upon at any time in the next few years."[1]

Education by "Polynesian Analogues"

During these years, Parsons thought of herself primarily as a feminist social reformer who used her ethnographic skills and her ethnological knowledge to educate people to observe and think about their own experience with greater immediacy and freshness. "She is naturally a reformer, not merely an iconoclast," she wrote of herself in the introduction to "Journal of a Feminist," "and she does appear to take her sex—but fortunately not herself—a little seriously." From the publication of her article "Supernatural Policing of Women" in the *Independent* in February 1912, she was determined to use anthropology to change the way the intellectual classes

Stonover Farm, 1990. Elsie did much of her writing in a cabin in the woods above the house.

thought—first of all about women, and then about age, race, and nationality. If there was the separation of thought processes from experience by an aura of emotion that the French anthropologist Lucien Lévy-Bruhl recently imputed to the "primitive" mind, comparative anthropology provided, in Parsons's opinion, an important solvent that helped bring people into more immediate contact with the world around them. Her own travels at this time had more of the quality of periodic jolts to keep her impressions fresh than of focused "scientific" expeditions. She is careful to note in her description of herself in "Journal of a Feminist" that "she has been of late years in many of the out-of-the-way parts of America—parts utterly foreign to the oblivious New Yorker—but . . . her last journey to the Old World was made eleven years ago."[2]

During this period, Parsons campaigned actively for cultural anthropology to be included as an essential part of a liberal education, as a necessary tool for social reform, and as an aid to clear thinking that could be applied equally to literate and nonliterate societies. In December 1913, as she was working out her ideas on sex and family, she was impressed by Robert Lowie's masterly refutation for a lay audience of the idea of racial inferiority. In particular, she was struck by Lowie's observation that children needed to be educated in cultural relativity with the same emotional intensity that they were now introduced to racist ideas. Early in the new year she wrote to Lowie, "You suggest a kind of propaganda that I've had for a long time at heart. Do you think we could do something practical? Dr. Flexner the other night was talking along the same line & he asked me if I knew of any ethnological primer. . . . Something that could be used in the schools." Lowie replied enthusiastically, suggesting the additional goal of educating "the anthropologically miseducated adult population, including perhaps the majority of biologists." "I have just read Sedgwick's article in the *Times!*" he added, referring disparagingly to the well-known scientist.[3]

This was probably the genesis of an elaborate plan Parsons drew up for a university extension school of ethnology. "Some degree of shutting-your-eyes-before-you-jump is necessary in social progress," she conceded in a draft proposal for the school, "but the jumper should at least know what he is jumping from. To be well educated, socially, one must know the history of the social habits, customs and ideas of one's community, and this of course necessitates knowledge of those of others."[4]

It is unclear how far Parsons pursued this plan. But she had attended her first American Anthropological Association meetings that December, and she presented an ambitious and innovative program for anthropology to Boas around that time. Introducing herself as a student of "certain aspects of folklore, of Pueblo Indian culture and of the culture of Western Civilization," Parsons suggested that literate and nonliterate peoples should be treated alike as subjects for anthropological study, observing that their artificial separation was a "remarkable, if unremarked, instance of folklore." This would require examining the magical elements in the mental habits of literate cultures—which she had done in *Old-Fashioned Woman* and was currently working out for *Fear and Conventionality*—as well as the scientific elements in the folklore of oral cultures. It would also involve studying the cultural history of both literate and nonliterate peoples and the ways the two interact in any specific instance of cultural contact. "Inquiry into problems of acculturation throughout the world," she pointed out in her first statement in an area she was to pioneer, "is handicapped by ignorance of the culture of the civilized members in the contacts. For example, in a study of Pueblo Indian witchcraft or Haytian voodoo, we are more handicapped by our ignorance about medieval Spanish than by our ignorance of Indian or Negro."[5]

The outbreak of war in Europe in July 1914 probably undermined Parsons's attempt to find support for the school of ethnology she envisaged. But she continued to use what *Evening Post* editor Simeon Strunsky approvingly called her "Polynesian analogues" in her books and popular articles, and she took whatever opportunity she could to push the educational use of anthropology. "What a crank you are about ethnology—I mean about popularizing it!" she has Herbert (disguised as "Lawyer") exclaim in a dialogue, "Making Ethnology Popular," in the *New York Tribune*. "What good does it do me to know that somewhere on the west coast of Africa they get married with as much fuss as my great-grandmother?" Ethnology is a way of sneaking in knowledge people don't want to face, the Ethnologist answers. "Lawyer—You, mean . . . we'll sit up and take notice of how we live here in New York? . . . Set people to comparing if you want them to change? . . . you'd popularize ethnology because you're a radical, is that it?"[6]

However skeptical Herbert was about the usefulness of ethnology, Elsie's style enjoyed a certain mode among the avant-garde. "Mrs. Parsons refers to the Australian Blackfellow," a critic complained to the *New Republic* in 1915, "and this, I know, carries with it as much authority nowadays as a reference to the lives of the saints did some years ago."[7]

Reconstructing Anthropology

As an avowed "propagandist," Parsons was interested in anthropology as a practical guide to action. She found it particularly useful in revealing how people think—in other words, as an insight into their psychology. When she began to contribute to scholarly journals again at the end of 1913, she drew on her popular work to comment on two psychological tendencies, avoidance and ceremony, that helped maintain distance and group cohesion in both "primitive" and "civilized" societies. These articles, and another she wrote on friendship in 1915, were published in the *American Journal of Sociology*. With their mixture of sociology, ethnology, and psychology and their spare, provocative style, they sat rather strangely in the scholarly journal. As editor Albion Small wrote her tongue-in-cheek, "We cogitated for a long time on the problem. . . . will not Mrs. Parsons's brilliancy in the company of our dry as dust style of material look like a diamond on a gentleman in overalls?" But they would have seemed even more out of place in the *American Anthropologist* or the *Journal of American Folklore*. Psychology and social reform were treated with suspicion by anthropologists, despite the fact that Boas had been advocating for years an understanding of the native mind, and that his whole program for reform of the discipline was based on a fierce desire for social justice. But, as his daughter Helene wrote to Alfred Kroeber in 1956, "He was a man of strong emotions, and great sensitivity, repressed because of his great fear of being subjective."[8]

Pliny Goddard, however, was anxious to move anthropology beyond the dry reports of fieldwork that filled the *American Anthropologist* and the methodological point-scoring that preoccupied the *Journal of American Folklore,* and he felt that the discipline had much to learn from Parsons. When he took over as editor of the *Anthropologist* in 1915, he lured Parsons away from the *American Journal of Sociology* with the promise of a de facto partnership. Delighted by her analysis of the psychology of contemporary ceremonial in the recently published *Fear and Conventionality,* he encouraged her to challenge Lowie's arguments in a recent article on ceremonialism. "Won't you discuss Dr. Lowie's paper?" he wrote in January 1915. "I am sure you have something to say in reply. You are going to help me make the Anthropologist more than a mere record of field work accomplished. When I said the other night *we* had the journal to play with I was not using an editorial plural."[9]

Goddard saw Parsons as a powerful ally in the cause of reconstructing cultural anthropology to emphasize individual choice, action, and innovation. Having taken the highly schematic evolutionary anthropology to pieces, Boas's students were busily reconstructing the discipline. Their "American School" had developed a distinctive approach to the studies of cultural diffusion that now replaced evolution as anthropology's central concern. Eschewing the sweeping reconstructions of historical time sequences favored by their European counterparts, they carried out detailed descriptions of culture areas, building a dynamic picture of the diffusion of cultural traits among neighboring groups through a painstaking comparison of evidence from material culture, ceremonial, social organization, recorded history, language, mythology, and folklore. Boas had always insisted that this more limited and focused version of the historical method necessarily involved "the interesting psychological problems of acculturation," that is, "what conditions govern the selection of foreign material embodied in the culture of the people and the mutual transformations of the old culture and the newly acquired material." But the psychological side of Boas's program had, until recently, been poorly developed. Now Goldenweiser, Radin, and Goddard were keen to investigate the relationship between a culture and its individual members; and Boas himself encouraged this trend by bringing the innovative social psychologist H. K. Haeberlin to the Columbia graduate program in 1914, and by encouraging the systematic collection of folklore and autobiography.[10]

The enthusiasm of the young New Yorkers for a psychologically oriented anthropology was challenged at the end of 1914 by Alfred Kroeber, the older son of the Boas school. Isolated in California, and struggling with grief at the death of his wife, Kroeber wanted to "get [back] in the game" and work out for himself what his rapidly changing discipline stood for. He was also aware of the precarious hold cultural anthropology had in the universities and museums—particularly in his own University of California at Berkeley—and realized that he and his colleagues had to explain their new project clearly to their fellow scholars, especially those in the natural sciences, if it was going to survive.

Kroeber threw down the gauntlet to both natural scientists and his fellow Boasians with a paper he sent to the annual meeting of the Anthropological Association in December 1914, the second meeting Parsons attended. Carefully distinguishing anthropology from biology and psychology, he asserted that the discipline had its own quite separate subject matter—culture—which, "though carried by men and existing through them, is an entity in itself." Kroeber noted privately that his purpose in emphasizing the structural aspects of culture was primarily political. "I'm trying to reach public opinion," he underlined. "I'm tired of anthropology being a charity orphan allowed to pick up a profusion of scraps until biologists or geographers or psychologists or Madison Grants take a fancy to having them again." "If you don't agree with me," he wrote Edward Sapir, "the greatest favor you can do me is to say so publicly. I don't know whether I'm right or wrong (though I have some strong convictions on the subject), but I am sure that the only progress is by forcing issues to a head."[11]

At the same 1914 meetings, Pliny Goddard suggested an alternative direction for cultural anthropology. In his address as president of the American Folklore Society, Goddard emphasized the importance of folklore for securing an unbiased view of the native standpoint, implying, therefore, that the investigation of individual psychological processes was not only an integral part of cultural anthropology, but should be its focus. Kroeber tried to goad his old friend into sparking a debate by taking a clear stand on the issue.

"I don't expect you to subscribe, nor write footnotes, nor contro-
vert," he wrote Goddard. "You've always displayed a certain fine-
ness in your work, which makes it seem your business to tackle
something that will have more effect on others. . . . What's the use
of being timidly modest? We don't live long."[12]

Although Goddard was constitutionally unable to take up
Kroeber's challenge directly, he did make the social structure versus
individual psychology debate the major methodological issue in the
Anthropologist under his editorship. Kroeber's challenge was eventually met by Sapir, who argued forcefully for the "psychologists"
in 1917 that "it is always the individual that really thinks and acts
and dreams and revolts." But the brilliant Sapir was personally
unhappy and preoccupied with administration in his Canadian position, and was toying with the idea of quitting anthropology altogether; and during the early years of the debate, Goddard felt in sore
need of energetic, articulate supporters. Alexander Goldenweiser,
usually in the lead in methodological arguments, was in a state of
personal disarray—the beginning of a lifetime of scandal in which
"peccadilloes hung like a fringe around his loins." And Paul
Radin—"that amiable trickster"—was equally unable to take a
lead. Of all Boas's students, Radin carried out most faithfully his
dictum to understand the native from within. As Goldenweiser put
it in 1933, "Dr. Radin . . . has admirably succeeded in being a
Winnebago but finds it more difficult to cease being one." But he
was, according to an affectionate Kroeber, "a constitutional neu-
rotic who needs gentleness and tactful steering." "He is a responsibility; but also a stimulus," Kroeber wrote Parsons ruefully in 1919.
"I think you might appreciate him—for a little while."[13]

Gathering in an Ally

Throughout 1915, Goddard persistently drew Parsons into the anthropological fold, hoping she would take a lead in championing
the psychological side of the debate. Reviewing *Fear and Conventionality* in the *Anthropologist,* he pointed out it was "only incidentally" the sort of book ordinarily reviewed in that publication; but
it employed a psychological methodology that had the potential to
enlarge American anthropology's narrow scope, which, in his opinion, was "too much confined at present to those phases of culture
that are independent of psychological causes." In May that year,
Parsons was one of the inner circle who contributed to the fund

Goddard collected to assist Boas with his work following his brush with cancer earlier that year. After a visit to Lenox, Goddard wrote to Parsons as a comrade-in-arms: "There is no reason why *I* should thank you for the Boas donation. It is a pleasure that some one feels as I do about him and his work." "I tagged you Sunday night for John," he added. "He may well know that his mother is worth considering, that she possess some authority when she speaks of human society."[14]

In 1915 Parsons was a prize catch for anthropology. *The Old-Fashioned Woman* and *Fear and Conventionality* made Parsons a central figure in the New York avant-garde. Her iconoclastic articles on the psychology of sexual and intergenerational relationships, and her provocative articles on war mentality, with their amusing and telling use of ethnology, appeared everywhere. As an outspoken public intellectual, she wrote on ethics for the *International Journal of Ethics;* on methods in the *Journal of Philosophy, Psychology, and Scientific Methods;* on education for *Pedagogical Seminary, School and Society,* and *Harper's Weekly;* on personal relationships for the *Masses;* on the Elders for *New Review;* on feminism for *Harper's Weekly;* on pacifism for the *Scientific Monthly;* and for a brief moment, she even flirted with psychoanalysis in the *Psychoanalytic Review.* She was also a charter member of the group of young intellectuals who wrote for the *New Republic,* the new, experimental "Journal of Opinion" funded by Dorothy Whitney Straight and edited by Herbert Croly, Walter Lippmann, Philip Littell, Francis Hackett, and Walter Weyl. Economist Clarence Ayres recalled in 1927 his ambition during these years "to make a pilgrimage to [her] shrine, like Carlton Parker paying a visit to Veblen." "And . . . when you did turn up for lunch at 421 West 21 Street [the offices of the *New Republic*]," he wrote of his youthful admiration, "I believe I actually sat agape straight through dessert, though on that occasion your irony was confined to refusing Mr. Croly's cigarettes!"[15]

A Professional Home

The collegiality of the young anthropologists became more and more important to Parsons during 1915. As the First World War made its influence felt in the United States, issues of racial intolerance began to replace sexual relations as her focus of attention; and the ugly racism of leading sociologists such as Edward A. Ross and

Frances Kellor and her Americanization program caused Parsons to break her already fragile ties with sociology. After her article on friendship appeared in September 1915, she never published in the *American Journal of Sociology* again. Under pressure of the war hysteria, her women friends were dividing between those who gave priority to suffrage or to pacifism. And at home, her life and Herbert's diverged radically.[16]

During 1915, Lucy Wilson was finally seeking a divorce, and Herbert was acting as her lawyer. No doubt feeling tense about the situation, Elsie spent as much time as she could at Lenox. She went to New York reluctantly, and even then she had her own set of friends. When Herbert expressed his unhappiness about this, Elsie was adamant, putting it in the principled terms she was articulating in print, rather than referring to Lucy Wilson. "I'm more than sorry that I've been hurting you," she wrote in April 1915. "I'll try to be more considerate, and yet I can't help thinking that freedom rather than consideration is the basis of any real relation between two persons." "As for the immediate point at issue," she went on, "the disposal of my time after 7.30 P.M., I can't concede that you have any *a priori* claim on it, for if I did, no matter how much I liked being with you, every evening spent with you would be an abhorrence. . . . I can do my work far better away from New York . . . and New York has little to offer me in exchange except its evenings. If I'm to get any satisfaction out of living there (and remember I do live there solely on your account and the children's) we had much better face the fact that many of our evening tastes are dissimilar, and not to be satisfied together. . . . why do we have to pretend to like the same people or the same amusements; what good does either get from that or what sense of friendship?"[17]

In a play Elsie had started in 1913 but had taken up again at this time, the two protagonists, a couple very similar to herself and Herbert, discuss the possibility of divorce. "I'd like you to combine the real relationship with her," the wife says to her husband, who is in love with another woman, "with the real fatherhood you have with the children, and a real friendship with me—you keeping the machinery of life as it is." But when Herbert wrote about his weekend activities with Lucy, including a motor ride with the children, she found it difficult to maintain such magnanimity. "Keep your 'cat' out of the family life, just for your own fun," she wrote venomously.[18]

Lucy Wilson's pending divorce and the enthusiasm of Goddard

and Goldenweiser for her psychological approach to ceremonialism pushed Parsons definitively into the field in the summer of 1915. In August 1915, she fled to the Southwest from an "absurdly upsetting" episode at Newport which preceded the newspapers' announcement of Huntington Wilson's presence in Reno "for divorce purposes." "My first post office address will be Gallup, New Mexico," she wrote Herbert on 7 August. "I'll outfit there. I've written Clara True to join me or send me on one of good Santa Clara men. Also Goddard has written about me to Kroeber, the man working at Zuñi for the Museum. I'll be in time for the 'dances' at Hopi."[19]

A week later she was in Zuni, after a nine-hour drive south from Gallup to the "glorious" valley in which the pueblo was situated. To her disappointment Kroeber, whom she had not yet met, had already left; but she made friends with Margaret Lewis, the Cherokee wife of the Zuni governor, who had come to the pueblo originally as a schoolteacher. This was the beginning of a fruitful collaboration between the two women. Parsons was entranced by the life of the pueblo and the possibilities it offered for the study of sex conventions and ceremonialism, and she never got to the Hopi reservation, where Robert Lowie was working that summer. She returned to the East triumphant after her two-week stay. "I've had a hard but accomplishful jaunt," she wrote Herbert, "and I return more in hand than I left. . . . In Zuñi I shall have a great opportunity for brief periods of field-work, the thing I've been hankering for for years."[20]

Over the next few months, as the Wilson divorce came closer, Parsons buried herself in her Zuni material. Her only break was a camping trip to Quebec with Grant LaFarge, during which she was transfixed with worry that she was once more pregnant. "This bit of camping may be my last for some time," she wrote Herbert, "for I have the impression that that muscular slip of yours may have consequences." "You have the laugh on me," she wrote with relief a few days after she returned to Lenox, "I'm menstruating. But what perturbation this month, first of all of uncertainty then of adjustment. And the idea as constantly in my mind as a lost article in John's. You may bless your stars that feelings-ideas have no obsessive hold on your mind."[21]

Throughout November, when Herbert traveled to Reno to arrange the Wilsons' divorce, Elsie threw herself into the activities and interests of her anthropological colleagues. As Herbert left for Baltimore to consult Lucy's doctors, she shared her notes with

Lowie, and planned a return trip to Zuni. And as Herbert took the train to Reno, she poured out nine articles on Zuni for the *Anthropologist*. At the end of November she began her long friendship with Boas, when he asked her to join the editorial board of the *Journal of American Folklore*. She in turn invited him to accompany her to the Southwest. "It is a sore temptation," Boas replied gratefully, "But . . . I must stick to my work. You know that I had a cancerous growth which was removed last spring. As time passes I feel more and more sure that it will not recur, but I feel it is my business to look out for my scientific collections and be prepared to leave them in such state that they will not be lost."[22]

Parsons returned to Zuni for two weeks in December 1915, this time to see the *shalako*, the great winter ceremony which became the centerpiece of her studies of Pueblo acculturation. While she was there she arranged for Margaret Lewis to keep a register of pueblo ceremonies over the next year. In committing herself to a long-term study of Zuni, Parsons was placing herself at the center of action in American anthropology. Since 1909, the principal anthropological focus of the American Museum of Natural History had been an archeological survey to establish a chronology of Southwestern native cultures. In 1915, Clark Wissler launched a major study of Pueblo social organization. He sent Lowie to the westernmost pueblos of the Hopi and Herbert Spinden to those along the Rio Grande, and invited Kroeber, who was anxious to move out of the Californian field during a year's sabbatical, to study Zuni family and clan systems. Spinden soon abandoned this work, but Kroeber's survey of Zuni and Lowie's of Hopi in 1915 and 1916 breathed new life into Southwestern ethnology. In 1916, Boas's student Leslie Spier joined Kroeber at Zuni to carry out an archeological study nearby. By the end of that summer, Kroeber was able to write to Parsons from Zuni, "You were missed this summer. We were eight of the profession here."[23]

Parsons's focus on ceremonialism at Zuni also meant that she was weighing seriously into the battle over structure and psychology. In a brief article written for the *Anthropologist* in response to Goddard's invitation just before she went to the Southwest in August 1915, Parsons sketched the psychological theory of ceremonialism she had elaborated in *Fear and Conventionality* the year before. "Many customs which have come to be explained as mere relics of the past can be understood far better as vital expressions of contemporary psychoses," she argued, applying to traditional anthropological preoccupations her observations of contemporary culture. Citing as an example "our chronic aversion to adaptation" and the elaborate rituals with which her contemporaries surrounded and cloaked major changes in their lives, she suggested that ceremonial was better thought of as "a shock absorber, which helps us to adjust ourselves to inevitable change."[24]

Parsons went to Zuni with this methodological controversy at the forefront of her mind. Investigating beliefs surrounding conception and pregnancy, she found that she was unable to explain those ideas solely in terms of contacts with neighboring cultures, but had to investigate as well the Zunis' psychological tendencies—to make certain choices and not others, to dispose of those choices in certain ways, and even not to choose, but instead to invent. On her return from New Mexico, she joined Lowie in championing the judicious use of a combination of methods. Turning once more to Tarde—her longtime guide in questions of cultural dynamics—she argued that "questions of transmission cannot be dealt with independently of questions of interference." "The historically minded ethnologist tends to use interference psychology as a kind of understudy," she pointed out, "bringing it forward when his principal—historical determinism—breaks down." But "when the ethnologist has used together in culture after culture the historical and psychological methods," she concluded, in a statement that encapsulated her lifelong method, "when he has worked with both of them upon the riddles of cultural interferences, and then brought his findings to the bar of individual psychology . . . then and only then can we hope for a science of society."[25]

Pliny Goddard was delighted that he had recruited Parsons to his cause. "When Kroeber gets back I hope to listen some time when you, he, and Lowie discuss the Southwest," he wrote, in anticipation of a good fight. When Kroeber and Parsons did finally meet just before she left for Zuni in December 1915, they immediately established the affectionate sparring relationship that characterized their long friendship. *Social Freedom* was just about to appear, and Parsons took advantage of the publicity she expected it to generate to write her article on popularizing ethnology for the *New York Tribune*. "I suspect you have in mind the liberalizing influence of an acquaintance with ethnic phenomena, and perhaps a certain detachedness of mind of some of our profession," Kroeber commented when she solicited his support. "I know of nothing more narrow-minded than the formulations of what is called the science of ethnology; and it is precisely these formulations, and little else, that would get into education. I have taught ethnology for fifteen years; and I have ended by cutting out all the ethnology." "All of which however is no reason why you shouldn't have a fine time at Zuñi," he added, "and I hope you do."[26]

Despite the cold water he threw on her "propaganda," Kroeber and Parsons liked each other immediately. She returned from Zuni just in time to give a paper at the International Congress of Americanists in Washington. A few days earlier, the Sunday *Tribune* had devoted a center-page spread to *Social Freedom,* and Clarence Day had called it "Big, calm, penetrating, effective." But Parsons was more excited by the anthropology meetings. The papers were not so interesting, she wrote Herbert, except those of Boas, Kroeber, and Goddard. "But more interesting was lunching with Kroeber and looking at the Zuñi exhibit with him in the Museum. I had Mr. & Mrs. Boas, Kroeber, Lowie & Goddard to dine with me."[27]

During the first half of 1916, when Kroeber completed his sabbatical at the museum, he and Parsons consolidated the close friendship that lasted until her death. Parsons was constantly in the public eye during this period, earning Kroeber's affectionate title, "Dear Propagandist." In January 1916, Floyd Dell called *Fear and Conventionality* "a delightful and dangerous book" and compared her gift "of being at once pleasant and profound, erudite and agreeable" with that of Thorstein Veblen. But her greatest triumph came in April, when she was invited to contribute to a symposium organized by the City Club of Chicago: "The Ideals of Contemporary Life." Speaking in the first of the symposium's four parts, Parsons shared the platform with George Perkins, captain of finance, political leader, and pillar of progressivism, and John Frey, labor editor, writer, and union leader. Taking "Society" as her subject, she was, according to Victor Yarros in the *New York Evening Post,* "satirical, ironic, biting, drily humorous, candid, and clever." Parsons told her large audience that feminism was administering the coup de grâce to fashionable society. Embellishing her account with her usual sharp observations of human absurdity, she asked: "Without boundaries, without leaders, without matrimonial baits, without means of accrediting or advertising itself through crisis ceremonials or through newspaper notoriety what hope of a future existence is there, we may ask, for the gynocratic caste?" "Society" was doomed to dissolution, she argued, and genuine forms of association based on community of tastes, interests, needs, were taking its place.[28]

"Mrs. Parsons's paper was full of digs and hits that made certain local society leaders squirm," Yarros reported. "But only a few permitted themselves to betray anger and leave the hall. The rest stayed and—laughed merrily at themselves and their tacit pretensions. They voted the paper a treat." "Elsie Clews Parsons gave a most brilliant paper in a symposium on ideals before the City Club," Judge Julian Mack wrote to Felix Frankfurter two days later. "Graceful, witty, sarcastic, brilliant in every way." "I was glad to escape the reporters this morning," Elsie wrote Herbert, never easy with this aspect of being a public intellectual. "I had hardly anticipated that nuisance." "Most of my jokes took," she added gratefully.[29]

During this same period, Parsons took a public stand on birth control that attracted considerable attention and alienated many of her feminist friends. Margaret Sanger had recently returned from Europe to face charges against her long-defunct anarchist journal, the *Woman Rebel*. At a pretrial dinner at the Hotel Brevoort, Parsons spoke of her own experiences, slightly disguised in a third-person account. "Of her six children she had lost two," she told the large audience, "largely she thought because of the misleading information given her by her physicians on conception control. The one child had been born after a long and trying journey, the other child too soon after the birth of the former. As a result of these bitter experiences, she learned that to insure the birth of her children under the most favorable circumstances she would have to become a criminal. She became one."

"Not long after she broke the law on her own account," Parsons continued, "she had the occasion to break it on account of another woman. She found that her country neighbor, the wife of a gardener, a woman of 25, was not convalescing as well as she should after the birth of her fifth child, and so my friend asked her own physician to take the case. . . . After operating he reported to my friend that . . . he had . . . patched her up, telling her that if she did not have another child for at least four years she would regain her health. 'Is that all you're going to tell her?' asked the lady. 'Yes' answered the doctor. 'It is not my business to tell her anything more. Why don't you tell her?' And the lady did."[30]

"This record of crime is not, I fancy, unique," Parsons concluded. "Many women have done for their own children and for a few other women what Margaret Sanger would do for many children and for many women." "Would it not be a good idea," she asked, in a challenge to feminists to speak out, "for other women to come forward & state what they had done in regard to this law & what they intend to do?"[31]

Parsons was bitterly disappointed with the response to her challenge. In a letter to the *New Republic,* she reported on her efforts to get a dozen "liberal minded" mothers to sign a statement that they approved of Mrs. Sanger's publication of birth control articles; that they believed that this information should be readily available; that they themselves had given birth control information; and that they had practiced birth control. Out of about fifty women she approached, only three agreed to sign all four articles, while six others would sign the first three. Some said they didn't know enough about the case; others left the question to the medical profession, ignoring the class bias of that solution, and the fact that giving advice was also unlawful for doctors.

But Parsons found the more direct refusals the most interesting and disturbing: " 'I'm just not the person for that sort of thing . . .' 'you're going to publish it in the newspapers! I couldn't stand that! . . .' 'I consulted with my son, and he objected very much to the publicity . . .' 'My husband says until he gets this lawsuit off his hands I must do nothing conspicuous . . .' 'My husband says it would be improper for me as the wife of a judge to sign . . .' 'My husband laughed when I read him the statement . . .' " "And who would deny," Parsons asked, "that the very need of public testimony on so private a matter, testimony that more than anything else would contribute to lift the taboo safeguarding the present law and the present practice of class discrimination—who would deny that this need of testimony is highly laughable?" But, this very private woman pointed out, as she did on many occasions during her life: "At times, testimony about the private life takes on a sufficiently public significance to free it from ridicule or the charge of bad taste."[32]

Parsons's impatience with her feminist friends' reluctance to speak out on controversial topics led to a distinct cooling of relations with many of them. In the second half of 1916, when much of their effort was focused on suffrage in the run-up to the presidential elections, she sensed that she had been ostracized. "I presume you were at Alice's party," she wrote Herbert soon after the elections. "She never asks me to her parties & you would not have been asked to this one had I been in town." "A's party was very nice," Herbert replied. "All asked after you, Rhodes about 'the lady who bears

your name' which Hackett said was a term he did not dare use."
"It is news to me that Alice never invites you," he added. "Why?"[33]

Parsons was more comfortable with her anthropology colleagues,
who were both admiring of and amused by her public stances. After
reading *Social Freedom,* Kroeber and Goddard decided that Parsons
had a dual nature. "Duality is the most certain numerical concept
in nature," Goddard teased her. "Your winter activities are propaganda and your summer ones research. There has been a growing
feeling that you might be a trinity (no capital this time). I am now
pretty certain you are an artist. . . . Kroeber says four is the sacred
number and that you are in part a Puritan," he added. "Little
Kroeber knows."[34]

Kroeber kidded Parsons about her interest in psychology and
what he called, with deliberate provocativeness, her "moralizing."
But he read her papers, giving critical praise, and challenging her
to take the detached view their circle valued, while appreciating the
concern with the human condition which drove her. When she asked
him to comment on the brief paper "A Zuñi Detective," in which
the sense of the "detective's" personality and of his gossipy community is conveyed as strongly and economically as his forensic methods, Kroeber replied, "It's a bully little paper. If you tried to make
it read as if you were an ethnologist, you fell down. Does that sting
or please?" "My stuff will be finished in two or three days, nicely
and impersonally embalmed behind glass," he wrote from the museum a week later. "It and I are delighted to be at your service. And
when you're all through and have squeezed us dry, I'm going to
exact a return—in moralizing." "As long as you are nice enough to
send me reprints and correct my Zuñi you may call me whatever bad
names you like—psychologist or even moralist," she shot back.[35]

While the rest of her new "tribe" treated Parsons with admiration
and affection tinged by awe, Kroeber's more intense regard for her
always had an edge of skepticism and challenge to which she responded with pleasure. To Kroeber she was never an abstraction—
the rich patron, as she became in later years, or the clever public
intellectual or the eccentric visionary. She was always Elsie, the
many-sided, complex person who was struggling to find her way in
the world. In other words, Kroeber always saw her and listened to
her, responding to her freshly in the manner she had hoped for, and
not found, in her marriage. Over the six months Kroeber was in
New York, he and Parsons learned to respect each other's work, as
well as to enjoy each other's company.[36]

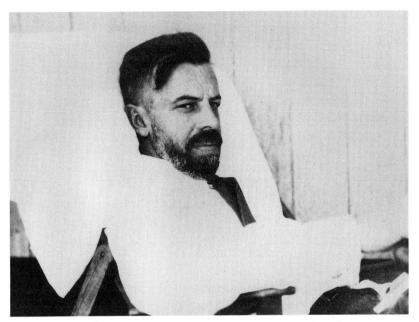

Alfred Kroeber sent Elsie this photograph from Hawaii in 1920. Elsie Clews Parsons Papers, American Philosophical Society Library.

As Lowie perceptively observed, Parsons had the ability, "akin to the pluralism of the historical ethnologist," to grasp the uniqueness of phenomena. He and Kroeber both recognized that this acute facility made Parsons a skillful and persistent fieldworker. She, for her part, found extremely attractive Kroeber's thorough, systematic observation, his almost poetic gift of expression, and his ability to grasp the essence of things through myriad details. What feminist could resist the attraction of Zuni when it was described as Kroeber did in *Zuñi Kin and Clan*? "The house belongs to the women born of the family," he wrote. "There they come into the world, pass their lives, and within the walls they die. As they grow up, their brothers leave them, each to abide in the house of his wife; but they and their children are constant visitors and intimate frequenters of the old home. Each woman, too, has her husband, or succession of husbands, sharing her blankets, and as her children begin to play about, their father's kin and household also resort to the house. So generation succeeds generation, the slow stream of mothers and daughters forming a current that carried with it husbands, sons, and grandsons. Now and then a new dwelling may be built by all the inmates, or for a girl of the house by an enterprising husband;

but in general the same walls, or re-erected ones on the same spot, compass the lives of woman after woman born within.''[37]

After spending another summer of intensive work at Zuni in 1916, Kroeber had a clear idea of the questions the Southwestern pueblos posed for the anthropologist. "Dear E.C.P.," he wrote as he left Zuni in August, "now I'm through . . . and the gate is wide open to your scruples. . . . The real work, though—and it's going to be a tough job—will have to be done between Acoma and Taos. Zuñi is too easy—a rich picking." Presenting his "Thoughts on Zuñi Religion" at the end of 1916, Kroeber made the three-part cultural distinction between the centrally located Zuni, the Rio Grande pueblos in the east, and the Hopi in the west that was the basis of Parsons's work over the next twenty-three years. "That the Pueblo civilization was substantially the same in every town, has always been assumed," he wrote, but "it begins to be evident that a great part of it has been borrowed back and forth in the most outright and traceable manner. The history of the cults and institutions of any one of these peoples therefore cannot be understood without a knowledge of the customs of the others: the problem is in its very nature a comparative one." Here was a task after Parsons's own heart—an absorbing and complex study of acculturation, focused not on Zuni, as she imagined in August 1915, but on the more difficult eastern pueblos.[38]

The teaching was not all one way. Parsons happily took on the role of "psychologist" in their circle; and she fought vigorously against the idea of the "superorganic" nature of culture that Kroeber was crystallizing during his New York stay. While he eventually argued his position against Sapir and Goldenweiser publicly in the pages of the *Anthropologist,* Kroeber and Parsons hashed out their differences in private conversations and letters. Defending himself against her criticisms of his "metaphysics" in May 1916, he pleaded, "Don't you see the entity developing itself? We are all still so impressed by the fact that there are human beings—perhaps because we have only so recently succeeded in abolishing God—that it may be hard. But just subtract all individuals and everything individual. If anything looms large then, you are entitled to a certificate of being a historian—or ethnologist. If there is only a blank left, you are what I call a psychologist." "If I may," he went on perceptively, "I should guess that you sense this residuum very keenly, but are so warmed up by the long and very real fight you have been in, that you think first, and perhaps only, of its reflex on the individual."[39]

Parsons enjoyed the serious but unacrimonious debate she had with Kroeber, the sort of logical duel envisaged by Tarde. Rereading his letter in the peace of Lenox a month later, she confessed that she was reacting against "what some decades ago took the place of supernaturalism in bringing assurance to men's minds—evolutionary theory. It does set me traps and with me it is a case of a burnt child dreading fire." "I confess to a sense of the residuum," she wrote Kroeber, "but I'm awfully suspicious of it." "We are all one on the evolution superstition," Kroeber replied. "But is it more profitable to smash the dear old idols or to look for new beliefs? I think we are agreed on that too. Of course it's easier to talk of new headway than to gain it; but you are the last one to be afraid to try."[40]

Parsons's parting shot in this private debate was a public one, in an "impious article" in the June *New Review* that Lowie and Goddard recognized immediately as aimed at Kroeber. The time is now ripe for new "futurist" gods, she wrote in "A Progressive God," and some ethnologists are welcoming them. "Mind evolves not, but culture does evolve, certain ethnologists are declaring. Culture is an entity, I heard one of them not long since asserting; culture is a self-determining entity—'call it God if you like.'" "I'm glad I was able to be pressed into service in a good cause," Kroeber wrote with amusement when he read the article, "but unfortunately the God part is mainly Goddard's. He wanted it that way and I wouldn't stick at a name."[41]

"It's a nice world, and nice to have friends in it," Kroeber wrote Parsons as he left New York in June 1916. "If you can remain gracious through all my blatancy and contradicting, I shall look forward with pleasure to accepting your next invitation to Lenox—in a year or in five." "Dear Mrs. Parsons," he wrote from Zuni later that month, "There are three of the trade in town now and we're not in each other's way, so if fancy takes you I hope you'll reconsider your decision not to interfere." When the field trip was over, and she had not joined them, he wrote regretfully from California, referring to her role as provocateur, "Three of us argued the relation of psychology and ethnology half the night and ended lamely in agreement. You might have saved us that ignominy."[42]

CHAPTER NINE

The End of the Conversation

AMERICA'S hesitating descent into what was at first called "the European War" formed a somber counterpoint to Parsons's increasing absorption into the world of anthropology. The outbreak of hostilities between Germany and the Allied countries of Great Britain and France in August 1914 caught Americans by surprise. Walter Lippmann and Harold Stearns were just setting out on a European tour when Austria declared war on Serbia, and Germany and then Russia and France mobilized at the end of July. They returned to London to join Norman Hapgood in witnessing Britain's declaration of war on 4 August. Randolph Bourne and Arthur Macmahon arrived in Dresden the day Austria declared war on Serbia, and they left for home from a mobilizing Denmark. And Lucy Clews, traveling in Europe, was finally located at the Ritz in London. Once Lippmann had recovered from the shock and worry of his immediate situation, he realized that the war changed everything. We see now, he wrote in his diary, "that all our really civilized effort is set in a structure of hard necessities." Liberalism could no longer concentrate entirely on local problems, he noted, but had to incorporate an understanding of national and world politics. Already, in August 1914, he was planning for the new world the end of the war would bring.[1]

The "Bust" Par Excellence

At first, Parsons wrote that December, "the war seemed unreal to me. The accounts I read might have been transcribed from ancient historical records as far as any realization of actuality they brought." But observing the excited and emotional reactions of her family, friends, and community in the quiet beauty of the Berkshire fall, she began to sense "an utterly mad, pervert universe." "War is 'a compelling idea' people like to fall back upon," she noted in

"Journal of a Pacifist," which had replaced her "Journal of a Feminist." "Paradoxical as it may seem, war is soothing." It is "an opportunity to enhance that sense of participation almost every one craves." Lissa, then thirteen years old and always social, was knitting a muffler "for the soldiers," as was the treasurer of a suffrage association at a New York dinner. Knitting "so warms the heart," Parsons observed. "It is an emotional outlet. It links the fair knitter to the great world movement."[2]

War is the "bust" par excellence, Parsons wrote in the *New Republic* in February 1915, anticipating the terms in which American soldiers characterized their "Great Adventure" in 1918. "It is the greatest of gregarious forms of excitement." The satisfactions of the collective response were so compelling, Parsons found, that people were impervious to reason. Quietly and persistently questioning Herbert and her friends about their fears of German invasion, she asked: Haven't we been struggling for years to have the children learn German? Don't we too have unnecessary regulations? (What, for instance, of the rule in Boston parks against lying down in a canoe?) Are we really a self-governing people, given our disenfranchised women and Negroes?[3]

Alarmed at the implications for rational discussion of this outbreak of emotionalism, Parsons asked in a letter to the *New York Times* in November 1914: "Is there not a need at present of somewhat clearer thinking on our part in regard to the duties and rights of a neutral people?" Our greatest duty, she argued, is to help form international public opinion on this war and on war in general. But we need to be clear about what public expressions are neutral. Demonstrations of emotion, such as an audience cheering the "Marseillaise," violate neutrality because they arouse antagonism and paralyze thought. Frank and unrestricted expression of critical opinion, on the other hand, is the greatest duty of neutrals. It is essential for belligerents to know what neutrals think of them, Parsons emphasized, where they place the responsibility for the war, what they think of the treatment of noncombatants, and most important of all to what extent they are distressed and aggrieved by the effects of the war on themselves. What is this war actually costing us in trade and in unemployment? How much of a drain is it on all our material resources? When we know this, she concluded, "when we realize too what we are being deprived of in the arts and sciences, how our collective attention is being diverted from progress to repair, how the war has given a setback to our social advance along

all its lines, we may begin to protest with a due measure of indignation against what I have heard euphemistically called the European
irregularities."[4]

Generally, however, Parsons held out little hope for clear thinking
from her own generation. Like many commentators since, she saw
the war as an old man's war, a creation of the Elders. The main
hope in checking militarism lay, she thought, in child-rearing practices. "It has always seemed queer to me that the most peace loving
people failed to see that playing at war is one of the best ways to
prepare for war," she noted in the "Journal" when the local minister
organized a war game between the Lenox boys and those of a neighboring town. She had always forbidden war toys and games, and
she strongly opposed the campaign for universal military training in
the schools. In "The Toy Soldier," published in June 1915, Parsons
pointed out that in the hand-wringing about America's unpre-
paredness for war there was no mention of "that profound and
ineradicable preparation made generation after generation in the
nursery," where the soldier is held up as a model of self-control,
obedience, and success. Because the idea of the soldier first enters the
mind as a "representation"—an idea with an aura of emotion—it is
difficult to think about it in a detached and innovative way. A mind
whose ideas are not free and untrammeled is not a thinking mind,
Parsons warned. In such a mind, "the toy soldier long after he has
been put away with other childish things lives on unchallenged by
reason, protected against competition, and by the realities of life
untested." Offering a moral equivalent for military experience, Parsons suggested that childbearing, exploration, the work of the engi-
neer and the conservationist provide better and more relevant examples to children of virtue, adventure, glamour, and heroism.[5]

Because they were "bullied by traditions," the Elders were not
capable of such lateral thinking. In "A Warning to the Middle-
Aged," published in the *New Review* the same month, Parsons attacked the domination of society by the old as an unnecessary and
harmful habit. "There is no place in our society, no respectable
place, for the old *qua* old," she asserted. On the contrary, "a search
for the fountain of youth," and with it an adaptability to changing
circumstances, has never been so imperative. "With that old man
who believed in staying young, with Cato of Rome, let us entirely
disagree to what was still in his days, he says, a highly commended
counsel, the counsel to become an old man early in order to be an
old man long."[6]

Attacking the Senile Codes

Parsons's call for youthful and innovative thinking in this unexpected crisis attracted the attention of the young man who had become America's spokesman for youth, Randolph Bourne. Bourne—
the "divine cripple" whose conversation made people forget his
misshapen body—had defended his generation in an article entitled
"The Two Generations" in the *Atlantic Monthly* in 1911, when he
was still a student at Columbia. In "Youth," published in 1912,
Bourne described with passion and flair the essence of youth, its
"constant susceptibility to the new," its "eagerness to try experiments," and its scorn for "the inertia of older men." "It is only the
young," Bourne argued, "who are actually contemporaneous; they
interpret what they see freshly and without prejudice; their vision
is always the truest, and their interpretation always the justest."[7]

Parsons and Bourne met early in 1915, probably at one of the
elegant *New Republic* lunches. Bourne's patron, *Atlantic Monthly*
editor Ellery Sedgwick, had recommended him to Herbert Croly,
one of the founders of this new journal of "radical" but not "social-
istic" opinion. When the *New Republic* issued its first number in
November 1914, Bourne was in place as a regular contributor. It is
not clear where Parsons first met Croly and his fellow editors, but
there were many ties of friendship among the Crolys, the Simkho-
vitches, the Norman Hapgoods, the Learned Hands, Parsons's
wealthy friends Charlotte Sorchan and Mabel Dodge, and the young
editor Walter Lippmann. In any case, she was an important representative of avant-garde opinion by the end of 1914, with a reputation for pungent broadsides against conventional thought and behavior. Bourne's contention in his first *New Republic* article that
"Thinking cannot be done without talking" was exactly in line with
Parsons's ideas, and although the editors sought out her clever,
subtle reviews, it was as a controversial conversationalist that they
most valued her. She was a regular member of the journal's luncheon group, often providing articulate opposition to their current
thinking. She always disliked Croly, but Lippmann and literary editor Francis Hackett became close friends who appreciated her advice
and criticism.[8]

Parsons and Bourne cemented their friendship at the Heretics, the
discussion group—founded by Alexander Goldenweiser and made
up mostly of social scientists—to which they both belonged.
Bourne's first surviving letter to her was soon after she stirred up

the group with her new sexual ethics in May 1915. "You have more good psychology to the inch than almost anything I have seen about militarism," he wrote in June in praise of a paper she prepared for the Committee on International Conciliation. "Do you know her?" he wrote his friend Elizabeth Shepley Sergeant after a weekend at Lenox. "If you are interested in rare persons, there she is. . . . After all I *am* an ethnologist, and she is a so clever and stimulating one that she sets one's thoughts tumbling all over each other. And such a fine adventurousness and command of life she radiates!"[9]

During the second half of 1915, when the *New Republic* began to advocate war preparedness after the sinking of the *Lusitania,* Bourne found Parsons a stimulating and fearless ally for his unremitting pacifism. Both viewed the war as part of a larger struggle between youth and age that encompassed sexuality and education as much as militarism. "I should like to believe that there is to be a concerted movement to nullify the senile codes, and lock up the old where they can do no harm," Bourne wrote Parsons, drawing her attention to Jane Addams's Carnegie Hall speech describing the war as an old man's war. Before she left for Zuni in August 1915, Parsons fired off a volley to the *New Review,* reporting in "War and the Elders" a conversation with an ethnographer friend after hearing Addams's speech. Just as the tribal elders and the chiefs make war magic, doctor the trails, anoint the weapons, and look for favoring omens, her friend observes, the older generation use the shibboleths of king, country, national honor, loyalty to empire, and patriotism to preserve the distinctions of sex, caste, and age. Bourne followed this up with a condemnation of "the older generation" in the *Atlantic Monthly*—which tolerated him, he confided to Parsons, as their "unique little radical pet." The older generation has grown weary of thinking, he wrote. "It has simply put up the bars in its intellectual shop-windows and gone off home to rest." "Where," Bourne asked, "are the leaders of the older generation in America who, with luminous faith and intelligence are rallying around them the disintegrated numbers of idealistic youth?"[10]

Impudent Traitors

One of the most alarming aspects of the American war mood to Parsons and Bourne was the demonization of the enemy, particularly the Germans, and by extension, German-Americans. Parsons and Bourne had both found stimulating friendship among their immigrant colleagues, and found it insupportable that these vivid individuals should be reduced to a demonic category such as "Hun." It was equally unacceptable that America should retreat from the "larger air" of cosmopolitanism that European immigration brought to America.[11]

Sociologist Edward A. Ross's *Old World in the New* preached an ethnocentricity late in 1914 that captured the nation's uneasiness about the cultural effects of the recent tide of immigrants. As the *Masses* noted tartly, "The science of anthropology . . . would have little tolerance of such generalizations on race as this one about the 'Black Portuguese': 'They are obviously negroid, lack foresight and are so stupid they cannot follow a straight line.' . . . Sometimes the spirit of Science fails to appear just where you have best reason to expect it." America's mood of racial intolerance was further inflamed in 1915 when *The Birth of a Nation* was screened to huge audiences and an appreciative White House. As *New Review* editor Paul Kennaday wrote to Parsons, "Have you seen The Birth of a Nation & the audiences? There you will find plenty of confirmation of your 'Bust' theory. And also confirmation that we are a society of savages."[12]

Fear and hysteria about "hyphenated Americans" were fueled in December 1915 by Woodrow Wilson's first preparedness speech, in which he spoke as much about patriotism as he did about preparedness. "There are citizens of the United States . . . born under other flags but welcomed under our generous naturalization laws . . . who have poured the poison of disloyalty into the very arteries of our national life," Wilson declaimed. "Such creatures of passion, disloyalty, and anarchy must be crushed out." As preparedness advocates talked of "Yank[ing] the hyphen" out of the immigrant population, a wave of enthusiasm for "Americanization" and immigration exclusion swept the country.[13]

When congressional debate on the preparedness bill began in March 1916, Bourne poured his vision of a "trans-national America" into an article for the *Atlantic Monthly*. Editor Sedgwick was profoundly shocked by Bourne's lack of allegiance to the "Anglo-Saxon ideal" but published the article because it was "the ablest and certainly the most interesting" thing he had written. Bourne characterized America as a country without a culture. It had the undemocratic nativism of the genteel English tradition of New England, but there was no shaping ethos: "In our loose, free country, no constraining national purpose, no tenacious folk-tradition and folk-style hold the people to a line." Given this absence, Bourne urged Americans to think of themselves as the first international nation, accepting the positive value of cultural and religious diversity. Only the American, he claimed, had the unique chance of becoming a "citizen of the world."[14]

As the country lumbered toward war with the passage of the National Defense and Naval Appropriations Acts in May 1916, Parsons and Bourne mulled over the perplexities of the "American" mania in Lenox. While Bourne developed his ideas in "Americanism" and "A Moral Equivalent for Universal Military Service," Parsons drew on *Fear and Conventionality* and *Social Freedom* for an article on the contradictions between being an American and being a citizen of the world. We are told that it is selfish not to be patriotic, she wrote. " 'In the less significant things be a man of the world, of course,' we say, 'but in what really counts, be an American.' " But is the current form of militaristic patriotism really unselfish? she asked. "If we feel that we cannot be 'safe' unless the group we belong to is 'safe,' is it anything but selfish in us to protect the integrity of our group?" "To be separated from the group, to differ from it, makes one uncomfortable, upset, lonely. Our gregarious impulse must be protected and indulged—at almost any cost. And so we proclaim ourselves family men, clannish, patriots. We are full of family feelings, we are 'good' husbands, 'good' wives, we are good churchmen, we are devoted to our country. All these feelings . . . are sublimations of the primal gregarious impulse, quite as self-gratifying an impulse as any other. And quite as regardless of others."[15]

A few weeks later, declining an invitation from Hunter College to give the commencement address on Americanization, Parsons put her position succinctly: "If I may address the students along the line of anti-preparedness and of anti-Americanization as Americanism is now preached I accept your invitation. I am for practical & definite pacifism in nursery & school & for democratic tolerance of all nationalities as against the melting pot propaganda. I am a bad speaker nor am I up to making a graceful ceremonial address & so must read. For these reasons & because my brand of Americanism is not in much favor, I believe, in school circles, please feel entirely at liberty to withdraw your invitation." "They will lose a few Zuni anecdotes and a few references to Anglo Saxon arrogance," she wrote Bourne.[16]

"You are the only other renegade Anglo-Saxon I know," Bourne replied. "The NR is getting—or F.H. [Francis Hackett] is—a little wary of my anti-Americanness and my peevishnesses, and my stock is running very low." But much to his—and editor Sedgwick's—surprise "Trans-National America" struck a chord in many readers. An invitation to speak before the Harvard Menorah Society, the Zionist society established by his friend Horace Kallen, and a week's visit to Parsons prompted Bourne to develop his ideas further. The only thing that kept American culture from aggressive nationalism was the "hyphenate," he argued as the Americanism campaign climaxed in the close-fought presidential race. Accordingly, the task now was to find a way to a "cultural self-consciousness" that was pluralistic enough to avoid "the price of terrible like-mindedness." In Bourne's opinion, the cosmopolitanism of Jewish Americans such as Kallen, Lippmann, and Louis Brandeis were concrete examples of the way the hyphenate American could help turn America into the first international nation.[17]

Searching for Cosmopolitan America

As Bourne's optimism rose with the reelection of Wilson on a platform that promised peace and internationalism, Parsons's spirits sank. "Life for a militant pacifist has been rather trying these past months," she wrote Kroeber in May 1917, "and if I hadn't had my Zuñi notes to write up & no end of Negro folk tales to edit—I'd be worse off than I am." The long campaign against militarism and ethnocentrism had, indeed, strengthened her commitment to anthropology. The readiness of even her fellow intellectuals to reduce Germans to the despised "Hun," and their acceptance of the use of force to preserve their own culture, focused Parsons's attention on the question that had fascinated her since she first read Gabriel Tarde in 1894—the problem of culture contact, or acculturation. In *Fear and Conventionality, Social Freedom,* and *Social Rule,* she had used a wide range of sources to draw sweeping conclusions about why people could not tolerate difference, and she had constructed a utopian vision of a society no longer divided by arbitrary sex, race, caste, and national classifications. Until 1914, her major preoccupation had been with sex and age differentiation. The horrors of cultural intolerance during World War I, inevitably expressed in terms of "race," forced her to turn her attention to the clash of cultures. What happens when cultures come into contact? By what processes can they reach an accommodation? Why are some aspects of one culture readily absorbed by another, while others are rejected? How can these processes be studied?[18]

During 1916, when she and Bourne were struggling to articulate their vision of a cosmopolitan America, Parsons embarked on a study of African-American folklore that she found extraordinarily helpful in tackling these issues. In December 1915, when she joined the editorial board of the *Journal of American Folklore,* Franz Boas had appointed her associate editor in charge of this work. In February 1916, Parsons made the first of many folklore-collecting trips during her long career—to the Bahamas, stopping off on the way in Guilford County, North Carolina, where the British Loyalists who had migrated with their household slaves to the Bahamas during the Revolution had originated. Parsons was anxious to stay close to home that summer because John, then thirteen years old, was going to board at his father's school, St. Paul's, in the fall. But with her usual resourcefulness, she found a rich field of study at her front door in Newport in the Portuguese-African population from the Cape Verde Islands. "Sunday I was fishing for folk-tales," she wrote John in July during a brief trip to a nearby town. "Went to a negro church to talk with the pastor and have him arrange a meeting with one of his Portuguese negro parishioners." Parsons found a "very helpful interpreter and teacher" in Gregorio Teixeira Silva from the island of Fogo, who arranged for her to interview a *saibo,* or magic worker. One Sunday morning found her sitting in a car in a Providence alley "where the windows are full of heads calling out to one another that she wants some one to tell stories." "Last night," she wrote Herbert, "I worked here till 11:30 with ease. Not as pleasant as a cranberry log cabin but much nicer than the slum of Fall River where we spent yesterday afternoon."[19]

Throughout the summer, Parsons threw herself into her collecting, working sometimes eleven or twelve hours a day, too absorbed, she told Herbert, to want to escape to the Adirondacks with him. "Tomorrow I take John's boat at New Bedford & go with Silva on a little trip to Nantucket returning Sunday night." By the end of August collecting had become "a bit of a grind," but she stuck to it for another ten days or so and took it up again in early October, after John left for St. Paul's. "Just before leaving New Bedford last night we stopped in at a sailor's dance," she wrote John. "There are three or four Portuguese Negro whalers in port. Such whirling I never saw except by tops. One of the musicians, a player on the guitar, had invited us."[20]

"You haven't written to me this summer," complained Randolph Bourne in September. "I hope it is because you are still doing folk-tales in some strange region or writing your folk-lore journal." Alfred Kroeber, back in California after his half year in New York, also tried to prod her into correspondence. Herbert, at Roosevelt's Oyster Bay house for the shooting of a Republican Party film, amused Alice Longworth with stories of Elsie's folklore expeditions. But the children rebelled against their steady diet of folktales: fifteen-year-old Lissa merely fell asleep, but John retaliated from school with a drawing of a Negro with frizzy hair with the inscription: "Dont get mad at this." Finally she and John came to an agreement: "If I cut out folk-tales, will you cut out football scores. . . . It's a very important part of the art of living to know what you can & what you can't make interesting to the other fellow." "You are probably buried in tales," Bourne wrote after a visit. "You must give me another chance at appreciating them."[21]

Although family and friends found it hard to share her enthusiasm, Parsons derived endless intellectual and emotional pleasure from folklore collecting. The study of folklore gratifies a sense of romance, she wrote in a review of *Uncle Remus Returns* in the *Dial*. "As there is romance in the wanderings of peoples over the globe, so is there romance in the wanderings of tales. It is exciting to recognize in an Apache tale from the Southwest or in an Indian tale from Penobscot Bay a tale you have heard the day before from a Cape Verde Islander on Cape Cod, a coincidence which may resolve for you an uncertainty whether the tale came from Europe or from Africa. Or, after comparing the forty-odd variants of a tale collected from American negroes and American Indians from the southeast to the northwest of the continent, it is exciting to hear the one recorded European version of the tale, a Spanish version, fall from the lips of a Sea Islands Negro in South Carolina."

Folklore collecting had another aspect that Parsons enjoyed immensely: it took her into the homes, lives, and minds of people who were normally inaccessible to outsiders. "It was due to the friendliness that is a by-product of collecting tales that, after two days and parts of two nights spent in story-telling in the cabin of James and Pinkie Middleton of Hilton Head, I was informed by my host," she wrote proudly, "that, had I stayed on in the house of the white man where Mr. Middleton and I had met, he would not have told me tales—'fo' no money, not fo' a week.' " "We hol' no communication wid dem," a companion added. "We don't boder wid dem an' dey don' boder wid us."

The important lesson that Parsons learned from collecting folklore was that good ethnography must be a reciprocal process. "On the whole the art of story-telling is wont to be practiced between equals. One hears quite often from the Whites of the South that the Negroes do not tell stories any more. And they don't—to their White neighbors. . . . Arrogance or condescension stand in the way of story-telling. . . . It takes something of an artist to listen to a folk-tale as well as to tell it, and between artists theories of social inequality do not obtrude." In all of her ethnographic work, Parsons did her best to get information through genuine and pleasurable interaction in which she and her informants shared information. Above all, she made sure that she gave her informants a good time— the secret, probably, of her success.[22]

The major payoff from the study of folklore was the insight it gave to the process of acculturation. As Melville Herskovits pointed out in his assessment of Parsons's work in 1943, her folklore studies were groundbreaking because they were driven by problems of cultural dynamics. Folklore was, for her, the study of cultural diffusion in process. She rarely made this explicit in her publications, which were essentially a stockpiling of tales and riddles so extensive that they comprised the bulk of published materials at the time of her death. But she did state her intellectual and political rationales clearly in her presidential address to the American Folklore Society in December 1919. Acknowledging her debt to Tarde's theory of imitation, Parsons outlined a program of research that took up where he left off. Tarde made little attempt to analyze why certain cultural variations or inventions "take" and others do not, she said; and he could not do so with the inadequate ethnological data available to him. The problem of cultural selection, she argued, requires the study of cultural variants; but these are rarely noted, particularly when they indicate the encroachment of another culture. The study of cultural processes requires the recording of all cultural manifestations, not just those that are "genuine" or "authentic." And it requires systematic restudy in order to observe change over time. "Until this is done," Parsons contended, "we cannot get all the help possible in determining not only what Indians and Negroes took from white story-tellers, but what they did not take, or, if taking, what did not stick in tradition"—important clues, she pointed out, to habits of mind.

"Whether or not in the future anthropologists will be called upon to direct cultural contacts or to suggest cultural experiments, seems doubtful," Parsons the public intellectual concluded. "Efforts to direct or control will probably continue to express merely group will-to-power, the desire to have people like yourself or to have them amenable to immediate group ends,—such efforts as are well exemplified in the current movement for Americanization or in bureaus of immigration or Colonial or foreign offices. However, if ever the desire for cultural inventiveness or experiment does arise in Administration circles,—desire based not only in tolerance for group differences, but in appreciation of their value,—the desire will fail of satisfaction unless attention shall have been paid meanwhile to the study of cultural variants, and unless anthropologists really learn something about cultural variation, whether due to foreign contact or to individual departure."[23]

The political events of 1916, with their accompanying crescendo of racism, as well as her experiences collecting folklore, sent Parsons back to the Southwest early in 1917 with new interests, a more clearly defined methodology, and a well-developed field technique. Her interests at Zuni two years before were feminist and psychological, involving the recording of ceremonials and conventions surrounding pregnancy, childbirth, child-rearing, and sex roles with the sharp eye she previously applied to New York society. When she returned in January 1917, those interests were still important, but they were subsumed under a more general concern with the dynamics of culture contact. In December 1915, she had witnessed the beginnings of the winter solstice dances—the *shalako* and the *mo'lawia* that immediately followed it. In 1917 she saw the end of the winter solstice ceremonials, including the rare *mahedinasha* and the *hilili,* a dance introduced from neighboring Acoma or Laguna about twenty-five years before and modified more recently by elements borrowed from the Hopi.[24]

Keen to compare Zuni ceremonial with that of other pueblos, Parsons persuaded Margaret Lewis and her husband, the former governor, to introduce her to his counterparts in neighboring Acoma. She had just seen Lewis pass on his cane of office in Zuni. In Acoma she hoped to witness the King's Day dance, the *hoinawe,* which celebrated the installation of officers there. They climbed the steep, narrow rock stairway that took them to the mesa-top pueblo—one of the most beautiful and interesting places in the world, Parsons thought when she first saw it. She was intrigued to find the people of Acoma more Americanized in dress and more thoroughly Christianized than the Zuni, following marriage and godparent customs that were unmistakably Spanish. In Acoma, Parsons noted, the Catholic character of All Souls' Day was recognized, whereas the Zuni asserted that what they called "the dead their day" had always been observed and was in no way Catholic.[25]

But the Acoma people were much more secretive about their rituals than the friendly and open Zuni. After five exhausting and frustrating days, in which she was excluded from the ceremonials she hoped to see, Parsons went on briefly to the nearby pueblo of Laguna. There she found shelter from a howling windstorm in the warm and comforting kitchen of Mrs. Eckerman, the wife of a former brakeman on the Santa Fe Railroad whose house had become a popular way station for people like Parsons staying overnight to catch the next day's train. Margaret Eckerman was the daughter of Gawiretsa of the Laguna Sun clan and Robert Marmon, the first American schoolteacher in the pueblo. Marmon and his brother, Walter, a surveyor, came to Laguna in the 1870s, married Pueblo women Marie Anaya (Gawiretsa) and Susie Reyes, and took a prominent part in the life of the town. When Mrs. Eckerman's Uncle Walter became governor of the pueblo, he persuaded the people, he told Parsons, "to give up their old ways." Margaret Eckerman's Indian family were prominent in the pueblo: her great-grandfather had been educated by priests in Mexico and was said to be the first Pueblo who could read; and her mother's brother, Giwira, was the religious leader and head of the fraternity that organized the great summer solstice ceremony.

Margaret Eckerman was just the sort of informant Parsons valued most, a knowledgeable insider-outsider like Margaret Lewis at Zuni, well-connected but modern and detached from the ceremonial life of the pueblo. What is more, her kitchen and well-run house and family provided the sort of relaxed setting in which Parsons thrived. "Opaque and devastating sandstorm without, but cheer and gaiety in our kitchen," she remembered later, "where Mrs. Eckerman was baking bread and interpreting at the same time." Margaret Eckerman's mother, Gawiretsa Marmon, had invited her friend Tsiwema (José) out from town, and "the old people gossiped of the old feud to my enlightenment—gossip as ever being more informing than interrogation. Then when the bread needed particular attention or the baby lapsed from her extraordinary goodness one of the little girls would take a turn interpreting." "Late in the afternoon Velma [Gawiretsa Marmon's granddaughter] interpreted a long folk-tale from beginning to end," Parsons remembered. "The children loved and respected their grandmother and they were proud to be able to interpret her stories and pleased to find in me too an appreciative auditor. The story of the Rabbit Huntress I had heard before and I have heard it since, but never as pleasantly as on that gale-swept day."[26]

Parsons found Laguna interesting as well as comforting. It had all the elements that intrigued her—the mixture of Pueblo and American culture, the internal feuds, the broken-down ceremonial, the strong remnants of Catholic ritual and morality. She never returned to Acoma, despite its physical beauty. As she wrote John on her return trip, "My last week has been so remote from luxury and so beset by physical miseries, one night until I dosed with salt water I thought I had ptomaine poisoning—with no aid in sight, & for several days I lost my voice & coughed so peculiarly I was sure it was tuberculosis, that at times I entertained quite favorably the idea of passing out. . . . High winds, sand laden, are bad for the throat particularly after nights of sleep broken by crying babies and by adults ceremonially wailing for a dead daughter. Besides I had to play scientific detective unusually vigilantly to get meagre facts, so suspicious are the Acomas of any White." But she was convinced by the trip that the pueblos provided the sort of comparative material she was looking for. "Did Margaret Lewis write you I was at Zuñi in January & of our trip to Acoma?" she wrote Kroeber in May 1917. "You suggested Acoma, you may remember. I doubt if it is as fruitful as you surmised. I only scraped it a bit of course, but its ceremonial life seemed more disintegrated than I had expected. From it & Laguna, however, I became convinced that comparative study of all the pueblos will be very fruitful indeed. I would like next to try out Cochiti or better still Sant Anna, going back to Acoma or rather, next time, to Acomita. I shall have friends in Acomita and away from Acoma they will be, I think, more communicative."[27]

The War to Save Civilization

Parsons did not return to the Southwest for another year, however. Back in New York, she found a city preparing for war. In March 1917, she came to the defense of Franz Boas, who had responded to the Columbia trustees' invitation to students to report unpatriotic faculty opinions in an address to his classes entitled "Preserving Our Ideals." "It has been popular in recent months," she wrote to the *New York Times,* "to draw a picture of what would happen to New York given a German invasion; but even the most imaginative of our futuristic artists have never pictured the University as efficiently 'prussianized' as the Columbia trustees now propose. That the trustees of a great American university should thus desire to violate the principle of academic freedom is tragic; that they should seek to check in the university the kind of political reference or discussion which may occur in any legislature, in any newspaper, at any public meeting, is grotesque, a bit of almost incredible buffoonery."[28]

The previous June, Parsons had met a "lonely bedraggled" Walter Lippmann at the "chaotic, banal, and sordid" Republican convention in Chicago. "Seek[ing] indefatigably" for new light, Lippmann found comfort in talks with Parsons and in her *Social Freedom,* which "came to [him] as a personal communication." "I have just read your 'Social Freedom' with great exulting," he wrote in August 1916. "It touched me more than anything I have read this year, and it is an enormous help to me in some work I'm doing." But when the United States finally declared war on 7 April 1917, she found her ideas hideously distorted. This would be a war to end all wars, Lippmann argued, congratulating intellectuals for urging entry into a war that was being fought for the highest ideals of internationalism, peace, and democracy. The war would bring about a "transvaluation of values as radical as anything in the history of intellect"; concepts like liberty, equality, and democracy would be reexamined "as fearlessly as religious dogmas were in the seventeenth century"; and there would be "a new fertility of invention." The war was no longer a national struggle for power; instead it was "a gigantic experiment in internationalism." "The democracies are unloosed," he exulted in an address before the Academy of Political and Social Science soon after war was declared, and the war "is dissolving into a stupendous revolution."[29]

Literally sickened by this travesty of her vision, Parsons retreated to Lenox, drawing comfort from her housekeeper, Mrs. Abernethy, and the children's nurse, Miss Carmody, "the two persons in my life who have given me the most sense of comfort, not altogether physical comfort either," she wrote Herbert. *"Don't show Mother this!"* fourteen-year-old John warned as he wrote his father how much he enjoyed his military drill.[30]

Parsons's response to despair was, characteristically, an attack on the "teleological delusions" of intellectuals like Lippmann who "willed" the war. "As long as our sense of progress gives us the glow religion once gave us, we will protect it," she lamented. "Witness the protection given [it] in these passing days. . . . The supreme horror of the war lay in its assault on our sense of progress. It threatened to break down our faith, as we said, in civilization." But we have recovered our faith by identifying the ends of war with those of civilization, and the war is now a war for civilization! Referring scornfully to a Lippmann editorial written just before the declaration of war, she observed, "The consequences of war, we daily hear, will be important and beneficent, a world more liberal and more peaceful will emerge—England will be class-free, Russia democratized, Europe purified, Feminism triumphant, Internationalism founded, and a Peace laid that will endure forever"—"even if it pass understanding," she added acidly.[31]

By the middle of May and a diet of "Zuñi in the morning, Cape Verde in the afternoon," Parsons was more detached and hopeful. "All your criticism of the League to enforce peace I agree to but as I dont take the plan very seriously I dont oppose it as you do," she wrote Bourne. "Peace or war is much more a matter of cultural patterns. . . . Hasn't 'Business' been resisting militarism quite a little the last few weeks? . . . I wouldn't be a bit surprised if we heard . . . when taxes really pressed, that since war promoted socialism, undermining the Constitution, we must make peace in order to protect democracy. 'Peace for Democracy' will sound just as noble and convincing as 'War for Democracy.' "[32]

Still feeling impelled to action, Parsons joined the organizing committee of the People's Council for Democracy and Peace, a radical antimilitarist organization that was soon accused of being "pro-German and disloyal," and she began a series of articles about the war. She sent Lippmann an article criticizing his crisis mentality. But by this time he was on his way to Washington, where he began his profoundly disillusioning war work; and the chances of publishing anything critical of the war effort diminished rapidly. A week after the declaration of war, the Committee on Public Information was set up, based on Lippmann's blueprint, to sell the war to America. As schools such as St. Paul's instituted military training, a conscription law was passed. In June, despite petitions from intellectuals such as Croly and Dorothy and Willard Straight not to sacrifice constitutional freedoms, Congress passed the sweeping Espionage Act.[33]

"This is the gloomiest day of all," Bourne wrote Parsons on 28 May 1917. After the horror of conscription, "now comes the censorship." " 'Speculation about possible peace is another topic which may possess elements of danger,' " he quoted despairingly. "Discussion is barred of our strangling of neutral countries. . . . Can you believe it? A complete suppression of speculation, criticism. The only relief is the amusing predicament the NR must find itself in, which only last week was calling for peace terms and this week roasts Lord Cecil, a member of His Sacred Majesty's Government. . . . It merely goes to show how powerless the individual is when he gets into a great 'culture-pattern' like the running of a war. . . . That is why the 'willing of American participation' was so fatuous and sinister. Croly and Lippmann, for instance, were obsessed with the idea of themselves controlling the war-technique in a democratic manner . . . everything polite, well-bred, humane, enlightened. They are now slightly aghast at the terrible forces they have unloosed. . . . I am acquiring a feeling of cold anger against the whole crowd, and I haven't been near the place for weeks."[34]

"It's a trying time since January 31," Kroeber wrote from California. But, he pointed out, "We've earned it. . . . We want our responsibility narrowed to a quadrennial choice between not more than two men. . . . Having solemnly or hysterically selected Dum over Dee, we shout hooray and send our sons to be shot when Dum decides that his theory of democracy demands it." "Do you remember when the Republic proclaimed that the Intelligenzia had done it," he went on, "that it was put over on a puzzled but willing people, and that it was up to the Intelligenzia to educate the people to what it was all about? Rather ambitious even for the Republic staff, but frank and truthful. The rest of the so-called I. [intelligentsia] haven't even sense and courage to see it, and fool themselves into thinking it's an uprising of national emotion. And as to the people—our theory of life is that if they want to be sheep following over a precipice, they're entitled to be."[35]

"Your article is delightful," Bourne wrote Parsons early in May when he read her excoriation of the intelligentsia in "Teleological Delusion." "The intellectuals must be exposed." He was planning his own denunciation of his colleagues in an "aggressive" article for Seven Arts. "Now that Croly has confessed 'who willed American participation,' we know who to find responsible, and they need expect no mercy," he wrote Parsons. "Last week I had dinner with the Kuttners and Lippmann. We three formed a strong coalition against W.L., and I never saw a man become so progressively depressed."[36]

Bourne's article bitterly blasted the complacent "socialists, college professors, publicists, new-republicans, and practitioners of literature" who supported American intervention. They might have worked to "clear the public mind of the cant of war" or used the war "for a great wave of education." Instead unconsidered action has taken the place of thought, and dissenters are being excommunicated. "Is there no place left," Bourne asked, for the "irreconcilable," the intellectual who "will not even accept the war with walrus tears?"[37]

President Wilson's Flag Day Speech of June 1917 damning the entire pacifist movement as traitors set off a vicious anti-alien reaction. Under the Espionage Act (and later the even more comprehensive Sedition Act), Americans embarked on what John Reed called "a regime of judicial tyranny, bureaucratic suppression and industrial barbarism." The government set up a nationwide spy system, maintained surveillance over the foreign-language press, infiltrated "dangerous" organizations, raided their premises without warrants, and destroyed their property. The June 1917 issue of *Mother Earth,* containing among other things a reprint of Bourne's "War and the Intellectuals," was confiscated. In November, when the Post Office halted publication of the *Masses,* the *Milwaukee Leader,* and the *New York Call,* Max Eastman joked despairingly: "They give you ninety days for quoting the Declaration of Independence, six months for quoting the Bible, and pretty soon somebody is going to get a life sentence for quoting Woodrow Wilson in the wrong connection."[38]

Patterns for Peace or War

"Patterns for Peace or War," published in James McKeen Cattell's *Scientific Monthly* in September 1917, but drafted soon after her return from the Southwest in February, was one of the few articles on the war Parsons was able to get published during this period. Its detached and deft analysis shows clearly the lessons she had learned from her folklore and anthropological work of the past year. Her friend Signe Toksvig, who married Francis Hackett in 1918, reading this article in the calm of 1923, pronounced it "marvelous, clairvoyant, that you should have written that in 1917."[39]

In "Patterns for Peace or War," Parsons coolly analyzed the war mood in terms of acculturation. Drawing on her Zuni observations, she suggested that cultural innovation probably depends on the preexistence of a cultural pattern into which the alien belief or practice may be fitted. If this is the case, she asked, how can we explain why the pacifist mood of the 1914 summer has been converted so thoroughly into the militaristic pattern of 1917? "The theory of militarism that physical compulsion should be the preferred way out of social misunderstanding or incompatibility has been fairly well acculturated throughout the country. In a remarkably short period a system that would suppress by physical means or quasi physical means minority opinion at home and conflicting opinion abroad has been adopted. The plans for international arbitration that in very recent years had been to the fore were readily dropped, discredited outright or deferred until after the war, to be embodied in that love child of militarism and pacifism, namely the League to Enforce Peace. At home, principles of toleration for minorities, of freedom of conscience, of freedom of speech, of *lehrfreiheit,* of no discrimination against 'race,' principles which for a comparatively longer period had been under cultivation in the United States, these principles were also dropped, dropped with a facility amazing to many."

Parsons reasoned that preexisting patterns in American life lent themselves to this leap into militarism: Negro disenfranchisement, segregation, and lynching; harsh treatment of Jews and immigrants from southern and southeastern Europe; "Americanization"; taboos on speech and thought; and a refusal to seriously examine inherited catchwords such as liberty, equality, and fraternity. Catchwords, in particular, make the new appear at one with the old, she argued. For example, by asserting that the flag is once more being used for "some old familiar, heroic purpose for which it has seen men, its own men, die on every battlefield upon which Americans have borne arms since the revolution," the President portrays this war as the latest in a series of wars for freedom—"As the Zuñi would say, 'it has been with us ever since we came up.'" Added to all these predisposing factors for militarism was the existence of a large number of "socially destitute and jobless" men, the sons and husbands of plutocrats and gynocrats, who are "peculiarly adrift in our society, having in it no particular place or power." Militarism in school or nursery, she claimed, quickly turns such a group into a militaristic caste.

Given these powerful patterns for militarism, are there also patterns working for peace, Parsons asked? Paradoxically, she found them among the plutocracy, the very persons she blamed for the war. "The declaration of war against Germany was essentially a declaration that American business would be protected," she argued. "But with the country actually at war, burdened with war, will American business continue to prosper?" "Under a heavy excess-profits tax business men would become pacifists. Under a confiscatory surplus income tax the plutocracy as a whole would turn pacifist." On the other hand, if the burden of the war fell on the people, a struggle might develop to put the burden of the war onto the class who willed the war. "Were anti-militarists to turn their attention away from peace terms to changing the distribution of the war burden at home their efforts could no longer be discounted as pro-German. . . . Then in self-defense the plutocracy might come to desire peace. Preserving the social order would seem more important than a war to end war. To make the country safe for plutocracy would become more urgent than to make the world safe for democracy." Parsons was not optimistic, however. She envisaged a future where an enlarged military served the plutocracy with a series of "little wars" that kept nationalism alive and distracted from antiplutocratic enterprises at home. In other words, she noted drily, "they will be wars for the good of 'backward' peoples."[40]

"You are rather startling in your mingled optimism and pessimism," Bourne wrote when he read the article early in August 1917. "I wish I could get your impersonal attitude. . . . I can't hope that the rich will become pacifists. The inflation of power which war gives them is so delightful that they will be willing to pay a large economic price for it. Having floated the Liberty Bond on the populace, they will not turn against a scheme which promises to leave them after the war the only capitalists in the world."[41]

The War at Home

Parsons found it harder to maintain her detachment as the war hit closer to home. As an unregenerate and outspoken pacifist— an "irreconcilable" to use Bourne's apt term—she found herself completely isolated in her family. To Lissa, sixteen years old and concerned as always about her social life, she was an intense embarrassment. "Lissa went with a 'mother' . . . to her home in Washington, Conn.," Parsons wrote Herbert a few days after the Flag Day speech. "Mrs. Hagin, it seems, was a girl painting at Mr. Chase's the same year I was there. . . . She stopped for Lissa in a motor. . . . It seemed civil & I had a curiosity so I went out to speak to her although Lissa, ashamed of me, begged me not to go. For unsophisticated elders it really must be tragic to have their children ashamed of them." A few months later, when she had Bourne as a guest and entertained what Van Wyck Brooks called a "noble army of my fellow-martyrs," Lissa kept to her room and would not join them.[42]

Even more devastating than Lissa's shame was Herbert's decision to join the army. "Sweetheart," he wrote a few days after the Lissa incident, "Monday afternoon I heard there was an army job I might get thru Stimson which would be interesting & in which I might be useful. So I wired him yesterday, came over on the night train, breakfasted with him at the Army & Navy Club, saw the man who can do the trick, was offered the job, & said yes. . . . It will be a big wrench, giving up everything & going." By the end of the month he was in Washington, at the War College, and by early August he had orders for active duty. At the end of November he knew he was going to France.[43]

Parsons's response was, predictably, to immerse herself even further in her work. Immediately after Herbert wrote about his army job in June 1917, she was planning her next trip to the Southwest, writing to Kroeber to find out when he intended to return to Zuni; and in September she took up her folklore collecting again. In October, when she moved back to Lounsberry—the large Harrison house they had recently inherited from Herbert's father—for the children's return to school, she drew around her the close-knit group of anthropologists who were, with the children, her principal source of pleasure and security. Even her friend and confidant Clarence Day could not work his usual magic. Clarence came out last night, she wrote Herbert the day he got his orders to go to France. "It may seem a queer taste, but Negroes and Indians for me. The rest of the world grows duller & duller. But for you and the children I would certainly spend little time in this part of it."[44]

Parsons made one more plea for civilized conversation before she left the fray. Appalled by academic dismissals at Columbia, court,

Lounsberry, whose quiet beauty Elsie always preferred to New York City.

congressional, and presidential support for the suppression of any sort of dissent, and the refusal of her fellow intellectuals to publish her own and Bourne's work, Parsons appealed for the right of the minority to be heard. In a letter to the *New York Tribune* she noted, in a caustic understatement, "There has been of late some discussion of suppression of speech and thought in circles liberal and conservative—if these somewhat archaic terms may still be used." What, she asked, should minority opinion do when it is met by unanimous suppression by the majority? Should it acquiesce or should it attempt to assert itself? Should it take "the proud and suspiciously arrogant position that if it is not tolerated it is not called upon to express itself?" Or should it "more humbly and sympathetically . . . continue to feel itself a part of public opinion and therefore obligated to self-expression?" "If your correspondents will throw light on this query," she ventured, "they may furthermore be good enough to consider, in case they advocate the second position, the question it in turn leads to: To what extent should the costs of expressing minority opinion be incurred, i.e. in loss of work, of position, of money, of friends, of health and of ease?"[45]

Resourceful in Compensations

In December 1917, Mabel Dodge took the train across the continent to Santa Fe, and then to Taos. "I want a vacation," she said to herself. "I've had a horrid time lately. I feel like a Change." New York had become dull and dangerous. Leaders of the Industrial

Workers of the World were in jail rather than in her long-defunct salon. Her young majordomo, Walter Lippmann, was now drawing up a blueprint, destined to be entirely disregarded, of the postwar world. Emma Goldman was about to begin a long prison term for conspiring to prevent draft registration, and in December 1919 she was deported as an undesirable alien. Heterodoxy members were under surveillance, and the group had to change their meeting place regularly. Elizabeth Gurley Flynn was under indictment for "conspiracy to hinder and delay certain laws of the United States." Marie Howe was questioned by "Secret Service Hounds." Fola La Follette suffered persecution for her father's stand against the war. As Mabel Dodge later told it: "People snubbed her, cut her, and behaved like idiot barbarians. She ceased to go about much but she generally came to Heterodoxy luncheons. . . . She would come in looking somewhat pale and pinched, but after an hour in that warm fellowship her face flushed and her muscles relaxed."[46]

Despite the comforting warmth of Heterodoxy, the conversation was finished. A medium saw Mabel Dodge surrounded by "dark people . . . dark faces—they are Indians, I guess. You are to help them—you are for them." Mabel Dodge did not save the Indians— they saved her—or to be more accurate, she made a more satisfying life for herself with what she found through Taos pueblo and Tony Luhan, the Pueblo she eventually married. As she put it, her life broke in two right then, and she entered into the second half, "a new world that replaced all the ways I had known with others, more strange and terrible and sweet than any I had ever been able to imagine." Elsie Clews Parsons would not be so ready to fit her life into the standard American conversion narrative. But she too took a decisive turn at the end of 1917, and for much the same reasons. The Indians were going to save her too, not through her conversion to their spiritual values, but by providing her with vital examples of the processes of acculturation.[47]

Looking back on this time in a consideration of Bourne's life and work after his untimely death at the end of 1918, Parsons remembered him as "the single American writer who succeeded, even partly, in expressing minority opinion about American participation in the war of 1914–1918." From the standpoint of 1920 she points out that Bourne (and she might have included herself) saw clearly in August 1917 what the Treaty of Versailles demonstrated—that, as he had put it, "in the war we are a rudderless nation, to be exploited as the Allies wish, politically and materially, and towed,

To Charles

I shouldn't have sneaked off like a thief in the night. I had a very luxurious day along, and a good deal of my spring list for the country got satisfied. I liked Krabbe. He seems a man's man, like all entomologists. I seem to have talked too much as usual, not giving him a chance.

Jo's recently come across a number of your pamphlets and articles, and wonders why you don't collect them and publish them as a book. They are too good and pertinent to let die, and you could get by with some of your war psychology (?) that the NR

did not print. Don't say that you are going to publish nothing but technical scientific stuff now. Re-read my review of you in the Dial, and see how much we need your point of new trend on all these modern problems. I wish you could be persuaded to think of it.

R. B.

to their aggrandizement, in any direction they may desire." The recent deportations and the exclusion of a minority party from political representation proved Bourne correct when he warned that "willing war means willing all the evils that are organically bound up with it." Bourne's sharpened eye was that of a man out of sympathy with his group, Parsons wrote; and the loss of sympathy came hard to him as to others—a reference no doubt to her own sense of isolation and desolation at the end of 1917. Going on to discuss Bourne's reluctant and gradual loss of faith in public opinion, Parsons revealed, by implication, her own profound disillusionment at that time with the possibilities for rational thinking among plutocrats, intellectuals, and workers alike. But, she said, Bourne was resourceful in compensations, and he continued to hope that out of the disgust at the frustrations and aridities of American life "there might be hammered new values." Though he had given up hope for the state, Bourne could still talk about American promise. But, again echoing her own trajectory, she thought that he would eventually have taken nation and country less seriously, indeed as a quite negligible part of "that range of modern culture that the individual must roam about in if he wishes to retain the sense of freedom or to think of himself, as A. A. Goldenweiser, our philosopher-anthropologist, has phrased it, as the carrier of culture rather than its freight."[48]

Opposite: Randolph Bourne to Elsie after a visit to Lounsberry, May 1918. Elsie Clews Parsons Papers, American Philosophical Society Library.

PART THREE

Trans-National America

Give him a leaf of corn in his hand—
Let him dance!
Dance, Domingo, dance!
Jesus won't care,
For a little while.

—Marsden Hartley, "The Festival of the Corn," 1920

War god image and feather sticks from shrine on *towa yallane*. Source: Elsie Clews Parsons, *Pueblo Indian Religion* (University of Chicago Press, 1939). Drawn from an image in the American Museum of Natural History of the younger brother Ahayu:da created by the Zuni Bear clan and originally from an altar-shrine on Corn Mountain.

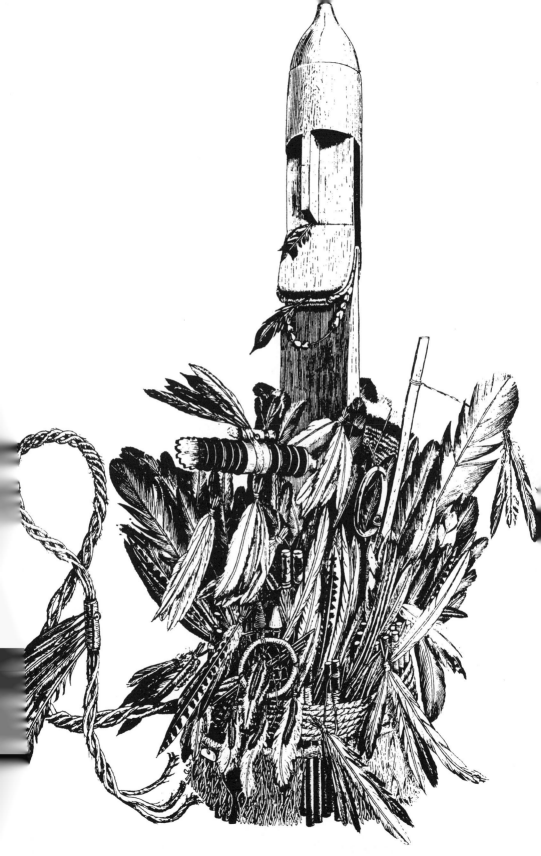

CHAPTER TEN

Saving Herself

HERBERT Parsons left for active duty in France on 25 January 1918. "My dear Children," he wrote in a long farewell letter in which he carefully enumerated his reasons for going. "I gladly give myself to combat the might-makes-right policy of Germany. . . . Germany drove our country into the war by her persistent and insolent violations of our international rights. . . . in the interest of the world's peace and right of self-government a stop had to be put to her aggrandisation." "England is the great liberalizing power," he continued. "Her application . . . of the principle that colonies have the right to govern themselves . . . has been the finest application the world has seen of enlightened government." "The world is going to be better after the war in many ways, if we win," he concluded. "For there will be a keener sense of justice. I hate war. I would not chose a military life except in such an emergency as the present [and] I hope that the Allies will form a league to enforce peace which by its international army/navy will compel nations to adjudicate disputes & abide by the judicial decisions of them. . . . may the spirit of Christ master you. Au revoir, Your father."

To sixteen-year-old Lissa he added, "Goodbye. I did not tell you when I was going lest it upset your plans. Enclosed is a rather solemn document which I wish you would send to John after reading it your self. Please ask him to return it to you and keep it to show to the little boys when they are old enough to understand, if in this horrible war anything happens to me. Probably nothing will. Have a good time. Your loving Father."[1]

"Father is off," Elsie wrote to John at school, "first to England then to France. May it seem rewarding to him! But why should one be so anxious to see imperialist France occupying Syria, or imperialist England, Bagdad, or imperialist Italy, Dalmatia? . . . Saturday I am off to the Southwest for a few weeks, say a month. Address, c/o Mrs. Eckerman, Laguna Station, New Mexico." She spent the rest of that week working at the museum. Kroeber was back in New York for the first half of 1918, and she walked with him in the park, and hosted Goddard and Professor and Mrs. Boas for dinner before the annual meeting of the Ethnological Society, of which she had become treasurer. Mac was six years old and attending the new experimental Lincoln School with Herbert Jr. Parsons felt she was able to leave them for a longer period than before under the supervision of her mother and Lissa, who was desultorily completing her final year at Brearley School. From the train, she wrote to Herbert, "I have a heavy program in SW, the Museum having definitely commissioned me to prepare a monograph on ceremonialism." Lucy Wilson—a voice, apparently, from the past—wrote Herbert too, from London: "Second only to my greatest wish, is that your duties might bring you to England before the end of April."[2]

Leaving New York

"Imagine yourself suddenly set down," wrote Malinowski of his arrival in the Trobiands in 1914, "surrounded by all your gear, alone on a tropical beach close to a native village while the launch or dinghy which has brought you sails away out of sight." Parsons could not manage to banish the world she was brought up in quite so splendidly as Malinowski during his wartime exile. But she did her best to do so intellectually from the end of 1917. When she wrote to Herbert in November of that year that she was abandoning New York for "Negroes and Indians," she meant it literally. From the beginning of 1918, she set out deliberately to strip herself of the whole language of Anglo-American life—the paraphernalia of unconscious understandings, theories, conventions, catchwords, and ideals that made up the intellectual equipment of the modern American. At the same time, she began systematically to build up her own clan, her own people, on the basis of the democratic principles she despaired of in her old life.[3]

In an unpublished article, probably written in 1918, Parsons portrays an escapee "from life in a vehement city, from a constant giving and taking of the thumb prints of an imperious propaganda," who has taken up the craft of bookbinding in a log cabin standing "where the sheer side of the wooded mountain yields to a slope of meadow." War is "the most exhausting form of social compulsion, a very climax of intolerance," she writes. "For me, and for many in my case . . . peace comes from a diversion of effort, from a change in the will to power." "Will it come by like ways to the peoples of Europe?" she muses, "*their* bookbinding will be on a vast scale. . . . what will be the spirit of reconstruction? Will it be the age-old spirit of . . . moral clubs, religious sandbags, industrial brass knuckles?" Or will it be "research and art and an economy rendered just and decent?"[4]

Parsons's "bookbinding" in 1918 took the form, ironically, of a meticulous comparative study of the war god shrines of Laguna and Zuni pueblos; and her log cabin was the American Southwest. On the day Herbert left for France, she was supervising the exquisite drawings of the feather sticks of the war god shrines at the museum; and this article—her first major anthropological publication—occupied her for much of the year. Its opening paragraph has the flavor of Malinowski's later and more famous lines: "About three miles southwest of Suwanee, a water and coal station on the Atcheson, Topeka and Santa Fe railroad," she wrote, "there arises from the plain what might be described as a great ant-hill, an inconspicuous and yet, from its detachment, an easily recognized and remembered spot. This hill or mound of about fifty feet or more sits about one mile from the mesas to the south and about eight miles from those to the north. About two miles to the east rises a detached mesa the Indians call *matsaiye,* and to the west stretches a vast plain beyond which southwesterly lies Acoma and northwesterly Laguna. On the northeast horizon rise the Sandia mountains, on the northwest, the San Mateo. Laguna is about sixteen miles away, and Masseta, an outlying settlement, twelve miles." She was a long way from New York.[5]

"War God Shrines of Laguna and Zuñi" is typical of the detailed work in which Parsons immersed herself during the years following America's entry into the war—relentlessly empirical, stripped as much as possible of theory and preconceptions, exact, exhaustive. In 1925 Robert Herrick, with grudging admiration, termed this work her "grains of sand." Her friend Signe Toksvig, begging Parsons in 1923 to return to her brilliant observations of human absurdities, called this work "noting down the difference between Tsola and Tsóla! (A very small squirrel & a tiny squirrel)." But to Parsons, it was stimulating and satisfying to note the difference between the butts of feather sticks—"flat at Zuñi (and Sia), pointed at Laguna (and among the Navaho)," we are told in one footnote. And it was also part of a long-term collaborative effort intended

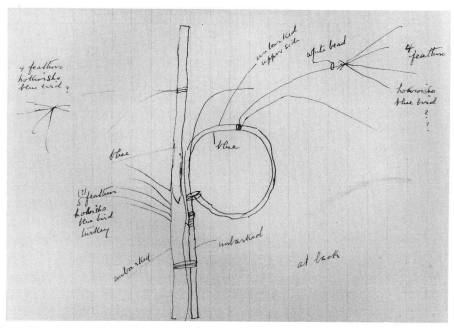

Drawing of a feather stick from Elsie's Zuni notebook. Redrawn, it appeared in her article "War God Shrines of Laguna and Zuñi." Elsie Clews Parsons Papers, American Philosophical Society Library.

to provide accurate knowledge about processes of acculturation—the historical conversation between cultures, to put it in Tarde's terms—and help build a community of scholars all contributing their expertise to the general pool of knowledge. Her project of finding a basis for social freedom was displaced from the "vehement city" to the mesas and plains of the Southwest, from the social engineers of the *New Republic* and the American Sociological Society to the more detached scholars of the Anthropological Association and the Folklore Society.[6]

Coordinating Work in the Southwest

In saving herself from the psychological ravages of war, Parsons was also intent on saving anthropology. Columbia University's less than enthusiastic support for the discipline diminished further during the war years, when Boas made no secret of his opposition to the university's suppression of free speech. Although he in no way endorsed Germany's position, he publicly opposed American entry into the war and deplored the wave of nationalism in a way that was interpreted as pro-German. Pliny Goddard's campaign to raise funds for Boas's work in 1915 and 1916 was a response to the cutback in support Boas was already experiencing. When student numbers fell off dramatically in 1917 and 1918 because of the war, Boas had to fight with steely determination to maintain financial support and faculty.[7]

At the same time, the American Museum of Natural History, with which Boas already had a strained relationship, was reducing its support for anthropological fieldwork. When Henry Fairfield Osborn became president of the museum in 1908, he worked energetically to turn it into a "positive engine" for the propagation of "socially desirable views," which he equated with "the principles and modes of evolution." During his twenty-five year presidency, he concentrated the museum's resources on evolutionary zoology, skillfully publicizing its "naturalists-explorers" and their adventures in the "wild places of the world."[8]

Anthropology did not fit well into this scheme. "Between ourselves," Osborn wrote a colleague in 1908, "much anthropology is merely opinion, or the gossip of natives. It is many years from being a science. Mr. Jesup and the Museum spent far too much money on anthropology." Nor did Boas's antievolutionary liberalism find an enthusiastic audience at the museum. Osborn and many of the trustees, including the lawyer-zoologist Madison Grant, supported theories of Nordic racial superiority that Boas and his students ardently and publicly opposed. An important target for the museum's educational project was the immigrant population, who needed, in the opinion of Osborn and his friend Theodore Roosevelt, to be educated in American values. During the preparedness campaign of 1916, superpatriot Osborn ordered all male employees to perform military drill in the museum's parking lot; and when the United States entered the war, he added bayonet drill to defend the museum against "barbarous Teutonic hordes." Robert Lowie and Leslie Spier found their positions increasingly precarious, and it was no doubt a relief for Lowie to exchange with Kroeber in 1918.[9]

In the difficult position of curator of anthropology at the museum, Clark Wissler was almost entirely dependent on the patronage of railway magnate Archer M. Huntington to continue his department's fieldwork in the Southwest. Pioneering archeological work had established a statistical method for dating archeological sites by pottery types. But Southwestern ethnography languished.

Huntington seemed to have lost his enthusiasm for the project by 1917. Writing to Parsons shortly after America's entry into the war, Boas commented unhappily, "It is very curious how little susceptible Mr Huntington is to scientific suggestions." A month later, apparently in response to Parsons's request for funds for a folklore expedition to Spain, Huntington was positively disapproving. "If I may be permitted to state a view with which perhaps you are not in accord," he wrote, "I think it is most unwise for anyone to undertake such work at this time. It is very pleasant and important work which you are doing and I wish you all the happiness that it can bring—but do you not think as little money as possible should be spent for the moment."[10]

In December 1917, Parsons told fellow Heterodite Elizabeth Gurley Flynn, who had appealed to her for help, that she had a personal income of $2,500—"an allowance from my father," she explained. This just covered her scientific work—field trips, secretary, and publication expenses. "My ability to be of service to any cause is limited—pecuniarily," she added. "To many of my acquaintances my circumstances are misleading." From the end of 1917, she resolved to use this income to promote collaborative work in Southwestern ethnology. Early in January 1918, she presented her plan to Clark Wissler, seeking the museum's support for an encyclopedia of Southwest culture. Arguing that "research in the Southwest is being done in a desultory, individualistic fashion," she suggested that a research program was needed to coordinate intensive, comparative work carried out on a cooperative basis. Topics would be assigned according to experience and interest. Researchers would keep in mind the data needed by their colleagues and would turn it over to them as required, while retaining the right to publish separately.[11]

Wissler, always suspicious of anything that might be associated with Boas, replied coolly to the proposition. "I should be glad if you could see your way clear to take up the question of ritualistic pattern among the Pueblos, beginning perhaps with the subject you have most in hand, namely, Zuni, and gradually extending your studies to a comparative view of ritualism in the Southwest. Unfortunately, I shall not be able to give you any financial support at present, but I take this opportunity to invite you to join with us as a volunteer worker," he replied, ignoring her wider project. But the master plan she laid out for collaborative work remained her guide throughout her career.[12]

Getting Life at Firsthand

When Parsons left for the Southwest early in February 1918, she had her year—and her future—mapped out. She wanted to see the two major kachina dance series at Zuni—the magnificent masked dances that celebrated the winter and summer solstices in February and September. She wanted to take a closer look at the intriguingly different eastern pueblos, beginning with Laguna, where she felt sure of a warm welcome from the Eckermans. And she wanted to visit the Hopi, the westernmost pueblos that sat like sentinels on three great mesas looking out over the Arizona plains.[13]

At Laguna, Parsons resumed the pleasant conversations in Margaret Eckerman's kitchen with Mrs. Eckerman's mother, her uncle Giwire, the old and feeble sun priest, and José, the joint sexton and raincloud priest—the Eckerman family's "Uncle Joe." She also paid daily visits to Margaret Marmon (Wana), a younger relative living in the pueblo proper, who gave Parsons the family genealogy. Wana's baby was two weeks old, and Parsons was able to continue her observations, begun at Zuni, of the beliefs and customs surrounding pueblo mothers and children.[14]

During this visit to Laguna, Parsons descended a thirty-foot ladder into a war god shrine near the pueblo. "The adventure of reaching it & finding the offerings it contains was thrilling to me," she wrote Herbert, implying that there were better excitements than those provided by war. "Living among Americans, White I mean not Indians, who have never heard of the Balkans and ask you if the Teutons are the English the war seems somewhat remote even when you find them reading with interest of the death of Vernon Castle, and scaring you with the rumored sinking of transports." "A cowman I had breakfast with," she added, "opined that conscripting such people was a more cruel act than any of the Indian acts in their wars."[15]

To John she wrote in more detail of her adventure, but the message was the same: "I read your letter in a motor loaded up with a 30 ft. ladder in sections, rope, nails, a shovel and a lunch. We were on our way to a ceremonial cave of the Indians, a war god shrine. It was sixteen miles from the pueblo & they still go to it to throw in arrows & feather sticks & rabbit clubs. The hole was like the crater of a volcano, the volcano being a hill of about sixty feet rising like a big ant hill from the plain, the mesas on either side far away, you would never guess the hole was inside. It was an amazing prison like place, impossible once in to get out. We found in it the skeletons of rabbits & other rodents & thirty or more snake skins or skeletons. You'd have enjoyed the climb & the excitement of getting off before the horseman who came up to see what we were about could reach us." "Do you remember," she went on, "my crying one day in the train because you were seeing the country I was so fond of only from a car window? I have somewhat of the same regret this afternoon in writing to you about that cave trip. You see more of what is left of pioneer life in one week in going about in this country than any amount of national park tripping or railroad travel."[16]

After ten days in Laguna, Parsons moved to Zuni in mid-February in time for the last three of the kachina dances presented by the six ceremonial clubhouses following the winter solstice ceremony. "We would go in at 8 P.M. &, according to rule, stay until the program ended, at 12.30 or 1 A.M.," she wrote John. "Such gorgeous masks, & lively stepping and singing! Still in spite of the extraordinary sight, after a day's hard work writing down tales or stealing feather sticks from shrines one did get tired. One night everybody in the audience was supposed to be whipped, the women on the back, the men on each arm & leg, whipped 4 times by 4 fiercely masked personages. It was to exorcise bad dreams or bad habits—pretty much like the early Christian practice of flagellation."[17]

After three weeks at Zuni, Parsons set out in a downpour for Hopi with her Zuni interpreter Leslie. "We were getting through when our gas gave out," she wrote John as she sat around a stove twelve miles south of Gallup with three Navajo and "a white woman who has been held up by the mud, in spite of travelling with four horses hitched to a schooner." "The road was so heavy that we used up 12 gallons where they usually spend three," she added. Three days later she wrote to Herbert from the train east of Albuquerque. "When I got to Gallup I was pretty much all in, I thought, tired, somewhat starved, & fighting sinus. So, the roads being impassible I was quite content to rest a day in that ever pleasing Page hotel & I resolved to take my last ten days easily. So at a large price I got the best motor in town to take me out to the Hopis. Three days later, i.e. today when I got in this train I was indeed all in, having spent the night in the wilderness on the back seat of the motor & at 6.30 A.M. having walked in 8 miles & wagoned in on a springless Navaho wagon, 8 miles. On top of 12 hours of motoring two successive days the tires had completely given out, likewise the pump. When we got to the Hopi Indian agency we learned that there was smallpox on the mesas, they were in quarantine & if I went in my stay would have to be at least 3 weeks, perhaps 6, perhaps 9 etc. . . . I felt rather responsible for my Zuñi boy, I was awfully tired, so I just turned back." A moral equivalent of war indeed! Her parting shot was directed at the war hysteria: "Up at the head of the canon where we spent the first night, near the agency, there were to be sure some charming people who spoke beautiful English, got out of bed to cook us a delicious supper & gave us clean & very comfortable bedrooms,—but they were Germans."[18]

Parsons's ten days at Laguna were her first sustained contact with the tangle of cultures represented in the eastern pueblos. Not only was Laguna more Hispanicized and Americanized than Zuni because of its comparatively recent settlement and its continuous contact with Mexicans and Americans, it was also a village of immigrants—from other pueblos and from intermarriage with the Navajo. In the preface to *Notes on Ceremonialism at Laguna* (1920), Parsons set out clearly what attracted her to Laguna's apparently disintegrated culture. Most ethnographers had ignored Laguna, dismissing it as a "hybrid and therefore uninteresting culture." But "such a preconception overlooks the tenaciousness and ubiquity of Pueblo Indian habits of mind or culture." Moreover, "the preconception is unscientific in its indifference to some of the most significant problems of ethnology, the problems of acculturation." Such a preconception, she asserted tartly, was explicable "only as a variant of the race snobbery which is ever seeking for pure races."[19]

Partner and Witch

Back in New York, Parsons was welcomed by "her" people—the children and her anthropological colleagues. John had come down with chicken pox, "one of the more frivolous of the contagious diseases," she wrote Herbert. Visiting him in the school infirmary she was surprised and pleased at his eagerness to see her; and she was delighted to find that his young teachers and nurse were socialist pacifists who read the *Liberator*—the journal that had replaced the banned *Masses*. "Nurse has read one of your books and seems wild about it," wrote a newly respectful John.[20]

"We need you back," Alfred Kroeber had written Parsons from New York two weeks after her departure for the Southwest. "The lunches—they come on Tuesdays again—have degenerated into shop gossip and swapping yarns." In 1918, Kroeber was forty-two years old, two years younger than Parsons. This half year in New York proved to be a watershed for him. During that period, he told his second wife, Theodora, years later, "I got over my *Sturm und Drang* which had overtaken me twenty years late. I learned not to be so solemn."[21]

Elsie was an important cause of Kroeber's sturm und drang, and an equally important part of its cure. When Kroeber came to New York in January 1918, he was determined to reorder his life. The previous fall he had completed his 995-page *Handbook of the Indians of California* and was more than ready to move in new intellectual directions. But his problems were emotional as much as intellectual. A major reason for returning to New York was to undertake psychoanalysis, for which he felt an "insistent" need. Parsons was also experiencing the intellectual and personal crisis of the "irreconcilable" intellectual, disapproved of by most of her friends, silenced by the media, unable to check the country's slide into war hysteria, intolerance, and oppression. Faced with the dramatic failure of civilized debate, of everything she stood for intellectually, she also had to withstand the personal blow of Herbert's departure for war service in France.[22]

The intellectual and personal empathy that had developed between Kroeber and Parsons since the end of 1915 made their relationship central at this crisis point in their lives. When she returned at the end of March 1918 from her exhausting visit to Laguna and Zuni, Parsons worked every afternoon at the museum, putting in order the collection of ceremonial objects she brought back with her and preparing specimens to be photographed and drawn for her articles. After she moved from her city house to the more relaxing Lounsberry early in May, Kroeber, Goddard, and Spier often came out for supper. Kroeber, who had no family to take him home, would stay overnight; and during the long intimate talks those visits allowed, their relationship deepened.[23]

Kroeber was emotionally very self-contained ("repressed" was the word he himself used in 1920). "He is emotionally very queer," Lowie wrote his sister Risa, "stunted perhaps as a result of his marital experiences, and altogether an incalculable quantity in this regard." But Kroeber found that he was able to discuss his personal problems candidly with Parsons, and he found her advice both unconventional and wise. "You'll find me changed," he wrote her sometime in May. "The shell is gone, and a thousand friendly indifferences have grown into gratitudes." "You'll laugh at the bread and butter letter—but I'll put it on the spiritual food and drink bestowed. You're wise and I'm a child; you have courage and I'm a fool; and I get and have nothing to give," he wrote after one of his visits. "Dear Mrs. Parsons" became "Dear Elsie" by the middle of May and quickly gave way to the cryptic notes without greeting or signature or the slightly mocking "Very Nice Elsie" that characterized their subsequent correspondence.[24]

We have only Kroeber's side of this correspondence. Her personal letters are missing from his papers, and where work and personal messages were combined, the personal parts have been carefully torn off. But for Kroeber, it is clear, Parsons became the "witch" who understood all and risked all. During the early months of their relationship, she encouraged him to overcome his ascetic and passive tendencies. "You're right. Asceticism is hateful," he wrote early in June. "I didn't say I had it. I claimed a streak of it, not boastfully, I think, but analytically. If it's there, I'm willing to have it cast out. And the way I like my food, and two glasses of wine when the company is right; and lying on my back, and killing time while it's sweet, prove the streak not very thick." When Elsie moved to Lenox with the children in June, Kroeber admitted to a "shred of proprietary sense" that made him glad he got a letter from her before Goddard. "No letter," he lamented a few days later. "Centrifugal mail velocities evidently exceed centripetal. There are several things I'd like awfully to say but my brain is ossified and I'll have to wait for expression."[25]

Kroeber enjoyed Parsons's balance of work and play. When he visited her at Lenox during June, he found the "long mornings of work and afternoons on Bald Top," with her listening to his "sermons on the mount," relaxing and invigorating. He responded happily to her invitation to spend July in Lenox, staying at the lodge of her neighbor Carol Phelps Stokes; but he was dismayed to find that he would have to share Parsons's company with her other male friends. As always, however, he admired Parsons's courage of her convictions. "If you can get the house, I'll be happy to tumble into it," he wrote after initially backing out of her invitation, "and whatever loneliness comes with it, will be good medicine." Grant was here last weekend, she wrote Herbert, and Kroeber this weekend.

"The two men are as different as two can be and comparisons amuse me. . . . Kroeber regrets you are not here to know, but I doubt if you would make much of each other."[26]

While Kroeber's main interest in Parsons was emotional, she was seeking in him a working partner. Despite Bourne's urgent plea for her to reread his March 1917 review of her in the *Dial* and "see how much we need your point of view turned on all these modern problems," she was determined, as he regretfully acknowledged, "to publish nothing but technical scientific stuff now." During the three weeks she and Kroeber were apart in June, they discussed her ideas on love and work by letter. Mockingly calling her "partner," as he always did when she insisted on their working relationship, he conceded, "Yes, partner, you're a varietist. . . . But I suspect you are reading yourself into others, and doubt whether most women are miserable for the want of it. . . . It takes an experience of change to cause that." Answering a letter written in late June, he agreed with her assessment that "most personal relations are a failure—not only mine but other people's," and that "Work is different." "The worth whileness of much of it may be questioned—mine, yours, everybody's—but a clean job is a clean job that no one can take away or undo its cleanness. And as for our work, each new bit of knowledge or each confusion resolved is that much for ever added. And if there is such a thing as progress, its essence is, or rests mainly on, knowledge."[27]

In December 1918, writing from Berkeley, Kroeber remembered the happiness of the two weeks he spent with Parsons in Lenox that July. "Elsie dear," he wrote. "Do you want to do me a real pleasure? Send me for Christmas your book with the sermon on the mount [*Fear and Conventionality*]. Elsie, it's not loneliness speaking, and I am not longing, but I do look back with great pleasantness on the flowers along the Hackensack, and the garden walk at Harrison, and the music room, and the cool dinners on the porch, and Lenox lying spread before us on the bald hill, and the many houred cabin, and the last paddle up the Housatonic to the little fire, in the dusk; and I am grateful and will never forget them." But the attempt to establish a more intimate relationship on Parsons's "varietal" terms failed, and Kroeber left hastily when LaFarge was expected, leaving her "needing comfort" and him with "no guarantee as to what the future will bring." Three days later, in the Adirondacks with his sisters, he was more resigned. "The more hours pass, the more I'm satisfied, both at the trial and failure. And as to what the future may bring, I really don't know, don't want to know, and am entirely serene about. That I have to thank you for." "I wrote for the Zuñi notebooks to be sent to you at Lenox by express," he ended, apparently resigning himself to the role of partner, not lover.[28]

During their time together at Lenox, Parsons and Kroeber decided to make a joint trip to Zuni in September, before he returned to California. But her insistence on keeping their plans private brought back his despair. "Honestly, Elsie, I learn your tactics awfully hard," he wrote late in August. "You're no doubt much the wisest, and circumstances have made you experienced: but every so often my insides balk and then I am depressed. I got blue in bed last night and it hung over. It's torture to want and not to, unless one takes the wanting deliberately with one's own hands and turns it into another channel; and then it always seems to me the diversion might as well be written on the wall. No one else takes a real interest in sublimation, and if they talk idly, it's idle. Talk goes on anyway." "So long, partner," he ended. "It's nice to be able to talk it off one's heart. . . . Once I'm away [from] here, I'll be better. I always like quick endings."[29]

Throughout the summer, Goddard envied Kroeber's growing intimacy with Parsons; and his realization that Kroeber was her preferred working partner was a blow. "Elsie dear," Kroeber wrote just before their departure for the Southwest, "Goddard ran true to dope. When Zuñi came up, his mind began to brew. While he gathered himself, I filled in about New York in September being an anticlimax, and the like. Then he shot his question in the very words: 'Are you going to Zuñi alone?' I parried: 'I knew you would ask that and you know I can't answer.' He laughed, flushed, looked sick—and away—and said: 'Well, it will be a climax.' It took some minutes to get over the look; so I stayed an hour . . . and we parted, I think, with undiminished affection. At the end I ventured to ask him to remember me to you and the laugh seemed to be genuine."[30]

"Zuñi is even more beautiful than usual—yellow blooms and marvellous sunsets," Elsie wrote Herbert a few days after she and Kroeber arrived. But their visit was not a success. Kroeber's return to his Berkeley "prison" was weighing on him, and the extraordinary sight of the Zuni men registering on War Registration Day reminded him of the possibility of being drafted. He wanted to recapture one more time at Zuni the exhilarating mixture of work and relaxation he had enjoyed with Elsie in Lenox. She instead

Alfred Kroeber to Elsie, July 1918. Elsie Clews Parsons Papers, American Philosophical Society Library.

wanted to bury herself in a well-defined program of work. She was determined to investigate the war god shrines she had not seen during her earlier visit. She wanted to take advantage of Kroeber's presence to carry out a census of one of the ceremonial societies to test his conclusion about the connection between Zuni clans and fraternities. And most of all, she wanted to see the summer dance series in the outdoor plazas that complemented the indoor series she had seen in February and March. An unexpected bonus on the last day of the series was a rare performance of the *olowishkya ia,* which was, according to Kroeber, "of the most astonishingly frank phallic character." To Herbert she wrote a positive assessment of the three weeks with Kroeber: "The partnership in work with Kroeber was most helpful and agreable. . . . Thanks to this visit he has put his knowledge of Zuñi language into shape or near shape for publishing a Zuñi grammar. My knowledge of the religious life has grown considerably. He has planned a joint paper on the comparative ceremonialism of the Pueblo peoples, and I look forward sometime to writing a book on 'Pueblo Indian Religion.' Meanwhile shaping up the notes accumulated on this trip will carry me well into the winter."[31]

Kroeber's first letter to her from Berkeley told a different story. "Dear Elsie, collaborator, and witch," he wrote, "What you said in the last 24 hours sent me off with a sense of Zuñi having been wasted. It was for you—I hadn't suspected because I was content, as such. It was that that threw you into robbing expeditions and the like, naturally enough, and that derailed me. I take the blame: I ought to have known. You did, though I don't think through greater experience." "Well, Elsie, old partner, good luck to you, and as much peace as your soul wants," he signed off, "and my thanks for a filled half year." Pondering their relationship a few days later, he mused, "It seems rather a tempestuous time at Zuni; in one aspect of the retrospect." A year later, when Goddard told him (no doubt exaggerating) that Elsie had cooked a meal for Boas on their trip to Laguna, Kroeber vowed that "if ever we go again to Zuñi, Hopi, or camp, I'll cook more than that for you, and the rest you'll cook for me—instead of robbing shrines at dusk and eating cold stuff in the dark." Flora Zuni, who worked with Kroeber that summer, was observant enough to note that the relationship between Kroeber and Parsons was more than professional. "He used to go to Towayalane [the Sacred Mountain] with Mrs. Parsons," she recalled in the 1960s, "and we thought that they went there to have a nice time." "It might have been true," a more skeptical, or perhaps more discreet, Margaret Lewis observed. "Who knows?"[32]

Parsons's adventures and work were not finished when Kroeber left for California at the end of September 1918. Some Zuni acquaintances were going to Houck's Tanks, thirty miles the other side of Gallup, to see the Navajo *nda* dance. Determined not to miss this opportunity to see a ceremony of the Pueblos' most important neighbors, she managed to get there in time for the performance. Sometime around midnight, she fell into a six-foot hole and sprained her ankle badly. "Shock, pain & inattention the rest of that night made me think I must be having quite a military experience," she wrote Herbert a few days later from Laguna. "Fortunately there was one Navaho family there with an automobile & my friend had attached me to them so in the morning they motored me to the rr. station & I made my way on here, hopping when necessary & supported when necessary by those willing arms the West so eagerly offers in any predicament. Here I am very comfortable with my old friends, the Eckermans, and I shall spend the week in bed instead of going to Cochiti."

Before she put herself out of action, Parsons watched the circle of about 500 Navajo, on horseback and in wagons, and the "girl" dance in which the young women attempted to pull the men from their horses in order to dance with them around the fire. It was part of the Navajo war dance and "The licence character was plain," she wrote Herbert, "altho no doubt the dance is not what it once was. . . . It was extraordinarily different from the Pueblo dances and general attitude." Also different was their attitude to women and guests. After a sleepless night with the family that was to take her to Gallup, Parsons wanted coffee badly. "My eyes actually filled with tears," she wrote, "when I found that in accordance with Navaho etiquette we women were expected to wait for our breakfast until the men had eaten theirs. . . . Pueblo Indians always feed their guests first and men and women eat together. No wonder the Pueblos consider the Navaho an outlandish lot!"[33]

"Grant turned up at Laguna intending to join me on the Cochiti trip," she wrote Herbert a week later from Harrison, "and he came back on the train with me." This was no doubt a disappointment for LaFarge, who had suffered all summer, seeing his role as Parsons's field trip and canoeing companion usurped by the attractive and more professional Kroeber. It was also a disappointment for Parsons, who missed the *cha'kwena,* the masked dance closely associated with the war gods, which was performed at Laguna as she lay immobilized by her swollen ankle. But Tsiwema (José)—the one remaining ceremonial priest since the death of old Giwire earlier that year—came to manipulate the swelling, and the following day he brought her some spruce twigs from the sacred mountain, Mt. Taylor, as a restorative.[34]

A page from Elsie's fieldnotes, describing her departure from Zuni for the Navajo dance where she injured her ankle, 30 September 1918. Elsie Clews Parsons Papers, American Philosophical Society Library.

Different Trajectories

Back in New York, Parsons found Randolph Bourne ostracized by the *Dial*, where he had temporarily found a refuge. "They censor all my reviews," he wrote in September 1918, "for fear my dark obscure cynicisms will get us all into trouble." She had missed the "excitement" of the draft raids and the raids on the Civil Liberties

Bureau, which was doing "absolutely legitimate work in protecting men unjustly drafted, and in keeping track of the offenses against freedom." "All the paraphernalia of a full-fledged military regime," he ended. "How I envy your absorption in serene scientific things!"[35]

With Herbert writing from the battlefield in France, however, Elsie buried herself even more in her work. She felt so out of sympathy with the community that she registered to vote only "as a sex expression and in recognition of past efforts, yours among others," she wrote Herbert. On election day, Lissa and the little boys looked through the window "to see Mother vote"; and on the way home her old friend from settlement days, the banker Meredith Hare, tried to persuade her that she could not escape from propaganda into science. "Well, I have escaped," she wrote Herbert, "& forever." Commenting on an unforgiving position she took in a recent review, Kroeber exclaimed in exasperated affection, "Oh Elsie, Elsie. I guess Bourne is right—I'm benevolent too. You're not; but you *are* nice." But Goddard, happy to have Elsie more or less to himself again, declared that she "grows more reasonable and human every day." The change, he decided, was "largely due to her turning her attentions so completely from the affairs of white society to her southwestern studies." "She even referred to Herbert as 'my husband' yesterday," he told Kroeber.[36]

Kroeber, lonely and suffering from dizzy spells in Berkeley, bowed to Parsons's insistence on their working partnership. "Elsie, you have been a lovely witch and will always be a splendid brother in arms," he wrote late in October, "But I prize the witch even more and regret her. Well then, let it be business." Their coauthored comparative ceremonial paper was destined never to be finished, however. Having no teaching or administrative duties, Parsons could pour all of the energy she had previously devoted to "propaganda" into this new and exciting field. Kroeber, on the other hand, was bored and disillusioned with anthropology, bitter about his treatment at Berkeley, where he was long overdue for promotion, and battling to maintain his mental and physical health. "I had an upset five days with my head," he wrote Parsons. "I'm not crowded by work, but there are enough things to be done, between teaching, editing, bossing the job, and jollying the old lady, to leave time very fragmentary. Zuñi speech progresses, though slowly; and the joint paper hasn't been touched. . . . When I scheme, it's something new—on the war, to be done after it's over. . . . it helps the sense that living a little longer can be worth while. I don't know if this can be called happiness; but it's as much as I've earned, I can see."[37]

"I agree with Boas," he wrote Parsons in December 1918. "We have no distinctive subject and no peculiar method. All our heritage can ever be, therefore, is some specialists' studies of the exotically primitive, and a point of view. The latter the world would sooner or later get without us. We are merely in a position to drive it along. I often feel that the only things that will last in our work are my Yokuto vowel mutations or some of the finer points in your Laguna ceremonialism. And those after all, while they give real pleasure in the doing, are hardly enough to sustain long a vivid interest in life." "The language hangs, our joint effort lags," he continued despondently. "Have a little patience. Once my steam is up again, I'll move; and I do think I see clearly the central problem of binding our two personalities into one team. We may not do it; I may be the first to bolt; but I think it's worth trying." Reminiscing about their time together that summer, he ended remorsefully, "if Zuñi fell below par, the fault is all mine. And I wish I could make it all up to you; but it doesn't seem for such things to be."[38]

"Witch dear," Kroeber wrote in February 1919, "Tell me something of yourself—your writing, your lame foot, new friends, Lissa and John, Herbert's return, the latest Russian music, a garden close if you have found one—anything to assure me that Elsie is still willing to be a person and a very feminine one to me. I live in the Faculty Club, detest the members as a mass . . . and generally am an anti-social being of distinctly little use . . . write sporadically instead of by steady habit; and waste much time. Can you picture me, or did Zuñi anticipate Berkeley?" "And when do you go southwestward next?" he added. "Will there be a Californian extension?"[39]

"You'll get the Zuñi language, and you'll get the Pueblo ritual organization paper that you no longer ask for," Kroeber assured Parsons wryly a year later. "After all, Elsie, you are new at this work and have two or three goodsized careers already behind you— sociology, propaganda, maternity—so that ethnology isn't much more than an excursion. But I've had nothing else in my life than ethnology, and if I don't play very right shall have nothing else. Therefore it is that other things just now take precedence: above all the economic margin that brings freedom. If I attain that even reasonably, my ethnology will get done, for I think I am faithful; if I don't, ethnology can be nothing but the last defence, which means it won't be done really worth while. Again, be patient. I don't really want money or position; I must have them. My indignities burn. I mean to have them burn me."[40]

Throughout this difficult period, Kroeber was studying psychoanalysis. In January 1920, he decided to take leave to establish a psychoanalytic practice. Two months later he wrote Parsons, "Time and again I've been on the point of writing you something about it, and would have been more than glad to talk to you; but one doesn't spread unformed decisions on paper. . . . So I haven't written at all, but I now look forward to talking." "If you have a mind," he asked, "will you go down the Hackensack with me Thursday, April 22? The trees ought to be at the peak of the spring about that day."[41]

If Kroeber anticipated disapproval from Parsons, he was not disappointed. She was angry that he was deserting anthropology just when it needed coordinated effort and will to save it from enemies inside and outside the discipline. After their April river trip, Kroeber wrote defensively, "I know I'm too much interested in myself. But . . . haven't you made it a little hard for me, Elsie, to be as interested in you as I did want to be? Perhaps it was a defence, or an antipathy reaction produced by myself, that made you put work in the foreground when I was surely more interested in Elsie the person than in Elsie the anthropologist. Before long I got the sense that you wanted nothing between us but shop."[42]

Two days later, he was relieved that she had vented her anger. "That was a hard letter," he wrote, "but I invited it and what you say is true. . . . Do you suppose it's fun giving up anthropology or thinking about it? That is no excuse for bravado about it; but it is a reason. What I'm doing is an admission of failure. But what choice have I? Would you have me dog on blindly?" But they continued to be out of sympathy, despite spending time together in Lenox. "Luck is surely breaking adversely between you and me," Kroeber wrote just before his return to California at the end of May. "I know what that means psychologically. But I am not going to be discouraged. Nor proud. Elsie, let's admit we have mismanaged and look into ourselves. We've both been lacking in sympathy. But don't let us allow that to stand and grow into new aloofnesses. . . . You'll hardly be at the lunch tomorrow; but if you are, and can find time for the Park, or tea, or anything else, you are going to be asked. I leave Thursday evening. If I don't see you before, it will be because I am awkward or you indifferent. I'll never let you be hostile again."[43]

They seem to have parted amicably. Two weeks later Kroeber

reported to Parsons, who was then at Hopi, on the departmental business that had absorbed him since his return. "Not much science, except indirectly by providing for other people. But tennis is a relief. And I remain reasonably content." He said nothing of his psychoanalytic venture, and was disappointed by the negative reactions of his other colleagues. "Why are you so silent on the notice of my new undertaking?" Kroeber wrote Edward Sapir in July. "You are the one man in the profession that I had counted on not to take the event either as a slap or as a morsel of gossip." "I wish you every possible good luck," Sapir replied. "I have no doubt you will make a brilliant success of it, though still a little gaping at your courage. I may as well confess that I have some notion of a certain limitation in your temperament that may impede." But Kroeber's defection remained a source of gossip and speculation.[44]

When Parsons returned from her second trip to Hopi just before Christmas 1920, she was infuriated by the letter from Kroeber turning over all his manuscripts on their joint paper. "Don't be harsh, Elsie," he pleaded. "Fortune set you in what you call a muck against which you had to wage a long fight for self-preservation; and the fight left its marks. It set me, and most others, into a condition that compelled mixing the pure motives of science with personal and sometimes base ones. . . . You are right; but be tolerant also."[45]

Absorption in Serene Scientific Things

Like Robert Lowie, Parsons preferred to fight her way out of the "muck" through anthropology rather than the "religious faith" of psychoanalysis. By the time Herbert was preparing to return from Europe in March 1919, Parsons was absorbed in her new world. "What news do you get of Russia?" she wrote Herbert. "All or almost all Russian news has been suppressed here." "Having at last seen the decrees of Nov. 1917 of the soviet government, I begin to realize that their plan is pretty much like my community plan when I was seeing visions a few years ago," she continued as if *Social Freedom* had been written in another life. "I predict that if Bolshevism appears to spread Business, Press, Government & the Intellectuals will not be content with only a part of the Amer. army in Russia. War without declaring war e.g. Amer. exploits in Mexico & Russia will make a curious chapter in history. I suppose that under cover of conceding a League of Nations to Wilson Eng. Fr. & It. will get what they want, & the League of Nations will prove to be merely a balance of power arrangement or a paper plan. There appears to be no spirit of internationalism either abroad or here. I have seen a letter from French anthropologists which expresses bitter nationalism. There is Wilson himself attacking German scientists in a speech at Rome. Liberals (not radicals) here are getting disgruntled over the failure of reconstruction plans in the U.S.A. I wouldn't be surprised if in the course of time the fruits of the war will taste bitter to them."[46]

At the end of January 1919, Parsons was named, along with Jane Addams, Emily Balch, and Marie Howe's husband, Frederic, in the infamous "Who's Who in Pacifism and Radicalism" drawn up by Military Intelligence. "The Editor of the Nation called me up asking me to join a meeting at his office to protest against the list of 62," Parsons wrote John. "I declined as I said I did not object to being on the list, it was a roll of honor. I did not deserve to be on it as I had done so little to express the minority opinion, there was little opportunity." "What you say about the scientific absorption that comes upon scientists in the field, makes me think of the rapt states musicians get into, or the blood-lust of dogs on the hunt," Clarence Day wrote her in February. "Dogs are usually immensely aware of each other—but not on the hunt. But scientists keep up their obliviousness longer."[47]

"An unobservant citizen might almost suppose she was one of us," Clarence Day wrote in an affectionate portrait of Parsons in the *New Republic* in July 1919. "She wears the usual tribal adornments, and bead-work, and skins, and she sleeps and eats in the family's big stone igloo near Fifth Avenue." But "what is civilization to us, is mere jungle to her: the houses and street cars are like underbrush that she must push through, to get to the places where her quarry is, and where she really wakes up." And "every now and then her neglect of some small ceremonial sets the whole tribe chattering about her, and eyeing her closely, and nodding their hairy coiffures or their tall shiny hats, whispering around their lodge-fires, evenings, that Elsie is queer."[48]

Having a "queer" mother was not at all satisfactory to Lissa, then eighteen years old and repeating her final school year after failing everything but algebra the year before. Looking for patrons for Boas's work, Parsons invited a wealthy potential donor to tea. "Mother," Lissa asked afterward, "why don't you have men like that come to the house instead of your old scientists?" Seven-year-old Mac, however, was loyal. "Wissler started a story last night,"

Lissa in 1920. Parsons Family Papers, Rye Historical Society.

Goddard wrote Kroeber of a visit to Parsons's house, "when 'Mack' said 'Wait a minute. Mother doesn't like war stories, do you mother?' You should have seen Elsie's pleased face." But even the loyal Mac suffered. Seventy years later he remembered running home in shock and confusion when his Lenox playmates turned on him, taunting him that his mother was "an IWW."[49]

Parsons's major link to the world of "propaganda" was broken in December 1918 with Randolph Bourne's death from influenza. "The death of Randolph Bourne is no small loss to the intellectual life of this country," she wrote to the *Evening Post*. "He was a critic of great ability in a community not only possessed of but few critics but unaware of the lack. Intolerant of intellectual sham and impatient of compromise, Randolph Bourne did not temper the facts for either friend or enemy—and he had both friends and enemies. Nor was he uncritical of the inadequacies he saw in himself, subject as he was to the depression of the artist. Companionship and good talk he cared much for, and he cared enough for his social relationships never to prostitute them to his worldly advantage. He talked as he wrote—with the restraint of unembarrassed skill and the certitude of sincere seeking. And for many of us as well as for himself he kept the light shining."[50]

Despite the shock of Bourne's death, Parsons attended the annual anthropology and folklore meetings at Philadelphia at the end of

December. They were "unusually interesting and full of sideshows," she wrote Herbert. "The men now take me as one of them." On the night before the meetings, she brought two warring factions together by inviting Boas and National Research Council president John Merriam to dinner to sort out their disagreements over the representation of anthropology on the council. To her delight she was elected president of the American Folklore Society; and she officially launched the Southwest Society, a "syndicalist experiment in the research workers running their own machinery & controlling their own funds," she explained to Herbert. "Thursday evening Elsie invited Boas, Merriam & myself to dinner and the two of them had it out," Goddard reported to Kroeber. "Elsie's wraps are in my office chair," he added with a small note of triumph. "She is Pres. Folklore." Learned Hand, writing pensively to Parsons on Christmas Eve about "the folly of man," envied her new calm. "Why are we all so scared?" he asked. "Why am I so scared? At what? I am glad that you persist calmly in not being so. It is pleasant to me, my friend, to know that you can live in our world without anxieties and disquietudes. That is certainly good evidence of 'adaptation to environment.' Unless of course you should be crushed for lack of fear. That I think will hardly be."[51]

CHAPTER ELEVEN

The Other Continents among Us

PARSONS threw herself into fieldwork in the Southwest in 1918 in reaction to an America that was chasing the chimera of racial purity. The American Southwest provided the perfect antidote to that absurd quest. Throughout the nineteenth century, the "Vanishing Indian" had served as a potent symbol of the inevitable destruction of the "primitive" by the forces of "civilization"—of "red" by "white." Whether through the segregationist philosophy of the 1830s or the assimilationist of the 1880s, American native populations were willed into extinction by removal or absorption. "Everywhere, at the approach of the white man, they fade away," Justice Joseph Story lamented in 1828. "We hear the rustling of their footsteps, like that of the withered leaves of autumn, and they are gone for ever." A century later, photographer Edward Curtis caught the continuing mood of elegy for a departed race in his evocative picture of a band of Navajo fading into the horizon.[1]

Department store heir Rodman Wanamaker dispatched his assistant Joseph Dixon on a series of expeditions between 1908 and 1913 to mark the death of the Indian. "Listen for the heavy footfalls of departing greatness," Dixon urged the American public in his book *The Vanishing Race.* "Watch the grim faces, sternly set toward the western sky rim, heads still erect, eagle feathers, emblems of victory, moving proudly into the twilight, and a long, solitary peal of distant thunder joining the refrain of the soul—and it is night." At the Panama-Pacific Exposition in San Francisco in 1915, where Dixon lectured three times a day, an enlarged version of James Earle Fraser's elegiac sculpture, *The End of the Trail,* won the gold medal.[2]

As the Americanization program got under way in 1916, the commissioner of Indian Affairs devised a bizarre citizenship ceremony for Native Americans—who were allowed to fight for "their" country but only selectively granted citizenship. After handing each male applicant a bow and instructing him to shoot an arrow, the secretary of the interior told him, "You have shot your last arrow. That means you are no longer to live the life of an Indian. . . . But you may keep the arrow; it will be to you a symbol of your noble race and of the pride you feel that you come from the first of all Americans." Then the secretary told him to put his hand on the handle of a plow: "This act means that you have chosen to live the life of the white man—and the white man lives by work." The hapless Indian was then presented with a leather purse, to remind him that "the money . . . from [his] labor must be wisely kept," a small flag, and a gold badge bearing the inscription "A Citizen of the United States." The record does not tell us what indignity was visited upon the female aspirant for citizenship, if indeed she was deemed "civilized" enough to merit it. In 1925, Zane Grey put the "dying Indian" mythology succinctly at the end of his *Vanishing American*. "[His] deeds are done," Grey's Navajo hero laments, "His glory and dreams are gone. His sun has set. Those . . . who survive the disease and drink and poverty . . . must inevitably be absorbed by the race that has destroyed him. . . . the white race will gain and the Indian vanish."[3]

A New American Aristocracy?

In the American Southwest, however, the Indian stubbornly refused to fade into the sunset. While the nomadic populations of the Plains were uprooted and decimated by Euro-American expansion, the settled agriculturalists of the pueblos of New Mexico and Arizona survived the invasion, just as they had survived colonization by Spaniards and Mexicans. And even the warlike and nomadic Navajo, whom Zane Grey so readily consigned to "Death, sleep, rest, peace!" reestablished themselves as seminomadic pastoralists, weavers, and silversmiths after their removal and incarceration during the 1860s.[4]

A consciousness that not all Native Americans were vanishing was brought to the American public by Frank Hamilton Cushing in his thrilling accounts of life in the Southwestern pueblo of Zuni from 1879 to 1884. Newspaperman Charles Lummis followed in Cushing's footsteps when he went to live in Isleta pueblo, just south of Albuquerque, from 1888 to 1892. There he befriended the Swiss ethnologist Adolf Bandelier, who lived in Cochiti pueblo near Santa Fe and had been surveying the "sedentary Indians of New Mexico" for the Archeological Institute of America since 1880. Bandelier's 1890 historical novel of Pueblo life, *The Delight Makers,* and Lummis's contemporary descriptions and photographs did much to popularize the idea of a living and vibrant Indian culture. After the two traveled together to Mexico and Peru in 1892, they wrote extensively about Spanish influence and culture in the Southwest. Bandelier's wife, Fanny, collected and translated several accounts of early Spanish explorers, beginning in 1905 with Alvar Nuñez Cabeza de Vaca's sixteenth-century journey from Florida to the Pacific.[5]

The cultures of the Pueblo and Navajo became the centerpiece of an intensive publicity campaign by the Atchison, Topeka and Santa Fe Railway after 1895. In contrast to the menacing Plains warrior, inevitably male, the Pueblo and the Navajo were more likely to be represented by the female artisan, whose work could be collected by discerning art lovers. The pottery, rugs, and jewelry of native artisans and the striking pueblo adobe architecture were incorporated into the interiors and buildings of the Harvey Houses that accommodated tourists at the Grand Canyon, Albuquerque, Santa Fe, and other destinations along the railway. And in "Indian Rooms" adjoining these hotels and railroad stations, museum-style exhibits and demonstrations of native artifacts established them as far superior to the memorabilia usually available to tourists.[6]

In 1921 two native-born New Mexicans, Erna Fergusson and Ethel Hickey, set up Koshare Tours, which became the enormously popular Indian Detours when the Harvey Company took them over in 1926. Koshare Tours and Indian Detours provided "insider" visits to Santa Fe and the pueblos by well-trained young women who knew the country and its peoples. Dressed in Navajo velveteen blouses, with silver concho belts, bracelets, and necklaces, the Indian Detour couriers were part of the exciting but unthreatening experience of "abroad at home" that the Southwest had come to symbolize.[7]

The Indian Detour couriers helped the tourist to see in the pueblos "not 'funny mud houses' and 'savage dances,' but the immemorial architecture and dramatic rituals of the oldest American Aristocracy," Charles Lummis wrote in 1928. His characterization of the Pueblos of the Southwest as an aristocracy whose art and architecture were equal to the great oriental and classical traditions was typical of many Americans seeking a source of cultural renewal in the period after the war. The idea was fostered by Edgar Hewett, the great impresario of the Southwest, who became director of the

Institute of Archeology's new American program in 1905. An astute politician, he successfully pushed the Preservation of American Antiquities Act through Congress in 1906 to "check archeological vandalism in the Southwest." From 1907, he directed both the Museum of New Mexico and the School of American Research and promoted a romantic mix of archeology, art, tourism, and politics from Santa Fe that infuriated more sober scholars such as Franz Boas. Through the pages of *El Palacio*, the museum's journal established in 1913, and the institute's *Art and Archeology*, Hewett disseminated his ideas and attracted artists, patrons, amateur archeologists, and collectors to the region. Indians were neither primitive nor inferior, he argued in *Art and Archeology* in December 1916. "Their ideals of right and practice of justice" match "the most exalted that civilization had brought forth," and their "masterpieces of art" are "worthy of presentation to the public in museums, galleries, and publications devoted to art and culture."[8]

By 1919, there was a critical mass of "Anglo" artists and writers living permanently in Santa Fe and Taos, or visiting frequently, who agreed with Hewett. Alice Corbin Henderson in Santa Fe and Mabel Dodge in Taos, central figures in the Chicago and New York avant-gardes before moving to New Mexico in 1916 and 1917, brought their friends to visit; and many stayed, delighted by the weather, the landscape, and the interesting and complex cultural milieu. In 1919, the first exhibitions of paintings by Pueblo artists were held at the Museum of New Mexico, with Mabel Dodge demonstrating her enthusiasm by purchasing the entire initial exhibit. The following year, the artist John Sloan included Pueblo paintings in the annual exhibition of the avant-garde New York Society of Independent Artists, whose catalog emphasized that "these inheritors of the most ancient traditions of our continent continue to express their ideas with a vitality and with a style that shows them to be a very far remove from anything like decline."[9]

The writers, artists, patrons, and collectors who settled in the Southwest during and after the war found a way of life and an aesthetic sensibility among the Pueblo and Navajo that they admired and envied. And they enjoyed the complexity of a society where several cultural groups lived side by side in apparent accommodation, seeing in this a model for the "trans-national America" Bourne and Parsons imagined in 1916. The shock—and pleasure—of this cultural mingling to a young easterner encountering the house Mabel Dodge built with her fourth husband, Tony Luhan, is beautifully conveyed by Miriam Hapgood DeWitt in her memories of Taos, written sixty years later. "I have never seen anything like it," she wrote of her first visit in 1929. "The house is built of adobe, local earth mixed with straw, as are all Mabel's houses and most others in Taos. The walls, windows and door openings and the fireplaces, molded by Indian women, show the touch of their bare hands. The beams of the ceiling are peeled trees; across them are laid saplings in a straight or herringbone pattern. The walls are painted with a white earth, tierra blanca, applied with a sheepskin; tiny bits of mica embedded in the earth reflect the light. At the St. Theresa house [Mabel's guest house] we enter the living-room. Under the very large paned window is a big day-bed covered by an embroidered spread and numerous cushions all in gay colors. A tin cage containing a large wooden parrot hangs near it and a Mexican tin chandelier for candles is suspended in the center of the room. The pine floors are covered with Indian blankets. On the walls are Mexican embroideries, Indian paintings, tin mirrors and a santo or two. The chairs are of wood covered with hide or brightly painted. There are a few old chests of Spanish Colonial design. All is lively, simple, comfortable and charming."[10]

Miriam Hapgood's brother Charles, who accompanied her, described to their parents, Neith Boyce and Hutchins Hapgood, the electrifying effect of their new surroundings. "This new country seems to me like the other side of the moon, nature being so different from anything I have ever imagined before that the similarities to my former way of living stand out in isolation, like a few scattered known words in a strange language." In this new and renewing environment, easterners such as the young Hapgoods found that they could, like Mabel Dodge, reinvent themselves in imaginative ways. As Edmund Wilson reported, rather disapprovingly, when he visited Santa Fe and Taos in 1931, he encountered there an "extraordinary population of rich people, writers and artists who pose as Indians, cowboys, prospectors, desperadoes, Mexicans, and other nearly extinct species." With a greater sense of play, Erna Fergusson urged the "Dude of the East" to "have your kind of a good time. Be yourself, even if it includes synthetic cowboy clothes, motor goggles and a camera."[11]

In the immediate postwar period, artists and writers who admired the Southwest struggled to find a way in which the strengths of Pueblo and Navajo culture could be incorporated into what made up "America," without patronizing, appropriating, or destroying the people who made those cultures. This was often done ineptly, as non-Indians articulated their quest in the inappropriate language of a previous era. "The richness of the whole is worthy of a great Oriental school, but this work is different from the Oriental and nearer to us: it is American!" exclaimed critic Walter Pach, at the same time as he talked of "true Primitives," "children of nature," and "instinct," and praised the "timeless" quality of Indian life which "must not change." The Indian was no longer dying, but he was still exotic, instinctual, and unchanging—still, in other words, very much a figure of the white imagination. As D. H. Lawrence put it in "Just Back from the Snake Dance—Tired Out," "The Southwest is the great playground of the White American. The desert isn't good for anything else. But it does make a fine national playground. And the Indian . . . he's a wonderful live toy to play with. More fun than keeping rabbits, and just as harmless."[12]

The Tangle and Fusion of Cultures

The work of Elsie Clews Parsons helped change the way Americans perceived the Pueblo peoples of the Southwest, and gave the advocates of trans-national America—and the Pueblo themselves—a new vocabulary to speak about Native Americans and their culture. Erna Fergusson pointed out in 1936 that the "Changing" Indian had, by then, replaced the "Vanishing" Indian as the dominant conception of America's native peoples. She could also have added that "Indian" was no longer the operative word: in place of the homogenizing singular was a plural and fuzzy-edged conception of Spanish Indians or Indian Americans—certainly Indians, not "*the* Indian."[13]

When Parsons went to the Southwest in 1917 to escape the Americanizing hysteria preceding entry into the war, she was looking for differences between the pueblos and ways in which various cultural influences combined and recombined. By investigating processes of acculturation in these Southwestern towns, which seemed to the casual observer so timeless and organic, she was determined to reassure New Yorkers or San Franciscans that the mixing of cultures did not necessarily mean culture clash or cultural disintegration. Instead of practicing salvage ethnography, Parsons's unsentimental focus was on the living, changing culture. As Kroeber remarked in 1923 of a visit Parsons made to the Micmacs of Nova Scotia, "Your impartiality makes me admire. Native, half-breed

Catholic, New York culture—if there is any favoritism of interest, you don't show it."[14]

"Processes are substantially the same, of course, in all cultures," he continued in a later letter, comparing his own preferences to hers. "I know that my predilection for the relatively pure ones is a wholly aesthetic matter, an expression of the classical streak in me, which has no place in science. . . . You, on the other hand, are enough of an individualist to be at bottom a bit anti-cultural, and when two civilizations get tangled and fuse their patterns perceptibly, it gives you a bit of satisfaction at the break-up of the patterns, as I feel shock." "Boas is right," he wrote ruefully: "at bottom I haven't the scientific temperament."[15]

Parsons's Southwestern work, though always low-key and relentlessly scholarly, guaranteed a maximum shock value for the racial purist, whether of the pseudoscientific Madison Grant variety or the romantic Santa Fe artist. Focusing on the religious ceremonials, so admired by artists and tourists for their "timeless" beauty and condemned by assimilationists for their savagery and obscenity, Parsons scrutinized them exhaustively for borrowings and adaptations from other cultures—between pueblos, from surrounding peoples, and from colonizing Spaniards and Americans.[16]

"If one were put to it to give the most outstanding single character of the complex culture of the Pueblo Indians of the Southwest," Parsons concluded in her second presidential address to the American Folklore Society in December 1920, "one would choose, I think, that facility, so notable throughout the tribes, for keeping definite cultural patterns in mobile combination,—a facility which, from an aesthetic point of view, results in style, and, from the standpoint of general culture, in vitality and durability. Were the pattern less definite or rigid, mobility of combination would mean cultural disintegration. Were there less mobility or elasticity, given such an encroaching culture as that of proselyting Spain or of the United States, industrializing, and intolerant of social dissimilarity, rigidity of pattern would mean cultural downfall and annihilation. Moreover, apart from the Conquistadores, Hispanic or of El Norte, interpueblo penetration of itself might well have led, not of course to cultural impermanence, but to cultural monotony. As it is, Pueblo Indian culture has succeeded both in adopting the alien and seemingly incompatible with but little sacrifice of its own nature or spirit, and in preserving heterogeneities from tribe to tribe."

"This character of fixed ideological unit, mobile in practical combination, is most clearly expressed in the ceremonial life," Parsons continued, describing that life as "a rich embroidery of ritual patterns." But it could also be seen in another aspect of social organization, the clan system—"that system of social relationship which in native theory is unchanging and unified, and in actuality a flux of many currents." "In Pueblo Indian tradition," she noted, "the clan is an original and immutable unit, its members coming up together from below when the world was to be peopled, migrating together, and settling down together when . . . the middle place . . . was reached; its association with ceremonial is also original and fixed; and equations between clans in different places are made either on identity of names or on resemblances seen between the eponymous clan beings." "In actuality," however, "the clan is a highly unstable group; its association with ceremonial is through a family connection which is necessarily precarious; and equations between clans of different places are conceptual or even fortuitous." In sum, neither the "timeless" ceremonials, nor the social organization associated with them, were fixed. Instead they were constantly changing responses to the environment, physical and human—the products of individual and communal adaptation and invention.[17]

Carefully identifying and comparing the numerous ritual elements that made up the Pueblo ceremonials (the flat feather-stick butts of Zuni and the pointed ones of Laguna of her "War God Shrines" paper, for instance), Parsons traced the development of markedly different ceremonial practice and social organization in the various pueblos. By February 1919, when she completed her analysis of Laguna and Zuni ceremonial and compared it with Kroeber's re-analysis of available information on other Keresan pueblos and Hopi, a three-part pattern of differentiation was clear. "Notable variations in the ceremonialism of the different tribes exist," she wrote in *Notes on Ceremonialism at Laguna*. Hopi ceremonial in the west was organized primarily around rainmaking, and Keresan in the east—such as at Laguna—around curing, while between the two at Zuni both types of organization flourished.[18]

By 1924, after she had carried out careful studies of ceremonial, clans, and families at Zuni, Laguna, and Jemez, a pueblo southwest of Santa Fe, Parsons was ready to state definitively the relationship she perceived between ceremonial organization, social organization, and house-ownership by women. "The Pueblo Indians of New Mexico and Arizona have the most complex culture, it is generally agreed, of any of the Indians of North America," she wrote in "The

Religion of the Pueblo Indians," a paper she gave to the International Congress of Americanists at the Hague that August, "and their culture has been one of the most resistant to disintegrating influence. Surrounded by predatory Indian tribes, and subject to the White race for three centuries, first to the Spanish Conquistadores and friars, then to American traders and Washington agents and school teachers, this population of ten thousand Indians, living in thirty towns scattered through a very large territory, have held their own to an amazing degree. Contrasted with their alien neighbors, Indian or White, whether economically as farmers, house builders, or craftsmen, or from the point of view of family, government, or religion, the Pueblos have appeared homogeneous."

"Yet from within the population presents wide variations," Parsons pointed out, painting the sweep of cultural differentiation from west to northeast, "from the all penetrating matrilineal clanship system of the Hopi through weak clans among the Keres and Tewa to no clanship at Taos; from an equally pervasive patrilineal moiety system among the Tewa there is variation to the barest ceremonial traces of moiety classification in the West, among the Hopi and at Zuñi. In the west the women own the houses; in the north-east the men, a mixed system of ownership prevailing in the towns between. In the west there are an efflorescent mask cult and an elaborate service of prayer-stick or prayer-feather offering, which diminish steadily to the east and north." Within each pueblo, moreover, Parsons found a number of separate but cooperating groups concerned with internal and external relations, war, hunting, weather control and fertility, and curing, in different combination and emphasis from pueblo to pueblo. "Not one boss in Zuñi, many bosses," she pointed out, quoting Nick Tomaka, "that Zuñi intellectual who is now governor." Similarly, in the Zuni pantheistic and ceremonial organization there was little hierarchy, everyone controlling their own sphere. The same supernaturals are found throughout the pueblos, Parsons noted, but their evaluation and significance vary greatly; and ceremonial was "a kind of ritual kaleidoscope" in which an elaborate variety of elements were combined and recombined.[19]

"I liked your summary," Kroeber wrote when he read Parsons's 1924 paper. "I liked it particularly for the quality which may do most to hinder its full recognition: compactness and close organization. To give its significance, it has to be read with a degree of concentration that we don't ordinarily bring to ethnology." "What struck me most was a sort of geographic non-partisanship," he added. "I find I had grown a set of biases—the Hopi were a fringe, and that sort of thing. Tentative judgments that had crystallized more than I realized, and determined not only emphasis but observation. The few pages corrected a lot of that."[20]

Pueblo and Spanish: New Wine in Old Bottles

Much of the distinctiveness that Parsons identified among the pueblos derived, in her view, from their different experience of inter-pueblo migration and of interaction with neighbors and Spanish and American colonizers. The Pueblos had always been migratory people, owing to the exigencies of warfare, famine, and internal feud; and, she pointed out, migrants are culture-carriers. Parsons had been interested in Laguna from her first visit because it was, like New York, a town of immigrants. It also provided an example, within living memory, of the sort of internal feud that led to the establishment of new towns. Throughout her work in the Southwest, Parsons paid close attention to these migrations and splits. Migrants, she noted, introduce new languages, novel building or handicraft techniques, and even major forms of social organization. Even small groups can bring new clans, new rituals, or new ceremonies that add complexity to the calendar. And long sojourns establish connections of hospitality and trade that remain strong after the visitors have returned home.[21]

From the time she first saw the masked kachina dances of the giant *shalako* at Zuni just before Christmas 1915, Parsons was intrigued by evidence of Spanish influence in Pueblo ceremonial. Her first deliberately comparative visits to Zuni, Acoma, and Laguna in February 1917, when the United States was moving inexorably toward war, confirmed her interest; and it was this particular example of the tangle and fusion of cultures that she pursued most tenaciously. As Frank Waters, one of the most persistent students and popular interpreters of Pueblo culture, commented many years later, Parsons's "special talent" was for detecting cultural affinities between Indian and Spanish ceremonies.[22]

In *Notes on Zuñi*, written immediately after her February 1917 trip, Parsons remarked on the Zuni capacity to assimilate foreign ceremonial. By 1919, when she knew more about other pueblos, she was convinced that "the Pueblo Indian is unsurpassable as a pourer of new wine into old bottles!" In 1927 and 1928, when she set out in detail her controversial argument for the Christian origin of the kachina cult—that most spectacular and "Indian" of Pueblo ceremonials—she noted that she had been struck from the beginning by the similarities between Pueblo and Spanish rites. Early in 1917, she suggested in a paper to the American Ethnological Society that the Pueblo office of governor was of Spanish origin. Discussing the celebration of All Souls' Day at Zuni, Acoma, and Laguna soon after, she observed that the Christian character of the day was recognized in Catholic Acoma; but in Zuni, where the church had been abandoned for a century, "the Zuñi assert that the day has always been observed by the people, and that it is in no wise a Catholic ceremonial." She drew these observations together in a paper on Christian rites in Zuni ceremonialism presented at the anthropology meetings in December 1917.[23]

During her brief visit to Acoma in January 1917, Parsons noted the prolonged Christmas celebrations, with their mixture of Catholic and Pueblo rituals. When she made her second visit to Laguna in February 1918, she took careful note of the equally lengthy Christmas festivities there, and questioned José, the sexton-cum-medicine-priest, about the meaning of the Nativity group that still sat in the church. At Zuni during the same trip, she sought information about the *santu* (saint), whose image was preserved despite the church's disestablishment. The *santu,* she discovered, was treated like a Zuni fetish, as a source of life, as a rain priest, and as an agent of fertility whose lying-in brought increase to the pueblo during the year. At Laguna, José told her a story about Jesus, but at Zuni elements of the Christian story seemed to be incorporated into that of a native culture hero. Observing a winter solstice kachina dance at Zuni during that same visit, she was struck by similarities between such Pueblo and Catholic rites as asperging, incensing, ceremonial fasting and continence, penitential or purificatory flagellation, soliciting alms or offerings, breathing upon or from (kissing) sacrosanct things, head washing, and name giving. Parsons's appreciation of the pervasive influence of Spanish Christianity in the pueblos was increased during the 1918 summer when she edited the ethnographic notes of Father Noël Dumarest, a French priest based at Peña Blanca from 1894 to 1900, where he was responsible for Cochiti, Santo Domingo, and San Felipe pueblos; and her determination to visit Cochiti with Grant LaFarge that October was foiled only by her injured ankle.[24]

By the end of 1918, Parsons had assembled the basic outline, if not the details, of the theory she stated at the end of her *Social Organization of the Tewa* in 1927 and set out fully in the paper "Spanish Elements in the Kachina Cult of the Pueblos," presented to the International Congress of Americanists in 1928. The kachina cult was an intricate mélange of Spanish and pre-Spanish beliefs and practices, she contended. A combination of Pueblo spirit rainmaker ideology and the burlesque practices of the Plains Indian war society had been hospitable to the ideologies and rituals of the Catholic saints and the religious dramas introduced by the Spaniards. "Kachina and saints are alike the dead," she argued in 1927, "sending rain, bestowing blessings, more particularly fertility, in crops and offspring, making cures. They have once lived among men, and some day there will be a second coming. To their images or representations (saints' figures, kachina dolls, kachina masks) even now they return. They expect offerings. They entertain vows. They confer personal names. Fasting and continence are expected of those they are to possess, whether *padre* or 'fathers' in retreat or kachina dancers."

The *shalako* ceremony is the Christmas–Kings' Day celebration of Zuni, Parsons argued; the coming of the giant masked *shalako* figures is the Zuni Christmas Eve; Shulawitsi, the boy kachina, is a Jesus figure; and the prayers of the native religious hierarchy represent midnight mass. The Koyemshi clowns of Zuni, an integral part of the kachina ceremonial, are derived, Parsons claimed, from the Spanish "grandfathers" (the *abuelos*) of the eastern pueblos and their Mexican neighbors. The Koyemshi origin tale has a distinctly Christian flavor, she pointed out, "a Zuñi variant of the story of Adam and Eve"; the Koyemshi are feared for their magic or witchcraft, a sure sign of Mexican influence; payments are made to Koyemshi impersonators, especially in sheep and store-bought goods, a sign of post-Spanish development; they practice a prolonged retreat and continence in Christian rather than Pueblo style; and they are a third clowning group over and above the two groups found in the other pueblos.[25]

Reconstructing the process of acculturation and the current efflorescence of the kachina cult at Zuni, Parsons suggested that it flourished initially in all pueblos where the Franciscans had influence: that is, in all except Hopi in the west, to which they did not return after they were driven out in 1680. "Presumably, in the beginning, the Friars contributed deliberately to the process of assimilation," Parsons surmised. "Finding their pagans given to dancing, war

Zuni *shalako* figure. Photo from Virginia More Roediger, *Ceremonial Costumes of the Pueblo Indians* (Berkeley: University of California Press, 1941).

dance or mimetic animal dance, would they not seek to substitute for these the religious dances of the Church? What better way of conversion where the difficulties of language must have been so great?" In the eastern pueblos, however, assimilation did not develop beyond a certain point. There, with the continuous presence of the missions and increasing numbers of Mexican neighbors, Catholic ideology and rituals held their own. At Zuni, on the other hand, Spanish influence was less pervasive and long-lasting, and Catholic theory and practice were made over more thoroughly than in the eastern pueblos. Parsons conjectured that when the mission withdrew from Zuni in the early nineteenth century, the native ceremonialists took over many of the priest's functions and the kachina cult blossomed: "From the same beginnings it had in the east—Saint day dance, the 'grandfathers,' the animal burlesque mask, and Spanish dramatization, the cult became too distinctive to be recognizable by either Mexican or Pueblo as of Spanish origin." "Even the Saint's cult at Zuñi has been described to me by old men as purely Pueblo," she observed. "The Saint, like other fetiches, including the indubitably Spanish canes of office, came up with them at the Emergençe." From Zuni, the assimilated ceremonial then spread to the Hopi, who encountered it for the first time in this form, and then back to the east in its new elaborated and "native" version as an apparently purely indigenous creation.

"The *kachina* cult spread from Zuñi," Parsons argued, "whence in fact it is still spreading, to the Hopi, through the associations with the immigrant group probably Keresan, that had settled at Sichumovi after living some time at Zuñi; to Acoma, where there was no resident missionary; to Laguna; likewise to the Eastern Keres, to Jemez, and, circling out, to the Tewa, and even to Isleta and Taos. No doubt even in the eighteenth century this process had begun, but it was in the first half of the nineteenth century . . . that a great impetus was given to the distribution." "At that time as a wholly native cult, the *kachina* cult met with opposition from the Church, and even in native circles," Parsons speculated. "Just as opposition from the Church drove the New Mexican *Penitentes* into hiding, so we may suppose there developed that secretiveness of the *kachina* cult which precludes all Mexicans from looking on at *kachina* dances, and in the East all whites."[26]

Nothing Is Over, Done, Finished

From 1922, when Parsons began work at Taos pueblo with a visit to her old friend Mabel Dodge, she was a major source of comparative anthropological information for Mabel and the group of artists, writers, and activists she had attracted to the Southwest. Over the next five years, as Parsons studied the Tewa pueblos along the Rio Grande between Santa Fe and Taos, she worked every winter from a dude ranch at Alcalde, near San Juan pueblo, and later from her own ranch near Santa Clara pueblo. She often visited Mabel, who was by then married to Tony Luhan; and she had many occasions to discuss her ideas with the artists and writers who flocked to the public dances at Taos and the Rio Grande pueblos over the Christmas season. Certainly the young Frank Waters took Parsons as his intellectual guide to the extent that he later visualized her in a kiva in the Hopi pueblo of Oraibi, taking notes on a Snake dance he attended in 1932, even though she was busily writing in Maine at that time.[27]

Whether she was really with him in Oraibi or not, it was Parsons's view of the vitality of Pueblo ceremonial that animated Waters's celebration twenty years later, if not his exuberant spirituality. "The bow is broken. The thing is all over, done, finished—one thinks," he wrote in *Masked Gods: Navaho and Pueblo Ceremonialism* in 1950. "When suddenly they come. Out of the kiva, out of myth and legend, out of the depths of America itself."

> They come filing into the open plaza, shuffling unhurriedly, in dusty moccasins, with their loose-kneed walk. A line of figures, part man, part beast, part bird. Bare bodies splotched with paint, sinuously bending at the waist. Wearing ceremonial kirtles, a ruff of spruce around the neck. Carrying gourd rattles and twigs of spruce. But staring with tiny or bulging eyes from great wooden heads—bird heads with long beaks, animal heads with large-toothed snouts, square heads, round heads, cloud-terraced heads hung with tufts of feathers and bearing the symbols of lightning and rain. . . . They are dancing. Barbarically beautiful, brilliantly colored. . . . No longer part man, part beast, part bird. But forces which sway squatting mountains, which shape the cloud terraces building overhead.

"Nothing is ever all over, done, finished," Waters realizes. "Seed and fruit, form and substance, deed and intention—everything fuses in a whirling circle that encloses an undivided, undifferentiated, ever-living wholeness."[28]

"Nothing is ever all over, done, finished" was also the message that Erna Fergusson extracted from Parsons's work in her influential *Our Southwest* in 1940. "Remarkable as the changelessness of Pueblo culture is," Fergusson wrote, "closer study reveals that insidious modifications are always going on, and always have been." Citing Parsons's "wonderfully detailed and scholarly" work, she pointed out: "Tribes, clans, and individuals have shifted about, taking their customs and their ceremonies with them. They have learned, stolen, even bought each other's rites and 'medicine.'" "How little Catholic are the Pueblos, baptized these four hundred years," Fergusson underlined. "And how much they have managed to affect their conquerors."[29]

The New School: Tying Up Knowledge with Liberalizing Policies

Parsons was well-placed, during the decade she worked in the Southwestern pueblos, to influence intellectuals' ideas about race, ethnicity, and identity. By 1919 she was, to the reading public, one of the best-known anthropologists in the United States. Clarence Day's portrait of her in the *New Republic* in July 1919 confirmed her reputation as an unusual "character" whose activities and opinions were newsworthy. In November of that year, Signe Toksvig summed up Parsons's influence as a feminist public intellectual in a retrospective review of *The Old-Fashioned Woman, Fear and Conventionality, Social Freedom,* and *Social Rule* in the *New Republic*. Applauding her "vision of a 'neo-humanism' that would 'set personality free from the overbearing rule of age-class, of sex-division, of economic and political class, of family and nation,'" Toksvig noted that the experts may frown on the popular side of Parsons's work. "But the inexpert reader can hardly help wanting to communicate his joy over the illumination which she throws on our own contemporary society by pointing out the similarities between Polynesia and New York. The total effect of her four books written for the laity is to make the ordinary American realize how mortgaged and enslaved is his present to the inglorious primitive past. . . . We may be incredulous, but the patient, impersonal, drily ironic evidence that Elsie Parsons piles up in these four books cannot be set aside by any except the angrily conventional. She is laconic, and she is irrefutable, at least so she seems to a non-ethnologist."[30]

But the final seal of approval came from that prince of iconoclasts, H. L. Mencken, who anointed her as the only social scientist worth attending to in a long article in his *Prejudices: First Series* (1919). Mencken did not think much of the social sciences. Sociology was "monkey-shine," and psychologists wasted their time on problems that were "petty and idle when they are not downright and palpably insoluble" and ignored those that were "of immediate concern to all of us, and that might be quite readily solved . . . by an intelligent study of data already available." "Why," for instance, "do the great majority of Presbyterians . . . regard it as unlucky to meet a black cat and lucky to find a pin? What are the logical steps behind the theory that it is indecent to eat peas with a knife? By what process does an otherwise sane man arrive at the conclusion that he will go to hell unless he is baptized by total immersion in water? What causes men to be faithful to their wives? . . . Why are women forbidden to take their hats off in church?" These questions were important, he pointed out, because "their solution would materially improve the accuracy of our outlook upon the world, and with it our mastery of our environment."

Dr. Elsie Clews Parsons—"a lady once celebrated by Park Row for her invention of trial marriage"—was, in Mencken's opinion, the only person apart from Nietzsche who came close to uncovering "the genesis of this, that or the other common delusion of man"; and he found her books, particularly *Fear and Conventionality*, "extremely instructive." "I know of no other work," he wrote, "which offers a better array of observations upon that powerful complex of assumptions, prejudices, instinctive reactions, racial emotions and unbreakable vices of mind which enter so massively into the daily thinking of all of us. The author does not concern herself . . . with thinking as a purely laboratory phenomenon, a process in vacuo. What she deals with is thinking as it is done by men and women in the real world."[31]

In the face of the attention she received, Parsons resisted all attempts to make "copy" of her. Those were the years when the Museum of Natural History was promoting its adventurer-scientists in an attempt to attract funds. When the museum published *Laguna Ceremonialism* in 1920, the Science News Service approached her for a story "woven around your personality." "Would it be possible to get data showing how you became involved in anthropological investigations," the bureau chief asked; "what your personal life was when living with the tribe investigated, and how the natives regarded your status as a white woman?" "Also," he continued in a manner that presumably appalled Parsons, "there is the matter of striking photos for illustrative effect. Perhaps you wore and had yourself photographed in the costumes, or ceremonial paraphernalia." "I think this fellow must be taking a liberty with your name," she wrote curtly on the letter to Wissler, who had suggested the story to the bureau, "& that you might like to know it. E.C.P."[32]

Parsons dealt summarily with reporters looking for titillating stories. But she had not lost her interest in promoting anthropology to the general public. In 1919 she returned to her role of public intellectual as an enthusiastic supporter of the Free School of Political Science. The Free School—later the New School of Social Research—was an experiment in higher education backed by her friends Charlotte Sorchan, Emily Putnam, Frances Hand, and Dorothy Straight. Caroline Bacon, a former Smith College professor, had brought together two groups who were deeply dissatisfied with the lack of intellectual freedom in the universities: Columbia academics James Harvey Robinson, Charles Beard, John Dewey, and Wesley Mitchell, and *New Republic* editors Alvin Johnson and Herbert

Croly. During the first half of 1918, they planned a cooperative research institute and school for adult professionals that would have no formal requirements, curricula, or degrees. They acquired six elegant houses backing onto one another on West Twenty-third and West Twenty-fourth Streets, near the *New Republic;* and Charlotte Sorchan applied her considerable architectural skills (and no doubt her fortune as well) to transforming the buildings into a school, giving it, in Alvin Johnson's words, "a seductive if modest personality" when it opened in the spring of 1919.[33]

The Free School was an attempt on the part of New York intellectuals to reclaim their role as independent and influential social critics after the devastation of the war years. Among the school's distinguished faculty were economists Wesley Mitchell and Thorstein Veblen and political scientists Graham Wallas and Harold Laski; and Parsons's generosity and influence ensured that Alexander Goldenweiser, finally dismissed from Columbia, found a more congenial and tolerant berth among what Columbia president Nicholas Murray Butler called "a little bunch of disgruntled liberals setting up a tiny fly-by-night radical counterfeit of education."[34]

Parsons's former Barnard dean, Emily Putnam, approached her in March 1919 to teach a course on "women and the social order" in the fall. Although she shared Putnam's criticism of the title as "bad science and worse feminism," she was keen to have anthropology included in the school's offerings. "At least why not change the name of the course to sex in the social order or sex in social organization?" she asked. "For the first twelve lectures I would suggest the title Sex in Ethnology, and in the first lecture the arbitrary character of this classification should be made plain, the arbitrariness both of separating sex facts from other social facts, and of restricting the social groups considered to those without historic records as ethnology is assumed to do and does do." "Given the course," she went on, "it might contain first an ethnographic survey of certain cultural groups—say Australians, Todas, Pueblo Indians, some West Coast African tribe, etc.,—and then summaries of the division of labor between the sexes, of the division of religion, arts, games, of the division of government, of kinship reckoning and of family organization." "But you see what a scrappy treatment ethnology would come in for," she concluded. "Wouldn't it be much better for the School to offer a general course in ethnology or anthropology extending through the year and given, let us say, by Dr. Boas or, if he would not, by Dr. Goldenweiser or one of the men of the Natural History Museum?"[35]

Parsons's students in "Women and the Social Order" included *New Republic* writer Signe Toksvig and an unhappily married and childless woman named Ruth Benedict, who was searching for something to do with her life. At the end of the semester, Parsons suggested that Benedict take a course with Alexander Goldenweiser. After two semesters with Goldenweiser, Benedict entered the Columbia graduate program and began the career that made her one of Boas's most famous students. "I expect you are where I was six weeks ago," Kroeber wrote Parsons in October 1919, "deep in getting courses going. . . . tell me something of the school. Nothing percolates here."[36]

In 1920 Parsons tried to persuade James Robinson to let her offer a course on folklore in New York City. "It would mean the assignment of each student to the study of a special immigrant group," she wrote after broaching the subject over a dinner with Goldenweiser and Goddard. "I know of a public school teacher in an Italian district who . . . would collect material in that Italian district. Another acquaintance, one of the leaders among the Negroes of New York would . . . collect Negro material." A few general lectures in comparative folklore would be thrown in, but the real point would be the fieldwork. "On the practical side of tying up knowledge with liberalizing policies, the side which it has always seemed to me you all are most interested in, the course might be thought of as one in Americanization, a study of what happens to the cultural traditions of the other Continents among us."[37]

But the Free School was already suffering from the division that split its organizers a year later—between those favoring policy-relevant studies and those seeking a general intellectual forum. Robinson was one of the former, and like many others Parsons was seeking to educate, he failed to see the relevance of folklore to public policy. "In view of our present limited income we ought to confine ourselves for the time being to those things which bear most clearly and obviously on present day problems," Robinson wrote Parsons. A year later, Croly, Beard, and Robinson had all resigned. For the "true teacher, the restless searcher-out of all things," a disappointed Beard wrote in the *Freeman,* the printed word provides a greater forum than the university, which is "obsolete for all except those engaged in cramming candidates for degrees."[38]

Real—Not Paleface Fancy—Indian Life

Parsons also returned to propaganda by the written word. In 1919, prompted by a request for a series of popular articles about Pueblo women, she had written a story that followed a Zuni girl through her life course. During Kroeber's Christmas visit to New York, he and Parsons discussed a volume of similar biographies to educate the public about Indian life and culture. At first Kroeber was skeptical, thinking that the book would "average rather low as science or literature." But his enthusiasm grew when he read Parsons's story. "I had no idea it would read so well," he wrote from Berkeley on his return. "The form has always seemed to me an essentially unattainable one, but your skill is astounding." "Radin is enthusiastic," he added. By February 1920, Parsons had interested B. W. Huebsch in publishing the collection with an introduction by Kroeber and illustrations by Grant LaFarge.[39]

Kroeber had been interested in life histories since he published "War Experiences of Individuals" in his Gros Ventre ethnology in 1908. But the life history genre was proselytized in anthropology by Paul Radin, who published a short annotated autobiography of a Winnebago in the *Journal of American Folklore* in 1913 and had another in press in Kroeber's California series. "Most ethnological memoirs lack 'atmosphere,'" Radin wrote in 1913, and represent the culture they seek to portray only by "the skeleton and bones." The only remedy, in Radin's opinion, was to allow native informants to give their own accounts. They would not give a well-rounded and complete account of a culture, he conceded, but they could present "an inside view of the Indian's emotional life" that was closed to the ethnologist. Radin had won Kroeber's affection and grudging regard while teaching at Berkeley the previous year; and Kroeber's interest in Parsons's attempts to capture native psychology through biography was no doubt stimulated by their discussions. In addition, a general interest in the possibilities of biography and autobiography for the social sciences was greatly increased by the publication of Thomas and Znaniecki's *Polish Peasant* between 1918 and 1920.[40]

"Well, you can thank your hundred percent persistence, my damned conscience, *and* the enforced idling of a sea voyage for the Mohave story," Kroeber wrote on his way to Hawaii in August 1920. "It's half written, and should be ready to type when I return. . . . It won't be very good as a story . . . but I think a fair picture of the culture." "My story grows and grows," he wrote on his return voyage. "You'll have to use the blue pencil. Tozzer [their Harvard colleague] hasn't done his: he seems to think there is something wicked in the undertaking." By Christmas, Parsons had elicited stories from most of her colleagues. "Surely they don't grow enthusiastic over your cooperative schemes," Kroeber replied when she complained of the laggards. "You hold them to their tasks, and they are all full handed, some lazy, others timorous. I shall always marvel at the way you drove them."[41]

The result of Parsons's editorial efforts, *American Indian Life: By Several of Its Students,* is a beautiful book in large format, with contributions from almost every anthropologist working in the United States at that time. Even M. R. Harrington, that most reclusive of American ethnologists, was among the writers of the twenty-seven life stories. The book was intended, Parsons said in the preface, to fill the gap between the "forbidding monograph," which "anthropologists themselves have been known not to read," and the legends of James Fenimore Cooper. "Appearances to the contrary, anthropologists have no wish to keep their science or any part of it esoteric. They are too well aware . . . that facilities for the pursuit of anthropology are dependent more or less on popular interest." But there was a cost to becoming popular—in time and energy, and often in integrity. In this book, she pointed out, she and her fellow anthropologists had attempted to disregard white myths about Indians. But it was even more difficult to eradicate their own tendencies to focus on the exotic rather than presenting a whole culture. The anthropologist's data, she confessed, often gave the impression that native life was "one unbroken round . . . of curing or weather-control ceremonials, of prophylaxis against bad luck, of hunting, or of war. The commonplaces of behavior are overlooked, the amount of 'common sense' is underrated, and the proportion of knowledge to credulity is greatly underestimated. In other words the impression we give of the daily life of the people may be quite misleading, somewhat as if we described our own society in terms of Christmas and the Fourth of July, of beliefs about the new moon or ground hogs in February, of city streets in blizzards and after, of strikes and battleships."[42]

What was new about this book, Kroeber pointed out in his introduction, was the attempt to describe the mental life of the people. "This psychology . . . is often expressed by the frontiersman, the missionary and trader, by the man of the city, even. But it has been very little formulated by the very men who know most, who have each given a large block of their lives to acquiring intensive and exact information." "To many of us," he wrote, "the writing of our tale has been a surprise and of value to ourselves. We had not realized how little we knew of the workings of the Indian mind on some sides, how much on others."[43]

"The Elsie book is stunning in its get-up and impressive in content," Kroeber wrote Parsons admiringly in June 1922, when he saw it complete with Grant LaFarge's striking illustrations. "I am interested how the reviewers will be disposed." The *New York Times Book Review* gave it a full-page spread. "Real, Not Paleface Fancy, Indian Life," the reviewer announced. Writing from "an abundance of knowledge touched with inspiration," these scientists were determined "to make you and me see as a living panorama the long history of the race," he wrote. "Mrs. Parsons has very nearly succeeded, in this expensive and handsome volume, in convincing us that the real scientist—or at any rate the passionate ethnologist—is a first-rate novelist." British anthropologist R. R. Marrett gave the volume somewhat amused but sincere praise in the *American Anthropologist.* "When a lady has piped to them," he noted facetiously, "the doctors have not refused to dance." In the *Nation,* philosopher Hartley Alexander gave the book its most sympathetic reading. It was frankly an experiment in publicity, he pointed out, "publicity of that higher sort which is partly an appeal for sympathetic understanding and partly an apologia for the special preoccupation of its authors. . . . The form is actuated by the desire of portraying both the outward dress and the inward intention of Indian life." "'American Indian Life' gamely, and in its degree splendidly, goes to the heart of the anthropologist's problem," he concluded, "striving to see whole and steadily its phase of our universal human lot."[44]

Carriers of Culture

From the start of her work on the Southwest, Parsons had wrestled with the problem of how to convey a culture's subjective meaning. Coming to this work under the somewhat suspect label of "psychologist," she demonstrated the skill with which she could observe elements of culture and the intricate paths by which they moved from one people to another. But she never forgot that culture is carried by people who choose, reject, adapt, and blend these elements. From the first, with her *Notes on Zuñi* (1917), Parsons was concerned to convey the inner life of the people whose culture she was studying. As she said to Lowie in 1922, she was attempting to combine the subjective, psychological picture with the objective one in her studies of Pueblo religion. "It's damn hard," she confessed. "Mary Kingsley . . . has snatches of subjective interpretation, but they are only snatches." Barbara Freire-Marreco, the British anthropologist who had worked in the Rio Grande pueblos, saw immediately what was new about Parsons's approach. *Notes on Zuñi* "impresses me with a sense of truth, and understanding, and solid real life," she wrote Parsons in 1918. "How excellent are your homely illustrations of ways of thinking and speaking! and how honestly you include the touches of Americanisation!"[45]

Parsons honed her working style at Laguna in 1919. There she applied the principle she had perfected during her folklore trip to the Sea Islands earlier that year—that the way to learn something is to know something—in other words, that information is best obtained through interaction. She was careful, therefore, to collect and publish whatever fragmentary materials she could. Parsons's footnotes were always filled with the gossip and conflicting opinions and points of view of the people she came into contact with, and the genealogies she collected during her 1919 Laguna visit provide all sorts of chatty information about pueblo life. During her subsequent visit in 1920, she made the collection of town gossip an integral part of her fieldwork procedure. "Like any other small town, Laguna is rife with gossip," she wrote in "Town Gossip: Personal Notes" in *Laguna Genealogies* (1923), "and the character of the gossip is pretty much that of a White townsman alert to the jobs and deals of his acquaintances and relatives and interested in the sicknesses and deaths, the love affairs, the family quarrels, and the goings and comings of his neighbors." At Zuni, she observed, much of the town gossip was about the public ceremonies. At Laguna, such gossip was less frequent, because religion figured less in the daily life of the pueblo.[46]

In "Town Gossip," Parsons brought the townspeople—and her interactions with them—to life in a series of brilliant, insightful word-pictures. Tsiwema, the medicine priest we met in 1917 as José the sexton, becomes "the ubiquitous sacerdotalist," with a "compelling personality, forceful, unscrupulous and avaricious, and of so vigorous a physique that even now, a man over seventy, he can out-walk in his expeditions to distant shrines men much younger,"

Tsiwema of Laguna. From a painting by W. Langdon Kihn. Elsie Clews Parsons, *Pueblo Indian Religion* (Chicago: University of Chicago Press, 1939).

and, incidentally, vigorous and attractive enough—"a distinguished figure, tall and grave, his thick hair encircled with a scarlet banda"—to be the reputed father of Margaret Marmon's (Wana's) newborn child. We see the unhappy home life of Tsiwema's near-blind assistant, Goty'iai, who is despised by his stepdaughter, Parsons's ungracious hostess Dzaidyuwi, in "a truly ludicrous illustration of the contempt of the manual laborer for the intellectual, the over-paid intellectual." But we also, in a more sympathetic moment, see Dzaidyuwi meeting her son on his return from school in Santa Fe, showing "the emotions familiar in the mother of a boy back from boarding-school," emotions, of course, that Parsons could identify with—at least in part. Then there is Hiedyedye, her Isleta-raised interpreter, a light-hearted and charming ladies' man with a "moody, forbidding, and ungracious wife" who, uncharacteristically for a Pueblo woman, rarely left his side. Like Tsiwema and Goty'iai, Hiedyedye combined Catholic and native religious duties, and we catch a glimpse of him taking the children on a Sunday school picnic to Mt. Taylor when he had to plant prayer sticks before the summer solstice ceremony.[47]

Parsons continued to provide charming and insightful accounts of the personal lives of her Pueblo friends and acquaintances in the prefaces, introductions, sections on personal life, and chatty footnotes of her articles and monographs. But she agreed with Edward Sapir—in a "little squib" at the end of his review of *American Indian Life* in the *Dial*—that "the bare recital of the details of any mode of life that human beings have actually lived" was more compelling than the most skillful reconstruction by another. Accordingly, her most innovative attempt to capture the psychology of a Pueblo is the *Pueblo Indian Journal* of "Crow-Wing," which she edited in 1921. Crow-Wing was the name she gave to her Hopi host, George Cochisi, who kept a journal of town life, at Parsons's suggestion, for the year following her December 1920 visit. Crow-Wing was the first of a series of men and women—most notably Eligio of Mitla, Mexico, and Rosita Lema of Peguche, Ecuador—whom Parsons used as exemplars of the acculturation process. He belonged to that choice class of informants, middle-aged men and women for the most part, who were "Americanized" sufficiently for ethnological work, but who still appreciated their own culture. Crow-Wing learned English at boarding school; but he refused to graduate with his class. "Graduation to his Indian way of thinking was an initiation, a rebirth into a new life, the American life, and that break with the old life, 'life as a regular Indian,' as he put it, [he] did not wish to make," Parsons explained in an article in *Century*. "And so he took what the school could give him, but on his own terms." He is likable, sympathetic, dependable, resourceful—a "hard man" who refused to do or tell certain things. "He absolutely refused at the end of our day's drive to try to find me an overnight lodging at hostile Hotavila," Parsons tells us; "but had I been forced to sleep out that cold night he would have stayed by me . . . and kept up a fire. No White person, he has assured me, will ever see the ancient Tewa mask of which he is trustee," and "he would not say a word, I have reason to surmise, to facilitate admission for any White to esoteric ceremonial."[48]

"The Hopi, in number 2200, live in seven towns, not counting a closely affiliated Tewa town, built on top of three widely separated mesas in northern Arizona," Parsons wrote in her introduction to Crow-Wing's *Journal*, "or, speaking to the traveller by rail, 'on the other side of the Painted Desert.' To the traveller the attractions of Desert and Towns have increased from year to year. Until the present century visitors were rare, but today they are not uncommon and automobile campers are drawn by the hundreds, even thousands, by the notorious Snake Dance. This host of sightseers, however, merely swarms and in a day or two departs, having chosen for their flight but one spectacular moment in the year-long calendar of Hopi ceremonials." "That calendar remains intact," she tells us, "unaffected by American automobilists or other American progressives, except in one town, feud-rent Oraibi."

Most aspects of Hopi ceremonialism had been carefully studied, Parsons noted. But there was one striking gap: there was little or no record of the ideas and feelings of the people. "This journal is peculiarly welcome," she pointed out, because "it fills psychological interstices." "The picture of the distinctive cultural setting and the impression of harmony and integrity of culture" set forth by Crow-Wing is "precious to the anthropologist . . . because it is indispensable in evaluating cultural factors." "To the lay reader," she added, ever alert to ways of influencing her own "people," "the picture may also be of value as revealing unsuspected ways of achieving happiness and well-being, ways often different from our own."[49]

CHAPTER TWELVE

Disciplinary Politics

WITH plans for joint work and the possibility of a more intimate relationship behind them, Parsons and Kroeber had settled into an affectionate friendship. "Shall I see you in the spring?" Kroeber wrote in February 1921. "I haven't lost the craving to stretch on earth. If it were now, I'd listen and listen to you, and answer and listen again. It would be pleasant . . ." The spring visit did go well. On the train west, Kroeber found that at last the prospect of returning to San Francisco held some attraction for him.[1]

During his visit, Kroeber had seen Lissa, who was planning to marry in the fall, after a year at Bryn Mawr devoted mainly to social life. Elsie was unhappy at this precipitous marriage to a young law student, Morehead Patterson, blaming it on Herbert's moralistic views on premarital sex. But Kroeber admired the twenty-year-old Lissa for "her firm edges" and her "quick spirit," finding her, as others did, a softer version of her mother. She was "pleasant to remember," he wrote Elsie, "and if you'll take it as implying participation only and not proprietorship, I'd like to congratulate you."[2]

"My congratulations on you'll be surprised what," Kroeber wrote in anticipation of his New York visit the following year. "I read again today the last chapter of Fear and Conventionality. I can't yet agree everywhere . . . but a something that underlies and shines through stirs me and wins me." Psychoanalysis and the resolution of his relationship with Parsons helped free Kroeber to begin his major statement on anthropology in the summer of 1921. "It comes out a strange mixture of the philosophical and the concrete," he wrote Parsons. "I lack Lowie's easy adaptability and picking an easy, useful way."[3]

By spring 1922, when Kroeber became anthropology's representative on the National Research Council, he was ready—somewhat reluctantly—to return to the disciplinary fold. "I half wish I had never agreed to anything," he wrote Parsons. "But ambition and thoughts of 'career' die hard." He finished the first draft of *Anthropology* that summer; and for the first time in many years, he was full of plans for new fieldwork. "You'll smile, and at the same time groan," he wrote in August, "because it slips before Zuñi: I'm going to make a stab at South America: our unworked Peruvian collection." "Where is psychoanalysis?" he asked wryly, "you'll laugh. I sometimes wonder too; but it pegs along. No allusion from Boas all summer; or to him. I'm freer with you."[4]

Defending Cultural Anthropology: The Southwest Society

Although Parsons's plans for cooperative work with Kroeber never came to fruition, there was another, more lasting, result of their long discussions at Zuni and elsewhere during 1918—the Southwest Society. "We started up the SW society yesterday," Parsons wrote Kroeber in November 1918, "& next week we'll get a constitution." Over the next twenty-five years, the Southwest Society funded the fieldwork, mostly in the American Southwest, Mexico, and the Caribbean, of numerous scholars in cultural anthropology, paid for secretarial and research assistance for Boas, financed the publication of the results of field trips, underwrote the *Journal of American Folklore,* and gathered together, edited, and published the diaries, field notes, and papers of previous scholars and observers. Although everyone acknowledged that the Southwest Society was a cover for Parsons's generosity, they cheerfully went along with the fiction of cooperative funding and paid their one dollar annual subscription; and friends such as Learned Hand and Clarence Day sent their subscriptions and joked about their participation.[5]

As long as Kroeber was involved in joint work with Parsons, he played an active role in planning the society's work. "I'll think over the approach to Spinden," he wrote in January 1919. "He will not accept Wissler's advice of publishing his notes: he is constitutionally incapable of it." Surveying "modern quality material" on the Southwest three months later, Kroeber observed: "Left to themselves these seven or eight authors will be struggling along with their publication over the next fifteen years. With their data in the hands of one person, two months would see ready for the press a complete digestion of S.W. kinship. Wissler will never bully his people into coming through. With your society as an instrument, you may cajole them all."[6]

The financial and organizing role of Parsons and her Southwest Society were crucial over the next few years, as Boas and his allies faced what George Stocking has called the scientific reaction against cultural anthropology. The American Museum of Natural History under Osborn had always been skeptical of, if not actively hostile to, Boas's work and cultural anthropology in general. During the war years, support for a more "scientific" anthropology was strengthened by the establishment of the National Research Council (NRC). Organized in 1916 to mobilize American science for military preparedness, the NRC focused its work in anthropology on eugenics and physical anthropology and, more or less bypassing the discipline, placed its Committee on Anthropology under the control of the geneticist Charles Davenport and the gentleman zoologist Madison Grant. In the immediate postwar period, Boas, urged on by Goddard and Lowie, fought for the discipline, and cultural anthropology in particular, to have a controlling voice in the committee. Boas did, in fact, persuade the NRC that anthropology's representatives should be elected by the American Anthropological Association; but ironically, this in turn made the affairs of the association, which had been run by Boas and his supporters for a number of years, much more problematic.[7]

These issues came to a head at the anthropology meetings in December 1919, ostensibly over the question of Boas's recent letter to the *Nation* accusing unnamed, but well-known, anthropologists working in Central America of spying for the United States during the war. A censure motion against Boas, which expelled him from the association's executive council and forced him to resign from the NRC, brought together in a temporary alliance all who opposed his approach to anthropology, all he had slighted in his campaign to remake the discipline, and all who saw him as a dangerous and unpatriotic foreigner. The following year these "counterrevolutionaries," as Stocking aptly calls them, attempted to gain control of the *American Anthropologist*. Goddard lost his position as editor, but the counterrevolutionaries did not win: a compromise candidate, John Swanton, took over until 1923, when Robert Lowie, the consummate Boasian, became editor—a position he held until 1933, when Leslie Spier continued the Boasian tradition.[8]

Central to this whole conflict was race. At the most obvious level, it was a conflict between the mainly immigrant—and Jewish—Boasians and the "true" Americans to whom they refused to be assimilated in the manner advocated by the Americanization program. At a deeper level, it was about how race was to be conceptualized and studied. In December 1918, NRC president John Merriam made a plea for a more relevant American anthropology, arguing that it could no longer afford to occupy itself solely with salvage work among the remnants of the indigenous population. Anthropology must follow American interests overseas; and at home, it must study the racial composition of the increasingly diverse population. This could best be done, in Merriam's opinion, in close cooperation with psychology, biology, and neurology. As Goddard interpreted this message, Merriam and his fellow scientists "felt that our cultural stuff was getting nowhere, that we aren't scientific anyway, that it is time to take things out of our hands and really get down to business."[9]

Over the next few years, the National Research Council attempted to put in place what Kroeber called in exasperation "Merriam's big 'Human Migrations' vagueness," and anthropologists who wanted funding had to tailor their research to the council's requirements. Melville Herskovits was unable to secure funding for fieldwork in Africa on cultural diffusion but won a three-year fellowship for an anthropometric study of African-Americans. Margaret Mead received a fellowship in 1926 to study adolescents in American Samoa, probably because she focused on its relevance for contemporary America. But Ruth Benedict was turned down in 1924, ostensibly because she was over the age limit of thirty-five (she was then just thirty-six), but probably because her focus on Native American culture was seen as hopelessly academic. Merriam's hopes of strengthening an alternative to Boas's cultural approach to questions of race were not realized, however. Control of the Anthropological Association was back in the hands of the Boasians by 1923, Kroeber and Lowie were important representatives of anthropology on the NRC during the 1920s and 1930s, and scholars such as Herskovits and Mead became leading opponents in the popular press as well as in scholarly circles of what Boas called "the Nordic nonsense." But the cultural anthropology that Herskovits and Mead popularized was not the constrained empiricism of Boas; instead, it took an open advocacy stance. The movement of this new generation of Boas students in the direction of what came to be called applied anthropology had much to do with the influence of Elsie Clews Parsons and her vision of the anthropologist as responsible public intellectual.[10]

A New Boas

Boas's problems in the immediate postwar period were not all of his enemies' making. His major work was done by 1911, when he was fifty-three years old. In 1915, he was treated for a cancerous growth on his cheek. His fear of a recurrence, combined with the threat of diminished resources due to the war, made him anxious to finish work on the material he had collected years before. Always extremely circumspect in coming to conclusions, he was paralyzed, in those years, by what Stocking calls the "mutual inhibition" of his scientific caution and his compulsion to assemble all available evidence. At a moment when some clear statement of the methods and contemporary relevance of cultural anthropology was needed to educate and counter the evolutionary scientists of the Museum of Natural History and the National Research Council, and to proselytize the "half-breeds" of the Anthropological Association, there was no one available to make it. Boas tried to do this in a chapter he read to a gathering that included Goddard and Parsons in December 1918. But his conclusion that "we have no distinctive subject and no peculiar method" was not likely to persuade anyone of cultural anthropology's usefulness. Nor was Lowie's equally negative message, in cultural anthropology's first book-length statement, *Primitive Society,* in 1920, that civilization was a "planless hodgepodge," a "thing of shreds and patches," going to convert the convinced evolutionist. As Kroeber put it in his review, although Lowie's book exemplified the best of the American (that is, Boasian) method, "As long as we continue offering the world only reconstructions of specific detail, and consistently show a negativistic attitude toward broader conclusions, the world will find very little profit in ethnology." Kroeber pointed out that people wanted explanations and applications of them to human conduct. "If we cannot present anything that the world can use, it is at least incumbent on us to let this failure burn into our consciousness."[11]

But Kroeber himself, and Boas's other favorite son, Edward Sapir, were enmeshed in personal problems, and the brilliant Goldenweiser was squandering his energies and moral capital. All three were also going through intellectual crises that would eventually mean breaking their filial ties to Boas and striking out in their own directions. "I rather think Boas should get it inside of him that we are not standing by him any less because we refuse to declare war on his

248 / Trans-National America

personal enemies. In fact he knows it now but cannot get over the habit of trying to have his own way," Kroeber wrote Goddard during the 1918 imbroglio. Kroeber's *Anthropology* (1923), which crowded out his work with Parsons and gradually weaned him from psychoanalysis, and Goldenweiser's *Early Civilization* (1922) were the products of this period of crisis and separation.[12]

Kroeber, always more attracted to generalization and more assimilated to "American" culture than the "hyphenates" and "renegades," argued for a strategy of accommodation. "Don't you think it's nearly time for us to establish positive relations with Madison Grant?" he suggested to Parsons after the 1918 meetings. "He's . . . too great an energy to be allowed to run wild and continue to work mischief. Some of him could be turned into good channels. Osborn does it in some measure; and perhaps you could. . . . I rather believe he will react pleasantly to frankness and courage. Goddard sees only the villain in him, Boas only the perverted scientist, Wissler is too timid except in the last ditch." For the same reason, he welcomed Wissler's *Man and Culture* (1923), which "Americanized" the concept of culture and made it acceptable to the wider scientific community. "Wissler's book looks as if it would be very valuable for its effect," Kroeber wrote to Parsons on its publication. "A lot of chemists and botanists are likely to learn from it what we are really about and what our technique is."[13]

Parsons, however, had her own ideas about how to save cultural anthropology. She resisted Kroeber's attempts to involve her in the politics of the National Research Council after she successfully brought the two sides together over dinner at the 1918 meetings. And, always uncompromising in her resistance to anything that even hinted at the evolutionary paradigm, she had no intention of seeking a modus vivendi with its propagandists. On the other hand, she was not willing to spend time and energy "dancing with Madison Grant's scalp," as the more hot-headed Goddard wanted to do. She had discovered long before that activity and change stimulated human invention and adaptation, while also providing a balm to the spirit. Her response to the impasse that Boas found himself in was not to urge compromise or battle, nor to embark on a program of institution building or infiltration. Instead she provided him with the means to reorient himself and put new life and relevance into the discipline. "I have a date with Boas May 20 to go to the southwest for the month to study Keresan language," she told Herbert in January 1919. "I put him off this January because of the children & your possible return."[14]

Parsons had tried to entice Boas back into the field once before, in 1915, in the aftermath of his operation and the outbreak of war in Europe. He turned down her invitation at that time, pleading the pressure of work. But by 1919 she was a valued colleague; his anxieties were more pressing; and he may well have agreed with her that a change in routine was necessary. Whatever his motivation, Boas spent a month in Laguna with Parsons that summer. She wrote Herbert from the train heading west that Boas was depressed over starvation in Germany and the prospect of an unsettled Europe, "but I have hopes that once in N.M. he will forget about it." "Although," she added, "he has ordered the Times sent on."[15]

Like most of Parsons's initiatives, her invitation to Boas had important payoffs for herself as well as for her guest. Kroeber had pointed out in "Thoughts on Zuñi Religion" in 1916 that "ethnology can make only halting or erroneous advances toward the solution [of the interconnections between pueblos] as long as it remains aloof from thorough acquaintance with the Pueblo tongues." Parsons had little hope of getting quick results from the secretive and quixotic J. P. Harrington, who had been studying the Tanoan languages of the Rio Grande pueblos for many years. What better then than to interest the country's leading linguist in the Keresan language spoken at Laguna, Acoma, and several Rio Grande pueblos?[16]

During this May 1919 visit to Laguna, Parsons hoped to make an intensive study of ceremonial. She had decided during her brief visit the previous October, when she was hampered by her sprained ankle, that she would have to live in the pueblo proper rather than three miles away in Mrs. Eckerman's agreeable house. "If I were ever to see even their public ceremonies," she concluded, "ceremonies to which all their own people were admitted, but no White, I would have to enlarge my circle of acquaintances and become an object of familiarity about town." But Laguna was not Zuni, for reasons Parsons was only just beginning to understand; and she and Boas found it inhospitable and secretive. Uncomfortably housed, they found themselves barred from the summer solstice ceremonies they hoped to see. After presenting their case to the pueblo governor and observing the preparations for the dance all day long, the war captain—the brother-in-law of their grudging hostess, Dzaidyuwi—came to inform them they could not attend. "It was a warm night,"

Parsons recalled two years later, "the windows of the house across the way were left open and from our terrace we could hear the singing of the *cheani* [priests]. . . . A connection drove in from Paraje, and Dzaidyuwi borrowed our last can of preserved pears to give him supper. He was an officer come to guard the ceremony against intrusion. . . . For an hour or so we sat listening to the singing and looking at the dark figures that now and then passed under the terrace, then the Professor betook himself to his paradym of baffling verbs and I in no agreeable state of mind went to bed."[17]

Despite the trip's discomforts and frustrations, the change of scene and interest apparently worked its magic on Boas, because he returned to the Southwest with Parsons the following year. In June 1920, they traveled together to Laguna, accompanied by Grant La-Farge as artist and photographer. Parsons and LaFarge continued on to Zuni for the summer solstice ceremonies and a week with the Hopi—Parsons's first visit despite previous attempts to get there—before rejoining Boas at Laguna.[18]

The pleasantness of her reception at Hopi reinforced Parsons's preference for the western pueblos. Flora Zuni "had the happy idea of giving me a photograph of her Hopi friend, George Cochisi, as a card of introduction," Parsons wrote later in the *Century*, "knowing as well as I how reassuring to any Pueblo Indian on meeting a stranger is the knowledge of having a common friend." The trip was a long one—thirty-six miles from Zuni to Gallup, and a hundred-odd miles to First Mesa. Calling, as always, at the post office–store that was in this case at the foot of the mesa, Parsons found Cochisi's aunt and proceeded up to the mesa-top town of Sichumovi with mail and aunt in tow. Cochisi gave them a room—the same one the movie star Douglas Fairbanks, somewhat to Parsons's dismay, had lived in a few weeks before. But she was reassured when, walking to the neighboring village of Walpi, she saw prayer sticks, a shrine, and a ceremonially buried eagle. And she soon found her apparently Americanized household "quite as uncontaminated as any Pueblo household I knew anywhere." "The singular-looking hoops which hung to a corner of my ceiling, and which I learned were a store-bought machine to teach a child to walk, interfered," she discovered, "in no way with original beliefs about hastening the child's development." In the roof there were prayer sticks, over her American bedstead a *shalako* shrine was fastened to the rafters, and under the American-style floorboards were prayer sticks made for the house when it was rebuilt to entertain the *shalako*. "It was the old story," she realized, "as old as Spanish occupation, of foreign goods and contrivances fitted into native concepts and habits of mind."[19]

That evening Sihtaimi, the head of the winter solstice ceremony, suggested that Parsons be adopted into his family, to disarm criticism of her presence. The next morning she had her hair washed ceremonially with yucca suds and her face rubbed with cornmeal in a ritual that washed away her old name and life and allowed her to start anew—an idea that was most congenial to her. As usual she did not waste a moment that could be used to gather information. On the arduous trip back to Zuni a few days later, a trip that was particularly trying because she was menstruating, she ranged over missing information with her host. "The Hopi ceremonial system and their general ways of life are far closer to the Zuñi than one would know from what has been published," she wrote Herbert, "so my fund of knowledge of Pueblo Indians is materially increased & coordinated in many particulars." "My own rite consisted of being taken into the community through baptism—head washing & name giving—and the acquiring of a father & a large number of aunts, Affly Yu yu huñöma or cloud-covered-falling-rain." A month later, back in Lenox, she was more ready to admit the difficulties of the trip: "Unwell, and having a very peaceful and enjoyable time, particularly when I recall the vicissitudes at this time a month ago," she wrote Herbert, "18 hours in a buggy, the first day, the second, training & motoring to Zuñi & up most all night watching a ceremonial from outside a window."[20]

After this second field trip, Boas wrote gratefully to Parsons, who was by then "My dear Elsie": "I do not know whether you appreciate how much the two summer trips that I owe to you have meant for me. Ever since I left the Museum in 1905 it has been a struggle for me to find opportunity for work in the field and after my various attacks of illness 1915 and 1916 I had given up all plans for new work and made up my mind to try to work out what I had done & thought over past years. It is not saying too much if I say that the new work has made me younger & reborn a good deal of my energy and enterprise, and for that I have to thank you."[21]

Over the next three years, Parsons, Boas, and his secretary (and later graduate student) Esther Schiff surveyed the Southwestern pueblos, Boas concentrating on language and the collection of texts, myths, and folktales, and Schiff and Parsons investigating ceremonial, social organization, acculturation, and Pueblo psychology. In

Winslow Station, Arizona
June 17. 1920

Drove out yesterday from the Hopi country —
didn't travel how many miles, that started at
5.30 — up at 4 — and got here at 11.30 P.m.
with me 1½ hrs off for stops. The last part
was rather trying; particularly as I saw unwell. However it was a real part of the
world to see — real Arizona desert, much of
it, of quite a different quality from New
Mexico I know, more desert and a greater
range of wonderful color. Besides I
had my Hopi host who was driving
to question — and I managed my rather
my information. The eight days in this
or rather two Hopi house made most

profitable. Two ceremonies on, except a little
one of my own, as the people were still participating their fields; but thanks to a happy
introduction — a photograph + messages — from
my Zuñi friend Flora, I got to work
at once, + on the best possible basis.

The Hopi ceremonial system and their
general ways of life are far closer to the
Zuñi than I would have from what
has been published, so my friend ? ?
knowledge of Pueblo Indians is naturally
increased + assimilated in many directions
large. — My own role consisted of
being taken into the community through
fatherhood — had involving + naming of many —
and the acquiring of a father + a large
— & child-wise — ? ?
[struck through] Yeye-hanoʻna
? : often
number of uncles —

1921 and 1922, Boas and Schiff worked in Cochiti, the northern-most Keresan pueblo whose ceremonial was described by Father Dumarest in the notes Parsons edited. Parsons, meanwhile, under-took the first full-scale description of a pueblo in nearby Jemez. In 1922 a relaxed Boas, a mellow Goddard, and students Esther Schiff, Gladys Reichard, and Ruth Benedict visited Kroeber at Berkeley after fieldwork at Laguna and Cochiti and "a delightful 10 days at Rito de los Frijoles, Acoma, Grand Canyon, Pasadena, Santa Bar-bara" with Mrs. Boas. "Boas and retinue are here," Kroeber wrote Parsons. "He looks very well and is at his sweetest."[22]

By getting Boas back into fieldwork, Parsons not only introduced him to the Southwest and its intellectual and methodological prob-lems, but also stimulated him to renew his fieldwork in the North-west and to attract new and innovative graduate students into the Columbia department. After teaching summer school at Berkeley in 1922, Boas and his wife went on to Portland, Seattle, and Victoria, where they spent two weeks with his old collaborator George Hunt. In 1924, he returned to Vancouver. "My dear Elsie," Boas wrote that year with mortality on his mind, "I wanted to ask you, if you would permit me to state in my will that all my unpublished Manuscripts should be turned over to you, without any obligation on your part, but in the hope that you would try to put them in the hands of people who might use them to best advantage, either for publication or for study." "I am still busy with my art book," he wrote Parsons in 1926, when she was traveling in Egypt. "I hope very much to finish it this month. . . . Thanks to you I have been able to make headway with the accumulation of the last twenty years or more." "Herskovits has not been reappointed as fellow of the National Research Council," he continued, filling her in on the department's students. "Ruth Bunzel is doing remarkably well. She is ambitious to learn the Zuni language & I have keen hopes of getting money for her to go south from Columbia. . . . Ruth Benedict is going to Europe this summer & intends to attend the Americanist Congress. . . . We do not know yet if Gladys [Reichard] is to receive her fellowship. . . . She has nearly finished her Navajo organization."

"At home we are just recovering from a long siege of the influ-enza," Boas ended, turning for a moment to more personal matters.

Opposite: Elsie to Herbert from Arizona, June 1920. Elsie Clews Parsons Papers, Ameri-can Philosophical Society Library.

Franz Boas climbing Mt. Taylor, New Mexico, with Laguna residents Solomon Day and Karl Leon, 1921. Esther Goldfrank Papers, Smithsonian Institution Photo No. 86-1324.

"Wissler has written a new book, Men & Nature or something like it, conceited and slovenly. Margaret Mead sends us many reports. I believe she is getting a good deal that will clinch the position that fundamental individual reactions depend upon cultural setting more than upon hereditary or innate characteristics." "I wonder when we shall see you back here," he ended affectionately. "I trust you are keeping well & that the new impressions keep your mind occupied. Yours as ever Franz Boas."[23]

In 1927, at the age of sixty-nine, Boas wrote Parsons en route to fieldwork in Portland, "It seems to me often very curious that after years of retirement I am again so in the midst of anthropological activities. The change is very largely due to your insistence. I had as fully made up my mind that I wanted to close off my work and I thought so definitely that I could not do any more, that it was quite a change of tack when I finally accepted your invitation to go to the southwest with you, and the stimulus received then has been permanent,—not withstanding all the sadness that has come over my life since."[24]

Becoming Papa Franz

An important part of Boas's rejuvenation was the close-knit group of graduate students—many of them women—who gathered around him during the 1920s. When he wrote to Parsons in 1926, "We miss you very much in our narrow circle," he was referring to a family-like group held together by ties of affection, gratitude, and professional respect, who met regularly—particularly at a Tuesday or Thursday lunch—and called Boas "Papa Franz," a far cry from the forbidding and distant figure of Lowie's student days.[25]

Boas's well-earned reputation as a mentor of brilliant women students came about as an accident of war, combined with his scrupulous sense of fairness, the effects of feminism, and Elsie Clews Parsons's generosity and determination. Between 1901 and 1915, Boas had seen eleven students through their Ph.D., the best-known being Kroeber (1901), Lowie (1908), Sapir (1909), Goldenweiser (1910), Radin (1911), Thomas Waterman (1914), and Fay-Cooper Cole (1915). Although feminist undergraduates such as Freda Kirchwey found his classes stimulating, he attracted only one female doctoral student in the prewar period, Laura Benedict, who graduated in 1914. During the war years, male enrollments in Boas's graduate classes fell off, but the number of women increased. "I have had a curious experience in graduate work during the last few years," he wrote Berthold Laufer at the Chicago Field Museum in 1920. "All my best students are women." In February 1918, his favorite student, Herman Haeberlin, died at the beginning of a promising career. Apart from Leslie Spier, a self-taught archeologist who entered the graduate program in 1915 and became Goddard's assistant at the museum in 1916, and his brilliant Mexican student Manuel Gamio, who was embroiled in the cultural politics of his revolutionary country, his other two students during those years were Martha Beckwith and Helen Roberts. Beckwith, who grew up on the island of Maui, wrote her dissertation on Hawaiian folklore in 1918. From

Elsie and colleagues at Lounsberry, mid-1920s. On the porch, Elsie (in shadow on left) talks with Pliny Goddard; on the steps are Margaret Mead, Esther Goldfrank, Franz Boas, and Mrs. Nelson. Elsie Clews Parsons Papers, American Philosophical Society Library.

1920, she was the guiding force behind the Folk-Lore Foundation at Vassar College. Although she published extensively on Jamaican and Hawaiian folklore and continued her affiliation with Boas, she seems never to have become part of the charmed circle that formed around him in the 1920s. Musicologist Helen Roberts found life and work in New York difficult, despite Boas's support and Parsons's financial help. She never finished her Ph.D., although she continued her anthropological work and taught—in what capacity it is not clear—at Yale from 1924 until she retired in 1936.[26]

When Leslie Spier completed his Ph.D. and moved to Seattle in 1920, Boas found he had only two graduate students left, both of them women—and they were very good indeed. Gladys Reichard and Erna Gunther went on to successful careers in anthropology,

Reichard at Barnard College and Gunther at the University of Washington. Boas found both women very agreeable when they enrolled in the program in 1919. "We had our first lunch with Boas last Tuesday. He seems happy with his two girls," Goddard wrote Parsons in October. The women attracted into the discipline in the immediate postwar period shared the "secure outsider" status of the men who had helped Boas make the revolution in American anthropology a decade earlier. And they shared Parsons's brand of feminism. Reichard, who had a Quaker background, came to graduate school at Columbia at the age of twenty-six. Like Parsons and Roberts, she established an immediate rapport with Boas, and their relationship remained close—a mixture of daughter and loving friend—for the rest of his life. She completed her M.A. in 1920, and the following year Boas had her appointed his assistant in anthropology at Barnard. In 1923, Parsons lured her away from the salvage work on language that Boas had laid out for her by financing fieldwork among the Navajo with Pliny Goddard. Gunther came from a German-American background. Drawn to anthropology by undergraduate courses with Boas, like Reichard she remained devoted to her mentor. In 1921, Parsons supported her fieldwork among the Havasupai, the Hopi's western neighbors, with her new husband Leslie Spier.[27]

From 1919, Parsons supplied the salary for a secretary for Boas. Esther Schiff, a Jewish-American who graduated in economics from Barnard in 1918, was the first to take the job. She had a taste of fieldwork, financed by Parsons, in 1920 when she joined Boas, Parsons, and LaFarge in Laguna and went on with them for brief forays into San Felipe, Santa Ana, and Isleta. She returned with Boas to Laguna and Cochiti in 1921 and 1922, each time funded by Parsons. She resigned as secretary and enrolled in the graduate program in the fall of 1922; and later that year she married Walter Goldfrank, a widower with two sons. Her new family put a permanent end to her graduate work; but in 1924, encouraged and supported by Parsons, she returned briefly to the field a few months after the birth of her daughter and made a difficult breakthrough in the secretive pueblo of Isleta. Schiff's replacement as departmental secretary, Ruth Bunzel, another 1918 Barnard graduate of middle European background, launched her long and rocky career when she accompanied Ruth Benedict to Zuni in 1924, also at Parsons's expense; and Parsons continued to support Bunzel's innovative work through all its ups and downs over the next twenty years.[28]

Esther Schiff with Karl Leon in Laguna, 1921. Esther Goldfrank Papers, Smithsonian Institution Photo No. 86-1306.

Boas's best-known student from the early 1920s was Ruth Benedict, who entered the graduate program in 1921 at the age of thirty-four. When she completed her Ph.D. the following year with a brilliant dissertation, she replaced Reichard as Boas's teaching assistant at Barnard while Reichard was on fellowship in California. Between 1923 and 1926, Parsons supported her as a research fellow of the Southwest Society and funded her fieldwork in Zuni and Cochiti in 1924 and 1925.[29]

Challenging Sexual Taboos

Parsons's support for these women scholars went much further than financial help, although that was crucial to their careers. Even more important was her breaking of the sexual taboos that prevented unmarried men and women working together in the field. Despite the inroads of feminism in advanced circles of American society, most men considered women a different, and somewhat dangerous, species. Helen Roberts gives a good insight into the problems women faced in a 1919 letter thanking Parsons for supporting her dissertation research on Native American music. Roberts recounts how Boas took her to the Field Museum to assure Berthold Laufer that she could transcribe records: Laufer's "aversion to women . . . was as fixed as the laws of the Medes & Persians," she wrote dejectedly. "His idea is that women are useful only as clerks or stenographers. There is other work there too, that he would give a man, if he could find him, but not to me. . . . There is some museum work here in Los Angeles which I would like to get—and it is one place where a woman would be considered—except with Dr. Boas. Surely no one could want more help or encouragement than he gave me."[30]

Parsons's many trips to the field with Kroeber, Boas, and LaFarge were deliberate attempts on her part to break down the sexual barriers that prevented men and women from being unselfconscious colleagues. Just as she had always insisted on friendship as a crucial relationship between men and women because it was relatively free of convention, Parsons also insisted that professional relationships should be free of artificial conventions that helped exclude women. And, as always, she demonstrated this by her own example. Although we know from their correspondence that her friendships with Kroeber, Boas, and LaFarge were of different orders of intimacy, Parsons gave no hint of this in her demeanor or conversation; nor would she allow others, at least in her presence, to treat any of those relationships as subjects of gossip or speculation. She had maintained in her discussions of the ethics of love affairs that the nature of a relationship should be a private matter between those involved. She kept to the same rule in her professional relationships. Aware of Goddard's proclivities for gossip—and jealousy—she insisted that Kroeber not discuss their Zuni plans beforehand; and afterward she talked about it as if it was the most natural thing in the world that she and Kroeber—the two experts on Zuni—should go to the field together. Her field trips with Boas, and her casual introduction of LaFarge during these trips, established the principle of privacy and reticence for men and women going to the field, helping to destroy a major stumbling block for women's careers. Without her example, it is unlikely that Gladys Reichard and Pliny Goddard would have been able to work together on the Navajo between 1923 and 1928; and it is unlikely that Boas would have

Esther Schiff Goldfrank's anthropology picnic, 1927. Gladys Reichard and Pliny Goddard are second and fourth from the right. From the left, the others are Nils Nelson, unidentified, Franz Boas, Esther Goldfrank, unidentified, Gertrude Boas, Robert Lowie, William Ogburn, and Mrs. Nelson. Esther Goldfrank Papers, Smithsonian Institution Photo No. 86-1312.

accepted so readily the love affair that developed between Reichard, his favorite student, and Goddard, his most loyal colleague.[31]

Parsons could not suppress all gossip, of course. "I smiled at the Navaho expedition," Kroeber wrote Parsons in 1923 when he heard she was funding Reichard and Goddard's field trip. "It looks as if the Southwest Society had the secondary aim of helping to liberate individuals." "Her explanation that he took her because he didn't have money enough to go alone is as sincere and candidly naive as she always is," he added the following month. "It is a world with amusing spots, even if most of the rest is futile." Goddard, always avid for gossip, wrote gleefully to Kroeber in 1925 about reports of Ruth Benedict's fieldwork in Cochiti where she "ran 3 shifts of informants who told her tales and myths 9 hours a day. The men made love to her evenings besides." Edward Sapir was more malevolent, particularly about a woman as self-confident and prominent as Parsons. "She needs psychoanalysis," he wrote of Parsons to his graduate student Leslie White in 1926, as White left for fieldwork she was financing. "You might solve her difficulties by having intercourse with her. Her interest in 'science' is some kind of erotic mechanism."[32]

But Parsons did give men and women the opportunity to assess each other as professionals. "Goddard won't clear up social organization," Kroeber added in his comment on the Navajo field trip. "It means handling crossed threads, and he likes sliding in a groove. Gladys is different, and I'll be interested to see how she handles something new like this. That girl is a workman." And despite Sapir's denigrating introduction, Leslie White soon discovered that Parsons was the generous and courageous colleague and friend whom he later absolved from his sweeping condemnation of the sterility of Boasian anthropology.[33]

Parsons was not always successful in winning over the men in the discipline, as Sapir's venomous comment demonstrated. She encountered particular obduracy in the "half-breeds" from Harvard, Alfred Tozzer and Alfred Kidder, whose impeccable Wasp credentials sat uncomfortably with their advocacy of Boas's methodology. Parsons first met Kidder in 1920, when he was excavating the Pecos ruins outside Santa Fe. Kidder thought highly of Kroeber's Zuni work and tried to persuade him to carry out a similar study of Jemez, the pueblo to which the surviving inhabitants of Pecos had migrated. Kroeber, preoccupied with psychoanalysis and bored with fieldwork, no doubt suggested Parsons for the job, as he did when Goddard wanted him to go to Taos for the museum. But the meeting between Kidder and Parsons did not go well. Grant LaFarge was probably with her—certainly he introduced his freshman son, Oliver, to Kidder and Tozzer at Harvard a few months later. "Have you scared Kidder or does he disapprove of you," Kroeber asked Parsons with amusement after the encounter. "You may be sure you brought it on your own head. . . . the kind of men that smile readily you have the least use for. Oh, partner, there is something or other you still have to learn." "I suspect you are paying the penalty that is so often exacted from me: trying to materialize an imagination, to realize an image," he continued, skeptical as always of her attempts to eliminate the sexual conventions surrounding male-female interactions. "Gibt's leider nicht [It can't be done]. But there's nothing quite so stirring as the grasping out after it; and I wish you luck."[34]

"You are in the face of something difficult when you try for contacts with people like Kidder and Tozzer," Kroeber warned Parsons. "Tozzer . . . does want to be medieval until he's assured that the modernism which is facing him hasn't marked his code for attack." "Don't blame them altogether," he counseled when Kidder dragged his heels in offering her the Jemez commission. "The current that carries them is directed to avoid the drastic. Most people would come to grief if they forced the battle as you can."[35]

Parsons began the Jemez study in 1921, still, apparently, without any firm commitment from Kidder that he would publish it in his series. "It's very amusing, your hate of New England and New England's terror of you," wrote Kroeber the following year. "Don't you realize that Kidder is *afraid* of you, Tozzer afraid of you, Dixon afraid of you? They put a good face on you, as well-bred drawing-room people put it on an enfant terrible; but they are wary all the time. You are a lady, so must be treated as one; but ladies don't talk of sex, and they would be ever so much more comfortable if you were a bit off-color and they could cut you. Indifference indeed! You may or may not know it, but you are getting a legitimate sadistic satisfaction out of making them wriggle. And I . . . get my fun out of watching you do it."[36]

Fighting the Boys' Club

Kidder was apparently satisfied with Parsons's monograph on Jemez. But he still did not count her among the "real" anthropologists and archeologists. In 1927, when he called a meeting of Southwest scholars to organize the Santa Fe based Laboratory of Anthropology, he wrote Boas, who had apparently remonstrated with him, "I am afraid I cannot manage to include Mrs. Parsons," and he relied on Boas to smooth matters over. For the next few years, the summer field trips sponsored by the laboratory were an important part of graduate student socialization and professional bonding, and Parsons fought to ensure that female students were not left out of what could readily become a boys' club.[37]

When she heard that women were being excluded from the first summer school in 1929, Parsons reacted angrily. "I am wondering why you have become so anti-feminist in regard to the Santa Fe Laboratory fellowships," she wrote Kroeber sharply. "But perhaps the girls have misinterpreted your manifesto, whatever it was. We understand it in Kidder who was subject to the boy boarding school influence at Cambridge, which you were free from." Sapir, now at the University of Chicago and remarried after his wife's death in 1924, came to Kidder's and Kroeber's defense. "I was surprised to hear Kidder quoted as wanting to exclude women. As a matter of fact, I understand he is taking along several on the archeological trip. . . . I wonder if you did not get a prejudiced or heated version of it all."[38]

"There are, of course, difficulties about a mixed party in the field," Sapir continued, revealing the prejudice Parsons was trying to eradicate, "but I hardly think Kroeber would have refused to take a woman if selected, nor do I think Cole, Dixon, and Kidder, who did the selecting, would have turned down a really strong woman candidate. The share that women are taking in scientific work, particularly in field work, is just a bit more of a problem, it seems to me, than some are willing to admit. The type of woman who really means business scientifically, like Gladys Reichard or Eva Horner or Ruth Bunzel, is welcomed by all, but I am afraid there are some—and they may be among the ablest intellectually— who create highly disturbing and embarrassing problems which are only beginning to be estimated at their true seriousness. It seems to me we have all been refraining, to a dangerous extent, from psychological honesty in these matters."[39]

"Sapir has forwarded me your letter," Kidder wrote Parsons. "I think you are a bit rough on me." "There are two aspects to this situation," he went on. "The first is that it is very difficult, under certain conditions, to attach women to field parties, particularly where the group must break up into small units for scattered investigations." "I have stated the position of the committee in an announcement of the award of fellowships . . . as clearly as possible," he pointed out. "The field work of the training course will be so arranged that any properly qualified woman can be taken care of at some time during her graduate career. This year it was obviously not feasible to attach women to Kroeber's party. He could only take five people at the outside, and if any women were to go there would have to be at least two. The male applicants, as it happened, for ethnology were, with one exception, all much better qualified than the women. You have been misinformed, I fear, in regard to Kroeber's attitude. He made no objection whatever, as far as I know, to women as such, but merely stated that it would be difficult for him to take them on for his proposed work on the Wallapai. I don't think I should be considered a persecutor of the sex, as three out of my five students at Pecos will be women." Kidder's second point was less elaborated, but more telling. "Much fewer professional positions (as field workers) are open to women," he wrote. "The ratio being, as nearly as I can figure it, after consultation with Tozzer and others, about one to four or five. Hence, it would seem unsound policy to select for training (in field work) women much in excess of that ratio."[40]

The bottom line was, of course, that Boas was the only male anthropologist who attempted to find positions for his female students on anywhere near the same basis as his male students. Parsons no doubt pointed this out to Kidder, because a further letter clearly addressed the larger question. "This business of women in anthropology is a perplexing one," Kidder wrote. "Looking at it from the point of view of anthropology, it is obvious that, for its own good, that discipline should draw its quota from the scientifically inclined women who pass through our universities; and it should also have the benefit of the special abilities possessed by women for typological analysis, and certain branches of sociological investigation. The trouble is not . . . that women are not well trained (for ⁹/₁₀ of the men are most inadequately prepared for their work), but that it is hard to provide professional positions for them. An anthropologist can make his living in one of two ways: either as a teacher; or as a staff member of a museum or research institution." "Anthropology is taught at so few women's colleges that there are very few professional jobs open," he went on, accepting the current wisdom that women could (or should) not teach male students; "and in the institutional field, women are handicapped by the fact that, whether justly or not, the heads of institutions feel that men are better qualified physically and temperamentally to head most ~~institutions~~ expeditions." "Another handicap," he added to this mother of four, "and a very real one from the administrator's point of view, is that a young woman, because of the likelihood of her marriage, is an unreliable element to build into the foundation of a staff structure."[41]

Kroeber was less willing to parade ambivalences before Parsons. "As to the summer," he wrote her in an addendum to other matters, "does anyone see me wanting to lead a little harem around an Arizona railroad town for two months? I do not know much about the student body in the various institutions, but I did know many of the men at Chicago and Harvard had gone in for archeology and that nearly all women who were studying were ethnologists. I don't think I have changed in views, but if ever Anthropology gets to be prevailingly a feminine science I expect to switch into something else. So, I think, will you!"[42]

"I have had my revenge! Personal, if not scientific," Gladys Reichard wrote Parsons from the Pecos Conference that concluded that

1929 summer program in the Southwest. "I have two kids with me neither of which is hard to look at, one of whom is really beautiful. One is Charlotte Leavitt, the student I told you about, the other is La Charles Goodman, daughter of Lorenzo Hubbell of Ganado. The latter is a senior at Univ. of Arizona, with a major in Archeology. She speaks Navaho." Not only were they beautiful, but they could take care of themselves: "we came in Carry [Reichard's car] with all living arrangements complete. Kidder said his idea of a 'good' person was one who travelled with a bedroll! Sapir's eight students plumped in on him without a blanket among them." Kidder had two parties, she reported, one all men and one all women. "The main contention of them all is that girls are all right, entertaining, etc. But no good in science because you can't do anything with them. Kroeber ends all remarks with 'Boas will place her.' It never seems to occur to any of them that if he can others might be able to were they sufficiently interested. All the men needed plenty of defense against my two girls. But that condition will probably be nothing in favor of their being taken on another year." "Kroeber's answer to your message," she concluded: "Tell Elsie I never was a feminist, & I'm not an anti-feminist now, appearances to the contrary notwithstanding."[43]

Cooling Women Out

The question of jobs for women continued to be a problem that Parsons could do little to alleviate. Working outside institutions, she could provide the means for women to be as well qualified and experienced as their male colleagues; but as any student of gender and work knows, qualifications are not enough to overcome institutionalized discrimination. Boas's struggle to have Ruth Benedict appointed at Columbia to a position appropriate to her standing and her failure to be appointed in his place have been widely discussed. Three less well known examples demonstrate the problem the women faced.[44]

In 1935, Kroeber's friend Hank Alsberg, director of the WPA Federal Writer's Project, was looking for a replacement for anthropologist Ralph Beals. "If you can use a girl," Kroeber wrote, "without full professional status, there is a very able one here, Jane Richardson, daughter of a Latin professor, ex-president of the English club, travel in Europe, perfect French, field experience with the Kiowa, half-way to her Ph.D. in Anthropology. About 27, suave, shrewd, excellent social manner, highly intelligent, of good stock and good breeding; slow in her output, but it's of the very best when it comes, form and substance. No formal administrative experience, but grand at knowing and handling people. Only reason I'd let you tempt her with your fleshpots is that she's a woman and therefore a regular anthrop. career is uncertain for her."

"There's a Columbia Ph.D. of uncertain age, menopause I'd guess," Kroeber added after first canvasing the dubious qualifications of a male candidate, "Ruth Underhill, who was a magazine writer before she came in, has done Papago and Mohave fieldwork, talks all the elevated last-minute jargon of higher anthropology, but can write—I recently saw a fine semi-popular ms. by her. Has a harsh voice and distracted passionate look and is not at all simpatico to me, and I judge not to most other people. She's had a couple of minor jobs with Collier and is now hanging around the Sells Papago agency waiting for a bigger one which he seems not quite ready to hand out. I think she has competence, and as one of the fellows to turn out usable copy she'd probably beat most others; but if it was my responsibility I'd probably not set her over other people." "She'd take $2500 with a leap, is my bet," he concluded this less-than-enthusiastic appraisal of a fifty-two-year-old woman who did not have, in his opinion, the "excellent social manner" and "good stock and good breeding" of his younger and less-qualified student, despite her Vassar and London School of Economics education.[45]

Parsons, by contrast, thought highly of Underhill, and assessed her qualifications for another ethnologist position at the Bureau of Indian Affairs dispassionately along with other more experienced male candidates. "Unfortunately no very outstanding person, qualified by training and experience, by administrative ability, and by general characteristics appears to be available," she wrote bureau head John Collier earlier that year. "Some of us talked about it quite a little and were agreed on [Ralph] Linton, if he would take it. Ruth Underhill too has since been mentioned. She is not as well known in the profession as Linton, but I think would be good." Parsons's assessment was accurate: Underhill went on to a fifty-year career in anthropology during which she was awarded honors from the Tohono O'Odham people as well as an honorary LL.D. by the University of Denver and a D.Sc. by the University of Colorado. In 1984, when Underhill was 101 years old, the president of the American Anthropological Association, Nancy Lurie, presented her with the association's special recognition citation for popularizing an-

Ruth Underhill, photographed by her friend Laura Gilpin in 1946. Laura Gilpin Collection, negative 3496.5, Amon Carter Museum, Fort Worth, Texas.

thropology in a responsible manner, for her work in applied anthropology and the study of women's roles, and for her scholarship and teaching.[46]

Although Edward Sapir thought highly of the work of Ruth Benedict and Margaret Mead, he found it difficult to view women in any way except through the lens of sex. His attitude to Mead, whom he wanted to marry in 1925, was protective. When she was preparing to go to Samoa that year, he tried to intervene with Boas to persuade her not to undertake what he saw as a risky adventure. Boas, to his credit, brushed Sapir's fears aside. "In my opinion Sapir has read too many books on psychiatry," he wrote Benedict; "he does not really know the subject and therefore always sees abnormal things in the most normal forms." As Ruth Underhill pointed out in 1981, looking back from her ninety-eighth year, "I was told that women were to take a second place in the world and be helpless behind men—be very useful and able, but not to push themselves forward." According to this formula, Sapir and Kidder were quite happy for wives to support their husband's scholarly work. Kidder's wife, Madeleine, for instance, assisted him with his study of pottery at Pecos, and she accompanied him in the field throughout his career. Such wifely support was seen as a bonus, especially if, as Underhill put it, the wife was "useful and able." When Sapir was trying to place his student Morris Swadesh, he recommended him to Kroeber, despite "a certain asperity of temperament." Mrs. Swadesh, he added, had just got her Ph.D. in linguistics. "At no extra cost to your department, or at very little extra cost," therefore, Kroeber "would be getting the benefit of another linguist."[47]

Mary Haas Swadesh apparently did not care to be her husband's appendage: when Sapir updated Kroeber on Swadesh's situation two years later, she was planning a divorce. But as Parsons pointed out years before, it was difficult to remove the identification of wife with husband. When Alexander Lesser was denied reappointment at Columbia in 1939, the position of his estranged wife was also endangered. "It is a bit ironic that Gene Weltfish should not be allowed to lecture at Columbia any more because she is the wife of Al Lesser with whom she no longer lives," Gladys Reichard remarked to Parsons.[48]

When able women did not come as part of a package with their husbands, they were not wanted. This was demonstrated most blatantly by Sapir in 1928 when he undercut a possible offer to Chicago graduate Charlotte Gower by the University of Michigan. Earle Guthe had tried to interest Ralph Linton in the position, Sapir wrote his former student Leslie White at the University of Buffalo, but Linton was not interested. "Then Charlotte Gower suggested herself to him and I understand Guthe . . . is inclined to make her an offer." "Because of her relation to us I am resisting my first impulse to take the initiative and write Guthe to get in touch with you," he went on. "But I think it would be quite all right for you to drop Guthe a note. . . . He may be able to make you a better offer than he is prepared to make to Charlotte." Leslie White became assistant professor of anthropology at the University of Michigan in 1930.[49]

Ruth Bunzel: A Case Study in Disciplinary and Sexual Politics

The elusive mixture of sexual innuendo, assumptions about women's place, and old boy networks, ethnicity, and individual personality that kept talented women out of permanent academic positions, despite Parsons's best efforts, is evident in the case of Ruth Bunzel. Bunzel was widely regarded as one of the best of the crop of graduate students who took anthropology in new directions during the 1920s. "I wish I knew what is to become of Bunny," Boas wrote Parsons in 1931, four years after she completed a brilliant and innovative Ph.D. "She is one of the best among the younger people but I do not know where there is an opening for her." Parsons had supported Bunzel's fieldwork since she first went to Zuni in 1924. Bunzel returned to Zuni every summer until 1929, learning the language and pioneering a more participatory kind of fieldwork. Parsons thought highly of her work and financed its publication in a series of very expensive volumes. In 1929, Bunzel was one of the few women who Sapir thought "really means business scientifically," even though he criticized her language ability when it suited him politically. She made an exploratory visit to Chiapas, Mexico, later that year in anticipation of applying for a Guggenheim award in 1930. After extensive conversations with Kidder, who had recently become director of the new Division of Historical Research of the Carnegie Institution of Washington (CIW), and Robert Redfield, who was working in Yucatán as part of the division's expanded Central American program, she was persuaded to take up her Guggenheim in Guatemala, where the CIW intended to initiate work.[50]

As Bunzel says in the foreword to *Chichicastenango,* the study that resulted from her Guatemalan work, it was planned originally as a general introduction and orientation to an interdisciplinary study of the Guatemalan Highlands involving geographers, agronomists, archeologists, linguists, historians, and cultural experts. Ignoring the bewildering social wars surrounding the Carnegie's agents in Guatemala, she settled into the ceremonial and market center of Santo Tomás Chichicastenango, where she boarded with the German priest, Father Rossbach. During two subsequent field trips of more than six months' duration, Bunzel helped Kidder and John Merriam—who was now chair of the Carnegie Institution—to formulate a large project for the area; and Kidder led her to believe that she would play an important role in its execution. But she soon became the object of scandalous gossip in Guatemala City—"that I was Padre Rossbach's mistress; that we had indulged in wild orgies at the Convent (our innocent whisky and soda!)," she told Parsons in 1934. And she was too critical of a young geographer, R. A. Atwood, the son of the president of Clark University and a colleague of Kidder's, who came to work in Chichicastenango. By early 1933, Kidder had decided Bunzel would not do as the Carnegie scholar and wrote her that there was no money to continue her work.[51]

Unknown to Bunzel, other arrangements were under way to fill the position she felt she deserved by dint of experience and expertise.

A rare photograph of the notoriously shy Ruth Bunzel, taken in 1985, when she was eighty-seven years old. Reproduced courtesy of the Wenner-Gren Foundation for Anthropological Research, Inc.

Robert Redfield had already offered the position to his student Sol Tax. A year later, as soon as his dissertation was turned in, Tax left for Guatemala and his appointment became public. Bunzel was shocked and humiliated at being passed over for a raw graduate with no experience or background in the area. Responding to Parsons's sympathetic inquiry, she reflected bitterly on "the hopelessness of getting anything done so long as human nature remains as it is," and she poured out the long unhappy story of her Guatemala experience. Aware that, like any whistle-blower, she would only harm herself even more by complaining of her treatment, she had kept it to herself. Now she found that, in order to justify Tax's appointment, slanders were circulating against her. As a skillful and sensitive fieldworker, she was particularly distressed that "the version of the incident now current in Chicago is to the effect that I had serious trouble with the natives—a tale made up by someone out of whole cloth."[52]

Summing up the whole experience, Bunzel made some shrewd observations about the nonacademic issues that kept women such as herself out of jobs. "Kidder, I think, was quite without guile in all this," she told Parsons. "He is naive to the point of fatuousness in his dealings with people. . . . So he permitted himself to be led around by the nose by a pair of social climbers and two half-baked boys who were defending their interests in a racket. To please them he pulled the keystone out of a carefully thought out plan and permitted the lazy, the incompetent and the venal to run the Guatemala project to their own advantage. He is right, of course. If it is to be run as a college on wheels (or wings?) with a lot of Best People running around looking at everyone else not working, I don't belong in it."

"What Tozzer had to do with this dirty business I can't make out," Bunzel continued, "especially since he has no official connection with the Carnegie Institution. But his interest may, perhaps, be inferred from a conversation I had with him about a year ago. . . . We were discussing the job situation in general and he remarked quite suddenly that of course I was in a very difficult position; but I was Boas' student and Boas would have to take care of me. He had his hands full with his own students, although the Carnegie Institution was a Godsend to Harvard, since he could place most of his students there. As for me, he knew I was not destitute, he knew I had a family and that they lived in a certain way, quite decently, and served good meals (sic!) and presumably they could take care of me. He felt no responsibility; if Boas thought I needed a job he would have to find it for me. This was said quite as bluntly as it is written here—you know Tozzer. I remarked that he was misinformed if he thought that my family could or would 'take care' of me; and anyway it was not for that that I had fitted myself for a career in anthropology."

"This has turned into quite a document," she concluded. "Please don't let it go out of your hands, or quote any part of it. Professor Boas does not know any of the details. He would be too outraged. When I urged you not to press this matter with Kidder or Tozzer I was thinking of my own interests. Both of them, I believe, give evidence of having bad consciences about this whole matter. . . . And you know how men feel towards those whom they have treated unfairly. [*insert:* they will not feel any better or more kindly if it is pointed out to them that I am better than Sol Tax] If only they didn't feel that they had to go to such lengths to justify their action! . . . It might improve the quality of work in Central America to have these scandals aired, but I don't want to offer my neck for martyrdom. Or do you think it's already in the noose? It looks so, doesn't it? Yours for Science Ruth L. Bunzel."[53]

The whistle was blown on Kidder's Central American operation a few years later—ironically, in a volume honoring Alfred Tozzer. But it was blown by one of their own, the young maverick Harvard professor Clyde Kluckhohn, when he classed current Mayan researchers with a scholar who "devoted his life to writing a history of the three-pronged fork." It is probably no coincidence that Kluckhohn was an old friend of Bunzel, who had befriended him when he was an undergraduate spending the summers with Navajo friends near Zuni during the 1920s. This was too late to save her career, however. Parsons continually put her name forward for research projects, and she taught on and off at Columbia for many years. (Like Ruth Underhill, she had a long, vigorous life and she did not die until 1990.) But she never obtained the tenured position warranted by the quality of her work.[54]

Diversifying Cultural Anthropology

Parsons did not support Reichard, Schiff, Benedict, and Bunzel because they were women, but because they were talented and professional. Always even-handed, she was just as generous to young male scholars. When the American Museum of Natural History withdrew funds from Leslie Spier's work with the Havasupai in 1919, she gave him financial help to complete it (and for his new wife, Erna Gunther). In later years, when he was an influential figure in the discipline and editor of the *American Anthropologist,* he put into practice the lessons he learned from the Southwest Society, devising ways to make research findings available to the scholarly community quickly and economically.[55]

As young men returned to the ranks of Boas's graduate students during the 1920s, Parsons was an important source of intellectual and financial support. In 1918, Boas had frightened off Ralph Linton, who had made the mistake of coming to see him in his military uniform. Linton's flight may also have been precipitated by Goddard's affair with his wife, who left him around that time. But a new generation of male students began to materialize in 1920 when Alexander Goldenweiser brought Melville Herskovits, "a bouncing, cheerful, unsquelchable extrovert" of Hungarian-German-Jewish background, into the Columbia program.[56]

As a lively member of the New York avant-garde, Herskovits fitted well into the Boas crowd. Interested from the beginning in race relations, he lectured at Howard University during 1925 and 1926, where he worked with Alain Locke and E. Franklin Frazier, and he was probably responsible for bringing Zora Neale Hurston to Barnard in 1926. In 1927, Herskovits found a permanent position in Northwestern University's sociology department. He found it difficult, however, to get funds for work on the African diaspora in the Americas. From 1928, Parsons encouraged Herskovits and his wife, Frances, to follow up her own work on African New World acculturation, financing extensive fieldwork in Surinam, Haiti, and West Africa over the next decade.[57]

Parsons also encouraged and financially supported Leslie White's work from his first venture into the field in Acoma as a graduate student in 1926. More than anyone else, White followed faithfully in Parsons's footsteps, completing the work she had begun in the Southwest with his studies of Acoma, San Felipe, Santo Domingo, and Zia. When he later pioneered a return to grand theory and became one of the most virulent critics of Boas and his "cult," he was careful to exclude Parsons from his condemnation. "Parsons published at least 3 descriptions of whole cultures," he wrote in her defense. "Boas never wrote a synoptic account of the Kwakiutl who were the object of almost 40 years of study. Also, Parsons did not shun generalizations and was not as hostile toward theory as a good disciple was supposed to be. . . . Elsie Parsons deviated greatly from the Boasian ideal."[58]

Over the twenty-three years of its existence, Parsons's Southwest Society financed the work of dozens of young scholars, giving them funds to do fieldwork when none was available elsewhere, supplementing slim resources in order to keep a promising person from slipping out of the discipline. As Robert Herrick put it in one of his more admiring descriptions of the character he based on Parsons:

> Jessica [Parsons] had first thoroughly opened his mind to the grandeur of the scholar's world, its selflessness and power of sacrifice and pure idealism. Ordinarily the scientist's, the scholar's devotion was tinctured by some trace of egotism, of conceit or ambition, but in Jessica where her work was involved he could discover no evidence of egotism. She would freely turn over to younger and less advantageously situated assistants results that had cost her much effort and time as well as money, provided that she deemed they could make a better use of the data than she could. As for the helping hand and purse she was noted throughout her narrow professional circle for her generosities. Many a worker's results would have gone unprinted except for Jessica's bounty, many a young and promising student would have been forced to give over valuable research for some teaching habit had it not been for Jessica's support. Nor did she make protegees of those she helped. On the contrary her hand was as free and open with persons she had cause to dislike as with friends. In fact as Redfield [Herrick] observed all the heroisms and virtues ordinarily spread thinly over the multiplex

exigencies of the personal life Jessica Mallory had concentrated on her professional occupations. As a man she would have been considered wholly admirable, it being taken for granted that to his scientific ends he had sacrificed the personal life.[59]

When Gladys Reichard made the same testimony to Parsons's generosity in 1943, she also emphasized Parsons's importance as a teacher—"the great monument of Elsie Parsons's career which does not and cannot stand forth obviously as do the titles of a bibliography." Although Parsons was a teacher in the formal sense for only a few brief years, Reichard pointed out, she had great influence on a large group of younger ethnologists by sponsoring an "incalculable" amount of research work that she followed through to publications "in which even a sentence of appreciation sometimes became embarrassing to her." Parsons's teaching, according to Reichard, "consisted in long talks with young people about their work; such conferences included well-taken criticism and advice. It was followed by intensive correspondence, a means of furnishing constant stimulation and new direction. Never did Dr. Parsons have the idea that money alone would do a job, although she was often sympathetic with the 'undeserving poor' and did not cut off funds because of youthful mistakes."

Reichard's final tribute to Parsons's "unique" method of furthering research pinpointed what was probably her most important contribution to American anthropology. "Never did she exert pressure on a worker or his theories," Reichard observed, "as might have been expected because of the subsidy." Just as the ideal of the settlement house as she and Mary Simkhovitch conceived it was to empower the individuals who made up the community in which it was situated, Parsons wanted to give young scholars the opportunity to develop their own interests and skills. Invention was always more important to Parsons than conformity, and much of anthropology's diversity during the 1920s and 1930s was due to her subtle encouragement of the rebellion of younger scholars against the tyranny of their elders—even such velvet-gloved patriarchs as Boas. Esther Schiff Goldfrank's comment in a 1985 interview encapsulates the spirit that Parsons encouraged in her protégés: "I just did what I wanted: I wrote when I wanted, I went for my research where I wanted, and I took exception where I wanted." Such a spirit did not always help those young scholars to get jobs, especially if they were women; but their experimental work gradually infiltrated

American anthropology, preventing the discipline from settling into either an old or a new orthodoxy.[60]

The Perils of Patronage: Parsons and Benedict

Almost all of the anthropologists who got their start with Parsons's help unfailingly praised her disinterested generosity and collegial attitude. The one major exception—Ruth Benedict—demonstrates some of the difficulties inherent in the patronage relationship. Benedict was introduced to anthropology by Parsons; but she was never attracted by Parsons's cool detachment and found the brilliant, more speculative style of Alexander Goldenweiser and Edward Sapir more congenial.[61]

If the normal channels for someone of Benedict's acknowledged ability had been open to her, her life and that of Parsons would have gone their separate ways. When Benedict submitted her Ph.D. in 1923, however, she had little prospect of employment. She had hoped to keep the position she had filled at Barnard during Gladys Reichard's California fellowship; but Reichard had first claim on it. Casting around for a place for Benedict, Boas pounced on Parsons's request for help in finding an assistant. Parsons's father had just died, and Boas knew she was now a wealthy woman in her own right. "I wonder whether it would not appeal to you to arrange the matter in a somewhat different way," he wrote after they had discussed her needs at the Thursday lunch, "namely to engage someone who would work out such notes as the genealogies to which you referred yesterday and to whom you would at the same time give the task of working out independently one of the big problems of the Southwest." "If a plan like this would appeal to you," he concluded, "I should suggest Mrs. Benedict as a possible candidate." This was not at all what Parsons had in mind. "It doesn't quite meet my personal need," she answered, "for there is work merely for a copyist which I wouldn't give her." But she acquiesced in Boas's request.[62]

This was a particularly sensitive time for Benedict. She had quickly distinguished herself in an intellectual field that she found particularly congenial; her new colleagues provided her with a sense of belonging that had long disappeared from her marriage; and she was at last succeeding in her quest for a rich and attractive "personality." But her hold on these hard-won achievements seemed tenuous. She found it humiliating to have to accept a fellowship from Parsons, whose work, wealth, and sexual morals she both disapproved of and envied. When Boas proposed what he called "a fellowship in SW folklore" funded by Parsons, Benedict developed what she described as the "worst sick headache I've had in years." "I know my subconscious staged it," she wrote in her diary. "Said nothing to Mrs. Parsons at lunch—nor she to me," she noted in her diary after the next Thursday lunch. "Dr. Boas said I was to approach her." "~~Couldn't Wrote Mrs. Parsons I'd take the job.~~ Wrote Mrs. Parsons I was interested," she recorded, clearly agonized, the next day. Her pride was not assuaged by a lunch with Pliny Goddard. "He took up Dr. Boas' worry about me for me. He said he supposed there'd always be these driblets of research but that was all he could see ahead for me.—I feel some capacity for making a place for myself, thank you! but on the elevated I was weary, and plain wept with vexation." "Found a letter from Mrs. Parsons with details—$1000 and a study of SW mythology," she wrote several days later. The next day she reluctantly gave in. "Wrote Mrs. Parsons I'd take the job," she noted curtly in her diary. The prospect of an independent income for the coming year had one positive side effect. "First Award No Red Tape Fellowship," she wrote, enclosing a check for $300, to Margaret Mead, whose father was balking at her return to do graduate work. The next day Benedict submitted her dissertation and attended the Thursday lunch, but all was ashes. "And oh, I am lonely," she wrote in her diary.[63]

Both Benedict and Parsons tried to make the best of their forced collaboration. Benedict worked diligently on the proposed concordance of Southwest folklore during 1923. She traveled to Zuni with Ruth Bunzel to record mythology and folklore in the summers of 1924 and 1925 and went on to Cochiti in 1925. Her quiet style suited her to work in the pueblos, as did Bunzel's, and she got good material. "Nick [Tomaka] and Flora [Zuni] both eat out of my hand this summer," she wrote Mead in 1925 of Zuni's two leading intellectuals. "Nick is invaluable—if I could only take his 'sing-songs' in text!" At Peña Blanca and Cochiti, where Parsons, Boas, and Goldfrank had difficulty in finding informants, she did not find "the spiked fence" they talked about, she wrote Mead. "I don't understand the openness with which they give me the stories." "He hopes I'll be another Mabel Dodge," she wrote of one of her informants; "he's all ready to take Tony's [Luhan's] part and I will say he's a better catch than Tony."[64]

It is not clear how long Parsons's fellowship to Benedict continued. Benedict was still working on the concordance in the spring of 1926; and it no doubt galled her to see Parsons sail off to "Abyssinia" with a lover in search of folktales while she toiled with card indexes and slips of paper in the Columbia library. In 1924 Boas appointed her assistant editor of the *Journal of American Folklore,* and in 1925 he handed the editorship over to her. If there was any salary attached to this position, it probably came from Parsons; so Parsons may have moved her support of Benedict to the more comfortable—and distanced—one of journal patron. As Sapir commented to Benedict in one of his many sour moments regarding Boas and Parsons, "I'm delighted to hear you're to have a secretary next season. Only an idealistic slave-driver like Boas would ever have expected you to do five or six jobs all at once. . . . And now, I presume Elsie is ready for a monument to her munificence, for no doubt she is to cough up the necessary funds for this new secretarial extravagance." The following January, Benedict noted in her diary: "Session with Elsie—she's providing an anthropological haven in the Sub!"[65]

Between 1923 and 1926, Benedict tried to get a fellowship from one of the new institutionalized sources of funding; but despite Parsons's forceful intervention, she was unsuccessful. Redoubling his efforts to create a position for her at Columbia, Boas managed to keep her on in a temporary capacity until she took over from him during his 1929–30 leave; and until his retirement in 1936 she was, as Margaret Mead put it, his indispensable "right hand." A new dean in 1931 recognized Benedict's importance to the department and finally appointed her assistant professor—"a grand scoop for feminism!" in Reichard's eyes, but "a modest and criminally belated acknowledgement of [her] services" to Edward Sapir, who had done nothing to help her find a position.[66]

From the beginning, Benedict's synthesizing intelligence took her far beyond the journeyman job of the concordance for which Parsons reluctantly hired her. As she became more integrated into the Columbia department and the profession through her teaching, her editorship, and her friendship with the rising star, Margaret Mead, Benedict's self-esteem rose and her intellectual gifts flowered. In the 1927 summer, her fieldwork with the Pima of Arizona brought her into contact with a culture very different from their Pueblo neighbors, and she began to formulate the Dionysian-Apollonian contrast of psychological traits that became the basis for her famous *Patterns of Culture*. From its first public articulation at the New York Congress of Americanists in September 1928 until its publication in 1934, Benedict was almost totally absorbed in working out this idea.[67]

Meanwhile, the unfinished concordance hung over her head, making her relations with Parsons more uneasy than ever. When *Zuñi Mythology* appeared in 1935, Parsons was pleased to find the long-awaited concordance—at least of the Zuni tales. But, as could have been expected, she disagreed with Benedict's highly generalized psychoanalytic interpretation. "*Psychological interpretation without accompanying analysis of distribution is ever precarious*," she wrote reprovingly in her review in the *Journal of American Folklore*, where she contrasted it with Bunzel's beautifully detailed autobiography of Lina Zuni. "I wish you might have had more satisfaction from it," Benedict wrote Parsons in response, "for you first made possible my work in Zuni."[68]

CHAPTER THIRTEEN

Jessica at Fifty

IN March 1925, when Elsie Clews Parsons was fifty years old, the novelist Robert Herrick described, in fictional form, the woman he had fallen in love with two years before. She was "a tall slight woman with waving blond hair . . . meditatively smoking a long cigarette of a peculiar shape which she held to her lips with tiny fingers of one hand . . . like a delicate, contemplative bird of prey, waiting with keen eyes, determining where next she would make her plunge, her swoop into the human pool to grasp with her slender hands the desired morsel that her mind coveted."

> She was fairly famous, intellectual, distinguished, in men's fashion, and yet as if to prove that she could do the women's thing too, with one hand, she had taken a husband, produced children, lived as others. Yet was never like others . . . [she] was comely, alluring in a delicate white and gold manner (with the sunlight evoking the nimbus of her flowing hair, bringing out the tawny warmth of her skin, lighting the jade depths of her roving eyes). And she was young, still something youthful to her, in spite of her long record as writer and mother known to all, something wilfully and mockingly youthful, superior to [other women] worn by their hearts.[1]

Over the course of their five-year relationship, from 1923 to 1928, Herrick was both fascinated and repelled by this woman who refused, unlike most other women he knew, to be "worn by her heart." He described her again and again, trying to capture the essence of this new kind of woman whose passion was for her work and for her children, and only secondarily for the men in her life. In 1926, as their relationship started to deteriorate, he began to formulate ideas for a novel he called "Jessica at Fifty," which became, finally, *The End of Desire,* published in 1932, four years after their affair ended.

Herrick introduced Jessica into his work from the beginning of his relationship with Parsons, making her one of the symbols

Elsie at San Gabriel Ranch, New Mexico, 1924, with her signature cigarette holder and lighter around her neck. Elsie Clews Parsons Papers, American Philosophical Society Library.

of modernism in *Chimes,* the account of the raw new University of Chicago that he sketched out during their first trip together to New Mexico in 1923. Reviewers of *Chimes* agreed that Jessica had "never been done before." "It is doubtful if fiction anywhere represents so convincingly the highly educated woman," one reviewer wrote. "If you have ever asked yourself the question: 'Does the higher education destroy femininity?'—Jessica Mallory is the answer. If you have never seen a woman like her you perhaps doubt whether a woman can be so, but Mr. Herrick makes you believe that Jessica Mallory is so." The young Jacques Barzun found Jessica "the most captivating" of the engrossing characters in *Chimes,* with an intellectualism which is really, he noted perceptively, "a convergence of the strongest emotions."[2]

New Directions

Herrick met Parsons in 1923 when she was ready to move in new directions in her life and work. She was forty-nine years old and had become a grandmother the previous year when Lissa—married too young and unwisely in her mother's opinion—had her first son. Over the past ten years, Parsons had established herself as an authority on the Southwest; she had challenged the taboo that prevented unmarried men and women from doing fieldwork together; and she had broken the dam on publication, the application of anthropology to contemporary problems, and experimentation with new methodologies. Her sweep through the pueblos of New Mexico and Arizona had carried out its therapeutic purpose both for herself and for the discipline. Now she hoped that work could be carried on by the younger scholars she helped and cultivated.[3]

Early in 1923, Parsons's father had died and left her a wealthy woman in her own right. With independent economic and professional status, Parsons now had the keys to the "republic of the spirit" she had sought since childhood. As Clarence Day wrote when he discovered she had sent money to Francis Hackett and Signe Toksvig, then writing in poverty in Ireland, "Elsie dear it's awfully satisfactory to know that you're rich. It's not often that just the right person is." In 1923, John was twenty years old and at Yale. In October of that year, Herbert and Mac, then fourteen and twelve, followed John to St. Paul's School, leaving Parsons free to spend longer periods in the field.[4]

What Parsons lacked in her new freedom was a companion for her travels. After Herbert returned from the war in 1919, their relationship took on a more tolerant and loving tone, with both apparently willing to go their own way and enjoy the brief periods they spent together. They had come to an agreement, probably at the time she began to work seriously in anthropology, that she should have primary responsibility for the children until the age of twelve. After that, their everyday care and major decisions such as schooling were Herbert's responsibility. From 1919, they seem to have put this agreement into effect. Respecting and protecting Elsie's professional status and personal predilections, Herbert took a greater share in caring for the children, introducing Lissa into social circles more agreeable to her than Elsie's, and taking Lissa and John to Europe the summer before John entered Yale and Lissa married. Their mutual concern over Lissa's marriage seemed to draw them closer in 1921, when, secure in their more flexible roles, Elsie was devising ways in which she and Herbert could combine "her Indians" with "his cowboys." Sometime during 1922 she ended her relationship with Grant LaFarge, and in 1922 and 1923, with Boas happily working with Esther Schiff, Gladys Reichard, and Ruth Benedict, she included more sedate trips with Herbert and the younger boys in her fieldwork plans.[5]

But life was flat without the stimulus of a love affair and a companion for the more interesting and arduous travel her work required. "You'll never fall in love with trying to," Parsons wrote the reluctant bachelor Robert Lowie in 1922, when he confessed his keen desire to be married. "Nor are dancing and book writing favoring circumstances since both are substitutes." "I'm not dancing, but unfortunately, I am book writing," she added, referring to the beginnings of her work on the encyclopedic *Pueblo Indian Religion* (1939). "You have more respect for, or faith in, marriage than I," she wrote Mabel Dodge on her marriage to Tony Luhan in 1923. "I admit it sometimes facilitates a situation, and that circumstances out of marriage may be just as awkward as in marriage. Still all but the very young have to have a pretty good excuse for getting married, it seems to me, unless they are just made that way."[6]

Signe Toksvig, sensing her restlessness, wrote from Europe, urging her to return to her commentary on contemporary society. "Clarence sent us a piece of yours which it seems odd that we hadn't read before, your 'Patterns for Peace or War,'" she wrote. "It is so full of penetration, of healthily bitter candor, but so divinely calm, so expressed in little, well directed nut-shells, each of which could make a book." Suggesting that Parsons consider living and working in Europe, Toksvig argued that she would be more appreciated there. In Europe she would be forced to write: "people would demand it. . . . It should be your exclusive business to think about human absurdities and to publish your thoughts. . . . I keep meeting people over here every one of whom would really delight you and whom you would delight. . . . Rebecca West, perhaps a bit intense but *alive*. . . . Dame Rachel Cravdy . . . the chief of the—Opium and White Slave Section! (We do meet queer people.) . . . She has the best English manners, which are, I think, a very superior brand, and . . . she's as keen and liberal and quaintly free as only a released Englishwoman can be." "She reminds one a little of you," Toksvig concluded, "because you *are* released English, you know. But much more so." But Parsons had found the sort of work that suited her. "You are wise to have made your work a creation among knowledgeable things," Toksvig replied to an uncharacteristically personal letter. "To make the things one cares about tell in the long run, is all that any art or science can do for you. . . . I am glad you said what you did. You commit yourself rarely, in regard to yourself."[7]

In 1923, Parsons began to turn her attention more fully to New World African culture. She had continued to collect African-

American folklore along the Atlantic Coast during the years she was absorbed in the Southwestern pueblos. In February 1919, she spent two weeks in the Sea Islands off South Carolina; and that fall she began to visit Hampton Institute, where faculty and students had been collecting folklore for several decades. The following spring, when she tried to convince James Robinson and the Free School of the contemporary relevance of folklore, Parsons told a Hampton assembly that she considered folklore an important means of understanding the contributions made by Africans to American culture. "There are quite a number of different kinds of people in this country. Some of them—White and Black—hope that the particular Negro gifts of gracious manners, of expressiveness in color and in music and in the spoken word—including the art of storytelling—will be, not withdrawn from American culture, or crushed out of it, but contributed to its enrichment."[8]

Parsons had long been a vocal critic of the ignorance and thoughtless racism of Americans in their relations with countries within their sphere of influence. She concluded her Hampton lecture by pointing out that work on folklore was urgently required in the Caribbean and Latin America. Later that year, she protested American attitudes in Haiti; and as the military occupation of Haiti and Santo Domingo became a major political issue, the idea of shifting her focus onto acculturation between Indians, whites, and Africans in the tangled threads of Caribbean cultures became increasingly attractive. The need for greater understanding and tolerance of New World African culture was brought home to her when she invited an African-American friend—probably NAACP secretary James Weldon Johnson—to tea. "Father must have been quite agitated by the white-muffler-wearing black man whom you brought home with you, as he wrote me all about him," wrote nineteen-year-old John in his usual sardonic manner. "I can imagine Lissa's comments, but will be hard put to it to guess Manga's [Lucy Clews's]. Perhaps if she hasn't found out yet, it would be best not to inform her. She would possibly say, ~~John~~ 'Henry, how unpractical your mother is.' How did you induce the ebony one (or was he a mulatto) (or possibly an octroon) to come on? I should think he would be afraid of a crank like you. Maybe—"[9]

Early in 1923, in preparation for this change in geographical and cultural focus—and possibly to inculcate some cultural relativism before he went off to his elite boarding school—she took twelve-year-old Mac with her on a two-week field trip to the Bermudas.

That summer Mac and Herbert Jr. accompanied her to Nova Scotia for a folklore expedition with African-American writer and graduate student Arthur Fauset, where she enjoyed the "combination of medieval French & Algonkian" during a visit to the Micmacs of Cape Breton.[10]

Sometime that year, probably as a result of her interest in the Haiti question, Parsons met Robert Herrick. A well-known novelist who wrote for the *New Republic* and the *Nation,* he was treasurer of the organization that pressed in 1920 for a Senate investigation of America's role in Haiti and Santo Domingo. Parsons was a close friend of Senator Medill McCormick, the Chicago newspaper magnate who chaired the subsequent inquiry; and Norman Hapgood, then editor of *Hearst's International,* was an old Harvard friend of Herrick's.[11]

Herrick was an acerbic observer of modern America, the idol of a generation of young writers for a series of novels that dealt candidly with American sexual and economic foibles. He was, according to Henry Seidel Canby, "a realist when realism was still unfashionable and a satirist when Americans did not like satire." Unfortunately for his friends, Herrick drew much of his material directly from life, and his first novel cost him the friendship of art historian Bernard Berenson, whom he portrayed cruelly after visiting him in Italy in 1895. Herrick was divorced in 1916 in a well-publicized case in which one newspaper ran the headline, "Wife of Former Technology Instructor Sick in Chicago and Her Illness Attributed by Friends to Breakfast Table Episodes—Peculiar Sex Views Figure in Case." The journalist failed to note that Herrick had already dissected the marriage and his wife's character defects in several novels.[12]

With their mutual interest in race relations, Herrick seemed the perfect companion for Parsons's Caribbean work. He had no family obligations apart from his adult son and, once he resigned from the University of Chicago at the end of 1923, no institutional obligations either. As a writer, he was mobile and busy, two important requirements for anyone who accompanied Parsons in the field. From late 1923 through 1927, Herrick accompanied her each spring in a comprehensive sweep through the Caribbean islands in search of folktales, "anthums," spirituals, and Christian-African ceremonials; and in the fall he traveled with her, somewhat more reluctantly, as she completed her survey of the Tewa pueblos along the Rio

Grande and of Taos and Isleta—the related pueblos to their north and south.

Observing Jessica

We know little of Parsons's perspective on this relationship. No correspondence between them is preserved in their papers, when almost everything else is; and Parsons never mentions Herrick in her letters to others. The only hint of a passionate relationship comes from a series of Elsie's poems that probably to refer to Herrick. But she seems to have initiated the relationship—at least if we can believe Herrick's fictionalized account. In his novel *Chimes,* sketched immediately after their first field trip to Alcalde, New Mexico, in the fall of 1923, Clavercin (Herrick) receives a curt note from Jessica (Parsons) inviting him to accompany her to a dude ranch in Colorado. " 'If you want to escape this dead town,' she wrote in her firm, small hand, 'why not come out to the mountains with me next week? Bring some work along as I shall be busy with proof. . . . I am taking the afternoon train on Thursday. Bring riding clothes.' " The time Clavercin and Jessica spend together in the mountains is not a conventional amorous adventure. She is busy with her work, and he is forced to concentrate on his own writing. At dusk, the long hours of work behind them, they ride together, Jessica giving to her recreation the same singleness of mind she does to her work. As the weeks pass, a sense of intimacy grows between them. Clavercin finds to his surprise that Jessica is an excellent companion, and that in their seemingly desultory conversations they cover much of the ground of human relations. He finds that her clear intelligence is extraordinarily stimulating, and that her reticence whets his imagination. "Something had crystallised within him," he discovers at the end of their unusual tryst, "a purpose, out of this fresh engagement with life."[13]

Parsons did enjoy the month she spent at San Gabriel Ranch outside Alcalde in November 1923. The ranch was on the site of the original Spanish capital, San Gabriel—a fitting place to study acculturation. The Tewa pueblo of San Juan was nearby. "An adobe house built around a patio, flowers, chili pendants to the columns of the porches," she described it to Herbert. "Above, the seven mountains & blue sky, mostly. Delicious food, a warm room, quiet at night, a few too many other guests. Not a horse yet, but I plan

Elsie at San Gabriel Ranch, New Mexico, 1924. Elsie Clews Parsons Papers, American Philosophical Society Library.

to soon. . . . A dude ranch indeed, and I stick to it. My informants are brought out from the pueblo." "I had some delightful rides, I worked with a San Juan story teller who was a great artist, and I got the material we needed to piece out the gaps in Pueblo ceremonial organization, better material, I incline to think, than Fewkes-Harrington keep hidden," she wrote Herbert at the end of the visit.[14]

Herrick was an astute and interested observer of relations between the sexes. *Together* (1908) and *One Woman's Life* (1913) dissected modern marriage in a manner almost worthy of Parsons, whose feminist writing he had always admired. The heroine of *Homely Lilla*, published in 1923, was a strongly sexed and capable woman thwarted in a tepid marriage; and *Waste*, which he completed at Alcalde, examined several types of modern women. As his portraits in *Chimes* and the novella "Magic" indicate, he was immediately fascinated with Parsons as a pure type of the modern woman.[15]

As Herrick explained to Parsons in his unpublished "Foreword to Jessica," probably written in 1926, his intention was "not to celebrate your charm or your intelligence, your human interest so to speak, except in one narrow way, that is so far as I can make you representative of many of your sisters of our day, of certain powerful tendencies that I have observed . . . in our modern life." What made Parsons modern for Herrick, and the aspect of her life and personality that he projected through Jessica, was "nothing less than the subjection of life, including men, to your own peculiar purposes. A subjection—and mark you this is the distinction which makes your Jessica Mallory significant, interesting, not through instinct or emotion, the wornout formula of the romantics, but through the mind." You, my dear Seknet, he wrote, giving her affectionately the name of the lion-headed wife of the god Ptah he had discovered at Luxor, "are miles in advance of the many eager Jessicas stumbling along this road to the great goal of freedom." "Just as you have thought yourself out triumphantly to all the freedoms that you now enjoy, and primarily the freedom of the spirit . . . so you are rapidly thinking yourself into power over others, over destiny. . . . In this process you will become necessarily more ruthless, perhaps even brutal and hard (from the old fashioned standpoint of men) as no doubt Jessica Mallory will often be accused of being. You will be less tender and melting in your amorous dealings with the other sex, less patient with their betises and always less 'sentimental'—making the sentiments ring true on your marble counters before you accept them as valid. In other words you will become the realistic sex . . . that bargains and demands good concrete values out of life, not dreams nor ideals nor the soft imaginings of poets and men!"

In making Jessica representative of a powerful modern tendency in relations between men and women, Herrick was confident that Parsons was "intelligent and active minded enough" to appreciate his intention. While "your less developed sisters will busy themselves with making a chronique scandaleuse out of my tale," he wrote, "you my dear wise woman are too subtle and self-assured to make the assumption that you are the one represented in this volume. . . . You, I am sure, will repudiate not passionately but superiorly the belief that any one, even your Creator, (were you conscious of having one) could wholly reveal yourself. . . . You are serenely convinced—impregnably—that it can't be done, that you have concealed yourself with too much skill, even from yourself, and have eluded the world." "I agree with you," he added. "At any rate I am not the one who could wholly penetrate the ramifications of that intricate and hidden personality."[16]

As Herrick predicted, Parsons seems to have been unconcerned that "the world" would construe his chronicles of Jessica's life as accounts of her own. She met Herrick at a time when her daughter's youthful marriage, reluctant motherhood, and contemplated divorce was forcing her to look closely again at sex relations—this time among the heirs to her generation of pioneers of sexual freedom. Herrick's son was going through a series of sexual disasters that paralleled those of Lissa; and one of the things that held the relationship between Parsons and Herrick together was their mutual fascination with the dynamics of sex relations, both their own and those of their children. Parsons was always willing to sacrifice her valued privacy to bring a needed point of view forcefully to public attention. In 1906, she used her privileged position to force public discussion of trial marriage, the control of conception, and divorce. In 1926, she was less inclined to take to the public platform, although she did so when invited. But she was still a committed public intellectual and welcomed Herrick's perceptive discussions of sexual relationships, even when they were not flattering to her. *Chimes and Wanderings,* the book of novellas Herrick published in 1925 based on his observations of Parsons in New Mexico and the Caribbean, were written and published long before the relationship ended in 1928. And "Jessica at Fifty" grew out of a joint project they embarked on in 1925, to be called "Tides," in which they intended to draw on the messiness of their children's sexual lives and the ebb and flow of their own relationship to discuss the dilemmas of modern relationships.[17]

Herrick's public and private musings on Jessica's character followed the contours of his relationship with Parsons. When their relationship began in the fall of 1923, he had just ended the second of two long affairs with wealthy married women; and when they set out for the Caribbean in February 1924, he and Elsie were virtually strangers to each other. In his "Diary" a year later, Herrick remembered the "highly imaginative and romantic expectations" he had of that trip. In "Stations of the Cross," a novella based on their experiences that spring, he evokes the fears and hopes with which he set out, the lingering memory of the warm-hearted and sacrificial lover he had recently broken with, and his despair over his new companion's separateness and apparent aloofness. It is only when she reveals her compassion and capacity to love when he suffers a tropical fever that he appreciates her as an individual, and not as the embodiment of a romantic ideal.[18]

The trip seems to have been successful on both a personal and professional level for Parsons and Herrick. They went by cruise ship to the southernmost point of the Lesser Antilles, the island of Trinidad, just off the coast of Venezuela, after a brief visit to Barbados. Then they proceeded north, in Parsons's preferred fashion, by steamer or mail boat schooner, from island to island, as fancy and the folklore trail took them. Herrick's fever in St. Lucia forced her to give up her plan to visit all the French islands. They settled instead in Morne Rouge, on the southern slopes of Mount Pelée in Martinique. "Out in the country, in the house of an old lady, White, very French, with a *bonne* to cook, wash etc, very comfortable," Parsons wrote Herbert. "Beautiful country, wooded peaks, & cup like valleys, with Pelée, green but still bare, to the North. . . . The folk lore is rich, and I am hard at work, with a one leg man who lost his leg from snake bite, in the morning teaching me idioms, & discussing customs and beliefs & in the afternoon or evening working the phonograph or recording stories from visitors of all kinds. When the old people fail, there is always a child at the door to speak *tim tim,* i.e. riddles."[19]

Parsons's one-legged tutor in Martinique was Félix Modock, an "extremely intelligent" small farmer who could write both French and Creole. "We learned much each from the other," Parsons wrote later, "so that after I left the island for several years he continued to record folklore." Parsons derived great pleasure from the moonlit nights spent in the yard of her house, surrounded by bamboo fence, jasmine and rose bushes, listening to the stories "told and sung naturally." During the day, she and Modock recorded tales and called on neighbors to collect riddles and listen for good storytellers. In contrast to the reticent and secretive pueblos, in island villages Parsons's visits inevitably attracted an "eager and clamorous" mob. At home, Louise, the *bonne,* "sang over her pots and authenticated traditions . . . when she was not too busy cooking or cleaning or gossiping or bickering with the *marchande* who brought us fish from the coast or milk or vegetables, those long striding, long necked girls who give their greatest charm to the island highways."[20]

When they returned to New York in April, Herrick wrote to his friend Robert Morss Lovett, "I had a good and profitable time away . . . wrote first draft of two novelettes, and planned a third which ultimately I shall put out as a book "Wanderings," also made progress towards my university novel, "The Pleasant Walks of Academe" [*Chimes*]. . . . Unfortunately I got a bilious fever a month ago, which has left me weak. . . . Have also some notes on the negro situation in the Antilles, which I shall use either for Nation or Century. An interesting ten weeks."[21]

Herrick returned from the weeks he spent with Parsons very much in love and anticipating further "spiritual fulfillments" and "intimacies." But he found, as Herbert had many years earlier, that he was only one of her many interests, to be fitted in as her busy schedule allowed. She was especially preoccupied that summer with the paper she was preparing for the International Congress of Americanists in the Hague, which laid out her general Southwestern framework and provided the backbone for its massive documentation in *Pueblo Indian Religion* (1939). During the summer, Parsons visited Herrick's home in York Village, Maine. Although she delighted in its comforts, its "enchanted garden," and the picnics and canoeing trips they enjoyed after she had done her morning's work, it was never more than that—"Another of Serena's Homes," as Herrick titled a chapter in *The End of Desire* (1932) in which "Jessica" became "Serena." To Herrick's dismay, Parsons placed professional commitments—"ambition"—before domestic felicity and had no qualms about leaving for Europe in August to present her paper. As Herrick put it with consternation when he mulled over that summer in February 1925, it was "her very great absorption in her professional work—and her vanity about it and all its perquisites, which probably moved her to Europe last summer more than anything else."[22]

When Parsons returned from Europe and Mac and Herbert Jr. were back in school, she and Herrick spent two weeks together at York that seem to have been the happiest of their relationship. She was relaxed and confident now that the threads of her Southwest work had been pulled together, and she looked forward to one or two more seasons filling in the details of the pattern she now saw clearly. Herrick was sure, however, that he had "wrought changes in her hidden character" by the physical comforts and sexual happiness he provided during those golden early fall days, and he set off on their second trip to Alcalde in November 1924 with "deeply tender and intimate" expectations.[23]

The trip proved a bitter disappointment, at least to Herrick. It is not clear what went wrong. Parsons told Leslie White a few years later that the second field trip to any area is disappointing and frustrating, and she seemed to hit more dead ends in her work that

Robert Herrick at San Gabriel Ranch, New Mexico, 1924. Elsie Clews Parsons Papers, American Philosophical Society Library.

year than she had previously. She had taken up the Rio Grande work reluctantly, only after it became clear that no one else was available to do it and that Fewkes and Harrington were not going to give her access to Matilda Stevenson's unpublished work. As she pointed out in her preface to *The Social Organization of the Tewa of New Mexico,* the Tewa were "past masters in the art of defeating inquiry"; and much as she enjoyed the comforts of San Gabriel Ranch, she found the secretive detective work entailed in her research there distasteful—and probably boring. After 1926, she gladly left this work to Leslie White. In 1924, she had persuaded Esther Schiff—now Esther Goldfrank—to leave her five-month-old daughter with "a good nurse" and return to fieldwork in Isleta pueblo. Despite her breakthrough in this pueblo renowned for its secrecy, Goldfrank decided not to continue the work, which Parsons felt obliged to finish. Herrick, however, seemed unable to appreciate Parsons's professional dilemmas and interpreted this "fatal visit to Alcalde" and subsequent visits in terms of his own increasing ill health and impotence and Parsons's indifference and disillusion with his company.[24]

Jealousy

From the end of 1924, their relationship became essentially a battle over her work. Herrick realized from the beginning that this was what was new about the woman that Parsons embodied. "All the romanticism in Jessica North's nature is gradually absorbed by her science," he noted in an early sketch for *Chimes* in January 1924. "This the new note of the story, the transference of the romantic passion not merely from love between the sexes or maternal love but also from religion and philanthropy to Science, which is the new passion." But he seemed unable to relate "the inexplicable facts of her intermittent interest and indifference, the rare times of tenderness and intimacy, the long periods of deadness even dislike, complete indifference," to this central passion.[25]

Herrick's own career was in eclipse by 1924. His novel *Waste*, published that year, was a critical success, but it had not sold. Parsons, on the other hand, was at the height of her powers, bringing to a successful conclusion her work on the Southwest, beginning to gather young scholars around her, and possibly most wounding, in demand as an authoritative commentator in Herrick's own field, relations between the sexes.

Between 1922 and 1924, Parsons had moved back into a kind of "distinguished guest spot" as a public authority on sexual mores. In 1922, she wrote on sex as one of the older of the thirty young modernists who contributed essays to *Civilization in the United States* at the invitation of editor Harold Stearns. In May 1924, she was one of the "intelligent observers" of "authority or at least of some restraint"—"not reformers like Stopes and Sanger who can't write"—selected by *Nation* editor Freda Kirchwey to discuss "the difficult problems of modern sex relations." Early in 1925, as she and Herrick were deciding whether to travel to the Caribbean again, Parsons was a featured speaker at another *Nation* dinner where she, Floyd Dell, and the newly divorced Alexander Goldenweiser spoke on the subject "Is Monogamy Feasible?"[26]

Herrick viewed the proceedings in retrospect with considerable distaste. "These monthly Radical [*Nation*] dinners had become a feature of the season for New York intellectuals," he wrote in *The End of Desire* in 1932. They attracted "not merely the riff-raff of studio apartments and the vagrant free lances of journalism, but college professors, doctors and lawyers, the more serious minded with a touch of daring in their speculations. . . . Hurd, the editor [Oswald Garrison Villard], was a good fellow, sincere, courageous if a trifle self-conscious as the standard bearer of revolt. . . . The little editress of *The Radical* at his right [Kirchwey] was . . . a perfect directory . . . of New York intellectuals and their temporary sex affiliations." "It was the heyday of psychological cults," Redfield, Herrick's hero observes caustically, and *The Radical* was always at the cutting edge of such enthusiasms. Scanning the assembled crowd he wishes that they were "healthier looking, more physically vigorous, with clearer complexions and smarter clothes, at least fresher." He notes a "febrile, nervous merriment, a bitterer note of appreciation" among the women present. "As yet women were too much concerned in winning their sexual freedom—or in having that freedom which they now enjoyed recognized publicly—to relish altogether the flippant air of ribaldry."

"Serena [Parsons] . . . was a considerable personage in this circle," Redfield observes, "infrequently as she appeared there." She was perfectly calm, collected, at her ease, with an air of personal distinction the other speakers lacked. "A gift from her Southern ancestors who did not believe in polygamy and polyandry, et al!" he notes with amusement. And she arouses in the audience "a curiosity due entirely to herself—to her youthful appearance, her fresh beauty, her reputation as a scholar and also as a woman of large means who might have taken the woman's commonplace way to social triumphs." " 'Who occupies what bedroom,' she said, with a sly curl to her upper lip and a toss upward of her dark head, 'no longer becomes a matter of current moment. . . . If a woman—as well as a man—is seen leaving a hotel at an early hour of the morning, her reputation is no longer irretrievably ruined.' This piquant phrasing elicited ripples of appreciative laughter. . . . It was in short . . . a plea for the sort of life with its eclectic couplings that she herself had, discreetly, pursued and enjoyed."

Serena "shot her shaft deftly, briefly," and "flushed by her triumph and . . . very lovely," was immediately surrounded. "Among the pressing women were couples of that new mating, just becoming recognized by the liberal minded as 'a problem,' " Redfield adds. "Some of these feminine couples were sufficiently well known to have won a sort of immunity; others were still guarded and furtive, shiveringly illicit. . . . there were present a not inconsiderable number of homosexuals, who had derived a certain indirect comfort from [her] words, feeling—quite justly—that relaxation anywhere in the sexual code must ultimately assist them in their peculiar search for pleasure."[27]

The account Herrick wrote in the days immediately after the *Nation* dinner was more personal. It was "one of those half-baked journalistic conceptions that could have emanated only from a crude feministic brain like Miss Kirchwey's," he wrote in a series of notes for "The Diary of an Intravert" (*sic*). But the evening was a triumph for Elsie. Somewhat to his surprise, he found that she "had the speaker's habit, the sense of audience . . . and clearly liked the performance." Her speech was "clear cut, definite . . . very clever of course, subtle, even sly in what it did not say." And she told the only witty joke of the evening—a story about John at Yale. Contemplating gloomily the effect of the evening on his waning self-confidence, he admitted that he was "distinctly less worth while, less provocative, less desirable, no doubt than at first, than in years past. I am getting to be shabby and shopworn goods, and my songs are vieux jeu, perhaps. . . . My Prestige has been steadily declining not merely with her, from controversy and exploration between ourselves, but objectively, what I count in the world, the little circle of the world that I touch. . . . The fact is that I was never at a lower point so far as writing, publishing, literary prestige and outlook go. Although we rarely touch on these matters, she is acute enough to divine the situation pretty accurately, and although I credit her with an unusual liberality and independence of evaluation no woman can be totally oblivious of these trappings."

"Am I going into decay?" he asked himself. "E. is generous enough to attribute the manifestations of such decay which she may notice, to ill-health, to 'poison'—but for how long? Either I must get started on the road of health mental and physical or inevitably she will lose interest." "She attributes the mental to the physical, as always," he went on. "Little does she consider how much the physical condition, even the low vitality sexually is due to the long mental strain of discouragements, defeats swallowed and put out of sight, but not forgotten in the subconscious. . . . Too often I suspect I have sought for Happiness as a compensation for failure in the arena, and perhaps looked for the approval of One to take the place of many! . . . What alarms me most now is sinking into a passive invalidism, indulging myself by withdrawing to my own quarters, lying on a lounge empty-minded, or reading, too slack to work—or to try to."

"She would not do that!" Herrick recognized. "If she were being torn by pincers of pain she would manage to do some 'grains of sand' and be better for it." In this depressed state of mind, he realized that Parsons was determined to go to the Caribbean whether he accompanied her or not, and that she would only tolerate his company, as she put it bluntly, "If you can be happy." "To which happiness she proposes to do nothing!" "She seems to have no thought of the risk to me in going into the W.I. [West Indies] or of anything except an agreeable method of accomplishing her one primary design,—to make her researches," he noted as they made their plans. "She admitted casually that she doubted if she ever would care to travel without this incentive." "In other words," he mused despondently, "I am permitted so long as I add anything to her enjoyment but she is ready for the final break at any moment, has envisaged what it would cost, and is quite ready to pay that cost rather than deviate from her own chosen way."

"There is another aspect," he continued: "by thus subordinating myself to her somewhat whimsical will, taking whatever she feels at the moment like giving, being subservient to her will, I degrade myself, lower my own self-respect—for surely such an unequal relation is not ennobling to either person." Herrick resolved to "detach [him]self from her image as compensation for other interests and achievements, steady recognition." But, he added, his romantic penchant asserting itself, "when I am with her she acts powerfully on me sexually and emotionally and it is very difficult for me not to become fluid and flamboyant in her hands, to pour myself out in adoration."[28]

As repeatedly happened over the next three years, Herrick's spirits rose as they planned the trip. Able to joke about the dark reflections of a few days before, he drew up a memorandum: "Field Trip, Number Three."

Imprimis: It is understood that the object of this Field Trip is SCIENCE, not love or pleasure or amusement or general culture—or anything else in the world. It is understood that R.H. is permitted to go along just so far as he recognises and observes this limitation. It is further understood that Dr. E.C.P. has definitely announced, recently, that this is the only kind of trip that she cares to take or proposes to take with said R.H. Therefore be it understood that

R.H.

must at all and any times efface himself when not wanted by Dr. E.C.P. & must subordinate all and any of his interests to the pursuit of Folk Lore, assist in every possible way the accomplishment of the objective of the Field Trip,—especially in regard to arranging for transportation, accommodations, baggage, etc. must accept the itinerary marked out by Dr. E.C.P. even if it should lead him into places dangerous for his health, and when Dr. P. is occupied with Folk Lore is not in any way to obtrude upon her notice, nor expect attention, consideration, personal or amatory.

His sole right and privilege is to depart when he has had enough, anywhere and any time when he so pleases.

Dr. E.C.P.

In consideration of the above Dr. E.C.P. agrees to permit said R.H. to "go along" (as long as agreeable to her) on the Field Trip, to make such business and travel arrangements as may seem good to her, to attend and care for her (when she feels like it) and in general to be a constant and faithful companion (when she needs one). She does not agree to be "loving" (except if and as and when it so pleases her, if at all) to be even amiable or companionable unless she so feels. She agrees on her part not to be wholly "marital" or "conjugal" in her treatment of said R.H. & to be as civil and conversational to him as she would be to a chance acquaintance, to permit him freely to care for her comfort and health, especially in case of illness, to permit him occasionally to speak of matters that are not strictly Folk Lore, even of Love, to "make love" to her not less than once every ten days on the average (provided it does not interfere with her "Hunt").

And further she specifically agrees not to compel said R.H. to sleep outside the protection of netting in a malarious country or to subject him to any unnecessary hardships and dangers in the exigencies of travel.

Lastly both understand and agree that if either or both decide to terminate the above arrangement, i.e. to part, there shall be no reproaches, ill-feelings or misunderstanding on the part of either one. . . . This exemplifies what Dr. E.C.P. approves as the highest type of sexual cooperation between mature men and women.[29]

Parsons replied with her own version of their agreement in "Memoranda for Travel in the World and in Life." A manifesto for modern sex relations, the "Memoranda" provides one of the few glimpses of this middle-age love affair from her perspective:

E.C.P. and R.H. are to encourage those shy creatures Shimana and Lapi [the pet names Herrick gave their more attractive selves] in ways well known for encouraging the shy: Taking their presence for granted, not questioning nor exalting nor analysing, only taking delight in their presence and showing it by gaiety and affection.

Lapi is to understand that when Shimana is content and interested and happy it is largely because he is there and sharing, and her interest however impersonal it appears at the moment does not exclude him but includes him. Shimana is to understand that the existence of personal interest without direct personal reference, with merely impersonal and indirect expression, is very hard for Lapi to credit, so she must be direct when she sees his faith ebbing.

Each is to take pleasure in the passing scene, in itself and as something to contribute to the other and to their shared experience. Each is to contribute to the systematic pursuits of the other as much as he or she can, and with real interest not merely with patience and long suffering. Clashes of time and place may have to be met by temporary separations to which no emotional meaning is to attach. As the nature of E.C.P.'s work is more systematic and exigent in the matter of time and place than the work of R.H. he is not to feel that she is being perverse and indifferent when she declines to play with him. Such pressure by him would destroy her pleasure both in her work and in his society, and as a much greater tax on her vitality than he appreciates, were likely to make her sick. E.C.P. on her part is to realise that R.H. wants to look after her and that his judgment is better than hers in looking after oneself, and she is to show gratitude to him for his care and solicitude by accepting his judgment when it goes against hers as much as she can make herself do. By showing her that he is really interested in her doing good work, not merely tolerant of her working, and that he wants to contribute to her work as work she is sure to feel a peculiar spontaneous kind of gratitude that may surprise him by its expressiveness.[30]

Their three-month field trip in 1925 was happy and productive. Based on the French island of Guadalupe after a quick sweep from San Juan through the Virgin Islands, Anguilla, St. Kitts-Nevis, Antigua, Montserrat, and some smaller islands, Herrick wrote in comfort while Parsons made collecting forays around the island. Herrick finished *Chimes* and the novellas that made up *Wanderings,* and he planned a book based on their travels. He and Parsons also began to exchange ideas for "Tides," which was to be their joint book on sex relationships. As Herrick put it in *The End of Desire,* rather more loftily than was actually the case in 1925, "the major concern in the sexual revolution now in process was not, as the radicals seemed to consider, with men and women . . . but with children, youths,—how they could be launched in life with normal appetites and habits. What mature people did with their lives, how much they might experiment or bungle, did not interest him, except when, as frequently was the case, the self-indulgence of the older generation had an immediate or indirect bearing on the aberrations of their young."[31]

A brief outline among Herrick's papers, which appears to have been prepared by Parsons, sets out their broad approach. A father and a mother, not married to each other, are sitting before the fire in a country home in early May. The first chapter is a conversation between the father and his son. The second, obviously drawn from Parsons's experience with Lissa, is a similar talk between mother and daughter. The outline includes the following scenes:

A. Scene when girl tells her intention of getting married, leaving college, etc. The mother's educational theory of life vs. the egotism of the young male. The risk of marrying a first love.
B. The week before the wedding; mother's suggestions about the coming intimacy.
C. Three years later, when certain risks forecasted in the previous talk have been realised.

Chapter 3 turns to the father and mother themselves, who tell each other about these talks and discuss "those perplexities that they did not meet," and "what can and cannot be 'got across' from one generation to the next, from one individual to another." They agree to try to write out these ideas during the summer.

In what seems to be a comment on Parsons's outline, Herrick suggested that they "imply a love relation between the elders which contrasts and fulfills the other one." This might prevent acknowledgment of authorship, he concedes, "but I am afraid that will be necessary in any event." "I think the additional interest and balance given to the book by the double experience,—the love of youth as seen by the mature, the fullness of mature love,—is worth trying for. Incidentally I'd like to demonstrate that the best love is the love of the full, mature fruited period,—the flame and the substance, as you pointed out in your poem!"

The proposed chapter heads—Approach, Conquest, Initiation, Privacy, and Creation—apparently composed jointly, suggest that this innovative sex education book would have closely followed the ideas Parsons formulated for the *International Journal of Ethics* and the *Masses* between 1913 and 1915. Under "Privacy"—that central tenet of Parsons's feminist sexual ethics—they noted: "The inner citadel of personality inviolable. The triangle of understanding, A approaching B through an objective point X, not by direct penetration." Under "Creation," they expressed in shorthand Parsons's modernist ideal of relationships: "The sense of life created as a child by both, nourished by both, shared in by both, making something in which both participate, something which is held in common, but is not a merging, a submission of one to the other. The loss sustained through the ideal of submissiveness on the part of one."[32]

Different Things in Different Places

In the midst of this rapprochement, in September 1925, the completely unexpected happened. Herbert Parsons died suddenly, in a freak accident at Stonover Farm. He was demonstrating a motor-driven bicycle he had just given Mac for his birthday, when it overturned on rough ground. He died at the House of Mercy Hospital, Pittsfield, of a ruptured kidney. Parsons was stunned. Her son Herbert says that the only time he saw his mother cry was when she returned from the hospital and told them that their father was dead.

Elsie mourned Herbert in her own way, lunching with Walter Lippmann and the two younger boys instead of attending the funeral, and not mentioning Herbert's death during the entire meal, according to Lippmann. Her composure almost came undone when she saw Herbert Jr. and Mac off to St. Paul's a week later; but Lissa, with her usual social sensitivity, made sure there was a letter waiting for her mother with the latest news of her new baby, born just before her father's death. John, twenty-two years old at his father's death, moved immediately into the role of financial organizer and confidant that he played for the rest of Parsons's life. "John has stood by with perfect discernment and devotion in every particular," Parsons wrote Lissa with a surprising acceptance of conventional sex roles, "showing that he intends to take Father's place by us in what ways he can."[33]

"We have read today in the American paper here the terrible news about Herbert," Signe Toksvig wrote from the Pyrenees, "It is so utterly incomprehensible. . . . I keep thinking how much he had to live for,—and how charming to us although we were of such differing opinions." "You are a stoic," she went on, cautious of expressing the deep emotion she felt. "Dear Elsie, the distance is long and the silences have been long but we do love you." "I have just brought myself to write to Elsie," Pliny Goddard wrote to Kroeber two weeks after Herbert's death. "I judged her by myself. I don't like intrusions and felt almost anything would be an intrusion." Writing to Elsie of Herbert's "combination of respect for freedom & adherence to conviction" and his "dislike of facade," Mary Simkhovitch also mused on Elsie's qualities. "I often think of you & your skilful handling of your own life, pursuing the ends you have in view with so fine a determination, & though I haven't seen you of late years I have never felt any separation. It certainly is a great mystery—how to live—how to think & then how to act, one can despise nothing but insincerity—& that often masks uncertainty of mind." "I think you have done a good job of your life," she concluded. "Children & your work—always fastening your attention on such light as you can find. I doubt if it makes any difference what one does—its the workmanship."[34]

Parsons would have left immediately for the Southwest if the situation of the younger boys and settling Herbert's affairs had allowed it. She finally got away early in November, missing the christening of Lissa's new baby, called Herbert after his grandfather. "Sunday we lunched at Manga's," John wrote his mother, "who said it was from interest, not curiosity that she wanted to know your whereabouts. Lissa planned to have her answer Mrs Patterson's query at the Christening 'Elsie? Why she's staying with the Zunis in New Mexico. You dont know the Zunis? A large family, older than most in New York, who get considerable attention from the president.'" "My program has been prospering," she wrote Lissa from San Gabriel Ranch, "not with 'the large family of Zunis,' but with another townsman whom I beguiled into coming here with me. . . . I ride horseback daily, and it has done me good. Most of all though the interest in my old job has been restorative. . . . The beauty of the country I have never succeeded in getting across to you or anyone who has not seen it for himself." "I am glad to know you are in the field, probably busy every minute and getting interesting material," Boas wrote on his return from Oslo, where he was at the time of Herbert's death. "It is the best we can do."[35]

Herbert's death changed the situation between Herrick and Elsie dramatically, throwing Herrick back into the alternating despair and resignation of the previous January. She was now free to marry. But Herrick found that she had no intention of changing their relationship in any way. In fact, he noted in an early outline for "Jessica at Fifty," she was caught by "a curious revived respect and regard for her dead husband, which she had not latterly felt while he lived and thwarted and irritated her." What is more, Herrick now had something even more serious to compete with than Parsons's

work—her children. Lissa was twenty-four years old when her father died; she had just become a mother for the second time; and
free of Herbert's moral objections, she soon left for France to establish grounds for the divorce she had been contemplating from almost
the beginning of her marriage. John was doing brilliantly at Yale,
his intense relationship with his mother heightened by her new de-
pendence on his practical assistance. Herbert and Mac, aged sixteen
and fourteen, were both at boarding school.[36]

For a number of years, under their agreement on their primary
care, Herbert had played an important organizational and social
role in the lives of the children. And Elsie believed, in any case, that
children should learn to make their own decisions, and she tried
not to intervene unnecessarily in their lives. Now, however, she had
to provide the solid framework for them that Herbert had supplied
in recent years; she had to be more constantly available during
Christmas and summer vacations for the younger boys; and she had
to help John in his career and Lissa in her tangled marital affairs.

That Christmas, Parsons had no reason and no desire to return
to New York. Mac and Herbert Jr. joined her in Alcalde for their
vacation, and she was able to see for the first time the mixture of
mimetic animal dances, maskless kachina dances, and Spanish
dances that marked the Christmas season in the northern pueblos.
When the boys returned to school in the 1926 spring, Parsons and
Herrick traveled to Egypt and the Sudan. She hoped to go overland
from Khartoum to Ethiopia—as Ruth Benedict noted with a touch
of asperity in her diary: "Elsie sails for 'Abyssinia' Sat." But persuaded by officials in Cairo not to attempt the journey, they hired
a dragoman and boat and traveled up the Nile, "following Arabic
folktales on their way into Africa," as Elsie wrote John. They put
in at villages normally not visited by tourists, "where the children
are mannerly & the *sheikh* gives you coffee and urges a dinner upon
you, & lets you smoke his water pipe & shows you—if the village
is Arab—his horse." "Also," she told John, "if you ask, his ladies
who kiss your hand, you in return kissing theirs. Later the story
tellers gather around the light you set up on the river bank and you
hear the origin stories of those you once heard in the Bahamas or
the Sea Islands & wondered where they came from, knowing they
were not European."[37]

Herrick returned from their Egyptian trip in April 1926 expecting
to be introduced to Parsons's family and hoping they would eventually marry. But Parsons found John, at least, hostile to her relation-

ship with Herrick. Ambitious and worldly in Herrick's opinion, John was set on an advantageous marriage and a successful legal career. He had no doubt been unhappy about the publication of *Wanderings* and *Chimes,* which was serialized in *Forum* in late 1925, and which came out just as his mother returned from Egypt, with its quite identifiable portrait of her and its less than flattering portrayal of his father. In an outline labeled "For Jessica at Fifty and Tides," Herrick notes that Jessica "is caught by the impossibility of getting back wholly into the social environment her son's ambitions require because she is always thought a little 'queer,'" and he plans to build into the story "the rather savage judgment of the son for the freedom she has taken in her life."[38]

Rather than planning a joint future with Herrick, however, Parsons set about organizing her family life to accommodate her own and her children's needs: "Otherwise they will be staying at Grantham [the Rocks] and rushing around on house parties," Serena explains to Redfield in *The End of Desire.* Early in June she found a house in North Haven, Maine, which became the family's summer home. "Your charming corner room . . . looks out to the Camden hills across the Thorough fare," she wrote John. "No end of small boats, including a motor boat . . . and a dinghy for the racing class, also canoe for the most beautiful canoeing waters." "I think you will enjoy it all very much. The schooner is a lovely boat, good sailer, good engine, excellent engine," she added, referring to the first of the schooners that added to the pleasure she and her family derived from their Maine summers. Parsons devoted July and August to the children and the completion of her 304-page *Tewa Tales,* fitting in visits to and from Herrick when her children were busy elsewhere. As Herrick put it in a draft of "Jessica at Fifty" that Parsons probably read, "he realized heavily that Jessica felt no more freedom because her husband had died than before, and saw no reason why it should change importantly their intimate relation."[39]

In September, after the younger boys returned to school, Parsons and Herrick took a cruise along the Maine coast, examining boats for the West Indies trip they planned for the winter; and Parsons paid several visits to York. In "Jessica at Fifty," Redfield meets the various members of Jessica's family over the course of the summer, but she gives no indication to them that he is anything more than one of her friends. Aware that he and Don (John) disliked each other at sight, she is chagrined when they encounter Don and a group of friends while cruising the coast of Maine. She would prefer "to keep different things in different places," she tells Redfield. When they return to Redfield's home, he presses her to marry him, but Jessica is quite definite: "I don't care to live openly together with any man," she tells him. "I never did in the past like it and there is no cause now why I should make a pretense." "Don't you want me with you?" Redfield asks. "Some times. Not all times," she replies. "I don't want any one all times. If we were married I'd have you often when I didn't want you and that would be as bad as now when I want you some times when I can't have you."[40]

Herrick wrote at the end of this chapter of "Jessica at Fifty" that "the conviction that the end had come to his brave hopes of a real marriage never left him from that hour." In December 1926, after a disastrous final trip to New Mexico and Arizona, when Parsons was busy finishing up her work on the Pueblos and their neighbors, Herrick ruminated on the months since they returned from Egypt: "What is evident is that she is largely, perhaps wholly indifferent," he wrote, "and ready for a break . . . Also that she has already lost almost all if not all of the charm with which my imagination once filled her." "My time of adoration and submission have passed," he added inaccurately, "and probably our intimacy is killed. When I return to New York it will be she who outwardly, as already in so many inward ways, will have left me. I do not raise a finger from this time on, but wait—as she waits."[41]

Parsons, in fact, was preoccupied with the children. Mac wrote lovingly from St. Paul's about his pride in the fact that his mother was an anthropologist "out in the wilds of New Mexico . . . with a Ph.D. and four years of Greek done in one." But John teased her with plans for his engagement to Fanny Wickes. "Lissa, Fanny, and Oui-Oui [her brother Henry's daughter Louise] are coming up for the Harvard game," he wrote her in New Mexico. "Last week I saw Cousin James' gem merchant in New York and purchased an emerald, with the aid and advice of Manga, Lissa and Oui-Oui. They stressed the importance of a stone that would 'make a show.' . . . I find myself quite keen on emeralds. They should fit admirably into the color scheme." "I hope your holiday with the Lady of the Emerald was wholly agreable," Parsons replied drily. "Engagement rings and Russian orphans (Lissa's devotion) don't appeal to me as much as some other things, but then Indians and Negroes have never especially appealed to you." Herrick suggests, somewhat melodramatically, in "Foreword to Jessica" that Elsie suffered considerable anguish over John's engagement: "young Edgar seeks his mate in another woman she could neither comprehend nor like and lets her perceive that all these years he has been judging her in his heart and finding her wanting as a woman, as a wife, as a mother, as a human being, admire and love her as he did." "She had failed him," Herrick writes, "her own created lover, her own flesh, as she had failed every male who had entered her life, and he had gone in search of the dream which she had openly ridiculed and secretly violated . . . A steadfast and enduring love."[42]

A field trip was always Parsons's antidote for pain; and if her grief was anything near as strong as Herrick suggested, it is not surprising that she set out with Herrick in November 1926 on a backbreaking trail through the pueblos, to the Pimas in Arizona, and through the Caribbean. That journey broke their health and permanently damaged their fragile relationship. They had decided to charter a schooner in order to give her boys a cruise over the Christmas vacation, and then to visit Haiti, Dominica, and some of the smaller islands—Marie Galante, Les Saintes, and Saba— "otherwise inaccessible only by dint of patient waits for very uncertain vessels." The trip did not start well, with Herrick unhappy at being dragged in discomfort through New Mexico and Arizona. After a three-week cruise through the Bahamas, John took the younger boys back to school, and Parsons and Herrick set off from Havana on an exhausting and ill-fated voyage.[43]

Herrick tells a dramatic story in *End of Desire* that seems to follow this voyage's misadventures closely. The climax of his account—and the scene of the hero's final disillusionment—comes at a Haitian "spirit" dance to which Redfield and Serena have been taken by Mack, a Cayman Islander who resembles Sam Holder, a charming "dock rat" Parsons hired as "runner" and interpreter. After crossing to a neighboring island in a leaky dugout canoe, Herrick's hero recounts, they follow a winding path through thick plantations of cocoa and bananas for an hour until they reach a little clearing. On a long table covered with a white cloth stand several bowls, two old glass decanters filled with rum, some colored pictures, a crucifix before which lies a branch of purple bougainvillea, and a plate of glass beads: "Serena examined the objects with care, listening to the explanations offered by Mack." She is then led to a broken armchair behind the altar. "Sitting there enthroned, her white face lighted by the leaping fire, and surrounded by eager black faces, she appeared very serious, solemn, a foreign priestess brought in to preside over pagan rites." After a goat is ceremonially killed and eaten, the dancing and singing begin, while Serena sits "alone, her eyes steadily fixed on the sweating nude bodies of the dancers." "Probably she considered it an important scientific opportunity!" her skeptical lover comments. The scene ends badly, with Serena having to be defended by Mack and rescued by her lover, who remarks coldly when they get to safety, "I don't know what Science has gained from that drunken spree, but we have lost a perfectly good cook!" But Mack is back the next day before they sail, with a bandaged arm in a sling. "This is pleasant, isn't it?" Serena says coolly as they get under way.[44]

Parsons's account was just as dramatic, but for more intellectual reasons. "During a recent folk-tale collecting trip to the south coast of Hayti," she wrote in the *Journal de la Société des Américanistes de Paris* in 1928, "I had opportunities to observe certain combinations of African paganism and French Catholicism of much interest to the student of acculturation, as well as to [the] West Indian folklorist or historian." "That this cult has heretofore passed undescribed in Hayti is probably due to the diversion of interest to one of its reputed features, ritual cannibalism or, in journalistic term, voodoo human sacrifice," she noted with her usual disapproval of racial snobbery, "the folklore of which is widespread among all foreigners, White and Colored, in Hayti as well as among Caribbean neighbors."

Setting out the information she gathered about the cult, Parsons described the spirit dance for Saint Peter that she attended with Sam, another lad, and a young woman—Sam's "keeper." Several of the participants became possessed, and there was much dancing. But there was no animal sacrifice. There was, however, a great deal of drinking, and as the evening wore on, quarrels broke out. A man picked a fight with Sam's "keeper" and was finally thrown out after a violent dispute. "As it was plain enough that there would be increase in ordinary drunkenness and decrease in extraordinary possession," Parsons explained, she decided they should start the two-hour walk back to town. Putting together what she had found about the spirit cult in Haiti, and what she knew about Spanish and French witchcraft, she deduced that much of what she observed was "in large part French rather than African." "French (and Spanish) necromancy, and Catholic and West Coast ritual and ideology," she concluded in an argument that was reminiscent of her analysis of the Pueblo kachina cult, "that is part of the weave from medieval

Europe and tribal Africa students have to unravel to understand Negro witchcraft and spiritualism in the New World."[45]

The End of Desire

Herrick's 1932 novel has them wrecked on the keys outside San Salvador. Certainly Parsons collected folklore on Watlings Island, the less exotic name given to that tiny cay. But, however the voyage ended, both Parsons and Herrick arrived back in New York ill. "I am now busy writing up notes of three field trips run into one," Parsons wrote Lowie in April 1927, "Pueblos, Pima, West Indian folklore French and English. In Hayti I found some interesting West Coast African cult survivals, which I will be describing for the Anthropologist." To Esther Goldfrank she was less sanguine. She was sorry to miss her party, she wrote in June. "I came back from the West Indies field trip this year considerably below par and with no energy to spare for anything except necessary chores, and that day I was especially low." "This Maine life has set me up wonderfully, as Westchester country never could," she wrote more cheerfully a month later from her summer home.[46]

Parsons never returned to the collection of African-American folklore, although she supported the comprehensive work of Melville and Frances Herskovits; and she never went to the Caribbean again. After 1927, she seems also to have confined her sailing to the waters of Maine. But the relationship with Herrick had not yet run its course, although Herrick's novel ends it with the shipwreck. More prosaically, the situation between them deteriorated during the 1927 summer when Parsons was preoccupied with John's wedding and with a visit to Chief Justice Taft in the interests of John's career. She was also completing her 309-page *Social Organization of the Tewa*, the fruit of the past four autumns in the Rio Grande pueblos. Herrick found the competition of her work and her children so stressful that he became convinced he had a heart condition and was about to die.[47]

When Herrick and Parsons made a final trip together to Majorca in the 1928 spring, he was in a mood of revulsion against all women: "For two months I have felt the same reaction on the streets of New York and in the cabs, buses, the quality of this womanworld of ours, its ugliness, its essential unintelligence," he wrote in what he prematurely called "My Last Book." "So far women with all their freedoms in this country have merely proved more conclusively than before the contentions of their opponents, their real inferiority as a sex, as persons." "To write thus," he went on, "seems to me myself almost sacrilege, I having maintained through the most of my sixty years an admiration for women, which has suddenly in old age come to an abrupt denial. The unspiritual, the ungenerous, the un-imaginative sex, and what we Victorians of my youth never sus-pected the unchaste, the sex obsessed sex. As soon as women are reasonably assured against social and physical results from cohabi-tation they are as wanton as men ever were, and I suspect that many dissatisfied married women crave merely a more abundant and more brutal sex indulgence—instead of the opposite as we used to think. Removed from the perils of child bearing—and the burdens— women become sly sensualists, with empty prostitute faces. And their instinct is to sell their bodies for what at the moment they want most. To this theme I shall often return in this my last book . . . But rather to the lack of imagination than to the sensuality, which I am naturally less interested in now than once."[48]

The end came imperceptibly. During their weeks in Majorca, Her-rick could hardly bring himself to write. "He was supposed to work also," he noted in "An Eighteenth Century Journey." "That was the understanding on which they cooperated in these excursions. . . . since he had been ill he had hardly worked at all, making his illness an excuse as he knew and supposed she thought. Any way it was stupid to work, to fill pages with typed lines when one's heart was not in it, and distinctly his was not in those meagre neatly typed pages, not in any of the subjects he had desultorily worked at the past five years, not overmuch in the places they had visited. In nothing, except in Elsie. Yes, too much in Elsie, too constantly in her."[49]

During the summer of 1928, Parsons was busy with her paper "Spanish Elements in the Kachina Cult of the Pueblos," the defini-tive statement on Spanish-Pueblo acculturation she was preparing for the International Congress of Americanists in New York that September. As usual, she took a cruise with the boys and had press-ing family problems to deal with—this time the question of whether seventeen-year-old Mac should play football. Feeling totally ne-glected, Herrick collapsed completely and retired to Florida with his devoted and efficient new housekeeper, who was willing to cod-dle him as Parsons never would. Confined to bed for the first month, but still apparently able to work, he wrote effortlessly every day. "Jessica at Fifty" quickly turned into *The End of Desire,* a devastating portrait of a "modern," self-centered woman, indulgent to her oldest son, but blind to the real needs of her other children. A new and completely fabricated subplot was added, playing into the current frisson over homosexuality; and Lissa was turned into an aviatrix à la Anne Morrow Lindbergh, the daughter of his Cornish friend Dwight Morrow. As Parsons commented when she read it in 1932, "I am not surprised that even if he did not think it was portraiture he was disinclined to see me while he was writing it."[50]

CHAPTER FOURTEEN

Other Americas

IN July 1928, Pliny Goddard was at the summer home he and Gladys Reichard had recently established, when he began vomiting violently. Before the tests ordered by Boas's physician son could be carried out, Goddard was dead, of an undiagnosed cancer of the stomach. Parsons, who was summering in Maine, wrote immediately to Gladys suggesting a field trip. As she wrote to Boas, "A new scene is an incredible help in distress of the spirit. . . . Time was when I wanted to get away from obsessing associations, and I thought she might feel that way." Two years later, when Mrs. Boas was killed in an accident, Parsons made the same suggestion, urging Boas to join her in Mexico. Deciding instead to "suffer in harness," Boas wrote affectionately to Parsons, "We each have our own way of meeting fate. . . . You have met fate bravely your way and so shall I."[1]

Parsons sought the solace of fieldwork herself in 1928 after the failure of her attempt at a loose but intimate companionship with Robert Herrick. By February 1929 she was in Mexico, striking out boldly in a new setting. But her turn to Mexico was not as quixotic or as personally motivated as it appears. During her visits to the Rio Grande pueblos and Taos in 1925 and 1927, she had been struck by the mixture of mimetic animal dances, Plains ceremonial, and burlesque of Christian practices that characterized Pueblo dancing during the Christmas season. Part of Parsons's intense excitement in Majorca in the 1928 spring—and no doubt one of the reasons Herrick felt neglected and de trop—was her discovery that Mexico was the central link in a chain that led from Majorca, where the religious dancing reminded her vividly of the Pueblo kachina cult, to the American Southwest. Examining the records of the San Francisco monastery at Palma, she found that Majorca supplied many of the early Franciscan missionaries to Mexico. The pioneering Antonio Llinás came from the Majorcan town of Artá, and

This San Juan Deer Dancer is typical of the mimetic dancing Elsie saw in the Rio Grande pueblos. Photo from Virginia More Roediger, *Ceremonial Costumes of the Pueblo Indians* (Berkeley: University of California Press, 1941).

half the Franciscans he recruited in the mid-eighteenth century were natives of "the very towns where religious dancing persists to this day"; and the Mexican mission house, in turn, supplied California and New Mexico with missionaries into the nineteenth century.[2]

Boas and the Mexican Renaissance

The International Congress of Americanists in New York in September 1928, where Parsons presented her landmark paper "Spanish Elements in the Kachina Cult of the Pueblos," brought her into contact with a number of people who drew her to Mexico. Presided over by Franz Boas, the congress attracted large delegations from Latin America, and it featured a number of sessions on cultural relations between North and South America and on Latin American ethnology, archeology, linguistics, and physical anthropology. Illustrated public lectures were given by Sylvanus Morley and Frans

Blom on excavations in the Mayan area, and Parsons's paper was one of five in a session on Spanish and French influences in the Americas. She shared the platform with Grant LaFarge's son Oliver, who explored the Yucatán and Guatemala with Blom in 1925, and with Frances Toor, the American-born editor of *Mexican Folkways,* a new journal dedicated to indigenous culture.[3]

The congress focused attention on Latin America, and especially on Mexico, at a time when interest in Mexico among North American intellectuals was at its height. Boas had been interested in Mexico since at least 1905, when he began moves to establish an archeological school there along the lines of the Archeological Institute of America's schools in Rome, Athens, and Palestine. Convinced that New World cultures represented as "much an inner unity as that of the Old World," he submitted a comprehensive plan for the study of cultural diffusion in Latin America to the Carnegie Institution in 1907. Boas's plan dovetailed with the Mexican government's attempts to modernize the country through educational reform. In 1910, they agreed to cooperate in the establishment of an International School of American Archeology and Ethnology. The school's opening coincided, however, with the beginnings of the Mexican Revolution. Although Boas spent a year as its director from 1911 to 1912, and his student Manuel Gamio carried on his work from 1913 to 1914, Mexico's political turmoil and the American invasion of Veracruz in the 1914 spring forced the school's suspension.[4]

Manuel Gamio remained Boas's principal contact in Mexico. During Boas's directorship, Gamio carried out the school's most important investigation, establishing by stratigraphic methods a chronology of preconquest cultures in the Valley of Mexico that is still accepted today. With his 1916 *Forjando patria* (Forging a nation), Gamio became a powerful force in the intellectual and cultural revolution that accompanied Mexico's political upheaval. Launching a program of applied anthropology designed to integrate the country's diverse ethnic communities, he planned "the redemption of the indigenous class" through a sociological and cultural project that would reflect and strengthen "the soul of the people." With the adoption in 1917 of a new Mexican constitution, Gamio headed what became the Dirección de Anthropología. From this position, he directed excavations and restorations at Teotihuacán that expanded to become a massive multidisciplinary community study intended as the basis for his program of cultural integration. When this study was published in five volumes in 1922 (and part of it submitted for his Columbia Ph.D.), its recommendations were already being implemented.[5]

Looking South

Revolutionary Mexico in the 1920s became a laboratory of political and cultural change for North Americans disillusioned by the failure of their hopes for a more tolerant and diverse United States. When the unknown writer Katherine Anne Porter arrived in Mexico City in 1920, Manuel Gamio was a central figure in the "Mexican renaissance" supported by the minister for education, José Vasconcelos. She and the other young Americans who flocked to Mexico were welcomed with a gay informality by the Mexican intellectuals and artists who were helping Gamio and Vasconcelos to improve popular education, stimulate folk art, and celebrate the Indians' rich cultural traditions, especially in striking public murals. Many of these young Mexicans had been educated in the United States—indeed, like Gamio, several key officials such as Moisés Sáenz and Adolfo Best Maugard were Columbia graduates or close associates of Boas.[6]

In 1922 Frances Toor, a former student of Berkeley borderlands historian Herbert Bolton, attended the Summer School for Foreigners, which had just been established at the National Museum. The museum's folk art exposition enchanted her, and she stayed on. In 1925 she began *Mexican Folkways,* an "artistic and beautiful" magazine designed to "present the masses of the Mexicans to the American people." "It is to treat of legends, dances, stories, superstitions, fiestas; in fact all of the expressions of the race soul of the Indian," Toor wrote Boas and Parsons, with whom she hoped to study. With Jean Charlot and Diego Rivera as its art editors, anthropologists such as Gamio, museum and education officials, and political commentators such as Carleton Beals as "Collaborators," *Mexican Folkways* became, for a short period, the showplace for *indigenismo.*[7]

In 1923, Toor was joined by Anita Brenner. Brenner, the daughter of Latvian Jews, was born in Aguascalientes, Mexico, but brought up in the United States, where her family had fled during the revolution. She returned to Mexico City to study at the National University, and the following year she was commissioned by the university to assemble an archive of indigenous arts. Together with the photographers Edward Weston and Tina Modotti, she explored Mexico, developing the knowledge and feel for Mexican art and life that she poured into a series of essays for American journals. As a twenty-four-year-old graduate student in the Columbia anthropology department in 1929, Brenner published these essays, along with Weston's and Modotti's photographs, in *Idols Behind Altars*. This brilliant account of what Brenner christened the "Mexican renaissance" introduced the Mexican muralists and Mexican indigenous art to a wider audience in the United States. At the end of her life, Brenner recollected the camaraderie of those years: "We were all . . . close friends," she wrote of the group of young Mexican and American intellectuals and artists gathered in Mexico City in the 1920s, "sort of looking for the same things, working in the same channels. And it was not like the social friendships of now, it was a revolutionary atmosphere, almost like a workshop atmosphere, so we could all get into each other's 'thing.' "[8]

American anthropological work in Mexico was stimulated by Manuel Gamio's arrival in "the United States of the North" in 1925 after he was dismissed from his central position in Mexico. From 1926 to 1929, he carried out a major study of Mexican immigration funded by the Social Science Research Council. As a counterpoint to Gamio's study, University of Chicago graduate student Robert Redfield was awarded a fellowship to study a Mexican community. His landmark work, *Tepoztlán,* based on an eight-month study of a town outside Mexico City, was published in 1930. Strongly influenced by the interest of his father-in-law, Robert Park, in the conflict of cultures brought about by urbanization, Redfield focused on current processes of social change in much the same way as Robert and Helen Lynd had in their study *Middletown* the previous year. In doing so, Redfield placed at the center of an anthropological study the interest in contemporary acculturation processes that was an insistent theme in Elsie Clews Parsons's work.[9]

While the young cultural radicals brought Mexico's "renaissance" to the attention of the American public, and Gamio and Redfield stimulated scholarly interest in immigration and acculturation, the activities of the Carnegie Institution of Washington in Yucatán aroused enormous popular interest during the 1920s and 1930s. Urged on by Sylvanus Morley, who had visited the Mayan ruins at Chichén Itzá in 1907 as a Harvard student of Alfred Tozzer, the CIW signed a contract with the Mexican government in 1923 for the excavation and restoration of that site. At the same time,

Tulane University sent Frans Blom and Oliver LaFarge—another Harvard student—to Mexico and Guatemala to explore preconquest sites. From the mid-1920s, American scholars, including Kroeber and Bolton at Berkeley, Sapir and Fay-Cooper Cole at Chicago, and Boas and Benedict at Columbia, scrambled to persuade foundations to fund research in Latin America. The Carnegie Institution, with its highly successful base in Mayan archeology, was, however, the only United States foundation that seriously promoted ethnological research in Mexico during this period. In 1929, seeking to broaden the disciplinary scope of its Middle America program, the CIW appointed Alfred Kidder to head the new Division of Historical Research. Kidder successfully exploited public interest in spectacular archeological finds in the Yucatán by orchestrating a well-publicized aerial reconnaissance by the United States ambassador's son-in-law, Charles Lindbergh. Although Kidder was better at publicity than interdisciplinary research, his appointment of Robert Redfield in 1930 to investigate the diffusion of urban culture in the Yucatán led to several important community studies, beginning with *Chan Kom* in 1934.[10]

Moving South

During the 1930s, American liberals looked to Mexico as a model for integrating indigenous populations without destroying their cultures. Mexican anthropology's fusion of intellectual and practical concerns fitted well with Elsie Clews Parsons's long-held view of the ethnological project. Attracted by this combination, she probably planned her spring 1929 visit to Mexico with Frances Toor during the September 1928 congress. But she kept quiet about her plans until she was ready to leave. The recent assassination of president-elect Obregón had threatened the country's precarious political stability, and Parsons's determination to go to Mexico despite its potential dangers may have precipitated the final break with Herrick. Between Christmas and New Year, she was reading Ruth Benedict's "Dionysian-Apollonian Southwest paper," which she thought was "very good," much to Benedict's surprise. Early in January, she was at the Bureau of American Ethnology in Washington, arranging publication of outstanding Southwestern work. On 28 January 1929, she wrote to Leslie White, whose study of Acoma was included in the volume, that she would be away "for a month or so, out of reach of mail." To Mabel Dodge Luhan she wrote after her return in April, "I was sorry not to see more of you this year. Not so long after that opera party I went to Mexico, for the winter."[11]

Parsons arrived in Mexico City less than two weeks after the tight-knit community of cultural revolutionaries was shaken by the assassination of Tina Modotti's lover, the young Cuban communist Julio Mella. His death marked the beginning of the end for the group. Their hero and supporter José Vasconcelos was defeated in humiliating fashion in the 1929 presidential elections and went into embittered exile; Modotti was deported early in 1930; Diego Rivera was expelled from the Communist Party and moved to the United States with his new wife, Frida Kahlo; and Mexico began a long period of political consolidation under the National Revolutionary Party. When Katherine Anne Porter returned to Mexico City in April 1930, she complained of corrupt bureaucrats and thick-skinned American entrepreneurs. What a "sink this country has become," she wrote in February 1931, with "every dumb, second-rate human being in the world" in Mexico to study the Indian and his art while "the Indian is in as bad a fix as ever."[12]

Although Frances Toor was Parsons's principal guide during her first Mexican trip, and Toor was one of the friends who helped Modotti through her highly publicized ordeal, Parsons mentioned nothing of these events in her letters home—concerned as always not to alarm her family. The direction of Mexican politics was hardly clear in February 1929, but she was, in any event, delighted with what she saw in Mexico City and the surrounding towns. Writing to John the day of a memorial gathering for Mella, she described traffic police chiefs banqueting near her in "gorgeous sombreros, besilvered black trousers, red buckskin jackets," the circus "in the handsomest red and white tent we agreed we had ever seen," and the game of pelota—"*fronton* as it is called here, played in a huge squash like court, with red bareta wearing bookies, mostly Spaniards, calling out the odds & catching the money bags . . . a stunning game!" She was meeting "the youth in the Museum and in the Department of Education. All so young, but never pompous or self-important . . . a warm and friendly spirit of cooperation prevails which is rare in N.Y. or Washington."[13]

"If the freedom from officialdom of the secretaryship of education, Rivera's frescoes (in the galleries of the great court) & the tide of visitors to the museum, workmen and peasants, represent new Mexico," Parsons wrote John, "something very much alive and promising is going on in the country." She met Diego Rivera and the young caricaturist Miguel Covarrubias, who showed her his film of religious dancing by the Yaqui of northwestern Mexico, and she became an enthusiastic supporter of *Mexican Folkways,* joining Toor, Rivera, Modotti, Covarrubias, Carleton Beals, Sáenz, and archeologist Alfonso Caso as a contributing editor. In the July-September issue, her article "Masks in the Southwest of the United States" was illustrated by a Hopi kachina from Covarrubias's collection.[14]

The day after the Mella memorial, Parsons and Toor set off on an extensive trip through the states of Mexico, Puebla, and Morelos to observe religious dancing during the Lenten period. They visited Carnival in the neighboring Pueblo towns of Huejotzinco and Santa Ana Xalminilulco, and in Huizquilucan, an Otomí town in the state of Mexico that Toor knew well. In Tlaxco they saw the dance-drama Las Tres Potencias. On the third Friday of Lent, they visited the sanctuary at Tepalcingo in the south of Morelos, where they saw a wide variety of religious dances. But probably the highlight of the journey was their visit to Chalma, the great Augustinian sanctuary, where they joined thousands of pilgrims to the miraculous shrine on the first Friday of Lent.[15]

Parsons's folkloric tour was brought to a sudden halt by a series of political uprisings. Back in Mexico City, she wrote reassuringly to John: "You are getting some scare headlines, I suppose. . . . Three generals 2 in the north, 1 in Vera Cruz, are uprising for reasons nobody knows and none but the Spanish-American group who have lost properties is in sympathy." "I infer it will be a matter of days rather than weeks," she concluded after giving him an amusing sketch of the local scene. "However, remember that Mac's Easter holiday begins April 3. If I am not back, had he not better spend it with you?"[16]

Parsons cooled her heels in the subdued luxury of a converted monastery in the suburb of San Angel, the San Angel Inn, which became her home away from home whenever she returned to Mexico City. The San Angel Inn was "celebrated for its excellent cuisine, quiet elegance, and delightful old gardens." Diego Rivera and Frida Kahlo built their famous double house with its organ cactus fence opposite the inn in 1933; and before their marriage in 1929, Frida lived with her family in the neighboring suburb of Coyoacán. In 1929, the inn's patio was a favorite eating spot for Mexicans and Americans alike. Parsons made friends with the gossipy owner and the "sweet little Mexican chamber maid who tells me riddles & fills

Elsie setting off from the San Angel Inn, Mexico City, February 1929. Elsie Clews Parsons Papers, American Philosophical Society Library.

my hot water bag very carefully." "This place is very pretty, the food delicious, & the Embassy visitors come out for refreshment," she wrote John, "Rublee, Paul Cravath, & now to complete the comedy of incongruities comes Wiley of the New York Times. His was the last train down from Laredo. I expect him to lunch with me tomorrow. The others here are the Winston Churchills who make water colors and live in terror of bandits and rebels . . . Mrs. Vincent (of the Rockefeller foundations) with some pretty southern girls who are flirting with some Mexicans, a Scotch youth who builds ships engines and races a Lincoln car over the country without knowing a word of Spanish, a Virginian New York lawyer who knows Spanish & is putting through an oil deal with 1000 Tatonaco Indians near Vera Cruz & is only too pleased that we liberals now see insurrection, 'annexation being an inevitable outcome, some time.' "[17]

Two weeks later, Parsons wrote serenely to John: "Home, Wednesday, & then visiting Lissa a couple of days in town. I came out of Mexico by the back door of Vera Cruz and New Orleans, a diversified and much pleasanter trip than by the north, just now

Frida Kahlo, San Angel Inn, Mexico City, February 1929. Elsie wrote her name "Frida Ribera" on the back of the photograph. Elsie Clews Parsons Papers, American Philosophical Society Library.

safer too." The trip was indeed diversified, though probably less than pleasant. Her diary records that she got to Vera Cruz by train, where she found a ship bound for New Orleans. When it finally set sail, it was seized by rebels. When she arrived in New Orleans four days later, she visited briefly with Oliver LaFarge at Tulane University and caught the train for New York. Undeterred by her misadventure, she wrote enthusiastically to John: "Consider a Christmas vacation for all of us: New Orleans (2 nights & a day) N. F. Co. boat to Puerto Barrios, Guatemala (2-3 days), Guatemala City & motor trip into the northwest high lands, & down to rail & on through southern Mexico, Mexico City & north. Possible in 3 weeks."[18]

Indian or Spanish?

Parsons found Mexico City and its surrounding towns "rich in tales as it is in other charming and interesting expressions of the human spirit." But she saw little that was recognizably indigenous. As she put it a few years later, "To the newcomer in Mexico City, at least to one interested in tribal culture, very little seems Indian; and yet he will hear references of all kinds to the Indian . . . and he will go from suburb to suburb or from town to town in the valley on the assurance that here they speak *idioma,* Indian idiom, very ancient are their customs, *muy indio,* very Indian." To Parsons it seemed that much of what she saw was derived from early Spanish customs. Religious folk dancing and other medieval forms "are preserved in Mexico as well as in Mallorca, perhaps better," Parsons wrote Kroeber after her return to New York in March 1929. "The Mexicans and their American journalist friends have a funny way of calling medieval ritual, Indian, partly as anti-Catholic propaganda, partly from ignorance of the medieval in Europe." Determined to tease out the elusive processes of Indian-Spanish acculturation, she found, as always, that she got her most useful information at first hand. On the way to Chalma, for instance, the donkey boy told her Adam and Eve stories that reminded her of the origin tale of the Zuni Koyemshi.[19]

When Parsons returned to Mexico in January 1930, she went straight to Oaxaca, a state whose population was almost entirely indigenous, where she established herself in the town of Mitla to learn about Mexican Indian life from the people themselves. Boas visited this southwestern state in 1912 and remembered the Mitla Inn fondly. But Parsons's choice of Mitla was probably prompted by Frances Toor, who wrote with delight of the ancient Indian town where "people converse in their musical Zapoteca tongue and tell tales of spirits who still linger around the old walls." Toor described Oaxaca in *Mexican Folkways* as a region crossed by sierras and valleys where the population spoke more than fifty dialects and the ancestors of the two principal groups, Zapotecan and Mixtecan, left highly developed ruins as evidence of a vigorous and complex preconquest culture. Parsons took to Mitla immediately. Indeed, how could someone so enamored of the tangle of cultures resist a town whose churches and houses appropriated stones from the ancient temples on which it was built, and whose bridge, half-stone, half-plank—neither Spanish nor Indian—seemed to symbolize mestizo culture?[20]

Personal reasons also encouraged Parsons to settle in for a long stay in Mitla. A draft note in her papers, possibly to Mabel Dodge Luhan or Clarence Day, the only friends she wrote to in so open a fashion, is the single clue to an unsatisfactory new relationship: "I'll never tell that G.P. but I'd like to tell you, what I am thinking of him," she wrote. "It's a hell of a mess. When I like him, he doesn't like me, and when he likes me, I don't like him. I could straighten it out if I had a chance, but I haven't a ghost of one—given his technique of paramount interests (family, paper, & polygymy) and his age, and his lack of ~~previous~~ experience—the poor timid dear fool with his silly talk about marriage and he ~~not having any~~ notion of what makes a happy relationship, either in or out of marriage. . . . So that's that. And I'm looking forward to going to Guatemala & Mexico with two boys of whom one at least lets me love him."[21]

As Parsons's final sentence intimated, she felt somewhat rejected, not only by her unnamed lover, but also by her sons. John was happily married, and he and Fanny were expecting their first baby. Since their marriage they had shared the Harrison home with her, but her concern for the privacy of lovers probably made her feel in the way in the newlyweds' household. The two younger boys were at Yale. Herbert, a serious twenty-year-old, was preparing for medical school. Mac, at eighteen very much like Parsons herself at that age, was in full-scale rebellion against the adult world in general and his mother in particular.[22]

After an arduous trip through Guatemala and southern Mexico with Mac and Herbert in December 1929, during which Mac conceded that they "would have been sunk" without her, Parsons arrived in Oaxaca early in 1930 in time to observe the cycle of New Year and Lenten ceremonial. On 14 January, she wrote to John from Mitla: "I am working now in a Zapotecan family. The climate is perfect, the inn comfortable. A full moon last evening over hills and a trickling river that reminded very much of Rio Grande country." Not only the geography but also the "low, self-contained voices [and] . . . the unhurried gait of the barefoot women with bowl or basket on their head, their small hands and feet, the quiet children playing adult, the composure of all the towns-people, their order and style" made her feel "sentimentally . . . at home." In Mitla as in Zuni, that "most endearing of all our southwestern pueblos," she was sure she would be *muy contenta*.[23]

Much of this contentment came from the friends she made in the small town of about 2,500 people. The family she referred to in her letter were the Santiagos—Petronila and her son Eligio. Petronila Santiago took Parsons into her patio one day when she encountered a herd of bulls running through the narrow streets of the town, whose organ cactus fences allowed no ready escape. As Ralph Beals noted when he was with Parsons in Mitla in 1933, "the only time I saw Elsie visibly frightened . . . was when, in the narrow streets, the cattle would be driven home down the street." The two women liked each other immediately, and Petronila's house became Parsons's second home in Mitla. Parsons was also impressed by Eligio, who was happy to act as her secretary, guide, and artist for two pesos a day—a handsome sum according to his envious brother. Eligio, who was then about thirty years old, became "a devoted servant, *muy caballero*, and a friend for life." His meticulous maps and drawings in *Mitla* testify to the care with which he set up his "office" in Petronila's kitchen. A "traveling man" like much of the town's male population, he was a knowledgeable guide in Parsons's exploration of nearby trade routes and villages; and he had a ready store of the tales that were a staple of trading life.[24]

The other important figure in Parsons's Mitla life was Angélica Quero y Toro, to whom *Mitla* is dedicated along with Eligio Santiago. "*Muchísimas gracias*," Parsons wrote, "to that most independent and competent of women" who ran the inn where Parsons lived during her three long visits in 1930, 1931, and 1933—"good Catholic and good Puritan, honest to a cent and ever careful of the morals of the town," despite her bobbed hair. Angélica and her family—her husband, Don Rafael, a "foreigner" from Oaxaca; the skilled housekeeper and nurse, Aunt Josefa, "who wears her hair down in braids, thick and black although she is sixty four"; her cousin, the dutiful Lidia; her son Dario, the endearing *anciano*—took Parsons into their lives, fed her teas and broths when she was sick, and introduced her to the intricacies of the social and ceremonial life of the town.[25]

Parsons's intimacy with the Quero family and the townspeople was literally jolted into a new phase when they shared the terrors of the major earthquake—*el grandote*—that devastated Mitla in January 1931. "I have slipped into all sorts of little personal relationships in this very agreeable town . . . and my book ought to be good," she wrote John. "Supper I eat now with the family. . . . They are all simple, sincere people with gentle manners, and as nice

Eligio Santiago, 1930. Elsie Clews Parsons, *Mitla* (Chicago: University of Chicago Press, 1936).

to me as can be." When Parsons returned with Ralph Beals in 1933, he was impressed by the inn—"a delightful partly and very little reconditioned Dominican monastery run by a fine mestizo couple"—and by Parsons's "obvious rapport with the inn keepers and the people of the town."[26]

La Sorpresa, the inn that was Parsons's home for her three seasons in Mitla, was a large stone house built by Angélica Quero y Toro's great-grandfather, with high-ceilinged rooms opening onto a pillared corridor around the patio. Its huge wooden portal looked out onto the tree-shaded plaza, with the market, the municipal offices, the school, and the jails—one for women and one for men—forming its other three sides. From her bench under the portal, Parsons could observe traders, pilgrims, and tourists who passed through the town, the women selling in the market, and the little girl peddlers; and she could gossip with the townspeople who visited the inn's shop and bar.[27]

Mitla was situated at the head of a valley that opened to the east

La Sorpresa, Mitla, 1930s. Elsie Clews Parsons, *Mitla* (Chicago: University of Chicago Press, 1936).

of the state capital, Oaxaca. This valley, about thirty miles long and two to twelve miles wide, held about twenty small towns plus Tlacolula, a large town at the end of the railway spur. The highway, traveled by service cars, sporadic buses, burros, and ox teams, ended at Mitla, seven miles beyond. Mountain trails then led through three passes north, east, and southeast, the last linking up eventually with the road to the Isthmus. Because it was the first of the valley towns reached by these trails, Mitla provided a cornucopia of riches for the ethnographer. "Sit in front of La Sorpresa and watch the traffic!" Parsons exclaimed as she described itinerant merchants selling mats and baskets, sugar cane, salt, oranges, lime, and pottery.[28]

But Mitla's position only twenty-six miles from the state capital also opened it to cosmopolitan influences. The town's population was growing, with one in every thirty an immigrant, and the many travelers brought to Mitla a comparative point of view and a curiosity about the outside world. Parsons found the Mitleyanos frank and open—indifferent on the whole to tradition, welcoming the motor truck and the corn mill. When the first loudspeaker disrupts the quiet commercial scene Parsons observes from her bench, advertising a new brand of cigarettes from the back of a truck, everyone is delighted, she notes, by the machinery and the handbills.[29]

A New Kind of Fieldwork

In Mitla, Parsons found conditions that allowed her to do the sort of ethnographic work she did best. She always enjoyed the give-and-take of personal interactions in the field and felt that she got her best information that way. But the secretive nature of the Southwestern pueblos, the exigencies of her young family, and the presence of sometimes impatient companions kept her field trips short and, in the Rio Grande pueblos, distressingly formal. Ruth Bunzel had shown, in her work at Zuni between 1924 and 1928, what a wealth of information could be gained by an ethnographer who lived and worked with the people she was studying. Unlike the rest of Boas's students, whose field technique, as Kroeber once put it, was to "walk up to an Indian with notebook in hand," Bunzel found accommodation with a Zuni family for the 1924 summer, put on a smock, and learned to make pots from the women whose approach to their craft she wanted to study. She returned to learn the Zuni language by the same method the following year; and over the five summers she spent there, she developed an extraordinary knowledge and understanding of the people's lives, their artistic productions, and their ceremonials. As Parsons wrote in an admiring review of Bunzel's *Zuñi Texts,* which included a rare autobiography of a Zuni woman—Bunzel's friend and hostess, Lina Zuni—"the portrait would not have been as finished, perhaps not have been drawn at all," without the author's intimate relationship with her informant and her language. Bunzel's guiding questions were those that had always been central to Parsons's work: "What is it like to be a Zuni? How does it feel to live in a culture so organized? Can we ever know how it feels?"[30]

Although the styles of the two women were very different—Bunzel quietly observant and Parsons energetically probing—Parsons had the opportunity in Mitla to put fully into practice the methodology she encouraged Bunzel to develop through her biographies in *American Indian Life,* her *Pueblo Indian Journal,* and the "Town Gossip" sections of her Pueblo studies. As Parsons put it in the preface to *Mitla,* "society in Mexico or anywhere else is not a tapestry to pick threads from and expect to find a new design in one's hand; and assimilation is one of the most subtle and elusive of social processes, which does not reveal itself by plucked threads, by isolated facts." She decided, therefore, "after visiting Huizquilu-can and many another town and going to fiestas and on pilgrimages or to a dance, a *baile típico,* wherever I heard of one, after being inquisitive about the organized cult of the saints, town government, calendars, curing and witchcraft, marriages and funerals, all in a comparative and yet loose-ended way . . . to try to tie up the threads by staying in one town until I learned something coherent about its people and its culture."[31]

Parsons quickly got to work, participating in the life of the community and gradually working out the complex systems of ceremonial and secular government through which mutual community obligations were sustained. Mitla's situation as a modernizing town surrounded by more traditional villages allowed Parsons to glimpse various levels of cultural change. In Mitla itself, both the communal government and the ceremonial life revolving around the elaborate institution of the *mayordomía,* or saint's day celebration, were rapidly attenuating. During her second visit in 1931, the innovative town president presented a film show in place of the more traditional entertainments that usually followed the bull-riding of the town's major saint's day celebration: "The high outer wall of the inn is used to show on," Parsons recorded. "A few benches are supplied, but most people sit on the ground. There are scenes of China and Spain, of rape, murder, and bullfight. . . . The chief hit is a trained dog doing his tricks in a Long Island palace. . . . 'A bad place for an earthquake,' comments somebody."[32]

When Parsons managed to reinstate the traditional Spanish piñatas in Mitla two years later, a blue-eyed Forestry Service chief from the Federal District who had been talking to her in French applauded this "very ancient custom, *muy indio.*" But she did see customs much closer to those of the preconquest culture when she rode with Eligio along the trade routes to the mountain towns. There a *curandera*—a medicine woman—breathed from her hands and made offerings in the four directions as the Pueblos did; town officials celebrated the *mayordomía* with highly ritualized drinking that had almost disappeared in Mitla; and people left hundreds of prayer images—miniature representations of their wishes for the coming year—at the base of La Cruz del Milagro on New Year's Eve in a scene that reminded Parsons of a similar Pueblo custom and of a ritual described by her much earlier predecessor, Francisco de Burgoa, in 1674.[33]

Between these two extremes, Parsons observed Mitla's system of town government—so similar to that of the Pueblos—which blended preconquest and early-eighteenth-century Spanish social organization. On New Year's Day 1931, she attended the passing of the canes of office to Mitla's new town officials. The custom of the canes derived from an early-eighteenth-century Spanish decree of representative government to its Indian subjects, she noted in an article in *Mexican Folkways*. With a town president "less indifferent to *los costumbres*, less anxious to be up to date, *muy moderno*," the occasion would have been more ceremonial. In the mountain towns, customs were preserved more thoroughly, as they were in the New Mexican pueblos where the canes were kept in the war chiefs' houses. During a visit to Oaxaca, Parsons recounts, she saw several men carrying large formal bouquets across the plaza. Later, when she saw them sitting outside the governor's office, they proved to be newly elected officials from towns around Mitla, come to pay their respects with flowers and formal speech. In the hands of the older men, she noted, were their canes of office, silver headed sticks of dark wood. "Canes gay with ribbons, white clothed figures, grave dark face, and the flowers, white, red, pink—it was a taking picture."[34]

To the Mayo and the Yaqui with Ralph Beals

After a season in Mitla and a Christmas spent in Uruapan in the western state of Michoacán, Parsons was keen to see more of Mexico's Pacific coast. Kroeber had just made a brief reconnaissance of northwestern Mexico for Berkeley's new Institute of Social Sciences. When Parsons wrote in January 1931 for advice, he suggested that Navajoa in southern Sonora would probably interest her most: "There are charming Mayo villages about 45 minutes drive out from town. You get more jolts, poorer food, and less native life by pushing into the rough hill country." "Then why not keep going until Berkeley," he continued, "make this mythical 'Elsie' a reality to our youngsters." Kroeber had married anthropology graduate student Theodora Kracaw, a mother of two young boys, in 1926, and now had two children of his own. "Look over Kroeber and what he has laid out for himself, in person," he urged. "You've side-stepped several invitations: this time I'm going to count on you."[35]

Parsons took up Kroeber's invitation the following December. Instead of going on to Mitla that winter, she planned to settle in Mazatlán on Mexico's Pacific Coast and write. In Berkeley she met Kroeber's former student, Ralph Beals, who had just returned from a field trip among the Yaqui and the Mayo, two Cahita peoples closely related to the native population of southern Arizona. It had been a frustrating experience for Beals because of problems making contact with the Yaqui, who were famous for their intense suspicion of outsiders. Discussing their mutual research interests at a party at the Kroebers, Parsons was fascinated to hear Beals talk about the Mayo and Yaqui clowns. Eager to compare them with those of the Pueblo, and to get some feeling for Cahita culture, Parsons decided to meet up with Beals when he returned to the field.[36]

The Yaqui and Mayo had resisted intruders for almost four centuries, during which they proved themselves masters of guerrilla warfare, renowned for their bravery. During the late-nineteenth-century Mexican land seizures, American developers and railroad men had driven them into the mountains. From there they remained a permanent thorn in the side of the government. In 1926, when it seemed that these fierce rebels could not be integrated into the newly imagined national community, a determined campaign to repress them was undertaken. Because they retained an uncompromising cultural identity, the Yaqui and the Mayo were of great interest to anthropologists; but their long history of conflict with Spaniards, Mexicans, and Americans alike made them hostile and dangerous subjects of study. Scholars in the history and geography departments at Berkeley—in particular Herbert Bolton and Carl Sauer—had been working in Sonora and Sinoloa for a number of years. Kroeber's 1930 trip was part of a Berkeley effort to define research problems and secure funding for work in the area. He returned convinced that investigators must have a command of Spanish, know the region's history, and be acquainted with Spanish-Mexican culture. Ralph Beals, in his opinion, was the only anthropologist qualified to do the job.[37]

When Beals set out on a two-year National Research Council fellowship to study acculturation among the Yaqui and Mayo, he had only a vague notion of what such a study might entail. Like other young scholars, he had the sense that acculturation studies were the wave of the future; and he was attracted by the way they seemed to confront current problems, in contrast to the abstracted salvage work with a "tribelet" that was standard dissertation fare. Beals was no stranger to Mexico. The son of struggling, idealistic socialist parents, he and his older brother, Carleton, had made their way to Mexico in 1918, when he was a seventeen-year-old schoolboy, in order to avoid the draft. Soon destitute, Ralph remained in Culiacán, Sinoloa, where he earned enough money to return to California, and eventually to school. Carleton pushed on to Mexico City, and over the next ten years became a major commentator on Mexican-U.S. relations and a central member of the *Folkways* group. In 1931 he published *Mexican Maze*, in which, among other things, he criticized the Mexican government for its willingness to destroy Yaqui culture in the name of national unity.[38]

Ralph Beals was critical of his brother's romanticization of Mexican Indian culture. The "romantic emotionalism" of Carleton Beals, Stuart Chase (who had just published a Rousseauean picture of Tepoztlán in his *Mexico: A Study of Two Americas*), and even Robert Redfield "seems out of place," he argued, "after the objectivity of modern ethnological studies has shown the Indian to be about as controlled by his culture as we are." "The Mayo is . . . primarily an empiricist," he pointed out in a manner that would have pleased Parsons. "What works is good; what works better so far as his experience goes, he will accept."[39]

After six weeks in Mazatlán, which was "as much of a Mexican Riviera as Nature, an American millionaire of Los Angeles, and a Spanish hotel keeper can achieve," Parsons made the twelve-hour train trip north along the tropical coast to Guaymas, Sonora. In early March 1932, she traveled down to Navajoa to join Beals in the town's one hotel, a simple colonial-style inn with plumbing "which worked so capriciously," Beals recalled, "that we were supposed to put toilet paper in the wire basket provided in order not to stop up the drains." Parsons found the town most unattractive—"a Mexican version of Anardarko, Oklahoma. Very dusty and now getting hot." But the similarities between the Mayos and Pueblos were so interesting, and Beals was such pleasant company, that she decided to stay on through the Easter week ceremonials.[40]

After three weeks in Navajoa, Parsons and Beals moved north to the Yaqui village of Estacion Vicam. The region the Yaqui had been reduced to was, in Beals's opinion, "unquestionably one of the most god-forsaken holes on the continent," and the hotel, with its dirt floor and cockroaches swarming in the toilet was "unspeakable." By the time Parsons left a week later, the temperature was hovering between 105 and 110, and they were tormented by dust storms. "All this Elsie took without complaint," Beals wrote admiringly. "As I was to learn later, she always wanted the best, but in the field, she translated this into the best the local environment afforded."[41]

There had been a serious uprising in the area in 1928; Beals had

been thrown out only a year ago, and it was still considered dangerous. An army officer was assigned to keep an eye on them, but
Parsons soon convinced him that they knew how to behave during
the ceremonials, essentially by following her long-established field
practice of being an unobtrusive participant in whatever was going
on. At the old town of Pitahaya, she insisted they get out of the car,
to which their escort had confined them; and they were soon re-
warded by the clowns inviting them to join the small group of
observers. After that they were allowed to go out unaccompanied
and were accepted at all ceremonials, to the extent that chairs would
be brought for them to watch the proceedings. Before they left, they
had been incorporated into the clowns' jokes and included in the
good-natured fun that leavened the ceremonial.[42]

Parsons's first glimpse of the Yaqui clowns—the Fariseos—
almost took her breath away. "It was the Fifth Friday," she wrote
in the *American Anthropologist* two years later, "the Fiesteros were
making the stations of the Cross at San Ignacio, and we had just
joined the procession of image-carrying women, the *rezador* and his
acolytes, and the group dedicated to the annual service, when the
Fariseos appeared on the scene to burlesque the devout and 'play'
around them." "Every new trick of bedevilment that was enacted
on the outskirt of that religious procession was one I had seen in
our Southwest. The Fariseos behaved just as would the Koyemshi
were there Catholic processionals at Zuñi which the Koyemshi had
to attend." "I gasped in amazement, inwardly," she remembered,
though outwardly "the dust was smothering."[43]

Parsons got on well with Beals. Their knowledge of American
indigenous cultures was complementary, and they spent long evenings over coffee and cigarettes arguing about anthropology. But
the young socialist and the older propagandist had much in common
apart from their work, and they often discussed the state of the
world, which, as Beals wrote Parsons's biographer and nephew Peter
Hare in 1978, "we both saw as not very good." Inevitably they
discussed the question of her wealth. She would willingly give it up,
she told Beals, if she thought it would do any good. But if it was
redistributed, it would not give more than a few pennies to the
poor. Instead she tried to use it for constructive and useful purposes.
"Such as," Beals added to Hare, "though she never implied it in
any way, helping a young anthropologist and his family through a
very difficult year."

They talked about still more personal matters. Beals was a loving husband and conscientious father of a young family, and his letters to his wife, Dorothy, were full of anxiety about their separation and advice about the children's problems. During their long talks, Parsons revealed her own anxieties and disappointments. "I learned about her children and her worries with them," Beals told Hare, "the disappointing daughter raised to be a liberated woman who wanted only to be a suburban wife and mother with her very conventional businessman husband, the older son now apparently well established but also somewhat of an establishment type, the younger son still at Yale and into all sorts of irresponsible undergraduate scrapes." Discussing Lissa's unhappy marriage, and no doubt thinking of the early years of her own marriage, Parsons remarked to Beals that she thought a person "who did not have the experience of eight or ten years of fairly comfortable living with another person was missing one of the big things in life, anyone who by very unusual circumstances had more than that was getting so much 'gravy' from life."[44]

"I want to approve your judgement of Elsie Clews Parsons as a field companion," Beals wrote Kroeber from Vicam after she left. "She was not only charming and entertaining but extremely helpful. Some of the leading questions she put from her Southwestern and southern Mexico experience opened up some very interesting leads. . . . As the situation stands now, I'm in an almost tearful state that I didn't keep on with the Yaqui. The truculent Yaqui is no myth, but he exists only when not properly approached and if he thinks you are a Mexican or associated with the Mexicans."[45]

"Easter week among the Yaquis was very interesting but pretty tough," Parsons conceded to John as she stopped off in an "exotic little paradise" in Chandler, Arizona, to recover. She needed all the strength she could muster to read Herrick's *End of Desire,* which was published while she was in Mexico. "It is a dull book," she decided. "He can't write narrative or . . . construct character or give a sense of life. Why a woman described directly as self-centred does not marry a man described indirectly as self-centred is too thin a theme. . . . The web of the snapshots with a lot of other stuff is curious. I suppose he thought putting in scraps of actual conversation, some of my rather threadbare captions and accounts of such personal habits as hours of work and book bags would give a verisimilitude of life. . . . I hope Lissa . . . will not think that I think she ever talked like the girl. . . . Of course Manga would not recognize

herself as a *sallow* old woman! . . . Fanny's putative Siamese father
. . . was the only thing in the book that made me laugh. Had Herrick
any humor he could have got a lot of laughs at my expense. Perhaps
you laughed at the book bag." "Well, enough of it," she wrote
philosophically to John. "It does leave a bad taste in the mouth
about the writer."[46]

Revived by her stay at Chandler, Parsons stopped off briefly at
Zuni. "I was delighted at last to have seen a kick-stick race," she
wrote Kroeber. "Do you remember one time at Zuñi when I went
around with you on a museum collecting trip, and among other
things you bought dance sticks held by the girls in the Thlahawe
ceremony, the people parting with them because, as they said, they
would never have that dance again? They held the Thlahawe this
summer and Margaret Lewis wrote it was most impressive, she had
never seen so much ceremony in one show." "I ran into Mrs. William Denman the other day and she told me about the Thlahewe
revival," Kroeber replied. "It quite stirred me up. It is the sort of
thing I should like to see if I did not have to be noting down all the
details."[47]

Real *Indians at Last: The Huichol of Tepic*

Before she left Vicam, Parsons offered Beals funding for further
fieldwork after his fellowship expired. A Mixe leader from the
mountainous region northeast of Mitla had asked her to extend her
study to his village. Fieldwork in this area required arduous travel
by horseback and on foot, and intrepid as Parsons was, she felt it
was a task for someone younger. "I would meet you at Tepic towards the end of November, you going on somewhat earlier . . . if
you wish to stop off among the Yaqui," she wrote in May 1932.
"You might even try to get into the mountain Yaqui country direct
from the border, without going through the military rigmarole. . . .
I really think you would be just as well off from a dietary point of
view in the mountains as on the railroad. . . . Then from Tepic to
Mexico City . . . Thence to Oaxaca, Mitla and you on to the Mijes.
Expenses and whatever stipend you consider proper."[48]

Parsons set off to meet Beals in Tepic early in November 1932.
Mabel and Tony Luhan had visited the area the previous year. "I
am leaving for Tepic," she wrote Mabel, "to try and see some of
that ritual Tony showed us in his film, then on to Mitla." "I am
glad you are publishing your Memoirs now," she added, "for I

don't see why you should leave the fun of it to your ghost." Two weeks later, she wrote from Tepic: "You said I would enjoy it and I have been doing so for ten days. Perfect weather, sun and clean air. . . . Church, plaza, hills, river—I think it is by far the prettiest town of the Republica." Tepic was "like coming upon a small forgotten pool left of a sea long since receded," Anita Brenner wrote in her Mexican guidebook that year. "The houses are full of what the galleons from Manila and the Philippines used to bring, and the fragile, priceless Chinese objects of art are owned by people unaware that time has made museum pieces of their possessions and indeed a museum of the whole town. . . . the barefoot sierra Indians slip indifferently through the streets and seem almost to erase and flatten out the walls, giving the Conquest and the centuries of white domination a queer unreality and the sense of a slight, nearly pointless incident now half forgotten."[49]

Here there are "*real* Indians, more so than the Yaqui," Parsons wrote Mabel. "Between them and the Pueblos we have already formed a good many links." "You would have liked these Indians," Beals wrote Dorothy. "The Huichol are alert, slightly amused at the attention they attract but otherwise indifferent to it. Our informant—native woven white trousers, the shirt open at the sides from armhole down, a little cotton apron fore and aft, obvious remnant of the old dress, wide brimmed, low crowned straw hat, a cross of red flannel on the top of the crown & four others on the brim, all stuck full of flowers, dabs of red paint on each cheek, coils of elaborate beads about his neck . . . beautifully woven bags hanging from strings about his neck, an elaborate sash (also hat & waist band, the woven-in designs resembling much Peruvian designs), and a string of little pouches about the hips, hair long & in a knot on back of the head, trousers rolled to the knees, thin dark muscular legs and light sandals—a piece of hide with thongs to hold it on—quite a gaudy figure as the various woven goods except shirt and pants are with designs in red and blue."[50]

Beals and Parsons had contacted their colorful informant in a *mesón*—a traditional inn with a communal kitchen. With the help of the innkeeper, they established friendly relations with Cora and Huichol traders who had traveled in groups for six or more days from their villages. At first Beals and Parsons visited in the evening, because the traders were doing business during the day; but later, when they had won the travelers' confidence, they worked with informants during the day while other members of the group did the trading.

Beals was impressed by Parsons's skill in establishing rapport with their informants. She was extraordinarily confident, Beals remembers, with no qualms about tackling anything in her poor Spanish. Sometimes the evening sessions became group affairs, he wrote in 1978, "almost a seminar with everyone crowding around and adding to the conversation." Beals himself had been singularly unsuccessful in his previous fieldwork. Recalling his first experiences fifty years later, he described Kroeber asking him what fieldwork he planned for the summer: "As the idea had not occurred to me, I fumbled for an answer until he remarked that the Nisenan (Southern Maidu) needed further study. . . . I was told to read what I could find . . . given some suggestions about keeping field notes in permanent bound notebooks, preferably with indelible pencil, told that there were Nisenan around Auburn and Colfax in the Sierra Nevada, and given the name of Billy Joe, who had once spent some weeks in Berkeley as a linguistic informant." Billy Joe turned out to be "an ethnographer's dream" who knew what anthropologists wanted; and Beals spent the summer taking down his dictation in the relative comfort of the ceremonial Round House.[51]

When Beals went to Mexico in 1930, he found conditions very different. This was no longer salvage anthropology, but work with a living culture: "People would not take time from their concerns with making a living and meeting the obligations of office and of ritual to spend long periods of time answering systematic but boring questions. Observations, often fragmentary and disconnected, friendships allowing one to visit and chat at odd hours, casual conversations, often with strangers, produced a much more fragmented and chaotic body of data, so that increasingly time had to be spent organizing and collating field notes, identifying lacunae, and devising methods of filling them. Analysis in the field became more important. The number of persons involved was many times greater, and many more communities had to be examined and compared. Where the Nisenan had been numbered in dozens, the Yaqui and Mayo were in the thousands. The problems of access and permissions even to enter some territories became important. Social structures proved much more complex than expected, and sometimes near fatal errors in judgment came from premature actions taken in ignorance." Beals recalled that Fay-Cooper Cole advised Robert Redfield to use a high-quality monograph such as Ronald Dixon's *The Maidu* as a model for his Mexican work. "When I got to Tepotzlán," Redfield told Beals, "I found I might just as well have read the Chicago Telephone Directory."[52]

Working with Parsons, Beals learned how to do fieldwork in an ongoing culture. In Tepic she demonstrated the secret of her success, which she learned from her early folklore expeditions and then applied in the Southwest pueblos—her standard technique of stimulating an entertaining exchange of information. "Elsie had brought a rare book by T. Preuss on the rituals of the Cora published in the last century," Beals wrote Peter Hare. "It had many fine illustrations of ritual objects and altars and shrines. These fascinated Cora and Huichol alike . . . and they always crowded around to look at the pictures, identifying objects, explaining how they are made, by whom, and for what they were used." "One gratifying verification for Elsie," he added, "was that the ritual arrows described and illustrated by Preuss were really prayer sticks such as are used by the Pueblo, made in the same way and used for the same purposes." "Another technique," Beals went on, "was to start her inquiries by posing some hypothetical situation and saying that in my pueblo—a vaguely presented synthetic entity drawn from the several pueblos in which Elsie had worked—under this situation my people do this or that, what do your people do? This always aroused interest and often the initial response would be to ask for more details of what went on in Elsie's village, but eventually they also told her what they did in their own village. And for good measure they might add in what they had seen or heard was a variant way of doing things in some other village." Summing up Parsons's approach, Beals pointed out that she tried to imagine every life situation and ask how it was dealt with: "not only the obvious life crises of birth, marriage, sickness and death but all the other problems of life. How do you know when to plant; how do you do it; do you say prayers, to whom, when and how. The stress always was upon the view that these are common problems we face and how can they best be dealt with." "She was particularly interested in ritual and the supernatural," Beals recalled. "Despite the difficulty of these areas she elicited a surprising amount of material in such a short time." "She did get enthusiasm," he concluded, "often with lively group sessions. One group I recall, delayed their departure for a half day so that we could conclude a session started the night before."[53]

Beals and Parsons were excited by what they learned in their "converaciones." The Cora and Huicholes were, as they had suspected, an important link between the Indians of southwest Mexico and the Pueblos of the American Southwest. As Beals wrote Dorothy after he and Parsons left Tepic, "The Cora *are a Pueblo people,* in all probability, but with much closer affiliations with Mexico (Aztec) and of course with the variation one would expect to find 1500 miles away. The remarkable thing is the closeness of the similarity, particularly in many of the fundamental ideas. Kivas, snake dance (this was a great find), ground altar, sand painting, the cult based in rain (we knew that), meal offerings, basically similar cosmogony and cosmology—Sun, earth—corn—moon—'Our Mother'—morning star war spirit, keeping heads of enemies (instead of scalps) . . . and offering them corn meal and prayer sticks for rain. . . . On the Mexican side Huicholes anoint with blood of animals killed for fiestas, four corn ears (cf. blood of Aztec sacrifices rubbed on idols of Sun, rain and corn deities!)." "I must confess a wild desire to do Cora and Huichol," the homesick Beals ended, "but not until you will go with me."[54]

Parsons was equally pleased. "My trip to Tepic was well worth while," she wrote Boas. "At last, real Indians, in psychology and culture! *And* they link up with the Pueblos in most interesting ways. The political organ. is just the same—including a lifelong war chief & assistant and lifelong *principales.* The cantadores cure by brushing with eagle feathers, by sucking, & by blowing. Another class of curanderos find the rag doll used to bewitch. (Undoubtedly this is derived from the *mono de cera* all the Mexicans thereabouts talk of.) The Gobernador has all his field work done for him; a cow from the communal herd is killed for church festivals, a deer for the *mitotes* of which the major are at New Year's for the Sun, before planting, after harvest. There is a June pilgrimage to a sacred mt. for rain & prayer-sticks are deposited. As Preuss says, the masks are impersonations of rain spirits, probably the dead." "Preuss' pictures were a great opening," she went on, "sticks for war, made by the war chief, for Morning Star, for Earth Mother, for Sun, for the Dead. There is a snake hunt, 5 turns to the East, & a dance by two groups carrying snakes around the altar; the snakes are released in the graveyard. The ceremonial house is used very much like a kiva; & in it is a ground altar of prayer-sticks & corn ears. Heads were taken & kept in a cave, the war chief making prayer-sticks for them, & they were or are prayed to for rain. Five days after they were brought in they were given corn meal. Five days after death the cantadore performs ritual, 5 miniature tortillas being given to the dead. Prayer-sticks for the family dead at All Souls." "I do wish we could think out a plan for publishing the remaining 3 vols.," she concluded, "following up the publication by systematic field work by some one who knows our Southwest cultures."[55]

Parsons and Beals left Tepic in the middle of December 1932, taking the spectacular train ride to Guadalajara, the train "winding and unwinding itself, worming and piercing the great inaccessible chaos of the Sierra." "Forgive the Southern Pacific its carelessness of your utter comfort," Anita Brenner asked her tourists, "for this magnificent bridging of America's formidable backbone." Parsons decided that Guadalajara was "unrewarding ethnologically" and they bumped their way to Lake Chapala, twenty miles to the south. There they settled into the inn, where Beals's room looked out across an arm of the lake to a tree-embowered house where D. H. Lawrence had stayed a few years before. "I have never been in such an enchanting place in my life," Beals wrote Dorothy. "If I had to pick just one place to go with you I'd certainly pick this."[56]

But Parsons did not go to Chapala merely for the scenery and to hear scurrilous gossip about Lawrence. She had learned that an interesting version of La Conquista was danced in the villages around the lake on Guadalupe Day. The two set off by boat to Ajijic, where they enjoyed being almost the only spectators at a performance that was done solely for the participants' pleasure. Parsons found the pueblocitos "unattractive, as squalid as Spanish towns." "They must have been settled by Spanish fishermen," she decided, "and god knows what became of the Zacateca population."[57]

Getting to Mexico City from Chapala proved to be something of an ordeal. "Yesterday we took a launch for two hours, walked half a mile, took an auto, and eventually wound up on the train to Mexico," Beals wrote Dorothy. "And what a train ride! Only the ropes put there for the purpose kept me from being precipitated from my upper berth." They settled into the luxury of the San Angel Inn and were soon caught up in a whirl of activities orchestrated by Frances Toor, Moisés Sáenz, and their colleagues at the education ministry. Beals (and perhaps Parsons) visited Gamio, who was in town, though still "one of the 'outs.'" Parsons took Beals to meet Zelia Nuttall in her beautiful old house and garden; and they dined with an embassy secretary so Parsons could "extract the inside dope about Mexico's withdrawal from the League of Nations." But by

Christmas, Beals was in hospital, recovering from the removal of a cyst in his groin. Parsons remarked that he "might just as well have had a baby—and nothing to show for it." But she saw to his welfare in every way, writing to reassure Dorothy, keeping him supplied with cigarettes and gossip, and paying the bill when it was over.[58]

A Violent Intellectual Crisis

To stave off boredom during his convalescence, Parsons encouraged Beals to begin a joint paper comparing the Yaqui, Mayo, and Pueblo clowns, continuing on paper their year-long conversation. Parsons began work with Beals in 1931 convinced that much of Pueblo ceremonial was acculturated Spanish—new wine in old bottles, as she often put it—and Beals, with his knowledge of Mexican history, was inclined to argue for the persistence of an aboriginal culture that extended from the Pueblos to Guatemala. In December 1932, he wrote Kroeber gleefully from Tepic: "Elsie is in the midst of a violent intellectual crisis brought on by reading Fanny Bandelier's translation of Sahagún. From her former position of believing the Pueblos largely Spanish, she is meditating a paper to prove the fundamental similarity of Pueblo and Aztec ceremonial. . . . In fact . . . she is inclined to be more anti-Spanish in her interpretations than I am." But Beals was also changing his position. "The Yaqui pascolas mask may also be from the *abuelo* [the Spanish "grandfather" clowns]," he wrote Dorothy, "although I have not even been willing to consider that until lately." And after observing the rituals at Lake Chapala, he admitted years later, "Elsie was beginning to make her point that a lot of contemporary 'Indian' was really warmed over Spanish or synchretized Spanish." "It's rather interesting how close the parallels are," Beals wrote Dorothy as he embarked on his half of their paper.[59]

"We think there is little if any doubt that between some of the so-called Grandfather or Abuelo clowns of the Pueblos, the Chapios, and the Chapaiyekas and Abuelos of Sonora there is an historical connection," Parsons and Beals agreed in "The Sacred Clowns of the Pueblo and the Mayo-Yaqui Indians." "In evidence are the association in New Mexico with the Matachina dance, the type of mask, the whip, and the association with Church fiestas." The Matachina, they argued, was probably the same dance that is called La Conquista and Los Moros elsewhere in Mexico—a European country dance introduced by the friars with varying degrees of dramatization and with or without colloquies according to the degree of hispanicization of the people they were dealing with. "Probably Mexican colonists around San Juan introduced the beclowned Matachina which spread to Taos and to some of the southern pueblos," they concluded. In all of these dances two masked clowns appear, carrying a whip; and like the dancers they play their parts for a vow, often made for sickness. "But were they all Spanish and introduced along with the country dance and the church fiesta?" Here Parsons and Beals agreed to differ. Parsons was inclined, at this stage, to argue that the Mexican and New Mexican clowns were derived from the devil clown of the European medieval miracle play and religious folk dances. Introduced by Spanish friars, they were easily accepted by the Indian population, who were sensitive to ridicule and gossip and familiar with the use of travesty to stimulate bravery in war or potency in domestic and political life. Beals, on the other hand, thought that the Yaqui and Mayo clowns were survivals of an aboriginal institution that the friars found easier to adapt than suppress.[60]

"I have read the joint paper by yourself and Ralph Beals with much interest," Robert Lowie wrote Parsons when they submitted it to the *Anthropologist.* "I cannot decide in favor of either one of you. . . . There are one or two specific features in European peasant ceremonial which are certainly startling. Haberlandt showed me a lightning frame from Austria at the Volksmuseum at Vienna that certainly resembled the Pueblo equivalent, and some of the Austrian peasant masks have at least a generic resemblance to Iroquois masks. Personally, I have a haunting sense of similarity between your Pueblo whippers' cowering children and the Austrian impersonators of a saint who appeared early in December. I . . . remember one episode where one of the maids disguised herself in this fashion and intimidated us children."[61]

Parsons's 1933 article "Aztec and Pueblo Parallels" indicated that she continued to revise drastically her views about Spanish influence. During her final visit to Mitla that spring, she carefully reread Fanny Bandelier's new translation of Sahagún's *History of Ancient Mexico*—the book that had begun her "intellectual crisis" the previous December. As Parsons tells us in the preface to *Mitla,* she found answers to many of her questions "no further afield than my own library, in a closer acquaintance with the patient friar to whom all students of the early cultures owe so much, Father Bernardino de Sahagún, first of American anthropologists." "In rereading Sahagún's History of Ancient Mexico," she wrote in "Aztec and Pueblo Parallels," "I have been struck by the number of parallels between Aztec and Pueblo cultures, some of which, as far as I know, have never been pointed out." Parsons went on to detail an extraordinary number of ways in which Aztec and Pueblo ceremonial were similar: impersonation of the gods, the use of masks by dance impersonators, the association of rain gods with the directions, with mountaintops, and with curing, curing by sucking or brushing, views of the afterlife, the concept of the drowned becoming rain or water spirits, war ritual concerning heads or scalps, fasting and continence, methods of exorcism, offering, and confession, road-guarding by snakes, the use of sacred canes, prayer sticks. As she concluded, "we get a general impression of Aztec ritual, blood sacrifice always apart, and I may add rites of intoxication, as strikingly similar to Pueblo ritual. Even when details vary, their general character remains the same, highly conventionalized and without patent explanation."[62]

The most surprising parallel for Parsons—because she had considered it so Spanish—was the similarity between the Zuni *shalako* and the Aztec twelfth-month ceremony. The Spanish made an impact where they were able to stimulate, or substitute for, aspects of ceremonial or communal organization that were already present, she concluded. Spanish use of masks stimulated the efflorescence of a preexisting Pueblo mask. The Spanish combined their system of town government with the Aztec system of communal service in a manner that still prevails in Mexico's smaller towns and among the Pueblos. And the Aztec institution of ceremonial sponsor folded smoothly into that of the Spanish godfather and godmother, the two combining in "one of the most interesting of all the expressions of acculturation in the social organization of hispanicized Indians."[63]

Parsons's fieldwork with Beals, and their long conversations about historical processes of acculturation in Mexico and the American Southwest, allowed her to work out the intellectual quandaries that had brought her to Mexico in 1929. Her long chapter in *Mitla*, "Indian or Spanish?" is the fruit of this process. "It seems clear to me," she concluded, "that among the hispanicized Zapoteca native modes of behavior which included language, forms of daily intercourse, habits of daily living, and ritual habits together with the emotions and some of the beliefs which have been integrated with these habits have outlasted everything else"—particularly for women. The important question—as it always was for Parsons—

was how these processes of adaptation, substitution, and resistance take place. Voluntary changes occur only when a new custom or belief is compatible with existing habits and emotions, she concluded after an exhaustive review of the evidence from Mitla. Forced changes are altered to fit, and whole complexes are adopted only when they can be fitted into an old form of behavior and are compatible with existing emotional attitudes. Parsons's study of Mitla confirmed, in other words, what she had observed of her own society for many years—that personal habits and emotional attitudes are obdurate and always the most resistant to change.[64]

PART FOUR

All Serene

Elsie at the wheel of her schooner, *Malabar V*, 1930s.
Gift to author from Mac Parsons.

CHAPTER FIFTEEN

Elsie's Lifework—*Con Amore*

DURING Parsons's final visit to Mitla in the 1933 spring, with the intricate patterns of Indian and Spanish cultural threads worked out to her satisfaction, she was able to concentrate on the sort of work she loved best—capturing the flavor of contemporary Mitla life. Allowing herself to be reabsorbed into "this vivid but very objective Mexico where the rest of your life falls away from you so completely," she moved decisively from being a diffusionist to being a modernist. "Just now I am describing it in some thing like what at college we called daily themes," she wrote John. A few weeks later she was engrossed in what had become her chapter on town gossip: it was getting quite novel-like, she wrote, "full of murder and intrigue and could not be published if there were a Mexican libel law or pueblo folk read books." From Mitla she wrote to George Young, who replied with amusement: "You seem to have been enjoying Mexico in your own way—which is the only way of enjoying anything. You were, I remember, one of those travellers that delighted in discomfort." "Yes—I would make good copy out of you," he concluded, no doubt referring to Herrick's book, "if I weren't a British Baronet."[1]

Parsons found much changed in Mitla after her two years' absence. Eligio had become *catrín* (citified), wearing a homburg instead of his broad-brimmed black felt hat, his shirt tucked in, rather than tied in front, and his trousers held up by a leather belt. He was also chewing gum. He was pleased to report that many changes had taken place since Parsons's last visit. A federal school had been established; the school children had made a garden in front of the town hall; a stage had been erected in the plaza; basketball was all the rage; and a plebiscite had been held to elect the town president at the direction of the state governor, who had also banned *mayordomías*. "*Ya es moderno,* now it is modern," Eligio told Parsons approvingly—"no more costly *mayordomías,* no more costly weddings. That is all over. Religion has died in Vera Cruz. Religion will die here. Calles is dictator and Calles is against the church. *Ya es moderno!*"[2]

But it was not as simple as that. The *mayordomía* of San Pablo still took place; the wax for the candles was weighed, still supervised by the alcaldes; the band played; the musicians were feasted; and the procession took place, although there were irregularities of procedure to keep within the letter of the law. Parsons found that the new *presidente* had added a basketball match to the festivities. "Regulation basket-ball," Parsons noted, "but in a Mitleyeno setting." The teams were escorted by the town band and the town officials; and they were accompanied by godmothers—*madrinas de listones,* godmothers of ribbons—who wore bandoleer-fashion the ribbons they bestowed on the winners. The band played through the game, and the players were given ritualistic drinks at the end. "A pretty piece of acculturation," Parsons concluded, "this game from the north which has swept the Republic: the first competitive game to be played in Mitla, with godmothers dressed as mestizas and behaving as Indians, with the town officials presiding and dispensing the quasi-ritualistic drink, with music and procession!"[3]

In the winter of 1933, Parsons returned to Lake Chapala to write, to the inn that had so delighted Beals the year before. Parsons herself appreciated "the rich brown hills, the clean little beach, the beauties of sunset and moonlight, delightful weather." "Are you planning a trip away?" she wrote Mabel Dodge Luhan in December 1933. "If you enjoyed swimming as I do I would suggest coming here. I see you in one of the little villas along the shore, making a home in your marvelous way. . . . I am occupying Witter Bynner's 'little house,' i.e. a corner bedroom in the lakeside hotel, with a balcony over the beach. After two weeks in a luxurious New York apartment it seems like paradise, a noisy one of course." "My season in Chapala, Jalisco, was quite pleasant," she wrote Kroeber on her return in May 1934, "and I finished my Mitla book."[4]

When Kroeber read the manuscript, he urged her to seek a commercial publisher, despite its bulk. "The material is fine, the writing plastic, and . . . you have ventured farther into both psychologizing and reconstruction than in the past. . . . I am confident you have the makings of a book. . . . Your last chapter in particular strikes me as having the general readability of Redfield's book besides penetrating considerably deeper into some problems. It seems a pity to bury work of this sort in a professional journal or technical monograph where only a few dozen people see it instead of the several thousands that a book might reach." The question was satisfactorily resolved at the anthropology meetings in December when Robert Redfield heard Parsons's paper on Mitla, and wanted to publish the book in his University of Chicago series. The Mitla manuscript was "extraordinarily interesting," he wrote her in March 1935. "It is certainly the fullest account we possess of a contemporary Latin-American people."[5]

A Modernist Text

Mitla: Town of the Souls is a modernist tour de force. Parsons uses the framework she established in her first full-scale description of a community—that of Jemez in New Mexico in 1925. The first chapter sets the scene, placing the town in its geographic and historical setting. Chapters on economic life, family and personal life, including town gossip, town government, ceremonial life, ritual, and folklore follow, then a comparative chapter on migrations and neighboring communities. But in *Mitla,* Parsons transforms this standard ethnographic framework into something quite different. The first chapter places us vividly in Mitla with Parsons, immediately aware of the various cultural strands—Zapotecan, Aztec, Spanish, and American—that have formed the community; and it introduces us into the lives of the people who will interpret it to us: the elderly Urbano, who can remember battles between the barrios that have now almost disappeared; Victor Olivera, the town president, in defiance of Mitleyeno custom, for the second time in succession—an Indian whose wife dresses *ranchera* and whose daughter is married to the son of the *hacendado,* a wealthy feudal overlord who is destined to be shot—and most important, the Quero family, who provide comfort, friendship, and information in equal quantities. The chapters on the economic, family, political, and religious life of Mitla show Parsons piecing its complex threads together like a detective as she participates in its daily rounds, never pretending to be anything but a curious visitor, but nevertheless one who is willing to be part of what she sees.

But it is Parsons's ninety-two-page chapter "Town Gossip" that moves *Mitla* beyond the standard ethnographic monograph: "In any systematic town survey much detail is necessarily omitted and life appears more standardized than it really is," she notes; "there is no place for contradictions or exceptions or minor variations; the classifications more or less preclude pictures of people living and functioning together." "In my last visit to Mitla I spent a good deal of time visiting and gossiping," she tells us, "and I would recall these scenes, as well as a few from earlier years, in order to convey personal aspects of the townspeople and some of the variability in their lives. We shall meet a family living in San Salvador, the barrio of *los tontos* [Redfield's term for 'the ignorant' or 'the traditional'], a family that is far from being *tonto,* and, in *El Centro,* in touch with its most sophisticated elements, a family that holds beliefs out of the distant past and eats off the floor. Described as a somewhat idle class, as individuals women will be seen doing all the work of the family. A folk tale will be told as by an Indian, but ending with a plea for praise no Indian would make; and we shall hear an old man speaking little or no Spanish telling Spanish folk tales and a young man speaking Spanish telling the most characteristically In-dian tales of all. The spinner who believes in the ancient goddess of weaving will be seen producing a garment that would suit the taste of only a *catrín,* perhaps a chauffeur from the city. We shall hear of a murder prompted by a kinswoman and unavenged by a kinsman, a twofold situation which would be most unlikely to occur in a community either *puro indio* or *puro Castellano.*"

"We will meet," Parsons promises, *"rancheros, Españoles,* who have become *indio,* and Indians who have become Castellanos, or mestizos; and there will be opportunities to note, in many particu-lars, some of them trifling and yet significant, the differences in attitude and opinion between the Indian and the mestizo or near mestizo; and the ways in which the Indian begins to go *catrín,* how he changes his dress, becomes a little ashamed of the *costumbres* and therefore close-mouthed about them, and takes on a more self-assertive disposition, reacting violently to emotional situations which as an Indian he would have avoided, and becoming critical of the system of communal service and of the exacting festivities of wedding or *mayordomía.*" "From these impressions will be im-parted," Parsons hopes, "some appreciation of the disposition of the townspeople, what they laugh at, what they are willing to talk about, and what they keep to themselves; what interests or gratifies them; the kind of behavior they condemn, the kind they commend or are indifferent about; how they feel about customs they know are lapsing"—in other words, "their manners and conventionali-ties," those almost instinctual behaviors she had been observing since she began watching her mother as a child.[6]

Incorporating many layers of voices, Parsons carefully and apparently effortlessly builds a picture of a culture that is constantly in process. The historical voices of Sahagún and Burgoa remind us that the Mitleyanos have been doing some of the things she observes at least since the Spanish conquest. The wide-ranging footnotes help us to see the panorama of settlement and resettlement, mingling aboriginal and European elements in varying ways; and they convey the diverse political and academic arguments that swirl around the meaning of race and culture in such a small, seemingly unimportant town. The older women, the *curanderas,* "God's spokesmen," and the *serranos* give us a picture of Mitla as it might have been in a previous generation, while the younger men, particularly Eligio, are voices of the future. The visitors, including Parsons herself, the Spanish outsiders, such as the padre and his sisters, and those half in and half out, such as Angélica, represent the diverse outside forces slowly stirring change. Like participants in a courtly dance, the people of Mitla seem to move through their days and years according to a timeless calendar, but Parsons makes us aware of the constant modifications of the steps in this dance, and the processes by which choices are made and not made—why this custom is rejected, that one accepted, another so completely assimilated to a previous form that its origin is virtually indistinguishable.

Parsons makes us aware of the individuality of each of the townspeople of Mitla. They are never "Indians": they are always Isadora, Remedio, Petronila, Eligio. And she herself does not try to *be* a Mitleyano, except to the extent that any immigrant or visitor wants to be accepted and included in the town's life. She is always herself, an individual with her own interests, needs, ideas, and beliefs, intervening in the lives of the people she meets, and ready to take responsibility for her actions. This is the source of *Mitla*'s verisimilitude and liveliness: Parsons is never just an observer, and the Mitleyanos are never mere curiosities whose customs are being noted. What we see is always an interaction. People may be amused, irritated, embarrassed, pleased, curious; but they are never puppets or objects.

The story Parsons constructs has no beginning and no end. The characters appear on stage fully formed, and they leave it to go on to unknown and uncertain futures. As in any modernist text, the reader has to do much of the work of constructing narrative and character. Parsons merely reports what she sees and does: it is up to us to do what we want with the material. All she is doing is

348 / All Serene

reporting town gossip, and we never find out whether Lorenza had her brother murdered, or if Eligio was really guilty of seduction, or who shot at Manuel Quero, and if it was a jealous husband. Nor do we know Eligio is married with an eight-month-old son until we turn to the genealogy at the back of the book. And Parsons draws few morals, except the modernist ones of tolerance and pragmatism.[7]

Science, Art, and Propaganda

When *Mitla* was published in September 1936, it was acclaimed by scholarly and general readers alike. "Naturally I turned first of all to the last chapter 'Indian or Spanish,' " Boas wrote Parsons immediately after he had received the book. "I think you have presented the whole problem of the process of assimilation admirably and if we had any sense, our ultraconservatives and ultraradicals might learn a lot from it. The former might see that under changed conditions change is unavoidable; the latter that an ideal cannot be imposed unless it fits in in many ways with the old scheme of life." Now retired and more openly propagandist, Boas expanded on this in his review in the *New Republic*. The book should be widely read because of its direct bearing on fundamental social and political questions, he wrote. "It shows that the attempt to remodel social life according to new dogmas or theories and to do away completely with the old is an impossible task, for the fundamental cultural attitudes can only be changed by very slow and laborious processes. It is equally instructive for the conservative who believes in the permanence of institutions, for it shows how easily the contents of culture are modified, and that under the pressure of outer and inner conditions they will yield no matter how strong the resistance may be—an observation that it will be well for us to take to heart."[8]

The reviewer in the *Christian Science Monitor* liked the book's "Main Street" approach, while the *Sun* considered it an "ethnological study of the first order." In the *Survey Graphic,* Gladys Reichard explained that "The author of *Mitla* is a sociologist by training and a seasoned anthropologist by conviction. Her research and field experience have convinced her that motives, attitudes, and forms of behavior may be largely explained by history and she believes that any attempt at social control should proceed from an awareness of all available historical data." "Her summary of the factors making for acculturation and of those resisting it is required reading for the sociologist," she concluded. In the *Barnard College Alumnae*, Reichard characterized the book as calm, factual, dryly humorous, and profoundly interesting. "The reader may stagger a bit in the first part of the mosaic," she warned, "but . . . will delight in the final chapters. . . . This is the kind of documented book which a layman feels *must* be relied upon."[9]

"How very kind of you it was to remember your little Chapala playmates!" poet Arthur Ficke wrote. "Sometimes I think that ethnologists, surgeons and alienists must be the only happy educated persons; for they confront, as scientific facts, the horrors of man's group-idiocies, his physical defects, his mental defects. . . . I quite honestly feel that all the world is insane except for . . . the people who combine a scientific approach to facts with a generous attitude toward persons. The horrid abysses of the religious mind and of the business mind frighten me to death. Well, I don't think that either one of those abysses will ever get you, *Doctora!*" On the envelope Ficke added, "Your chapters IX, X, are a great work of art—surprising in a book of science."[10]

Mitla appeared in the midst of a raging disciplinary argument about the legitimacy of acculturation studies. In 1935, the Social Science Research Council Committee on Personality and Culture marked the importance of this "new" field by setting up the Special Committee on Acculturation. Its members, Robert Redfield, Melville Herskovits, and Ralph Linton, were asked to examine research, "formulate an outline of promising frontiers of inquiry," and list "immediately feasible research problems needed to fill gaps and to advance frontiers." Their findings were published in the *American Anthropologist* early in 1936; and in 1938, Herskovits published a book-length consideration of the field in which he surveyed its history and reviewed several important studies, led off by *Mitla*.[11]

The implications for anthropology of a plethora of acculturation studies were raised by *Anthropologist* editor Leslie Spier in a letter to Parsons in November 1935, asking her to review Redfield and Villa's *Chan Kom*. "My question is whether acculturation studies belong properly to the field of anthropology at all. . . . In my view we had better stick to our own field, traditionally limited to preliterate peoples, else we will find that what few jobs and what little money we have for work is going to be expended on things that had better be left to the sociologists who will look after the field anyway." "This is really a practical matter," he explained. "I can see the *Anthropologist* being swamped with acculturation studies, leaving no room for strictly anthropological articles. What I would like to have is some expression of opinion, in print, to serve as a guide. I may get up at the Andover meeting and ask for the opinions of all who have them." Spier did bring the matter up at the anthropology meetings in December 1936. The meetings confirmed that acculturation did indeed have a place in anthropology, and the pages of the *Anthropologist* over the next few years attest to its enormous vogue.[12]

Parsons was never interested in labels, or in championing any methodological orthodoxy, and she declined Spier's request. But *Mitla* provided grist for those of her followers who were more inclined to enter the fray. In a review in *Annals of the American Academy of Political and Social Science,* Herskovits praised *Mitla* for its bold and comprehensive approach to "the most baffling and most intriguing problem of contemporary ethnology." "Current controversies as to whether or not acculturation should be studied in terms of traits or of psychological reactions to the total situation are ignored," he notes; "but there is such a mobilizing of cultural elements with reference to their provenience, and, despite a modest disclaimer of psychological competence, so telling an analysis of the mixture of motivations that underlie the objective manifestations of the culture, that the dispute becomes pointless."[13]

Serenity

With the writing of *Mitla* out of the way, Parsons spent the summer of 1934 as usual in Maine finishing the appendices of A. M. Stephen's *Hopi Journal* and keeping house for Herbert Jr.—"and for visiting grandsons." "All my young appear to be thriving," she wrote to Mabel Luhan. Lissa had remarried in June that year. Mac was in Germany, where he had been studying and traveling since graduating from Yale the previous year. Herbert was due to graduate from Harvard Medical School in 1935 and was applying for an internship in surgery at the Presbyterian Hospital, where his father had been a trustee. Ever active on behalf of the children's careers, Parsons wrote to two influential acquaintances for their support. "Herbert is his father over again in character and spirit," she wrote to hospital trustee William Williams, "particularly in devotion to what he has faith in. The faith is somewhat different, since young Herbert is scientifically, rather than legally, minded, but the capacity for self devotion is just the same."[14]

John on *Malabar V*, 1933. Parsons Family Papers, Rye Historical Society.

Herbert Jr., 1930. Parsons Family
Papers, Rye Historical Society.

Mac on *Malabar V*, 1933. Parsons Family papers, Rye Historical Society.

With the future of at least three of her children attended to, Parsons set out once more in the winter of 1934 for the peace of Chapala—this time to tackle the mammoth task of drawing together all the threads of her work on the Southwest. Carnival that year found her deep into her writing. "Last night the Carnival Queen and her party and brass band were about to leave the verandah below my window at 1 A.M. when the American poets from the other end of the beach arrived and whooped it up until 3 A.M. I learned that cotton can't keep out a brassband," she wrote John. Nevertheless she was cheerful. The postboy called her "Elissa Parson my friend," she swam every day, and she was getting on with her book. "All told I have eight vols. to see through the press during the next two years, which makes me feel like a slave."[15]

Perhaps Parsons had too much work and too little play that winter, because she arrived back in Harrison ill at the end of April 1935. She was now sixty years old, and she may have begun to feel the effects of the kidney disease that helped cause her sudden death six years later. Whatever the reason, she did not go abroad again until she made a tourist trip to Greece in 1938; and she made no more field trips until she visited Ecuador in 1940—and she insisted that she began that visit as a tourist. New York was more attractive in those years anyway. Mac, now aged twenty-four, was back from

Europe, and Parsons arranged for Ogden Reid to give him a job on the *Herald Tribune*. He also needed a home, so Parsons took over Lissa's apartment at 320 East Seventy-second, "an ugly, but comfortable place, with two very competent maids." Her old friends Betty Goodwin and Meredith Hare—married now for a number of years—lived in an apartment nearby at 340 East Seventy-second: "pretty as you might suppose," she told Mabel Luhan. "For the first time in about fifteen years I have wintered in New York, and for the first time in my life kept an apartment. A novel adventure, good and bad, made because of Mac. . . . Life with a journalist is novel, too." Lissa and her new husband, Jack Kennedy, had remodeled the farmhouse at Lenox and used the apartment for their occasional visits to New York. Parsons's summers were spent in Maine, where Herbert met his future wife, Margot Worrall, whom he married in 1936. In the fall, Parsons often visited Lissa in Lenox, and she was always welcome at the Harrison house where John and Fanny lived with their growing family.[16]

Parsons found to her surprise that New York life, shorn of the social obligations of politician husband and young children, was pleasant and compatible with sustained work. She had struggled throughout her life for a serenity that came from a balance of engrossing work and stimulating, but unforced, companionship. She found this in her summers in Maine, where the children's visits gave her enjoyable respites from the more mechanical tasks of tabulating and indexing she kept for that season. Now she discovered that this same uncluttered existence was possible in New York. During those relatively untroubled years, as she moved between New York, Maine, and Lenox, she made her gifts to anthropology, the two meticulously and generously edited volumes of the *Hopi Journal of Alexander M. Stephen,* published in 1936, and the two encyclopedic volumes of *Pueblo Indian Religion,* published in 1939. In the 2,692 pages of these books, the fruit of twenty-five years of collaborative work, she gave thanks to the mode of thought and the colleagues who saved her from despair and cynicism, and summed up the lessons for freedom and tolerance she discovered in anthropology.

A Hopi Treasure Trove

The *Hopi Journal of Alexander M. Stephen* was the fruit of the serenity Parsons found in her Maine summers. She had purchased Stephen's notebooks for $500 in 1923 from Stewart Culin of the

Brooklyn Museum, who had acquired them after Stephen's death in 1894. They were a veritable treasure trove. Stephen was an Edinburgh graduate who came to the United States in 1861. After service in the Civil War, he found his way to Keam's Canyon, Arizona, where he married a Navajo woman. Having learned his wife's language, he was an invaluable assistant and guide to Bureau of American Ethnology investigators between 1882 and 1894. The bulk of his notebooks dated from 1891 to 1894, when he systematically recorded the ceremonial and daily life of the Hopi on First Mesa. Some of his accounts had been published by the bureau; but their sexual and scatological content had been severely edited, as Parsons points out with disapproval in her preface.[17]

Parsons does not report how many pages of notebooks Stephen left; but her edited version fills over a thousand pages. The notebooks were written in pencil, but luckily for Parsons, few words were illegible, even when they were written in a kiva or in inclement weather; and, Leslie White added in his 1938 review, she was spared "the tortured labor of deciphering poorly written field notes, for Stephen wrote a good hand." They were also written under severe stress, because Stephen was dying, probably of tuberculosis. "His account of his 'cure' by Yellow Bear of the Poshwĭmkya doctors ranks with the fidelities of other scientific adventurers who kept their journal to the gallant end," writes the admiring Parsons.[18]

Parsons conceived the *Hopi Journal* as "primarily a biography of ceremonial, doing for the ceremonial round of the year what a day book would do for personal biography." Stephen's notebooks were invaluable for such a task. He was an insider who enjoyed access that "will never again be afforded," Parsons comments enviously. He lived in both Hopi and Tewa households. He could communicate with most of his neighbors in Navajo, and he was learning Hopi. The elders talked to him comparatively freely; he was initiated into three societies; and he had access to kiva life. The notebooks also recorded, less systematically, a great deal of material on the general culture, including perceptive observations on gender. Parsons illustrated the *Journal* with some of Stephen's hundreds of black and white and colored drawings and a dozen of his maps, including a Tewa horizon calendar.[19]

Parsons worked on the *Hopi Journal* each summer from 1927, when she finished her monograph on Tewa, until 1934. "Did I tell you that I was editing Stephen's Journal, patient work, but a thrilling record of the ceremonial life of thirty or forty years ago on First

Mesa," she wrote Lowie in November 1927, as she made her last visit to Hopi. "I am glad you are publishing your Hopi notes. . . . I am still editing the Stephen's Hopi Journal," she reported two years later from Maine. "Also my Lesser Antilles & Hayti French and English negro folklore (3–4 vols) Kiowa tales in proof; and Isleta monograph for the Bureau, Spanish folklore from Mexico. Busy enough. Besides the sailing life with the boys, which is very agreeable." By the end of summer 1931, she had finished editing the journal proper and had arranged with Boas to publish it in the Columbia anthropology series. During the 1934 summer she completed the appendices, and in February 1935 she was finishing the proofs and index at Chapala.[20]

Parsons's editorial contributions to the two volumes are substantial. She organizes the material as a ceremonial calendar, beginning with the December winter solstice ceremony and ending with the *wu'wuchim,* or initiation, ceremony in November. For each ceremonial she assembles the entries for each year, usually 1891 to 1893, but often including 1888 or 1894, and sometimes going back as far as 1885. She introduces each ceremonial with an essay setting out current understandings, describing Stephen's contribution, placing it in the context of other scholarship, and indicating areas for research. Stephen's notes are liberally footnoted by Parsons to provide clarification, commentary, and comparative information and references. A preface sets out the circumstances of Stephen's life and work, and an introduction provides an outline of Hopi history and culture, their relations with whites and other Indian peoples, their social and ceremonial organization, and the contribution of Stephen's work to the understanding of Hopi culture and society.

On top of these normal editorial tasks, which she carries out with her usual energy and precision, Parsons adds an encyclopedic series of appendices, a glossary, a bibliography, and a carefully detailed index that turn the volume into a comprehensive reference work for Hopi scholarship. These lovingly compiled "grains of sand" underline the fact that the *Hopi Journal* was Parsons's great offering to all those who shared her passion for careful and sympathetic observation of the world's diversity. Parsons's favorite appendix, and the one she considered the most important, is the "Who's Who" in which she provides thumbnail sketches of all the townspeople mentioned by Stephen and other observers through an index of references in the text. The Hopi social system is "far from being the automatic machine it almost inevitably appears from the way it has been hitherto described," she points out in her introduction; and she hoped that the "Who's Who" would stimulate Hopi biography. Robert Lowie found it immediately useful when he dipped into the *Hopi Journal* in January 1937: "Many thanks for the two fine volumes. . . . I began using your "Who's Who" . . . with very gratifying results. . . . I wonder whether systematic utilization of this record will not shed a good deal of light on these Pueblos as personalities." "I expect to use the Journal a great deal," he added; "you have put us all under great obligations. I am now eagerly looking forward to your Pueblo Religion."[21]

In his review of the *Hopi Journal* in 1938, her longtime collaborator Leslie White commented that "Dr. Parsons' contribution to this *Journal* in its published form has been tremendous, much greater, probably, than will be generally appreciated. . . . the enormous industry, patience and pains, and vast knowledge of the Southwest which she has lavished upon the *Journal* have contributed in large measure toward making it one of the most valuable and usable works in our entire literature on the Pueblos." It will, he attested, "remain a veritable treasure house as long as the study of Pueblo ethnology shall last," primarily because it provides, in conjunction with more recent studies, "a means for gauging the magnitude, velocity, and direction of culture change among the Hopi."[22]

Pueblo Indian Religion *and the Aryan Delusion*

Pueblo Indian Religion, Parsons's major preoccupation between 1934 and 1937, addresses precisely that question of "the magnitude, velocity, and direction of culture change"—or acculturation, as it was generally called by the mid-1930s—for all of the pueblos. Parsons began sustained work on the manuscript during the 1934–35 winter at Chapala. By the end of 1936, it was ready to send out for comments. "I worked all summer on Pueblo Indian religion and I am working on it now," she wrote Lowie in October. "The more I do the more there is to do, it sometimes seems. . . . Pretty soon I'll be having copies of manuscript in shape to send out for criticism and I am counting on you as a critic." By early 1937, it had been accepted by the University of Chicago Press. When series editor Redfield received the final manuscript in December 1937, he wrote Parsons that he was "more proud than ever" that they were publishing this "land mark of science."[23]

Pueblo Indian Religion was published in May 1939, just as the world was poised for the century's second great war. Three months later, on 1 September 1939, Germany invaded Poland and Britain, and France declared war on Germany. Hitler's military adventures were accompanied and justified by claims about the superiority of racially pure "Aryans," exemplified by the German "race," the need to return all Germans to the "Fatherland," and to assure them living space, if necessary by conquest and by removal of "inferior" races.

The harassment of Jews and book-burnings in service to the "Aryan" cause after Hitler rose to power in 1933 had mobilized American liberals. Franz Boas, feeling tired and old at seventy-four, nevertheless threw himself into the battle, the culmination of his lifelong struggle against the "Nordic nonsense." Determined to "prevent a similar state of mind developing in this country," he fought against the spread of anti-Semitic ideas and for the preservation of freedom of speech and belief. After his retirement in 1936, Boas devoted much time and energy to popularizing his work on race. As he wrote feelingly to Parsons soon after the outbreak of the Spanish Civil War in 1936, "Can a leopard ever change its spots? . . . I still feel the urge to act when my knowledge entitles me to represent my view. . . . I cannot keep out of the fight between individualism and the attempt to subjugate all reason to an emotionally fermented group consciousness. . . . It is at present an almost hopeless fight. . . . But all this is no reason to give up the fight and to supply at least ammunition to those who know best how to use it." "Papa Franz is getting smaller and more shrivelled every day," the more fatalistic Gladys Reichard wrote Parsons in 1939. "He is still doing too much to save a world which I doubt is worth saving, but he thinks it is and that is I suppose the important thing."[24]

In her pacifist writings between 1914 and 1917, Parsons had warned of the dangers of stimulating a false sense of nationalism in the service of particular class and ethnic interests—at that time those of the Anglo-American plutocracy who stood to benefit from American participation in the "European War." Her last piece of journalism before she submerged herself in the Southwest in 1918 was a biting indictment of the enthusiasm for "Americanization" that accompanied the promotion of nationalist sentiment. Using M. E. Ravage's account of his transformation into an "American," she pointed out that the end product was an individual—"not a Missourian, and not a New Yorker, East Side or West Side or Morningside, indeed not the product at all, thank God! of those Americanizers who would purify the newcomer of the dross of the Old

World and improve him by making him as much like themselves as can be."[25]

Twenty years later, Parsons again saw a world about to be convulsed by ethnonationalism—the aftermath, as she had predicted in 1917, of World War I. Her response was not to return to the popular "propaganda" she had left behind—at least temporarily—in 1918. Nor did she join Boas, Benedict, and Bunzel in their impassioned public opposition to fascism and anti-Semitism. As she wrote Lowie in 1938, commenting on the chapter on Boas in his recent *History of Anthropological Theory*, "You do not mention his ardor in combating the scientific fallacies which bolster up social injustices. This has been more marked, of course, in recent years but it was always there and is an essential part of his make-up. On a picture he gave me a year or two ago he wrote: 'Elsie Clews Parsons fellow in the struggle for freedom from prejudice.'" "I began that way and he ends that way," she concluded. "I suppose somewhere our trails crossed." "And now a repetition of the Great War to take one back," she wrote Kroeber on the eve of war in August 1939. "But I am wiser even if the world isn't, and expect less." "But no doubt I'll still feel outraged, on occasion," she added. "We'll pass over the war," Kroeber replied. "At least while we can. Last September, it upset me; but I had that behind me when she broke now. So far at any rate: I won't boast."[26]

Parsons instead poured her hatred of intolerance into her work. As Francis Hackett wrote her a month after Germany invaded his beloved Denmark in 1940, "I imagine you as reinforced in your conviction that war is a waste of human spirit and an avoidable evil if only one controls herd instinct and hatred." "I incline to believe there must be police," he ventured. Twenty years after she commended Ravage's "remarkable sketch . . . of contacts between diverse cultures," Parsons completed the task she had set herself that year—to use anthropology to uncover the processes of culture contact. Learned Hand had envied the certainty Parsons derived from her anthropological work at the end of 1918, when he himself was in despair about "the folly of man." In 1940, when she sent him *Pueblo Indian Religion*, he marveled again at her steadfastness of conviction and purpose. "That is Elsie's life-work," he ruminated in a strangely worded letter that sounded like a diary entry. "It is a job well-done, and it was done *con amore*. I think she took up anthropology because she was always disposed to look at folks from a little distance, anyway." "Why was she so disposed?" he asked himself. "Ah, that you never found out. Maybe you couldn't; probably she doesn't know. . . . People say it is because she doesn't care; but . . . it is more than that. But she's one of the most interesting people you know. It's a pity you have always been so much afraid of her."[27]

Encyclopedia and Guide

Pueblo Indian Religion is several books. Parsons's intention, when she outlined it to Wissler in 1918, was to prepare an encyclopedia of Pueblo culture. She also resolved that it would be a collective effort, partly to demonstrate how scientific work can and should be done, and partly to provide a model of how individual and collective interests could be harmonized. Faithful to her intention, Parsons incorporated in the volume's 1,275 pages nearly all the knowledge that she and other scholars of the Southwest had accumulated on ceremonial organization, the spirits, cosmic notions, ritual elements, the ceremonial calendars, the ceremonies, the towns, the history of the peoples of the region, and their contacts with and influence by foreigners, whether Aztec, Navajo, or white. Every description made of a ceremonial is included. Every town is described. The text is meticulously footnoted; there is an exhaustive bibliography; and the intricate network of cultural elements is broken down in a sixty-page index so that researchers can follow up any element with ease, whether it is acculturation (half a column), eagle feather (thirty-six mentions), or kachina (three columns). To emphasize even more that this was an ongoing project—still a work-in-progress despite its size—Parsons included an appendix listing research in progress and subjects still to be tackled. At this level, *Pueblo Indian Religion* is a comprehensive reference work, bringing together everything that had been done on the pueblos and organizing it for future researchers. "The reader who is not satisfied with bald outlines must do some work for himself," she warned in modernist fashion, "re-reading early chapters after he has read later ones, and reading with patience discursive reports of ceremonies that become lifeless in table or summary." "In the back of my own mind, salting the labor of description, has lain the theme of cultural change. . . . The problems, no doubt, will change or present themselves differently to others."[28]

At a second level, *Pueblo Indian Religion* is a regional study of the indigenous peoples of the American Southwest. "To assemble and compare our ceremonial data is my primary purpose," Parsons wrote in the preface. "After a visiting acquaintance of many years among all the Pueblos, as well as among other peoples who might contribute to a comparative point of view, I would try to draw the threads together, for myself and, I hope, for others, both for students of the Southwest and for students of cultural problems at large." "There are still too many gaps in our knowledge to write a general book," she argued: "certain pueblos have been barely described at all; only two of the four stock languages have been published, and language as a key to history has been completely ignored; there is little comparative study of handicrafts and arts, little comparative physical data, and studies of the individual in relation to culture are meager. Of Pueblo social organization we have learned but recently that there is a far wider range of variation than we had supposed, and variation in material culture or in social psychology may be expected. Pueblo archeology is still at loose ends."[29]

Despite this disclaimer and its precise title, *Pueblo Indian Religion* provides a breathtaking overview of the whole sweep of Pueblo history, with its migrations, feuds, alliances, its contacts, hostile and friendly, with neighbors, invaders, and traders, its adaptations, inventions, enthusiasms, and resistances. This is because Parsons saw Pueblo religion as "an instrument of life," as the means by which the Pueblos classified and interpreted their world. To Parsons, religion was "less antithesis to science than it is science gone astray," and an important means, therefore, of understanding habits of life and mind.[30]

These habits of life and mind are evoked in *Pueblo Indian Religion* through the accumulation and organization of vividly observed detail. As Parsons warned, the reader must do the work: "The trail must be followed, the details mastered, before generalizations can be properly enjoyed." Despite, or perhaps because of, its encyclopedic richness, the book has a wealth of generalizations; and as Parsons implies, the reader's appreciation of their acuity grows with familiarity with this or that element of ritual, the history of a town, the finer details of a ceremonial, the pattern of colors or the disposition of feathers on a prayer stick.[31]

At the same time, there is a calm center to *Pueblo Indian Religion* formed by Parsons's considered conclusions. These are not presented as truth, but as her understandings after two decades of careful observation and unhurried contemplation of the available data. Like the book's encyclopedic details, these conclusions are presented as a gift to the reader—a contribution to the conversation by someone with wide and deep experience of the phenomena under discussion. Different observers or historians see things in different ways, she emphasized at the beginning of her summary chapters, and they have different opportunities for observation. Cushing, she noted—"the poet and craftsman"—did not see the same facts at Zuni as the museum collectors who were there at the same time. Thirty years later, Kroeber devoted himself to studying aspects of Zuni life that had by then become more significant—language and social organization. "Cushing, Stevenson, and Kroeber—to these three would any culture look alike!" "Is Zuni ritual less intricate than Hopi," Parsons asked, "or is it merely that part of its complexity has not been recorded?" How much of the apparent difference between eastern and western pueblos results from the baffling inequality of conditions for inquiry between the two? And how much of the perceived similarity among the pueblos is due to the Pueblos' own blindness to their differences?[32]

Despite these qualifications, Parsons presented her conclusions with the authority of someone immersed in the data who has carefully and thoroughly sifted them through a discriminating intelligence. What is more, her conclusions concerned the questions she had long been asking: What keeps a culture alive and vital? How does a culture adapt smoothly to change? Why are some innovations accepted and others rejected? How can individuality be reconciled with social responsibility?

Many years before it was published, the project that culminated in *Pueblo Indian Religion* had helped to reorient anthropology. The work and stance it synthesized facilitated and influenced the intellectual direction and professional careers of Leslie Spier, Gladys Reichard, Ruth Bunzel, Leslie White, Ralph Beals, Morris Opler, Mischa Titiev, and more obliquely, Melville Herskovits, Ruth Benedict, and Esther Goldfrank. The published papers and monographs that systematically built up the book's pattern and argument had long before turned anthropologists' attention to questions of acculturation, to the use of historical records, to an interest in psychology and life histories, and to a self-consciousness about fieldwork and the "knowledge-gathering" process. When it was published, therefore, the long final chapters "Variations and Borrowing" and "Other Processes of Change" were Parsons's personal contributions to the discipline's cutting edge.

Parsons began a 200-page discussion of the processes of change with the thesis that "Borrowing from other groups . . . is a foremost factor in cultural variation." Among the Pueblos this process takes place between pueblos as well as from neighboring native cultures and from whites. Towns borrow from other towns through various forms of visits, through formal purchase or exchange of ceremonial, and, more fully and exactly, by marrying in or by immigration. But cultural contact does not necessarily mean borrowing, and change does not occur only through contact with other cultures. Parsons therefore devoted her most interesting, final, chapter to the processes of resistance, innovation, and acculturation—the fitting of a borrowed element into an existing organization in a way that often transforms it.[33]

"Resistance to taking over an alien trait or indifference to it is greatest when there is nothing resembling it in the culture of the potential borrower," she observed, "or when the new trait clashes with an existing trait or is incompatible with the spirit of the culture." There is less resistance to the adoption of one or two traits than to the adoption of a complex of traits that requires new organization. Several important features of Catholicism, for example, did not "take" among the Pueblos: the conception of a high god, the Jesus story, particularly the story of the Crucifixion with the dogma of redemption, and concepts of hell and heaven. In the Pueblo pantheon, Parsons pointed out, the spirits were not hierarchical but departmental, an organizational principle inhospitable to the conception of a supreme being. Even where the Dios was given prayer sticks, as at Acoma, the offering was always made in tandem with one to the underground Mother. The concept of redemption was similarly quite alien to the Pueblos, as was the idea of personal sin, with the result that penance and confession never "took." And the rite of fasting for penance was not followed because fasting was already conceptualized as a means of compelling results or obtaining power. Likewise, Pueblo beliefs that life after death was a continuation of this life, and that Spirits did not reward or punish, were incompatible with Catholic dogmas of hell and heaven.[34]

Innovations nevertheless occurred constantly in the kachina cult, Parsons noted, because it was very receptive to novelty: new impersonations, dances, songs, new details of costume or decoration. One of the most important ways in which the ceremonial became ever more complicated—or involuted, as she termed it—was by splitting-off or budding. A kachina's personality was constituted through the form and decoration of the mask, the mask feathers and other ornaments, body paint, details of costume, objects carried, posture, gait, behavior, and his call. Any change in these particulars created a new kachina with a new name. Through involution, Parsons argued, variety and change were accomplished without an accompanying sense of change. It was change "within the constitution"—not revolution, and not mutation. Change by involution characterized all the ritual arts of the Pueblo, she observed, and it characterized Pueblo ceremonialism as a whole. New goods often meant not only new customs, but also dead customs. Such disintegration was often combated by substitution, whereby the functions of an extinct group were transferred to another group or undertaken by persons called upon to fill a lapsed office on a temporary basis. Borrowed elements that were not well integrated into ceremonial life, on the other hand, readily lapsed; in effect, they were aborted.

Parsons concluded that the Pueblos displayed a greater cultural vitality than other Native Americans, despite the inroads of Spanish and American culture, and that the culture of the western Pueblos appeared to be more intact than that of the eastern. "As long as people are working or playing with their cultural patterns, their way of life appears integrated, sincere and vital. . . . Once the urge to involute is arrested, the desire to elaborate design or apply it, decadence of a sort sets in." "The saint's-day dance has been put into the Acoma origin myth without any mention of the saint or the slightest hint of foreign derivation," she noted in a final illustration of that culture's vitality: "Iyatiku [the Mother] wanted the people to have a good time, with everybody taking part in a free, public show, so she engaged Kashale as impresario and called it a thanksgiving dance." "Enough to make Fray Juan Ramirez turn in his grave!" Parsons ended with amusement. "Apostate Acoma!"[35]

CHAPTER SIXTEEN

A Modernist Death

"**WHAT** a rather uncanny feeling it gives one to be at the end of an epoch," Mary Simkhovitch wrote Parsons in 1940, anticipating the fortieth anniversary of Greenwich House. The previous November she and Parsons had attended the fiftieth anniversary of Barnard College. But neither had come to the end of her active life. Simkhovitch published her biography in 1938, looking back, at the age of seventy-one, over the years when she and Parsons were building their experimental institutions and families. But she did not retire from the directorship of Greenwich House until 1946, and she continued as vice-chairman of the New York City Housing Authority until her death in 1951. In May 1940, Parsons was sixty-five years old and had just returned from a field trip to Ecuador. Before she left on that trip, she was elected first vice-president of the American Anthropological Association—in effect the president-elect for 1941.[1]

When Parsons returned to New York in 1940, it seemed in many ways the end of an era. Marie Howe, Heterodoxy founder and leading spirit, had died in 1934 while Parsons was in Chapala; and she was not back in time to attend the memorial held in Alice Duer Miller's home, where her old friends and associates Vira Whitehouse, Floyd Dell, James Weldon Johnson, Charlotte Perkins Gilman, and Mary Ware Dennett were among those who paid tribute to the feminist pioneer. Inviting Parsons to speak in 1937, Mary Knoblauch noted that Heterodoxy's last speaker had been Elizabeth Gurley Flynn, "who has been absent also, much too long." Parsons began to attend that long-lived discussion group again; but, like much else, Heterodoxy received its deathblow with the onset of war in the early 1940s.[2]

Clarence Day, crippled by the arthritic disease that had tormented him for many years, died in 1935, just as he was finding happiness in what his friends saw as a "miraculous" marriage and fatherhood.

Mabel Luhan had completed her memoirs—now acknowledged as classic accounts of the modernist milieu. Alice Duer Miller was rich and famous, a regular at the Algonquin Round Table, and a successful screenwriter. Margaret Sanger's campaign to legalize birth control finally made a major breakthrough in 1936 with Judge Augustus Hand's decision in *US v. One Package of Japanese Pessaries*. But Katharine Dexter McCormick continued to support the search for a "fool-proof" contraceptive through the Neuroendocrine Research Foundation she established at Harvard Medical School in 1927, partly to seek a cure for Stanley's schizophrenia. Elsie seems to have lost touch with her old friend during the First World War, which Katharine had actively supported. Elsie followed birth control developments closely, however, and she would surely have hailed as one of the century's great feminist triumphs the oral contraceptive developed by 1960 as a result of Katharine's scientific acumen and financial support. She would also have applauded Katharine's provision, four years before her death in 1967 at the age of ninety-two, of first-class residential accommodation for women students at MIT, where many had been barred from the education she received there on the excuse that no housing was available.[3]

Parsons's old New York crowd was scattered or dead by the late 1930s. Betty Goodwin and Merry Hare lived nearby; but they spent much of their time in Colorado Springs, where Betty helped establish the Fountain Valley School and the modernist Fine Arts Center. Walton Martin and Charlotte Sorchan divided their time between their town house in Turtle Bay Gardens, long European trips, and their Cornwall home. Parsons saw Mabel Luhan when she came to New York, and Signe Toksvig and Francis Hackett on their regular visits from Denmark. Walter Lippmann disappeared from their circle after his divorce and remarriage, but she regularly saw Judge Learned Hand. And she and George Young—from 1930, Sir George—resumed their friendship in 1929 when he delivered the Lowell Lectures in Boston.[4]

Parsons's eccentric brother Henry died in 1937, and an exhibition of his sculpture was held at the Metropolitan Museum in 1939. She had not seen him since 1926, when she visited Lissa at Henry's chateau outside Cannes on her way to Egypt and was relieved, after a short visit, to be quit of "the Riviera and of Henry and his harem." She seems to have totally ignored his family's adventures in the Anglo-American fast set. Parsons's children, on the other hand, had settled into steady careers, marriages, and families by 1940.

John—lawyer, writer manqué, and staunch Republican—amused her with the witty poems he published in the *Herald Tribune* under the headline "Talk among the Tories"—as a counter to her radicalism, he teased. Herbert was a neurosurgeon, and he and Margot had three children. Mac had married the frivolous and much-married Renée Oakman in 1938, partly as a rebellion against his mother, he confessed years later; and their son was born the following year. Like her mother-in-law, Renée was interesting and notorious enough to be immortalized in a novel—John Marquand's *Wickford Point*—in 1939; but Marquand was "much kinder than Herrick," John commented to Parsons.[5]

The family's greatest sorrow was the deafness and retardation of John and Fanny's oldest son, Richard, whose treatment Parsons experimented with and advised on in her usual pragmatic and reticent way, offering suggestions from "Dr. E. C. Parsons, observer of human beings along various (not psychoanalytic) lines." When their second son, John, was born early in 1938, the strain on Fanny was intense, and Parsons urged John to send her to Florida with her mother, "where *she knows nobody and does not want to know them*" and "will feel completely at ease and relaxed." Every woman feels psychic strain somewhat the second to third month after childbirth, she added, remembering the stresses that surrounded the births of her younger children—and perhaps her older ones as well.[6]

An unexpected outcome of Richard's tragedy was the development of a new and comfortable relationship between Elsie and Lissa. Concerned as always not to be in the way when her children had emotional problems to work out, Parsons tactfully stayed with Lissa at Stonover Farm in the fall of 1937, when Fanny was pregnant with John Jr. To their mutual surprise they got along well, and Parsons spent each fall at Stonover until her death four years later. As Lissa wrote to Alfred Kroeber in response to his obituary of Parsons in 1943, "Given the milieu in which I grew up, she was rather intimidating, you know, as the mother of a little girl!" "As I grew older," she continued, "we both came to know each other as individuals, and I think that partly, just because of the early water over the dam, became as friendly and companionable as two such diverse individuals can. I miss her, & always shall."[7]

The devastating hurricane that destroyed much of the Rhode Island and Connecticut coastline in October 1938 swept away two important links to Parsons's past. The green water came within three feet of the crest of the hill on which the Rocks was built, as

Lucy Clews, now eighty-six years old, sat calmly with Lissa enjoying the storm. But the foundations and retaining walls of the beloved summer retreat of Parsons's youth were destroyed, and the grounds covered with sand and boulders, and the family decided not to rebuild. That same storm destroyed the LaFarge home at Saunderstown, where Grant LaFarge, immobilized by heart disease, was carried to a car, then driven through lashing winds and falling trees to a safe spot, where the family cook still managed to serve boiled lobster. LaFarge died soon after. There is no indication in Parsons's correspondence that she kept in touch with her former lover; but the storm that hastened his death and destroyed her family's Newport "cottage" linked them one last time.[8]

Robert Herrick also died in 1938. Ironically, his end came in the Caribbean, in the midst of a new and exacting job as government secretary for the Virgin Islands. The Caribbean travels with Parsons that he wrote about so bitterly in his fiction also resulted in a series of highly regarded articles on colonial policy and race relations. Ernest Gruening, an influential friend from the days when they both wrote for the *Nation,* had pressed Herrick's appointment on a reluctant Harold Ickes in 1935. But, revived in health by a new affair with Mabel Churchill, the wife of novelist Winston Churchill, Herrick was a great success. As Ickes noted in his diary after Herrick's death, "I doubted his ability for this job, but he has performed wonderfully. . . . Although a man of great personal dignity, he was a real democrat at heart and he had a feeling of sympathy for, and understanding of, the Negroes of the Islands." In his last printed words, Herrick expressed the hope that we "may be the people first to discover the way into the new life, the new conceptions of evolving personality." Perhaps Parsons had a more lasting influence on him than he cared to acknowledge.[9]

"Don't forget me altogether," Alfred Kroeber wrote Parsons in August 1939, complimenting her on *Pueblo Indian Religion.* In an affectionate mix of nostalgia and professional and personal gossip, the two friends brought each other up to date. "Tell me something about your family," Parsons wrote from Maine. "Until this week my camp house here has been full: Herbert on his month's vacation from the New York Hospital, his wife and two children, infant daughter and an enchanting two and a half year old son; John and his big daughter; Mac and his wife. A rejuvenating time!" "I have started a book on theory the sub-title of which is: An Essay on Anthropologic *Philosophy:* A fling into a wider world that I have been enjoying all summer," she told him. "You took it, of course, years ago, as your 'Anthropology' indicates, and rumor goes that you have taken it just lately. Tell me about it." "When I return to Zuni I think of you, and Mexico also," Kroeber responded. "I have [a volume] on culture growth . . . but two publishers have turned it down and a third will. . . . I ought to know better than to do synthetic work; but something drives me to it." "Clifton is in college, striding easily after wasting a year to mature," he continued in a delightful characterization of his young family. "Ted is finishing high school, and the smart, possessed, handsome and reliable one of the crew. Karl I can't describe—he's probably too much like me at 12, except he's neither timid nor shy." "Ursula has the best brain of the bunch," he wrote of the future author Ursula Le Guin, "without an illusion, rigorous, precise, negativistic, affectionate—potential tragic material, I sometimes fear."[10]

Kroeber's volume, finally published in 1944 as *Configurations of Culture Growth,* was, like *Pueblo Indian Religion* for Parsons, the culmination of his life's work. A comparison of the two makes it clear why their joint project of many years before never got off the ground. Kroeber's 846-page book is just as packed with evidence. But his is a study of "the rise and fall of civilizations"—as he put it in a statement to Harcourt Brace, it was Spengler with evidence. Kroeber was interested in the historical sweep of cultures, and in the patterned recurrence of periods in which "genius" flowered. Parsons, by contrast, focused on a limited area and time period; and she was more interested in the ragged edges of cultures, the apparently disintegrating, the melding. She found patterns, but she did not expect them to be predictable or to repeat themselves. And for her, genius was not a group phenomenon. Instead, the genius was an innovative individual who placed herself or himself outside of society and from there moved a culture in new and unexpected directions. Beside a quotation from Kroeber's *Anthropology* in which he outlined his idea of the "superorganic," she wrote, sometime in 1939, "Twaddle!"[11]

With the completion of *Configurations of Culture Growth* in 1938, Kroeber entered the final phase of his professional life. He had completed the tasks he set himself, and he had achieved the professional recognition he longed for in 1920. After 1938 he enjoyed the role of elder statesman, tolerantly engaged with, but not engrossed by, the efforts of younger anthropologists to once more reshape the discipline.[12]

The New Young Turks

Parsons was not quite so ready to turn to musing on the anthropological enterprise as she suggested to Kroeber in August 1939. The New York anthropological scene had changed dramatically since her return to New York in 1934. Franz Boas had retired, reluctantly, in 1936, at the age of seventy-eight. In 1931 he had tried to lure Kroeber and Sapir back to New York to replace him. But the call came too late: Kroeber was settled in Berkeley with a young family and a flourishing department; and Sapir was about to move from Chicago to Yale. By 1936, Sapir's health was deteriorating; he suffered a heart attack in 1937 and died, age fifty-four, in 1939. After a period of vacillation, during which Ruth Benedict acted as head of department, the Columbia authorities finally passed her over and appointed Ralph Linton as professor of anthropology, provisionally in 1937 and permanently in 1938.[13]

Linton's appointment was a deliberate attempt to counteract the influence of Boas and his students in the department, who were seen by the conservative Nicholas Murray Butler as dangerous radicals. There had been no love lost between Linton and Boas since the famous military uniform incident after the war. In 1937, Linton stood for an anthropology, a teaching philosophy, and a personal style that differed markedly from Boas and Benedict's. A deep enmity sprang up between Linton and Benedict; the more radical of Boas's appointees, such as Alexander Lesser and Gene Weltfish, were dismissed; and former Boas students dependent on his goodwill for year-to-year positions, such as Ruth Bunzel, found themselves in precarious situations.[14]

Linton brought with him to Columbia Kroeber's former student Duncan Strong. Strong was the first of the many graduate students who worked with Kroeber as the Berkeley department began its steep climb to eminence during the 1920s, and he remained his favorite. He was "totally simpatico" to Kroeber, who admired his old-family savoir faire, his drive, and his imagination and organization in tackling concrete problems. "In many ways he is the antithesis of Warner," Kroeber told Tozzer by way of complimenting Strong in 1934, "no propaganda, few abstractions, no frothing about methods." Parsons appreciated these qualities too; and Strong, going through a period of personal turmoil reminiscent of Kroeber's twenty years before, found Parsons's intelligent and detached views and her zest for life and work as healing as his mentor had. Parsons and Strong immediately became firm friends. During 1938 and 1939, Parsons's most frequent companions were Strong and George Vaillant and Junius Bird, the two Latin American experts at the museum. In late February and early March 1938, for instance, her appointment calendar shows that she attended *Rigoletto* with the Birds on Friday, 25 February, *Mice and Men* with Strong that Saturday night, had tea with the Birds on the Sunday, dinner with the Vaillants and Strong before a meeting at the museum on Monday, lunch with Linton at the Faculty Club on Tuesday, dinner with Vaillant on Saturday, 5 March, and dined that Sunday with the Birds.[15]

"I wish you had been with me in Crete last year," Parsons wrote Kroeber in 1939. "I tried to beguile Duncan Strong into going. That young man is very much mixed up, and nobody seems to be in a position to straighten him out." "Duncan is adrift," Kroeber answered. "My guess is that he'll work hard only when he has the anchorage of domesticity. As a bachelor he lets the world distract him randomly. I don't think he needs Crete; he needs the right wife. Sorry, but that's how some of us males are." Parsons had no more desire to play the wife than she had twenty years earlier with Kroeber; but she enjoyed the conversation just as much. And Parsons's friendship was important to Strong. "I did want to write," he says in a Christmas 1939 letter, "and tell you that getting to know you—and the many nice things I have done with you, constitute one of the nicest things New York has had to offer."[16]

Strong had much in common with Parsons intellectually and professionally. Like her, he was interested in fringe populations and the mix of cultures; his approach was historical and distributional, like hers, and he shared her ability to synthesize large bodies of data into a vigorous and coherent whole; and like her, he was an assiduous and colorful fieldworker who combined field research with documentary evidence. During a brief teaching stint in Nebraska, he did pioneering work on the Great Plains Indians which uncovered an unexpected mixture of village and nomadic cultures. But Strong's major enthusiasm was for Central America, where he worked in Honduras on Mayan frontier cultures. In 1940, when Parsons visited Peru, Ecuador, and Bolivia, he was planning to begin excavations in Peru.[17]

Duncan Strong was one of the young archeologists who were attempting to bring ethnology, archeology, and history together to solve problems of acculturation in a manner that Parsons had tried unsuccessfully to suggest to Alfred Kidder in 1920. In 1937, when Strong was chair of the committee to appoint a new director of the Laboratory of Anthropology and to redefine its objectives, Parsons found they were very much in accord; and she was happy, for the first time in her dealings with the laboratory, with the policies pursued by the new director, Scudder Mekeel. Through Strong she came into contact with Clyde Kluckhohn, who, with Strong, was leading the Young Turks who were edging Kidder and his fellow "antiquarians" out of their central place in American archeology. Parsons was enthusiastic about the more ethnologically oriented archeology that Strong and Kluckhohn stood for, and turned her attention to ways to coordinate her work with theirs.[18]

A New Field: Ecuador

Robert Lowie had been pressing unsuccessfully for a handbook of South American Indians for many years. Finally, in 1939, his former student Julian Steward was able to mobilize the resources of the Bureau of American Ethnology for the mammoth project, which resulted in the publication of the seven-volume *Handbook* between 1946 and 1950. Parsons, who had funded his fieldwork at Hopi in 1928, immediately wrote Steward her approval of the project. "I plan to fly to Peru late this winter and would be glad to have any chore wished on me," she added, her philosophy project apparently forgotten. Steward had recently done fieldwork in Ecuador and Peru and suggested that she study acculturation in Ecuador's northern highlands. There were barely a handful of ethnographic studies of South America at that time, almost none of them historical. Here was a chance for Parsons to again pioneer a field.[19]

Parsons had just been elected first vice-president of the American Anthropological Society at the December 1939 meetings and was thus slated for elevation to president the following year. This was an irregular step: there were four vice-presidents, and usually they progressed from fourth to first and then to president. In effect, Earnest Hooton from Harvard, Duncan Strong, and Ruth Benedict had stepped aside and allowed Parsons to take precedence. There is no evidence from her correspondence or from published accounts how this had been organized. None of her numerous correspondents refer to it as anything out of the ordinary. But it is clear that, with the publication of *Mitla* and *Pueblo Indian Religion,* the scope and originality of her work had been brought home to the profession at large. The younger scholars who had worked closely with her all knew how innovative and suggestive her work had been from the outset. Now those who knew only the wealthy patron or the legendary (and perhaps eccentric) fieldworker, saw that she had blazed the trail for almost all of the "new" developments in the discipline: acculturation studies, biography and autobiography, ethnohistory, community studies, and applied anthropology. The new Young Turks brashly pushing the discipline in new directions—Herskovits, White, Kluckhohn, Redfield, Strong—were her admirers, and they even read her early feminist work with enjoyment and interest. Leslie White liked *Fear and Conventionality* the best. "I have been puzzling myself about the nature of etiquette," he wrote Parsons in 1931. "It is amazing to me that this tremendously important phase of all human society should be so neglected by anthropologists." Clyde Kluckhohn, the enfant terrible of anthropology in the early 1940s, found to his surprise that he sat down and read all four of her self-styled "youthful vision[s] of a different world" from cover to cover. "I had a lot of fun with them," he wrote Parsons in January 1941, "and not only amusement—I learned a good deal—both in odd ethnographic items and, even more important, I learned with some sense of shame (but it is good for me) that some conceptions were not quite so new in the world as I imagined." "May I say that I take more than a casual pleasure in the fact that you are this year's president of the Anthropological Association?" he added.[20]

The young anthropologists were not the only ones who gained a new appreciation of Parsons during these New York years. Harold Stearns had returned from his "thirteen years' French Sabbatical," and in 1937 he was planning a new edition of *American Civilization,* to be called *America Now.* Parsons was one of the few original contributors he asked to participate. New York was not like the old Jones Street days, he lamented, but he found Parsons just as amusing when they lunched together at the Algonquin. Her views had apparently not lost their piquancy in print either: when the book was reviewed in the *Herald Tribune* in 1938, Gerald Johnson remarked on "Mrs Elsie Clews Parsons' sparkling essay on the family." Parsons had declined to write again on sex: it was "old hat" and démodé, and would be like having an article on cooking or the training of babies, she told Stearns. "Even for our children," Stearns remarked in his introduction, "any residual mystery about it appears to have vanished."[21]

People don't talk about sex any more, Parsons noted in her article. "Do what you like, marry or 'live in sin'. . . but don't talk about it; nobody is interested." There had been slight changes in mating and childbearing practices during the last two decades, she observed—the age at marriage had risen, the divorce rate had increased, the birthrate had dropped—but clear thinking was not responsible for these changes. Knowledge about conception had increased and spread, but there was no more distinction made between private sex and public childbearing than there was "when Mrs. Sanger was not an international figure and the medical profession was content to be supine on any social relationship." Pictures of childbirth were still condemned as private obscenities, and the Catholic clergy could still talk about birth control "breaking the dam against lust" or about "totalitarian sex" and find an audience—"even one that doesn't laugh."

Turning from youth and sex, Parsons looked at her own generation. With the continued demise of the extended family, she asked, what do the aging do? Drawing on her own recent experience in Greece, she pictured them taking to the road "like philosophic Hindus in the final stage of life . . . carrying their rice bowl by trailer or in that priceless invention for the aging, especially aging women, the cruise boat." Noting the disproportionately large number of elderly women and the accumulation of wealth in their hands—and no doubt thinking of her mother—she observed that these women spend more, but give less to welfare or educational groups. To remedy the situation she suggested—not entirely tongue-in-cheek—a tax on old ladies who "have" for the benefit of those who "have not," or at least for educating girls to look ahead to middle age and diversify their interests. What the future held for the family was uncertain, she concluded: "sociological prediction . . . is a rash pursuit, so many unexpected things can happen." All that was certain was that the world was changing—so why not prepare for it by encouraging young people "to take pleasure in the unexpected and to prize every hour and day, every place, and every person as good and valuable in themselves?"[22]

Peguche

Parsons's plan to work in South America probably predated the announcement of Steward's revival of the South American *Handbook*. In 1935, Lowie had decided to focus on this area, and she and Lowie exchanged information about Mexican–South American parallels from that time. "We must all collaborate in an attempt to discover what features are pan-American in range," he wrote while reading *Mitla* in 1936. Lowie was teaching a course on the Americas for the first time that year; his collaborator, Curt Nimuendajú, was sending him "priceless stuff about his N.E. Brazilian Ge-tribe, whose social organization presents some analogies to the Hopi"; and the young Swiss anthropologist Alfred Métraux, who had worked with several South American tribes, was visiting Berkeley. "The general picture . . . is certainly Mexicanlike," Parsons wrote of Métraux's work on the Tupinamba. "I am very much interested indeed in the idea of collaboration for the Pan American range, particularly in ritual." In December 1938, when the South American anthropologist de la Fuente visited New York for the anthropology meetings, Parsons's appointment calendar shows that she entertained him several times; and with Ralph Beals staying as her house guest, there were no doubt many discussions of Latin American research.[23]

Parsons left for Peru, Bolivia, and Ecuador in March 1940, armed with an introduction from Strong to Julio Tello, Peru's principal archeologist. It is not clear how long she spent in Peru, or whether she ever got to Bolivia. When she arrived in Ecuador, the wife of the British minister put her in touch with Juan Gorrell, an American businessman who farmed a valley south of Otavalo, a town of about 10,000 in the highlands seventy miles northeast of the capital, Quito. Gorrell introduced her to Rosita Lema from Peguche, an Indian community on the outskirts of Otavalo. Rosita, a vivacious and intelligent young woman who was about to give birth to her second child, brought her brother and daughter to school in Otavalo each day. As Parsons recounted it to Reichard, she could not resist the opportunity that Peguche offered. "I went there at once and stayed until it was time to come home!"[24]

Ecuador was an ideal place to study culture contact. The Indian states of Ecuador had been the northernmost outposts of the Inca empire, brought briefly under Inca rule at the end of the fifteenth century. When the Spaniards conquered the region in 1531, they put in place the *encomienda* system that virtually enslaved the Indian population. After three centuries of Spanish rule, followed by another century's domination by the 50 percent of the population who considered themselves white, half the Ecuador Indians were landless. Some worked as *peones* on whiteowned haciendas, others in towns or as independent agricultural laborers, while those with enough land to support them lived almost completely separate lives in communities like Peguche, where whites were not welcomed.

Peguche was a scattered community of 122 households of weavers, traders, and farmers, in which most people owned a housesite and a field. Rosita Lema was "the most enterprising person in all Peguche," Parsons discovered, but she had never been across the valley to a neighboring Indian town. She had little or no knowledge of the world outside her community: the people of Peguche had a relationship of economic convenience with the white town, but they never sat in its plaza, they kept to their side in its churches, and only one Indian girl and a few Indian boys attended its Spanish-speaking schools. Mexico, the United States, and even Peru were totally unknown to her; and she had no conception of a world without "Spaniards."[25]

Rosita Lema was thirty years old when Parsons met her in 1940. As the portrait of her with baby Matilde by Bodo Wuth in the front of Parsons's book on Peguche attests, she was a striking figure, with a mobile, intelligent face, beringed fingers, and wide stiff felt hat. Rosita was a central person in the limited contacts that were developing between the white town and the Indian community. Spinners and weavers such as Rosita and her husband fulfilled a recent demand for woollen ponchos, tweeds, and homespuns for the local and city market. This new source of revenue created a social group with a different, more independent relationship with whites. They began to acquire city goods, their children went to school, and they often traveled long distances to dispose of their goods. But they still maintained Indian dress, language, and beliefs.

Rosita's brother was one of the fifteen Indian boys who attended the Christian Brothers' School in Otavalo, and her daughter was the only girl at the convent school. A devout Catholic, Rosita feasted the Sister when she paid parochial visits; her husband José was the alcalde of the church; and they organized work parties for church repairs. She traded with whites in Otavalo and even in Quito, and she had whites as godparents for her children. As Parsons observed, "White connections seem worth while to Rosita, and more than anyone else in Peguche she understands how to make and keep them."[26]

Alert, observant, and curious about her world, Parsons found Rosita a "telling example" to her neighbors, "an illustration of the opportunities for acculturation through unusual personality"—

Rosita Lema with baby Matilde, Peguche, 1940. Elsie Clews Parsons, *Peguche* (Chicago: University of Chicago Press, 1945).

"indeed," she remarked, "one of the most outstanding instances I have ever observed." With her sense of personal distinction, she reminded Parsons of Flora Zuni, who had been an important friend and informant for both herself and Ruth Bunzel. Rosita saw herself as a self-made woman. She experimented continually with anything new she came in contact with, whether it was foreign medicine, an unknown fruit, or foreign fabrics or dyes.[27]

When Parsons returned to New York in May 1940, she wrote enthusiastically to Lowie: "Back from Ecuador. . . . I spent two months . . . working in a hamlet of about 1000 Quechua-speaking Indians only three miles out from a very attractive White town. Quite early I began to think that the Indians of this valley might be descendents of Inca colonists and now I am piling up Peruvian parallels. The relations between Indians and Whites or near Whites are also a matter of great interest. . . . Just now I am having a grand time rereading Garcilasso de la Vega. What a charming book from many points of view!" The following February she was "digesting the Peruvian chroniclers who have been read more by archeologists than by ethnologists." "For an acculturation study," she told Lowie, "Garcilasso is rich. . . . When I asked Dr. Boas who had first described pitch accent among American Indians he did not know it was Garcilasso," she concluded with amusement.[28]

Parsons returned to Peguche in September 1941. But the field trip was distressing in many ways. She was alarmed and disconcerted to find Rosita bundled up in bed, listless and uninterested in anything. She had been ill for a year, vomiting during and after nursing Matilde. The children no longer went to school. Rosita, obsessed with her illness, no longer worked or traded. "Poor Rosita!" Parsons wrote in distress. "*Pobricita,* perhaps she is 'the most intelligent Indian in Ecuador' . . . but there are situations native wit or personal wisdom cannot cope with; and maybe one of these is severe anemia given no adequate medical attention . . . and given cultural pressures that would handicap even an able and devoted doctor or nurse, particularly if uninformed about them." Without knowledge of Indian home life, any form of medical advice will remain ineffectual, she concluded sorrowfully.[29]

Death

Parsons returned to New York at the end of November, just in time to finish her presidential address and attend to the final arrangements for the Anthropological Association annual meetings. Gladys Reichard found her in excellent spirits but glad to be back. She had felt the discomforts of fieldwork more than usual, and as Gladys put it in a letter to Kroeber, "We decided on analyzing the situation that there were more discomforts than usual." Parsons attended a council meeting of the American Ethnological Society on Wednesday night, 10 December, in apparent good health. The next day she was taken to the New York Hospital for observation and was operated on immediately for appendicitis. She seemed to be recovering well during the following week, as she worked with Fred Eggan, the Anthropological Association secretary, on final arrangements for the meeting. Suddenly on the night of 18 December, uremia, or kidney failure, set in, and as Reichard put it, "she simply slept away." "You will doubtless have heard the shocking news of Elsie's death before you get this," Reichard wrote Kroeber, "but I thot you might want to know a little more than you read in the newspaper." "She had her presidential speech ready," she ended, after giving particulars of Parsons's last days, "I have it now—& I think it ought to be read, don't you?"[30]

"Dr. Elsie Clews Parsons Is Dead: Anthropologist and Sociologist," Mac Parsons wrote bravely in an obituary in the *Herald Tribune* the next day. Her death may not have been quite the shock to her family that it was to colleagues and friends. Ever since she left for Jemez in 1921 feeling "a curious form of nervousness," she had made or revised her will several times before going to the field; and in 1926, before leaving for Egypt, she had written explicit instructions for cremation and avoidance of ceremonial after her death. Despite her obvious energy and resilience, she was often ill when she returned from field trips. She was particularly unwell when she returned from the ill-fated Caribbean cruise in 1927, and in the summer of 1930 she was ill for some weeks with a kidney problem. After that time, her family were especially anxious about her trips. She told Beals in 1932 or 1933 that she had to conceal her plans to allay their anxiety until she was settled in whatever foreign place she was visiting. She made no field trips after her 1933 season in Mitla and, after two winters writing in Chapala, did not go abroad again until her trip to Greece in 1938. Before she left for Greece, she revised her will. Lounsberry was to go to John, Stonover Farm to Lissa, the Maine house to Herbert, and the schooner, *Malabar V,* to the three boys. An annuity was provided for Mary Carmody, the nurse who had seen her through all six childbirths. Five thousand dollars was set aside for the American Folklore Society for the publication of *Taos Tales* and the third volume of Antilles folklore. The remainder was to go to the four children. In 1940, as she was preparing to leave for her "tourist trip" to South America, she left clear instructions in case of her death. "Dear Lissa," she wrote,

> Our thoughts being on death, I enclose a memorandum on my own. E.C.P.
>
> Directions after death
> If convenient, cremation (ashes left at crematory), otherwise, if not convenient, burial, but not in a cemetery and without grave stone.
> No funeral, and no religious services whatsoever.
> Relatives requested not to wear mourning.
> Will in charge of Mr. Wright of Parsons, Closson & McIlvaine.
> January 31, 1926
> O.K. 1940 [signed Elsie Clews Parsons][31]

The scanty evidence of Parsons's medical history suggests that she probably suffered from some kind of kidney infection at least from the time of her third pregnancy in 1905, that this was the cause of the deaths of her two babies at birth, and that this was what caused her sudden collapse after what seemed to be routine surgery. She was not well during the second half of her last two pregnancies in 1909 and 1911. During the 1909 pregnancy, she was anxiously monitoring the presence of protein in the urine. She was ill for at least three months after Herbert was born, and she nearly died after Mac's birth in 1911. It seems that this "indefatigable" researcher was battling chronic ill-health, as well as social convention, throughout most of her career.[32]

Four days before Parsons's operation, on Sunday, 7 December 1941, the Japanese attacked Pearl Harbor, making it certain that the United States would declare war the next day. That evening hundreds of New Yorkers listened to the eighty-two-year-old John Dewey speak on "lessons from the war in philosophy" in a lecture series planned months earlier. Before he spoke, Dewey's thoughts turned back to the First World War and his disastrous decision to support America's military intervention. We do not know if Parsons was in Dewey's audience; but we do know that sometime late that evening she wrote to her son Mac with the restrained passion that was so characteristic: "I have been thinking about Father," she wrote without preliminaries. "Lissa and I have often wondered during these wars what his reactions would have been. This evening I have been thinking of him in several connections." She then went on to tell Mac about Herbert's campaign for Congress during their honeymoon, and his lying down from fatigue for the first and only time in his life the day of his defeat. "The next time he ran for office he was elected," she added, perhaps thinking of the thirty-year-old Mac. "He was thirty one years old." "There are times when I miss Father awfully," she concluded in her abrupt way. "This is one. I feel like talking about him. The next best thing is writing. Affly E.C.P." The next day Congress declared war on Japan; on 11 December, the day Parsons was hospitalized, Germany and Italy declared war on the United States; and on the day of her death, 19 December, Congress extended military conscription to men between the ages of twenty and forty-four. A month after her death, her three sons were in the armed forces—John in the Navy, Herbert in the Army Medical Service, and Mac in Naval Intelligence. Herbert had signed up immediately, telling his mother "that everyone was going & he would have to also." John Parsons told Peter Hare in 1976 that his mother didn't seem to object to her sons' plans for going to war; but of course she had brought them up to make their own decisions.[33]

Prospects: A Posthumous Presidential Message

Elsie Clews Parsons managed to ignore boundaries and circumvent ceremony even in death. Mac told Peter Hare in 1976 that they carried out her instructions: she has no gravestone and she was not buried anywhere, although the graves of Herbert and their deceased children—John and Lissa—were in the cemetery of the Lenox Congregational Church. Her death was fittingly modernist in other ways as well. She died striding into the future, as it were, with her presidential address ready to deliver in one week's time, and the results of two seasons' fieldwork written up ready for publication. The presidential address was not the summing up of a lifetime's work, but the beginning of a new project on anthropological theory; and her work with Rosita Lema in Peguche was left, like a gripping detective serial, with the denouement signaled, but still uncertain.[34]

Parsons's presidential address, "Anthropology and Prediction," was read on 29 December 1941 by Gladys Reichard. "Next to desires of subsistence and reproduction the urge to know ahead of time seems to be in the lead," Parsons observed. "Uncertainty is painful, the hardest of all things to bear . . . which may be why concepts of fate and preordainment develop, why both science and divine revelation are popular." The only differences between lettered and unlettered peoples in this regard are what they want to know and their means of finding out. "You may look into a crystal or into a microscope for a lurking witch or for bacilli. . . . You choose a proper mate—a Water person if you are an Earth person— and a propitious wedding day or, as the Committee on Social Adjustment of the Social Science Research Council suggests, you look up in a matrimonial expectancy table your matrimonial risk."[35]

Parsons pointed out that anthropologists were not immune to this desire for prediction. This has led, she commented with her usual dislike for labels, to a number of trends: functionalism "which by emphasizing certain familiar aspects of investigation felt that it had given birth to something quite new"; cultural anthropology, again "a new name for something old"; personality study, a "courtship of psychology without as yet much prospect of reciprocity in union"; acculturation study "bent on squeezing out of cultural contacts . . . more secrets, it is said, than the diffusionists were after"; and child study, "a new battlefield to fight over in order to determine why we behave as human beings, or why we don't."[36]

"What is *our* market? Who wants our goods?" she asked, referring to Fay-Cooper Cole's call for anthropologists to "sell their goods." Medicine, which is much better packaged for the market, is still the province of vested interests; and already demands have been made on anthropology to favor special groups—White Skin, Nordic, Gentile, National. So far, anthropology has not had enough prestige for its stamp of approval to be required on Aryanism or the Yellow Peril or the incapacity of the Negro or the ethics of the White Man's Burden. This may change with the war, she warned, and anthropologists may look back with yearning to "the good old days when they were poor but proud, independent because obscure, free because nobody cared very much what they did." Nevertheless, Parsons believed, as she always had, in anthropology as an important guide to social change. But, she warned, if we really want to make the drastic move from legislation by public opinion to psychological conditioning, "it better not be haphazard or just by rule of thumb." "If we object to being a divided, name-calling people, let us achieve understanding of what makes people like-minded before we develop a program of unification or standardization."

Basic to the responsible application of anthropology to social problems, in Parsons's opinion, was education, and the first obligation upon applied anthropologists was to popularize anthropology through teaching, particularly in the schools, by popular lectures, and by informed best-sellers. She warned that this was not easy, because people have little interest in other cultures. Popularizers had to be practical acculturationists and find something compelling to tie their message to. As the urge to know the future is so strong, she suggested, why not talk about knowledge of cultural processes as "a possible means of foreknowledge, indicating what may happen—many possibles—but also what cannot happen, the impossibles."

Summing up her thoughts on selling the discipline's skills, Parsons envisaged a world guided by her idea of a responsible anthropology. In such a world, foresight would develop through increased knowledge, not through faith or divination, which are by their nature concerned with special interests and social control: "So I conclude with a prediction, demonstrating once more that to predict is human."[37]

A Positive Creed

Obituaries seem almost out of place for someone who continued to live, through her newly published words, for months and years after her death. *Peguche, Canton of Otavalo, Province of Imbabura, Ecuador: A Study of Andean Indians* was published in 1945 by the University of Chicago Press. Its central focus and raison d'être is Rosita Lema. If anything tempted the vacationing Parsons to stay in Otavalo, it was this young woman, so like herself at thirty. In her "town gossip" chapter, "In Peguche Houses," Parsons vividly portrays the changing culture of the town through the eyes of Rosita, this Ecuadorean "inventor of the future." As Paul Radin wrote in a review that was his final tribute to Parsons, "Her method was always the same, to study the life of a group as it was reflected in the life histories of a few selected individuals with whom she had established an intimate rapport." "Her study," in his opinion, was "perfect" within the limitations imposed. "It will remain, for many years to come, a model of what can be done by the new method of approach to the study of acculturation, of which she was one of the founders."[38]

Parsons detested any sort of ceremonial tribute. But, because of that, she appreciated all the more the genuine word of appreciation, gratitude, and affection. As she said to Kroeber in 1916, "You certainly know how to have compliments valued by one who doesn't particularly care for compliments at all." Kroeber did not disappoint her in death; nor did her other memorialists, Gladys Reichard, Leslie Spier, and Franz Boas. All paid tribute to the pathbreaking and definitive quality of Parsons's work. But they gave equal weight to her life and personality. "Elsie Clews Parsons was fascinating," Gladys Reichard states flatly. "If one trait in her sturdy character were to be stressed more than another it must be her absolute regard for truth. She had her own ethical ideals, other people had theirs. She could understand and tolerate such differences, but the overlap, the *sine qua non* was a demand for honesty, of which the greatest part was self-honesty." "She could face any fact," Reichard recalled, "no matter how damaging it was to self-complacency; she could not deal with a liar; she pitied him if he lied only to himself. . . . This fundamental rule of her life sometimes led to misunderstanding on the part of others, because she followed it through with consummate consistency, and most people do not like consistency when it affects their own prejudices." She was able to maintain a tolerance "so magnanimous as to be almost more than human," Reichard explained, because her keen intuition and honesty were mellowed by a sense of humor that had to be experienced to be appreciated; and she had an innate simplicity that allowed her to be at home in any company. Concluding on a personal note, Reichard remembered with affection that Parsons's idea of complete comfort was "to have *at the same* time a cigarette, a cup of coffee, and an open fire."[39]

Leslie Spier pointed out that the essential story of Parsons's life and thought can never be caught by any recital of positions or bibliography. Instead it is found in her consistent desire "to understand others, the trammels of their conventions," and in "a positive creed—by which she lived rigorously—to allow the utmost freedom of self expression to every individual, herself included." "This was no mere ideal," he emphasized, "for she acted on it simply and directly, ignoring the empty forms of manners, neither for or against them. It appeared in her desire to help fellow anthropologists as individuals: institutional weight and official status were rigorously excluded in her shrewd estimates. Her attitudes were grounded in intensity of feeling but were dispassionate in expression. She was wise, tolerant, and reticent."[40]

Parsons "forged her own convictions, often slowly, sometimes painfully," Kroeber recalled of his old friend; and "their temper represented self-trial, experience, resolution, and tenacity against which contrary views were likely to shatter, especially if based on shallow enthusiasm or alloyed with facile dexterity or any ingredient of pretense. . . . She was ruthless toward sentimentality, weakness, and sham; yet never needlessly unkind. She knew the foe as a foe, but wasted no vindictiveness on him; she probably never really experienced the active gratifications of hate. . . . She valued control preeminently: first in herself, next in others. Therefore, she trained her judgment to be unsparing, and sometimes seemed more coldly reasoned in her motivations than was actually the case. Toward the young and the dependent she was uniformly helpful, provided they were not parasitic." "She was an unflinching person," he concluded, "grappling and pushing steadfastly toward what seemed to be the fundamentals." And, he added in an assessment that would have pleased her, "she was an increasingly serene one, devoid of vanity, pettiness, and disturbing turmoil. The serenity was manifest in her erect carriage, chiseled features, level look, and slow direct smile."[41]

Elsie Clews Parsons was "one of those whose scientific insight shapes their life," wrote Franz Boas, who more than any person created the context for her professional life. "Conscious through her studies of the far-reaching influence of tradition, she was . . . an enemy of all catch phrases that beguile us and skeptical of the beautiful words that promise a better future, but that are not liable to be kept by those who glibly pronounce them." Because she insisted that "freedom of mind and willingness to forgo old accustomed prejudice must be attained before we can hope for a better future," she was, Boas concluded in a final tribute to Parsons the public intellectual, "in every way a power for good in our society."[42]

EPILOGUE

BY CATHARINE R. STIMPSON

BORN to affluence and privilege, Elsie Clews Parsons rejected the ease and indulgences of both. She fought to have a vital life and succeeded. She was adventurous in mind and body, courageous, original, creative. She also had her complexities and limits. One sign of a vital life is the quality of the memories it inspires. She deserves the immense integrity, clarity, sweep, and fullness of this new and unmatched biography.

After her death on 19 December 1941, Parsons received tributes and admiring obituaries. After World War II, historians of anthropology never wholly neglected her. The emergence of women's studies in the late 1960s increased interest in her career. However, *Elsie Clews Parsons* proves how much more there was for subsequent generations to know. So doing, it provokes readers to ask obvious questions: *why* did anthropology push Parsons toward the margins of its records, *why* did modern intellectual and cultural history tend to forget her? Because she was a woman? Because her circumstances both permitted and forced her to work outside of the academy? Because, in her free-ranging independence, she bends any grid of interpretation out of shape?

As Desley Deacon demonstrates, to ignore Parsons is to ignore important elements in the history of modernity. Indeed, a biography of Parsons, that is, the writing of a life, is inseparable from an aeonography, that is, the writing of a time. To ask what Parsons saw, heard, touched, smelled, wanted, thought, and taught is to grasp how very much was at stake in the invention of the modern. Like others, she wanted to kill the nineteenth century—in part because its conventions were killing her. Recently, I had an experience that symbolized for me how suffocating the nineteenth century must have seemed for rebels like Parsons. I was in a Victorian house that had been restored and refurbished to a fare-thee-well. After one evening, I felt that if I had to walk by one more fringe, one more furbelow, one more swirling pattern, I would run screaming out into the open, crying for fresh air, purity of line, a new design for living.

For Parsons, modernity meant crafting a new moral, political, social, and cultural architecture. Both women and men could embody a radical set of modern values: cultural pluralism, a "transnational America" that reflects this pluralism, the tolerance that pluralism demands, cultural diffusion and mobility, empiricism, freedom, egalitarianism between the genders and among the races, honesty, and "sexual plasticity." First sociology, then cultural anthropology were the academic disciplines that could accommodate, though sometimes uneasily, Parsons' modern temperament.

Today, many of us think of ourselves as postmodern. We believe that the world changed, although not completely and not for everyone, after World War II. We speak of our global economy, culture, and communications, and often do so on e-mail. We analyze, often skeptically, modernity's master narratives. The more affluent among us go as tourists or as owners of second homes to the sites—the Southwest, for example—that field-workers once studied with their local informants. The anthropology that Parsons helped to found and lead has also changed. It asks more persistently about meaning, acts of interpretation, the relationships of power between the anthropologizing Self and the anthropologized Other.

How postmodern would Parsons have been? No doubt, she would have been on e-mail. No doubt, she would have been sympathetic to the questions of contemporary anthropology. However, she might have remained a stubborn empiricist. All of this is speculation. What we have here, in our hands, is *Elsie Clew Parsons: Inventing Modern Life.* It is a book of consequence, not only because it will become the standard narrative of a consequential life, but because it reminds us that the project of modernity is incomplete. We have inherited but not fully used its inventions. Postmodernity will be the poorer if, in yet another bout of historical amnesia, we allow these inventions to rust and crumble.

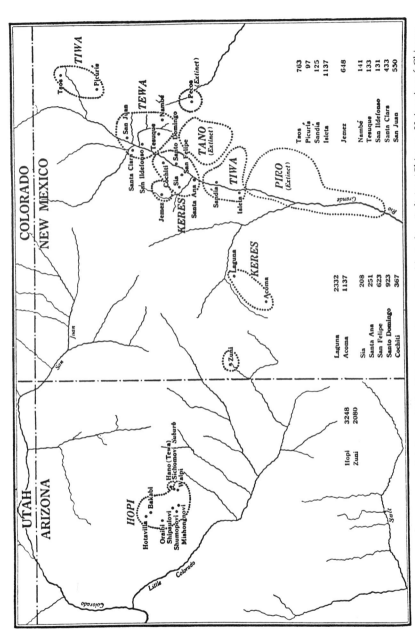

The pueblos of New Mexico and Arizona, 1937. Elsie Clews Parsons, *Pueblo Indian Religion* (Chicago: University of Chicago Press, 1939).

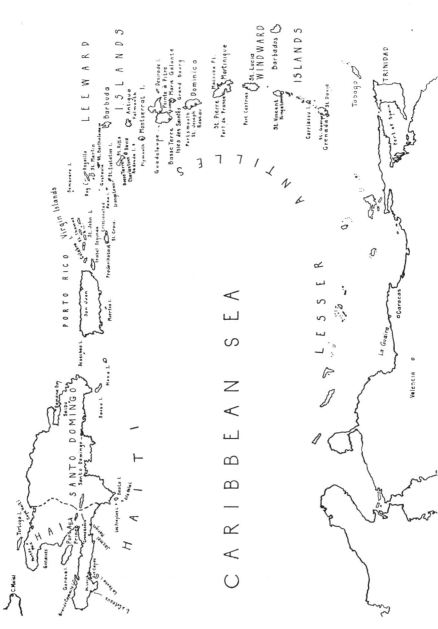

The Caribbean, 1933. Elsie Clews Parsons, *Folk-Lore of the Antilles, French and English*, part 1 (American Folklore Society, 1933).

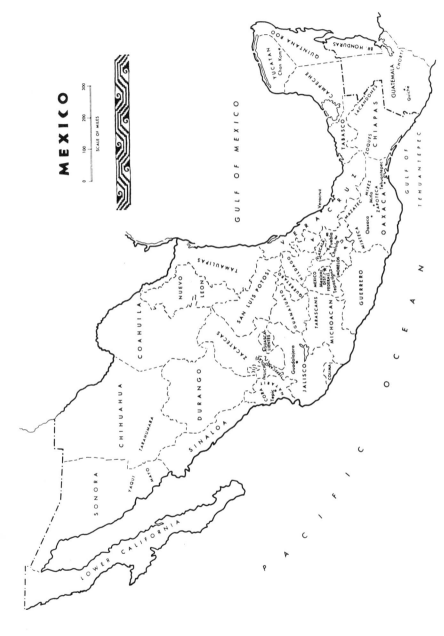

Mexico, 1936. Elsie Clews Parsons, *Mitla* (Chicago: University of Chicago Press, 1936).

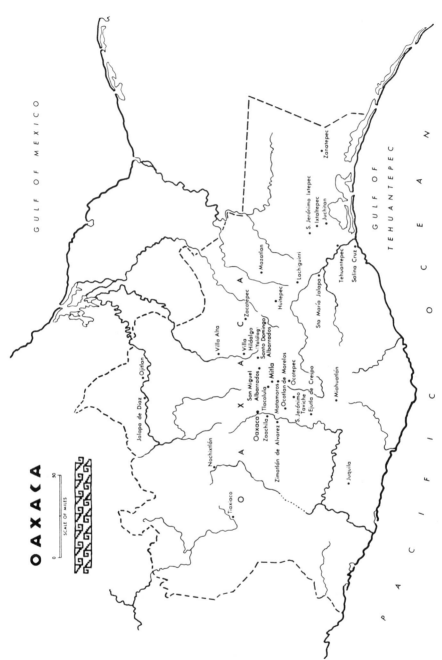

OAXACA

SCALE OF MILES

0   50

GULF OF MEXICO

Ojitlán •

Jalapa de Díaz •

Nochixtlán •

Tlaxiaco •

Zimatlán de Alvarez •

Oaxaca •
Zaachila •

San Miguel
Albarrados •
Tlacolula •

Matamoros •

S. Jerónimo
Taviche •

Ejutla de Crespo •

Ocotlán de Morelos •
Ocotepec •

Mitla •

Santo Domingo
Albarrados •

Villa
Hildalgo
Yalalag •

Villa Alta •

Zacatepec •

Huitepec •

Mazatlán •

Lachiguiri •

S. Jerónimo Ixtepec •
Ixtaltepec •
Juchitán •

Zanatepec •

Sta María Jalapa •

Tehuantepec •

Salina Cruz •

GULF OF
TEHUANTEPEC

Miahuatlán •

Juquila •

P A C I F I C   O C E A N

Oaxaca, 1936. Elsie Clews Parsons, *Mitla* (Chicago: University of Chicago Press, 1936).

NOTES

Abbreviations

AA	*American Anthropologist*
AAA	American Anthropological Association
ADM	Alice Duer Miller
AFLS	American Folklore Society
AJS	*American Journal of Sociology*
ALK	Alfred L. Kroeber
AMNH	American Museum of Natural History
ASR	*American Sociological Review*
BAE	Bureau of American Ethnology
DAB	*Dictionary of American Biography* (New York: Scribner, 1932–1964).
DNB	*Dictionary of National Biography* (London: OUP, 1885–1990).
EC	Elsie Clews
ECP	Elsie Clews Parsons
FAW	Robert McHenry, ed., *Famous American Women: A Biographical Dictionary from Colonial Times to the Present* (New York: Dover, 1983).
FB	Franz Boas
GLF	Grant LaFarge
Golla	Victor Golla, ed., *The Sapir-Kroeber Correspondence: Letters between Edward Sapir and A. L. Kroeber, 1905–1925* (Berkeley: University of California Survey of California and Other Indian Languages, 1984).
GR	Gladys Reichard
GY	George Young
HC	Henry Clews
HP	Herbert Parsons
ICA	International Congress of Americanists
JAFL	*Journal of American Folklore*
JD	Josephine Dexter
JEP	John E. Parsons
KD	Katharine Dexter
KDM	Katharine Dexter McCormick
LC	Lucy Clews
MDL	Mabel Dodge Luhan
MFW	*Mexican Folkways*
MKS	Mary Kingsbury Simkhovitch

NAW	Edward T. James et al., eds., *Notable American Women, 1607–1950: A Biographical Dictionary,* 3 vols. (Cambridge: Belknap Press, 1971).
NAW Mod	Barbara Sicherman et al., eds., *Notable American Women, the Modern Period: A Biographical Dictionary,* vol. 4 (Cambridge: Belknap Press, 1980).
NAWSA	National American Woman Suffrage Association
NCAB	*National Cyclopedia of American Biography* (New York: J. T. White, 1898–1984).
NMB	Nicholas Murray Butler
NR	*New Republic*
NRC	National Research Council
NYEP	*New York Evening Post*
NYH	*New York Herald*
NYHT	*New York Herald Tribune*
NYT	*New York Times*
NYTr	*New York Tribune*
NYW	*New York World*
PG	Pliny Goddard
RB	Randolph Bourne
RB Letters	Eric J. Sandeen, ed., *The Letters of Randolph Bourne: A Comprehensive Edition* (Troy, N.Y.: Whitston Publishing Company, 1981).
RH	Robert Herrick
RHL	Robert H. Lowie
RLB	Ralph L. Beals
SD	Sam Dexter
SSRC	Social Science Research Council

Archival and Oral History Sources

ADM Papers	Alice Duer Miller Papers, Barnard College Archives
ALK Papers	Alfred L. Kroeber Papers, Bancroft Library, University of California, Berkeley
APS	Elsie Clews Parsons Papers, American Philosophical Society Library
Barnard College Archives	
Columbiana Collection	
	Columbiana Collection, Columbia University
CSS Papers	Community Service Society Papers, Columbia University Rare Book and Manuscript Library
FB Papers	Franz Boas Professional Papers, American Philosophical Society Library
GR Papers	Gladys Reichard Papers, Museum of Northern Arizona
HP Papers	Herbert Parsons Papers, Columbia University Rare Book and Manuscript Library
KDMA	Katharine Dexter McCormick Papers, MIT Archives
KDMM	Katharine Dexter McCormick Papers, MIT Museum

LPK   Lissa Parsons Kennedy [Mrs. John D. Kennedy], Columbia University Oral History Collection, 1962
LW Papers   Leslie A. White Papers, Bentley Historical Library, University of Michigan
MDL Papers   Mabel Dodge Luhan Papers, Beinecke Library, Yale University
MKS Papers   Mary Kingsbury Simkhovitch Papers, Schlesinger Library, Radcliffe College
RB Papers   Randolph Bourne Papers, Columbia University Rare Book and Manuscript Library
RH Papers   Robert Herrick Papers, University of Chicago Library Special Collections
RHL Papers   Robert H. Lowie Papers, Bancroft Library, University of California, Berkeley
RHS   Parsons Family Papers, Rye Historical Society
RLB Papers   Ralph L. Beals Papers, National Anthropological Archives, Smithsonian Institution

Interviews with Herbert Parsons Jr. and McIlvaine Parsons

Prologue

1. HP to ECP, 28 Nov. 1924; EC to SD, 13 Dec. 1893, APS; Edward Bellamy, *Looking Backward* (Boston: Ticknor, 1888); Gertrude Stein, *Wars I Have Seen* (New York: Random House, 1945), 21. The American Philosophical Society (APS) holds two Elsie Clews Parsons collections: (1) Ms. Coll. no. 29 (1880–1980, 26.25 ft.) contains the bulk of her personal and some professional correspondence, lectures and manuscripts, research notes and notebooks, financial papers, and photographs, as well as a small collection of Herbert Parsons's papers and materials for Peter H. Hare, *A Woman's Quest for Science: Portrait of Anthropologist Elsie Clews Parsons* (Buffalo: Prometheus Books, 1985); (2) APS 572/P25 (1835–1944, 12 ft.) contains professional correspondence ca. 1921–41, notebooks, and manuscripts. A third collection is the Parsons Family Papers (1832–1982, ca. 20 cubic ft.), Rye Historical Society (RHS). For description of APS 572/P25, see finding aid; Gladys Reichard, "The Elsie Clews Parsons Collection," *APS Proceedings* 94 (1950): 308–9; and J. Stephen Catlett, ed., *A New Guide to the Collections in the Library of the American Philosophical Society* (Philadelphia: American Philosophical Society, 1987), nos. 861 and 863. For APS Ms. Coll. no. 29, see Timothy Wilson and Carla B. Zimmerman, *Elsie Clews Parsons Papers: Guide to the Collection* (Philadelphia: APS Library, 1992), and Catlett, *Guide,* no. 862. The most comprehensive accounts of ECP's life and work are Hare, *A Woman's Quest for Science;* and Rosemary Lévy Zumwalt, *Wealth and Rebellion: Elsie Clews Parsons, Anthropologist and Folklorist* (Urbana: University of Illinois Press, 1992). See also Barbara A. Babcock, " 'Not Yet Classified, Perhaps Not Classifiable': Elsie Clews Parsons, Feminist/Anthropologist" (paper presented at the AAA meetings, 1988); introduction to *Pueblo Mothers and Children: Essays by Elsie Clews Parsons,*

1915–1924, ed. Babcock (Santa Fe: Ancient City Press, 1991); Babcock and Nancy J. Parezo, *Daughters of the Desert: Woment Anthropologists and the Native American Southwest, 1880–1980, an Illustrated Catalogue* (Albuquerque: University of New Mexico Press, 1988), 14–19; Paul Boyer, "Elsie Clews Parsons," *NAW;* Elizabeth L. Capelle, "Elsie Clews Parsons: A New Woman" (M.A. thesis, Columbia University, 1977); Desley Deacon, "Elsie Clews Parsons: New York Woman" (paper presented at the AAA meetings, 1988); and " 'Is Elsie Clews Parsons Good Enough to Teach?' " (paper presented at the ASA meetings, 1989); Mary Jo Deegan, "Elsie Clews Parsons," in *Women in Sociology: A Bio-Bibliographical Sourcebook,* ed. Deegan (New York: Greenwood Press, 1991), 320–26; Judith Friedlander, "The Life and Work of Elsie Clews Parsons" (paper presented at the AAA meetings, 1986); and "Elsie Clews Parsons," in *Women Anthropologists: Seclected Biographies,* ed. Ute Gacs et al. (Urbana: University of Illinois Press, 1989); Ramón Gutiérrez, introduction to ECP, *Pueblo Indian Religion,* vol. 2 (Lincoln: University of Nebraska Press, 1996); Louis A. Hieb, "Elsie Clews Parsons in the Southwest," in *Hidden Scholars: Women Anthropologists and the Native American Southwest,* ed. Nancy J. Parezo (Albuquerque: University of New Mexico Press, 1993), 63–75; Barbara Keating, "Elsie Clews Parsons: Her Work and Influence in Sociology," *Journal of the History of Sociology* 1 (fall 1978): 1–10; Alfred L. Kroeber, "Elsie Clews Parsons," *AA* 45 (1943): 252–55; Louise Lamphere, "Feminist Anthropology: The Legacy of Elsie Clews Parsons," *American Ethnologist* 16 (1989): 518–33; Nancy Oestreich Lurie, "Elsie Clews Parsons," *International Encyclopedia of the Social Sciences,* ed. David L. Sills (New York: Macmillan, 1968); Morris Opler, "Elsie (Worthington) Clews Parsons," *The New Encyclopaedia Britannica* (Chicago: University of Chicago Press, 1943–1973), Micropaedia; Gladys Reichard, "Elsie Clews Parsons," *JAFL* 56 (1943): 45–56; Rosalind Rosenberg, *Beyond Separate Spheres: Intellectual Roots of Modern Feminism* (New Haven: Yale University Press, 1982); Leslie Spier, "Elsie Clews Parsons," *AA* 45 (1943): 244–51; Pauline Turner Strong, introduction to ECP, *Pueblo Indian Religion,* vol. 1 (Lincoln: University of Nebraska Press, 1996); Leslie A. White, "Elsie Worthington Clews Parsons," *DAB.*

2. Friedrich Nietzsche, quoted in Frederic Jameson, foreword to *The Postmodern Condition,* by J.-F. Lyotard (Minneapolis: University of Minnesota Press, 1984), xii.

3. See *The Education of Henry Adams: An Autobiography* (New York: Time Inc., [1907]), 16–20, 67, for the reaction of this scion of an old political family to Washington life in 1868.

4. Anna was born in 1830 and Amanda (Puss) in 1840. Their parents, John Atwood Tomlinson (1794–1861), a wealthy medical practitioner, and Eliza Morris Thompson (1800–1865) of Harrodsburg, Kentucky, had ten surviving children of thirteen born between 1817 and 1842. During the 1850s, several settled in Keokuk in the new territory of Iowa, where they they met up-and-coming lawyer Belknap. Belknap served with Sherman during the war, rising to the rank of brigadier-general. He married Puss's sister Caroline in 1868. In October 1869, he was appointed secretary of war by President Grant. Caroline died in December 1870, three months after giving birth to a son, whom she committed to the care of Puss, whose

husband, John Bower, had just died. The baby died six months later. See ECP, "Family Faculties," APS; *Keokuk (Iowa) Gate City,* 5 Mar. 1876. For Carrie's death see *NYT,* 30 Dec. 1870; 1 Jan. 1871, 1; 2 Jan. 1871, 8. For Keokuk see Margaret Sanborn, *Mark Twain: The Bachelor Years, a Biography* (New York: Doubleday, 1990), 99.

5. Louis Auchincloss, *The Vanderbilt Era: Profiles of a Gilded Age* (New York: Collier, 1989), 46; *NYW,* 2 Jan. 1876, 1; *NYT,* 2 Jan. 1876, 1. For Puss Belknap's "charming grace and manner" as she welcomed guests at her New Year's Day party in 1876, see Rebecca Felton, *Country Life in Georgia in the Days of My Youth* (Atlanta, 1919), 135.

6. *NYT,* 3, 7, and 10 Mar. and 21 July 1876; 14 and 17 Oct. and 21 Nov. 1890; *DAB.* See William McFeely, *Grant: A Biography* (New York: W. W. Norton, 1981), 426–28; Gore Vidal, *1876: A Novel* (New York: Random House, 1976), 157–62.

7. *The Diary of James A. Garfield,* ed. H. J. Brown and F. D. Williams (East Lansing: Michigan State University Press, 1967), vol. 3, quoted in McFeely, *Grant,* 242–43; *NYW,* 13 Mar. 1876, 1, and 18 Mar. 1876, 8. See also Vidal, *1876,* 16; Mark Twain and Charles Dudley Warner, *The Gilded Age: A Tale of Today* (1873; New York: Trident Press, 1964).

8. *New York Evening Express,* 2 Mar. 1876; *NYW,* 3 Mar. 1876; *NYT,* 3 Mar. 1876. See also *NYT,* 4, 5, 6, 7, 8, and 10 Mar. and 21 and 26 July; *Keokuk (Iowa) Gate City,* 5 Mar. 1876.

9. *NYW,* 3 Mar. 1876; *Trenton Gazette,* quoted in *NYW,* 4 Mar. 1876, 6.

10. *NYT,* 5 Mar. 1876, 1, and 6 Mar. 1876, 5; *NYW,* 3 and 5 Mar. 1876. See also *Chicago Tribune,* reported in *NYW,* 8 Mar. 1876, 5. For masculinization of politics, see Paula Baker, "The Domestication of Politics: Women and American Political Society, 1780–1920," *American Historical Review* 89 (June 1984): 620–47; and Desley Deacon, "Politicizing Gender," *Genders* 6 (fall 1989): 1–19. For women lobbyists, see Twain and Warner, *Gilded Age;* Adams, *Education;* B. Bardes and S. Gossett, *Declarations of Independence* (New Brunswick: Rutgers University Press, 1990).

11. See Baker, "Domestication of Politics"; Deacon, "Politicizing Gender"; Ruth Bordin, *Woman and Temperance* (New Brunswick: Rutgers University Press, 1990). For important studies of women working within this new political culture, see Ellen Fitzpatrick, *Endless Crusade: Women Social Scientists and Progessive Reform* (New York: OUP, 1990); Estelle B. Freedman, *Maternal Justice: Miriam Van Waters and the Female Reform Tradition* (Chicago: University of Chicago Press, 1996); Kathryn Kish Sklar, *Florence Kelley and the Nation's Work: The Rise of Women's Political Culture* (New Haven: Yale University Press, 1995); and Theda Skocpol, *Protecting Soldiers and Mothers: The Political Origins of Social Policy in the United States* (Cambridge: Harvard University Press, 1992).

12. In 1847, Anna Tomlinson (1830–1909) married William Hord Worthington (1828–1862), son of John Worthington (1802–1868) and Frances Ann Slaughter (d. 1829), and grandson of Gabriel Slaughter, Kentucky governor in 1816, and of Edward Worthington and Eliza Given Madison, whose father's cousin James was U.S. president 1809–17, and whose uncle George was Kentucky governor after 1816. Lucy Madison

Worthington was born in Harrodsburg in 1852. William Hord Worthington died at Corinth in 1862. Anna married Robert Fermor Bower, the brother of Puss's first husband, in 1864. Preoccupied with a new family, she left Lucy's "coming out" to Puss, who probably found her a useful chaperone in the period between Caroline's death in 1870 and Puss's marriage to Belknap in 1873. In 1872, the *New York Times* noted that Secretary Belknap was assisted at his New Year's Day reception by his sister-in-law Mrs. Bower (Puss) and her niece Miss Worthington (Lucy). See *NYT,* 2 Jan. 1872, 8. For inaugural ball where Lucy and Henry probably met see *NYT,* 6 Mar. 1873, 1. For Lucy's deprivations as a child, see LC to ECP, Sun. [1906?], APS; LPK, 9.

13. LPK, 3–4, 7–9; interview with Dr. McIlvaine Parsons, May 1990; Henry Clews, *Twenty-Eight Years on Wall Street* (New York: Irving Publishing, 1888). For Lucy's recreation of herself, see Robert Herrick, *The End of Desire* (New York: Farrar and Rinehart, 1932), 75.

14. ECP, "Family Faculties," APS; Clews, *Twenty-Eight Years on Wall Street.*

15. LPK, 8–9. See T. F. Dawson, *Life and Character of Edward Oliver Wolcott, Late a Senator of the United States from the State of Colorado* (New York: Knickerbocker Press, 1911); *DAB; NCAB.* See C. Bancroft, *The Melodrama of Wolhurst* (Denver: Golden Press, 1952), for his large estate.

16. ECP, "My Washington Journal," 2 Mar. 1905, RHS. See also Herrick, *End of Desire,* 23 and 89, for this "sentimental and conventional southern lady" who "rambled off to Europe as often as she could manage it, dragging thither one of her children as chaperon." See "Mr. and Mrs. Wolcott to Part," *NYT,* 6 Mar. 1899, 10, for his divorce from Frances Wolcott, whom he married in 1891; and Frances Wolcott, *Heritage of the Years* (New York: Minton, Balch, 1932).

17. LPK, 10–11.

18. Herrick, *End of Desire,* 89; ECP, "Family Faculties," APS; LPK, 1–2; Stephen Fiske, *Off-hand Portraits of Prominent New Yorkers* (1884; New York: Arno Press, 1975); ECP to HP, 26 July 1909, APS.

19. Adams, *Education,* 67; also Herrick, *End of Desire,* 89.

Chapter One

1. Leslie Spier, "Elsie Clews Parsons," *AA* 45 (1943): 244–51; ECP, "The Imaginary Mistress" (1913), 1, APS.

2. Alice Belknap to EC, 27 Jan. 1890; 17 Nov. 1889; 7 Apr. 1890, APS. See also 22 Feb. and 7 Dec. 1889, APS.

3. LC to HP, 17 Aug. 1901, RHS; LC to ECP, 19 Aug. [1901]; LPK, 33; LC to EC, [20 Aug. 1888] and 24 Sept. 1889, APS. See ECP, "The Journal of a Feminist, 1913–1914," 102, APS.

4. ECP to HP, 16 Oct. and 20 Sept. 1905, APS. See Edith Wharton, *The House of Mirth* (1905; New York: Library of America, 1985), which was based on mutual friends, the Ogden Reids, and their circle.

5. Edith Wharton, *A Backward Glance* (1933; London: Century Hutchinson, 1987), 7, 2, 5, 22–25.

6. Ibid., 6, 20–21, 56–57; ECP, "American 'Society,' " pt. 1 (1916), 186. See Louis Auchincloss, *The Vanderbilt Era* (New York: Collier, 1989), 9–10, 45; and Edith Wharton, *The Age of Innocence* (1920; New York: Library of America, 1985), for old New York.

7. ECP, " 'Society,' " pt. 1, 185; Wharton, *Backward Glance*, 82–83. For intricacies of calling, see ECP, *Fear and Conventionality* (1914), 98–106; and "Journal of a Feminist," 100–101.

8. Wharton, *House of Mirth,* and *Age of Innocence*, 1081; Auchincloss, *Vanderbilt Era*, 43–52. For policing see also Wharton, *Backward Glance,* 24, 65, 77; for divorce, "Autres Temps . . . ," in *Roman Fever and Other Stories* (1911; New York: Macmillan, 1964), 233–76.

9. ECP, "Sex and the Elders" (1915).

10. Gertrude Stein, *The Making of Americans* (Paris: Contact Editions, 1925); Mary Lynn Broe, "My Art Belongs to Daddy: Incest as Exile, the Textual Economics of Hayford Hall," in *Women's Writing in Exile,* ed. Mary Lynn Broe and Angela Ingram (Chapel Hill: University of North Carolina Press, 1989); Louise DeSalvo, "To Make Her Mutton at Sixteen: Rape, Incest, and Child Abuse in the Antiphon," in *Silence and Power: A Reevaluation of Djuna Barnes,* ed. Mary Lynn Broe (Carbondale: Southern Illinois University Press, 1990); Christina Stead, *The Man Who Loved Children* (1940; New York: Henry Holt, 1968). For similar family dynamics, see Joyce Antler, *Lucy Sprague Mitchell: The Making of a Modern Woman* (New Haven: Yale University Press, 1987); Dee Garrison, *Mary Heaton Vorse: The Life of an American Insurgent* (Philadelphia: Temple University Press, 1990); Emma Goldman, *Living My Life* (1931; New York: Dover, 1970); Anzia Yezierska, *Breadgivers* (1925; New York: Persea, 1975).

11. ECP, "American 'Society,' " pt. 2 (1916), 214–15; Wharton, *Backward Glance,* 55.

12. Wharton, *Backward Glance,* 9; Van Wyck Brooks, "A Reviewer's Notebook," *Freeman,* 1 Dec. 1920, 287.

13. Henry James, *The Bostonians* (1886; Bantam Books, 1984), 240–43.

14. Wharton, *House of Mirth,* 7, 70–71. See Desley Deacon, "The Republic of the Spirit: Fieldwork in Elsie Clews Parsons's Turn to Anthropology," *Frontiers* 12, no. 3 (1992): 12–38. For excessive sex-distinction, see Charlotte Perkins Gilman, *Women and Economics* (1898; New York: Harper and Row, 1966).

15. See L. Stewart to EC, 1888–90; and M. L'Herbette to EC, 26 Dec. [1888], APS.

16. See EC's corres. with Alice Belknap, Dolly Potter, Miss Colton, and L. Luftis, 1885–90, APS. Cf. Wharton, *Backward Glance,* 48.

17. Alice Belknap to EC, 22 Feb. 1889; EC to Aimée Lawrence, 23 Sept. 1890, APS; Leslie Bright to EC, 5 Aug. [1892], RHS. For school, see EC, notebook; Large Album; M. Millard to EC, 6 Jan. 1890; EC to Miss Colton, [Sept. 1890?]; also corres. with Mme Ruel, HC, Abby Vaillant, Lucette Banks, Aimée Lawrence, F. C. and M. H. Addams, 1885–88, APS. For social life, see Large Album and corres. with Alice Belknap, Florence Westervelt, Amy Townsend, and Maude Stewart Lee, 1889–90, APS.

18. Aimée Lawrence to EC, [Aug. 1890], APS; Ralph Waldo Emerson,

"Self-Reliance" and "Circles," in *Essays: First Series,* vol. 2 of *The Collected Work of Ralph Waldo Emerson* (1841; Cambridge: Belknap Press, 1979), 27–51 and 179–90; J. M. Brinnin, *The Third Rose: Gertrude Stein and Her World* (New York: Addison-Wesley, 1987), 262–63. See also Bright to EC, 12 Nov. [1894], RHS. Cf. Mary Kingsbury Simkhovitch, *Here Is God's Plenty: Reflections on American Social Advance* (New York: Harper and Brothers, 1949), 156.

19. ECP, *The Old-Fashioned Woman* (1913), 285; Kathryn Kish Sklar, *Catharine Beecher* (New York: W. W. Norton, 1976); Helen Lefkowitz Horowitz, *Alma Mater: Design and Experience in the Women's Colleges from Their Nineteenth-Century Beginnings to the 1930s* (New York: Knopf, 1985). See also LPK, 13; EC to HP, 14 Aug. 1900, APS; ECP, "On Sending a Daughter, Willy Nilly, to College," in "Little Essays in Lifting Taboo" (1904–7), APS. For one of Elsie's set who did go to college, see Henry Wise Miller, *All Our Lives: Alice Duer Miller* (New York: Coward-McCann, 1945). For her mother banning books by the "common" Harriet Beecher Stowe, see Wharton, *Backward Glance,* 43, 64–76.

20. EC to J. Vatable, 4 [Apr. 1890?] and [1890], APS. See also ECP to HP, 14 Aug. 1900, APS; ECP, "Friendship, a Social Category" (1915); "Journal of a Feminist," 102; and "Selfishness" (1916?), APS. For Barnard, see Annie Nathan Meyer, *Barnard Beginnings* (Boston: Houghton Mifflin, 1935); Alice Duer Miller and Susan Myers, *Barnard College: The First Fifty Years* (1939); R. L. Taylor, "The Doctor, the Lady, and Columbia University," *New Yorker,* 23 and 30 Oct. 1943.

21. For Bobby's death, see ECP, "Family Faculties," and corres. with HC Jr., Miss Colton, Maude Stewart Lee, F. C. Addams, Anne Cameron, Sigmund Cohn, Beatrice (Bend), and Aimée Lawrence, 1890. For tour, see passenger lists, 3 Jan. and 27 June 1891, APS. For family claim, see ECP, "A Plan for Girls with Nothing to Do" (1905); Jane Addams, "The Subjective Necessity for Social Settlements," in *Philanthropy and Social Progress,* ed. Jane Addams et al. (1893; Montclair, N.J.: Patterson Smith, 1970), 1–26. For psychosomatic illness from conflict between family and outside interests, see Allen F. Davis, *American Heroine: The Life and Legend of Jane Addams* (New York: OUP, 1973); Charlotte Perkins Gilman, *The Yellow Wallpaper* (1892; Old Westbury, N.Y.: Feminist Press, 1973).

22. Ella Weed to EC, 16 June 1892; Alice Belknap to EC, [Nov. 1892?], RHS. See card, instructor in Greek, Newport, summer 1891; F. Thompson to EC, 2 Oct. [1891?]; schedule [1892?], in Large Album; Columbia College Entrance Examinations, 1892, APS; N. McCrea to HC, 13 May 1892; HC to EC, 2 June 1892, RHS. For Brearley, see Bertha Williams to EC, 5 Jan. 1899, RHS.

23. ECP, *Old-Fashioned Woman,* 285; LC to EC, 25 Oct. 1897, RHS. See also LC to EC, 21 Sept. 1897, RHS; ECP, *Fear and Conventionality,* 55. Elsie's daughter, Lissa, reports that "Grandfather was very proud of her intellectual capacity" (LPK, 13); but for his opinion that women's place was in the home see Henry Clews, "Shall the Suffrage Be Given to Women?" in *Financial, Economic, and Miscellaneous Speeches and Essays* (New York: Irving Publishing Company, 1910), 268–69; and "Woman in Politics, Nature, History, Business, and the Home," speech to National

Society of New England Women, Feb. 1910, cited in Rosemary Lévy Zumwalt, *Wealth and Rebellion: Elsie Clews Parsons, Anthropologist and Folklorist* (Urbana: University of Illinois Press, 1992), 36–37.

24. LC to EC, 13 June 1897, APS.

25. Alice [Belknap] to ECP, 2 Jan. 1905, RHS; ECP to LC, 24 Aug. 1908; LC to EC, 13 June 1897, APS. See Bright to EC, 5 Aug. [1892], RHS, on the grand tour: "if I only could have had your force and have studied no matter what happened and entered Barnard as you will this Fall!"

26. HC to EC, 30 July 1892, RHS. See also HC to EC, 10 June 1897; JD to EC, 3 Feb. [1895], RHS; Rosalind Rosenberg, *Beyond Separate Spheres: Intellectual Roots of Modern Feminism* (New Haven: Yale University Press, 1982), 12.

27. See Owen Wister, *Roosevelt: The Story of a Friendship, 1880–1919* (New York: Macmillan, 1930).

28. See SD to EC, 19 Dec. 1893; Helen Benedict to EC, 25 Apr. 1900; Grant LaFarge, poem, 3 July 1918, APS; KD to EC, 21 Dec. [1894], RHS; Robert Louis Stevenson, *Across the Plains* and *The Silverado Squatters*, in *From Scotland to Silverado* (1883); and *In the South Seas* (1890) (letters to *New York Sun*).

29. *Travels with a Donkey in the Cévennes* (1879), in *Complete Works of Robert Louis Stevenson*, Swanston Edition, 1:208. See Richard Aldington, *Portrait of a Rebel: The Life and Work of Robert Louis Stevenson* (London: Evans Brothers, 1957). Cf. ECP, "Unwritten Sumptuary Law," in "Little Essays" (1904–7), APS.

30. ECP to HP, 4 Aug. 1909, APS. See also ECP to HP, 24 July 1907 and 9 Sept. 1913, APS; ECP to MDL, 30 Aug. 1922, MDL Papers.

31. Wharton, *Backward Glance*, 44–45; LC to EC, [20 Aug. 1888], APS. See photographs and memorabilia, Large Album; corres. with Aimée Lawrence, Lispenard Stewart, and James Gerard, 1888–90, APS.

32. Dolly Potter to EC, 11 Sept. 1892, RHS. See ECP, "Friendship"; "Journal of a Feminist," 115, APS. For Potter family, see "Alonzo Potter," "Henry Codman Potter," "Horatio Potter," and "Robert Brown Potter," *DAB*.

33. See "Wirt Dexter," *DAB*. Sam was born in 1867. For his family see "Samuel Dexter, 1726–1810"; "Samuel Dexter, 1761–1816," *DAB*; "Katharine Dexter McCormick, 1875–1967," *NAW Mod*.

34. SD to EC, 19 Dec. and 25 Oct. 1893; EC to SD, 6 Feb. 1894, APS.

35. EC to SD, 27 Sept. 1893; SD to EC, [after 28 Sept.] and 25 Oct. 1893; EC to SD, 22 Oct. and 13 and 24 Dec. 1893, APS. See also EC to SD, 17 Oct. 1893; SD to EC, 6 Nov., [13 Oct.], and 13 Dec. 1893, APS.

36. EC to SD, 27 Sept. 1893, APS. See SD to EC, 19 Dec. 1893 and 18 Mar. 1894, APS. For chaperones, see ECP, "Feminism and Conventionality" (1914), 48; and *Fear and Conventionality*, 29.

37. EC to SD, 19 Nov. and 13 Dec. 1893; 13 Jan., 13 Mar. and 12 Apr. 1894, APS; L. D. Blake and H. A. Keyser, *Petition for Equal Suffrage*, letter, and convention call, 26 and 27 Feb. 1894, and leaflets, RHS. See also EC to SD, [22? and 27? Dec. 1893], 3 A.M. and 1 A.M. after balls, APS.

38. SD to EC, 1 May 1894; JD to EC, May and June 1894, RHS. Sam

died 4 May 1894. His mother endowed a set of gates at Harvard in his memory.

Chapter Two

1. Kirk Brice to EC, 5 Sept. 1894, RHS. See also Leslie Bright to EC, 17 Aug. and 12 Nov. 1894, RHS.

2. KD to EC, 13 Mar. 1895, RHS. See JD to EC, 26 Oct. 1896; and EC corres. with KD and JD, 1894–96, RHS. For Katharine's career that culminated, through tragic byways, with the development of the contraceptive pill sixty years later, see James Reed, "Katharine Dexter McCormick," *NAW Mod,* and *From Private Vice to Public Virtue* (New York: Basic Books, 1978), 334–45; Ellen Chesler, *Woman of Valor: Margaret Sanger and the Birth Control Movement in America* (New York: Simon and Schuster, 1992), 429–52.

3. JD to EC, 14 Apr. [1895], RHS.

4. Harry Elmer Barnes, in an editorial note to Clarence H. Northcott, "The Sociological Theories of Franklin Henry Giddings: Consciousness of Kind, Pluralistic Behavior, and Statistical Method," in *An Introduction to the History of Sociology* (1948; Chicago: University of Chicago Press, 1965), 763–64, ranks Giddings with Durkheim and Weber. See Franklin H. Giddings, *The Principles of Sociology* (New York: Macmillan, 1896).

5. G.D.G.C. [Goddard Chase] to EC, [June 1895], APS. See schedule [Nov. 1894]; second term report, 7 June 1895, APS. For Bryn Mawr, see Helen Lefkowitz Horowitz, *The Power and Passion of M. Carey Thomas* (New York: Knopf, 1994); "Emily James Putnam, 1865–1944," *FAW.*

6. Franklin H. Giddings, *Democracy and Empire: With Studies on Their Psychological, Economic, and Moral Foundations* (1900; Freeport, N.Y.: Books for Library's Press, 1972), 24–25, quoted in A. J. Vidich and S. M. Lyman, *American Sociology: Worldly Rejections of Religion and Their Directions* (New Haven: Yale University Press, 1985), 107–8; Charles E. Merriam, "Merriam's Early Experiences as a Graduate Student of Political Science," 28 Nov. 1949, Charles E. Merriam Papers, University of Chicago Special Collections, quoted in R. W. Wallace, "The Institutionalization of a New Discipline: The Case of Sociology at Columbia, 1891–1931" (Ph.D. diss., Columbia University, 1989), 121. See also Giddings, "The Ethics of Social Progress," in *Philanthropy and Social Progress,* ed. Jane Addams et al. (1893; Montclair, N.J.: Patterson Smith, 1970), 210–46.

7. Thomas Bender, *New York Intellect* (New York: Knopf, 1967); Wallace, "New Discipline." For sociology and settlements, see Mary Jo Deegan, *Jane Addams and the Men of the Chicago School, 1892–1918* (New Brunswick: Transaction Books, 1988); J. T. Carey, *Sociology and Public Affairs* (Beverly Hills: Russell Sage, 1975); S. J. Diner, *A City and Its Universities: Public Policy in Chicago, 1892–1919* (Chapel Hill: University of North Carolina Press, 1980). For the larger context of the development of sociology, see Dorothy Ross, *The Origins of American Social Science* (New York: Cambridge University Press, 1991).

8. See KD to EC, 9 Dec. [1894], RHS; EC, notice of meeting at Barnard, 21 Feb. 1895, to consider representation of Barnard in College Settlements Association, APS; JD to EC, 25 May [1895], RHS, re Jane Addams; Jean

Tatlock to EC, 2 June [1895], RHS, re "College, University Settlement, Kappa and all your other 'irons' "; Jane Robbins to EC, 26 Oct. 1895, RHS; *Barnard Annual* 1895 and 1896.

9. Jane Robbins, "The First Year at the College Settlement," *Survey,* 24 Feb. 1912, 1801. See Jane Addams, "The Subjective Necessity for Social Settlements" and "The Objective Value of a Social Settlement," in Addams et al., *Philanthropy and Social Progress,* 1–26 and 27–40; Ann Firor Scott, introduction to *Democracy and Social Ethics,* by Jane Addams (1902; Cambridge: Belknap, 1964).

10. R. A. Woods and A. J. Kennedy, eds., *Handbook of Settlements* (New York: Charities Publication Committee, 1911); College Settlements Association reports, *Commons;* Teresa Corcoran, "Vida Scudder," *NAW Mod;* and Vida Scudder, *On Journey* (1937); "Katharine Lee Bates," *FAW;* Barbara Miller Solomon, "Emily Greene Balch," *NAW Mod;* and Mercedes M. Randall, *Improper Bostonian* (New York: Twayne, 1964); Mary Jo Deegan, "Women and Sociology, 1890–1930," *Journal of the History of Sociology* 1 (1978): 11–34; J. P. Rousmaniere, "Cultural Hybrid in the Slums: The College Woman and the Settlement House, 1889–1894," *American Quarterly* 22 (1970): 45–66; Allen F. Davis, *Spearheads for Reform: The Social Settlements and the Progressive Movement, 1890–1914* (New Brunswick: Rutgers University Press, 1984); Jill Ker Conway, *The First Generation of American Women Graduates* (New York: Garland, n.d.).

11. Mary Kingsbury Simkhovitch, *Neighborhood: My Story of Greenwich House* (New York: Norton, 1938), 60–74, esp. 70–71, 78; and *Here is God's Plenty* (New York: Harper and Brothers, 1949), 171.

12. Lillian D. Wald, *The House on Henry Street* (1915; New Brunswick: Transaction Publishers, 1991), 133, 84. See Addams, *Democracy and Social Ethics,* 180–81; D. Rosenstein, "The Educational Function of the Social Settlement in a Democracy," *School and Society,* 29 Sept. 1917, 369; A. Thomas Jr., "American Education and the Immigrant," *Teachers College Record* 55 (1953–54): 253–67.

13. Quoted in Diane Ravitch, *The Great School Wars* (New York: Basic Books, 1974), 173, 146, and see 148–67 for 1896 reform bill, the 1897 establishment of the first three high schools, and the 1901 revised charter under the mayoralty of Seth Low. For seminar see NMB to EC, 20 May 1897, APS. See also Nicholas Murray Butler in *Educational Review* 8 (June 1894); and Butler, ed., *Education in the United States* (Albany, 1900).

14. Lawrence A. Cremin, *The Transformation of the School* (New York: Vintage, 1961), 86–87; Sol Cohen, *Progressivism and Urban School Reform: The Public Education Association of New York City, 1985–1954* (New York: Teachers College, 1964); M. I. Berger, *The Settlement, the Immigrant, and the Public School* (New York: Arno, 1980). For College Settlement activities, see Jane Robbins, "School Playgrounds in New York" and "The Settlement and the Public School," *Outlook,* 31 July 1895 and 6 Aug. 1910; Simkhovitch, *Neighborhood, Here is God's Plenty,* and "The New Social Science Put into Practice," *Harper's Bazaar,* 25 Dec. 1897, 1088; also "College Settlement Extension in New York," *Public Opinion,* 9 Nov. 1900, 587.

15. EC, "On Certain Phases of Poor-Relief in the City of New York"

(1897). For friendly visiting, see EC to Miss Decker, 28 Nov. [1896] and 7 Jan. [1897]; Charity Organization Society, Annual Report, 1896–97, CSS Papers; Simkhovitch, *Neighborhood*, 60. For clubs see EC, large ms. on New York history; corres. with Stanford White, HP, Frank Kelley, and Robert Woods, 1896–99, RHS; Association for Improvement of the Condition of the Poor, Annual Reports, CSS Papers; Winifred Buck, *Boys' Self Governing Clubs* (1903; New York: Macmillan, 1912). See also William James, *Principles of Psychology* (1890), *Talks to Teachers* ([1892]1899), and *The Will to Believe* (1897); John Dewey, "Interest as Related to the Training of the Will" (1896), "Ethical Principles Underlying Education" (1897), and "My Pedagogic Creed," *School Journal* 54 (1897): 77–80. For Julia Richman (1855–1912), see NMB to EC, 9 Mar. 1896, RHS; Richman, "The School as a Social Center," *Charities Review*, 8 Apr. 1905, 646; Selma C. Berrol, "Julia Richman: Agent of Change in the Urban School," *Urban Education* 12 (Jan. 1977): 361–81; Berger, *The Settlement*, 91–92. For Teachers College, see "Grace Hoadley Dodge," *FAW*. For EC's school plan of two years earlier, see EC to HP, 20 Apr. 1899, APS; President's Report (1899), cited in Cremin, *Transformation*, 175. The Speyer School of Columbia Teachers College opened in 1902. See Howard Woolston, "Social Education and the Public Schools," *Charities Review*, 1 Sept. 1906, 570–78. For agreement with family, see EC to HP, 20 Apr. 1899, APS. Family opposition probably prevented her from taking up the headship of Friendly Aid House in 1898, which then went to Mary Kingsbury. See Mary Hewitt to EC, 2 July 1897, RHS. EC could not do doctoral work in sociology because it was located in the School of Political Science, which did not accept women. See Wallace, "New Discipline."

16. K. [Wadamoris?] to EC, 3 Dec. 1899, RHS; Ralph [Paine?/ Parry?] to EC, 5 Oct. 1897, RHS, from the Philadelphia *Press*, re doing "an expedition"—the first of many attempts to make copy of her; Bessie Davis to EC, [Dec. 1894]; JD to EC, 3 Feb., 25 May, and 19 June [1895]. See also 20 Jan. and [Apr.] [1896], RHS. For Cinderella Dance, see Ellis to EC, 8 Feb. 1895, RHS.

17. LC to EC, 21 Sept. 1897, RHS. For Tarde, see Alice Sterne to EC, 13 Oct. 1896, RHS; ECP to HP, 1 Nov. 1896, APS; and Giddings to EC, 20 Dec. 1897, RHS, re publication.

18. Alice Chase to EC, 23 July and 7 Aug. 1895; Caroline Brombacher to EC, 3 Aug. 1895, RHS; Liggett to EC, 15 June 1896; also 8 Oct. 1895, RHS.

19. ECP, "The Study of Variants" (1920), 87. See ECP, *The Laws of Imitation*, by Gabriel Tarde (1903). For concept of "legislator," see Zygmunt Bauman, *Legislators and Interpreters: On Modernity, Post-Modernity, and Intellectuals* (Ithaca: Cornell University Press, 1987). ECP's is still one of only two translations of Tarde's work into English. *Les Lois sociales: Esquisse d'une sociologie* (Paris, 1898) was translated in 1899 by H. C. Warren, assistant professor of experimental psychology, Princeton, with a preface by J. M. Baldwin, whose child development studies were strongly influenced by Tarde.

20. Tarde, preface to *Laws of Imitation*, xviii, and "L'Accident et le rationnel en histoire d'après Cournot," *Revue de Metaphysique et de Morale* 13 (1905): 334, quoted in A. C. Taymans, "Tarde and Schumpeter: A

Similar Vision," *Quarterly Journal of Economics* 64 (Aug. 1950): 611–22, esp. 613; C. Bouglé, "Un Sociologue individualiste: Gabriel Tarde," *Revue de Paris*, 15 May 1905, 313. See Franklin H. Giddings, introduction to *Laws of Imitation*; T. N. Clark, introduction to *Gabriel Tarde on Communication and Social Influence: Selected Papers* (Chicago: University of Chicago Press, 1969); G. Guy-Grand, "Gabriel Tarde, 1834–1904," in *Encyclopedia of the Social Sciences*, ed. Edwin R. A. Seligman (New York: Macmillan, 1930–35). For debate with Durkheim, see Steven Lukes, *Emile Durkheim* (Harmondsworth: Penguin, 1975), 303–11.

21. Tarde, preface to *Laws of Imitation*, esp. xxiv. See review of *L'Opposition universelle*, *Monist* 8 (1898): 142–44.

22. Gabriel Tarde, *L'Opinion et la foule* (1898; Paris: Alcan, 1922), selection reprinted in *Selected Papers*, 297–318, esp. 307–8; see Clark's introduction, ibid., 56–58. For Tarde's utopia, see *Fragments d'histoire future* (1905); English ed., *Underground Man*, preface by H. G. Wells (London: Duckworth, 1905).

23. ALK to ECP, 19 Sept. 1916, APS.

24. Alice Sterne to EC, 30 Oct. 1896, RHS; Carroll Smith-Rosenberg, "Mary Kingsbury Simkhovitch," *NAW Mod;* Kathleen Marquis, "Mary Melinda (Kingsbury) Simkhovitch, 1867–1951," finding aid, Schlesinger Library. For Friendly Aid House, see Edith Kendall, "Warren Goddard House," *Unitarian*, Apr. 1908.

25. Smith-Rosenberg, "Simkhovitch." See Mary Kingsbury, "Women in New York Settlements," *Municipal Affairs*, Sept. 1898, 458–62; Mary [Kingsbury] Simkhovitch, "Friendship and Politics," *Political Science Quarterly* 17 (June 1902): 189–205; "Settlement Organization," *Charities and the Commons*, 1 Sept. 1906, 566–69; *The City Worker's World in America* (New York: Macmillan, 1917); *Neighborhood; Group Life* (New York: Association Press, 1940); and *Here Is God's Plenty*.

26. ECP to Lewis Chanler, copy with ECP to HP, 2 July 1906, APS. White was shot 25 June 1906. See P. R. Baker, *Stanny: The Gilded Life of Stanford White* (New York: Free Press, 1989).

27. EC to SD, 2 Feb. 1894; White to EC, [Apr. 1985?], APS.

28. JD to EC, 24 Aug. 1895, RHS; Helen Benedict to EC, 9 July 1896, RHS; White to EC, [Mar. 1897] and 16 Aug. [1896]: "My dear & Honorable Bachelor of Arts"; and [Apr. 1896], RHS. For fishing trip, see ECP to HP, 29 May and 18 June 1897; HC to EC, 10 June 1897; photo album, photos in Kodak envelope, and mounted photos by James Breese, RHS.

29. "Herbert Parsons," *NCAB;* "John Edward Parsons, 1829–1915," *DAB*.

30. See Fanny Wickes Parsons, "A Visit to the Parsons House," *Rye Historical Society Newsletter*, May 1986, 9–15, and Oct. 1986, 9–14. The Lenox house has been demolished, though the farmhouse, Stonover Farm, is still lived in. The Harrison house belongs to ECP's grandson David Parsons, son of Herbert Parsons Jr.

31. HP to Children, 12 May 1918, APS. See also JD to EC, 20 Dec. 1894; Holken Abbott to EC, 27 Dec. 1894; KD to EC, 22 Jan. 1895; HP to EC, 16, 17 and 26 May, 4 and 16 Aug. 1895; Helen Benedict to EC, 20 June and 8 Oct. 1895; [Alonzo Potter] to EC, [Aug. 1895]; Eleanor [Cross] to EC, 9 Oct. [1895], RHS.

32. HP to EC, 10 July 1896, APS. See HP to EC, 8 and 11 Nov. 1895; 5 and 15 May 1896; Walton Martin to HP, 20 July [1896]; Abbott to EC, 15 Oct. 1896, RHS; HP to EC, [Nov. 1896]; LC to HP, Sept. 1897, APS.

33. Edward Parsons to HP, 28 Dec. 1896 and 14 Apr. 1897, APS; Robert Herrick, *Chimes* (New York: Macmillan, 1926), 10, 146; White to EC, [Mar.] 1897, RHS. See HP to EC, 7 Feb., 31 Mar., 11 and 27 Apr., and 12 May 1897, APS. Herrick, *Chimes,* 15, gives some hint as to why Herbert was more attractive to Elsie than her Boston admirers: " 'As a Yale man,' " he seemed to be saying, 'I am not supposed to be as refined, as finished a product as they make about Boston, but I am more virile and American than your kind, less of a dilettante, better adapted to understanding the great public and making my place in a thoroughly American environment like this one. I am not as intolerant and unsympathetic as you are likely to be. I can understand different sorts of superiority, while you admit only your own kind.' "

34. LC to EC, 25 Oct. 1897, RHS. See EC, "The Status of the Study of Pedagogics in the American College and University" (1898); HC to EC, 10 June 1897, RHS.

35. EC to HP, 20 July and 5 Aug. 1897, APS.

36. LC to EC and HC to EC, 22 Aug. 1897, APS. See also EC to HP, 9 July, 5 Aug., and 7 Sept. 1897; HC to EC, 13 Aug. 1897; LC to EC, 21 Sept., 25 Oct., and 5 Nov. 1897; HP to EC, 25 Aug., 1, 2, 7, 10, and 11 Sept. 1897; Walton to HP, 28 Aug. and 3 Sept. 1897; HP to LC, 31 Aug. 1897; LC to HP, 14 Sept. 1897, RHS.

37. EC to HP, 5 Aug. and 7 Sept. 1897, APS.

38. HP to Children, 12 May 1918, APS; EC to HP, 5 May and 30 June 1898, APS. See also 28 June and 2 Aug. 1898. For war see HP to EC, 27 Jan., 22 Feb., 13 and 29 Apr. 1898, RHS. Herbert did not serve in the war, but see photograph of him in military uniform, RHS.

39. EC to HP, 29 Apr. 1899, RHS. See Giddings to EC, 17 Apr. 1899, RHS; EC to HP, 20 and [21] Apr., [4 and 10 May] 1899, RHS; EC to HP [May] 1899, APS. See EC, *Educational Legislation and Administration of the Colonial Governments* (1899): superviser N. M. Butler; advisers colonial historian H. L. Osgood, sociologist F. H. Giddings. For fellowship see corres. with L. Eudy, N. McCrea, HP, Giddings, Y. Weizenhoffer, 22 Apr. 1899–29 May 1900; EC, "Hartley House Fellowship," draft, RHS; and "Field Work in Teaching Sociology" (1900); Barnard College, announcement, 1899–1900, Barnard College Archives; Wallace, "New Discipline," 175–208.

40. For illness, see Edward Castle to EC, 12 May 1899, RHS. For reconciliation, see EC to HP, 19 and 21 June, 16 and 17 July, and 21 Aug. 1899, APS. For oral examination in education, philosophy, sociology, and statistics on 15 May 1899 by Nicholas Murray Butler, J. McKeen Cattell, and Franz Boas, and notification of pass, see NMB to EC, 16 May 1899, in Large Album, APS. Boas apparently examined Elsie in statistics, although there is no evidence that she studied with him, or that she ever used statistics in her work. At least in 1897–98, statistician Richard Mayo-Smith refused to accept Barnard students, and Wallace's table of student enrollments do not show any Barnard students in his courses. See Alice Sterne to EC, 13 Oct. 1896, RHS; Wallace, "New Discipline," 406–7.

NOTES TO PAGES 46–50 / 407

41. EC, "Field Work in Teaching Sociology," 159, 164–68; M.H. [M. Halbwachs], review of Elsa G. Herzfeld, *Family Monographs,* in *L'Année Sociologique* 10 (1905–6): 605–8, esp. 605: "Ces vingt-quatre monographies de famille ont été établies par Miss Herzfeld suivant la methode que pratiquent à Barnard College les étudiants en sociologie: elle consiste à insister sur la psychologie des groupes plus que sur leur caractère économique, et se propose non de dresser des budgets de famille, mais de reproduire en toute sa complexité et son détail l'histoire et la vie des ménages étudiés. L'auteur faisait à ces familles des visites régulières, pour les encourager à l'épargne, comme 'penny provident collecter': ce lui fut l'occasion de pénétrer réellement dans leur intimité." See "Instruction in the Observation of Social Facts According to the Le Play Method of Monographs on Families," translated by Charles A. Ellwood, *AJS* 2 (Mar. 1897): 662–88; ECP, *The Family* (1906), 9–19; and appendix, 359–64, for questionnaire on family relations compiled by Dr. Albert Hermann Post for the International Society for Comparative Law and Ethnography, Berlin. ECP's source was Steinmetz, *Rechrsverhältnisse von eingeborenen Völkern in Afrika und Ozeanien* (Berlin, 1903). The students were from Giddings's Sociology 15: "Principles of Sociology." The class, open to seniors and graduate students, had two graduates, ten seniors, one junior, and one special student. For publication by one of her students, see Elsa G. Herzfeld, *Family Monographs: The History of Twenty-Four Families Living in the Middle West Side of New York City* (1905); C.R.H. [Henderson], review, *AJS* 11 (Jan. 1906): 706.

42. For Alice's experiment, see EC to HP, 21 Aug. 1899, APS. For her wedding to Harry Miller on 5 Oct. 1899, see ADM Papers. For school inspectorship, see L. C. Butler to EC, 13 July 1899, RHS. For decision to marry, see EC to HP, 20 Apr. 1900, APS; Parsons family to EC, 4 May and May 1900; Constance Parsons to EC and Sheldon to EC, 16 May [1900], RHS. See Robert Herrick, "Chapter Six, Cooperation versus Combination," 66–76, from early version of *End of Desire* (1926?), RH Papers: "Jessica had had a hard struggle to go to college. . . . Another family battle to go on into the graduate school and take a doctorate. . . . possibly that was the reason for her prompt marriage to Dean Mallory. . . . Has she ever loved Mallory? Redfield answered this query yes and no alternately through the period of his intimacy."

Chapter Three

1. Rosalind Rosenberg, *Beyond Separate Spheres: Intellectual Roots of Modern Feminism* (New Haven: Yale University Press, 1982), 12; Helen Lefkowitz Horowitz, *The Power and Passion of M. Carey Thomas* (New York: Knopf, 1994).

2. Dean Putnam to Brownell, 13 Apr. 1900. See Mar. 1929 note by Annie Nathan Meyer about holding Putnam to promise of resigning if pregnant, Barnardiana File C Admin. (corres., 1888–1911, trustee corres., committee reports; also Dean Putnam's resignation), Barnard College Archives. For Miller, see Stanley J. Kunitz and Howard Haycraft, eds., *Twentieth Century Authors: A Biographical Dictionary of Modern Literature* (New York: H. W. Wilson, 1942), 958–59. For Jacobi (1842–1906), see

Ruth Putnam, ed., *Life and Letters of Mary Putnam Jacobi* (New York: G. P. Putnam's Sons, 1925). Her husband's nephew was anthropologist Franz Boas. For Croly (1829–1901) see *FAW*. Her son Herbert was founding editor of the *New Republic*.

3. Carlotta Russell Lowell to EC, 3 June 1900; A. R. Cross to EC and Annie Nathan Meyer to EC, 7 June 1900, RHS.

4. Sarah Cohen to EC, 19 July 1900; James Reynolds to EC, 23 July 1900; Jane Robbins to EC and Susan Walker to EC, 1 June [1900], RHS. Walker was head of the Women's University Settlement and later, as Susan Fitzgerald, mother of at least two children.

5. Edward Westermarck, *The History of Human Marriage* (London: Macmillan, 1891); C. Wright Mills, "Edward Alexander Westermarck and the Application of Ethnographic Methods to Marriage and Morals," in *An Introduction to the History of Sociology*, ed. Harry Elmer Barnes (1948; Chicago: University of Chicago Press, 1965), 654–67, esp. 663.

6. Edward Carpenter, *Love's Coming of Age* (1896), in *Edward Carpenter: Selected Writings* (London: GMP Publishers, 1984), 1:96.

7. Ibid., 103. See Jan Marsh, *Back to the Land* (London: Quarter Books, 1982), 17–23. In the final chapter of *The Family* (1906), ECP draws on Carpenter's "Marriage, a Forecast" (1897) for the idea that divorce should depend only on mutual consent, the state interfering only in the provision for offspring. She also seems to have found the outdoors and the beauties of nature sexually stimulating, a taste that Herbert did not share.

8. Havelock Ellis, *The New Spirit* (London: Bell, 1890), 129.

9. Sections of Ellis's *Sexual Inversion* (Leipzig, 1896; London, 1897) appeared in the American medical press prior to its troubled British publication, followed by *The Evolution of Modesty, The Phenomena of Sexual Periodicity,* and *Auto-Eroticism* (Leipzig, 1899). See "The Study of Sexual Inversion," *Medico-Legal Journal,* Apr. 1894, 148–57; "Sexual Inversion in Women," *Alienist and Neurologist,* Apr. 1895, 148–58; "Sexual Inversion in Man" and "A Note on the Treatment of Sexual Inversion," *Alienist,* Apr. 1896, 115–50, and July 1896, 257–64; "Sexual Inversion in Relation to Society and the Law," *Medico-Legal Journal,* Dec. 1896, 279–88. Because of censorship in Britain, these and later volumes by Ellis were published by the Philadelphia medical publishers F. A. Davis from 1901 to 1910. See *Studies in the Psychology of Sex,* vol. 1, *The Evolution of Modesty, The Phenomena of Sexual Periodicity, Auto-Eroticism* (Philadelphia: F. A. Davis, 1900); vol. 2, *Sexual Inversion* (1901). See also *Affirmations* (London: Walter Scott, 1898).

10. James Mark Baldwin, *Mental Development in the Child and the Race,* 2d ed. (1895; New York: Macmillan, 1903), 4, 5; S. E. Wiltse, "A Preliminary Sketch of the History of Child Study in America," *Pedagogical Seminary* 3 (Oct. 1895): 190, quoted in Nathan G. Hale Jr., *Freud and the Americans* (New York: OUP, 1971), 105. See also Baldwin, *Social and Ethical Interpretations in Mental Development: A Study in Social Psychology* (New York: Macmillan, 1897); R. H. Mueller, "A Chapter in the History of the Relationship between Psychology and Sociology in America: James Mark Baldwin," *Journal of the History of the Behavioral Sciences* 12 (1976): 240–53.

11. ECP, "A Plea against Nursery Paraphrases," 2, in "Little Essays in

Lifting Taboo" (1904–7), APS; Herrick, "The Story of Jessica Stowe" (1924), RH Papers. Edward A. Ross, who coined the term "race suicide" in 1901, defined it in *Foundations of Sociology* (1905) as the process whereby the "higher race quietly and unmurmuringly eliminates itself rather than endure individually the bitter competition it has failed to ward off from itself by collective action." A 1904 lecture series published as *Sin and Society* (Boston: Houghton Mifflin, 1907) attracted the attention of Roosevelt who applied the term to women in attacking the low birth and increased divorce rates in 1905. See Linda Gordon, *Woman's Body, Woman's Right* (New York: Penguin, 1990), 133, 139; Ross to Lester Ward, 22 Oct. and 22 Nov. 1906; and Ward to Ross, 1 Apr. 1907, in B. J. Stern, ed., "The Ward-Ross Correspondence IV, 1906–1912," *ASR* 14 (1949): 88–119, esp. 98, 101–2.

12. ECP, "Pertinent to the Simple Life," 2; "Unwritten Sumptuary Law," 3, 4; "On the Domestic Service Problem," 1; and "Caste and the Unproductive Activities of the American Woman," 1, 3, 4, in "Little Essays." Thorstein Veblen, *The Theory of the Leisure Class* (1899; New York: Penguin, 1981). ECP was also reading Hugo Munsterberg, *The Americans* (New York: McClure, Phillips, 1904), when she wrote these essays.

13. EC to HP, 15 Aug. 1898, APS; HP to EC, 28 July 1900; ECP to JEP Sr., 23 Sept. 1904, RHS.

14. ECP to JEP, 17 Mar. 1926. See ECP to HP, 2 Sept. 1909, APS.

15. LC to HP, 2 Aug. 1900; *NYH*, 2 Sept. 1900, APS.

16. See EC, "Field Work in Teaching Sociology." For honeymoon, see corres. Sheldon-HP-EC, RHS; and Howard Cushing-EC-HP, 31 July–14 Aug. 1900, APS. For politics, see HP to EC, 29 July–29 Aug. 1900 and voting card, RHS; ECP to Mac Parsons, 7 Dec. 1941, copy fr. Dr. McIlvaine Parsons.

17. ECP, "The Journal of a Feminist, 1913–1914," 118, APS.

18. HP to ECP, 6 Dec. 1900; Giddings to ECP, 20 June 1901, RHS. For Archeological Institute, see McCrae to ECP, 31 Oct. 1900; for Women's Municipal League, J. S. Lowell to ECP, 27 Mar. 1901, RHS.

19. LC to HP, 21 July; also 7 July 1901; "Diary of Elsie Parsons from the day of her birth, Tuesday, August 6, 1901," RHS. The diary breaks off with the sending of the telegrams (including HP to HC Jr.) and is never resumed. For Miss Carmody, see esp. ECP to HP, 9 May 1917, APS.

20. ADM to ECP, 7 Aug. 1901; MKS to ECP, 9 Aug. 1901; LC to HP, 7 Aug. 1901, RHS. See also LC to HP, 21 Aug. 1901, APS.

21. HC to ECP, [11 Sept. 1901], RHS; ECP to MDL, 24 Aug. 1922, MDL Papers; ECP to HP, 1 Mar. 1907, APS. See also HP to ECP, 26 Feb. 1907; ECP, notes misc. no. 2 [1908], APS; E. Crockett to ECP, 20 Aug. 1901; JEP Sr. to HP, 25 Aug. 1901, RHS. See ECP, "Sex and the Elders" (1915), for episode re breastfeeding probably based on her straitlaced father-in-law; also Robert Herrick, *The End of Desire* (New York: Farrar and Rinehart, 1932), 50. For education board, see ECP to NMB, draft, 19 Nov. 1901; NMB to ECP, 20 Nov. 1901; Mrs. A. Dodge to ECP, [ca. 30 Nov. 1901], RHS.

22. See ECP, notes re jobs to do, [end May 1902], RHS; MKS to ECP, [Jan.? 1902], RHS; MKS to Edith and E.K. to MKS, [May?] 1902, Schle-

singer Library. For other differences with Friendly Aid House, see Carroll Smith-Rosenberg, "Mary Kingsbury Simkhovitch," *NAW Mod.* For new settlement see MKS-ECP corres., 25 May–[Aug. 1902], RHS; Mary Kingsbury Simkhovitch, *Neighborhood: My Story of Greenwich House* (New York: Norton, 1938), 87–89. The Cooperative Social Settlement Society had Elsie's friend and Newport neighbor Bishop Henry Potter, Catholic layman Eugene Philbin, Carl Schurtz, Jacob Riis, Felix Adler, and Robert Fulton Cutting as incorporators, Professor Seligman and Edward Devine as managers, Paul Kennaday as treasurer, and Elsie's friend, banker Meredith Hare, on the board.

23. MKS to ECP, 13 July 1903, RHS.

24. Katharine Coman to ECP, 5 Nov. [1903], RHS. For appointment see Catalogue, 1902–3, Columbiana Collection; R. W. Wallace, "The Institutionalization of a New Discipline: The Case of Sociology at Columbia, 1891–1931" (Ph.D. diss., Columbia University, 1989), 175–208. For John see HP to JEP, 15 Aug. 1903; for social hall, MKS to ECP, 29 Oct. 1903; Tom Hastings to ECP, 2 Nov. 1903, RHS. See Tarde, *The Laws of Imitation* (1903). For a summary of ECP's positions in 1904, see HP, "Memorandum for Montee Cutler" (1904), HP Papers. For continuing work with students, see Elsa Herzfeld to ECP, 20 June; ECP to Herzfeld, Aug. 1903; Herzfeld to ECP, 14 June 1904, RHS; Paul Kellogg to ECP, June 1905; Herzfeld, *Family Monographs: History of Twenty-Four Families Living in the Middle West Side of New York City,* with preface by ECP (1905); C. R. Henderson, review, *AJS* 11 (Jan. 1906), 706; director, Greenwich House, Report, Oct. 1904 and Jan. 1906, CSS Papers; Herzfeld Naumberg, *West Side Rookery* (1906); Simkhovitch, *Neighborhood,* 131. For Greenwich House during ECP's association see Simkhovitch, "The Settlement and the Public School," *Commons,* May 1903; "Playgrounds and Public Parks," *Commons,* Nov. 1903, 10; "The Public School: Its Neighborhood Use," *Commons,* Sept. 1904, 406–17; and "The Enlarged Function of the Public School," in *National Conference of Charities and Correction Proceedings* (1904), 471–86. For Committee on Social Studies with Columbia economist Henry Seager, political scientist E. R. A. Seligman, and Franklin Giddings, see director, Greenwich House, Report, 19 Oct. 1904, CSS Papers. For studies carried out under its auspices including Louise Bolard, "Wage Earners' Budgets" (1903), Herzfeld Naumberg, *West Side Rookery* (1906), Mary Ovington, *Half a Man* (1911), see Simkhovitch, *Neighborhood,* 150–51. John Dewey chaired the Greenwich House Committee on Education. See Dewey, "The School as Social Center," *National Education Association Journal of Proceedings* (1902), 381; Allen F. Davis, *Spearheads for Reform: The Social Settlements and the Progressive Movement, 1890–1914* (New Brunswick: Rutgers University Press, 1984), 77–81; ECP to Florence Kelley, 27 Dec. 1903; 3 Jan. 1904, RHS; Kelley to ECP, 11 Dec. [1904?]; J. G. Phelps Stokes, "Public Schools as Social Centers, *Annals of the American Academy of Political and Social Science* 21 (May 1904): 460; M. McGuire to ECP, 25 Apr. 1905, APS. For College Settlements Association, see Susan Fitzgerald [Walker] to ECP, 11 June, 1 July 1902, RHS; Helen Phelps Stokes to ECP, 10 Apr. [1903?] and [n.d., when ECP was in Washington, D.C.], APS. For recipients of College Settlements Association fellowships, see Mary B. Sayles, "Housing Conditions in Jersey

City," *Annals of the American Academy of Political and Social Science* 20 (1903): 139–50, and "The Work of a Woman Tenement House Inspector," *Outlook,* 12 Sept. 1903, 121; Lucille O'Connell, "Frances Kellor," *NAW Mod;* Alvin Johnson to ECP, 4 Sept 1902; K.C. [Katharine Coman] to ECP, 5 and 17 Nov. 1903; Helen Thayer to ECP, 11 Apr. 1904; Emily Putnam to ECP, 3 Aug. 1904, RHS; E. M. Lewis, "Mary Van Kleeck," *NAW Mod;* for Sayles, see Davis, *Spearheads,* 66. For faculty advisory council and fellowships committee of School of Philanthropy, see Edward Devine to ECP, 25 Feb. and 10 Mar. 1905, RHS, and 26 Dec. 1906, APS; School of Philanthropy to ECP, 10 Sept. 1906, APS. Charity Organization Society general secretary Devine became Schiff Professor of Social Economy in March 1905. For invitation to join Jane Addams, Margaret Robins, and Jacob Riis on the National Charities Publication Committee, whose investigations led to the Pittsburgh Survey, see Paul Kellogg to ECP, 27 Oct. 1905, RHS; Graham Taylor to ECP, 17 Dec. 1906, APS.

Parsons appears to have begun her career as philanthropist by donating her salary to female scholarship. For financial support for a woman Fellow in History, see NMB to ECP, 6 May 1902, RHS; and for donation of $300 to Barnard Library, Anna Ware to ECP, 20 Apr. [1903?], RHS. For her general financial situation see ECP to JEP Sr., 23 Sept. 1904, RHS: "At present I run the household on an allowance of $6000 a year. Herbert makes me a personal allowance of $1800. The allowance of $2500 from my father has formed a part of our savings account. . . . As I give away at least half of my personal allowance $1000 is an ample allowance for me. Of our assured income of $7500, we should have still $1500, for the savings account or for an emergency fund. Herbert could use his congressional salary for his personal and political expenses so that, *as far as that goes,* it seems to me that Herbert could afford, irrespective of an income from law, to be a Congressman. As to the future, I hold certain views which would make it extremely distasteful to me ever to increase our present scale of living whatever our income might be. (As a matter of fact even our present expenditure is not determined by our income as we must give away between ⅓ & ¼ of it) If Herbert becomes a successful lawyer, he will have more to give away. If he becomes a successful politician, his public service will be an equivalent—if not more than an equivalent—for what would be, as a lawyer of large income, his philanthropic gifts and activities."

25. ECP, "Penalizing Marriage and Child-Bearing," 4–5, in "Little Essays." For an editorially censored version, see *Independent* (1906). See also ECP, "Sex and the Elders." See Neith Boyce's fictionalized account of her first pregnancy in 1902 in *The Bond* (New York: Duffield, 1908), and "Selections from *The Bond,*" in *Intimate Warriors: Portraits of a Modern Marriage, 1899–1944: Selected Works by Neith Boyce and Hutchins Hapgood,* ed. Ellen K. Trimberger (New York: Feminist Press, 1991), 39–132, esp. 43–49.

26. Robert Herrick, *Chimes* (New York: Macmillan, 1926), 106, also 7, 14–15, 47–50, 87–88; "Chapter Six, Cooperation versus Combination," 66–76, 115–16, from early version of *End of Desire* (1926?), RH Papers.

27. MKS to ECP, Nov. 1904, RHS. See HP, "Memorandum for Montee Cutler"; voting card, "To the Voters of the 13th Congressional District";

and policy statement after election, HP Papers. For illness, see ECP-HP-Giddings-Brice-LC-MKS corres., 20 Oct.–Nov. 1904, APS and RHS.

28. ECP, "Girls with Nothing to Do: A Rejoinder from Mrs. Parsons" (1905); Edith Wharton, *The House of Mirth* (1905; New York: Library of America, 1985), 71. See ECP to HP, 5 June 1904, APS, for reading with great enjoyment Wharton's *Descent of Man* (New York: Scribner's Sons, 1904).

29. Herrick, *Chimes,* 107–8; ECP, *The Family,* notes to lectures. See ECP to HP, 13 June 1904, APS, for working on textbook.

30. ECP, introduction to *The Family,* 1–19, and 358.

31. See ECP, "My Washington Journal," RHS; and Rosemary Lévy Zumwalt, *Wealth and Rebellion: Elsie Clews Parsons, Anthropologist and Folklorist* (Urbana: University of Illinois Press, 1992), 68–73, for Asian trip with Secretary of War William Taft and "Memoirs of Washington & Outlying Provinces: By a Political Wife" (1906).

32. ECP, "A Plan for Girls with Nothing to Do," "The School Child, the School Nurse, and the Local School Board," "The Aim of Productive Efficiency in Education" (1905), and "Division of Labor in the Tenement-House" (1906). See also Celia Parker Woolley, Anna Garlin Spencer, Emily V. Hammond, Frances Greeley Curtis, Sadie American, and Cynthia West-over Alden, "Girls Who Have Nothing to Do," *Charities,* 4 Mar. 1905, 520–23; S.W.H., letter to editor, *Charities,* 16 Sept. 1905, 601–2; Edith Eustis, "Why Should Girls Have Nothing to Do?" and editorial, "Mrs. Parsons, Mrs. Eustis, and the 'Girl with Nothing to Do,'" *Charities,* 16 Sept. 1905, 1083–86 and 1080–81; and Dr. Hamilton, "Is the Settlement a Permanent Institution?" *University Settlement Studies,* Jan. 1906, 131.

33. ECP, "The Imaginary Mistress" (1913), 1, APS.

34. ECP, "Penalizing Marriage and Child-Bearing" (1906).

35. ECP, "Sex Morality and the Taboo of Direct Reference" (1906).

36. Review of *The Family, Athenaeum,* 13 Apr. 1907, 445–46.

37. ECP, "The Religious Dedication of Women" (1906), the first volley in a lifelong battle with religious conservatism, traced the Christian idealization of celibacy—one of the many cases in which religion preserves outgrown social practices—to the custom of dedicating women to the gods. See Helen Montgomery, *Western Women in Eastern Lands* and *Handbook of Suggestions to Accompany the Text-book* (New York: Macmillan, 1910); Joan Jacobs Brumberg, "The Ethnological Mirror: American Evangelical Women and Their Heathen Sisters, 1870–1910," in *Women and the Structure of Society,* ed. Barbara J. Harris and Jo Ann K. McNamara (Durham: Duke University Press, 1984), 108–28. For the scientific basis of the notion of white superiority inherent in these accounts, see Cynthia Russett, *Sexual Science: The Victorian Construction of Womanhood* (Cambridge: Harvard University Press, 1989).

It is not clear how successful ECP was in achieving these objectives. Peter H. Hare, *A Woman's Quest for Science: Portrait of Anthropologist Elsie Clews Parsons* (Buffalo: Prometheus Books, 1985), 20, notes that 3,904 copies of *The Family* had sold by 1918.

38. ECP, *The Family,* 334–54.

39. ECP's son was born 2 Apr. 1906 and died 4 Apr. 1906. For baby's birth and death and ECP's illness for two and a half weeks before, see HP

to ECP, 29 Mar. 1906; HP to Dr., 30 Mar. 1906; ECP, "Family Faculties," APS; and Gertrude Pinchot to ECP, 28 June [1906?], APS, suggesting intestinal poisoning. ECP became pregnant again about 11 May 1906. She seemed to suspect she was pregnant in ECP to HP, 18 July 1906, APS. See also 26 July 1906. See 8, [13], 15, and 22 Aug. 1906 for being confined to bed because of flow; and Mary Carmody to ECP, 14 Aug. 1906, APS. See ECP to HP, 20 Aug. 1906, APS: "It is ridiculous how much I long for a baby. . . . it seems to me that I shall never quite regain my old *joie de vivre* until I have, *we* have, a baby." For Harry Thaw's murder of White 25 June 1906, see P. R. Baker, *Stanny: The Gilded Life of Stanford White* (New York: Free Press, 1989). See ECP to HP and HP to ECP, 26 June 1906; ECP to Lewis Chanler, 30 June 1906; *NYTr,* 2 July 1906; HP to ECP, 2 and 24 July 1906; ECP to HP, 26 July 1906, APS.

40. See G. A. Harrison, *A Timeless Affair: The Life of Anita McCormick Blaine* (Chicago: University of Chicago Press, 1979); James Reed, "Katharine Dexter McCormick," *NAW Mod.* For Stanley's socialism, see R. W. Ozanne, *A Century of Labor-Management Relations at McCormick and International Harvester* (Madison: University of Wisconsin Press, 1968).

41. G. Stanley Hall, *Adolescence: Its Psychology and Its Relations to Physiology, Anthropology, Sociology, Sex, Crime, Religion, and Education* (New York: Appleton, 1904), 2:122–23.

42. Heywood C. Broun and Margaret Leech, *Anthony Comstock: Roundsman of the Lord* (London: Wishart, 1928), 227–36, 249–56; Theodore Schroeder, "A Unintentional Contribution to the Erotogenetic Interpretation of Religion," cited in Ralph E. McCoy, *Theodore Schroeder, a Cold Enthusiast: A Bibliography* (Carbondale: Southern Illinois University Press, 1973), 26, for Craddock; and "From the Free Speech League's Attorney," in *The Persecution and the Appreciation: Brief Account of Moses Harman* (Chicago: Lucifer Publishing, 1907), 15–17. *Lucifer's* open letter column was a national forum for women's sexual problems. See M. H. Blatt, *Free Love and Anarchism* (Urbana: University of Illinois Press, 1989); Hal Sears, *The Sex Radicals: Free Love in High Victorian America* (Lawrence: Regents Press of Kansas, 1977).

43. See D. M. Rabban, "The Free Speech League, the ACLU, and Changing Conceptions of Free Speech in American History," *Stanford Law Review* 45 (Nov. 1992): 47–114; Alice Wexler, *Emma Goldman: An Intimate Life* (New York: Pantheon Books, 1984), 116–18, 138.

44. *NYH,* 17, 18, 19, and 30 Nov. 1906; *New York Evening Sun,* 17 Nov. 1906; *Sun,* 18 Nov. 1906; "Criticised by Clergy: Dr. Morgan Dix Describes Mrs. Parsons's Book as 'Outrageous'," *NYTr,* 18 Nov. 1906, 4; *World,* 19, 22 Nov. 1906. See also "Suggests Trial Marriages: Mrs. Clews Parsons in 'The Family' Recommends a Radical Change," *NYT,* 17 Nov. 1906, 1; "Marriage on Trial: Elsie Clews Parsons Advocates Startling Reforms in New Book," in "For and About Women," *NYTr,* 17 Nov. 1906, 5; "Dr. Dix on Trial Marriages: Rector of Trinity Says Mrs. Parsons's Views Are Barbarous," *NYT,* 18 Nov. 1906; "Perilous Transportation" (report on Herbert Parsons's campaign for better public transport), *NYTr,* 18 Nov. 1906, 8; "Dr. Dix Speaks Out to Save the Home: Rector of Trinity Protests against Loose Marital Relations, First Duty to the Child, The Home Is Its Predestination, He Says—When That Goes, Social Order

Goes Also," *NYT,* 19 Nov. 1906, 5. But see on same page: "Wants Wider Divorce Laws: The Rev. M. C. Peters Says They Should Embrace Drunkenness." See also "Dr. Dix on the Home, Attacks Its Enemies, Says Future of State Depends on Sanctity of Marriage" and "Dr. Carsons on Divorce: Says Remedy Is To Be Found in Better Home Life," *NYTr,* 19 Nov. 1906, 12; "Calls Trial Marriage Barbarous: Bishop Coleman Says Any One Favoring It Should Be Considered an Outlaw," *NYTr,* 20 Nov. 1906, 11. For cuts made to "Penalizing Marriage and Child-Bearing," see ms., APS, with Elsie's notation to Herbert: "To be printed soon in the *Independent* 'softened down,' writes the editor." Omitted: "The time regulation of pregnancies is important to working women. Here again women are handicapped by educational inadequacies and by taboo in general upon knowledge of the temporary prevention of conception" and "I believe, however, that direct instruction [in the time regulation of pregnancy] will be much more of a check upon than an encouragement of race-suicide."

45. ECP, "Little Essays," 1–4.

46. Theodore Schroeder to ECP, 26 Feb. 1906, APS; *Arena,* Jan. 1907, 105–7. See A. Maddaloni, "Theodore Schroeder: Personal Impressions," in McCoy, *Schroeder,* 5–10; Hutchins Hapgood, "A Cold Enthusiast," *New York Globe and Commercial Advertiser,* 15 Oct. 1912; reprinted as *A Cold Enthusiast* (Riverside, Ct.: Hillacre, 1913).

47. ECP to HP, 24 Apr., 19 and 25 June 1907, APS. See also 30 Apr., 1 May, 18 June 1907, APS. The baby was born 11 Feb. 1907 and lived only two hours. See HP to ECP, 26 Feb. 1907; ECP to HP, 27 Feb. and 1 Mar. 1907; ECP, notes misc. no. 2 [1908], APS. ECP appears to have had an operation on 4 May after trying some "black pills." See ECP to HP, 24 and 30 Apr., 1 May 1907, APS. For reviews of *The Family,* see Dr. Allan McLane, *Putnam's Magazine,* Feb. 1907, 557; *Outlook,* 20 Apr. 1907, 899; *Saturday Review,* 1 June 1907, 689; Mary Bush, *Journal of Philosophy, Psychology, and Scientific Methods* 4 (15 Aug. 1907): 467–70; F. M. Davenport, *Political Science Quarterly* 22 (1907): 744; Franklin H. Giddings, *Educational Review* (Sept. 1907): 202.

Chapter Four

1. William James, "The Energies of Men," *Philosophical Review* 16 (Jan. 1907): 1–20, esp. 13, 17–19, delivered at Columbia in December 1906. See ECP to HP, 23 Mar. 1907, APS. For writing, see ECP's review of *Kinship Organizations and Group Marriage in Australia,* written for *Charities and the Commons* between June and August 1907; and G. P. Putnam's Sons to ECP, 4 Feb. 1907, APS, for plans for a "study of Religious Dedication of Women" that became *Religious Chastity* (1913). In 1905, ECP started "My Washington Journal." Entries for 1905 and 1908–10 are in RHS; and "Congressional Junket in Japan" was written in fall 1906 as the first chapter of "Memoirs of Washington & Outlying Provinces: By a Political Wife," which apparently was never completed. See "Congressional Junket," 385 n. 1, 385–86. Among ECP's papers is a four-page manuscript, "A Suggestion for Ethnography in the Philippines" (1907?), APS. In "Washington Journal," 2 Mar. 1905, ECP describes ar-

ranging for facilities to work in the Library of Congress and her expectations of meeting Alice Fletcher, the president of the Anthropological Society of Washington. In ECP to HP, 16 Apr. 1907, APS, she describes attending a meeting of the Anthropology Association, but Miss Fletcher was not there. In 1905–6, Fletcher suffered a breakdown, probably over the marriage of her colleague and adopted son, Francis La Flesche, and the departure of her longtime companion, Jane Gay. Fletcher spent the second half of 1906 in Mexico, and in April 1907 was embroiled in the scandal over Francis's divorce which consumed that year. See Joan Mark, *A Stranger in Her Native Land: Alice Fletcher and the American Indians* (Lincoln: University of Nebraska Press, 1988), 291–324, esp. 311.

2. ECP to HP, 24 Apr. 1907, APS. See HP to ECP, 26 Feb. 1907; and ECP to HP, 27 Feb. 1907, APS.

3. ECP to HP, 24 Sept. 1907, APS. For poor health, see 19 June–17 Sept. 1907. For trip see HP to ECP, 24, 29, and 31 July 1907, APS; HP to secretary to president, 10 Sept. 1907, HP Papers; F. W. Hodge, *Handbook of American Indians, North of Mexico*, 2 vols. (59th Cong., 1st sess., 1905–1906, House document no. 926, pt. 2), BAE Bulletin 30 (Washington, D.C., 1907–10).

4. ECP to HP, 25 Mar., 18, 24, 27, and 29 Sept., 7 Oct. 1908, APS. See HP to ECP, 27 and 29 July 1908, for trip; ECP to HP, 27 Aug. 1908, for menstruation; [Fitz] to ECP, 27 Oct. 1908, [Sept. 1911], and [1 Aug. 1909]: "Last September really was the best month I've ever had in my life. . . . sincere thanks for the new pathways which you opened for last winter." For Katharine, see ECP to HP, 18 June 1909; 30 Sept 1908, APS; G. A. Harrison, *A Timeless Affair: The Life of Anita McCormick Blaine* (University of Chicago Press, 1979), 161–62.

5. ECP to HP, 10 Oct. 1908; also HP to ECP, 4 Oct. 1908, APS.

6. See *AJS* 11 (1906): 555–69, 681–82; and 12 (1907): 579–81, list of members, 735–38; Bernhard J. Stern, ed., "The Ward-Ross Correspondence III, 1904–1905," and "The Ward-Ross Correspondence IV, 1906–1912," *ASR* 13 (1948): 82–94, and 14 (1949): 88–119; Howard Quint, "Wilshire's Magazine," in *The American Radical Press, 1880–1960*, ed. Joseph R. Conlin (Westport, Conn.: Greenwood Press, 1974); Hal Sears, *The Sex Radicals* (Lawrence: Regents Press of Kansas, 1977), for Walker, who was jailed for his "free marriage" with Lillian Harman, daughter of *Lucifer* editor Moses Harman.

7. Notes misc. no. 2, [1908], APS. See ECP, "Higher Education of Women and the Family" (1909). She is probably referring to *Religious Chastity* (1913).

8. ECP to HP, 29 Dec. 1908; 1 Jan. 1908 [1909], APS. For papers by Sumner, Ross, Gilman, Morrow, and Devine, see *AJS* 14 (1908–9). See review of Ross, *Social Psychology* in *AJS* (1908–9): 681. See ECP to HP, 17 Mar. 1909, APS: "Having just read part of that Pittsburgh Survey I have decided to sell out my steel stocks."

9. ECP, "The Imaginary Mistress," 2–3, APS. See HP to ECP, 25 June 1908; Lucy Wilson to ECP, 13 Aug. 1908, APS; ECP, appt. cal., 20 and 23 Apr. 1909, RHS; HP to Huntington Wilson, 15 May 1909, HP Papers; ECP to HP, 15 June 1909; HP to ECP, 15 and 28 July 1909, APS.

10. ECP, "Washington Journal," 5 Mar. [1910], RHS; HP to ECP, 18 and 19 July 1909; ECP to HP, 19 July 1909, APS.

11. Lucy James [Wilson] to HP, 30 Mar. 1918, HP Papers; ECP, "Imaginary Mistress," 13. See HP to ECP, 14–31 July, 2 and 18 Aug., 17 Sept. 1909, APS. For jealousy, see ECP to HP, 28 July, 3 and 4 Aug. 1909; HP to ECP, 29 July 1909, APS. For anxiety about the presence of protein in her urine, see ECP to HP, 3 Aug. 1909, with Dr. Herter to ECP, 30 July 1909, APS.

12. ECP to HP, 4 Aug. 1909, APS. For Alice Duer Miller, see Henry Wise Miller, *All Our Lives* (New York: Coward-McCann, 1945), 81–83; ECP to HP, 4 June 1903, 13 Nov. 1905, 16 Oct. 1906, APS; ECP to NMB, 14 Nov. 1905, RHS, suggesting Alice or Mary Simkhovitch for Barnard dean.

13. See ECP to HP, Feb., 3 Mar., and 4 May 1910; 7 Mar. and 12 and 25 July 1911, APS; "Washington Journal," 13 and 21 Jan., 7, 10, 21, and 23 Feb., and 5 and 18 Mar. [1910], RHS. There is no evidence that the relationship was ever consummated sexually. In fact, Herbert's idealization of Lucy seems to have been a major source of pain and frustration for Elsie.

14. ECP to HP, 14 Apr. and 18 June 1909, APS. See also 28 July and 1 Sept. 1909; and 18 and 25 May 1910, APS.

15. See "Washington Journal," 9 Dec. 1908, 12 and 30 Jan. and 19 Feb. [1910]; ECP, appt. cal., 23 and 24 Apr. and 2 May 1909, RHS; ECP to HP, 26 Mar. 1908; GY to ECP, 30 [Jan.] 1909, APS.

16. According to Geoffrey Winthrop Young, *The Grace of Forgetting* (London: Country Life, 1953), 40, 230, George (1872–1952) was the first to codify Ottoman Law; he helped to draft the new Weimar Constitution; and he and his wife organized, and he himself led, the mountain rescue and relief measures during the Spanish Civil War.

17. Archie Butt, *Taft and Roosevelt: The Intimate Letters of Archie Butt, Military Aide* (Garden City, N.Y.: Doubleday, Doran, 1930), 1:70; ECP, appt. cal., 2 May 1909, RHS; GY to ECP, 10 Nov. 1910, 1 Mar. 1914, APS. For the Young family, see B. Williams, "Sir George Young, Third Baronet, 1837–1930," *DNB, 1922–1930;* Wayland Young, "Edward Hilton Young, First Baron Kennet, 1879–1960," and Arnold Lunn, "Geoffrey Winthrop Young, 1876–1958," *DNB, 1951–1960;* Geoffrey Dearmer, "(Edith Agnes) Kathleen Kennet, Lady Kennet, 1878–1947," *DNB, 1941–1950;* Baroness Kathleen Bruce Young Kennet, *Self-Portrait of an Artist* (London: Murray, 1949).

18. GY to ECP, 12 July 1910, APS.

19. ECP to HP, 7 May 1911, APS; Robert Herrick, *The End of Desire* (New York: Farrar and Rinehart, 1932), 56.

20. GY to ECP, 17 May 1912; ECP to HP, 1, 26, 30 June 1910, APS. See ECP to HP, 27 and 30 June 1910, APS, for her relationship with the children and with her mother. See ECP to HP, 26 July 1910, and HP to ECP, 27 July 1910, for disagreement over John's seeing her naked. See ECP to HP, 20 Sept. 1910, APS, quoting Lissa: "The only thing I could say about you are that you are rather tall, that you like to write books and go without clothes."

21. ECP, "The Accident of the Forester," 1–2, in "In the Southwest"

(1921), APS. See HP to ECP, 19 July, 7 Aug. 1910; ECP to HP, 5 Aug. 1910, APS. True earlier befriended Matilda Coxe Stevenson, who did pioneering anthropological work at Zuni and the Rio Grande pueblos from 1879 until her death in 1915. By 1910 they were bitter enemies engaged in litigation over money. See Nancy J. Parezo, "Matilda Coxe Stevenson: Pioneer Ethnologist," in *Hidden Scholars: Women Anthropologists and the Native American Southwest,* ed. Parezo (Albuquerque: University of New Mexico Press, 1993), 38–62, esp. 52–53.

22. ECP, "Accident of the Forester," 3–6.

23. Ibid., 6. For loss of ring, see Peter H. Hare, *A Woman's Quest for Science: Portrait of Anthropologist Elsie Clews Parsons* (Buffalo: Prometheus Books, 1985), 130, based on HP's diary, 23 Aug. 1910. See also Miss Carmody to ECP at Grand Canyon, 8 and 19 Aug. 1910; HP to JEP, 21 Aug. 1910, fr. Yosemite; ECP to HP, 27 Aug. 1910, fr. Reno, APS.

24. ECP to HP, 6 Aug. 1912; HP to ECP, 7 Aug. 1912; ECP to HP, 22 Oct. 1910, APS. See also ECP to HP, 7 and 9 Mar. 1911; HP to ECP, 8 Mar. 1911, APS.

25. ECP, "American Ethnology SW," APS. See ECP to HP, 8 Sept.–23 Nov. 1910; Mar.–Oct. 1911; GY to ECP, Sept. 1910–Jan. 1912, APS. For *Religious Chastity* (1913), see ECP to HP, 15 and 31 Oct, 1910; F. Hitchcock to ECP, 29 Dec. 1910, APS.

26. For Mac's birth on 31 August, see ECP to HP, 25 and 28 Aug. 1911; HP to ECP, 28 Aug. 1911; C. H. Aldrich to ECP, 2 Sept. 1911, APS. For near death, see ECP to HP, 11 Oct. 1918. For travels, see ECP to HP, 2–29 Feb., 3 Apr., 28 Aug. 1912; ECP to JEP, 29 Feb. 1912; ECP, "Hayti Misunderstood" (1912). For new book, see "The Supernatural Policing of Women" (1912); H. Holt to ECP, 8 July 1912; GY to ECP, 24 Mar., 17 May, 9 Aug., 13 Sept. (cont. 10 Oct.) 1912. For reading Havelock Ellis and Nietzsche, see ECP to HP, 26 June and 31 July 1912, APS.

27. ECP to HP, 4 Aug. 1912. See also ECP to HP, 26 June 1912; HP to ECP, 26 June and 1 July 1912; Lucy Wilson to ECP, 9 July 1912, APS.

28. HP to ECP, 4 Aug. 1912, APS.

29. ECP to HP, 6 Aug., also 7 Aug. 1912, APS. The second book ECP refers to is *Religious Chastity,* which was in press, but not published.

30. HP to ECP, 7 Aug., also 6, 8 and 9 Aug. 1912, APS.

31. ECP, "Imaginary Mistress," 16–17; also ECP to HP, 6–[26] Aug. 1912; HP to ECP, 12 Aug. 1912; MKS to ECP, 8 Sept. 1912, APS.

32. ECP to HP, 12, 18, and 20 Sept. 1912, APS. See also 9 and 11 Sept. 1912, APS; ECP, "From Paharito Ranch to Taos and Back," 8, in "In the Southwest."

33. True to ECP, 18 and 20 Oct. 1912; GY to ECP, 25 Nov. 1912, APS. See description of ride with Baca in ECP, "From Paharito Ranch to Taos and Back."

34. ECP, "Imaginary Mistress," 19–20. For completion of this account see ECP to HP, 9 Sept. 1913; GLF to ECP, 13 and 14 Oct. 1913, APS. The introduction (1–2), supposedly written by her literary executor after her death, explains that she is publishing the account, found among the papers of this famous intellectual woman, of the breakup of her marriage. She is publishing it, she explains, to elucidate what has always been an

enigma to her friends; and, more important, so that "the outside world will no longer be able to gloat over her as one more intellectual gone astray because of her brains"; as "an expression of personality"; and because it "lucidly and with perfect honesty" deals with "the question of human monopoly"—"one of the pages of life we modern folk are becoming vastly perplexed over." The account itself starts: "It occurs to me that if I write it out in an orderly way—talk it out I can't for his sake and because—I just can't, the obsession I feel taking hold of me again may be easier to get rid of. I have come to dread the obsessive quality of the situation more . . . than any other feature of it."

35. ECP, "Imaginary Mistress," 20. See ECP to HP, 21 Nov. 1912, APS.

36. ECP to HP, [13 Jan.] 1913; HP to ECP, 18 Jan. 1913, APS. See FB to ECP and FB to J. Engerrand, 14 Dec. 1912, FB Papers. Engerrand had just replaced Boas as director of the recently established International School of American Archeology and Ethnology in Mexico City, where Boas spent 1911–12. Boas had been on ECP's Ph.D. orals committee, and she had asked him—apparently without success—to write a defense of *The Family* early in 1907. See FB to ECP, 1 Jan. 1907, APS.

37. ECP to HP, 10 Mar. 1911; GY to ECP, 25 Nov. and 30 Dec. 1911. See John L. Stephens, *Incidents of Travel in Yucatán,* 2 vols. (New York: Harper and Bros., 1843). See also GY to ECP, 28 Nov. 1911, [Jan. 1912], 26 June, 15 and 27 July, 1 Aug. 1913; ECP to HP, 7 and 9 Mar., 18 Apr. 1911; HP to ECP, 8 Mar. 1911, 23 and 29 July 1913; Helen Young to ECP, 13 Sept. 1913, APS; ECP, "Imaginary Mistress," 18.

38. ECP, "Imaginary Mistress," 21–25. See ECP to HP, 16 and 21 Jan. 1913, APS. Harvard graduate Sylvanus Morley had been working in Yucatán and Guatemala as Fellow in Central American Archeology of the Archeological Institute of America since 1909. In 1913, he and Jesse Nusbaum were photographing for the 1915 San Diego Exposition. ECP may have met him in Santa Fe, where he was based. Rosemary Lévy Zumwalt, *Wealth and Rebellion: Elsie Clews Parsons, Anthropologist and Folklorist* (Urbana: University of Illinois Press, 1992), 280, says that ECP explored Chichén with Morley and Balch. See R. L. Brunhouse, *Sylvanus Morley and the World of the Ancient Mayas* (Norman: University of Oklahoma Press, 1971), 49–56. In "Imaginary Mistress," 28, the narrator is a famous American archeologist living in a beautiful villa in Mexico City a là Zelia Nuttall—a glimpse into ECP's fantasy world in 1913.

39. Robert Herrick, "The Story of Jessica Stowe" (1924), RH Papers. See ECP to HP, [14], 15, and 18 Feb. 1913; HP to ECP, 14 and 15 Feb. 1913; Balch to ECP, 4, 7, and 21 Feb., 25 June 1913, APS.

40. ECP to HP, 16 June 1913, [14 Feb. 1913], re divorce, APS; ECP, "Imaginary Mistress," 16, 18, 25–27. See ECP to HP, 18 Feb. 1913, APS, fr. Lenox: "I am well started on my new book ['Imaginary Mistress'?] & each day waste less time on obsessions." For play see "In New York State" (1913–15); Francis Hackett to ECP, 28 Apr. 1915, APS. See Herrick, "Story of Jessica Stowe": "Marriage outwardly successful, inwardly hollow and dead. Her husband has a real passion for her but does not satisfy her sexually and being of a simpler but more ardent and idealistic nature rather bores her. . . . she is forty, her children are well on in school, she . . . has

had several skittish flirtations, and has been a good deal talked about for advanced ideas and peculiar conduct."

Chapter Five

1. Melville J. Herskovits, *Franz Boas* (Clifton: Augustus M. Kelley, 1973); J. M. Kennedy, "Philanthropy and Science in New York City: The American Museum of Natural History, 1868–1968" (Ph.D. diss., Yale University, 1968), 134–44. See also George W. Stocking Jr., *Race, Culture, and Evolution: Essays in the History of Anthropology* (New York: Free Press, 1968); and *The Shaping of American Anthropology, 1883–1911: A Franz Boas Reader* (New York: Basic Books, 1974); Regna Darnell, "American Anthropology 1879–1920: From the Bureau of American Ethnology to Franz Boas" (Ph.D. diss., University of Pennsylvania, 1969); Curtis Hinsley, *Savages and Scientists: The Smithsonian Institution and the Development of American Anthropology, 1883–1911* (Washington, D.C.: Smithsonian Institution, 1981).

2. Herskovits, *Boas,* 22–23.

3. Theodora Kroeber, *Alfred Kroeber: A Personal Configuration* (Berkeley: University of California Press, 1970); Regna Darnell, *Edward Sapir: Linguist, Anthropologist, Humanist* (Berkeley: University of California Press, 1990); Paul Radin, "Robert H. Lowie, 1883–1957," *AA* 60 (1958): 358–75; Harry Hoijer, "Paul Radin, 1883–1959," *AA* 61 (1959): 839–43.

4. Wilson D. Wallis, "Alexander A. Goldenweiser," *AA* 43 (1941): 250–55; Alexander Goldenweiser, "Alexander Solomonovich Goldenweiser," *Encyclopedia of the Social Sciences,* ed. Edwin R. A. Seligman (New York: Macmillan, 1931–35); Alexis Goldenweiser to Leslie White, 3 Mar. 1956, LW Papers.

5. Robert Lowie, "Relations with Boas," RHL Papers; William James, "The Social Value of the College Bred," *McClure's,* Feb. 1908, from a 1907 speech; Robert Brym, *The Jewish Intelligentsia and Russian Marxism* (London: Macmillan, 1978), 55–57, 92–93; Hutchins Hapgood (James's former student), *The Spirit of the Ghetto* (1902), 39–40, quoted in Ross Posnock, *The Trial of Curiosity: Henry James, William James, and the Challenge of Modernity* (New York: OUP, 1991), 7.

6. Robert Lowie, "Reflections on Goldenweiser's 'Recent Trends in American Anthropology,'" *AA* 43 (1941): 151–63; M. R. Cohen, *A Dreamer's Journey: The Autobiography of Morris Raphael Cohen* (Boston: Beacon Press, 1949).

7. See Robert Lowie, "Reminiscences of Anthropological Currents in America Half a Century Ago," *AA* 58 (1956): 98, for "an intimate conversation with Ostwald" after a seminar of Cattell's.

8. R. F. Murphy, *Robert H. Lowie* (New York: Columbia University Press, 1972), 102–3, quoting Lowie, "Reminiscences"; Lowie, "Boas"; and "Letters from Ernst Mach to Robert H. Lowie," *Isis* (1947): 65–68. See Henri Poincaré's *La Science et l'hypothèse* (1903), Wilhelm Ostwald's *Vorlesungen über Naturphilosophie* (1902); RHL to Risa Lowie, 27 Oct. 1929, RHL Papers: "I do not consider Dewey a great man like James—he

is too little developed on the aesthetic & cognate sides . . . with the Vermont farmer sticking out a bit too much."

9. Robert Lowie, "Ernst Mach," *NR*, 9 Apr. 1916, 335–37; J.-F. Lyotard, *The Postmodern Condition* (Minneapolis: University of Minnesota Press, 1984), xxiv; Mach, quoted in P. Frank, "The Importance of Ernst Mach's Philosophy of Science for Our Times," in *Ernst Mach: Physicist and Philosopher,* ed. R. S. Cohen and R. J. Seeger (Dordecht: D. Reidel, 1970), 219–34.

10. Ernst Mach, *Analysis of the Sensations* (1886), quoted in R. von Mises, "Ernst Mach and the Empiricist Conception of Science," in Cohen and Seeger, *Ernst Mach,* 245–70, esp. 263.

11. Ralph Barton Perry, *The Thought and Character of William James* (Boston: Little, Brown, 1935), 2:56, 60. Cf. Mach, *Science of Mechanics* (1883) and *Analysis of the Sensations* (1886), and Nietzsche, *The Will to Power* (London: T. N. Foulis, 1909), nos. 252, 289, 287, 291; and see Frank, "Ernst Mach's Philosophy of Science," 232–33. R. W. Clark, *Einstein* (New York: World Publishing, 1971), 37–39, 54, 159–61; see 53–55, 73–103, for a similar reading group to the Pearson Circle. M. Bradbury and J. McFarlane, eds., *Modernism: A Guide to European Literature, 1890-1930* (New York: Penguin, 1991), esp. 122, 622; R. J. Thornton, " 'Imagine yourself set down . . .': Mach, Frazer, Conrad, Malinowski, and the Role of Imagination in Ethnography," *Anthropology Today* 1 (Oct. 1985): 7–14; H. Hickman, *Robert Musil and the Culture of Vienna* (London: Croom Helm, 1984); K. M. Jensen, *Beyond Marx and Mach: Aleksandr Bogdanov's Philosophy of Living Experience* (Boston: D. Reidel, 1978); R. S. Cohen, "Ernst Mach: Physics, Perception, and the Philosophy of Science," in Cohen and Seeger, *Ernst Mach,* 126–64, esp. 156–60.

12. Robert Lowie, "Social Organization," *AJS* 20 (July 1914): 68–97, esp. 68.

13. Robert Lowie, "Science," in *Civilization in the United States: An Inquiry by Thirty Americans,* ed. Harold Stearns (New York: Harcourt, Brace, 1922), 151–62, esp. 154, 160–61.

14. RHL to Risa Lowie, 12 Aug. 1908 and 29 Dec. 1910, RHL Papers.

15. ALK to ECP, 5 May 1916 and 14 July 1923, APS; Robert Lowie, "The Methods of American Ethnologists," *Science* 34 (1911): 604–5, and "American and English Methods in Ethnology," *AA* 14 (1912): 398–99; also critique by British-trained Wilson D. Wallis, 178–86. See also Lowie, "Boas"; Alfred L. Kroeber, "Pliny Earle Goddard," *AA* 31 (1929): 1–8; George W. Stocking Jr., "Clark Wissler," *DAB,* suppl. 4. For Lowie, see RHL to Risa Lowie, 27 July 1906 and 21 July 1907, RHL Papers. For Sapir, see ALK to Sapir, 30 Aug. 1910, in Golla. For Radin, see Sapir to ALK, 20 Nov. 1911 and 15 May 1913; and Golla, 47, 55. For Goldenweiser, see RHL to Risa Lowie, 29 Dec. 1910, RHL Papers; Sapir to ALK, 29 Apr. 1911 and 15 Jan. 1913; Golla, 57, 79. For Boas-Wissler antagonism, see Kennedy, "Philanthropy and Science," 76–155, esp. 141–44, 149; Leslie White to Wissler, 10 July 1943; Wissler to White, 19 July and 31 Mar. 1943, LW Papers: "never sympathized with Boas' deep hostility to biological science and his contempt for most psychological research"; remained "agnostic" on the race question, "seeing no reason

for being cocksure there were no significant differences yet to be discovered"; found Boas's "unswerving belief in something like the 'freedom of the will,' a feeling that man could do what he liked at any time," unscientific. "Boas considered me a heretic. . . . He felt that I was too schematic to be a good anthropologist."

16. Alexander Goldenweiser, "Totemism: An Analytic Study," *JAFL* 23 (1910): 179–293; Paul Radin, "History of Ethnological Theories," *AA* 31 (1929): 9–33, esp. 15; Robert Lowie, "A New Conception of Totemism," *AA* 13 (1911): 189–207. See W. Shapiro, "Claude Lévi-Strauss Meets Alexander Goldenweiser: Boasian Anthropology and the Study of Totemism," *AA* 93 (1991): 599–610, for "observer-dependency" of Boasian social theory and links with postmodern thought.

17. Goldenweiser, review of *Primitive Paternity*, by Edwin Hartland, *AA* 13 (1911): 598–606, esp. 605–6; Robert Lowie, "On the Principle of Convergence in Ethnology," *JAFL* 25 (1912): 24–42.

18. Lowie, "Social Organization," 68–69, 87; Berthold Laufer, "Methods and Principles," *AA* 20 (1918): 87–89. See Robert Lowie, *Culture and Ethnology* (New York: Douglas C. McMurtrie, 1917).

19. Robert Lowie, *Primitive Society* (New York: Horace Liveright, 1920), 13, 441.

20. Claude Lévi-Strauss, *Tristes Tropiques* (1955; New York: Atheneum, 1963), 63, quoted in Murphy, *Lowie*, 76.

21. Pliny Goddard, *Indians of the Southwest*, AMNH Handbook 2 (New York, 1913). The first known letter from ECP to PG, dated 15 Feb. 1913, just after her return from Yucatán, was sent to her nephew-biographer Peter Hare from the AMNH files. For ECP's introduction to the group, see GR to ALK, 23 Mar. 1942, ALK Papers: "I have discussed it with Boas and have emphasized his influence on her, but he demurs and says she had it before he met her. He says she once told him that she got interested in the Pueblos while on a tourist trip with Herbert. Papa Franz says he met her thru Goddard and I am wondering if, after the trip to the Southwest, she went to the Museum and met him that way"; ALK to GR, 26 May 1942, ALK Papers: "Elsie told me she got into Anthropology through an invitation from a friend who had a ranch in New Mexico, I think in the Rio Grande Valley. She went for a visit and got interested in a neighboring pueblo. On her return she went to the American Museum and got acquainted with Goddard, who encouraged her. . . . Psychologically, of course, the development was allied to her early work in sociology. I think she was by nature primarily a high grade field worker, but sociology failed to give her this opening, and when she happened to run across it through anthropology it was just what she wanted"; RHL to GR, 10 Apr. 1942, RHL Papers: "I clearly remember meeting Elsie at the Museum through Goddard. He told me then that her interest had been aroused in Southwestern Indians through a tourist trip. . . . she and I were joint members of various groups, such as the Dinner Club and another group which considered psycho-analysis in relation to human behavior. Ogburn, Jelliffe and a few others also belonged to the latter organization."

22. Kroeber, "Goddard," 5, 6.

23. Ibid.; Pliny Goddard, "The Relation of Folk-Lore to Anthropology," *JAFL* 28 (1915): 18–23.

24. ECP, "The Imaginary Mistress" (1913), 1, APS.

25. ECP to HP, 18 Sept. 1912; ECP to PG, 15 Feb. 1913; Clara True to ECP, 5 Apr. 1913, APS; ECP, "From Paharito Ranch to Taos and Back," in "In the Southwest" (1921), APS; ECP, review of *A Psychological Study of Religion,* by James H. Leuba (1912). See *Current Anthropological Literature* 1 (Dec. 1912) for founding by AAA and AFLS to promote "fair and fearless opinion on new works from a modern scientific point of view."

26. James Leuba's review of *Religious Chastity,* in *Current Anthropological Literature* 2 (Oct.–Dec. 1913): 229–30, pronounced it "thorough," "vivacious," and "elegant." For New Mexico, see PG to ECP, 10 and 27 Oct. 1913; ECP to HP, 1, 2, and 16 Oct. 1913; ECP, "The Journal of a Feminist, 1913–1914," 1–29 Oct. 1913; and "Pedro Baca and I go Visiting," in "In the Southwest."

27. PG to ECP, 8 Nov. 1913 and 2 Feb. 1914, APS.

Chapter Six

1. Henry F. May, *The End of American Innocence* (1959; New York: Columbia University Press, 1992), remains the best of the numerous books on this milieu; but see also Robert M. Crunden, *American Salons: Encounters with European Modernism, 1885–1917* (New York: OUP, 1993).

2. Edna Ferber, *A Peculiar Treasure* (New York: Doubleday, Doran, 1939), 188–91; George Middleton, *These Things Are Mine* (New York: Macmillan, 1947), 110.

3. H. L. Mencken, *The Philosophy of Nietzsche* (Boston, 1908); Umbro Apollonio, ed., *Futurist Manifestos* (New York: Viking, 1973).

4. *New York Evening Sun,* 13 Feb. 1917, 10, quoted in Carolyn Burke, "Mina Loy, 1882–1966," in *The Gender of Modernism,* ed. Bonnie Scott (Bloomington: Indiana University Press, 1990), 230–38, esp. 230.

5. Nancy Cott, *The Grounding of Modern Feminism* (New Haven: Yale University Press, 1987), 13–16, 289; also 15, where Cott quotes Edna Kenton, "Feminism Will Give—Men More Fun, Women Greater Scope," *Delineator,* July 1914, 17.

6. ECP, "The Journal of a Feminist, 1913–1914," Mar. 1914, 102, APS.

7. Margaret Chanler to EC, 23 July 1899, RHS; Karen Offen, "Defining Feminism: A Comparative Historical Approach," *Signs* 14 (autumn 1988): 119–57; bibliography, *AJS* 4 (May 1898): 879; Charlotte Perkins Stetson [Gilman], *Women and Economics* (Boston: Small, Maynard, 1899). For use of "feminism" by American psychologist G. Stanley Hall and Dutch sociologist Steinmetz see ECP, *The Family* (1906), 33, 355–58.

8. Elaine Showalter, "Inez Leonore Haynes Gillmore Irwin," and Sharon Hartman Strom, "Maud May Wood Park," *NAW Mod;* Eleanor Flexner, "Harriott Eaton Stanton Blatch," *NAW;* Harriott Stanton Blatch and Alma Lutz, *Challenging Years: The Memoirs of Harriott Stanton Blatch* (New York: G. P. Putnam's Sons, 1940), esp. 93, 98; Ellen DuBois, "Working Women, Class Relations, and Suffrage Militance, 1894–1909," *Journal of American History* 74 (June 1987): 34–58; Nancy Schrom Dye, *As Equals and as Sisters: Feminism, Unionism, and the Women's Trade*

Union League of New York (Columbia: University of Missouri Press, 1980), 90–97.

9. ECP, "Journal of a Feminist," Jan. 1914, 85; ECP to HP, 16 June and 25 Aug. 1909; NAWSA (Mass.) to ECP, 7 July 1908, APS; Christopher Lasch, "Mary Coffin Ware Dennett," *NAW;* Susanne Wilcox, *Independent,* 8 July 1909, 62–66, for Nietzsche's influence on the suffrage movement. For ECP's membership of the College Equal Suffrage Association publication committee which sponsored Helen Sumner's 1909 report on Colorado suffrage, see Caroline Lexow [Babcock] to ECP, 22 June and 19 July 1906, and 14 July 1908, APS.

10. ECP to HP, 26 July and 18 Aug. 1909, with copy ECP to Taft, and 25 Aug. 1909, APS. Taft pleaded his wife's illness and did not attend. See Taft to ECP, 19 Aug. 1909, APS.

11. Mabel Potter Daggett, *Delineator,* Jan. 1910; HP to ECP, 7 May 1911, APS; ECP, "Journal of a Feminist," Jan. 1914, 85. For New York organization, see Ronald Schaffer, "The New York City Woman Suffrage Party, 1909–1919," *New York History,* July 1962, 269–87. For parade, see Blatch, *Challenging Years,* 129, 133, 179; *NYT,* 10 May 1911; *Harper's Weekly,* 20 May 1911 and 11 May 1912; Middleton, *These Things Are Mine,* 120–28.

12. For Men's Suffrage League, see Max Eastman, *Enjoyment of Living* (New York: Harper and Brothers, 1948); and HP corres. with Eastman and *NYT,* Oct.–Nov. 1909, HP Papers. Herbert Parsons was New York County committee chair 1905–10, and again from 1914; delelegate to the state convention from 1904, and to the national convention 1908, 1912, 1916, and 1920; delegate-at-large to the state constitutional convention 1915; chair of the industrial relations committee and member of the committees on state finances and rules; and member of the national committee for New York State 1916–20, and of the executive and campaign committees. See *NCAB.* For 1914 state convention, see sec. Men's Suffrage League to HP, 28 Feb. 1914, HP Papers; and HP to ECP, 16 Aug. 1914, APS. For ECP's brief visit to the convention, see ECP to HP, 17 Aug. 1914, and ECP, "Journal of a Feminist," 125, APS. For Whitehouse, see Blatch, *Challenging Years,* 217–18, 240; Jane E. Ward, "Vira (Boarman) Whitehouse, 1875–1957," finding aid, Schlesinger Library; ECP, "Journal of a Feminist," 128, APS; HP-ECP corres., Aug. 1914–Oct. 1917; and Whitehouse to ECP, Nov. 1917, APS.

13. Theodore Schroeder, "A Symposium of Woman's Suffrage," *International,* May 1911, 93–94; cf. ECP, "The Lesser Evil" (1916), 215, and "Slogan for Chicago Newspaper," June 1916, notes misc., APS. For Harper, see ECP to HP, 23 May 1908 and 25 Aug. 1909, APS. For articles, see Women's Political Union to ECP, 7 June 1912; ECP to HP, 29 May 1912 and 23 July 1913, APS; ECP, *NYH,* 17 Oct. 1915. For Choate and march, see ECP to HP, 26 and 19 Oct. 1915, with Louis Wiley to ECP, 18 Oct. 1915; HP to ECP, 19 and 28 Oct. 1915; Francis Hackett to ECP, [19] and 23 Oct. and [Oct.] 1915; "The Banner Woman Suffrage Parade," *Masses,* Oct.–Nov. 1915.

14. Alice Wexler, *Emma Goldman: An Intimate Life* (New York: Pantheon Books, 1984), 122–30, esp. 122, 124.

15. Ibid., 195–210, esp. 195 for *New York Sun,* 2 May 1909; Emma

Goldman, "The Tragedy of Woman's Emancipation," in *Anarchism and Other Essays* (New York: Mother Earth, 1911); "Woman Suffrage," in *Emma Goldman: The Traffic in Women and Other Essays on Feminism*, ed. Alix Kates Shulman (Ojai, Calif.: Times Change Press, 1970), 51–63, esp. 63; Ellen Chesler, *Woman of Valor: Margaret Sanger and the Birth Control Movement in America* (New York: Simon and Schuster, 1992); Hutchins Hapgood, "Emma Goldman's Anarchism," *Bookman*, Feb. 1911, 639–40; Goldman, "Why and How the Poor Should Not Have Children," *Mother Earth*, Apr. 1911, 2, described condoms, recommended cervical caps and diaphrams that could be bought in drugstores, suggested three homemade methods—suppositories, douches, and a cotton ball dipped in borated vaseline—advised against the rhythm method, but defined the safe period as the two weeks before menstruation.

16. Walter Lippmann, "The Most Dangerous Man in the World," *Everybody's*, July 1912, 100–101; James to Bergson, 13 June 1907, in Ralph Barton Perry, *The Thought and Character of William James* (Boston: Little, Brown, 1935), 2:354–56; review of Lippmann's *A Preface to Politics* (New York: Mitchell Kennerley, 1913) in *Annals of the American Academy of Political and Social Science* 51 (Jan. 1914): 270. See Randolph Bourne to Prudence Winterrowd, 16 Jan., 10 Apr., and 18 May 1913, *RB Letters*, for a "never to be forgotten little supper" with Bergson.

17. Henri Bergson, *Mélanges* (Paris: Presses Universitaires de France, 1972), 843–75; Gertrude Stein, *The Making of Americans* (Paris: Contact Editions, 1925), 499, 923; and *Wars I Have Seen* (New York: Random House, 1945), 21, quoted in Lisa Ruddick, *Reading Gertrude Stein* (Ithaca: Cornell University Press, 1990), 135; Marion Cox, *Forum*, May 1913, 548–49, esp. 548. For an illuminating discussion of modernism, patricide, and Stein's feminism, see Ruddick, *Reading Gertrude Stein*, 55–136. For Florence, see Mabel Dodge Luhan, *European Experiences* (New York: Harcourt, Brace, 1935), 337–43; Carolyn Burke, "Becoming Mina Loy," *Women's Studies* 7 (1980): 136–50.

18. Dora Marsden, *Freewoman*, 23 Nov. 1911, 3, and 14 Dec. 1911, 64; Weaver to [Marsden], winter 1911–12, quoted in *New Freewoman* publicity, in Jane Lidderdale and Mary Nicholson, *Dear Miss Weaver* (London: Faber and Faber, 1970), 53–54; Rebecca West, "The 'Freewoman,'" *Time and Tide*, 16 July 1926, 648–49, and "Spinster to the Rescue," *Sunday Telegraph* (London), 11 Nov. 1970, 12, reprinted in Scott, *Gender of Modernism*, 573–80; Les Garner, *A Brave and Beautiful Spirit: Dora Marsden, 1882–1960* (Aldershot: Avebury, 1990); Bruce Clarke, *Dora Marsden and Early Modernism: Gender, Individualism, Science* (Ann Arbor: University of Michigan Press, 1996). West began her career on the *Freewoman*. See *Freewoman*, 9 Sept. 1912, 346–48, and Bonnie Kime Scott, "Rebecca West, 1892–1983," in *Gender of Modernism*, 560–69, for the cutting review of H. G. Wells's *Marriage* which began their liaison.

19. Dora Marsdon, *Freewoman*, 23 Nov. 1911, 1–2; cf. ECP, "The Supernatural Policing of Women" (1912).

20. Frances Maule Bjorkman, *Forum*, Oct. 1912, quoted in *Current Opinion*, Jan. 1913, 47–48; Middleton, *These Things Are Mine*, 116, 130; Margaret Anderson, *My Thirty Years' War* (New York: Horizon Press, 1969), 149–50; Floyd Dell, *Homecoming* (Port Washington: Kennikat

Press, 1969), 234; and *Women as World Builders: Studies in Modern Feminism* (Chicago: Forbes and Company, 1913).

21. Elizabeth Gurley Flynn, "Heterodoxy to Marie," 1920, Inez Haynes Irwin Papers, Schlesinger Library; Mabel Dodge Luhan, *Movers and Shakers* (New York: Harcourt, Brace, 1936), 143; both quoted in Judith Schwarz, *Radical Feminists of Heterodoxy: Greenwich Village, 1912–1940,* rev. ed. (Norwich, Vt.: New Victoria Publishers, 1986), 1. Marsden's message was taken up enthusiastically by Edna Kenton's Greenwich Village friends, particularly by members of the "Fighting Twenty-Fifth," the branch of the NAWSA led by Marie Jenny Howe. Probably at Kenton's suggestion, Marsden's editorial "Bondwomen" was issued in 1912 as a NAWSA pamphlet; and Howe's use of street theater, art, and publicity-grabbing mass meetings fitted Marsden's prescription to combine joy, will, and passion. Edna Kenton and Mary Dennett, another *Freewoman* reader, were two of the original twenty-five Heterodoxy members.

22. Schwarz, *Heterodoxy,* 7, also 17, for Jakobi quote; Frederic C. Howe, *The Confessions of a Reformer* (New York: Scribner, 1925), 240. As assistant to Rev. Mary Safford, the president of the Iowa Suffrage Association in Sioux City, and, after her marriage in 1904, as an activist in city politics and the National Consumer's League in Cleveland, Marie Howe formed close friendships with fellow Heterodites Lucy Huffaker and Susan Glaspell, reform-minded politician Senator Robert La Follette and his wife Belle and daughter Fola and free speech advocates Lincoln Steffens and Gilbert and Netha Roe. In New York, she immediately put her organizing skills to work for the suffrage movement, where she met Mary Heaton Vorse, Crystal Eastman, Mary Dennett, Henrietta Rodman, and other talented women who later joined Heterodoxy. See also Hutchins Hapgood, *A Victorian in a Modern World* (Seattle: University of Washington Press, 1972), 332–33; Luhan, *Movers and Shakers,* 143–44, 526–27.

23. RB to Prudence Winterrowd, 28 Apr. 1913, *RB Letters.*

24. Marie Howe, *An Anti-Suffrage Monologue* (New York: NAWSA, 1913); "Feminism," *New Review,* Aug. 1914, 441. See *NYT,* 18 Feb. 1914, 2, and 21 Feb. 1914, 10 and 18; ECP, "Journal of a Feminist," 18 Feb. 1914, 99–101, APS; Frederic Howe, *Confessions,* 240; Middleton, *These Things Are Mine,* 125–30.

25. For the Cosmopolitan Club see ECP, "Journal of a Feminist," Jan. and [14 Feb.] 1914, 76 and 70–71; for problem plays, 27 Jan. and Mar. 1914, 68 and 75; for feminist mass meeting and Lucy Clews, 18 Feb. and Mar. 1914, 99–102; for Betty Sage, Jan. and Mar. 1914, 76–77, 108, and 117–19; for Charlotte Sorchan, 26? Nov. 1913, 47–48; for Walton Martin, Mar. 1914, 117; for Vira Whitehouse, 3 Aug. and Aug. 1914, 121 and 128; for Learned Hand, Jan. 1914, 78; for Norman Hapgood, 13 Nov. 1913, 42–43; for Clarence Day, Dec. 1913, 49–54; for their discussion parties, Dec. 1913 and Jan. 1914, 56–61 and 76.

26. For "salvage ethnology," see Brian W. Dippie, *The Vanishing American: White Attitudes and U.S. Indian Policy* (Middletown, Conn.: Wesleyan University Press, 1982), 232, quoting Boas (1909). The French anthropologist Lucien Lévy-Bruhl had recently elaborated the difference between the "savage" mentality and the "civilized." See Lévy-Bruhl, *Les Fonctions mentales dans les sociétés inférieures* (Alcan, 1910); review by

Alexander Goldenweiser, *AA* 13 (1911): 121–30; Alfred Kroeber, "The Morals of Uncivilized People," *AA* 12 (1910): 437–47; Franz Boas, "The Mind of Primitive Man," *JAFL* 14 (1901): 1–11; and *The Mind of Primitive Man* (New York: Macmillan, 1911). For a projected series of articles that were never published, see ECP, "Primitive & Tenement House Man" (1905–7); ECP [to *Outlook*?], [June 1905]; notes with reference to Boas, "Mind of Primitive Man" (1901), APS; *Atlantic Monthly* to ECP, 19 May 1906; Livingston Farrand to ECP, 1 June 1906; *Outlook* to ECP, 23 June 1906, RHS; ECP, preface to her student Elsa Herzfeld's *Family Monographs* (1905); and Herzfeld, "Superstitions and Customs of the Tenement-House Mother," *Charities and the Commons*, 5 Aug. 1905, 983–86. For observations of her friends, see ECP to HP, 19 June 1905: "Eunice has the same point of view as many savage women. The prevention of conception is however a rather more refined method than female infanticide"; and ECP to HP, 20 Aug. 1906, APS: "Florence asked me the other day 'Did you mind the baby dying?' It made me think of the primitive state of mind that favored infanticide as a natural occurrence."

27. For evolutionary paradigm, see Cynthia Russett, *Sexual Science: The Victorian Construction of Womanhood* (Cambridge: Harvard University Press, 1989); Joan Jacobs Brumberg, "The Ethnological Mirror: American Evangelical Women and Their Heathen Sisters, 1870–1910," in *Women and the Structure of Society*, ed. Barbara J. Harris and Jo Ann K. McNamara (Durham: Duke University Press, 1984), 108–28. For current fascination with the primitive, see Marianna Torgovnick, *Gone Primitive* (Chicago: University of Chicago Press, 1990); Edith Wharton, *The House of Mirth* (1905; New York: Library of America, 1985), 7.

28. ECP, *Old-Fashioned Woman*, v–vi. Cf. "Suffrage and Feminism" (1917), 1.

29. Boas, "Mind of Primitive Man," 1.

30. Paul Radin, "Personal Reminiscences of a Winnebago Indian," *JAFL* 26 (1913): 293–318; *The Winnebago Tribe* (1923; Lincoln: Bison Book, 1970), written in 1913, preface dated 11 May 1916; "Religion of the North American Indians," *JAFL* 27 (1914): 335–72.

31. William James, "The Importance of Individuals," in *The Will to Believe and Other Essays in Popular Philosophy* (1890; New York: Longmans, Green and Co., 1897), 270, quoted in Perry, *Thought and Character*, 2:212; "On a Certain Blindness in Human Beings," in *Talks to Teachers on Psychology* (New York: Henry Holt, 1899), 229–64; *The Principles of Psychology* (New York: Henry Holt, 1899), 2:674–75, quoted in Perry, *Thought and Character*, 2:266; Robert Louis Stevenson, "The Lantern-bearer," in *Across the Plains* (1892).

32. Hapgood's work was inspired by his friend Josiah Flynt Willard, the delinquent (and alcoholic) nephew of Woman's Christian Temperance Union president Frances Willard, who turned his experiences as a runaway youth into studies of "the tramp-world" that emphasized observation and firsthand experience as the proper basis for theories about crime. See Willard, *Tramping with Tramps* (New York: Century, 1900); and Hutchins Hapgood, *Spirit of the Ghetto* (1902); *Autobiography of a Thief* (1903); *The Spirit of Labor* (1907); *An Anarchist Woman* (1909); and *Types from City Streets* (1910). Although Hapgood struggled to free his portraits from

sentimentality, moralizing, and sensationalism, he was still, as he put it in his own autobiography in 1939, "a Victorian in the modern world." The autobiographies in Hamilton Holt's volume were published in the *Independent* between 1902 and 1906. Strongly influenced by Franklin Giddings, who regularly wrote editorials under his editorship, Holt worked throughout his life to break down barriers of race, ethnicity, nationality, and education. The *Independent*'s literary editor, scientist Edwin Slosson, set out in an introduction the book's aim to be useful as sociology—"not merely to satisfy our common curiosity as to 'how the other half lives.'" "If Plutarch had given us the life stories of a slave and a hoplite, a peasant and a potter, we would willingly have dispensed with an equivalent number of kings and philosophers. Biography and demography are equally useful, the former more vivid, the latter more comprehensive." See Werner Sollors, "From the Bottom Up," foreword to *Life Stories of (Undistinguished) Americans as Told by Themselves,* ed. Hamilton Holt (New York: Routledge, 1990). For Thomas, see review, *AJS* 12 (1906): 273–74; W. I. Thomas and Florian Znaniecki, *The Polish Peasant in Europe and America,* vols. 1 and 2 (1918), 3 (1919), 4 and 5 (1920) (reprint, New York: Knopf, 1927). Znaniecki translated Bergson into Polish 1912–13. Thomas and Znaniecki believed that "personal life-records, as complete as possible, constitute the perfect type of sociological material." Accordingly, the first two volumes of *The Polish Peasant* comprised fifty series of letters used to describe Polish peasant society, and the third volume was the autobiography of an immigrant peasant—some 3,000 pages of human documents in all.

33. Stein broke from the intellectual domination of her brother and began her lifelong relationship with Alice B. Toklas; Wharton finally dissolved her empty marriage; Vorse found herself the sole breadwinner for her young family when her estranged husband died and her mother disinherited her; and Boyce had to choose between the lover who gave her freedom and her husband, who wanted her to personify his ideal of Woman. See R. W. B. Lewis, *Edith Wharton* (New York: Fromm International, 1985); Dee Garrison, *Mary Heaton Vorse* (Philadelphia: Temple University Press, 1989); Neith Boyce, *The Bond* (New York: Duffield, 1908); [Hutchins Hapgood], *The Story of a Lover* (New York: Boni and Liveright, 1919); Boyce and Hapgood, "Enemies," *The Provincetown Plays: Second Series* (New York: Frank Shay Publishers, 1916), 105–6; and letters and poems in Ellen Trimberger, ed., *Intimate Warriors: Portraits of a Modern Marriage, 1899–1944* (New York: Feminist Press, 1991); Stein, *The Making of Americans; Matisse, Picasso, and Gertrude Stein* (Paris: Plain Edition, 1933); "Portrait of Mabel Dodge at the Villa Curonia," *Camera Work* 24 (June 1913): 3–5; *Tender Buttons* (New York: Claire Marie, 1914).

34. Gertrude Stein, *Bee Time Vine* (1922), 7, quoted in Elyse Blankley, "Beyond the 'Talent of Knowing': Gertrude Stein and the New Woman," in *Critical Essays on Gertrude Stein,* ed. Michael J. Hoffman (Boston: G. K. Hall, 1986), 196–209, esp. 201; Georg Simmel, "The Sociological Significance of the 'Stranger'" (1909), reprinted in *Introduction to the Science of Sociology,* ed. Robert E. Park and Ernest W. Burgess (Chicago: University of Chicago Press, 1921), 322–27; Mary Heaton Vorse, "The

Quiet Woman," *Atlantic Monthly,* Jan. 1907, 86–87; *Breaking In of a Yachtsman's Wife* (1908); *The Very Little Person* (Boston: Houghton Mifflin, 1911); *Autobiography of an Elderly Woman* (New York, 1974); Edith Wharton, *The Custom of the Country* (1913; New York: Library of America, 1985). Cf. Patricia Hill Collins, "Learning from the Outsider Within: The Social Significance of Black Feminist Thought," in *Beyond Methodology,* ed. M. M. Fonow and J. A. Cook (Bloomington: Indiana University Press, 1991), 36–59.

35. William James, *Psychology: Briefer Course* (1961), 39, 8, and "The Hidden Self," in *A William James Reader,* ed. Gay Wilson Allen (Boston: Houghton Mifflin, 1971), 93, 181; both quoted in Ruddick, *Reading Gertrude Stein,* 16–19.

36. Franz Boas, "The Ethnological Significance of Esoteric Doctrines," *Science* 16 (1902): 872–74, reprinted in *Race, Language, and Culture* (New York: Macmillan, 1940), 312–15; H. L. Mencken, "The Genealogy of Etiquette," *Prejudices: First Series* (New York: Knopf, 1919), 150–70, esp. 156; ECP, *Fear and Conventionality* (1914), xiv, and "Interpreting Ceremonialism" (1915), 601, 603.

37. The unpublished manuscripts are in APS.

38. RHL to Radin, 2 Oct. 1920, RHL Papers.

39. ECP, *Social Freedom* (1915), 1; *Social Rule* (1916), 2; "The Aversion to Anomalies" (1915).

40. ECP, *Social Rule,* 54–55; Ernst Mach, "Introductory Remarks: Antimetaphysical," in *The Analysis of Sensations and the Relation of the Physical to the Psychical* (New York: Dover, 1959), 1–37, esp. 13–14, 16, 23–24.

41. ECP, "Journal of a Feminist," Apr. 1914, 115. Parsons was responding to a talk given to the Columbia Feminist Forum by Dr. Oscar Riddle of the Carnegie Laboratory, Cold Spring Harbor, whose sex research suggested to her that "sex is not an [in]eradicable, immutable character in any given individual."

42. ECP, *Social Freedom,* 105–6; *Fear and Conventionality,* 209–13, 216–17; cf. Luhan, *Movers and Shakers,* 39.

43. Judith Ryan, *The Vanishing Subject: Early Psychology and Literary Modernism* (Chicago: University of Chicago Press, 1991), 226.

44. Ernst Mach, "The Economical Nature of Physical Inquiry," in *Popular Scientific Lectures* (1895), 197, quoted in R. J. Seeger, "On Mach's Curiosity about Shockwaves," in *Ernst Mach,* ed. R. S. Cohen and R. J. Seeger (Dordecht: D. Reidel, 1970), 60–61. ECP, "Feminism and Conventionality" (1914), 48–49; cf. "Supernatural Policing of Women" (1912) and *Fear and Conventionality,* 205–18, esp. 210.

45. ECP, *Social Rule,* 2; *Social Freedom,* 25; "Friendship, a Social Category" (1915). For marriage, see "One," in *The Old-Fashioned Woman* (1913), and "Avoidance" and "Teknonymy" (1914).

46. Desley Deacon, "The Republic of the Spirit: Fieldwork in Elsie Clews Parsons's Turn to Anthropology," *Frontiers* 12, no. 3 (1992): 12–38.

47. Robert Herrick, "The Story of Jessica Stowe" (1924), RH Papers.

48. RHL to ECP, [after 5 Feb. 1916], APS; ECP to RHL, 6 Jan. 1938, RHL Papers.

49. Perry Anderson, "Modernity and Revolution," in *Marxism and the Interpretation of Culture,* ed. L. Grossberg and C. Nelson (Urbana: University of Illinois Press, 1988), 317–33, esp. 326.

Chapter Seven

1. PG to ECP, 2 Feb. 1914 and 8 Nov. 1913, APS.
2. *Current Opinion,* Aug. 1913, 113–14; *Harper's Weekly,* 16 Aug. 1913; Ford, *NYH,* 1 Jan. 1916; M. D. Marcaccio, *The Hapgoods* (Charlottesville: University Press of Virginia, 1977), 116, 124–25, 223. See ECP, "The Journal of a Feminist, 1913–1914," APS, esp. 13 Nov. 1913, 43–44, for *Harper's* cover, 1 Sept. 1913, featuring "Unmarried Mothers." For rejection of articles, see Hapgood to ECP, 19 and 24 Sept., 24 Oct., 11, 18, and 26 Nov. 1913, 2 Feb. 1914, APS; and "The Woman Who Did" (1915) for one he accepted.
3. ECP, "Journal of a Feminist," Newport, 19 Aug. 1913, 10.
4. The talk was published as "Marriage and Parenthood—a Distinction" (1915). For discussion of these issues, see ECP, "Journal of a Feminist," 13 Nov. 1913 and 27 Jan. 1914, 43–44 and 64; Hapgood to ECP and PG to ECP, 2 Feb. 1914; James Robinson to ECP, 8 Feb. 1914, APS. For rejection, see *Atlantic Monthly* to ECP, 2 Mar. 1914; Francis Hackett (*New Republic*) to ECP, 28 Apr. 1915; Walter Lippmann (*New Republic*) to ECP, 3 May 1915, APS. For acceptance, see James Tufts to ECP, 2 Apr. 1915, and ECP to Tufts, 13 May 1915, APS. See also ECP, "Sex and the Elders" (1915); "School," review of *A History of the Family as a Social and Educational Institution,* by Willystine Goodsell (1916); and review of *A Social History of the American Family,* by A. W. Calhoun (1918).
5. ECP, "When Mating and Parenthood Are Theoretically Distinguished" (1916), 211, 213–15. See critique by Mary Willcox Glenn, 217–22, and James Tufts's wishy-washy observations, 223–40. For a negative response, probably from some Heterodoxy members, to increasing women's responsibility (rather than enforcing greater male responsibility), see ECP, "Feminism and the Family" (1917).
6. ECP, "Feminism and Sex Ethics" (1916). For Herbert's (Amos's) reactions to these ideas, see "Journal of a Feminist," 1 Jan. 1914, 73–74; for Learned Hand's (Judge), Jan. 1914, 78. See also "Meetings" (1915), 11; and RB to ECP, 3 Aug. 1916, APS.
7. ECP, "Privacy in Love Affairs" (1915). For Heretics, see J. Salwyn Schapiro to ECP, 7 May and 27 June 1915; RB to ECP, 17 June 1915; Goldenweiser to ECP, 8 July 1915, APS. A typed sheet (1915?), APS, lists members: Bourne, Evans Clark (Freda Kirchwey's husband), Henderson Deady, Herman Defrem (Henrietta Rodman's husband), Adolf Elwyn, Goddard, Goldenweiser, Alyse Gregory, Alcan Hirsch, Harry Hollingworth, Leta Hollingworth, Charlotte Howell, Herschel Jones, Edward Kasner, Arthur Kellogg, Freda Kirchwey, Alfred Kuttner, Margaret Lane, Winthrop Lane, David Mitchell, William Montague, Helen Parkhurst, Maurice Parmelee, Elsie Clews Parsons, Henrietta Rodman, Benoy Sarkar, Salwyn Schapiro, Theodore Schroeder, and Inis Weed.
8. ECP, "Sincerity in Love Affairs" (1915), APS. It is not clear why this was not published. See Floyd Dell to ECP, [July 1915], APS.

9. ECP, "Must We Have Her?" (1916). For the formulation of these ideas, see "Journal of a Feminist," Mar. 1914. See also letter to editor, "Separate Invitation—Not Divorce" (1916); NR to ECP, 22 May 1916; HP to ECP, 6 Oct. 1916; ECP to HP, 10 Oct. 1916; "Selfishness" (1916?), APS; and Signe Toksvig to ECP, 3 Mar. and 4 Apr. 1922, RHS. For long discussions with Bourne see ECP to HP, 24 and 26 May 1916; RB to ECP, 13 June and 4 July 1916, APS; RB to Dorothy Teall, [21 Apr. 1916], in RB Letters.

10. For LaFarge (1862–1938) see DAB, suppl. 2; Owen Wister, Roosevelt: The Story of a Friendship (New York, 1930); Oliver LaFarge, "Salt Water," in Raw Material (New York: Houghton Mifflin, 1945), 23–35.

11. GLF to ECP, 29 July 1913, APS. For return from Yucatán, see ECP to HP, [14] Feb. 1913, and HP to ECP, 14 Feb. 1913, APS. For beginning of relationship, see GLF to ECP, [Apr.] 1913, APS. I have been unable to locate any of ECP's letters to GLF.

12. Royal Cortissoz, "John LaFarge," DAB; John LaFarge, S.J., The Manner Is Ordinary (New York: Harcourt Brace, 1954), 4, 7; Oliver LaFarge, "Old Man Facing Death," in Raw Material, 36–48, esp. 37–38.

13. ECP, "Journal of a Feminist," Newport, 20 Aug. 1913, 10–11.

14. "Journal of a Feminist," [26 Nov. 1913], 47–48. Cf. "The Sin of Being Found Out" (1915); and "The Near Conjugal" (1916); Hackett to ECP, 7 May [1915], cont. of 28 Apr., APS. Sorchan divorced her husband and married her longtime lover and ECP's friend, Walton Martin, in 1921.

15. "Journal of a Feminist," New York, 27 Nov. 1913, 49–50.

16. Ibid., 28 Nov. 1913, 51–54. See Eastman, "Marriage under Two Roofs," Cosmopolitan, Dec. 1923, in Crystal Eastman on Women and Revolution, ed. Blanche Wiesen Cook (New York: OUP, 1978), 76–83.

17. See GLF corres. and poems, 1918, APS.

18. Grant LaFarge, "Rivers and Recollections" (1920?), 23–27, APS.

19. GLF to ECP, 23 Dec. 1913, APS.

Chapter Eight

1. ECP to HP, [31 July] and 2 Aug. 1914, APS. See also ECP, "The Journal of a Feminist, 1913–1914," 3 Aug. 1914, 121; Laurie Hughes to ECP, 2 Aug. 1914, APS.

2. ECP, introduction to "Journal of a Feminist," 3–4; Lucien Lévy-Bruhl, Les Fonctions mentales dans les sociétés inférieures (Alcan, 1910).

3. Robert Lowie, "The Inferior Races from an Anthropologist's Point of View," New Review, Dec. 1913, 934–42; ECP to RHL, 6 Feb. 1914, RHL Papers; RHL to ECP, 7 Feb. 1914; New Review to ECP, 20 Feb. 1914, APS; ECP, "Ethnology in Education," New Review, Apr. 1914. For General Education Board secretary Abraham Flexner, who planned the experimental Linclon School of Teachers College that Herbert and Mac attended from 1917, see "Journal of a Feminist," 90. For Sedgwick, see Gail Bederman, Manliness and Civilization (Chicago: University of Chicago Press, 1995), 159–63.

4. ECP, "The School of Ethnology [Social History]: A University Extension School" (1914?), RHS.

5. ECP to FB, draft, [Dec. 1913?], APS.

6. Strunsky to ECP, 27 Oct. 1914, APS; ECP, "Making Ethnology Popular" (1916).

7. Philonous, "A Contribution Criticised," *NR,* 20 Mar. 1915, 183.

8. ECP, "Avoidance" (1914); "Teknonymy" (1914); Small to ECP, 3 Dec. 1913, APS; Helene Yampolsky to ALK, 18 May 1956, ALK Papers.

9. PG to ECP, 25 Jan. 1915, APS. See Robert H. Lowie, "Ceremonial in North America," *AA* 16 (1914): 602–31. With the encouragement of Goddard and Goldenweiser, ECP "got in the game" for the first time in 1915 by challenging the major spokesman for the structural school, British anthropologist W. H. R. Rivers. In "Avoidance in Melanesia" (1916), her first article for the *Journal of American Folklore,* written in June 1915, she argued that avoidance could not be explained, as Rivers tried to, without considering the psychology of boundary maintenance; and we cannot even ask the right psychological questions unless we have a clear idea of those processes in our own society—an argument that she reiterated in the article "Home Study in Ethnology" in the *American Anthropologist* (1915). See Goldenweiser to ECP, [7 May 1915], APS; Lowie, review of Rivers's *Kinship and Social Organization, AA* 17 (1915): 329–40.

10. Franz Boas, "The Growth of Indian Mythologies," *JAFL* 9 (1896): 11, quoted in ECP, "Two Methods in Ethnological Hypothesis" (1915), APS. For Haeberlin's promise, see Boas, "In Memoriam: Herman Karl Haeberlin," *AA* 21 (1919): 71–73.

11. Alfred L. Kroeber, "Eighteen Professions," *AA* 17 (1915): 283–88; ALK to Sapir, 24 July 1917, in Golla. Kroeber's urging persuaded Sapir to discuss the logic and methodology of historical reconstruction in his classic *Time Perspective in Aboriginal American Culture: A Study in Method,* Geological Survey, Canadian Department of Mines, Memoir 90, Anthropological Series 13 (1916) and his definitive *Language: An Introduction to the Study of Speech* (New York: Harcourt, Brace, 1921). Kroeber did not attend the meetings himself, so ECP did not meet him until December 1915.

12. Pliny Goddard, "The Relation of Folk-Lore to Anthropology," *JAFL* 28 (1915): 18–23; ALK to PG, draft, 11 Feb. 1915, ALK Papers. The portion quoted was scratched out, but it probably reflected an ongoing conversation.

13. Alvin Johnson to Leslie White, 11 Aug. 1955, LW Papers; W. Fenton, "Sapir as Museologist," in *New Perspectives in Language, Culture, and Personality,* ed. W. Cowan, M. Foster, and K. Koerner (Amsterdam: J. Benjamins, 1986), 228; Alexander Goldenweiser, review of *Social Anthropology,* by Paul Radin, *AA* 35 (1933): 349; ALK to Edward Sapir, 11 July and 17 Aug. 1919; ALK to ECP, 18 Aug. 1919, ALK Papers. See Sapir, "Do We Really Need a 'Superorganic'?" *AA* 19 (1917): 441–47. See also Goldenweiser's comment, 447–49; H. K. Haeberlin, "Anti-Professions: A Reply to Dr. A. L. Kroeber," *AA* 17 (1915): 756–59; Goldenweiser to ECP, July 1915, APS; ALK to Sapir, 28 Nov. 1915 and 23 Oct. and 4 Nov. 1917; Sapir to RHL, 26 June, 10 and 23 July 1917; Sapir to ALK, 29 Oct. 1917, in Golla; ALK to Goldenweiser, 23 Oct. 1917, ALK Papers; Kroeber, "The Possibility of a Social Psychology," *AJS* 23 (1918): 633–51. See Goldenweiser, *History, Psychology, and Culture* (New York: Knopf, 1933), 158–63, for full discussion and bibliography.

In 1914, Goldenweiser was accused of taking an Iroquois mistress—
"from one of our best Christian families, not one of the Longhouse people"—and was barred from the Iroquois reservation where he had been
doing fieldwork since 1911. By all acccounts, he was a talented fieldworker
who danced and sang with his hosts, reciprocating by playing sonatas on
the piano he brought with him and taking his Iroquois friends to the opera
in Niagara Falls. But the Baptist elders on the reservation considered him
"a brilliant scoundrel." As a successor put it, "AAG ignored such mundane
requirements as accounting for time and money, repaying loans, and other
conventions expected of civil servants." He was dismissed and became
persona non grata in Canada. In New York, as Lowie remembered it,
"while his first wife was at a maternity hospital, Goldenweiser borrowed
money right and left,—obstensibly to meet the requisite expenses. Actually
he needed the money for an affair. Apart from these escapades, G. failed
to return books to the University Library and did not pay his bills at the
Faculty Club. At one time he was jailed for non-support of his wife and
child." In that imbroglio, Goldenweiser lost all chance of securing the
permanent position he expected at Columbia. Meanwhile, he made a precarious living and borrowed from Parsons, among others, to support his
family, and perhaps his lovers. See Fenton, "Sapir," 228–29; RHL to Leslie
White, 21 Feb. 1956, LW Papers. See also Sapir to ALK, 29 Apr. 1911
and 15 May 1913, in Golla; Goldenweiser to Sapir, 9 June 1914, quoted
in Fenton, "Sapir"; Goldenweiser to ECP, 28 and 30 Jan. 1918, APS; RHL
to Risa Lowie, 8 Sept. 1925, RHL Papers.

14. Pliny Goddard, review of ECP's *Fear and Conventionality*, *AA* 17
(1915): 343–44; PG to ECP, 18 May 1915, APS. For psychology vogue,
see Max Eastman, "The First Few Books," *Masses*, Apr. 1915, 22; ECP,
"Discomfiture and Evil Spirits" (1916).

15. Clarence Ayres to ECP, 6 Apr. 1927, APS. Ayres wrote regularly
for the *New Republic* in 1922–29. See *Science: The False Messiah* (India-
napolis: Bobbs-Merrill, 1927); and W. Breit and W. P. Culbertson Jr., eds.,
Science and Ceremony: The Institutional Economics of C. E. Ayres (Austin: University of Texas Press, 1976). Thanks to Mark Smith for information on Ayres. For *New Republic* see Hackett to ECP, 28 Apr. and 7 May
1915; Lippmann to ECP, 3 May 1915, APS.

16. ECP, "The Will to Power among Sociologists" (1915), APS; "Gregariousness and the Impulse to Classify" (1915); Ross, *The Old World in
the New: The Significance of the Past and Present Immigration to the
American People* (New York: Century, 1914); A. J. Vidich and S. M.
Lyman, *American Sociology: Worldly Rejections of Religion and Their
Directions* (New Haven: Yale University Press, 1985), 156–61, 164–65
for Ross; for Kellor, Ellen Fitzpatrick, *Endless Crusade: Women Social
Scientists and Progressive Reform* (New York: OUP, 1990), 130–65,
esp. 159–61.

17. ECP to HP, [5 Apr. 1915]; also 21, 24 Apr. 1915, APS. For Nassau
trip, ECP to HP, 27 and 29 Feb. 1915, APS. For possible flight to Spain,
ECP to HP, 9 Apr. 1915, APS. For divorce, see ECP, "Imaginary Mistress"
(1913), 13–14; HP to ECP, 31 Dec. 1914, 22 April, 19 May, and 27 July
1915, APS.

18. ECP, "In New York State" (1913–15); ECP to HP, 26 May 1915; also Francis Hackett to ECP, 28 Apr. 1915, APS.

19. ECP to HP, 31 and 7 Aug. 1915; see also ECP to HP, 5 Aug. 1915; HP to ECP, 26 Aug. 1915, APS.

20. ECP to HP, 15 and 31 Aug. 1915, APS. ECP was at Zuni 14–28 Aug. 1915. The modern spelling is "Zuni," but ECP and her colleagues usually spelled it "Zuñi."

21. ECP to HP, 17 Sept., 1 and 5 Oct. 1915; Grant LaFarge, "Rivers and Recollections" (1920?), 5–6, APS. LaFarge, probably unaware of Parsons's preoccupation, found the trip disappointing. "It is none too easy to describe the frustration of that camp," he wrote in "Recollections." "You were introduced to two varieties of tent—the Baker, which was your house, while I had the tiny green-gray 'Forester.' There was a pretty portage up to a lonely little lake, where we watched for moose; there was a delicious beach for swimming. . . . But moose there were none. . . . And there was no fishing. Then came awful weather, gales of wind and wet snow. . . . So it was a poor outcome of my dreams of showing you the pleasures of Canadian wilds."

22. FB to ECP, 24 Nov. 1915; also FB to ECP, 23 Nov. 1915; ECP to FB, 23 and 25 Nov. 1915, APS. For work see ECP to RHL, [7] Nov. 1915; RHL to ECP, 9 Nov. 1915; ECP to HP, 15 and 17 Nov. 1915; PG to ECP, 20 Nov. 1915, APS; "A Few Zuñi Death Beliefs and Practices" (1916); "The Zuñi Adoshlĕ and Suukĕ" (1916); "The Zuñi Ła'mana" (1916); "Mothers and Children at Zuñi, New Mexico" (1919).

23. ALK to ECP, 9 Aug. 1916, APS. For Zuni see ECP to HP, 17 Nov., 8 and 22 Dec. 1915, APS. For AMNH see ALK to PG, draft, 11 Feb. 1915; Wissler to ALK, 23 Feb. 1915, ALK Papers; Wissler, general introduction to *The Archer M. Huntington Survey of the Southwest: Zuñi District,* AMNH Anthropological Papers 18 (New York, 1919); and "Survey," in J. M. Kennedy, "Philanthropy and Science in New York City: The American Museum of Natural History, 1868–1968" (Ph.D. diss., Yale University, 1968), 173–74. For Lowie at Hopi, see *Robert H. Lowie, Ethnologist: A Personal Record* (Berkeley: University of California Press, 1959), 67; RHL to Risa Lowie, 27 June, 23 Aug. 1915, and 20 Aug. 1916, RHL Papers.

24. ECP, "Interpreting Ceremonialism" (1915). See PG to ECP, 25 Jan. and 19 Apr. 1915, APS; also ECP, "Journal of a Feminist," 27 Jan. 1914, 75; ECP to RHL, 5 Feb. 1916; RHL to ECP, [after 5 Feb. 1916], APS; ECP, "Holding Back in Crisis Ceremonialism" (1916); "Ceremonial Reluctance," [before 8 Feb. 1914]; "Puppet of the Ceremonial," [Apr. 1914]; review of *The Primitive Family as an Educational Agency,* by J. A. Todd (1914); "Feminism and Conventionality" (1914); "The Ceremonial of Growing Up" (1915); "Ceremonial Impatience" (1918).

25. ECP, "Two Methods in Ethnological Hypothesis." For *AJS* rejection following decision not to publish anthropology, see W. I. Thomas to ECP, 28 July 1917, APS; but see ALK to Edward Sapir, 23 Oct. 1917, in Golla; and Kroeber, "Possibility of a Social Psychology." See also ECP to RHL, 28 Oct. 1915; RHL to ECP, 5 and [7?] Nov. 1915, RHL Papers; RHL to ECP, 9 Nov. 1915, APS; Robert Lowie, "Psychology and Sociology," *AJS*

21 (1915): 217–29; Alexander Goldenweiser, review of Durkheim, *AA* 17 (1915): 719–35; James Leuba, "Sociology and Psychology," *AJS* 19 (1913): 323–42.

26. PG to ECP, 20 Nov. 1915; ALK to ECP, 3 Dec. 1915; see also *NYTr* to ECP, 13 Jan. 1916, APS.

27. Day to ECP, [26] Dec. 1915; ECP to HP, 29 Dec. 1915, APS. See "Youth to Wrest Sceptre from the Elders: Elsie Clews Parsons Foresees Rebellion of Young Blood against Domination by Graybeards—a Roman Parallel," *NYTr,* 26 Dec. 1915, v, surrounding Alice Duer Miller's regular column "Are Women People?"; ECP, "Zuñi Conception and Pregnancy Beliefs" (1917); ECP to HP, 22 Dec. 1915, fr. Gallup, APS.

28. Floyd Dell, review of ECP's *Fear and Conventionality, New Review,* 1 Jan. 1916, 17–18; Victor Yarros, *NYEP,* 2 May 1916; ECP, "American 'Society,'" pt. 1; pt. 2, esp. 215.

29. Julian Mack to Felix [Frankfurter], 28 Apr. 1916; ECP to HP, 28 Apr. 1916, APS. See also Town Crier, "Library Table," clipping, 6 Jan. 1917, APS.

30. For her neighbor, see ECP to HP, 16 Oct. 1906, fr. Lenox, APS: "the children and I walked to call on Mrs. Frankfurt. She has been improving, but now she thinks she may be pregnant again, & Armstrong told her to have no more children for four years, but of course did not tell her *how.* I shall give him a piece of my mind; for it may be her death or at any rate wrecked health." ECP herself became pregnant again in April 1907 six weeks after her previous confinement, so her information was apparently not very reliable.

31. ECP, "Remarks at Sanger dinner," Jan. 1916, APS.

32. ECP, "Wives and Birth Control" (1916). See also "The Lesser Evil" (1916); review of Katherine Anthony, *Feminism in Germany and Scandanavia* (1916); "Feminism and Sex Ethics" (1916); *Harper's Weekly* to ECP, 18 Jan. 1916; F. W. Stella Browne to ECP, 21 Apr. 1916; James Tufts to ECP, 10 Apr. [May] 1916, APS.

33. ECP to HP, 15 Nov. 1916; HP to ECP, 19 Nov. 1916, APS. Herbert is referring to writers Harrison Rhodes and Francis Hackett.

34. PG to ECP, 26 Jan. 1916, APS. See ECP, "The Favorite Number of the Zuñi" (1916), for significance of four.

35. ALK to ECP, 19 Sept., 24 Jan., 1 and 3 Feb. 1916, APS; ECP to ALK, 2 Feb. 1916, ALK Papers; ECP, "A Zuñi Detective" (1916). See *Folk-Lore* (British journal) to ECP, 6 Mar. 1916, APS, for rejection, apparently agreeing with Kroeber.

36. See ALK to ECP, 24 Jan., 20 Mar., and 11 June 1916, APS; ECP to ALK, 6 Feb. and 3 June 1916, ALK Papers.

37. RHL to ECP, [after 5 Feb. 1916], APS; Kroeber, *Zuñi Kin and Clan* (New York, 1917), 47–48. For ECP's feminist interests, see the beautifully produced *Pueblo Mothers and Children: Essays by Elsie Clews Parsons, 1915–1924,* ed. Barbara A. Babcock (Santa Fe: Ancient City Press, 1991), especially Babcock's insightful introduction. For ECP's fieldwork skill, see ALK to GR, 26 May 1942, GR Papers.

38. ALK to ECP, 9 Aug. 1916, APS; Alfred L. Kroeber, "Thoughts on Zuñi Religion," *Holmes Anniversary Volume* (1916; New York: AMS

Press, 1977), 269–77, esp. 276. See also ECP, *Pueblo Indian Religion* (1939), xiii.

39. ALK to ECP, 5 May 1916, APS. See Kroeber's analysis of organic and social evolution in "Inheritance by Magic," *AA* 18 (1916): 19–40, Goldenweiser's reply, "Use Inheritance and Civilization," and Kroeber's retort, "Heredity without Magic," *AA* 18 (1916): 292–94 and 294–96. Kroeber followed this in 1917 with his famous paper "The Superorganic." Taking a strong stand for a social structural rather than a psychological approach to culture, Kroeber emphasized the superorganic, superindividual, superpsychological nature of cultural phenomena. In doing so, he minimized the individual's role in determining historical outcomes and separated anthropology quite clearly from psychology. See "The Superorganic" *AA* 19 (1917): 163–213; ALK to ECP, 24 June, 19 Sept., and 23 Dec. 1916, APS. For its acceptance, see PG to ALK, 3 Nov. 1916, ALK Papers.

40. ECP to ALK, 3 June 1916, ALK Papers; ALK to ECP, 11 June 1916, APS.

41. RHL to ECP, 18 May 1916, APS; ECP, "A Progressive God" (1916); ALK to ECP, 28 June 1916, APS. See also ALK to ECP, 31 Mar. and 19 Sept. 1916, APS.

42. ALK to ECP, 11 and 28 June, 9 Aug. 1916, APS, probably referring to Spier, Goddard, and Lowie. In August 1916, when he wrote the preface to his *Zuñi Kin and Clan,* Kroeber acknowledged his debt to "exceptionally stimulating conferences" with Mrs. Elsie Clews Parsons, "whose series of intensive ethnological and psychological studies of the Zuñi are well known" (41). For the continuing discussion see ALK to ECP, 5 Oct. and 23 Dec. 1916; 20 May and 24 June 1917; Knight Dunlap to ECP, 2 Dec. 1916, with ECP notation, APS; ECP to ALK, 11 May 1917, ALK Papers. ECP had the last word in "The Teleological Delusion" (1917). See ALK to ECP, June 1917, APS: "If you've written better, I don't remember. . . . In the end I'll have to take back having called you a psychologist, I expect."

Chapter Nine

1. Ronald Steel, *Walter Lippmann and the American Century* (London: Bodley Head, 1980), 71–73, esp. 73. See Bruce Clayton, *Forgotten Prophet: The Life of Randolph Bourne* (Baton Rouge: Louisiana State University Press, 1984), 115–16; ECP to HP, 2 Sept. 1914; HP to ECP, 9 Sept. 1914; ECP, "The Journal of a Pacifist," 4 Nov. 1914, 22–23, APS.

2. ECP, "Journal of a Pacifist," 1 Dec. 1914, 36; 18 Oct. 1914, 1–3; Dec. 1914, 31, APS. But ECP did march "in that grotesque peace parade down Fifth Avenue" while Lissa wondered what good it would do. See "Journal of a Pacifist," 18 Oct. 1914, 1; "The Journal of a Feminist, 1913–1914," [27 Aug. 1914], 129; ECP to HP, 27 Aug. 1914, APS. "Journal of a Pacifist" (77 pp.) begins 18 Oct. 1914 and ends 18 Mar. 1915.

3. ECP, "On the Loose" (1915); "Journal of a Pacifist," Oct. 1914, 9–12; 2 Nov. 1914, 20; and 4 Nov. 1914, 22–23. "Great Adventure" was Roosevelt's phrase. See David M. Kennedy, *Over Here: The First World War and American Society* (New York: OUP, 1980), 184–85, for young men's eagerness to get to the front.

4. ECP to editor, *NYT,* 9 Nov. 1914, APS.

5. ECP, "Journal of a Pacifist," 18 Oct. 1914, 1; "The Toy Soldier" (1915), 92, 94. See "Journal of a Pacifist," 1 Dec. 1914, 35–36, for volunteer school cadets killed in action; 4 Feb. 1915, 66, for debate ECP attended at John's school on military drill; Mar. 1915, 73–74, for war toys; also "The Dragon's Teeth" (1915); "Japan and Preparedness" (1915), APS. See Kennedy, *Over Here,* 33, 51–52, on outdated ideals and tactics.

6. ECP, "To Abolish War" (1915); "A Warning to the Middle-Aged" (1915). See also "Journal of a Pacifist," Nov. 1914, 33.

7. Goldenweiser to ECP, 12 Mar. 1920, APS; Randolph Bourne, "The Two Generations," *Atlantic Monthly,* May 1911, and "Youth," *Atlantic Monthly,* Apr. 1912, reprinted in *The Radical Will: Randolph Bourne, Selected Writings, 1911–1918,* ed. Olaf Hansen (New York: Urzen Books, 1977), 93–105, esp. 96–99, 101, 105.

8. Bourne quoted in Clayton, *Forgotten Prophet,* 121. ECP probably met Lippmann (1889–1974) when he helped Mabel Dodge organize her "evenings." See LPK for Lissa Parsons Kennedy's memory of ECP attending all of these, and of being taken to *New Republic* lunches. See also Mabel Dodge Luhan, *Movers and Shakers* (1936; Albuquerque: University of New Mexico Press, 1985), 68, 89, 92, 118. See ECP, "Journal of a Pacifist," Dec. 1914, 46, reporting her attack over dinner on the editor of a weekly, probably Lippmann, who had advocated preparedness. For Francis Hackett (1883–1962), see obituary, *NYT,* 26 Apr. 1962, 33. For affectionate portrait of Croly's friend and adviser Learned Hand, a close friend of Charlotte Sorchan and Walton Martin, see Hackett, *American Rainbow* (New York: Liveright, 1971), 289–91. See Mary Kingsbury Simkhovitch, *Neighborhood: My Story of Greenwich House* (New York: Norton, 1938), 209, for Bourne playing piano at Greenwich House parties.

9. RB to ECP, 17 June 1915, APS; RB to Elizabeth Shepley Sergeant, 15 Nov. 1915, in *RB Letters.* See ECP, "In the Nursery—Militarism or Pacifism?" (1915), APS; L. Hollingsworth Woods, American League to Limit Armaments, to ECP, 11 and 16 Jan. 1915, APS.

10. RB to ECP, 19 July 1915 and 9 Sept. 1915, APS; Randolph Bourne, "The Older Generation," *Atlantic Monthly,* Sept. 1915, 385–91, reprinted in Hansen, *Radical Will,* 159–68. See ECP, "War and the Elders" (1915); also "Anti-Suffragists and the War" (1915). For speech on return from women's peace meeting in the Hague, see Jane Addams, "The Revolt against the War," *Survey,* 17 July 1915, reprinted in *Women at the Hague,* ed. Addams, Emily G. Balch, and Alice Hamilton (New York: Macmillan, 1915), 55–81; *New York Globe and Commercial Advertiser* and *NYT,* 12 July 1915; Richard Harding Davis, letter to editor, *NYT,* 13 July 1915; ECP, "Women and War," letter to editor responding to Davis and editor Louis Wiley, "Alcohol and the Bayonet," *NYT,* 23 July 1915; ECP to Wiley, 24 July 1915; Wiley to ECP, 26 July 1915, APS. For Addams's account, see *Peace and Bread in Time of War* (New York: Macmillan, 1922), 134–51, reprinted in *The Social Thought of Jane Addams,* ed. Christopher Lasch (New York: Irvington, 1982), 233–46.

11. Randolph Bourne, "Trans-National America," *Atlantic Monthly,* July 1916, reprinted in *History of a Literary Radical and Other Essays,*

ed. Van Wyck Brooks (New York: B. W. Huebsch, 1920), 266–99, esp. 288–90. See also ECP to RHL, 28 Oct. 1915, RHL Papers; ECP, "A Novel's Ethnology" (1915).

12. "Race Nonsense Again," *Masses*, Dec. 1914, 20; Kennaday to ECP, 5 Mar. 1915, APS. See Edward A. Ross, *The Old World in the New* (New York: Century, 1914).

13. Clayton, *Forgotten Prophet*, 189–90.

14. Sedgwick to RB, 30 Mar. 1916, quoted in David A. Hollinger, "Ethnic Diversity, Cosmopolitanism, and the Emergence of the American Liberal Intelligentsia," *American Quarterly* 27 (May 1975): 133–51, esp. 134; Bourne, "Trans-National America," 281, 297.

15. ECP, "Selfishness" (1916). See also RB to ECP, [2 June] 1916, on his return to New York; ECP to HP, [28 Oct.] 1916, APS; Randolph Bourne, "A Moral Equivalent for Universal Military Service," *NR*, 1 July 1916, 217–19; and "Americanism," 23 Sept. 1916, 197.

16. ECP to Prof. Montague, draft, [June 1916]; ECP to RB, 14 June 1916, APS.

17. RB to ECP, 4 July and 3 Oct. 1916, APS; Bourne, "The Jew and Trans-National America," *Menorah Journal,* Dec. 1916, 277–84, reprinted in *War and the Intellectuals,* ed. Carl Resek (New York: Harper Torchbooks, 1964), 124–33. See also RB to Alyse Gregory, 10 Nov. 1916, in *RB Letters;* RB to ECP, 21 Nov. 1916, APS. Cf. ECP to HP, 27 Oct. 1916, APS, after Bourne's visit, commenting on Hughes's speeches and quoting Munsterberg to the effect that the spread of *Kultur* meant the spread of nationalism in general. See also ECP to JEP, 7 Nov. 1916, APS, on Hughes's apparent election, that there is something shameful about electing a man on "an exclusively American policy." Hughes did not in fact win the election. The next morning the nation discovered that Wilson was the victor.

18. ECP to ALK, 11 May 1917, ALK Papers.

19. ECP to JEP, 13 July 1916; ECP to HP, 20, 27 and 31 July; also on back of Lissa to ECP, 12 July 1916, APS. For Silva, see ECP, "Ten Folk-Tales from the Cape Verde Islands" (1917). See also Franz Boas, "Notes on Mexican Folk-Lore," *JAFL* 25 (1912): 204–60; FB to ECP, 23 and 25 Nov. 1915, 29 July and 5 Aug. 1916; ECP to HP, [24] and 27 Feb. 1916, APS; Boas, *JAFL* 30 (1917): 270. See also ECP's works for the years 1917–23 cited in the bibliography.

20. ECP to HP, 20, 24, and 30 Aug. and 7 Oct. 1916; ECP to JEP, 7 Oct. 1916; also 9 Oct. 1916, APS.

21. RB to ECP, 7 Sept. and 21 Nov. 1916; JEP to ECP, 12 Oct. 1916; ECP to JEP, 27 Oct. and [11 Nov.] 1916, APS. See also ALK to ECP, 19 Sept. 1916; HP to ECP, 8 Sept. 1916, APS.

22. ECP, "Joel Chandler Harris and Negro Folklore" (1919), 492. See ECP, review of *The Black Border* (1922), for importance of accurate transcription of African-American speech and not "out-dialecting" dialect.

23. ECP, "The Study of Variants" (1920), 90. See Melville J. Herskovits, "Some Next Steps in the Study of Negro Folklore," *JAFL* 56 (1943): 1–7, esp. 2.

24. ECP, "The Zuñi Mo'lawia" (1916); and "Register of Ceremonies

from December 23, 1915, to December 5, 1916," "Shalako, 1915," "Mahedinasha, 1917," "Hilili, 1917," "Newekwe and Koyemshi," and "Decay in Ceremonialism," in *Notes on Zuñi,* pt. 1 (1917).

25. See ECP, "The Governor of Zuñi," in "In the Southwest" (1921), APS; "Installation of Tapup and Sipoloa Shiwanni, 1917," in *Notes on Zuñi,* pt. 1; "Pueblo-Indian Folk-Tales, Probably of Spanish Provenience" (1918); "A Few Zuñi Death Beliefs and Practices" (1916), 250. For Acoma, see "In the Room Below," in "In the Southwest"; "All-Souls Day at Zuñi, Acoma, and Laguna" (1917). The Spaniards had settled at San Gabriel opposite San Juan pueblo on the Rio Grande in 1598. In 1680, the Pueblos united to expel them. The churches were destroyed; but the Pueblos were at the mercy of the Apaches and Navajos, now on horseback. In 1692, the Spaniards returned, and a period of struggle between Pueblos and Spanish and pueblo against pueblo ensued, followed by peaceful collaboration. After Mexican independence in 1821, church influence waned throughout the pueblos, especially at Zuni, which had experienced Spanish incursion since 1540. In 1846, the pueblos became part of the United States. The Hopis resisted Spanish colonization most successfully.

26. ECP, "Laguna Lodging Houses," esp. 3, 6, in "In the Southwest." See also "Notes on Acoma and Laguna" (1918). See Leslie Marmon Silko, *Storyteller* (New York: Seaver Books, 1981), for her family, esp. 254–56, for ECP's and Boas's visits; and Esther Schiff Goldfrank, *Notes on an Undirected Life: As One Anthropologist Tells It* (Flushing, N.Y.: Queens College Press, 1978), 43–44, for the Eckermans and their hotel in 1920.

27. ECP to JEP, 1 Feb. 1917, APS; ECP to ALK, 11 May 1917, ALK Papers.

28. ECP to editor, *NYT,* 9 Mar. 1917, APS. See Franz Boas, "Patriotism," in *Race and Democratic Society,* ed. Ernst Boas (New York: J. J. Augustin, 1945), 159–69; FB to ECP, 7 and 10 Mar. 1917, APS.

29. Lippmann to ECP, 23 June 1916, APS; Lippmann, editorial, *NR,* 24 June 1916, 182; Steel, *Lippmann,* 103; Lippmann to ECP, 9 Aug. 1916, APS. See also RB to ECP, 15 June 1916; Lippmann, "At the Chicago Conventions," *NR,* 17 June 1916; Floyd Dell, review of *Social Freedom, Masses,* June 1916, 24–25. For war, see Lippmann, "The Great Decision," *NR,* 7 Apr. 1917, 280; "Who Willed American Participation?" *NR,* 14 Apr. 1917, 308–10; "The World Conflict in Its Relation to American Democracy," *Annals of the American Academy of Political and Social Science* (July 1917). The night before war was declared, ECP and Hackett attended the Negro plays written by Bourne's pacifist friend Ridgley Torrence and produced by Emilie Hapgood, and Bourne saw them the evening of the declaration of war. See ECP to HP, 2 Apr. 1917, APS; Bourne, letter to editor, *NYTr,* 10 Apr. 1917, 10: "It was Good Friday. And it was the day of the proclamation of war. As the solemn tones pealed out in the last play Simon, the Cyrenian, with its setting for the Crucifixion—'They that take the sword shall perish by the sword'—you could hear the audience catch its breath as it realized the piercing meaning of this heroic little drama of non-resistance played before a Christian nation that was going into a world war on the very day that its churches celebrated devoutly the anniversary of this very warning."

30. ECP to HP, 20 Apr. and [9 May] 1917; JEP to HP, 23 Apr. 1917;

also 6 Apr. 1917, APS, re craving a gun. As an adult, JEP became a collector and expert on guns.

31. ECP, "The Teleological Delusion" (1917). See ECP to RB, [22 May] 1917, RB Papers, dating it before RB to ECP, 9 May 1917; and ALK to ECP, 24 June 1917, APS; Lippmann, *NR*, 31 Mar. 1917.

32. ECP to RB, 22 May 1917, RB Papers.

33. Blanche Wiesen Cook, "Woodrow Wilson and the Antimilitarists, 1914–1918" (Ph.D. diss., Johns Hopkins University, 1970), 207–8. For People's Council, see Louis Lochner to ECP, 13 June 1917, APS. For article, see ECP to RB, 22 May 1917, RB Papers. ECP, "In Terms of Crisis" (1917), APS, was never published. See ECP to [Lippmann?], [22 May 1917]; Alvin Johnson to ECP, 29 May and 27 Aug. 1917; *NR* to ECP, 23 June 1917, APS. See also John Luskin, *Lippmann, Liberty, and the Press* (Tuscaloosa: University of Alabama Press, 1972), 36–38; Steel, *Lippmann*, 116–27; Arno J. Mayer, *Political Origins of the New Diplomacy, 1917–1918* (New York: H. Fertig, 1969), 349–50. The Selective Service Act passed 18 May 1917. Lippmann's housemates at 1727 Nineteenth Street included Parsons's old Washington friends Eustace Percy, back as the British ambassador's right-hand man, and Philip Kerr, later Lord Lothian and Britain's envoy to the UN. Lippmann returned to New York as executive secretary of a secret committee of experts, including Vladimir Simkhovitch, charged with gathering data to guide postwar peace negotiations. See Steel, *Lippmann*, 128–54.

34. RB to ECP, 28 May 1917, APS. See also Carol S. Gruber, *Mars and Minerva: World War I and the Uses of the Higher Learning in America* (Baton Rouge: Louisiana State University Press, 1975), 82, 157–62.

35. ALK to ECP, 20 May 1917, APS.

36. RB to ECP, 9 May and [June] 1917, reply to 22 May 1917, APS.

37. RB to ECP, 9 May 1917, also 28 May 1917, APS; Randolph Bourne, "The War and the Intellectuals," *Seven Arts,* June 1917, reprinted in Hansen, *Radical Will,* 307–18. Cf. Waldo Frank editorial, "American Independence and the War," *Seven Arts,* April 1917; and ECP, "Place-Fellowship," in *Social Freedom* (1915), 65–82. See Clayton, *Forgotten Prophet,* 211–12, for Mencken's attribution of the editorial to Bourne.

For *Seven Arts,* see RB to ECP, [May 1917], reply to 22 May 1917; Bourne, "Below the Battle," *Seven Arts,* July 1917, 270–71 (written at Lenox: see RB to ECP, May and June 1917, APS); Bourne, "The Collapse of American Strategy" *Seven Arts,* Aug. 1917, 409–24 (probably written at Lenox), reprinted in Hansen, *Radical Will;* James Oppenheim, "The Story of the *Seven Arts,*" *American Mercury,* June 1930, 156–64. Neither Bourne nor Van Wyck Brooks felt comfortable in the "psychoanalytic" atmosphere of *Seven Arts.* Early in May, they began planning a new journal for "pro-democratic, pro-hyphenate, pro-Negro, anti-Puritan, anti-English Americans" including ECP, Max Eastman, Ridgley Torrence, Floyd Dell, Lee Simonson, Theodore Dreiser, and Harold Stearns. See RB to ECP, 9 May, 13 June, and 1 Sept. 1917; Brooks to ECP, 27 June 1917, APS.

38. Reed and Eastman, quoted in Steel, *Lippmann,* 124–25. For speech see *NYT,* 15 June 1917. See also RB to ECP, [July] and 1 Sept. 1917; ECP to HP, 13 July 1917; Hackett to ECP, 28 Aug. 1917, APS; Donald Johnson, *The Challenge to American Freedoms: World War I and the Rise of the*

American Civil Liberties Union (Lexington: University of Kentucky Press, 1963), 58–63, 91; G. T. Tanselle, "Faun at the Barricades: The Life and Work of Floyd Dell" (Ph.D. diss., Northwestern University, 1959), pt. 1, 191–201; Leslie Fishbein, *Rebels in Bohemia: The Radicals of the Masses, 1911–1917* (Chapel Hill: University of North Carolina Press, 1982), 24–29; Mark Graber, *Transforming Free Speech* (Berkeley: University of California Press, 1991), 98–100.

39. Signe Toksvig to ECP, 26 Aug. 1923. See also Clarence Day to ECP, 1 Oct. [1917] and 15 Sept. [1924?], APS.

40. ECP, "Patterns for Peace or War" (1917); R. Torrence to ECP, 28 Feb. 1917, APS.

41. RB to ECP, [ca. 7 Aug. 1917], APS.

42. ECP to HP, [17 June] 1917, also 5 Oct. 1917; Brooks to ECP, 6 Oct. 1917, APS. See also RB to Waldo Frank, [2 Oct.] 1917, *RB Letters;* ECP, "It Costs" (1917), for Mac breaking his arm putting up a flag.

43. HP to ECP, 20 June 1917; also 28 and 29 June, 10, 16, and 19 July, 8 Aug. and 21 Nov. 1917, APS.

44. ECP to HP, 21 Nov. 1917, APS. See ALK to ECP, 24 June 1917; ECP to HP, 5 and 12 Sept., 5, 24, and [22] Oct. 1917; FB to ECP, 24 Oct., 23 and 28 Nov., and 21 Dec. 1917; PG to ECP, [Oct.] 1917; Day to ECP, 21 Dec. 1917, APS: "I'm damned if I get one word out of you, you Circe, in answer. Well, what do I care? You never say anything much to me anyway—except about Zuni's when I turn in desperation to them and unlock you on that side if I can't upon others—so I end with my head as full of Zuni's as it once was of hair and have to comb them out all the evening and drop them down my big air-shaft."

45. ECP, "The Minority" (1917). See replies from E. O. Marshall, "Trust Majorities," and H.K.M., "Faith in Majorities," letters to editor, *NYTr,* 7 and 10 Dec. 1917. Cf. ECP, "In Love and War," in "War Essays" (1915–18), APS; and Alvin Johnson (*New Republic*) to ECP, 24 Dec. 1917, APS. ECP was responding to Princeton professor Philip Marshall Brown, "War's Intellectual Anarchism, an Explanation of the Pacifist's Delusions," *NYT,* 2 Dec. 1917. At Columbia, Nicholas Murray Butler announced a wartime moratorium on academic freedom. Three students were convicted under the Conspiracy Act for writing a pamphlet supporting draft resistance. In October, James McKeen Cattell and Henry Wadsworth Dana were dismissed for sedition, treason, and opposition to the effective enforcement of the laws. See RB to ECP, [July] and [5 Oct.] 1917, APS; ALK to PG, 2 Oct. 1917, ALK Papers; Bourne, "Those Columbia Trustees," letter to editor, *NR,* 20 Oct. 1917, 328–29; [Franklin Giddings], editorial, *Independent,* supporting dismissals, cited in Gruber, *Mars and Minerva,* 206. For dismissals at Smithsonian, see FB to ECP, 23 Nov. 1917, APS. For rejections of articles, see Dell (*Masses*) to ECP, [Aug. 1917?]; Cattell (*Scientific Monthly*) to ECP, 19 Oct. and 1 Dec. 1917; *North American Review* to ECP, 31 Dec. 1917, APS; RB to E. Benjamin, 26 Nov. 1917, *RB Letters.* ECP's rejected articles included "Vicariousness in Wartime" (n.d., notes written after Sept. 1917), "Faith in War," "Blaming Somebody, Poorer in Faith," "Rationalization in War Time," and "War Wilfulness" (after Aug. 1917), in "War Essays"; "International Representation"; and "Patriotism," with notes for *Masses,* APS. For enthusiastic assessment of

this work see RB to ECP, [May 1918], APS. See Teachers' Defense Committee to ECP, 8 and 15 Jan. 1918, APS, re ECP joining its Citizens' Committee.

46. Mabel Dodge Luhan, *Edge of Taos Desert: An Escape to Reality* (Albuquerque: University of New Mexico Press, 1987), 6; and *Movers and Shakers*, 144; Sara Josephine Baker, *Fighting for Life* (New York: Macmillan, 1939), 246; Robert La Follette to Belle Case La Follette, 12 Jan. 1919, quoted in Judith Schwarz, *Radical Feminists of Heterodoxy* (Norwich, Vt.: New Victoria Publishers, 1986), 40–47; Kennedy, *Over Here,* 91–92, 263–66; Alice Wexler, *Emma Goldman: An Intimate Life* (London: Virago, 1984), 143–44, 230–37, 265–76. For possibility of ECP's mail being opened, see Day to ECP, 21 Dec. 1917, APS.

47. Mabel Dodge Luhan, "The End of That," in *Movers and Shakers,* 533–34; and *Edge of Taos Desert,* 6.

48. ECP, "A Pacifist Patriot" (1920). For comment, see editorial, "The 'Unmitigated Intellectual,'" clipping, [*NYTr?*], [Feb./Mar.? 1920]; and Goldenweiser to ECP, 12 Mar. 1920, APS.

Chapter Ten

1. HP to Children, 25 Jan. 1918; HP to Lissa, 26 Jan. 1918, APS.

2. ECP to JEP, 29 Jan. 1918; ECP to HP, 3 Feb. 1918, APS; Lucy James [Wilson] to HP, 12 Feb. 1918, HP Papers. See also ECP to HP, 28 Jan. 1918, APS. See Lucy James to HP, 27, 28, and 30 Mar. 1918, HP Papers, for end of the long-attenuated friendship: after Lucy's plea—"Answer two questions (1) Do you want letters or do they irk you? (2) what address?" —there are no more letters.

Lissa sat for entrance examinations for Bryn Mawr early in June. See ECP to HP, 18 May 1918, APS: "Her attitude towards college is hostile, towards school it is bitter. Next year will be trying but I have faith that once she is in college with choices open to her she will take a little more to intellectual interests. At any rate she must be given the chance. Socially, she is becoming quite efficient and charming, and to me more and more companionable." See ECP to HP, 3 June 1918, for exams; and 13 June 1918, APS, reporting that "Lissa passed algebra but no other—English 44."

3. Bronislaw Malinowski, *Argonauts of the Western Pacific* (New York: E. P. Dutton, 1922), 4; ECP to HP, 21 Nov. 1917, APS. For a lightly fictionalized account of her deacculturation see ECP, "In the Southwest" (1921), APS.

4. ECP, "After the War" (1918?), APS.

5. ECP, "War God Shrines of Laguna and Zuñi" (1918), 381.

6. Robert Herrick, "Diary of an Intravert" (1925), RH Papers; Signe Toksvig to ECP, 26 Aug. 1923, APS; ECP, "War God Shrines," 381.

7. See Franz Boas, "The Mental Attitude of the Educated Classes," *Dial,* 5 Sept. 1918, 145–48; letter to editor, *Nation,* 26 Oct. 1918; "Nationalism," *Nation,* 8 Mar. 1919, 232–37; and Esther Schiff Goldfrank, *Notes on an Undirected Life: As One Anthropologist Tells It* (Flushing, N.Y.: Queens College Press, 1978), 2–4, for her observations of Boas as his student in 1918 and secretary in fall 1919, and 222 n. 4, for other public

statements. For decline in student numbers at Columbia and Berkeley, see PG to ECP, 26 July 1918; ALK to ECP, 9 Oct. 1918, APS; PG to ALK, 4 Oct. and 20 Nov. 1918, ALK Papers. For finances and faculty, see Boas corres., Apr.–July 1918, esp. FB to Virginia Gildersleeve (Barnard dean), 18 Nov. 1918, FB Papers.

8. H. F. Osborn to Madison Grant, 10 Feb. 1909, and to H. C. Bumpus, 17 July 1908; and AMNH press releases, 22 Mar. 1928 and 17 Sept. 1924, quoted in J. M. Kennedy, "Philanthropy and Science in New York City: The American Museum of Natural History, 1868–1968" (Ph.D. diss., Yale University, 1968), 154, 162, and 157.

9. Osborn to W. B. Scott, 22 May 1908, and "Report on the Effect of World War I," quoted in Kennedy, "Philanthropy and Science," 163 and 189. For Osborn's policies, see 156–222. For poor relations, see FB to Osborn, 27 Apr. 1918, FB Papers; and FB to ALK, 6 Jan. 1908, ALK Papers, re the possibility of finding a position in New York: "all our former hopes and aspirations have gone. . . . neither the Museum nor the University will develop within a measurable time. The University . . . does not contemplate any research work, and has no means for [it]. . . . there are still a number of students who come here to get their training, because there has been a certain demand for our students. . . . but unless more opportunity for field-work is given . . . this will also cease. . . . your California work and the work in Chicago are about the only things . . . going, setting aside the special work done in Washington: and . . . neither . . . are so firmly established that they can be looked upon as permanent. . . . we always have to reckon on a complete change of interests, such as we have experienced here." Spier left in 1920 first for Berkeley and then the University of Washington; and Lowie left permanently for Berkeley in 1921. For Madison Grant, chairman of the New York Zoological Society and trustee of the AMNH in 1918, see *The Passing of the Great Race,* rev. ed. with preface by H. F. Osborn (1916; New York: Charles Scribner's Sons, 1918); Franz Boas, "Inventing a Great Race," review of 1916 edition, *NR,* 13 Jan. 1917, 305–7; Robert Lowie, review of later edition, *Freeman,* 25 Jan. 1922, 476–78, and rejoinder to objector, 29 Mar. 1922, 66.

10. FB to ECP, 12 June 1917; Huntington to ECP, 9 July 1917, APS. See Kennedy, "Philanthropy and Science," 173–76, citing Clark Wissler to ALK, 12 Sept. 1918; Wissler, "Annual Report of the Department of Anthropology" for 1910 to 1922; and "A Survey of the American Museum," first version, 1942–43, AMNH Archives, which Kennedy describes as highly personal and extremely critical of Osborn; Wissler, general introduction to *The Archer M. Huntington Survey of the Southwest: Zuñi District,* AMNH Anthropological Papers 18 (New York, 1919); Wissler to ALK, 23 Feb. 1915, ALK Papers.

11. ECP to Elizabeth Gurley Flynn, 10 Dec. 1917; ECP to Wissler, 3 Jan. 1918, APS. See also Flynn to ECP, 6 and 13 Dec. 1917, APS. For Fransiscan Fathers, *An Ethnologic Dictionary of the Navaho Langauge* (Arizona: St. Michaels, 1910), as a model, see ECP to S. Culin, [ca. 9 June 1918], APS. For folklore funding see FB to ECP, 16 Oct. 1919, APS: "American Folk-Lore is certainly indebted to you for a large amount of valuable work, that you are making possible"; and corres. Aurelio Espinosa–FB–ECP, beginning 20 Feb. 1920, FB Papers and APS.

12. Wissler to ECP, 21 Jan. 1918; also 9 Jan. 1917 [1918], APS.

13. See ECP to HP, 3 Feb. 1918, APS, en route to Chicago.

14. See ECP, *Notes on Ceremonialism at Laguna* (1920), 87; *Laguna Genealogies* (1923), 139; "Mothers and Children at Laguna" (1919). For José see "Nativity Myth at Laguna and Zuñi" (1918); *Laguna Genealogies,* 260–64; and W. Langdon Kihn painting in ECP, *Pueblo Indian Religion* (1939), opp. 32.

15. ECP to HP, 16 Feb. 1918, "En route from Laguna to Gallup, New Mexico, hence either to Zuñi or to the Hopi country," APS.

16. ECP to JEP, 16 Feb. 1918, APS. Vernon Castle of the popular dance team Irene and Vernon Castle was killed on military duty.

17. ECP to JEP, 8 Mar. 1918, APS. See also ECP to HP, 8 Mar. 1918, APS; ECP, *Winter and Summer Dance Series in Zuñi in 1918* (1922), 177, 190, 187–88. Grant LaFarge may have accompanied her on this trip. Margaret Lewis remembers an artist with her one year who was not allowed to sketch the dances. See Triloki Nath Pandey, "Anthropologists at Zuni," *APS Proceedings* 116 (15 Aug. 1972): 321–37, esp. 329.

18. ECP to JEP, 8 Mar. 1918; ECP to HP, 9 Mar. 1918, "three days later," APS.

19. ECP, *Notes on Ceremonialism at Laguna,* 87. Keresan languages are spoken at Acoma and Laguna and the eastern pueblos Cochiti, Jemez, San Felipe, Santa Ana, and Santo Domingo.

20. ECP to HP, 9 Mar. 1918, also 23 Mar. 1918; JEP to ECP, 17 Mar. 1918, APS. See also ECP to JEP, 9 Mar. 1918; and JEP to ECP, 11 Mar. 1918, APS.

21. ALK to ECP, 15 Feb. 1918, APS; Theodora Kroeber, *Alfred Kroeber: A Personal Configuration* (Berkeley: University of California Press, 1970), 104.

22. ALK to Sapir, 17 July 1921, ALK Papers, in Golla. See also Kroeber, *Kroeber,* 104–18.

23. See ECP to HP, 5 Apr., 2, 9, and 21 May, 4 and 6 June 1918, APS. See ALK to ECP, Sun. [early June?] and [early June?] 1918, APS, for staying overnight.

24. ALK to ECP, 26 Jan. 1920, APS; RHL to Risa Lowie, 1 Mar. 1918, RHL Papers; ALK to ECP, Wed. [May?], [May?], [29? May], [June], [ca. 9 June] 1918, APS.

25. ALK to ECP, 12 and 9 June, and [early June] 1918; also 11 June, Sat. [Aug.], and 8 Aug. 1918, APS.

26. ALK to ECP, 22, 25, and 17 June 1918; ECP to HP, 13 June 1918, APS. For June visit plans, see ALK to ECP, 9, [10?], and 12 June 1918; for retrospect and July plans, see 17, 21, 22, 25, and 30 June 1918, APS. See also ALK to ECP, 11, [18?], and [19?] June 1918, APS. For Kroeber's reputation as an infrequent letter writer, see Edward Sapir to ALK, 21 Nov. 1918, ALK Papers, in Golla.

27. RB to ECP, [May] 1918; ALK to ECP, 30 and 28 June 1918, APS. See Bourne, "A Modern Mind, Review of Elsie Clews Parsons, *Social Rule,*" *Dial,* 22 Mar. 1917, 239–40.

28. ALK to ECP, 18 Dec. 1918; Sat. 10 A.M. [20], and 23 July 1918, APS. See also Fri. [19], 24, and 28 July, and 2 Aug. 1918; ECP to HP, 14 July 1918; and ALK to Sapir, 6 and 17 July 1918, fr. Lenox, in Golla: "I

would send you [ECP's] regards if she did that sort of thing." See also LaFarge, "Lines upon the Selection of Samples for a Lady's Robe de Nuit," 22 July 1918; and "Elsie, Time, and the Map," 24 July 1918, APS.

29. ALK to ECP, Sat. [late Aug.] 1918, APS. See also 6 Aug. 1918, APS: "Very dear Elsie: I like to say it, so break rules." For Southwest plans, see ECP to S. Culin, [ca. 9 June]; Culin to ECP, 10 June 1918, APS, arranging to edit notes made by Father Dumarest on Cochiti, 1890–1900; ALK to ECP, 24 July, 18, 20, 23, 29 Aug., and Tues. [late Aug.] 1918; ECP to HP, 5 Sept. 1918, "En route to Zuñi, N.M.," APS.

30. ALK to ECP, Fri. [late Aug. 1918], APS. See also ALK to ECP, [early June?] 1918, APS.

31. ECP to HP, 10 and 26 Sept. 1918, also 13 Sept. 1918, APS; ALK to FB, 16 Sept. 1918, FB Papers. See ECP, *Winter and Summer Dance Series*, 190–99.

32. ALK to ECP, 9 and 14 Oct. 1918, 10 Aug. 1919, APS; Pandey, "Anthropologists at Zuni," 330. It is not clear what caused the agitation they refer to. But it was probably ECP's intense disappointment that their collaboration had not been a true partnership, and that Kroeber remained unaware of this. Only one interpreter, Leslie, was available, and he was monopolized by Kroeber, with whom he had a long working relationship. At loose ends and frustrated by her lack of progress, ECP apparently insisted on turning their evening visits to the hills outside Zuni into investigations of the war god shrines, while Kroeber wanted to unwind and enjoy these last evenings together in a more personal way. See ECP to HP, 10 and 13 Sept. 1918, APS; and ALK to FB, 16 Sept. 1918, FB Papers, for her frustrations and problems. ECP, "The Price of Fear—at Zuñi," in "In the Southwest," may describe one of these expeditions. For information gathered during this field trip, see "War God Shrines," 390, 402–5; "Census of the *Shi'wanakwe* Society of Zuñi" (1919); "Teshlatiwa at Zuñi (1919).

33. ECP to HP, 3 Oct. 1918, APS; ECP, "The Dance North of Houck's Tanks," 9, in "In the Southwest." See also "Note on Navajo War Dance" (1919); ALK to ECP, 14 Oct. 1918, APS: "You surely have use of a guardian after 6 P.M. At least I have the satisfaction of not feeling entirely wasted, in all my brakings and cautions."

34. ECP to HP, 10 Oct. 1918, APS. See also ECP, "Where the Chief Lives," in "In the Southwest"; *Laguna Ceremonialism*, 108 n. 1; LaFarge, "The Amorous Humorist Accepts the Sage Counsel of the Gipsy Queen . . . ," 3 July 1918, APS. See ECP to FB, 16 Oct. 1918, FB Papers, for her Laguna visit and their plans to visit there together the next summer.

35. RB to ECP, 12 Sept. 1918, APS.

36. ECP to HP, 16 Oct. and 6 Nov. 1918; ALK to ECP, 18 Nov. 1918, APS; PG to ALK, 20 Nov. 1918, ALK Papers. See HP to ECP, 15 and 17 Oct. 1918, APS.

37. ALK to ECP, [ca. 21] and 14 Oct. 1918, also 2 Nov. 1918, for illness, and [Feb.] 1919, for grievances with Berkeley, APS.

38. ALK to ECP, 18 Dec. 1918, APS, after she wrote him about a party where Boas read a chapter of his work-in-progress.

39. ALK to ECP, 22 Feb. 1919, APS.

40. ALK to ECP, 26 Jan. 1920, APS.

41. ALK to ECP, 8 Mar. 1920, APS.

42. ALK to ECP, Tues. [4 May] 1920, APS. See also 5 Apr. 1920, APS.

43. ALK to ECP, 6 and 24 May 1920, APS. ECP was about to leave for Hopi. ECP's letter to Kroeber, like all her personal letters, is not among his papers.

44. ALK to ECP, 10 June 1920, also 25 May 1920, APS; ALK to Sapir, 14 July 1920; and Sapir to ALK, 4 Oct. 1920, ALK Papers, in Golla. See also ALK to Sapir, 29 July 1920, in Golla; ALK to PG, 27 July 1920; and PG to ALK, 20 Sept. 1920, ALK Papers; ALK to ECP, 2 Aug. 1920, APS; ALK to Sapir, 17 Jan. 1921, in Golla. See ALK-Sapir corres., 23 May–20 Nov. 1921, in Golla, re Sapir's wife's mental illness.

45. ALK to ECP, 25 Dec. [1920], APS.

46. RHL to Radin, 2 Oct. 1920, RHL Papers; ECP to HP, 5 Jan. 1918 [1919], APS.

47. NYT, 25 Jan. 1919, 1 and 4; ECP to JEP, 29 Jan. 1919, with "Deplores Pacifist List," NYT, 28 Jan. 1919; Day to ECP, 14 Feb. 1919; also HP to ECP, 6 Feb. 1919, APS.

48. Clarence Day, "Portrait of a Lady," NR, 23 July 1919, 387–89, reprinted in Peter H. Hare, A Woman's Quest for Science: Portrait of Anthropologist Elsie Clews Parsons (Buffalo: Prometheus Books, 1985), 15–18. See ALK to ECP, 14 Sept. 1919, APS, for her colleagues' reactions.

49. ECP to HP, 4 Feb. 1919, also 14 Jan. 1919, APS; PG to ALK, 20 Nov. 1918, ALK Papers; information from Dr. McIlvaine Parsons, 1994. For Herbert's return, see ECP to JEP, 24 Mar. 1919, APS. See HP-ECP corres., 29 May–23 Sept. 1919, for struggle with Lissa over Bryn Mawr entrance exams; and ECP to HP, [9 Dec. 1919], APS: Lissa "is amazingly shrewd worldy wise and yet not on the make in the unforgiveable way— yet." Compare HP to ECP, 22 June 1919, for John's history prize.

50. ECP, letter to editor, NYEP, 24 Dec. 1918; also ECP to HP, 25 Dec. 1918, APS.

51. ECP to HP, 28 Dec. 1918; Learned Hand to ECP, 24 Dec. 1918, APS; PG to ALK, 30 Dec. 1918, ALK Papers. See Constitution and By-Laws of the Southwest Society, APS; "Report of the Secretary-Treasurer of the Southwest Society," ALK Papers; and AA 20 (1918): 464–65.

Chapter Eleven

1. Joseph Story, quoted in Brian W. Dippie, The Vanishing American: White Attitudes and U.S. Indian Policy (Middletown: Wesleyan University Press, 1982), 1; Edward Curtis, The North American Indian, ed. F. W. Hodge, 20 vols. (Cambridge, Mass.: The University Press, 1907–30), first folio supplement.

2. Joseph Dixon, The Vanishing Race: The Last Great Indian Council (Garden City, N.Y.: Doubleday, Page, 1913), 38, quoted in Dippie, Vanishing American, 211–19, esp. 211.

3. Dippie, Vanishing American, 193–94, quoting "A Ritual of Citizenship," Outlook, 24 May 1916, 161–62; Zane Grey, The Vanishing American (New York, 1925), 294, quoted in Dippie, 210. Until they were granted general citizenship in 1924, Indians could gain citizenship through land allotment or as members of the Five Civilized Nations. See Dippie, 192–96.

For a definitive account of the way Americans mythologized the Indian see William H. Goetzmann and William N. Goetzmann, *The West of the Imagination* (New York: W. W. Norton, 1986).

4. Grey, *Vanishing American*, 294, quoted in Dippie, *Vanishing American*, 210.

5. See Jesse Green, ed., *Zuni: Selected Writings of Frank Hamilton Cushing* (Lincoln: University of Nebraska Press, 1979); P. T. Houlihan and B. E. Houlihan, *Lummis in the Pueblos* (Flagstaff: Northland Press, 1986); Adolf Bandelier, *The Delight Makers,* introduction by C. F. Lummis (New York: Dodd, Mead, 1890); Stefan Jovanovich, "Adolf Bandelier: An Introduction," in Harcourt Brace edition (1971).

6. T. C. McLuhan, *Dream Tracks: The Railroad and the American Indian, 1890–1930* (New York: Abrams, 1985); Barbara A. Babcock, " 'A New Mexican Rebecca': Imaging Pueblo Women," *Journal of the Southwest"* 32, no. 4 (1990): 400–37.

7. D. A. Remley, *Erna Fergusson* (Austin: Steck-Vaughn, 1969); Marta Weigle, "Exposition and Mediation: Mary Colter, Erna Fergusson, and the Santa Fe/Harvey Popularization of the Native Southwest, 1902–1940," *Frontiers* 12 (1991): 117–50; and "From Desert to Disney World: The Santa Fe Railway and the Fred Harvey Company Display the Indian Southwest," *Journal of Anthropological Research* 45 (spring 1989): 115–37.

8. Charles Lummis, "The Golden Key to Wonderland," in *They Know New Mexico* (AT and SF Railway, 1928); Edgar Hewett, quoted in W. J. Rushing, "Native American Art and Culture and the New York Avant-garde, 1910–1950" (Ph.D. diss., University of Texas at Austin, 1989), 89; Hewett, "America's Archeological Heritage," *Art and Archeology,* Dec. 1916, 257, quoted in Rushing, 109–12. See also Rushing, *Native American Art and the New York Avant-Garde: A History of Cultural Primitivism* (Austin: University of Texas Press, 1995). For Hewett-Boas feud, see Beatrice Chauvenet, *Hewett and Friends* (Santa Fe: Museum of New Mexico Press, 1983); FB-ALK corres., 1909–13, esp. FB to ALK, 10 Apr, 1910; FB to president and council, Institute of Archeology, 24 Dec. 1909, ALK Papers.

9. "The Indian Exhibit," *Fourth Annual Exhibition of the Society of Independent Artists,* exhibition catalog (New York, 1920), quoted in Rushing, "Native American Art and Culture," 97. For a selection of material on the Southwest migration, see Mabel Dodge Luhan, "Paso Por Aqui!" *New Mexico Quarterly* 21 (1951): 137–46; Lois Rudnick, *Mabel Dodge Luhan* (Albuquerque: University of New Mexico Press, 1984); and "Re-Naming the Land: Anglo Expatriate Women in the Southwest," in *The Desert is No Lady,* ed. Vera Norwood and Janice Monk (New Haven: Yale University Press, 1987); Shelley Armitage, "Red Earth: The Poetry and Prose of Alice Corbin," *El Palacio,* winter 1987, 36–44; Sanford Schwarz, "When New York Went to New Mexico," in *The Art Presence* (New York: Horizon Press, 1976), 85–94; Elizabeth Shepley Sergeant, "The Santa Fe Group," *Saturday Review of Literature,* 8 Dec. 1934; E. L. Wade, "The Ethnic Art Market in the American Southwest, 1880–1980," in *Objects and Others,* ed. George W. Stocking Jr. (Madison: University of Wisconsin Press, 1985); Marsden Hartley, "Tribal Esthetics," *Dial,* 16 Nov. 1918, 399–401; and "Aesthetic Sincerity" and "America as Land-

scape," *El Palacio*, 9 and 21 Dec. 1918, 332–33 and 340–42; Mary Austin to Hewett, 10 Oct. 1918, in Chauvenet, *Hewett*, 140; and Austin, introduction to *The Path on the Rainbow: An Anthology of Songs and Chants from the Indians of North America*, ed. G. W. Cronyn (New York: Boni and Liveright, 1918).

10. Miriam Hapgood DeWitt, *Taos: A Memory* (Albuquerque: University of New Mexico Press, 1993), 5.

11. Ibid., 5; Wilson to C. Gauss, 31 July 1931, in Edmund Wilson, *Letters on Literature and Politics, 1912–1972*, ed. Elena Wilson (New York: Farrar, Straus and Giroux, 1977), 210; Erna Fergusson, "The City Incongruous," in *Fiesta Program* (1928), 19, quoted in Marta Weigle and Kyle Fiore, *Santa Fe and Taos: The Writer's Era, 1916–1941* (Santa Fe: Ancient City Press, 1982), 29.

12. Walter Pach, "Notes on the Indian Water-Colours," *Dial*, Mar. 1920, 343–45, esp. 344; D. H. Lawrence, "Just Back from the Snake Dance—Tired Out," *Laughing Horse*, Sept. 1924. For overviews, see R. H. Frost, "The Romantic Inflation of Pueblo Culture," *America West*, Jan.–Feb. 1980, 4–9, 56–60; Michael Castro, *Interpreting the Indian: Twentieth-Century Poets and the Native American* (Albuquerque: University of New Mexico Press, 1983).

13. Erna Fergusson, "Crusade from Santa Fe," *North American Review* 242 (winter 1936–37): 376–87, esp. 376. For overview, see Dippie, *Vanishing American*, 273–96.

14. ALK to ECP, [Sept.] 1923, APS. See ECP, "Half-Breed" (1924).

15. ALK to ECP, 18 Oct. 1923, APS.

16. Cf. Madison Grant, *The Passing of the Great Race* (New York: Charles Scribner's Sons, 1916); Frost, "Romantic Inflation." For defense of Pueblo dances against immorality charges, see John Sloan, "The Indian Dance from an Artist's Point of View," *Arts and Decoration*, Jan. 1924, 17; Mabel Dodge Luhan, "A Bridge between Cultures," *Theatre Arts Monthly*, May 1925, 300; and "Awa Tsireh," *The Arts*, June 1927, 298; Elizabeth Shepley Sergeant, "Earth Horizon," *Nation*, 29 June 1927, 714–16.

17. ECP, "The Pueblo Indian Clan in Folk-Lore" (1921), 209, 215. For response see Sapir to ECP, 7 Apr. 1922, APS, discussing "pattern" and "form"; and ALK to ECP, 26 June 1922, APS, agreeing even where she disposes of his inter-Pueblo clan scheme. Cf. ECP, review of *Zuñi Kin and Clan*, by A. L. Kroeber (1918).

18. ECP, *Notes on Ceremonialism at Laguna* (1920), esp. preface, 88.

19. ECP, "The Religion of the Pueblo Indians" (1924), 140, 143, 144. See also *The Pueblo of Jemez* (1925). For Tomaka, who died in 1932, see ECP, *Pueblo Indian Religion* (1939), 64–65.

20. ALK to ECP, 16 Nov. 1924, APS.

21. ECP, *Pueblo Indian Religion*, 14–18; *Notes on Ceremonialism at Laguna*, 88, 108–12; *Laguna Genealogies* (1923), 142–45; *Jemez*; "The Laguna Migration to Isleta" (1928); "Early Relations between Hopi and Keres" (1936).

22. Frank Waters, *Masked Gods: Navaho and Pueblo Ceremonialism* (Albuquerque: University of New Mexico Press, 1950), 273. For a similar assessment, see Leslie Spier, "Elsie Clews Parsons," *AA* 45 (1943): 249.

23. ECP, "Notes on Isleta, Santa Ana, and Acoma" (1920), 62 n. 3; "All-Soul's Day at Zuñi, Acoma, and Laguna" (1917), 496. See *Notes on Zuñi*, pt. 2 (1917), 229; "The Office of Governor at Zuñi" (1917); "Christian Rites in Zuñi Ceremonialism" (1917), APS; also "Installation of Tapup and Sipaloa Shiwanni, 1917," in *Notes on Zuñi*, 264–77; *Pueblo Indian Religion*, 597–99, 860; "Pueblo-Indian Folk-Tales, Probably of Spanish Provenience" (1918); ECP to JEP, 1 Feb. 1917, APS; ECP to ALK, 11 May 1917, ALK Papers; ECP to RB, 22 May 1917, RB Papers; FB to ECP, 12 and 28 June 1917, APS. For 1915 interest, see ECP, *The Social Organization of the Tewa of New Mexico* (1929), 281; and "Spanish Elements in the Kachina Cult of the Pueblos" (1930), 582.

24. See ECP, "Notes on Acoma and Laguna" (1918); "Nativity Myth at Laguna and Zuñi" (1918); *Notes on Zuñi*, 153, 170–71, 266; "Increase by Magic: A Zuñi Pattern" (1919); "Isleta, Santa Ana, and Acoma," 58; "Spanish Elements," 582; ECP, trans. and ed., *Notes on Cochiti, New Mexico,* by Father Noël Dumarest (1919), 183, 228; "Der spanische Einfluß auf die Märchen der Pueblo-Indianer" (1926); "Spanish Influence in Pueblo Indian Folktales" and "Culture Hero and War Gods," large table, APS; ECP to JEP, 8 Mar. 1918; ECP to HP, 26 Sept. and 3 Oct. 1918, APS; ECP to ALK, 14 Oct. 1918, ALK Papers; ALK to ECP, 2 Nov. 1918, APS.

25. ECP, *Social Organization of the Tewa*, 280; "Spanish Elements," 584. See also "Newekwe and Koyemshi" and "Ceremonial Continence," in *Notes on Zuñi*.

26. ECP, "Spanish Elements," 596–98. See also *Social Organization of the Tewa*, 283.

27. E.g., ECP to MDL, 10 Oct. 1922, MDL Papers: "I've been picking out reprints . . . so you'll come in for another flood. I wish you could see your pictures . . . J's 'uncle' next to the San Domingo Koshare and a Hopi-made Koyemshi 'doll' above—ethnologically a very correct company"; and 29 Apr. 1929: "It does interest me as descriptive of Spanish marriage customs which you and Tony will say are Indian. There are no clans at Taos, only societies. . . . The gift of boots and blankets *is* Indian. Historical and ethnological considerations apart, it is a very pretty description." For acculturation, see also ECP to FB, 11 July 1920, FB Papers; ECP, "Witchcraft among the Pueblos: Indian or Spanish?" (1927); *Isleta, New Mexico* (1932), 303–5. See Waters, *Masked Gods*, 304–16, where he implies ECP was present in August 1932, when she was in Maine; and Waters to Paul Walter Jr., University of New Mexico Press, 19 June 1950, explaining that he wrote her in to add color. Thanks to Tommy Meyers for this letter. See ECP to Leslie White, 2 July 1932, fr. Maine: "I wish I were with you for the August ceremonies [at Oraibi]. I have always wanted to see not so much the Snake-Antelope but the Flute ceremony"; and 16 Aug. 1932, APS, fr. Maine: "With both Antelope chief and Snake chief gone to Hotavila, how in the world did they carry on the Snake-Antelope ceremony?"

28. Waters, *Masked Gods*, 165–66. See 273, 304–20, 360, for ECP.

29. Erna Fergusson, *Our Southwest* (New York: Knopf, 1940), 287–91. See also *Dancing Gods: Indian Ceremonials of New Mexico and Arizona* (New York: Knopf, 1931).

30. Signe Toksvig, "Elsie Clews Parsons," *NR,* 26 Nov. 1919, 17–20. See Clarence Day, "Portrait of a Lady," *NR,* 23 July 1919, 387–89.

31. H. L. Mencken, "The Genealogy of Etiquette," in *Prejudices: First Series* (New York: Knopf, 1919), 150–70, esp. 150–60. Mencken had been a fan of Parsons's for a long time. In *The Philosophy of Friedrich Nietzsche* (Boston: Luce, 1908), 184, he notes that Nietzsche's proposal of trial marriage "when it was proposed years later by an American sociologist, caused all the uproar which invariably arises in the United States whenever an attempt is made to seek absolute truth."

32. W. H. Ballou to ECP, 5 Nov. 1920, with ECP note to Wissler, APS.

33. Alvin Johnson, *Pioneer's Progress* (New York: Viking, 1952), 272–88, esp. 277.

34. H. R. Mussey, "An Independent College of Political Science," *Nation,* 11 May 1918, 559–60; James Harvey Robinson, "A New Educational Adventure," *Nation,* 7 Sept. 1918, 264–65, and in the same issue, A. Meiklejohn and F. A. Hand, letters to editor, 266; Herbert Croly, "A School of Social Research," *NR,* 8 June 1918, 167; James Harvey Robinson, "The New School," *School and Society,* 31 Jan. 1920, 130–31; Johnson, *Pioneer's Progress,* 284, for W. I. Thomas and John Watson joining the faculty in 1923; Thomas Bender, *New York Intellect* (New York: Knopf, 1967), 298–302. ECP probably contributed Goldenweiser's salary. For fight to keep him at Columbia, see letters of support from Harry Barnes, Martha Beckwith, C. H. Northcott, Theresa Mayer, and Emily Balch to Boas; and corres. FB-NMB-Columbia officials-anthropologists, Apr.–May. 1918, FB Papers, when he was reappointed one more year; ECP-FB corres., 1918–19, for attempts to find and fund a position; Esther Schiff Goldfrank, *Notes on an Undirected Life: As One Anthropologist Tells It* (Flushing, N.Y.: Queens College Press, 1978), 4, for "unexplained cancellation" of his position in April 1919; Sapir to RHL, 12 May 1919, RHL Papers, for appointment at the Free School where he taught until his 1925 divorce scandal; Sapir to RHL, 25 Mar. 1926, RHL Papers: "It's going to be terribly difficult for Goldie to get a regular job in America. The ugly truth of it is he's become taboo in all academic circles." For ECP's help getting his *Early Civilization: An Introduction to Anthropology* (New York: Knopf, 1922) published, see B. W. Huebsch to ECP, 21 Feb. 1920, APS. For Goldenweiser, Dorothy Straight, Sorchan, and Frances Hand, Learned Hand's wife, see Leslie White to Bruce Bliven, 25 Mar. 1969; and Bliven to White, 29 Mar. 1969, LW Papers.

35. ECP to Putnam, 26 Mar. 1919, APS. ECP planned to use the salary to fund "certain enterprises of the Folk-Lore Society."

36. ALK to ECP, 8 Oct. 1919, also 22 Feb. and 14 Sept. 1919; ECP to HP, [28 Sept. 1919], APS. ECP, "New School Course, Woman and the Social Order," RHS, contains twelve lectures and students' weekly question sheets.

37. ECP to Robinson, draft, [ca. 16 Mar. 1920]; also Goldenweiser to ECP, 12 Mar. 1920, APS. ECP probably referred to NAACP secretary James Weldon Johnson with whom she was protesting misinformation about Haiti. See Johnson to ECP, 21 Oct. 1920, APS. For Herbert Parsons's criticism of the New School, see HP to Charlotte Sorchan, 22 Mar. 1920, HP Papers.

38. Robinson to ECP, 12 Mar. 1920, APS; "A Suggestion from Professor Beard," *Freeman*, 20 July 1921, 450–51. ECP's friend Alvin Johnson became director in 1923 and reorganized it as a school of adult higher education. See Johnson to ECP, 26 June 1923, APS; Johnson, *Pioneer's Progress*, 278–81; and *An Autobiographical Note* (New York: Knopf, n.d).

39. ALK to ECP, 2 Aug. and 26 Jan. 1920, APS. See ECP, "Waiyautitsa of Zuñi, New Mexico" (1919); Huebsch to ECP, 21 Feb. 1920; also ALK to ECP, 8 Mar., [27 Apr. or 4 May], 28 Sept., 25 Oct., 5 and 16 Nov. 1920, APS. The original article was rejected, possibly by *Century*, because it mentioned prostitution. See T. R. Smith to ECP, 21 Oct. 1919, APS. ECP may have begun her "literary" account of her fieldwork experiences, "In the Southwest" (1921), at this time.

40. Paul Radin, "Personal Reminiscences of a Winnebago Indian," *JAFL* 26 (1913): 293–318, esp. 293; also *The Autobiography of a Winnebago Indian*, University of California Publications in Anthropology and Archeology 16 (1920), 381–473, esp. 383; *Crashing Thunder: The Autobiography of an American Indian* (New York: D. Appleton, 1926), esp. x; Alfred L. Kroeber, *Ethnology of the Gros Ventre*, AMNH Anthropological Papers 1 (New York, 1908), 141–281; W. I. Thomas and Florian Znaniecki, *The Polish Peasant in Europe and America*, vols. 1 and 2 (Chicago: University of Chicago Press; Boston: Richard C. Badger, 1918); vols. 3, 4, and 5 (Boston: Richard C. Badger, 1919 and 1920).

41. ALK to ECP, 2 and 12 Aug. and 25 Dec. 1920, also 30 May 1921; and ECP to RHL, 19 May 1921, APS.

42. ECP, *American Indian Life* (1922).

43. Alfred L. Kroeber, introduction to *American Indian Life*, 5–16.

44. ALK to ECP, 26 June 1922, APS. The book sold for $10. See reviews by John M. Oskison, *NYT Book Review*, 18 June 1922, 16; R. R. Marett, *AA* 25 (1923): 266–69; and Hartley Alexander, *Nation*, 13 Sept. 1922, APS. For a recent reconsideration, see Kamala Visweswaran, *Fictions of Feminist Ethnography* (University of Minnesota Press, 1994), 2–3. LaFarge's illustrations and notes were the swan song of their relationship.

45. ECP to RHL, 19 Oct. 1922, RHL Papers; Barbara Freire-Marreco to ECP, 7 Apr. 1918, APS.

46. ECP, "The Town" and "Town Gossip: Personal Notes," in *Laguna Genealogies*, 235–48 and 260–79, esp. 260. See also "Isleta, Santa Ana, and Acoma," 56.

47. ECP, *Laguna Genealogies*, 139–40, 260–69, 272–74; "Mothers and Children at Laguna" (1919).

48. Sapir to Benedict, 22 Oct. 1923 [1922], in *An Anthropologist at Work: The Writings of Ruth Benedict*, ed. Margaret Mead (Westport, Conn.: Greenwood Press, 1977), 159; Edward Sapir, "A Symposium of the Exotic," *Dial*, Nov. 1922, 568–71; also ALK to ECP, [Nov. 1922], RHS. For Cochisi, see ECP, *A Pueblo Indian Journal, 1920–1921* (1925), 5–11, esp. 7; and "A Hopi Ceremonial" (1920), 178. See also "The Hotavilla Revival," in "In the Southwest," where ECP calls him John Köchasi; Cochisi to ECP, 22 May 1922, APS; ECP, check to Cochisi, 8 June 1922, RHS; ECP, *Hopi and Zuñi Ceremonialism* (1933), 5. ECP worked again with Cochisi, a descendant of Tewa immigrants, when she studied the

Tewa pueblos in 1923–27. See ECP to Goldfrank, 25 Nov. 1924, in Goldfrank, *Notes,* 27; ECP, *Tewa Tales* (1926), 6–7. He also worked with Ruth Bunzel. For personal lives see preface, "Historical and Contemporary Relations," "Day In and Day Out: Household Sketches," in *Pueblo Indian Journal,* xi–xiv, 1–10, 52–55; *Mitla* (1936); *Peguche* (1945).

49. ECP, *Pueblo Indian Journal,* 5–6, 10. For articles for a nonspecialist audience, see "Getting Married on First Mesa, Arizona" (1921); "Fiesta of Sant' Ana, New Mexico" (1923); "Half-Breed" (1924); "A Romantic in Bengal and in New York" (1925); "Curanderos in Oaxaca, Mexico" (1931); "Spring Days in Zuñi, New Mexico" (1933); "Some Mexican Idolos in Folklore" (1937); "Filipino Village Reminiscence" (1940), all in *Scientific Monthly.* She also reviewed Lowie's and Wissler's important statements on anthropology for the *New Republic* in 1920 and 1923.

Chapter Twelve

1. ALK to ECP, 12 Feb. and 30 May 1921, APS.
2. ALK to ECP, 16 Oct. and 30 May 1921, 26 June 1922, APS. See HP to ECP, 24 Mar. 1921, APS, for Lissa's engagement. For her marriage, see "Miss Elsie Parsons Married in Lenox," *NYT,* 11 Sept 1921, 21. ECP left for the Southwest immediately, finally feeling "free of a curious form of nervousness I have had the past week." See ECP to HP, [14 Sept. 1921], fr. Chicago; and Robert Herrick, *Chimes* (New York: Macmillan, 1926), 298: "her usual mental medicine did not work. A dozen times she took out from her bag a book or a bit of ms. or a copy of the Review . . . but she could not concentrate. . . . over the water came a vivid picture of May's [Lissa's] small, unformed face. . . . 'She would not stick to her college work, although I warned her,' Jessica thought, 'and now she has nothing but her emotions to meet life with.' . . . Something remotely like misery settled into her own mood." See also ECP, "Getting Married on First Mesa, Arizona" (1921), 128, for comment on marriage as an institution; and ALK to ECP, [late 1921], APS: " 'What more telling comment on wedding ceremonial—anywhere?' made me smile. We won't argue it nor even tease; but the fervor with which you hate all ritual makes me realize how little I know about you after all. There are so many other things to hate—and tolerate—that there must be a reason for your choice; but I'm as much in the dark as five years ago. Perhaps you too." For first months of marriage, see Lissa to HP, 28 Sept. 1921, RHS; ECP to HP, 19 Oct. 1921, APS. For HP's and ECP's differing views, see ECP, "Prospects," in "The World Changes: An Essay in Anthropologic Philosophy" (1939–41), 5; APS: "The keenest minded lawyer of my acquaintance condemned his own daughter to chastity while she was a young woman." In Herrick, *The End of Desire* (New York: Farrar and Rinehart, 1932), 95, May complains: "[Mother] told me I had better live with Roy [Morehead] first, and she would tell me how not to have consequences—a nice way for a mother to act!"

Herrick described May as "a slightly smaller replica of [Jessica] whose very gesture and expression differed totally from the original. It was as if by some necromancy Jessica had shrunk several sizes and an entirely new personality had been installed in her long finely shaped body . . . voluble, almost gushing where Jessica was self-contained, passive. She gesticulated much with her cigarette while Jessica had a repose which was monumental. And Little May went bravely forth to meet a situation, while her mother held herself guardedly in reserve. . . . While Jessica's mind worked slowly, but with power and precision and she would sometimes pause whole minutes between phrases to to get her idea formulated exactly to her scrupulous mind, May chattered on recklessly, lightly. See "Chapter Five, Bargains and Compromises," early version of *End of Desire* (1926?), 51–52, RH Papers.

3. ALK to ECP, [Apr.] 1922, RHS; and 16 Oct. 1921, APS.

4. ALK to ECP, [Apr.] 1922, RHS; and 30 Aug. 1922, APS; also [Feb. 1923], RHS, for feeling "he never belonged in" the NRC. See Alfred L. Kroeber, *Anthropology* (New York: Harcourt, Brace, 1923). For completion see ALK to ECP, 19 Jan. 1923, RHS. The preface is signed 22 Jan. 1923.

5. ECP to ALK, 13 Nov. 1918, postscript to 12 Nov. 1918, ALK Papers. See "Report of the Secretary-Treasurer of the Southwest Society December 28, 1918"; *Constitution and By-Laws of the Southwest Society;* "Elsie Clews Parsons: Secretary and Treasurer, in Account with The Southwest Society" (1918–23); ECP to HP, 12 and 28 Dec. 1918; Learned Hand to ECP, 2 Jan. 1919; Clarence Day to ECP, 17 and 29 June 1919, APS; FB to Livingston Farrand, 4 Dec. 1918; and to J. Walter Fewkes, 11 Dec. 1918, FB Papers. For first recipient J. Alden Mason, see ALK-ECP corres., Oct. 1918–Jan. 1919; Mason to FB, 17 Oct. 1918 and 5 Mar. 1919, FB Papers; Edward Sapir to ALK, 19 Jan. 1919, ALK Papers.

6. ALK to ECP, 30 Jan. and 28 Mar. 1919, APS. See 19 Jan. 1919 for joint plan to make a test case by asking Clark Wissler or Herbert Spinden himself for Spinden's Tanoan-Keresan data on religion; and 23 Apr. 1919, APS. Kroeber's list: Published: the Franciscans on Navajo, Freire-Marreco and Harrington on Tewa, Kroeber on Zuni and Mohave, Gifford on Yuma and Cocopa. "Collected but unavailable because unpublished": Lowie on Hopi, Parsons on Keresan, Radin on Cochiti, Spinden and Harrington on Tanoan pueblos, Goddard on White Mountain, San Carlos, and Mescalero Apache, Mason on Papago, and Spier on Walapai and Yavapai.

7. George W. Stocking Jr., "The Scientific Reaction against Cultural Anthropology," in *Race, Culture, and Evolution: Essays in the History of Anthropology* (New York: Free Press, 1968), 270–307. See PG to ALK, 12, 18, and 30 Dec. 1918; ALK to PG, 15 Dec. 1918, ALK Papers; FB corres. with Tozzer, H. R. Mussey (ed. *Nation*), Wissler, Hrdlička, Kroeber, G. E. Hale, E. G. Conklin, and William Ogburn, 30 Dec. 1918–18 Mar. 1919; FB, circular letter and "List of people [incuding ECP] to whom was sent the circular letter, dated January 17 [1919], asking for a statement of problems to be sent to the Research Council," FB Papers.

8. See Franz Boas, "Scientists as Spies," *Nation,* 20 Dec. 1919, 797 (written 20 Oct.), for Herbert Spinden and Sylvanus Morley; reprinted in *The Shaping of American Anthropology, 1883–1911: A Franz Boas Reader,* ed. George W. Stocking Jr. (New York: Basic Books, 1974), 336–37. For the larger conflict, see Stocking, "Scientific Reaction"; PG to ALK, 28 Oct. 1919 (also to Tozzer, Sapir, and Speck); ALK to PG, 4

Nov. 1919, ALK Papers; RHL to Wissler, 9 Nov. 1919, RHL Papers: "the Association is divided by a far-reaching difference as to principles and ideals. Last Christmas we were treated to the degrading spectacle of several men who are anthropologists only by courtesy [Dixon, Kidder] threatening to eject the foremost representative of our science from the Association. . . . I feel that no scientific bond unites me with Messrs. Seville, Judd, Spinden, et al. The sensible thing is to strengthen the American Ethnological Society into a truly national body which, if the Anthropologist falls into unworthy hands, shall definitely dissociate itself from the Association and run an independent publication"; RHL to Wissler, 18 Nov. 1919, RHL Papers; ALK to ECP, 16 Nov. 1919, APS: "Scraps of anthropo-political fur are raining even here. . . . Goddard has no votes, and Lowie is making a bad situation worse by his infantile blustering." For outcome see ALK to Sapir, 27 Dec. 1920; PG to ALK, 1 Jan. 1921; and J. Alden Mason to ALK, 11 Dec. 1956, ALK Papers. For Esther Schiff's view as secretary, see Esther Schiff Goldfrank, *Notes on an Undirected Life: As One Anthropologist Tells It* (Flushing, N.Y.: Queens College Press, 1978), 4–17.

9. PG to ALK, 12 Dec. 1918, ALK Papers. See PG to ECP, 16 July 1919, APS, for an "insane" Spinden who "told me how bad Prof Boas had been during the war and how much worse we native Americans had been who had made friends with the Germans"; and ALK to ECP, 14 July 1923, APS, for Wissler's opinion of them as "queer foreigners or half foreigners."

10. ALK to ECP, [May? 1923], APS. See G. E. Simpson, *Melville J. Herskovits* (New York: Columbia University Press, 1973); Margaret M. Caffrey, *Ruth Benedict: Stranger in This Land* (Austin: University of Texas Press, 1989), 111–12. See "Charles Merriam and Technical Expertise," in Mark C. Smith, *Social Science in the Crucible* (Durham: Duke University Press, 1994), 84–119, esp. 93; and B. D. Karl, *Charles Merriam and the Study of Politics* (Chicago: University of Chicago Press, 1974), 130, for John Merriam, and for founding of the Social Science Research Council and the NRC-SSRC Committee on Scientific Aspects of Human Migration.

11. George W. Stocking Jr., "Ideas and Institutions in American Anthropology: Toward a History of the Interwar Period," in *Selected Papers from the* American Anthropologist, *1921–1945* (Washington, D.C.: AAA, 1976), 1–44, esp. 5; ALK to ECP, 18 Dec. 1918, APS (for Boas); Robert Lowie, *Primitive Society* (New York: Boni and Liveright, 1920), 441; Alfred L. Kroeber, review of *Primitive Society, AA* 22 (1920): 377–81, esp. 380. For "breeds" who kept a foot in both camps see PG to ALK, 28 Dec. 1918, ALK Papers. See also reviews of Lowie by Sapir, *Freeman,* 30 June 1920, 377–79; and ECP, "Primitive Society" (1920); ECP to HP, 6 Dec. 1918, APS; Sapir to RHL, 11 and 25 May and 5 Nov. 1920, 2 and 15 Feb. 1921; RHL to Radin, 2 Oct. 1920, RHL Papers; RHL to ECP, 9 Aug. 1920, APS. For AMNH cutbacks, see ALK to ECP, 8 and 22 Feb. 1919; PG to ECP, 14 and 21 Oct. 1920, APS.

12. ALK to PG, 15 Dec. 1918; also ALK to ECP, 11 Nov. 1919, ALK Papers. For illness and mental breakdown of Sapir's wife, Florence, see Sapir to RHL, 29 Feb. 1920, RHL Papers; Sapir to ALK, 24 Nov. 1921, ALK Papers. For his "at-cross-purposes-with-oneself type of temperament," see Sapir to RHL, 12 Aug. and 29 Sept. 1916, in *Letters from Edward Sapir to Robert H. Lowie,* ed. Robert H. Lowie (privately printed,

1965). See ECP's 1923 review of Goldenweiser, *Early Civilization: An Introduction to Anthropology* (New York: Knopf, 1922).

13. ALK to ECP, 19 Jan. 1919 and [June?] 1923, APS. For Wissler's influence in the social sciences, see Wissler, foreword to *Middletown,* by Robert S. Lynd and Helen M. Lynd (New York: Harcourt, Brace, and World, 1929); and Smith, *Social Science,* 134, 140.

14. PG to ALK, 28 Dec. 1918, ALK Papers; ECP to HP, 14 Jan. 1919, APS. For field trip plans, see also ECP to FB, 16 Oct. 1918, FB Papers. For NRC, see ALK to ECP, 19 and 30 Jan., 8 and 22 Feb. 1919, APS; FB to Tozzer, 30 Dec. 1919, FB Papers. For ECP criticism of Wissler, see ALK to ECP, 25 Apr. and 14 July 1923; ECP to HP, 12 June 1923, APS; ECP, review of Wissler, *Man and Culture* (1923).

15. ECP to HP, 28 May 1919, APS. See FB to ECP, 25 June 1925, APS, for 1915 expectation of death, and FB corres., 1919–20, FB Papers, for preoccupation with Europe.

16. Alfred L. Kroeber, "Thoughts on Zuñi Religion," in *Holmes Anniversary Volume* (1916; New York: AMS Press, 1977), 269–77, esp. 276. Keresan was spoken in the Rio Grande pueblos of Santa Ana, San Felipe, Santo Domingo, Cochiti, and Zia.

17. ECP, "Laguna Lodging Houses," esp. 7, 11, in "In the Southwest" (1921). See ECP to HP, 3–25 June 1919, APS; ECP, *Laguna Genealogies* (1923), 139–40. Dzaidyuwi is the only person ECP ever seems to have actively disliked. For Esther Schiff's description of Dzaidyuwi (Jennie Day), see Schiff to ECP fr. Laguna, Fri. [ca. 9 June] 1922, RHS, and Goldfrank, *Notes,* 45–46.

18. See ECP to HP, 26 June 1920, APS. ECP was in Zuni 2–8 and 17–20 June and at Hopi 8–16 June. See ECP, *Hopi and Zuñi Ceremonialism* (1933), 94; and account of Laguna and the malfunction of LaFarge's camera that spoiled all his photographs, in Goldfrank, *Notes,* 46–57.

19. ECP, "A Hopi Ceremonial" (1920). See also *A Pueblo Indian Journal, 1920–1921* (1925), 9, for Cochisi; "Hopi Mothers and Children" (1921); ECP to HP, 8 June 1920; HP to ECP, 9 June 1920; ALK to ECP, 10 June 1920, APS; D'Arcy McNickle, *Indian Man: A Life of Oliver La Farge* (Bloomington: Indiana University Press, 1971), 29–37.

20. ECP to HP, 17 June and [21 July] 1920, APS. For Laguna 20–26 June and San Felipe, Santa Ana, and Albuquerque (Isleta) 26 June–5 July, see ECP to HP, 26 June 1920; FB to ECP, 9 July 1920, APS; ECP, "Third Degree at Lamy," in "In the Southwest"; "Notes on San Felipe and Santo Domingo" (1923); "Further Notes on Isleta" (1921), 149. For Esther Schiff's account when she joined Boas 17–30 June, see Goldfrank, *Notes,* 40–58, esp. 44, 47–50, 52–58, for ECP and LaFarge.

21. FB to ECP, 9 July 1920, APS. See also dedication in Boas, *Keresan Texts,* Publications of the American Ethnological Association 8, pt. 1 (New York, 1928), and ECP's response in Goldfrank, *Notes,* 24.

22. FB to ECP, 28 July 1922; ALK to ECP, 26 June 1922, APS. See also ALK to ECP, 30 Aug. 1922, APS; and Schiff (Goldfrank) account, with ECP to Schiff in Laguna, Sept. 1921, fr. Gallup, and ECP to Schiff in Cochiti, 15 June 1922, fr. Lenox; also Schiff 1921 photographs, including Boas and Laguna residents Solomon Day and Karl Leon climbing Mt. Taylor, and Schiff at Laguna, in Goldfrank, *Notes,* 24–26, 55–64, 83–92;

Schiff to ECP fr. Laguna, Fri [ca. 9 June] 1922, RHS. These photographs and one of the Quintana family, Cochiti, are reproduced in Barbara A. Babcock and Nancy J. Parezo, eds., *Daughters of the Desert: Women Anthropologists and the Native American Southwest, 1880–1980* (Albuquerque: University of New Mexico Press, 1988), 30–37. Potter Helen (Quintana) Cordero was six years old when Schiff lived with her family. Her famous storytellers depict her grandfather Santiago Quintana, gifted storyteller, member of one of the clown societies, friend and informant to Bandelier, Curtis, Parsons, and Benedict. See Benedict to Mead, 3, 5, and 8 Sept. 1925, in *An Anthropologist at Work: The Writings of Ruth Benedict,* ed. Margaret Mead (Westport, Conn.: Greenwood Press, 1977), 298–302; Barbara A. Babcock and Guy and Doris Monthan, *The Pueblo Storyteller: Development of a Figurative Ceramic Tradition* (Tucson: University of Arizona Press, 1986).

23. FB to ECP, 12 June 1924 and 28 Mar. 1926, APS.

24. FB to ECP, 20 June 1927, APS. Boas's son and daughter had recently died.

25. See Goldfrank, *Notes,* 39–40, where she begins calling him "Papa Franz" after their field trip to Laguna in 1920; also 91, for FB and Mrs. Boas to Schiff, 7 Aug. 1922, for "Papa Franz" and "Mama Franz."

26. FB to Berthold Laufer, 24 July 1920, FB Papers. See Schiff's account as undergraduate student, secretary, and graduate student from 1918, in Goldfrank, *Notes,* 1–21; Laufer to FB, 17 July 1920; FB to Leslie Spier, 23 July 1920, FB Papers; Sara Alpern, *Freda Kirchwey: A Woman of the Nation* (Cambridge: Harvard University Press, 1987), 10, 15, 38–39; FB corres., 1918–20, esp. B. Freire-Marreco to FB, 10 Apr. 1918; Mussey (ed. *Nation*) to FB, 21 Dec. 1918, FB Papers; Laura Watson Benedict, "Babago Myths," *JAFL* 26 (1913): 13–63; Boas, "In Memoriam: Herman Karl Haeberlin," *AA* 21 (1919): 71–73; H. Basehart and W. W. Hill, "Leslie Spier," *AA* 67 (1965): 1258–78; Martha Warren Beckwith, "Hawaiian Folklore" (Ph.D. diss., Columbia University, 1918); publisher's preface to *Basketry of the San Carlos Apache Indians,* by Helen Heffron Roberts (1929; Glorieta, N.M.: Rio Grande Press, 1972). Boas's letter continues: "if Mr. Skiff is still as much set against employing women as formerly, there is, of course, no help for that. If you should be able to employ a woman, I should recommend Miss Erna Gunther. . . . She is not as mature as Spier, but she knows quite a little about North America and is very energetic." Laufer had offered the assistant curatorship to Spier. Laufer to FB, 27 July 1920, FB Papers, re Spier's refusal makes no reference to Gunther.

27. PG to ECP, 1 Oct. 1919, APS. For Reichard (1893–1955) see FB to GR, 20 May and 11 July 1919, FB Papers; *Barnard College Alumnae Monthly,* Nov. 1950; obituary, *NYT,* 26 July 1955; Barnard College, *Memorial Booklet* (1955), with tributes from Bunzel, Frederica de Laguna, Mead, and bibliography by Nathalie Woodbury; Goldfrank, *Plateau* (1955), 48; and *JAFL* 69 (1956): 53–54; Marian W. Smith, *AA* 58 (1956): 913–16; Joan Mark, "Gladys Reichard," *NAW Mod;* Eleanor Leacock, in *Women Anthropologists: Selected Biographies,* ed. Ute Gacs et al. (Urbana: University of Illinois Press, 1989). For Gunther (1896–1982), see Spier to ECP, 29 June 1920 and 7 Jan. 1921, APS: "I have high hopes that Erna

will always feel fully free to develop as she chooses"; Viola Garfield and Pamela T. Amoss, obituary, *AA* 86 (1984): 394–99; and Amoss, in Gacs et al., *Women Anthropologists.*

28. See Goldfrank, *Notes.* For Bunzel (1898–1990), see Triloki N. Pandey, "Anthropologists at Zuni," *APS Proceedings* 116 (15 Aug. 1972): 321–37; David M. Fawcett and Teri McLuhan, in Gacs et al., *Women Anthropologists;* autobiography, and Robert Murphy, obituary, *Anthropology Newsletter,* Mar. 1990, 4 and 5.

29. Caffrey, *Benedict,* 95–113, esp. 103–4, for dissertation, and 105–110, for ECP fellowship. For her introduction to anthropology, see ECP, New School lectures, fall 1919, 1, RHS.

30. Helen Roberts to ECP, 3 Aug. 1919, APS. For continuing support, see FB to ECP, 3 May 1929, APS.

31. For the beginning of this relationship, see ALK to ECP, 26 June and 28 July 1922, APS; 30 Aug. 1922 and [Feb. 1923], RHS. For funding see FB-ECP-GR corres., 28 July–21 Dec. 1922; FB-GR-PG-ECP corres., 27 Jan. 1923–29 June 1925; ECP checks to GR: 3 Jan. 1923, $108; 16 Aug. 1923, $200; ECP checks to PG: 6 Aug. 1923 and 29 Oct. 1923, $100; 2 Nov. 1923, $700; 7 Jan. 1924, $200, RHS.

32. ALK to ECP, [Sept.] and 18 Oct. 1923, APS; PG to ALK, 30 Sept. 1925, ALK Papers; Sapir to White, 30 June 1926, LW Papers. Sociologist Pitirim Sorokin made a similar remark on Alexandra Kollontai's "sexual satyriasis" in *Leaves from a Russian Diary* (New York: E. P. Dutton, 1924), 59, quoted by Mary Jo Deegan, "Alexandra Kollontai, 1872–1952," in *Women in Sociology: A Bio-Bibliographical Sourcebook,* ed. Deegan (New York: Greenwood Press, 1991), 231–38, esp. 236. After he remarried in 1925, Sapir was increasingly moralistic about sex. See Sapir, "The Discipline of Sex," *American Mercury* 16 (1928): 417; "Observations on the Sex Problem in America," *American Journal of Psychiatry* 8 (1928): 529; Sapir to Benedict, 29 Sept. 1927 and 29 Apr. 1929; Benedict to Mead, 29 Dec. 1928, in Mead, *Anthropologist at Work,* 185–86, 195–96, 95; also Benedict to Mead, 8 Sept. 1925, 301–2, for her own account of Cochiti.

33. ALK to ECP, 18 Oct. 1923, APS. See also ALK to Sapir, 3 Mar. 1924, in Golla. For White's attack on Boas, see account of 1939 anthropology meetings in Goldfrank, *Notes,* 151–55; White, "The Ethnography and Ethnology of Franz Boas," *Bulletin of the Texas Memorial Museum* 6 (1963); and "The Social Organization of Ethnological Theory," *Rice University Studies* (fall 1966); White to Peter Hare, 29 Aug. 1973, APS.

34. ALK to ECP, 2 Aug. 1920, APS. See also ALK to ECP, 11 Nov. 1919; Kidder to ECP, 19 Jan. and 14 May 1919; ECP to HP, 26 June 1919, APS; ECP to ALK, 4 July 1920, fr. Pecos, ALK Papers; McNickle, *Indian Man,* 29–30; R. B. Woodbury, *Alfred V. Kidder* (New York: Columbia University Press, 1973).

35. ALK to ECP, 28 Sept. 1920 and 26 Jan. 1920 (for Tozzer); also 13 Mar. 1921, APS. Kroeber retained an affection for Tozzer after he taught at Berkeley in 1919.

36. ALK to ECP, 29 Jan. 1922, RHS. For Jemez, see ECP to HP, [16] and 29 Sept. 1921; "Memo for H.P.," [Sept. 1921], APS.

37. Kidder to FB, 31 May 1927, FB Papers, quoted in Caffrey, *Benedict,*

261. The laboratory, discussed in 1926 and planned at the first Pecos Conference, Aug. 1927, received Rockefeller funding for five years from 1928. An anonymous gift paid for fieldwork training in archeology, ethnology, and linguistics, and ten to twelve scholarships. See *Science* 66 (1927): 489–91; Benedict to Mead, 29 Dec. 1928, in Mead, *Anthropologist at Work*, 95. For Jemez, see Kidder to ECP, 21 and 26 Apr. 1924, APS; ECP, *The Pueblo of Jemez* (1925); "Relations between Ethnology and Archeology in the Southwest" (1940); D. R. Givens, *Alfred Vincent Kidder and the Development of Americanist Archeology* (Albuquerque: University of New Mexico Press, 1992), 63–64, 148, and Kidder notes (1957), quoted 143–44.

38. ECP to ALK, 26 Mar. 1929, ALK Papers; Sapir to ECP, 27 Mar. 1929, APS. University of Chicago student Eva Horner was one of Kidder's field group.

39. Sapir to ECP, 27 Mar. 1929, APS.

40. Kidder to ECP, 30 Mar. 1929, also 2 Feb. 1929; and ECP to Kidder, 14 Mar. 1929, APS.

41. Kidder to ECP, 8 Apr. 1929, APS.

42. ALK to ECP, 13 Apr. 1929, APS. See also 11 June 1918; 2 Dec. 1921; 3 Apr. 1929, APS.

43. GR to ECP, 25 Aug. 1929, APS.

44. See Caffrey, *Benedict*.

45. ALK to Hank Alsberg, 7 Dec. 1935, draft, ALK Papers.

46. ECP to John Collier, 18 Jan. 1935, APS. Ruth Underhill (1883–1984) was appointed to the Soil Conservation Service to head the Papago survey team. She transferred to the Bureau of Indian Affairs in 1937, where she was associate, then supervisor, of education from 1938 to 1945. See Underhill, *Autobiography of a Papago Woman*, AAA Memoirs 46 (Menasha, Wis., 1936); *Singing for Power: The Song Magic of the Papago Indians of Southern Arizona* (Berkeley: University of California Press, 1938); ECP's admiring review (1939); Joyce Griffen, in Gacs et al., *Women Anthropologists;* Babcock and Parezo, *Daughters of the Desert*, 72–75, with 1946 Laura Gilpin photo. For a former student's jaundiced view of Kroeber, see Patricia J. Knobloch, "Isabel Truesdell Kelly, 1906–1983," and for the different experience of Jane Richarson Hanks (b. 1908), see May Ebihara, in Gacs et al., *Women Anthropologists*.

47. FB to Benedict, 16 July 1925; also FB to Mead, 14 July 1925; and Benedict to FB, 18 July 1925, FB Papers, quoted in Mead, *Anthropologist at Work*, 288–91; Griffen, "Underhill," 359; Sapir to ALK, 17 June 1935, ALK Papers. For Sapir's relationships with Benedict and Mead, see Caffrey, *Benedict;* Regna Darnell, *Edward Sapir: Linguist, Anthropologist, Humanist* (Berkeley: University of California Press, 1990); Margaret Mead, *Blackberry Winter* (1972; Sydney: Angus and Robertson, 1981); Mead, *Anthropologist at Work*.

48. GR to ECP, 11 Oct., also 27 Oct. 1939, APS: "Gene Weltfish never had an appointment. She was only in Extension and last year when Al was told he could not even teach in Extension, she was also told that she could not teach there. . . . Hawkes was spiteful . . . because of the way Al talked to him at the time of the Boas rumpus. . . . Al has got himself another girl . . . and she never did have anything to do with Hawkes, but she has to

suffer indirectly." Weltfish (1902–1980) taught in the School of General Studies until dismissed in 1953 for suspected communist affiliation. Her next university position was at Fairleigh Dickinson in 1961. See Ruth E. Pathé, in Gacs et al., *Women Anthropologists;* "Biographical Note," to Alexander Lesser, "Franz Boas," in *Totems and Teachers,* ed. Sydel Silverman (New York: Columbia University Press, 1981), 32–33; FB to ECP, 22 Feb. 1930, APS. See Sapir to ALK, 5 Aug. 1937, ALK Papers, for Swadesh.

49. Sapir to White, 15 Mar. 1928, LW Papers.

50. FB to ECP, 10 Feb. 1931; Sapir to ECP, 27 Mar. 1929, APS. See also Benedict to FB, 12 June 1929, FB Papers; FB to ECP, 22 Feb. 1929; Bunzel to ECP, [ca. 24 June 1930], 16 July and [July] 1934; Bunzel-ECP-Stirling corres., Nov. 1929–June 1930, APS; Bunzel, *The Pueblo Potter: A Study of Creative Imagination in Primitive Art* (New York: Columbia University Press, 1929; reprint, New York: Dover, 1972); *Zuñi Ceremonialism, Zuñi Origin Myths, Zuñi Ritual Poetry,* and *The Nature of Katchinas,* BAE Annual Report 47 (Washington, D.C., 1932), 467–1006; *Zuñi Texts* (New York: G. E. Stechert, 1933); "Zuñi," in *Handbook of American Indian Languages,* ed. Franz Boas (1933), 535–88.

51. Bunzel to ECP, 16 July and [July] 1934, APS. See Bunzel, *Chichicastenango: A Guatemalan Village* (Locust Valley, N.Y.: J. J. Augustin, 1952). For CIW and Kidder, see Givens, *Kidder,* and Woodbury, *Kidder,* esp. 63 for Atwood. I am grateful to Betty Hannstein Adams for information on Father Rossbach, whom she knew as a girl growing up in Guatemala.

52. Bunzel to ECP, 16 July 1934, APS. See R. A. Rubinstein, ed., *Fieldwork: The Correspondence of Robert Redfield and Sol Tax* (Boulder: Westview, 1991).

53. Bunzel to ECP, 16 July 1934, APS. Bunzel was so angry that she did not publish her brilliant *Chichicastenango* until 1952. See foreword for an account of her fieldwork somewhat mellowed by time.

54. Clyde Kluckhohn, "The Conceptual Structure in Middle American Studies," in *The Maya and Their Neighbors,* ed. Clarence L. Hay et al. (New York: Appleton-Century, 1940), 41–51; Woodbury, *Kidder,* 74; Fawcett and McLuhan, "Bunzel"; ECP to ALK and to Collier, 14 and 18 Jan. 1935; to Scudder Mekeel, 25 Jan. 1938, APS.

55. Spier to ECP, 29 June 1920 and 7 Jan. 1921, APS. See also ECP to ALK, [19] Oct. 1918; ALK to Sapir, 7 Dec. 1918, ALK Papers; ECP, *Notes on Zuñi,* pt. 1 (1917), 151; RHL to ECP, 27 Nov. 1933. For General Series in Anthropology as an alternative to the laboratory "country club," see Spier to ECP, 1934–41, APS. For financial support of his editorial work, see ECP to Spier, 9 Apr. 1934 and Spier to ECP, 20 Apr. 1934, APS.

56. Simpson, *Herskovits,* 3, quoting Mead. See Adelin Linton and Charles Wagley, *Ralph Linton* (New York: Columbia University Press, 1971); ALK to ECP, 30 June 1918, APS, for Goddard affair. Herskovits took courses at the Free School with Goldenweiser and Veblen fall 1919 after completing his B.A. at the University of Chicago.

57. After completing a trait-distribution dissertation on the cattle complex in East Africa in 1923, Herskovits received an NRC fellowship in

1926 for an anthropometric study of African-Americans. See Melville Her-skovits, *The American Negro: A Study in Racial Crossing* (New York: Knopf, 1928). For new direction see his "Acculturation and the American Negro," *Southwestern Political and Social Science Quarterly* 8 (1927): 211–25; "Race Relations in the United States," *AJS* 34 (1929): 1129–39, and "Race Relations, 1929," *AJS* 35 (1930): 1052–62. From 1927–29, he served on the abortive SSRC Sub-Committee on Race Differences, which was disbanded in 1930. For ECP funding, see FB-ECP-Herskovits corres., 1929–30, 1936 and 1937, APS; FB to Benedict, 21 Oct. 1930, in Mead, *Anthropologist at Work*, 403–4.

Hurston did anthropometric measurement for Boas in Harlem as a Bar-nard undergraduate in 1926. For Association for the Study of Negro Life fellowship to collect folklore in her native Florida see FB-Woodson-ECP-Hurston corres., 1926–27; R. E. Hemenway, *Zora Neale Hurston* (Ur-bana: University of Illinois Press, 1977), 68–106.

58. White to Peter Hare, 29 Aug. 1973, APS. See White to ALK, 27 Feb. 1947, ALK Papers; Leslie A. White, *The Acoma Indians*, BAE Annual Report 47 (Washington, D.C., 1932); *The Pueblo of San Felipe*, AAA Memoirs 38 (Menasha, Wis., 1932), 1–69; *The Pueblo of Santo Domingo, New Mexico*, AAA Memoirs 43 (Menasha, Wis., 1935), 1–210; *The Pueblo of Santa Ana, New Mexico*, AAA Memoirs 60 (Menasha, Wis., 1942), 1–360; *The Pueblo of Sia, New Mexico*, BAE Bulletin 184 (Wash-ington, D.C., 1962), xi: "I began my fieldwork among the Keres under the tutelage of Dr. Parsons, and she gave me generously of her time and vast knowledge for many years. I would like to dedicate 'The Pueblo of Sia, New Mexico' to her memory."

59. Robert Herrick, "Chapter Six," early version of *End of Desire* (1926?), RH Papers.

60. Gladys Reichard, "Elsie Clews Parsons," *JAFL* 56 (1943): 45–48, esp. 47–48; Goldfrank, interview with Jennifer Fox, *Daughters of the Desert Oral History Project*, 3 July 1985 (New York Video Recording: Wenner-Gren Foundation), quoted in Charles H. Lange, "The Contribu-tions of Esther S. Goldfrank," in *Hidden Scholars: Women Anthropologists and the Native American Southwest*, ed. Nancy J. Parezo (Albuquerque: University of New Mexico Press, 1993), 221–32, esp. 232. For Goldfrank's continuing association with ECP, see Goldfrank, *Notes*, 26–35, 177–78, 208–221. For Reichard's pathbreaking work, funded by Parsons, see ECP to GR, 26 Nov. 1927, GR Papers; GR-ECP-FB corres., 29 May 1930–2 Oct. 1936, GR Papers, FB Papers, and APS; Reichard, *Social Life of the Navajo Indians* (New York: Columbia University Press, 1928); *Spider Woman: A Story of Navajo Weavers and Chanters* (New York: Macmillan, 1934); *Navajo Shepherd and Weaver* (New York: J. J. Augustin, 1936); *Dezba, Woman of the Desert* (New York: J. J. Augustin, 1939); *Navajo Medicine Man: Sandpaintings and Legends of Miguelito* (New York: J. J. Augustin, 1939); Reichard and Franc Newcomb, *Sandpaintings of the Nav-ajo Shooting Chant* (New York: J. J. Augustin, 1937); Reichard, unpub-lished ms. on her Navajo work (n.d.); "A New Look at the Navajo," GR Papers; "Course in Language and Thought," *NYT*, 14 Feb. 1937; and *Barnard Bulletin*, 24 Feb. 1943, GR Papers; W. H. Lyon, "Gladys Reichard at the Frontiers of Navajo Culture," *American Indian Quarterly* 13 (spring

1989): 137–63; Louise Lamphere, "Gladys Reichard among the Navajo," in Parezo, *Hidden Scholars,* 157–88. For resistance to her work see ALK to ECP, 11 Nov. 1926, APS; PG to ALK, 16 Feb. 1927; Sapir to ALK, 11 Feb. and 16 Apr. 1927, ALK Papers; FB to ECP, 20 June 1927, APS; Benedict to Mead, 29 Dec. 1928, in Mead, *Anthropologist at Work,* 95–96; GR to FB, 26 and 29 Aug. 1929, FB Papers; GR to ECP, 25 Aug. 1929, 22 and 24 Feb. 1930, APS; Darnell, *Sapir,* 252–57. For recent recognition, see Gary Witherspoon, *Language and Art in the Navajo Universe* (Ann Arbor: University of Michigan Press, 1977); and "Language in Culture and Culture in Language," *International Journal of American Linguistics* 46 (1980): 1–13.

61. Caffrey, *Benedict,* 92–99, 103; for ECP, 95–97, 101; Sydney Hook, Ruth Benedict, and Margaret Mead, "Alexander Goldenweiser: Three Tributes," *Modern Quarterly* 11 (1940): 31–34.

62. FB to ECP, 9 Feb. 1923; ECP to FB, 10 Feb. 1923, APS; also FB to RHL, 13 Feb. 1923, FB Papers; Mead, *Anthropologist at Work,* 341–43; Caffrey, *Benedict,* 106–8. When Sapir read Benedict's dissertation, he recognized a talent "more inspiring" than that of Goldenweiser or Waterman. See Sapir to Benedict, 25 June 1922, in Mead, *Anthropologist at Work,* 49–53.

63. Benedict, diary, 12–20 Feb. and 8 Mar. 1923; for Mead, 8 Feb. and 7 Mar. 1923, in Mead, *Anthropologist at Work,* 57, 65–67; FB to GR, 6 Mar. 1923, FB Papers; Mead, *Blackberry Winter,* 113–14, 119; Caffrey, *Benedict,* 106–7, 114–15.

64. Benedict to Mead, 15 Aug., 1 and 8 Sept. 1925, in Mead, *Anthropologist at Work,* 292–302. See also PG to ALK, 30 Sept. 1925, ALK Papers. For mythology, see Benedict to ECP, 13 Aug. 1923, APS; and to FB, 16 Sept. 1923, FB Papers; ECP, $500 check to Benedict, 14 Oct. 1923, RHS; FB to ECP, 12 June 1924, APS; Bunzel to FB, 6 and 30 Aug. 1924, FB Papers; Mead to Benedict, 30 Aug.–16 Sept. 1924; Benedict to Mead, 11–29 Aug. 1925, in Mead, *Anthropologist at Work,* 285–95.

65. Benedict, diary, 18 and 21 Jan. 1926, and Sapir to Benedict, 14 June 1925, in Mead, *Anthropologist at Work,* 75–76, 180. Caffrey, *Benedict,* 107, says the Southwest Society fellowship was for two years.

66. GR to ECP, 17 Mar. 1931, APS; Sapir, quoted in Caffrey, *Benedict,* 260. For funding see F. Lillie to ECP, 23 May 1924; E. Armstrong to Benedict, 23 Apr. 1926, in Caffrey, *Benedict,* 366; Sapir to Benedict, 11 May and 21 Oct. 1926, in Mead, *Anthropologist at Work,* 183–85; and 16 Mar. 1926, cited in Caffrey, *Benedict,* 260; FB to Beardsley Ruml (Rockefeller Foundation), 16 Mar. 1927, requesting funds to establish positions for female academics in women's colleges and for position of associate in coed universities for research and graduate teaching; FB-Benedict-Columbia corres., Nov. 1927–Feb. 1931, FB Papers; FB to ECP, 28 Feb. 1931, APS, for struggle to keep anthropology afloat under Dean Woodbridge: "About 4 or 5 years ago I hoped to get Sapir for linguistics but that also fell through, because they preferred the Sanskritist Grey. Two years ago the Trustees asked for a two years budget and I recommended the appointment of Kroeber and Sapir as well as of Ruth Benedict. Of course nothing happened. . . . the new Dean surprised me with the news that they provided in the budget for both Kroeber and Sapir and for an

associate professor. . . . In the meanwhile Sapir has been called to Yale.
. . . Kroeber's acceptance is still doubtful. . . . Ruth Benedict's fate is still
in the balance, but I hope I'll get a regular appointment for her."

67. See FB to ECP, 16 Sept. 1927, APS; Benedict to FB, 8 July 1928,
FB Papers; and to Mead, 21 Sept. 1928, in Mead, *Anthropologist at Work*,
94; Benedict, "Psychological Types in the Cultures of the Southwest"
(1928), *ICA Proceedings* (New York, 1930), 527–81. For ECP's unexpectedly favorable reaction, see Benedict to Mead, 29 Dec. 1928, in Mead,
Anthropologist at Work, 311. As Caffrey, *Benedict*, 156, points out, ECP,
in a review of Lowie's *Primitive Religion* (1925), characterized the Hopi
as "objective-minded" and their Plains neighbors as "subjective-minded"
in a duality similar to Benedict's. ECP's paper for the 1928 AAA meetings,
"Ritual Parallels in Pueblo and Plains Cultures" (1929), emphasized the
similarities of Pueblo and Plains cultures without denying important differences. For differentiation between generations, see Mead's advice to Benedict (1933), in Mead, *Anthropologist at Work*, 335–36: write it with "no
Boasian-Lowie-ish-Germanic scraps in it"; Benedict, *Patterns of Culture*
(New York: Mentor Book, 1934); and ECP to RHL, 1 Mar. 1937, RHL
Papers: "One does not have to spend a summer in Zuni or even go there
to know that Benedict's Patterns of Culture is over-standardized, just as
are countless other travel books or critiques on national traits."

68. ECP, review of *Zuñi Mythology*, by Ruth Benedict, and *Zuñi Texts*,
by Ruth Bunzel (1937), 108; Benedict to ECP, 19 June 1937, APS. See
Zuñi Mythology, 2 vols. (New York: Columbia University Press, 1935).
Cf. criticism in FB to Benedict, 23 Aug. 1934, in Mead, *Anthropologist at
Work*, 411.

Chapter Thirteen

1. Robert Herrick, "A Plot of Fair Women," 14 Mar. 1925, Dolé—Les
V-Bains, Guadeloupe, RH Papers.

2. Robert Herrick, *Chimes* (New York: Macmillan, 1926); reviews in
NYEP, 10 May 1926, and *Detroit News*, 13 June 1926; Jacques Barzun,
Columbia Spectator (1926), typed copy, RH Papers. See handwritten list
identifying fictional and real-life characters, RH Papers. Jessica is identified
as "Mrs. Elsie Clews Parsons imposed on the position of Mrs. George
Vincent."

3. For Lissa's unwelcome pregnancy, see Lissa to ECP, 8 and 20 Jan.
1922, RHS; ECP to HP, [20] and 22 June 1922; ALK to ECP, 26 June
1922; HP to ECP, 7 Aug. 1922, APS. For birth of Rufus Patterson, see
ECP to MDL, 24 Aug. 1922, MDL Papers.

4. Clarence Day to ECP, 22 June 1925, APS. For Henry Clews's death,
see obituary, *NYT*, 1 Feb. 1923; ECP to MDL, 6 Feb. 1923, MDL Papers;
Giddings to ECP, 6 Feb. 1923; ALK to ECP, [Feb.] 1923, RHS. See HP to
ECP, 17 July 1923, APS, re "large estate check deposited." For St. Paul's,
see ECP to JEP, 28 Oct. 1923, APS; and ECP to HP after a visit, [6 Nov.
1923], RHS. ECP helped Hackett and Toksvig with money a number of
times while he was writing what became the very successful *Henry the
Eighth: A Personal History* (New York: Horace Liveright, 1929). See Francis Hackett to ECP, 12 Dec. 1928, for finishing this 784 pp. "psycho-

history," and 20 Feb. 1929, APS, for its Book of the Month Club selection: "I couldn't have pulled through unless you had saved us."

5. ECP to HP, [14 Sept. 1921], APS, just after Lissa's wedding. Dr. McIlvaine Parsons told me about the agreement concerning the children in July 1994. See ECP to HP and HP to ECP, 1 Sept. 1920, re anniversary; HP to ECP, 9, 14, 17 June, 7 Sept. 1920, and 20 Aug. 1923; and ECP to HP, 15 Aug. 1923, re children; HP to ECP, 8 July–6 Aug. 1921, APS, for Europe; Barnabas to ECP, 11 May and 27 June 1922, RHS; HP-ECP corres., 27 June–18 July, APS; and ECP to MDL, 10 Aug. 1922, MDL Papers, for family trip to Southwest; HP to W. Phillips, 25 Feb. 1925, HP Papers: "Mrs. Parsons is interested in her scientific work and does not deviate for things such as that in which you are interested." For LaFarge see, "My Island," 11 Feb. 1921, and hon. degree, Princeton, 21 June 1921, APS—the last evidence of the relationship in ECP's papers.

6. ECP to RHL, 19 Oct. 1922, RHL Papers; ECP to MDL, 8 May 1923, MDL Papers.

7. Signe Toksvig to ECP, 26 Aug. 1923, APS; and 20 Jan. 1924, RHS.

8. ECP, "The Value of Folk-Tales," 10 Mar. 1920, APS, quoted in Rosemary Lévy Zumwalt, *Wealth and Rebellion: Elsie Clews Parsons, Anthropologist and Folklorist* (Urbana: University of Illinois Press, 1992), 205; see also 190 and 197. See JEP to ECP, 19 Feb. 1920, re their Hampton visit previous fall; ECP to HP, 27 Jan., 4, [10], and 13 Feb. 1919; ECP to HP, 26 Mar. 1920, APS. For folklore trips, see ECP, "Folk-Lore of the Cherokee of Robeson County, North Carolina" (1919); "Folk-Lore from Aiken, South Carolina" (1921); "Folk-Lore from Elizabeth City County, Virginia," with A. M. Bacon (1922); *Folk-Lore of the Sea Islands, South Carolina* (1923); "Joel Chandler Harris and Negro Folklore" (1919); Clarence Day Jr., "Portrait of a Lady," *NR*, 23 July 1919, 387–89; and Grant LaFarge, "Rivers and Recollections" (1920?), APS.

9. JEP to ECP, 26 Jan. 1921, APS ("Manga" was the family's pet name for Lucy Clews). See ECP, "Americans in Haiti," letter to editor, *NYT*, 18 Oct. 1920, 14; *NYEP*, 20 Oct. 1920; James W. Johnson to ECP, 21 Oct. 1920, APS; ECP, "Hayti Misunderstood" (1912). Cf. Franz Boas, "Nationalism," *Dial*, 8 Mar. 1919, 232–37. See also ECP, "American Snobbishness in the Philippines" and "Remarks on Education in the Philippines" (1906); and "Congressional Junket in Japan: The Taft Party of 1905 Meets the Mikado" (1906). For New School, see ECP to James Harvey Robinson, draft, [ca. 16 Mar.] 1920, APS.

10. ECP to JEP, 8 Aug. 1923, APS. For Bahamas, see interview with Dr. McIlvaine Parsons, 1991; ECP to MDL, 18 Mar. and 28 Apr. 1923, MDL Papers; Day to ECP, 28 Mar. 1923; and ECP to Day, 9 Apr. 1923, RHS. See ECP, "Lecture Folk-Lore at Home," [Philadelphia, Mar. 1923], with notes on back re Fauset; Arthur Huff Fauset, notes for Hare, Aug. 1970; ECP to HP, [6], 16, and 18 July 1923; ALK to ECP, 18 Oct. 1923, APS; Fauset, "Folklore from the Half-Breeds in Nova Scotia," *JAFL* 38 (Apr.–June 1925): 300–315; and *Folklore from Nova Scotia*, AFLS Memoirs 24 (New York, 1931); ECP, "Half-Breed" (1924), and "Micmac Folklore" (1925). Fauset (b. 1899) also made folklore trips to the South in 1926 and the Lesser Antilles in 1927 financed by ECP. ECP wrote a children's folklore series, illustrated by Clarence Day, for his sister, novelist

and *Crisis* literary editor, Jessie Fauset. See Day to ECP, 4 Aug. [1921], APS; ECP, "Wolf and His Nephew" (1921). "Negress Novelist Honored at Dinner," *World*, [Dec. 1922?], APS, on publication of Fauset's *There Is Confusion* (New York: Horace Liveright, 1922), gives family background. For Hampton folklore, see Ray Sapirstein, "The View within the Mask: The Illustrated Poetry of Paul Dunbar and Photography at Hampton Institute" (M.A. thesis, University of Texas at Austin, 1994); Edith Dabbs, *Face of an Island: Leigh Richmond Miner's Photographs of St. Helena Island* (New York: Grossman Publishers, 1971).

11. See "Memoir . . . Relating to the Republic of Haiti under the American Occupation," *Nation*, 25 May 1921; Ernest Gruening, *Many Battles* (New York: Liveright, 1973), 93–103.

12. Henry Seidel Canby, quoted in "Robert Herrick, April 26, 1868–December 24, 1938," in *Twentieth Century Authors: A Biographical Dictionary of Modern Literature*, ed. Stanley J. Kunitz and Howard Haycraft (New York: H. W. Wilson, 1942), 644–65; clipping (1916), RH Papers. See Herrick, *The Gospel of Freedom* (1898), *Together* (1908), and *One Woman's Life* (1913); Ernest Samuels, *Bernard Berenson* (Cambridge: Belknap Press, 1979), 266–67. See also Alfred Kazin, *On Native Grounds: An Interpretation of Modern American Prose Literature* (New York: Harcourt, Brace and World, 1942), 121–27; Blake Nevius, *Robert Herrick: The Development of a Novelist* (Berkeley: University of California Press, 1962).

13. Herrick, *Chimes*, 210, 221; serialized in *Forum*, Dec. 1925. See ECP, Poems, APS. For beginning of relationship, see also Herrick, "Diary of an Intravert," New York, 24 Jan. 1924 [1925], 5, RH Papers; "The Stations of the Cross," in *Wanderings* (New York: Harcourt Brace, 1925), 73–150, esp. 74–75. For rides, see ECP, *The Social Organization of the Tewa of New Mexico* (1929), 238–47.

14. ECP to HP, 17 Nov. and 4 Dec. 1923, fr. Lamy, N.M.; also 8, [9], 10, and [22] Nov., 3 and 5 Dec. 1923, APS. See RH to Robert Morss Lovett, 23 Nov. 1923; Herrick, "Pleasant Walks in Academe," outline for *Chimes*, 2 Dec. 1923, RH Papers; ECP, $272 check to San Gabriel Ranch, 4 Dec. 1923, RHS; PG to ECP, 27 Nov. 1923, APS. For attempts to obtain for editing and publication Stevenson's Tewa-Taos notes left to Harrington on her death in 1915, see ALK to ECP, 11 Nov. 1919 and 2 Aug. 1920, APS; ECP to Fewkes, 24 Apr. and 3 Dec. 1922; Swanton to ECP, 11 Mar. and 27 Apr. with Harrington to Swanton, 28 Mar. 1922; Fewkes to ECP, 23 Dec. 1922, RHS; Nancy J. Parezo, "Matilda Coxe Stevenson: Pioneer Ethnologist," in *Hidden Scholars: Women Anthropologists and the Native American Southwest*, ed. Parezo (Albuquerque: University of New Mexico Press, 1993), 38–62.

15. See Herrick, "The Story of Jessica Stowe," 4 pp., and "Pleasant Walks of Academe," New York, 15 Jan. [1924], 2 pp., sketches for "A University Novel," RH Papers. "Magic," in *Wanderings*, 3–70, based in New Mexico, draws on Herrick's observations of ECP in fall 1923. See "Magic," Bathsheba, Barbados, 17 Feb.? [1924]; and "Theme for Story," [19 Mar. 1924], RH Papers.

16. Herrick, "Foreword to Jessica" (1926?), papers relating to "Tides," RH Papers.

17. For Lissa's failing marriage, see ECP to HP, [6 Nov. 1923]; Patt[erson] to ECP, 8 Nov. 1923, RHS; HP to ECP, [9 May 1924], APS. For Herrick's reconstruction, including Herbert's opposition to divorce, see *The End of Desire* (New York: Farrar and Rinehart, 1932), esp. 95–96.

18. Herrick, "Diary," 4 Feb. [1925], 16, RH Papers; cf. 8 for the "miracle of her tears"; "Stations of the Cross," 133. For other sketches during this period, see early versions of "Magic," dated Bathsheba, Barbados, 17 Feb.?, 19 Mar., and June [1924]; "The Adventures of Ti Chat," Morne Rouge, Martinique, 6 Apr. 1924, and other versions of "The Adventures of Ti Chatte," in *Wanderings*, 151–254; and "The Further Adventures of Ti Chatte," York Village, Maine, 1925, RH Papers.

19. ECP to HP, 25 Mar. 1924, APS. For fever, see Herrick, "Diary," 8, 16; "Stations of the Cross," 132–38; RH to Lovett, 20 Apr. [1924], RH Papers.

20. ECP, preface to *Folk-Lore of the Antilles, French and English*, pt. 1 (1933), vii; unpublished preface, APS, quoted in Zumwalt, *Wealth and Rebellion*, 195. See Modock to ECP, 26 Oct. 1926, and other corres., APS.

21. RH to Lovett, 20 Apr. [1924], RH Papers. See Herrick, "Diary," [26 Jan. 1925], 13, for negotiations with Harcourt, Brace.

22. Herrick, "Diary," New York, 24 Jan. 1924 [1925], 17, 5, RH Papers; *End of Desire*, 41–68 and 177–209. See also early versions, dated York Village, July and Aug. 1924, RH Papers, of "The Passions of Trotsky," in *Wanderings*, 255. ECP presented "The Religion of the Pueblo Indians" in the Hague, 12–16 Aug. 1924. On the evidence of a story told me by Herbert Parsons Jr. about a trip to Spain with his mother while Mac and Herbert Sr. toured the French battlefields, Herbert, Herbert Jr., and Mac probably accompanied her.

23. Herrick, "Diary," New York, 24 Jan. and 4 Feb. [1925].

24. ECP to Leslie White, 16 Aug. 1927, LW Papers. See account in Esther Schiff Goldfrank, *Notes on an Undirected Life: As One Anthropologist Tells It* (Flushing, N.Y.: Queens College Press, 1978); ECP to Goldfrank, 25 Nov. 1924, in Goldfrank, *Notes*, 27; Goldfrank to FB, 30 Nov. 1924, fr. Isleta, FB Papers; ECP to JEP, 23 Nov. 1925; and ECP to Goldfrank, 24 Nov. 1925, APS; Goldfrank, "Isleta Variants: A Study in Flexibility," *JAFL* 39 (1926): 71–78; ECP to Goldfrank, 17 June and 1 July 1927; and Benedict to Goldfrank, 9 July 1927, in Goldfrank, *Notes*, 29; ECP, *Isleta, New Mexico* (1932).

For ECP's controversial fieldwork technique, which she found distasteful but necessary because of the secretiveness of the Rio Grande and Taos pueblos, see ECP, preface to *Social Organization of the Tewa*, 7–9; *Taos Pueblo* (1936), 14–16, 117–20; Leslie White, "Prefatory Note," *The Pueblo of Santo Domingo*, AAA Memoirs 43 (Menasha, Wis., 1935), 1–210, esp. 7–8; *The Pueblo of Santa Ana*, AAA Memoirs 60 (Menasha, Wis., 1942), 1–360, esp. 9–11; and *The Pueblo of Sia*, BAE Bulletin 184 (Washington, D.C., 1962), 6–10; Esther Schiff Goldfrank, *The Artist of "Isleta Paintings" in Pueblo Society*, Smithsonian Contributions to Anthropology 5 (Washington, D.C., 1967); and Goldfrank, *Notes*, 208–20. For reactions from anthropologists of Santa Clara and San Juan background, see Edward P. Dozier, review of Parsons, *Isleta Paintings*, ed. Goldfrank,

AA 65 (1963): 936; Alfonso Ortiz, review of Goldfrank, *The Artist of "Isleta Paintings," AA* 70 (1968): 838–39. ECP treated all religious beliefs—European or Pueblo—as sociological, not sacred phenomena. Likewise, she treated Pueblo fear about divulging religious secrets as a psychological characteristic to be examined and understood socially and historically like any other. She also saw the Pueblos as divided over this, as over other issues; and she emphasized always the constantly changing nature of beliefs and legitimate behaviors. See *Fear and Conventionality* (1914); "A Few Zuñi Death Beliefs and Practices" (1916), for witchcraft cases 1898–99 and 1910–11; "The Zuñi A'Doshlĕ and Suukĕ" (1916), for discipline by fear; *The Scalp Ceremonial of Zuñi* (1924), 5: "The warrior part of the town hierarchy, at Taos and elsewhere, is conspicuous today as a police for the preservation of custom, more particularly for that wall of secrecy which the Old Men know so well is their soundest bulwark against foreign attitudes of mockery or coercion." For studies of fear, see her "Teshlatiwa at Zuñi" (1919); and "The Price of Fear—at Zuñi" and "The Third Degree at Lamy," in "In the Southwest" (1921), APS. For controversy caused by her work, especially in Jemez and Taos, see Zumwalt, *Wealth and Rebellion,* 240–57. For current controversy, and a comprehensive bibliography, see Pauline Turner Strong's introduction to vol. 1 of ECP's *Pueblo Indian Religion* (Lincoln: University of Nebraska Press, 1996), for a critical assessment of her techniques; and Ramón A. Gutiérrez's introduction to vol. 2 for a more sympathetic discussion. For an example of the politics surrounding issues of anthropology and colonialism in the pueblos, see William L. Merrill, Edmund J. Ladd, and T. J. Ferguson, "The Return of the *Ahayu:da:* Lessons for Repatriation from Zuni Pueblo and the Smithsonian Institution," *Current Anthropology* 34 (Dec. 1993): 523–67. My understanding of these issues has profited enormously from discussions with my colleague Pauline Turner Strong.

25. Herrick, "Pleasant Walks of Academe," New York, 15 Jan. [1924], RH Papers; "Diary."

26. Kirchwey to Oswald Garrison Villard, 7 Sept. 1923; and Kirchwey, "Are We Better than Starfish?" *Nation,* 23 Apr. 1924, 470, quoted in Sara Alpern, *Freda Kirchwey: A Woman of the Nation* (Cambridge: Harvard University Press, 1987), 48–52, esp. 48, 49. See ECP, "Changes in Sex Relations" (1924), 551–53; "Sex" (1922). For *Civilization in the United States,* see Lewis Mumford, *Sketches from Life* (Boston: Beacon, 1982), 352, 365–68, who called it "a bit of preliminary housecleaning and rubbish-removing, before our generation moved in." See also Mumford, "The Art of Love," *Freeman,* 8 Nov. 1922, 213–34, commenting on ECP's article; ECP to MDL, 10 Aug. 1922, MDL Papers: "see what you have escaped"; Harold Stearns, *The Street I Know* (New York: Lee Furman, 1935); George W. Stocking Jr., "Ideas and Institutions in American Anthropology: Thoughts Toward a History of the Interwar Years," in *Selected Papers from the* American Anthropologist, *1921–1945* (Washington: AAA, 1976), 32–33.

27. Herrick, *End of Desire,* 117–27. See ECP, "Is Monogamy Feasible?" (1925), RH Papers. Cf. account by Kirchwey's husband, Evans Clark, in Alpern, *Kirchwey,* 54; "Nation Dinners," advertisement, *Nation,* 10 Dec. 1924, 631; notices (14, 21, and 28 Jan. 1925) that the dinner was

sold out by 12 Jan. and 450 reservations turned away; Kirchwey, *Nation*, 7 Jan. 1925, iii; and "The Personal Note: Memoirs of Nation Publishers and Editors," *Nation*, 20 Sept. 1965, 32; Sapir to Benedict, 7 Feb. 1925, in *An Anthropologist at Work: The Writings of Ruth Benedict*, ed. Margaret Mead (Westport, Conn.: Greenwood Press, 1977), 171–73.

28. Herrick, "Diary," 24 Jan. [1925], 2, 4; 25 Jan. [1925], 10–12; 4 Feb. [1925], 16–17, RH Papers. For other sketches during this period, see "Notes by the Way," 22 Jan. 1925; "The Storm," [ca. 25 Jan. 1925]; notes on ECP as Jung's "extravert-thinking type," [ca. 27 Jan. 1925]. For reviews of *Waste*, see Carl Van Doren, "Forty Years in the Wilderness," *NR*, 23 Apr. 1924, 235; J. W. Krutch, "Idealism and Despair," *Nation*, 28 May 1924, 588.

29. Herrick, "Field Trip, Number Three," [16 Feb. 1925], RH Papers.

30. Herrick and ECP, "Memoranda for Travel in the World and in Life," 16 Feb. 1925, RH Papers.

31. Herrick, *End of Desire*, 132–33. See ECP, preface to *Folk-Lore of the Antilles*. For Herrick's writing, see "Plot of Fair Women"; "Ti Chatte," 1 Apr. [1925]; "If One Cares," At Sea, [18–20 Apr. 1925], RH Papers. See "Diary," 25 May 1925, for Macmillan agreement re *Tides, Pictures from the Caribbean, Pleasant Walks in Academe* (*Chimes*); and 29 and 30 June and 13 Aug. 1925 for movie rights for *Wanderings*.

32. ECP and Herrick, "Tides," [25 Apr.? 1925], including handwritten "Points for E.C.P.," RH Papers. See various other versions and papers relating to "Tides," esp. ECP?, "The Inviolable," in "Tides," 2 June [1925]; Herrick, "For Jessica at Fifty and Tides" (1926?), RH Papers. For generations see Herrick, *End of Desire*, 39–40. For father-son conversation see "Tad," in *End of Desire*, 24–40. See ECP, Poems, APS; also Herrick, *End of Desire*, 63–65. For Redfield reading a chapter of *Tides* to Serena, see *End of Desire*, 159–60; for putting aside after a disastrous summer, see 280–81.

33. ECP to Lissa, 25 Sept. 1925, APS: "A copy of Father's will has come. You, John, and I are executors. I have directed the office to send you a copy in Newport; and that legal training of yours may help you to understand the language of the esoterics who composed it. In the Office Mr. Carnochan is representing the estate. Considerable detail will be done with Father's secretary, Mrs. Harding." See ECP to JEP, 4 Nov. 1925, APS. Herbert Parsons died on 16 Sept. 1925. For his death and Lippmann, see Peter H. Hare, *A Woman's Quest for Science: Portrait of Anthropologist Elsie Clews Parsons* (Buffalo: Prometheus Press, 1985), 41, 66, 167.

34. Toksvig to ECP, 18 Sept. 1925, RHS; PG to ALK, 30 Sept. 1925, ALK Papers; MKS to ECP, 22 Nov. 1925, APS.

35. JEP to ECP, 16 Nov. 1925; ECP to Lissa, 25 Nov. 1925; FB to ECP, 26 Nov. 1925, APS. See ECP to MDL, 13 Oct. 1925, MDL Papers, for Southwest plans.

36. Herrick, "For Jessica at Fifty and Tides," 6. See also *End of Desire*, 47–68, 273–74; *Chimes*, 298.

37. Benedict, diary, 21 Jan. 1926, in Mead, *Anthropologist at Work*, 76; ECP to JEP, 2 Mar. 1926. See also [30] and 31 Jan, 13, 17, and 27 Mar. 1926; ECP to Lissa, 1 Mar. 1926; FB to ECP, 28 Mar. 1926, APS; FB to Sapir, 7 May 1926, LW Papers; ECP to MDL, 14 Mar. 1926, MDL

Papers; Herrick, "Silhouettes from Egypt" and "Sight Seeing in Egypt," RH Papers.

38. Herrick, "For Jessica at Fifty and Tides," 6. See also ECP to JEP, 3 Dec. 1925 and 17 Mar. 1926, APS; Herrick, *End of Desire*, 17–22, 83–84.

39. Herrick, *End of Desire*, 58; ECP to JEP, 9 June 1926, APS; Herrick, "Jessica at Fifty," RH Papers. For cruise with boys, see Sapir to Leslie White, 30 June 1926; ECP to White, 14, 17, and 31 July, and 8 and 23 Aug. 1926, LW Papers. For *Tewa Tales* (1926), see RHL to ECP, 28 Sept. 1926, APS.

40. Herrick, "Part Two, The Schooner," 8; and "Chapter Two, The Return," 12–13, in "Jessica at Fifty," RH Papers. See also "Cooperation versus Combination," 66–76, esp. 66, and "The Slack of the Tide," in early version of *End of Desire* (1926?), 40–46; "Leaves from the Diary of a Wanderer, 1926, 1927," RH Papers; *End of Desire*, 16, 51–52, 57, 65–100, 104, 179, 213–15.

41. Herrick, "Chapter Two, The Return," 14; "Diary of a Wanderer." See also *End of Desire*, 281–82.

42. Mac to ECP, 17 Nov. 1926; JEP to ECP, 17 Nov. 1926; ECP to JEP, 30 Nov. 1926, APS; Herrick, "Foreword to Jessica," RH Papers. See also *End of Desire*, 102–3.

43. Preface, quoted in Zumwalt, *Wealth and Rebellion*, 194. See also ECP, preface to *Folk-Lore of the Antilles* (1933); ECP to JEP, 19 Oct. 1926; and 20 Jan. and 19 Feb. 1927; JEP to ECP, 17 Nov. 1926, APS; ECP, "Spirituals and other Folk-Lore from the Bahamas," "Spirituals from the 'American' Colony of Samana Bay, Santo Domingo," and "Lord Bateman" (1928); *Folk-Lore of the Antilles, French and English*, pt. 2 (1936); Herrick, "Diary of a Wanderer"; and "The Return," in early version of *End of Desire* (1926?), RH Papers; *End of Desire*, 336, 349–54.

44. Herrick, *End of Desire*, 337–48.

45. ECP, "Spirit Cult in Hayti" (1928), 157, 165, 167–72, 179.

46. ECP to RHL, 4 Apr. 1927, RHL Papers; ECP to Goldfrank, 17 June and 1 July 1927, in Goldfrank, *Notes*, 29; also ECP to White, 8 Apr. 1927, APS. See Herrick, *End of Desire*, 365–69; ECP, "Spirituals and other Folk-Lore," 454, 456, 486; "Spirit Cult in Hayti," 157, for St. Lucia boys (Sam?) shipwrecked in San Domingo; and *Folk-Lore of the Antilles, French and English*, pt. 3 (1943); Herrick, "Chapter One, The Cruise," 6–7, in "My Last Book," Jan. 1928, RH Papers; Nevius, *Herrick*, 311.

47. Herrick, "The Cruise," RH Papers. For *Social Organization of the Tewa*, see ECP to RHL, 11 Nov. 1927, RHL Papers; ECP to White, 8 July 1928, LW Papers.

48. Herrick, "The Cruise," 6, 3–4.

49. Herrick, "An Eighteenth Century Journey," Mar. 1928, RH Papers.

50. ECP to JEP, 3 Apr. 1932, APS. For Congress and paper, see ECP to White, 8 July 1928, LW Papers; ECP to FB, 1 Aug. 1928, FB Papers; ECP to JEP, [25 Sept. 1928], APS. For football, see Mac-ECP-Drury corres., 21 Sept.–1 Oct. 1928, APS; Hare, *A Woman's Quest for Science;* and Herrick, *End of Desire*, 76–80, 135, 146–47, 242–52. For Herrick, see Nevius, *Herrick*, 311–43; RH to Lovett, 18 May and 24 May 1930; and 22 Mar. 1931. "Themes and Notes for 'Jessica at Fifty'" (1928–29), RH Papers, outlines the new theme. For current interest in homosexuality, see

Serena's defense in *End of Desire*, 140–41; M. H. Dobkin, *The Making of a Feminist: Early Journals and Letters of M. Carey Thomas* (Kent, Ohio: Kent State University Press, 1979), 86–87; Lorine Pruette, "The Flapper," in *The New Generation: The Intimate Problems of Modern Parents and Children*, ed. V. F. Calverton and S. D. Schmalhausen (New York: Macauley, 1930). Among ECP's colleagues, see Margaret M. Caffrey, *Ruth Benedict: Stranger in This Land* (Austin: University of Texas Press, 1989), for Benedict's relationship with Mead and her lesbian partnerships; and Sapir's disapproval in "The Discipline of Sex," *American Mercury* 16 (1928): 417; "Observations on the Sex Problem in America," *American Journal of Psychiatry* 8 (1928): 529; Sapir to Benedict, 29 Apr. 1929, in Mead, *Anthropologist at Work*, 195.

Chapter Fourteen

1. ECP to FB, 16 July 1928; FB to ECP, 1 Jan. 1929 [1930], APS. See also ECP to FB, 1 Aug. 1928; FB to ECP, 18 July 1928; GR to ECP, 12 Oct. 1928, APS: "Your note . . . moved me more deeply than I can say. As if you hadn't done enough for us already! Just the evening before I had . . . given up hope of having any of Dr. G's books. . . . So you can imagine—you can anyway or you would not have thot of the most understanding thing you could do—what your note meant to me." Probably at Parsons's expense, Reichard returned to the Southwest during the 1929 summer. By the following year, again funded by Parsons, she was launched on a major study of Navajo weaving and language in the course of which she lived with the extended family of Miguelito and Maria Antonio and participated in their daily life. See GR to ECP, 22 and 24 Feb. 1930; and 6 July 1930, APS, for a flavor of the fieldwork experience: "I know you say a field-trip is neutral & one is neither happy or unhappy [but] There is a peace which comes to us at evening when the air is cool & the sun sets, the mountains become purple rose and blue—we are high in cedar & pinon country, a most comfortable setting—& night settles down with the sheep in the corral; & the stars & the moon & the air! Most people would hate the quiet—it *is* quiet—but I love it. It is the sort of thing some writers (a few) have gotten across, but somehow needs experiencing. My trip is half over, the only fly in my ointment is that the time passes too quickly."

2. ECP, "Spanish Elements in the Kachina Cult of the Pueblos" (1930), 598, 602–3. For pueblo dance, see *The Social Organization of the Tewa of New Mexico* (1929).

3. LaFarge, "The Ceremonial Year at Jacaltenango"; and Toor, "Textiles of the Otomí Indians," in *ICA Proceedings* (New York, 1930).

4. Boas to Huntington, 20 Jan. 1906, in George W. Stocking Jr., ed., *The Shaping of American Anthropology, 1883–1911: A Franz Boas Reader* (New York: Basic Books, 1974), 301–3. See Ricardo Godoy, "Franz Boas and His Plans for an International School of American Archeology and Ethnology in Mexico," *Journal of the History of the Behavioral Sciences* 13 (1977): 228–42; Zelia Nuttall to FB, 11 Oct. 1928, FB Papers, for attempt to revive School. Gamio completed his Columbia M.A. 1909–11; see FB to Bandelier, 15 Nov. 1909; FB to M. Saville, 17 Dec. 1909, FB Papers.

5. Manuel Gamio, *Forjando patria* (1916; Mexico City: Editorial Porrúa, 1982), 124, quoted in T. F. Walsh, *Katherine Anne Porter and Mexico* (Austin: University of Texas Press, 1992), 49. See Gamio, "Teotihuacán, Mexico" (Ph.D. diss., Columbia University, 1922); *La Población del Valle de Teotihuacán,* 5 vols. (Mexico City: Secretaría de Educación Pública, 1922; reprint, 1979); Helen Delpar, *The Enormous Vogue of Things Mexican* (Tuscaloosa: University of Alabama Press, 1992), 96–97; P. Henríquez Ureña, "The Revolution in Intellectual Life," *Survey Graphic,* May 1924, 165–66.

6. For director of the National Preparatory School Sáenz, who gained an M.A. at Columbia Teachers College in 1921, see Walsh, *Porter,* 141; Delpar, *Enormous Vogue,* 46. For Best Maugard, who developed the "Mexican drawing" system based on preconquest motifs while drawing pottery for Boas in 1911, see Walsh, *Porter,* 5, 26–27; Delpar, *Enormous Vogue,* 132–33; Best Maugard, *A Method for Creative Design,* ed. Porter (New York: Knopf, 1926); and "Art in the Public Schools," *Survey Graphic,* May 1924, 170–71. Porter accompanied Best Maugard to Mexico in 1920 after meeting him in New York in 1919. During 1921, she saw the return of Diego Rivera armed with a manifesto urging Mexican artists to seek models in ancient Indian painters and sculptors. In December, he received his first mural commission, and in 1922 José Clemente Orozco began painting frescoes in the National Preparatory School. See Porter, "Where Presidents Have No Friends," *Century,* July 1922; José Vasconcelos, "Educational Aspirations," *Survey Graphic,* May 1924, 167–69; Walsh, *Porter,* 50, 67–68, 92.

7. Frances Toor, "Editor's Foreword," *MFW,* June–July 1925, 3; Toor to FB, 1 Apr. 1925, FB Papers. See also Toor to ECP, 1 Apr. 1925, APS; FB to Toor, 9 Apr. 1925; Gamio to FB, 15 Apr. 1925, FB Papers; Gamio, "The Utilitarian Aspect of Folklore," *MFW,* June–July 1925, 6–7; ECP, letter to editor, *MFW,* Oct–Nov. 1925, 4; Gladys Reichard, review of *MFW, JAFL* 40 (1927): 212; Delpar, *Enormous Vogue,* 18–20, 36, 72–73; Summer School advert., *Survey Graphic,* May 1924, 189. The Exposition of Popular Art—the "true national culture"—was organized by artist Roberto Montenegro and Best Maugard's brother-in-law, National Museum director Jorgé Enciso, who established a permanent department of indigenous arts at the museum.

8. Anita Brenner, "A Mexican Renaissance," *The Arts,* Sept. 1925, 127–50; Margaret Constantine, *Tina Modotti* (New York, 1975), 65. See Brenner, *Idols Behind Altars* (1929; Boston: Beacon Press, 1970), esp. introduction and 206–7, 235–36; Susannah Joel Glusker (Brenner's daughter), "Anita Brenner: A Mind of Her Own" (Ph.D. diss., Union Institute, 1995); Weston, *The Daybooks,* vol. 1., *Mexico* (Millerton, N.Y.: Aperture, 1973). For graduate work 1927–30, see Brenner-FB corres., Nov. 1925–1930, FB Papers; "Vita," in Brenner, "The Influence of Technique on the Decorative Style in the Domestic Pottery of Culhuacan" (Ph.D. diss., Columbia University, 1930).

9. For Gamio's dismissal, see Toor, *MFW,* June–July 1925, 30. Gamio's work was supported by the Committee on Scientific Aspects of Human Migration, which emerged from John Merriam's "big immigration vagueness" disparaged by Kroeber in 1922. See Gamio, *Mexican Immigra-*

tion to the United States (Chicago: University of Chicago Press, 1930); Robert Redfield, *Tepoztlán, a Mexican Village: A Study of Folk Life* (Chicago: University of Chicago Press, 1930); Robert and Helen Merrell Lynd, *Middletown* (New York: Harcourt, Brace, and World, 1929); Delpar, *Enormous Vogue,* 114–16. See Mark C. Smith, *Social Science in the Crucible* (Durham: Duke University Press, 1994), 125–42, for influence of Veblen, Rivers, Radcliffe-Brown, and Wissler on the Lynds and Robert Lynd's influence as secretary of the SSRC.

10. R. L. Brunhouse, *Sylvanus G. Morley and the World of the Ancient Mayas* (Norman: University of Oklahoma Press, 1971); [Blom and LaFarge], *Tribes and Temples* (New Orleans: Tulane University, 1926); Delpar, *Enormous Vogue,* 99–118. See Benedict to FB, 12 June 1929, FB Papers; *An Anthropologist at Work: The Writings of Ruth Benedict,* ed. Margaret Mead (Westport, Conn.: Greenwood Press, 1977), 400–401; FB to ECP, 22 Feb. and 13 July 1929; Sapir to ECP, 27 Mar. 1929; Kidder to ECP, 30 Mar. 1929; Benedict to ECP, 17 Sept. 1929; ECP to Benedict, 21 Sept. 1929, APS.

11. Benedict to Mead, 29 Dec. 1928, in Mead, *Anthropologist at Work,* 95; ECP to Leslie White, 28 Jan. 1929, LW Papers; ECP to MDL, 29 Apr. 1929, MDL Papers. For secrecy, see RLB to Hare, 31 July 1978, APS. For assassination and the Christero war protesting laws prohibiting political activity by priests and imposing nonreligious education in church schools, see Carleton Beals, *Mexican Maze* (Philadelphia: Lippincott, 1931). For the application of the Mexican model in the U.S., see Delpar, *Enormous Vogue,* 120–24.

12. Porter to Dorothy Day, 17 Feb. 1931, in Walsh, *Porter,* 145. See ECP, passport, APS; Margaret Hooks, *Tina Modotti* (San Francisco: Pandora, 1993), 4–7, 196–99; Hayden Herrera, *Frida* (New York: Harper and Row, 1983); José Vasconcelos, *A Mexican Ulysses* (Bloomington: University of Indiana Press, 1963); Carleton Beals, "Mexico's New Leader," *NR,* 11 Dec. 1929, 62–64.

13. ECP to JEP, 10 Feb. 1929, APS. See Hooks, *Modotti,* 167–76.

14. For Rivera see ECP, Mexico Notes, APS; and Rosemary Lévy Zumwalt, *Wealth and Rebellion: Elsie Clews Parsons, Anthropologist and Folklorist* (Urbana: University of Illinois Press, 1992), 281. For Covarrubias see ECP, "Spanish Elements," 583 n. 4; Hooks, *Modotti,* 175. Covarrubias visited Taos summer 1929 and may have shown ECP his kachina collection when he returned to New York. See Adriana Williams, *Covarrubias* (Austin: University of Texas Press, 1994). For articles, see Toor to ECP, 4, 8, and 26 Apr. and 12 June 1929, APS; and ECP, "Masks in the Southwest of the United States" (1929).

15. See ECP, "On the Travels of Folk Tales and One Tale from the State of Puebla" and "Masks," with photograph of "Devil wearing an old paste mask in carnival, Huizquilucan, Mexico," and other articles in *MFW* (1929); "Spanish Elements," notes, 583–90; "Folklore from Santa Ana Xalmimilulco, Puebla, Mexico" (1932). For carnival, etc., see Anita Brenner, *Your Mexican Holiday* (1932; New York: G. P. Putnam's Sons, 1947), esp. 157, 185, 190–91. For Chalma, see Erna Fergusson, *Fiesta in Mexico* (New York: Knopf, 1942), 47–68; and Frances Karttunen, *Between Worlds: Interpreters, Guides, and Survivors* (New Brunswick: Rutgers Uni-

versity Press, 1994), 192–214, for Luz Jiménez, artists model for the cultural revolutionaries, who took them and their visitors to her native Milpa Alta, just south of Mexico City, and to Chalma. A pilgrimage to Chalma by Brenner, Toor, and Jean Charlot in 1925 took seventeen hours in the saddle the first day and from dawn to noon the next.

16. ECP to JEP, 6 Mar. 1929, APS. For this "military ripple" see Sáenz, in "The Mexican Situation discussed by Moisés Sáenz and Guy Stevens," Foreign Policy Association Luncheon, New York, Apr. 6, 1929, 18 (Stevens was director of the Association of Producers of Petroleum in Mexico).

17. Advert. in *MFW*, Oct.–Nov. 1925, 1; ECP to JEP, 6 Mar. 1929, APS. See also ECP, "Folklore from Santa Ana Xalmimilulco, Pueblo" (1932), 358, for maid; Herrera, *Frida*, 179–80, 98–100. For touring sites with AMNH and CIW archeologist George Vaillant, associate of Alfonso Caso who was working at Monte Albán near Mitla, see ECP to ALK, 26 Mar. 1929, ALK Papers.

18. ECP to JEP, 24 Mar. 1929, APS. See ECP, Mexico Notes, APS; and Zumwalt, *Wealth and Rebellion*, 280–81.

19. ECP, "On the Travels of Folk Tales" (1929), 352; preface to *Mitla* (1936), v; ECP to ALK, 26 Mar. 1929, ALK Papers.

20. Toor, *MFW*, Oct.–Nov. 1925, 5. See also Apr.–May 1926; *Frances Toor's Guide to Mexico* (1935), 163–64; FB to ECP, 22 Feb. 1930, APS; Boas, "Notes on Mexican Folk-Lore," *JAFL* 25 (1912): 204–60. For tangle of cultures see ALK to ECP, 18 Oct. 1923, APS; ECP, *Mitla*, 1, 3, 5, and photograph opp. 6. See also Adolf Bandelier, *An Excursion to Mitla,* Papers of the Archeological Institute of America, American Series 2 (Boston, 1884); Frederick Starr, "Notes on the Ethnography of Southern Mexico," *Proceedings of the Davenport Academy of Sciences* 8 (1899–1900): 102–198, and 9 (1900–1903): 63–172. Modotti and Weston stayed at the Mitla Inn in 1925. They found it "Not half bad" in contrast with the filthy one in Tlacolula which Ralph Beals also complained about in 1933. Weston, whose "Escusado" (1925) is one of his great photographs, was particularly impressed by La Sorpresa's, which was "like a throne. One ascended several steps and felt quite regal sitting there. And there was no way to shut out others who aspired to like heights." See Weston, *Daybooks*, vol. 1, 4 July 1925; also Oct. 30–Nov. 14, 1925.

21. ECP, [Dec. 1929], APS. The "G.P." may be her old friend Walton Martin, who had married Charlotte Sorchan in 1921. For a recent letter from their home, see ECP to RHL, Aug. 1929, RHL Papers.

22. See ECP to JEP, 14 Jan. 1930, APS, fr. Mitla, on Fanny's birth: "I hope everything is going very smoothly. Such queer unexpected things, unforseen discomforts for the most part, do happen in child bearing." See Mac's letter to ECP, 21 May 1929, APS, expressing his ambivalence about her visiting St. Paul's for "Last Night": [Herb and I] "hate the idea of any sort of fuss . . . just as you fear the possibility of Manga making any sort of fuss over you on your departure to a foreign land."

23. ECP to JEP, 14 Jan. 1930. See ECP, passport, APS; *Mitla,* vii–viii, 266–78.

24. RLB to Hare, 31 July 1978, APS; ECP, *Mitla,* 59. For adult yard or field worker's wage of fifty centavos a day, see *Mitla,* 62; for Eligio, x, 425, 397, 10–11, 59–63; and ECP, "Zapoteca and Spanish Tales of Mitla,

Oaxaca" (1932), 277–78. For Petronila, see ECP, "The Institution of the Mayordomía" (1930), 73.

25. ECP, *Mitla*, x, 390–91.

26. ECP to JEP, 4 Feb. 1931; RLB to Hare, 31 July 1978, APS; also RLB to Dorothy Beals, 15 Jan. 1933, RLB Papers. See ECP to FB, 5 Feb. 1931, FB Papers; ECP to MDL, 1 and 18 Feb. 1931, MDL Papers; FB to ECP, 28 Feb. 1931, APS; ECP, *Mitla*, 22–23, 118–20, 123–24, 148–49, 205–6, 402–3, 417–19, 462–66; photographs opp. 23, 32. For quake in Mexico City 16 Jan. 1931 and Eisenstein flying to Oaxaca to film, see Walsh, *Porter*, 144. Beals was wrong about the inn's history as a monastery. He notes in 1978 that it was by then the Frissell museum.

27. ECP, *Mitla*, 9, 14–15, 60–62, and photographs following 8, 32, and 52.

28. Ibid., 60–61, also 3. For Mixe, see 365–69, 374–79, and photograph opp. 378.

29. Ibid., 10, 14–15, 60–61.

30. ECP, review of *Zuñi Mythology,* by Ruth Benedict, and *Zuñi Texts,* by Ruth Bunzel (1937); Bunzel, foreword to *Chichicastenango* (Locust Valley: J. J. Augustin, 1952), esp. xx, for comparison of her field methods and experience with other Boasians. See also Bunzel to ECP, [ca. 24 June 1930], APS, for beginning work in Chichicastenango; GR to ECP, 6 July 1930, APS, for similar methodology. Only Goldenweiser's fieldwork among the Northern Iroquois from 1911–12 is comparable. Mead spent several months in Samoa in 1925 and sought the same sort of intimacy with informants; but she lived with a missionary family and was primarily concerned with what the culture revealed about American society.

31. ECP, *Mitla*, vii. By "assimilation," ECP referred to what we would now call "acculturation." See definitions, viii–ix; and Melville Herskovits, *Acculturation* (New York: J. J. Augustin, 1938).

32. ECP, *Mitla,* 239–49, esp. 245–46.

33. Ibid., 248. See Francisco de Burgoa, *Geográfica descriptión* . . . (Mexico, 1674); ECP, "Zapotecan Prayers at New Year" (1930), 44–45, sketches by Eligio; "Increase by Magic: A Zuñi Pattern" (1919); "Spanish Elements," 589 n. 26a; "Institution of the Mayordomía," 74 and 76–78. The *mayordomía* during the fiesta of Mitla's major patron saint, San Pablo, included fireworks on elaborate cane frames that reminded ECP of *shalako* masks.

34. ECP, "The Canes" (1932). See *Mitla*, 168–75 and 155, and 181 for Starr's 1899 account. For town government, see 154–82 and photographs following 154.

35. ALK to ECP, 4 Jan. 1931, APS. During the 1920s, ALK did archeological work in Mexico City with Gamio and in Peru. See ALK-ECP corres., 26 June 1922–11 Nov. 1926, APS, RHS, and ALK Papers; Alfred L. Kroeber, "Cultural Relations between North and South America," *ICA Proceedings* (New York, 1930), 5–22.

36. ECP to ALK, 8 May, 6 June, and 30 Nov. 1931, ALK Papers; ECP to JEP, 13 Dec. 1931, APS; ECP to RHL, 17 Sept. 1931, RHL Papers; FB to ECP, 18 Nov. 1931, FB Papers; ECP to RLB, 1 May 1932, APS. ECP visited the Luhans at Taos on the way. For plans to meet, see RLB to ALK,

11 Jan. 1932; ALK to RLB, 12 Jan. 1932, ALK Papers; RLB to ECP, 17 Jan. and 13 Feb. 1932; RLB to Hare, 31 July 1978, APS.

37. Alan Knight, *The Mexican Revolution* (Cambridge: Cambridge University Press, 1986), 2:372–75; ALK to Sapir, 18 Apr. and 10 May 1930; Sapir to ALK, 5 May 1930, ALK Papers. See also Sapir to ALK, 18 Feb. 1931; ALK to Sapir, 24 Feb. 1931; and ALK to E. Day, 2 Oct. 1935, ALK Papers; ECP to ALK, 4 May 1933, APS.

38. Beals completed his Ph.D. at Berkeley in 1930 with a library dissertation on the ethnology of northern Mexico before 1750. See Walter Goldschmidt, "Ralph Leon Beals, 1901–1985," *AA* 88 (1986): 947–53, esp. 948–9; Beals, "Julian Steward: The Berkeley Days," *Julian Steward Anthropological Society* 6 (1979): 3–15; "Fifty Years in Anthropology," *Annual Review of Anthropology* 11 (1982): 1–23, esp. 6–9; and "Acculturation," in *Anthropology Today*, ed. Alfred L. Kroeber (Chicago: University of Chicago Press, 1952), 621–41, esp. 621–22; Carleton Beals, *Mexican Maze*, 186–88; John A. Britton, *Carleton Beals: A Radical Journalist in Latin America* (Albuquerque: University of New Mexico Press, 1987), 14–18, 94–99, 149. Ralph Beals says Kroeber considered "acculturation" a "fad" word in 1929. See ALK to Guggenheim Foundation, 7 Dec. 1933, ALK Papers: "ethnological studies in Mexico are of necessity what in this country it is customary to call acculturation studies, even if the ultimate objective is a reconstruction of the primitive ethnography." Melville Herskovits first used the term in the title of an AAA paper in Dec. 1928; but he used it earlier in the *Southwestern Political and Social Science Quarterly* 8 (1927): 211–25, probably as a result of his association with Boas and ECP, who had used it for years.

39. Ralph Beals, "Aboriginal Survivals in Mayo Culture," *AA* 34 (1932): 28–39, esp. 28, 37; Stuart Chase, *Mexico: A Study of Two Americas* (New York: Macmillan, 1931).

40. ECP to JEP, 20 Jan. and 20 Mar. 1932; also 28 Jan. and 21 Feb. 1932, fr. Mazatlán; 2 Mar. 1932, fr. Guaymas; RLB to Hare, 31 July 1978, APS. See also ECP to Tony Luhan, 11 Apr. 1932, MDL Papers.

41. RLB to Hare, 31 July 1978. See ECP to Leslie Spier, 9 Apr. 1934, APS.

42. RLB to Hare, 31 July 1978, APS.

43. ECP and Beals, "The Sacred Clowns of the Pueblo and Mayo-Yaqui Indians" (1934), 491. See 500–507 for the Fariseos, Diablos, and Soldados (Yaqui "Chapaiyeka"), who are recruited through vows, e.g., as a result of sickness, for good crops, to avoid drought or pest. They guard Christ's image and his servitors during Lent, police attendance at ceremonies, enforce taboos, and punish moral crimes, wearing masks and observing abstinence. They dance with Pilate and his group, with a final performance Easter Saturday when the Pascolas and Deer dancers drive them from the church and their costumes are burned.

44. RLB to Hare, 31 July 1978; also 19 Dec. 1978, APS. See RLB to Dorothy Beals, 1 and 29 Nov., 7 and 16 Dec. 1932, RLB Papers: "We talk mostly about anthropology but also about the deteriorations and compensations of age, bringing up children, marriage relations, and exhaustively gossip about other anthropologists and mutual friends." See JEP to

ECP, 18 Aug. 1932, APS: "Dear Doctor, Knowing your aversion for thank you notes, I am entrusting this epistle to a brave man and good sailor who is willing to think that the Pope leads a jolly life. He should therefore be able to withstand your telling him that among the Ubangi the bread and butter letter is unknown. Even the fact that with the Pishi-Wishi it is customary to throw a stone at one's host on departure should not disturb him. As the Winter People put it, I have had good sail, eat, sleep—many times. Of all the fish that swim in the sea give me the fin of an ox. Please see that my rubber boots (two pair) are put away for another season. I will bet both pair however that I will come back again for more of the same." For Mac's twenty-first birthday party see ECP to JEP, 2 Sept. 1932, fr. North Haven: "There never was such a birthday party—in our family. Two cakes . . . melon, lobster, filet of beef with mushrooms, sweet potatoes, tomato jelly salad, peach ice cream, cocktails, sherry or sparkling Burgandy, champagne, whiskey or brandy, liquers. . . . yesterday . . . Mac & I were second boat and led the fleet through a short passage that had never been taken before. But we came in third. Business tomorrow." For a glimpse of his life at Yale, see Mac to ECP, 14 Dec. 1932: "Life has been wonderful and gives signs of continuing so. Only I envy you Mexico, if that's where you are, and miss you. I study . . . play squash furiously . . . take frequent weekends in NYC in my beautiful automobile and get arrested . . . write News editorials in sixty minutes. . . . I fall in love again, but with the same girl. . . . I lunch or tea with Lissa, & John and Fanny. I listen to Manga on the divine right of kings. . . . I pay most of my bills. . . . I write letters . . ."

45. RLB to ALK, 7 Apr. 1932, ALK Papers. Cf. RLB to ECP, 13 Feb. 1932, APS, fr. Ciudad Obregón: "All the arrangements have been made for me to visit the wild Yaquis in the hills near here but the Mexican army authorities so far will not hear of my making the trip. If I can I think I will do it for a few days. I should of course like to stay longer there but the conditions are bad. . . . But I think substantially as good work can be done among the settled Yaquis here in the valley. Vicam is probably the best town to work, it being the only one with a hotel of a sort." For ECP's influence, see RLB to ECP, 26 Apr. 1932; ECP to RLB, 1 May and 22 July 1932, APS.

46. ECP to JEP, 31 Mar. and 3 Apr. 1932; also 2 Mar. 1932, APS. Robert Herrick, *The End of Desire* (New York: Farrar and Rinehart, 1932), had a brief *succès de scandale*. According to an advertisement in Herrick's papers a first print run of 3,500 and a second of 2,500, ordered because of prepublication reviews, sold in a few days after "big" reviews; there was a third printing of 5,000, and paper was ordered for a fourth. For reactions by feminist friends of Herrick and ECP, see Neith Boyce, "The Eternal Feminist," *NR*, 9 Mar. 1932, and Mabel Dodge Luhan, "Decline of the Male," letter to editor, *NR*, 20 Apr. 1932. For reviews sympathetic to the Herrick character, see Harry Hansen, "The First Reader," *World-Telegram*, 5 Jan. 1932; and "Books in Brief," *Nation*, 9 Feb. 1932, 291–92: "The woman is one of the most disagreeable, hateful creatures in recent fiction."

47. ECP to ALK, 7 Oct. 1932, ALK Papers; ALK to ECP, 15 Oct. 1932, APS; ECP, "Spring Days in Zuñi, New Mexico" (1933).

48. ECP to RLB, 1 May 1932, APS. See RLB to Dorothy, 6 Feb. 1933, RLB Papers; RLB to ALK, 7 Apr. 1932, ALK Papers; RHL to ECP, 26 Apr., 11 and 13 July, and 12 Sept. 1932; ECP-ALK corres., Aug. 1932–June 1933, APS and ALK Papers. Beals told Hare, 19 Dec. 1978, APS, that his $100 a month was the first stipend, as distinct from field expenses, that ECP paid; but she had paid a fellowship to Benedict earlier.

49. ECP to MDL, 12 Nov. and 1 Dec. 1932, MDL Papers; Brenner, *Mexican Holiday*, 36. See ECP to MDL, 18 Feb. 1931, MDL Papers; Mabel Dodge Luhan, *Intimate Memories: Background* (New York: Harcourt, Brace, 1933); also ECP to JEP, 2 Dec. 1932, APS. For the Luhans' first trip to "old Mexico," see ECP to JEP, 15 Dec. 1930, APS: "His braids make him a conspicuous figure in a city where they try to forget they were ever Indian"; and ECP to Leslie White, 7 Feb. 1931, LW Papers: "Tony speaks Spanish like a Mexican herder."

50. ECP to MDL, 1 Dec. 1932, MDL Papers; RLB to Dorothy, 18 Nov. 1932; also 23 and 27 Nov. and 4 Dec. 1932, RLB Papers. For abandoning a trip to the Cora in the Sierra, see RLB to Dorothy, 18 Nov. 1932, RLB Papers: "Everyone holds up his hands in horror at the thought of a woman making the trip. Five to six days riding, 8 or 9 hours a day, sleeping in *rancherías,* eating where one can, over very rough trails, doesn't sound too good for Elsie"—or for himself, as he was feeling wretched with a cold. See also RLB to ALK, 6 Dec. 1932, ALK Papers: "Elsie drew the line at a mountain trip—five or six days on horseback—and the country does look damnably rough."

51. RLB to Hare, 31 July 1978, APS; Beals, "Fifty Years," 6–9.

52. Ibid.

53. RLB to Hare, 31 July 1978, APS. See also ECP to MDL, 18 Feb. 1931, MDL Papers, for Preuss; ECP to Leslie Spier, 9 Apr. 1934, for Beals's lack of fieldwork technique. See ECP, notes to Leslie White, on White to ECP, 11 Oct. 1935, APS: "Everybody likes [Beals]. He is not a first class field worker, not the insistent detective type."

54. RLB to Dorothy, 7 and 9 Dec. 1932, RLB Papers. For details, see RLB-Dorothy corres., 12 Nov.–16 Dec. 1932, RLB Papers; RLB to ALK, 6 Dec. 1932, ALK Papers.

55. ECP to FB, draft, [Dec. 1932], APS. See also ECP to ALK, 16 Dec. 1932, ALK Papers. Cf. ECP to R. Zingg, July 1934, APS: "I hope you plan a thorough description of the Huichol before testing theories, otherwise you will put yourself in the class of Lumholtz and Preuss who have been, at least Preuss, the despair of anthropologists for years"; ECP to ALK, 7 Jan. 1935, ALK Papers, re publication of Zingg by the Laboratory of Anthropology.

56. Brenner, *Mexican Holiday*, 36–37; RLB to Dorothy, 10 Dec., also 9 Dec. 1932, RLB Papers. For Lawrence, see Witter Bynner, *Journey with Genius* (New York: John Day, 1951).

57. ECP to MDL, 26 Dec. 1933, MDL Papers. See also RLB to Dorothy, 13 or 14 Dec. 1932, RLB Papers.

58. RLB to Dorothy, 13 Dec. 1932–24 Jan. 1933 (esp. 13 or 14 and 24 Dec.), 7 Jan. 1933, RLB Papers. See ECP to Dorothy, 1 Jan. 1933, RLB Papers; RLB to Hare, 31 July and 19 Dec. 1978, APS.

59. RLB to ALK, 6 Dec. 1932, ALK Papers; RLB to Dorothy, 7 and 30

Dec. 1932, and 7 Jan. 1933, RLB Papers. For their debate, see RLB to ALK, 7 Apr. 1932, ALK Papers; RLB to ECP, 13 Feb. 1932; ECP to RLB, 22 July 1932, APS; Fray Bernardino de Sahagún, *A History of Ancient Mexico, 1547–1577,* books 1–4, trans. Fanny R. Bandelier (Nashville, 1932).

60. ECP and Beals, "Sacred Clowns," 508–9, 506. See also RLB to ECP, 22 June 1934; Leslie Spier to ECP, 12 Mar. and 7 Apr. 1934; ECP to RLB, 20 Aug. 1934, APS.

61. RHL to ECP, 27 Nov. 1933, APS.

62. ECP, *Mitla,* viii; "Some Aztec and Pueblo Parallels" (1933), 611, 621. See RHL to ECP, 31 May 1933; RLB to ECP, 22 June 1933, APS; ECP to White, 23 Aug. 1933, LW Papers. See ECP, *Pueblo Indian Religion* (1939), for extensive Aztec references.

63. ECP, "Some Aztec and Pueblo Parallels," 625–27, 611, 629, 630. See also ECP to RLB, 20 Aug. 1934, APS, thanking him for Robert Ricard, *La "Conquete Spirituelle" du Mexique* (Paris: Institut d'Ethnologie, 1933), in which she found "a new point of view in regard to the friars withholding confession and the last sacrament instead of trying to get them across. The failure of these to 'take' had seemed puzzling."

64. ECP, *Mitla,* 479, 536. See preface, vi.

Chapter Fifteen

1. ECP to JEP, 2 Feb. and 10 Mar. 1933; GY to ECP, 28 Mar. 1933, APS. Young had recently succeeded to the baronetcy on his father's death. ECP's letters to John begin: "You will think I am exaggerating, but truly, I enjoy your letters more than anything else in this vivid but very objective Mexico," and "I have your letter of March 1, which makes me feel like starting homeward." For Beals's week with ECP in Mitla, see RLB to Hare, 31 July 1978, APS; RLB to Dorothy, 15–30 Jan. 1933, fr. Mitla, and 18 Feb. 1933, fr. Mixe country, RLB Papers. His Mixe work provides one of the many comparative strands that gives *Mitla* its extraordinary richness. For publication of his Mixe material, see ECP to ALK, 7 Jan. 1935, ALK Papers; Beals, "Modern Serpent Beliefs in Mexico," *MFW* 8 (Apr.–June 1933): 77–82; "Problems in the Study of Mixe Marriage Customs," in *Essays in Anthropology Presented to A. L. Kroeber* (Berkeley: University of California Press, 1936); and *Ethnology of the Western Mixe Indians,* University of California Publications in Anthropology and Archeology 42, no. 1 (1945), 1–176. ECP hoped to fund Beals and Bunzel for work on the Cora and the Huichol, but stock market losses cut her income and Boas already had plans to send Otto Klineberg to the Huichol. See ECP to ALK, 4 May 1933, ALK Papers; ALK to ECP, 22 May 1933; RLB to ECP, 22 June 1933; and RHL to ECP, 12 Nov. 1933, APS; ALK to Guggenheim Foundation, 7 Dec. 1933, ALK; also FB to ECP, 21 July 1931; Mischa Titiev to ECP, 23 Mar. 1936, APS, re "Note on parallels between the Cora-Huichol and the Pueblos." Ralph Beals, along with Julian Steward, Paul Radin, and Mischa Titiev, did ethnohistorical research in the National Park Service run by Kroeber's friend Hank Alsberg until ECP helped him to get an offer from Leslie White at University of Michigan in 1935. But he went to the psychology department at UCLA in 1936, where he insti-

tuted an anthropology and sociology program that became a separate department under his leadership in 1940. He returned to the Tarascan area near Lake Chapala from 1940–41 to do a community study of Cherán as part of a joint U.S.-Mexican project. See Beals, "Fifty Years"; Goldschmidt, "Beals"; White to ECP, 11 and 20 Oct. 1936; RHL to ECP, 17 Oct. 1936; RLB to ECP, 17 Nov. 1937 and 23 Jan. 1939, APS; ALK to Alsberg, draft, 7 Dec. 1935, ALK Papers.

2. ECP, *Mitla* (1936), 397–98. See photographs of Eligio before and after, following 396.

3. Ibid., 398–400, 249–50. See also ECP to JEP, 2 Feb. 1933, APS.

4. ECP to MDL, 26 Dec. 1933; also 12 Jan. 1934, MDL Papers; ECP to ALK, 12 May 1934, ALK Papers.

5. ALK to ECP, 27 Dec. 1934; also ECP to RLB, 20 Aug. 1934; B. W. Huebsch to ECP, 29 Oct. 1934; Robert Redfield to ECP, 4 Mar. 1935, also 16 Aug. and 19 Dec. 1935, APS; ECP to ALK, 7 Jan. 1935, ALK Papers.

6. ECP, "Town Gossip," in *Mitla*, 386–478, esp. 386–87.

7. C. M. Leslie, *Now We Are Civilized* (Detroit: Wayne State University Press, 1960), went to Mitla wanting to know if Eligio and Petronila were still alive but unfortunately neglects to tell us.

8. FB to ECP, 3 Sept. 1936; Franz Boas, "A Mexican Village," *NR,* 10 Mar. 1937; also ECP to Benedict, 6 Nov. 1936, re her review in *NYHT,* APS.

9. H.B.N., *Christian Science Monitor,* 2 Sept. 1936; *Sun,* 6 Dec. 1936; Gladys Reichard, "Indian or Spanish?" *Survey Graphic,* Jan. 1937; and *Barnard College Alumnae,* Feb. 1937. See also *Scientific Monthly,* Nov. 1936; Oliver LaFarge, *Saturday Review of Literature,* 16 Jan. 1937; Clark Wissler, *Journal of Social Philosophy,* July 1937, 284–85; *World Affairs,* June 1937.

10. Arthur Ficke to ECP, 14 Sept. 1936. See also MDL to ECP, [1936], APS.

11. *SSRC Annual Report* (New York, 1934–35), 23–24; Robert Redfield, Ralph Linton, and Melville Herskovits, "Outline for the Study of Acculturation" (1936), reprinted as "Memorandum for the Study of Acculturation," *AA* 38 (1936): 149–52, and in Herskovits, *Acculturation* (New York: J. J. Augustin, 1938). See G. E. Simpson, *Melville J. Herskovits* (New York: Columbia University Press, 1973), 84–92, for later history; and Adelin Linton and Charles Wagley, *Ralph Linton* (New York: Columbia University Press, 1971), 51 for significance of the "Memorandum."

12. Leslie Spier to ECP, 16 Nov. 1935, APS.

13. Herskovits review, *Annals of the American Academy of Political and Social Science,* Mar. 1937, APS. Cf. ECP, "Two Methods in Ethnological Hypothesis" (1915), APS. See also Beals review, *AA* 39 (1937): 681–82; and Robert Redfield's in *MFW,* July 1937, 70–72. For a more critical assessment, see Sol Tax, *ASR* 2 (1937): 135–36.

14. ECP to MDL, 18 May 1934, MDL Papers; ECP to Williams, 30 Nov. 1934, APS. See also ECP to RLB, 20 Aug. 1934, APS; Mac to Lissa, 27 June 1934; ECP to James Sheffield, 30 Nov. 1934, APS (Sheffield was a former ambassador to Mexico whose policies ECP disapproved of strongly).

15. ECP to JEP, 2 Mar. 1935, APS. See also ECP to ALK, 7 Jan. 1935,

ALK Papers; ECP to MDL, 25 Jan. 1935, MDL Papers; ECP to RHL, 22 Feb. 1935, RHL Papers.

16. ECP to MDL, 16 Mar. and 15 Sept. 1936, MDL Papers. For illness, see Spier to ECP, 29 Apr. 1935; for Mac and Ogden Reid, Ogden Mills to ECP, 17 Sept. 1935, APS.

17. ECP, preface to *Hopi Journal of Alexander M. Stephen*, 2 vols. (1936), xxi; review (unidentified), APS. Stephen assisted Mindeleff's study of Hopi building and Fewkes's Hemenway expedition. ECP sounded Stewart Culin out about editing the journals at the anthropology meetings hosted by the Brooklyn Museum in 1921, following her Hopi fieldwork in 1920 and 1921. See ALK to ECP, 1 Jan. 1922, RHS; ECP to MDL, 28 Nov. 1922, MDL Papers; ECP, $500 check to Culin, 16 Apr. 1923; Culin to ECP, 17 Apr. 1923, RHS.

18. ECP, *Hopi Journal,* xxiv; Leslie White, review, *AA* 40 (1938). ECP, incidentally, also wrote with a clear hand.

19. ECP, *Hopi Journal,* xx–xxii, li–lii.

20. ECP to RHL, 11 and 12 Nov. 1927, APS; 7 Aug. and 8 Oct. 1929. See also ECP to RHL, 17 Sept. 1931, RHL Papers, and 22 Feb. 1935, APS; ECP to FB, 15 Oct. 1931 and 6 Jan. 1933; FB to ECP, 18 Nov. 1931, 3 Jan. 1933, and 6 Nov. 1936, FB Papers; ECP to Benedict, 6 Nov. 1936, APS, for publication. See ECP, ed., "Hopi Tales," by Alexander M. Stephen (1929); and review of *Notes on Hopi Clans* and *Hopi Kinship,* by Robert H. Lowie (1931).

21. ECP, introduction to *Hopi Journal,* xlix–l; RHL to ECP, 31 Jan. 1937, APS. See appendix 3 for "Who's Who." ECP also prepared a "Who's Who in Isleta," which she omitted from *Isleta, New Mexico* (1932) to protect her sources. Esther Goldfrank included it in *The Artist of "Isleta Paintings" in Pueblo Society,* Smithsonian Contributions to Anthropology 5 (Washington, D.C., 1967), 19–26. See Esther Schiff Goldfrank, *Notes on an Undirected Life: As One Anthropologist Tells It* (Flushing, N.Y.: Queens College Press, 1978).

22. White review (1938).

23. ECP to RHL, 24 Oct. 1936; Redfield to ECP, 13 Dec. 1937, APS. See Redfield-ECP corres., Jan. 1937–June 1939; also Leslie Spier to ECP, 29 July 1936, APS; ECP to RHL, 8 Jan., 10 May, 23 July, and 9 Nov. 1937, RHL Papers; RHL to ECP, 20 May, 19 and 31 July, and 13 Aug. 1937, APS; 27 Aug. 1937, RHL Papers; and 3 Jan. 1938, APS; White to ECP, 4 Apr. 1938, APS.

24. FB to ECP, 11 Sept. 1936; GR to ECP, 27 Oct. 1939, APS. See also FB to ECP, 3 Sept. 1936, 18 Oct. 1938, and 22 Oct. 1940, APS. For Boas arguments, see "Nordic Propaganda," *NR,* Mar. 1934; "Aryans and Non-Aryans," *American Mercury,* June 1934; "Race Prejudice from the Scientist's Angle," *Forum,* July 1937; "Science in Nazi Germany," *Survey Graphic,* Aug. 1937; and other articles in *Race and Democratic Society* (New York: J. J. Augustin, 1945); also Margaret M. Caffrey, *Ruth Benedict: Stranger in This Land* (Austin: University of Texas Press, 1989), 282–91; Melville Herskovits, *Franz Boas* (New York: Charles Scribner's Sons, 1953); George W. Stocking Jr., "Anthropology as Kulturkampf: Science and Politics in the Career of Franz Boas," in *The Uses of Anthropology,* ed. Walter Goldschmidt (Washington: AAA, 1979); M. Hyatt, *Franz Boas,*

Social Activist: The Dynamics of Ethnicity (New York: Greenwood Press, 1990), 144–50; Sara Alpern, *Freda Kirchwey: A Woman of the* Nation (Cambridge: Harvard University Press, 1987), 113. See "Scientists Form Group to Help Save Democracy" and interview with Einstein, *NYHT*, 31 Dec. 1938 and 14 Mar. 1939; and "Prof Percy Bridgman Slams Door on Science from Totalitarian Countries," *Fort Meyers News-Press*, 26 Feb. 1939, clippings, APS.

25. ECP, review of *An American in the Making*, by M. E. Ravage (1918).

26. ECP to RHL, 6 Jan. 1938, RHL Papers; ECP to ALK, 31 Aug. 1939, ALK Papers; ALK to ECP, 30 Sept. 1939, APS. See ECP, "Patterns for Peace or War" (1917); Robert Lowie, *The History of Anthropological Theory* (New York: Farrar and Rinehart, 1937). For private indignation about Roosevelt's "war psychology a la Wilson" and "moralizing for the world" in response to the Japanese invasion of China, see ECP to JEP, 13 Oct. 1937, APS: "A country that excludes Orientals better not talk about what they do."

27. Francis Hackett to ECP, 13 May 1940; Learned Hand to ECP, 24 Dec. 1918 and 9 Feb. 1940, APS.

28. ECP, *Pueblo Indian Religion* (1939), 1:xiii–xiv. See ECP to Wissler, 3 Jan. 1918, APS. *Pueblo Indian Religion* has just been reprinted by University of Nebraska Press (1996) with introductions by Pauline Turner Strong and Ramón Gutiérrez.

29. ECP, *Pueblo Indian Religion*, xiii, xii.

30. Ibid., x–xii, esp. x, xi. Cf. *Social Rule* (1916).

31. ECP, *Pueblo Indian Religion*, xiii–xiv.

32. Ibid., 939–44, esp. 939.

33. Ibid., 968–69.

34. Ibid., 1085, 1097, 1101–4, 1122–24, 1127.

35. Ibid., 1127, 1131, 1150, 1165. For Ramirez, who built a church at Acoma ca. 1629, see *Pueblo Indian Religion*, 881; for Kashale, the Acoma clowns, 885.

Chapter Sixteen

1. MKS to ECP, 31 May 1940. See Mrs. F. Thurber to ECP, 18 Mar. 1940, APS; Margaret Mead, *Blackberry Winter* (Sydney: Angus and Robertson, 1981), 252–53; Mary Kingsbury Simkhovitch, *Neighborhood: My Story of Greenwich House* (New York: W. W. Norton, 1938); Carroll Smith-Rosenberg, "Mary Kingsbury Simkhovitch," *NAW*.

2. Mary Knoblauch to ECP, 5 Mar. 1937, writing at the suggestion of the experimental educator Elisabeth Irwin. See ECP, appt. cal., 17 Mar. and 14 Apr. 1938, APS; Judith Schwarz, *Radical Feminists of Heterodoxy* (Norwich, Vt.: New Victoria Publishers, 1986), 97–102.

3. Mabel Dodge Luhan, *Intimate Memories: Background* (1933), *European Experiences* (1935), *Movers and Shakers* (1936), and *Edge of Taos Desert* (1937). Alice Duer Miller's long poem *The White Cliffs* (1940) extolling Britain's resistance had sold 200,000 copies when she died in 1942. For birth control, see *NYHT*, 28 Mar. 1938 and 2 Jan. 1939; and *NR*, 20 Apr. 1938, 324–26, clippings, APS; David M. Kennedy, *Birth*

Control in America: The Career of Margaret Sanger (New Haven: Yale University Press, 1970), 248–51; James Reed, "Katharine Dexter McCormick," *NAW Mod.* MIT's Stanley McCormick Hall was dedicated in Oct. 1963. Katharine left $5 million to Stanford Medical Center "for the encouragement and assistance of women in pursuing the study of medicine, in teaching medicine, and in engaging in medical research," $5 million to Planned Parenthood, and $1 million to the Worcester Foundation for Experimental Biology.

4. Signe Toksvig to ECP, 24 Apr. 1939 and 12 Jan. 1940; Hand to ECP, 9 Feb. 1940, APS. For Lippmann, see MDL to ECP, 7 Nov. 1937, APS. For Sorchan, see Mabel Detmold, *The Brownstones of Turtle Bay Gardens* (New York, 1964). For Betty Hare, see Jane Elkind Bowers, "Gender and Geography" (seminar paper, University of Texas at Austin, 1994). Since 1912, Young had published a series of distinguished books on the Balkans, Portugal, Germany, Constantinople, Egypt, and Spain. See GY to ECP, 30 Jan. 1929, 25 June and 27 Oct. 1930, 11 Sept. 1932, and 28 Mar. 1933, APS.

5. ECP to JEP, 2 Mar. 1926, APS. For Henry Clews Jr., see obituary, *NYT*, 29 July 1937; JEP to ECP, 18 Oct. 1937 and 10 May 1939, APS; Metropolitan Museum of Art, *Exhibition of Sculpture by Henry Clews, Jr.* (1939); "Never-Never Land," *Time*, 31 July 1939, 32; Beatrice Gilman Proske, *Henry Clews, Jr., Sculptor* (Brookgreen, S.C., 1953). He dedicated his play, *Mumbo Jumbo* (New York: Boni and Liveright, 1923), to "my beautiful and beloved Mother, and my beautiful and beloved Wife." See admiring review in *NYT Book Review*, 22 Apr. 1923. He married the recently divorced Louise Morris Gebhard in 1901, and after their divorce in 1910, the recently divorced Marie Elsie Whelen Goelet. He had two children, Henry and Louise, from his first marriage and a son, Madison, from his second. For his family, see *NYT*, 26 Aug. 1930, 25; 13 Feb. 1937; and 8 May 1939; obituary, Mrs. Henry Clews, *NYT*, 16 Apr. 1959, 33; and interview with Dr. McIlvaine Parsons, 20 May 1991. His chateau, La Napoule, which he transformed with his sculpture, is now the La Napoule Art Foundation of the University of the State of New York. For ECP's family, see appt. cal., 22 July 1938; JEP to ECP, 24 Sept. 1940; for birth of Marnie and Peter (David) to HP Jr. and Margot, Toksvig to ECP, 17 May 1939; HP Jr. to ECP, 1 Mar. 1941, APS.

6. ECP, Report to Mr. and Mrs. John E. Parsons on their son Richard, 21 June 1939; ECP to JEP, [21 Mar.] 1938. See also ECP to JEP, 26 Sept. 1937; JEP to ECP, 5 Jan. 1938; Margaret Mead to ECP, 4 June 1939; ECP to JEP, 6 July 1939, APS.

7. Lissa to ALK, 30 Nov. 1943, ALK Papers. See ECP to JEP, 13 Oct. 1937, APS.

8. For the Rocks, see LPK, 18, and JEP to ECP, 3 Oct. 1938, APS. See Oliver LaFarge, "Salt Water," in *Raw Material* (New York: Houghton Mifflin, 1945), 23–35, esp. 30–35; and "Old Man Facing Death," 36–48; D'Arcy McNickle, *Indian Man* (Bloomington: Indiana University Press, 1971), 115, 127–28; obituary, *NYT*, 12 Oct. 1938, 27.

9. L. J. Budd, *Robert Herrick* (New York: Twayne, 1971), 120–21; Ernest Gruening, *Many Battles* (New York: Liveright, 1973), 183–85. See Herrick, "The Race Problem in the Caribbean," *Nation*, 11 and 18 June

1924, 675–76, 699–700; "Advising U.S. to Get Out of Haiti, Prof. Herrick Accuses Marines," *NYW*, 10 Apr. 1927, 11E; and "Magic, Black and White," *NR*, 30 Jan. 1929, 298–99.

10. ALK to ECP, 24 Aug. 1939, APS; ECP to ALK, 31 Aug. 1939, ALK Papers; ALK to ECP, 30 Sept. 1939, APS. These are the last letters from Kroeber in ECP's papers.

11. Theodora Kroeber, *Alfred Kroeber: A Personal Configuration* (Berkeley: University of California Press, 1970), 170–74, esp. letter to Harcourt, Brace, 170; ECP, "Prospects," in notes for "How the World Changes: An Essay in Anthropologic Philosophy" (1939–41), esp. 1, APS. See Alfred L. Kroeber, *Configurations of Culture Growth* (Berkeley: University of California Press, 1944).

12. See J. H. Steward, *Alfred Kroeber* (New York: Columbia University Press, 1973).

13. NMB to FB, Nov. 1935, APS; H. P. Robbins to ECP, 7 May 1936, APS; Kroeber, *Kroeber*, 155–57; Regna Darnell, *Edward Sapir: Linguist, Anthropologist, Humanist* (Berkeley: University of California Press, 1990); Margaret M. Caffrey, *Ruth Benedict: Stranger in This Land* (Austin: University of Texas Press, 1989), 276–77.

14. See FB to Columbia dean, 28 Jan. 1937, FB Papers, re unsuitability of Linton and recommending Benedict, Strong, Lesser, or Herzog; Adelin Linton and Charles Wagley, *Ralph Linton* (New York: Columbia University Press, 1971); GR to ECP, 11 and 27 Oct. 1937; RHL to ECP, 20 May and 31 July 1937, APS; FB to Benedict, 24 Oct. and 20 Dec. 1937, in *An Anthropologist at Work: The Writings of Ruth Benedict*, ed. Margaret Mead (Westport, Conn.: Greenwood Press, 1977), 413–14, 416, also 128; Linton to Benedict, 19 June 1939, in Caffrey, *Benedict*, 277.

15. ALK to Tozzer, draft, 4 Dec. 1934, ALK Papers; ECP, appt. cal., 25 Feb.–6 Mar. 1938, APS. For Columbia department, see ALK to Duncan Strong, draft, 14 Nov. 1936; for department when Linton left for Yale, see Strong to ALK, 31 Nov. 1945, ALK Papers.

16. ECP to ALK, 31 Aug. 1939, ALK Papers; ALK to ECP, 30 Sept. 1939, APS; Strong to ECP, [Dec. 1939], APS. See also Strong to ALK, 10 Feb. 1942, ALK Papers: "I agree with your comments in regard to Elsie. Being in New York I felt it as an extremely personal loss and have been much more deeply affected than I would have expected. She was a most unusual and very interesting person."

17. Ralph Solecki and Charles Wagley, "William Duncan Strong, 1899–1962," *AA* 65 (1963): 1102–11.

18. Clyde Kluckhohn, "The Conceptual Structure in Middle American Studies," in *The Maya and Their Neighbors*, ed. Clarence L. Hay et al. (New York: Appleton-Century, 1940), 41–51. See Strong-Mekeel-Kluckhohn-Opler-ECP corres., 7 June 1937–28 Nov. 1941, APS; ECP, "Relations between Ethnology and Archeology in the Southwest" (1940; written 1938); and "A Pre-Spanish Record of Hopi Ceremonies" (1940). For her unhappy experience on the laboratory publications committee see ECP-ALK-Kidder-Spier-Tozzer corres., 8 May 1931–14 Jan. 1935.

19. ECP to Steward, 26 Nov. 1939, APS. See Steward to ECP, 27 Nov. 1939 and 26 Feb. 1940, cited in Rosemary Lévy Zumwalt, *Wealth and Rebellion: Elsie Clews Parsons, Anthropologist and Folklorist* (Urbana:

University of Illinois Press, 1992), 300; Julian Steward, ed., *Handbook of South American Indians,* BAE Bulletin 143, 7 vols. (Washington, D.C., 1946–50), esp. preface to vol. 2, *The Andean Civilizations* (1944), xxvi. For Steward, see P. J. Bohannan and M. Glazer, eds., *High Points in Anthropology* (New York: Knopf, 1973), 319–20.

20. White to ECP, 8 May 1931; Kluckhohn to ECP, 12 Jan., also 22 Jan. 1941, APS. See AAA Program, Chicago, 27–30 Dec. 1939; Philadelphia, 27–30 Dec. 1940; Setzler to ECP, 31 Dec. 1940, APS; *AA* 42 (1940): 373. For election to executive committee with Redfield and Linton, see Redfield to ECP, 6 Jan. 1937 and Setzler to ECP, 3 Jan. 1938, APS. For Benedict as first woman admitted to the chain of command in 1938 and as president in 1946, see Caffrey, *Benedict,* 281. For 1910–44 see Betty J. Meggars, "Recent Trends in American Ethnology," *AA* 48 (1946): 176–214. For ironic comment on her own up-to-dateness, see ECP to ALK, 8 Sept. 1939, ALK Papers.

21. Harold Stearns, introduction to *America Now: An Inquiry into Civilization in the United States by Thirty-Six Americans* (1938), x, ix; Gerald Johnson, *NYHT Books,* 6 Nov. 1938, 2, ix. See Stearns to ECP, 3 and 13 Aug., 19 and 31 Dec. 1937, APS.

22. ECP, "The Family," in Stearns, *America Now,* 404–6, 408.

23. RHL to ECP, 26 July 1935 and 17 Oct. 1936, APS; ECP to RHL, 24 Oct. 1936, RHL Papers. See also RHL to ECP, 25 Mar. and 28 Oct. 1936; ECP, appt. cal., 7 and 13 Dec. 1938; AAA Program, N.Y., 27–30 Dec. 1938, APS.

24. Gladys Reichard, "Elsie Clews Parsons," *JAFL* 56 (Jan.–Mar. 1943): 45–48, esp. 47. See ECP, *Peguche* (1945), 149; [?] to Victor Eastman Cox, Francisco A. Uribe (son-in-law of *hacendada* of Cusin), Juan Marios Jr., Minister and Mrs. Bullock; "Notes on Letters for Mrs Parsons" and "ECP notes," in "South American Trip"; Strong to ECP, 20 Feb. 1940; Lissa to Colley, 1 Mar. 1940, APS.

25. ECP, *Peguche,* 7–13, esp. 13.

26. Ibid., 150; John Murra, "The Historic Tribes of Ecuador," in *The Andean Civilizations,* 785–821, esp. 819–20. Murra draws heavily on ECP for his description of highlands society. See photographs from ECP's Ecuador work following 814.

27. ECP, *Peguche,* 151, 163, 150.

28. ECP to RHL, 21 May 1940 and 10 Feb. 1941, RHL Papers; Garcilaso de la Vega, *Comentarios reales, que tratan del origen de los Incas* (Lisbon, 1609).

29. ECP, *Peguche,* 169. For trip see E. Tweedy to ECP, 28 Sept. 1941; JEP to ECP, 6 Oct. 1941, APS.

30. GR to ALK, 19 Dec. 1941, ALK Papers. See Eggan to ECP, 17 Dec. 1941; FB to ECP, 25 Nov. 1941, APS.

31. *NYHT,* 20 Dec. 1941; ECP to HP, [14 Sept. 1921]; ECP to Lissa, 11 Feb. 1940, APS. See ECP, "Memo for H.P.," [19 Sept. 1921?]; ECP to JEP, 4 Sept. 1930; FB to ECP, 10 Feb. 1931; Leslie Spier to ECP, 29 Apr. 1935; Last Will and Testament of Elsie Clews Parsons, dated 26 May 1938, admitted to probate 22 Jan. 1942; RLB to Hare, 31 July 1978, APS. See also obituary, *NYT,* 20 Dec. 1941; and for AFLS bequest, *NYT,* 10 Jan. 1942, 18.

32. ECP, "Family Faculties"; C. A. Herter to ECP, 30 July 1909, with ECP to HP, 3 Aug. 1909; ECP to HP, 11 and 14 Nov. and 16 Dec. 1909; Fitz to ECP, 2 and 16 Dec. 1909; Dr. Paddock to HP, 30 Aug. 1911; ECP to HP, 1, 4, and 12 Oct. 1911; LPK, 12–13, APS. See "Pregnancy," in *The New Encyclopaedia Britannica* (Chicago: University of Chicago Press, 1974).

33. ECP to Mac, 7 Dec. 1941, postmark 8 Dec., 1 P.M., copy fr. Dr. McIlvaine Parsons; Lissa to ALK, 30 Nov. 1943, ALK Papers; Hare note, 3 Aug. 1976, APS. For Dewey, see John Patrick Diggins, *The Promise of Pragmatism* (Chicago: University of Chicago Press, 1994), 1–2.

34. Hare note, APS; ECP, "The World Changes" (1939–41) (160 pp.), with final chapter "Prospects," APS.

35. ECP, "Anthropology and Prediction" (1942), 338–39. See AAA Draft Program, Andover, 27–30 Dec. 1941, APS. ECP was responding to a 30 July 1939 SSRC report questioning the usefulness of inquiries "of no substantial social value, either in promise for the future or relevance for the present." See draft AAA resolution deploring the report; ECP to ALK, 31 Aug. 1939, ALK Papers, APS; E. E. Day, foreword to *An Appraisal of Thomas and Znaniecki's "The Polish Peasant in Europe and America,"* by Herbert Blumer, SSRC Bulletin 44 (New York, 1939), viii, reporting that the Committee on Review of Policy's recommendation that "intellectual leadership in the facilitation and coordination of research in the social sciences be reasserted as the dominant and controlling purpose of the Council" was sharply opposed by members and resolved itself into an appraisal of six social science works, of which this was the first. For the policy implications of her Ecuador work see ECP, "Memo on Relations with Spanish America," 15 June 1940, APS. The Society for Applied Anthropology was organized in 1941.

36. ECP, "Anthropology and Prediction" (1942), 339.

37. Ibid., 341, 343–44. See Cole, "The Relation of Anthropology to Indian and Immigrant Affairs."

38. Paul Radin, *Hispanic American Historical Review*, May 1946, 245–46. John Murra and Anibal Buitron prepared *Peguche* for press and ECP's children paid for its publication.

39. ECP to ALK, 6 Feb. 1916, ALK Papers; Reichard, "Elsie Clews Parsons," 48. For ECP Memorial Number see *JAFL* 56 (Jan.–Mar. 1943), which contains Reichard's obituary, ECP's bibliography, and articles by Herskovits, Beals, Goldfrank, and Aurelio Espinosa, whose Hispanic folklore collection ECP subsidized generously. The *AA* issue with Spier's and ALK's obituaries also fittingly published articles on acculturation and applied anthropology from the centenary celebrations of the American Ethnological Society.

40. Leslie Spier, "Elsie Clews Parsons," *AA* 45 (1943): 244–51, esp. 245.

41. Alfred L. Kroeber, "Elsie Clews Parsons," *AA* 45 (1943): 252–55, esp. 255.

42. Franz Boas, "Obituary: Elsie Clews Parsons," *Science*, 23 Jan. 1942, 89–90, esp. 90.

The following list is chronological within years and includes selected
unpublished works.

1896 [Elsie W. Clews.] "The History of the Monroe Doctrine from 1822 to
1861: A Study on Public Opinion." Manuscript. American Philosophical
Society Library.

1897 [Elsie W. Clews.] "On Certain Phases of Poor-Relief in the City of
New York." M.A. thesis, Columbia University.

1898 [Elsie W. Clews.] "The Status of the Study of Pedagogics in the
American College and University." *Journal of Pedagogy* 11 (Jan.):
51–60.

1899 [Elsie W. Clews.] *Educational Legislation and Administration of the
Colonial Governments.* Columbia University Contributions to Philoso-
phy, Psychology, and Education 6. New York: Macmillan. Reprint, New
York: Arno Press, 1971.

1900 [Elsie W. Clews.] "Field Work in Teaching Sociology." *Educational
Review* 19 (Sept.): 159–69.

1903 Trans. *The Laws of Imitation,* by Gabriel Tarde, with an introduction
by Franklin H. Giddings. New York: Henry Holt and Company. Translated from *Les Lois de l'imitation,* 2d ed. (Paris, 1895).

1904–7 "Little Essays in Lifting Taboo." Manuscript. American Philo-
sophical Society Library.
"The Aim of Productive Efficiency in Education."
"Caste and the Unproductive Activities of the American Woman."
"A Compromise Plan for Girls with Nothing to Do."
"A Failure in Democracy." [On marriage.]
"The Injured Party?" [On illegitimacy.]
"Lax or Brittle Marriage?"
"Literary Censorship for Boys and Girls."
"On Sending a Daughter, Willy Nilly, to College."
"On the Domestic Service Problem."
"Penalizing Marriage and Child Bearing."
"A Plea against Nursery Paraphrases."
"Pertinent to the Simple Life."
"Some Anonymous Causes of Divorce."
"Some Inconsistencies of Home Education." [On sex roles.]
"The Taboo of Direct Reference."

"Unwritten Sumptuary Law."

"What Are Girls to Do?"

"Why Every Woman Should Have Something to Do."

1905 "A Plan for Girls with Nothing to Do." *Charities* 13 (4 Mar.): 545–49.

"The School Child, the School Nurse, and the Local School Board." *Charities* 14 (23 Sept.): 1097–104.

"Girls with Nothing to Do: A Rejoinder from Mrs. Parsons." Letter to the editor. *Charities* 15 (28 Oct.): 124–25.

Preface to *Family Monographs: The History of Twenty-Four Families Living in the Middle West Side of New York City,* by Elsa G. Herzfeld. New York: James Kempster Printing Company.

"The Social Settlement and the Future." Letter to the editor. *Charities and the Commons* 15 (25 Nov.): 255–56.

"The Aim of Productive Efficiency in Education." *Educational Review* 30 (Dec.): 500–506.

1905–7 "Primitive & Tenement House Man" ["A Derelict of Progress" or "Primitive Custom in Modern Culture: The Ethnolgic Parallel"]. Manuscript. American Philosophical Society Library.

1905–10 "My Washington Journal." Manuscript. Rye Historical Society.

1906 "Division of Labor in the Tenement-House." *Charities and the Commons* 15 (6 Jan.): 443–44.

"Penalizing Marriage and Child-Bearing." *Independent* 60 (18 Jan.): 146–47.

"American Snobbishness in the Philippines." *Independent* 60 (8 Feb.): 332–33.

[On Americans in the Philippines.] Letter to the editor, *New York Evening Post,* [May?]. Manuscript. American Philosophical Society Library. "The Religious Dedication of Women." *American Journal of Sociology* 11 (July): 610–22.

"Sex Morality and the Taboo of Direct Reference." *Independent* 61 (16 Aug.): 391–92.

"Remarks on Education in the Philippines." *Charities and the Commons* 16 (1 Sept.): 564–65.

"Congressional Junket in Japan: The Taft Party of 1905 Meets the Mikado." Published posthumously in *New-York Historical Society Quarterly* 41 (Oct. 1957): 385–406.

The Family: An Ethnographical and Historical Outline with Descriptive Notes, Planned as a Text-book for the Use of College Lecturers and of Directors of Home-reading Clubs. New York: G. P. Putnam's Sons.

"Social Solidarity: The Plea of a 'Parlor Socialist' " ["Municipal Ownership as Social Education" or "A Plea for Municipal Ownership"]. Manuscript. American Philosophical Society Library.

1907 Review of *Kinship Organizations and Group Marriage in Australia,* by Northcote W. Thomas. *Charities and the Commons* 18 (20 Aug.): 580.

"A Suggestion for Ethnography in the Philippines." Manuscript. American Philosophical Society Library.

1909 "Higher Education of Women and the Family." *American Journal of Sociology* 14 (May): 758–63.

1912 "The Supernatural Policing of Women." *Independent* 72 (8 Feb.): 307–10.

"Hayti Misunderstood." *Independent* 72 (12 Sept.): 322–24.

Review of *A Psychological Study of Religion: Its Origin, Function, and Future*, by James H. Leuba. *Current Anthropological Literature* 1 (12 Dec.): 282–85.

1913 [John Main, pseud.] *Religious Chastity: An Ethnological Study*. New York. Reprint, New York: AMS Press, 1975.

The Old-Fashioned Woman: Primitive Fancies about the Sex. New York: G. P. Putnam's Sons. Reprint, Ayer, 1974.

"The Imaginary Mistress." Manuscript. American Philosophical Society Library.

1913–14 "The Journal of a Feminist, 1913–1914." "With an introduction and notes by Elsie Clews Parsons." Manuscript. American Philosophical Society Library.

1913–15 "In New York State." Manuscript. American Philosophical Society Library.

1914 "Avoidance." *American Journal of Sociology* 19 (Jan.): 480–84.

"Ceremonial Reluctance." Manuscript. [Feb.] American Philosophical Society Library.

"Teknonymy." *American Journal of Sociology* 19 (Mar.): 649–50.

Review of *Ehe und Ehereform*, by Von Romundt Chasté. *American Journal of Sociology* 19 (Mar.): 697–98.

"Ethnology in Education." *New Review* 2 (Apr.): 228–29.

"Puppet of the Ceremonial." Manuscript. [Apr.] American Philosophical Society Library.

Review of *The Primitive Family as an Educational Agency*, by J. A. Todd. *Science* 39 (1 May): 654–56.

"Feminism and Conventionality." In *Women in Public Life*, ed. James P. Lichtenberger. Special issue of *Annals of the American Academy of Political and Social Science* 56 (Nov.): 47–53.

"Feminism and Men." Manuscript. [Nov.] American Philosophical Society Library.

[On neutrality.] Letter to the editor, *New York Times*, 9 Nov. Manuscript. American Philosophical Society Library.

Fear and Conventionality. New York: G. P. Putnam's Sons.

1914–15 "The Journal of a Pacifist." Manuscript. American Philosophical Society Library.

1915 "To Abolish War." Letter to the editor. *New York Times*, 10 Jan., sec. 3, 2.

"Links between Religion and Morality in Early Culture." *American Anthropologist* 17 (Jan.–Mar.): 41–57.

"The Reluctant Bridegroom." *Anthropos* 10 (Jan.–Apr.): 65–67.

" 'On the Loose.' " *New Republic*, 27 Feb., 100–101.

"Nursery Bugaboos." *Pedagogical Seminary* 22 (Mar.): 147–51.

"The Aversion to Anomalies." *Journal of Philosophy, Psychology, and Scientific Methods* 12 (15 Apr.): 212–19.

"The Will to Power among Sociologists." Manuscript. [Apr.] American Philosophical Society Library.

"Meetings." *Masses* 6 (Apr.): 11.

"Unconscious Feminism." Letter to the editor. *New York Times*, 28 Apr., 12.
"Sex and the Elders." *New Review* 3 (1 May): 8–10.
"The Dragon's Teeth." *Harper's Weekly*, 8 May, 449.
"Home Study in Ethnology." *American Anthropologist* 17 (Apr.–June): 409–11.
"A Warning to the Middle-Aged." *New Review* 3 (1 June): 62–63.
"The Toy Soldier." *Educational Review* 50 (June): 91–94.
"Nursery and Savagery." *Pedagogical Seminary* 22 (2 June): 296–99.
"In the Nursery—Militarism or Pacifism?" Manuscript. [June.] American Philosophical Society Library.
"Japan and Preparedness." Manuscript. [June.] American Philosophical Society Library.
"Facing Race Suicide." *Masses* 6 (June): 15.
"Privacy in Love Affairs." *Masses* 6 (July): 12.
"Sincerity in Love Affairs." Manuscript. [July.] American Philosophical Society Library.
"Marriage and Parenthood—A Distinction." *International Journal of Ethics* 25 (July): 514–17.
"Women and War." Letter to the editor. *New York Times*, 23 July, 8.
"Ceremonial Consummation." *Psychoanalytic Review* 2 (July): 358–59.
"Interpreting Ceremonialism." *American Anthropologist* 17 (July–Sept.): 600–603.
"Forbidden Stories." *New Review* 3 (1 Aug.): 165.
"War and the Elders." *New Review* 3 (15 Aug.): 191–92.
"The Strawberry Patch." *Masses* 6 (Sept.): 8.
"The Woman Who Did." *Harper's Weekly*, 11 Sept., 255.
"The Ceremonial of Growing Up." *School and Society* 2 (18 Sept.): 408–11.
"Gregariousness and the Impulse to Classify." *Journal of Philosophy, Psychology, and Scientific Methods* 12 (30 Sept.): 551–53.
"Friendship, a Social Category." *American Journal of Sociology* 21 (Sept.): 230–33.
"Marriage and the Will to Power." *Psychoanalytic Review* 2 (Oct.): 477–78.
"A Novel's Ethnology: Review of *The Pastor's Wife*, by the author of 'Elizabeth and her German Garden.'" *New Republic*, 23 Oct., 314–15.
"Circumventing Darwinism." *Journal of Philosophy, Psychology, and Scientific Methods* 12 (28 Oct.): 610–12.
"Anti-Suffragists and War." *Scientific Monthly* 1 (Oct.): 44–46.
"Two Methods in Ethnological Hypothesis." Manuscript. [Oct.] American Philosophical Society Library.
"The Sin of Being Found Out." *New Review* 3 (15 Dec.): 361–62.
"A Communication in Regard to 'The Discovery of Time.'" *Journal of Philosophy, Psychology, and Scientific Methods* 12 (23 Dec.): 713–15.
Social Freedom: A Study of the Conflicts between Social Classifications and Personality. New York: G. P. Putnam's Sons.
1915–18 "War Essays." Manuscript. American Philosophical Society Library.
"Blaming Somebody, Poorer in Faith."

"Faith in War."
"In Love and War."
"International Representation."
"Patriotism."
"Rationalization in War Time."
"Vicariousness in Wartime."
"War Wilfulness."
1916 "Seniority in the Nursery." *School and Society* 3 (1 Jan.): 14–17.
"The Near Conjugal." *New Review* 4 (15 Jan.): 39–40.
"Making Ethnology Popular." *New York Tribune*, 30 Jan., sec. 5, 1.
"When Mating and Parenthood Are Theoretically Distinguished." *International Journal of Ethics* 26 (Jan.): 207–16.
"Holding Back in Crisis Ceremonialism." *American Anthropologist* 18 (Jan.–Mar.): 41–52. Reprinted in *The Golden Age of American Anthropology: The Growth of the Science of Man on the North American Continent as Told by Those Who Laid the Foundations*, ed. Margaret Mead and Ruth L. Bunzel (New York: George Braziller, 1960), 547–52.
"The Lesser Evil." *Harper's Weekly*, 26 Feb., 215.
"Ironies of Death." Review of *The Brocklebank Riddle*, by Hubert Wales. *New Republic*, 11 Mar., 159–61.
"Wives and Birth Control." Letter to the editor. *New Republic*, 18 Mar., 187–88.
"Feminism in Germany and Scandanavia." Review of *Feminism in Germany and Scandanavia*, by Katherine Anthony. *New Review* 4 (Mar.): 82–85.
"Ideal-Less Pacifism." *New Review* 4 (Apr.): 115–16.
"Rough House." *Forum* 55 (Apr.): 454–56.
"A Few Zuñi Death Beliefs and Practices." *American Anthropologist* 18 (Apr.–June): 245–56.
"Avoidance in Melanesia." *Journal of American Folklore* 29 (Apr.–June): 282–92.
"Americans They Have Met." Letter to the editor. *New York Times*, 30 May, 8.
"Selfishness." Manuscript. [May.] American Philosophical Society Library.
"Must We Have Her?" *New Republic*, 10 June, 145–46.
"A Progressive God." *New Review* 4 (June): 181–82.
"Primitive Improvidence." *Journal of Philosophy, Psychology, and Scientific Methods* 13 (6 July): 371–74.
"Separate Invitation—Not Divorce." Letter to the editor. *New Republic*, 22 July, 307.
"Discomfiture and Evil Spirits." *Psychoanalytic Review* 3 (July): 288–91.
"Feminism and Sex Ethics." *International Journal of Ethics* 26 (July): 462–65.
"The Zuñi Mo'lawia." *Journal of American Folklore* 29 (July–Sept.): 392–99.
"The Zuñi A'Doshlĕ and Suukĕ." *American Anthropologist* 18 (July–Sept.): 338–47. Reprinted in *Selected Papers from the* American An-

thropologist, *1888–1920*, ed. Frederica de Laguna (Washington, D.C.: AAA, 1960), 638–47.
"Heroes of the Sea." Letter to the editor. *New Republic*, 9 Sept., 144.
"Zuñi Inoculative Magic." *Science* 44 (29 Sept.): 469–70.
"Mysticism in War." *Scientific Monthly* 3 (Sept.): 285–88.
"Marriage: A New Life." *Masses* 8 (Sept.): 27–28.
"The Zuñi Ła'mana." *American Anthropologist* 18 (Oct.–Dec.): 521–28. Reprinted in *Pueblo Mothers and Children: Essays by Elsie Clews Parsons, 1915–1924*, ed. Barbara A. Babcock (Santa Fe: Ancient City Press, 1991), 39–47.
"A Zuñi Detective." *Man* 16 (Nov.): 168–70.
"Engagements." *Masses* 9 (Nov.): 14.
"School." Review of *A History of the Family as a Social and Educational Institution*, by Willystine Goodsell. *School and Society* 4 (16 Dec.): 934–36.
"American 'Society.' " Pt. 1. *New Republic*, 16 Dec., 184–86.
"American 'Society.' " Pt. 2. *New Republic*, 23 Dec., 214–16.
"The Favorite Number of the Zuñi." *Scientific Monthly* 3 (Dec.): 596–600.
"Crime and Perversion." *Medical Review of Reviews* 22:191–92.
Social Rule: A Study of the Will to Power (New York: G. P. Putnam's Sons).
1917 "Injustice to Haitians." Letter to the editor. *New York Times*, 7 Jan., 2.
"Suffrage and Feminism." Speech given to the North Side Equal Suffrage Association, Chicago, January 1917. American Philosophical Society Library.
"Ceremonial Friendship at Zuñi." *American Anthropologist* 19 (Jan.–Mar.): 1–8.
[On Columbia trustees.] Letter to the editor, *New York Times*, 9 Mar. Manuscript. American Philosophical Society Library.
"Haiti." *Crisis* 13 (Mar.): 216–17.
"Reasoning from Analogy at Zuñi." *Scientific Monthly* 4 (Apr.): 365–68.
"Tales from Guilford County, North Carolina." *Journal of American Folklore* 30 (Apr.–June): 168–200.
"Notes on Folk-Lore from Guilford County, North Carolina." *Journal of American Folklore* 30 (Apr.–June): 201–8.
"Tales from Maryland and Pennsylvania." *Journal of American Folklore* 30 (Apr.–June): 209–17.
"Folk-Tales Collected at Miami, Fla." *Journal of American Folklore* 30 (Apr.–June): 222–27.
Ed. "Four Folk-Tales from Fortune Island, Bahamas," by W. T. Cleare. *Journal of American Folklore* 30 (Apr.–June): 228–29.
"Ten Folk-Tales from the Cape Verde Islands." *Journal of American Folklore* 30 (Apr.–June): 230–38.
"Riddles from Andros Island, Bahamas." *Journal of American Folklore* 30 (Apr.–June): 275–77.
"In Terms of Crisis." Manuscript. [May.] American Philosophical Society Library.

"Why Holidays." Review of *Rest Days: A Study in Early Law and Morality*, by Hutton Webster. *New Republic*, 2 June, 140–41.

"Zuñi Conception and Pregnancy Beliefs." In *Proceedings of the Nineteenth International Congress of Americanists, 1915*, ed. F. W. Hodge, 379–383. Washington, D.C. Reprinted in *Pueblo Mothers and Children: Essays by Elsie Clews Parsons, 1915–1924*, ed. Barbara A. Babcock (Santa Fe: Ancient City Press, 1991), 29–37.

Notes on Zuñi. Pts. 1 and 2. Memoirs of the American Anthropological Association 4, 149–226, 227–327. Lancaster, Pa. Reprint, Periodicals Service.

Review of *Rest Days: A Study in Early Law and Morality*, by Hutton Webster. *American Anthropologist* 19 (July–Sept.): 423–24.

"The Office of Governor at Zuñi." *American Anthropologist* 19 (July–Sept.): 454–56.

"The Teleological Delusion." *Journal of Philosophy, Psychology, and Scientific Methods* 14 (16 Aug.): 463–68.

"The Shame of Being a Baby." *School and Society* 6 (22 Sept.): 355–56.

"The Religion of Middle-Age." Review of *God the Invisible King*, by H. G. Wells. *Masses* 9 (Sept.): 29.

"Patterns for Peace or War." *Scientific Monthly* 5 (Sept.): 229–38.

"It Costs." *Masses* 9 (Oct.): 35.

"Feminism and the Family." *International Journal of Ethics* 28 (Oct.): 52–58.

"All-Souls Day at Zuñi, Acoma, and Laguna." *Journal of American Folklore* 30 (Oct.–Dec.): 495–96.

Review of *The Wonder*, by J. D. Beresford. *New Republic*, 10 Nov. 1917, 53–56.

"The Minority." Letter to the editor. *New York Tribune*, 4 Dec., 8.

"The Antelope Clan in Keresan Custom and Myth." *Man* 17 (Dec.): 190–93.

"Provenience of Certain Negro Folk-Tales." Pt. 1, "Playing Dead Twice in the Road." *Folk-Lore* 28 (Dec.): 408–14.

"Christian Rites in Zuñi Ceremonialism." Paper read before the American Ethnological Society. American Philosophical Society Library.

1918 "A Pilgrim Interprets the Promised Land." Review of *An American in the Making: The Life Story of an Immigrant*, by M. E. Ravage. *Dial* 64 (31 Jan.): 107–9.

Review of *Zuñi Kin and Clan*, by A. L. Kroeber. *American Anthropologist* 20 (Jan.–Mar.): 98–104.

"Ceremonial Impatience." *Journal of Philosophy, Psychology, and Scientific Methods* 15 (14 Mar.): 157–64.

"Pueblo-Indian Folk-Tales, Probably of Spanish Provenience." *Journal of American Folklore* 31 (Apr.–June): 216–55.

"Nativity Myth at Laguna and Zuñi." *Journal of American Folklore* 31 (Apr.–June): 256–63. Reprinted in *The Golden Age of American Anthropology: The Growth of the Science of Man on the North American Continent as Told by Those Who Laid the Foundations*, ed. Margaret Mead and Ruth L. Bunzel (New York: George Braziller, 1960), 552–59.

"Notes on Acoma and Laguna." *American Anthropologist* 20 (Apr.–June): 162–86.

"Ceremonial Defloration." *Psychoanalytic Review* 5 (July): 339–40.

"The American Family." Review of *A Social History of the American Family from Colonial Times to the Present,* by Arthur W. Calhoun. *Dial* 65 (5 Sept.): 160–61.

"Provenience of Certain Negro Folk-Tales." Pt. 2, "The Pass-word." *Folk-Lore* 29 (Sept.): 206–18.

"War God Shrines of Laguna and Zuñi." *American Anthropologist* 20 (Oct.–Dec.): 381–405.

"Randolph Bourne." Letter to the editor, *New York Evening Post,* 24 Dec. Manuscript. American Philosophical Society Library.

"After the War." Manuscript. [Dec.] American Philosophical Society Library.

Folk-Tales of Andros Island, Bahamas. Memoirs of the American Folklore Society 13. Lancaster, Pa. Reprint, Periodicals Service.

1919 "Mothers and Children at Laguna." *Man* 19 (Mar.): 34–38. Reprinted in *Pueblo Mothers and Children: Essays by Elsie Clews Parsons, 1915–1924,* ed. Barbara A. Babcock (Santa Fe: Ancient City Press, 1991), 69–78.

"Teshlatiwa at Zuñi." *Journal of Philosophy, Psychology, and Scientific Methods* 16 (8 May): 272–73.

"Joel Chandler Harris and Negro Folklore." Review of *Uncle Remus Returns,* by Joel Chandler Harris. *Dial* 66 (17 May): 491–93.

"Increase by Magic: A Zuñi Pattern." *American Anthropologist* 21 (July–Sept.): 279–86. Reprinted in *Pueblo Mothers and Children: Essays by Elsie Clews Parsons, 1915–1924,* ed. Barbara A. Babcock (Santa Fe: Ancient City Press, 1991), 59–68.

"Census of the *Shi'wanakwe* Society of Zuñi." *American Anthropologist* 21 (July–Sept.): 329–35.

"Folk-Lore of the Cherokee of Robeson County, North Carolina." *Journal of American Folklore* 32 (July–Sept.): 384–93.

Ed. "Folk-Tales from Students in the Georgia State College." *Journal of American Folklore* 32 (July–Sept.): 402–5.

Ed. "Folk-Tales from Liberia," by Richard C. Bundy. *Journal of American Folklore* 32 (July-Sept.): 406–27.

"Riddles and Proverbs from the Bahama Islands." *Journal of American Folklore* 32 (July–Sept.): 439–41.

"A West-Indian Tale." *Journal of American Folklore* 32 (July–Sept.): 442–43.

"The Provenience of Certain Negro Folk-Tales." Pt. 3, "Tar Baby." *Folk-Lore* 30 (Sept.): 227–34.

"Note on Navajo War Dance." *American Anthropologist* 21 (Oct.–Dec.): 465–67.

"Mothers and Children at Zuñi, New Mexico." *Man* 19 (Nov.): 168–73. Reprinted in *Pueblo Mothers and Children: Essays by Elsie Clews Parsons, 1915–1924,* ed. Barbara A. Babcock (Santa Fe: Ancient City Press, 1991), 79–87.

"Waiyautitsa of Zuñi, New Mexico." *Scientific Monthly* 9 (Nov.): 443–57. Reprinted in *American Indian Life: By Several of Its*

Students, ed. Parsons (New York: B. W. Huebsch, 1922), 157–73; and in *Pueblo Mothers and Children: Essays by Elsie Clews Parsons, 1915–1924,* ed. Barbara A. Babcock (Santa Fe: Ancient City Press, 1991), 89–106.

Ed. *Notes on Cochiti, New Mexico,* by Father Noël Dumarest. Memoirs of the American Anthropological Association 6, 134–234. Lancaster, Pa.

"Vitance." *L'Anthropologie* 29:289–95.

1920 "Notes on Isleta, Santa Ana, and Acoma." *American Anthropologist* 22 (Jan.–Mar.): 56–69.

"Accumulative Tales Told by Cape Verde Islanders in New England." *Journal of American Folklore* 33 (Jan.–Mar.): 34–42.

"Spanish Tales from Laguna and Zuñi, New Mexico." With Franz Boas. *Journal of American Folklore* 33 (Jan.–Mar.): 47–72.

"Three Games of the Cape Verde Islands." *Journal of American Folklore* 33 (Jan.–Mar.): 80–81.

"The Value of Folk-Tales." Lecture. [10 Mar.] American Philosophical Society Library.

"A Pacifist Patriot." Review of *Untimely Papers,* by Randolph Bourne. *Dial* 68 (Mar.): 367–70.

"The Study of Variants." *Journal of American Folklore* 33 (Apr.–June): 87–90.

"Americans in Haiti." Letter to the editor. *New York Times,* 18 Oct., 14.

Notes on Ceremonialism at Laguna. Anthropological Papers of the American Museum of Natural History 19, 85–131. New York.

"Primitive Society." Review of *Primitive Society,* by Robert H. Lowie. *New Republic,* 3 Nov., 245–46.

"A Hopi Ceremonial." *Century* 101 (Dec.): 177–80.

1921 "Folk-Lore from Aiken, South Carolina." *Journal of American Folklore* 34 (Jan.–Mar.): 1–39.

"Folk-Lore of the Cape Verde Islanders." *Journal of American Folklore* 34 (Jan.–Mar.): 89–109.

"Tale and Song from Virginia." *Journal of American Folklore* 34 (Jan.–Mar.): 125.

"A Narrative of the Ten'a of Anvik, Alaska." *Anthropos* 16 (Jan.–June): 51–71.

"The Family in Russian Soviet Law." *Freeman* 3 (20 Apr.): 130–32.

"Further Notes on Isleta." *American Anthropologist* 23 (Apr.–June): 149–69.

"Note on the Night Chant at Tuwelchedu Which Came to an End on December 6, 1920." *American Anthropologist* 23 (Apr.–June): 240–43.

"The Pueblo Indian Clan in Folk-Lore." *Journal of American Folklore* 34 (Apr.–June): 209–16.

"Hopi Mothers and Children." *Man* 21 (July): 98–104. Reprinted in *Pueblo Mothers and Children: Essays by Elsie Clews Parsons, 1915–1924,* ed. Barbara A. Babcock (Santa Fe: Ancient City Press, 1991), 107–19.

"Getting Married on First Mesa, Arizona." *Scientific Monthly* 13 (Sept.): 259–65. Reprinted in *Pueblo Mothers and Children: Essays by Elsie*

Clews Parsons, 1915–1924, ed. Barbara A. Babcock (Santa Fe: Ancient City Press, 1991), 121–31.

"The Provenience of Certain Negro Folk-Tales." Pt. 4, "Missing Tongues." Folk-Lore 32 (Sept.): 194–201.

"Wolf and His Nephew." The Brownies' Book 2:281–87.

"In the Southwest." Manuscript. American Philosophical Society Library.

"The Accident of the Forester."

"The Dance North of Houck's Tanks."

"From Paharito Ranch to Taos and Back."

"The Governor of Zuñi."

"The Hotavilla Revival."

"How My Head Was Washed at Sichumovi."

"In the Room Below."

"Laguna Lodging Houses."

"Pedro Baca and I go Visiting."

"The Price of Fear—at Zuñi."

"Third Degree at Lamy."

"Where the Chief Lives."

1922 "Die Flucht auf den Baum." Zeitschrift für Ethnologie 54 (Jan.): 1–29.

"Sex." In Civilization in the United States: An Inquiry by Thirty Americans, ed. Harold E. Stearns, 309–18. New York: Harcourt, Brace and Company.

"Hidden Ball on First Mesa, Arizona." Man 22 (June): 89–91.

Ed. American Indian Life: By Several of Its Students. Illustrated by C. Grant LaFarge. New York: B. W. Huebsch. Reprint, Lincoln: University of Nebraska Press, 1991. Also published as North American Indian Life: Customs and Traditions of Twenty-Three Tribes (New York: Dover, 1992).

"Folk-Lore from Elizabeth City County, Virginia." With A. M. Bacon. Journal of American Folklore 35 (July–Sept.): 250–327.

"Tar Baby." Journal of American Folklore 35 (July–Sept.): 330.

"From 'Spiritual' to Vaudeville." Journal of American Folklore 35 (July–Sept.): 331.

Review of The Black Border, by Ambrose E. Gonzales. Journal of American Folklore 35 (July–Sept.): 332–33.

Ed. "Contributions to Hopi History: 'Oraibi in 1883,' by Frank Hamilton Cushing; 'Oraibi in 1890,' by J. Walter Fewkes." American Anthropologist 24 (July–Sept.): 253–83.

"Contributions to Hopi History: 'Introduction'; 'Oraibi in 1920'; 'Shöhmo'pavi in 1920.'" American Anthropologist 24 (July–Sept.): 253, 283–98.

Winter and Summer Dance Series in Zuñi in 1918. University of California Publications in American Archeology and Ethnology 17, 171–216. Berkeley: University of California Press.

"Klu-Klux-Klanning Indians." Manuscript. [Nov.] American Philosophical Society Library.

"Pueblo Indian Parallels: An Ethnologic Study in Behaviours and Psychology." Manuscript. American Philosophical Society Library.

1923 "Fiesta of Sant' Ana, New Mexico." *Scientific Monthly* 16 (Feb.): 178–83.

"The Hopi Buffalo Dance." *Man* 23 (Feb.): 21–26.

"Folk-Lore at Home." Lecture. [Mar.] American Philosophical Society Library.

Laguna Genealogies. Anthropological Papers of the American Museum of Natural History 19, 133-292. New York.

"The Hopi *Wöwöchim* Ceremony in 1920." *American Anthropologist* 25 (Apr.–June): 156–87.

"The Origin Myth of Zuñi." *Journal of American Folklore* 36 (Apr.–June): 135–62.

Ed. "Origin Myth from Oraibi," by Frank Hamilton Cushing. *Journal of American Folklore* 36 (Apr.–June): 163–70.

"Zuñi Names and Naming Practices." *Journal of American Folklore* 36 (Apr.–June): 171–76.

Review of *Man and Culture,* by Clark Wissler. *New Republic,* 20 June, 103–4.

[On "Joint Grandparent Day."] Letter to the editor, *New York Tribune,* 10 Sept. Manuscript. American Philosophical Society Library.

"Notes on San Felipe and Santo Domingo." *American Anthropologist* 25 (Oct.–Dec.): 485–94.

Review of *Early Civilization: An Introduction to Anthropology,* by Alexander A. Goldenweiser. *American Anthropologist* 25 (Oct.–Dec.): 568–70.

"Navaho Folk Tales." *Journal of American Folklore* 36 (Oct.–Dec.): 368–75.

"The Provenience of Certain Negro Folk-Tales." Pt. 5, "The House-keepers." *Folk-Lore* 34 (Dec.): 363–70.

Folk-Lore from the Cape Verde Islands. Pts. 1 and 2. Memoirs of the American Folklore Society 15. Published in cooperation with the Hispanic Society of America. Cambridge, Mass., and New York.

Folk-Lore of the Sea Islands, South Carolina. Memoirs of the American Folklore Society 16. Cambridge, Mass., and New York. Reprint, Periodicals Service.

1924 "Half-Breed." *Scientific Monthly* 18 (Feb.): 144–48.

"Changes in Sex Relations." *Nation,* 14 May, 551–53. Reprinted in *Our Changing Morality,* ed. Freda Kirchwey (New York: Albert and Charles Boni; reprint, New York: Arno, 1972), 37–49.

The Scalp Ceremonial of Zuñi. Memoirs of the American Anthropological Association 31. Menasha, Wis. Reprint, Periodicals Service.

"Tewa Kin, Clan, and Moiety." *American Anthropologist* 26 (July–Sept.): 333–39.

"The Religion of the Pueblo Indians." *Proceedings of the Twenty-First International Congress of Americanists, 1924,* 140–61. The Hague.

"Tewa Mothers and Children." *Man* 24 (Oct.): 148–51. Reprinted in *Pueblo Mothers and Children: Essays by Elsie Clews Parsons, 1915–1924,* ed. Barbara A. Babcock (Santa Fe: Ancient City Press, 1991), 133–39.

1925 *The Pueblo of Jemez.* Papers of the Southwestern Expedition 3. New Haven: Yale University Press for Department of Archeology, Phillips

Academy, Andover. Reprint, New York: AMS Press.

A Pueblo Indian Journal, 1920–1921. Memoirs of the American Anthropological Association 32. Menasha, Wis.

"Is Monogamy Feasible?" In *Speeches: The Nation Dinner, January 23, 1925.* Pamphlet in Robert Herrick Papers. University of Chicago Special Collections.

"Micmac Folklore." *Journal of American Folklore* 38 (Jan.–Mar.): 55–133.

"Bermuda Folklore." *Journal of American Folklore* 38 (Apr.–June): 239–66.

"Barbados Folklore." *Journal of American Folklore* 38 (Apr.–June): 267–92.

Review of *Primitive Religion,* by Robert H. Lowie. *American Anthropologist* 27 (Oct.–Dec.): 562–64.

"A Romantic in Bengal and in New York." *Scientific Monthly* 21 (Dec.): 600–612.

1926 "The Ceremonial Calendar of the Tewa of Arizona." *American Anthropologist* 28 (Jan.–Mar.): 209–29.

"Cérémonial Tewa du Nouveau Méxique et en Arizona." *Journal de la Société des Américanistes de Paris* 18:9–14.

Tewa Tales. Memoirs of the American Folklore Society 19. New York. Reprint, with a foreword by Barbara A. Babcock, Tuscon: University of Arizona Press, 1994.

"Der spanische Einfluß auf die Märchen der Pueblo-Indianer." *Zeitschrift für Ethnologie* 58:16–28.

1927 "Witchcraft among the Pueblos: Indian or Spanish?" *Man* 27 (June): 106–12; (July): 125–28.

1928 "Notes on the Pima, 1926." *American Anthropologist* 30 (July–Sept.): 445–64.

"The Laguna Migration to Isleta." *American Anthropologist* 30 (Oct.–Dec.): 602–13.

"Spirituals and other Folk-Lore from the Bahamas." *Journal of American Folklore* 41 (Oct.–Dec.): 453–524.

"Spirituals from the 'American' Colony of Samana Bay, Santo Domingo." *Journal of American Folklore* 41 (Oct.–Dec.): 525–28.

"Lord Bateman." *Journal of American Folklore* 41 (Oct.–Dec.): 585–88.

"Spirit Cult in Hayti." *Journal de la Société des Américanistes de Paris* 20:157–79.

1929 *The Social Organization of the Tewa of New Mexico.* Memoirs of the American Anthropological Association 36. Menasha, Wis. Reprint, Periodicals Service.

Ed. "Hopi Tales," by Alexander M. Stephen. *Journal of American Folklore* 42 (Jan.–Mar.): 1–72.

"On the Travels of Folk Tales and One Tale from the State of Puebla." *Mexican Folkways* 5 (Jan.–Mar.): 71–77.

"Masks in the Southwest of the United States." *Mexican Folkways* 5 (July–Sept.): 152–57.

"Ritual Parallels in Pueblo and Plains Cultures, with a Special Reference to the Pawnee." *American Anthropologist* 31 (Oct.–Dec.): 642-54.

Kiowa Tales. Memoirs of the American Folklore Society 22. New York.

1930 "Zuñi Tales." *Journal of American Folklore* 43 (Jan.–Mar.): 1–58.

Ed. "Tales and Riddles from Freetown, Sierra Leone." *Journal of American Folklore* 43 (July–Sept.): 317–21.

"Proverbs from Barbados and the Bahamas." *Journal of American Folklore* 43 (July–Sept.): 324–25.

"Ring Games and Jingles in Barbados." *Journal of American Folklore* 43 (July–Sept.): 326–29.

"Zapotecan Prayers at New Year." *Mexican Folkways* 6 (Jan.–Mar.): 38–46.

"The Institution of the Mayordomía." *Mexican Folkways* 6 (Apr.–June): 72–78.

"Ritual for a Little Angel." *Mexican Folkways* 6 (July–Sept.): 141–45.

"Spanish Elements in the Kachina Cult of the Pueblos." *Proceedings of the Twenty-Third International Congress of Americanists, 1928,* 582–603. New York.

1931 "Curanderos in Oaxaca, Mexico." *Scientific Monthly* 32 (Jan.): 60–68.

"Laguna Tales." *Journal of American Folklore* 44 (Jan.–Mar.): 137–42.

Review of *Notes on Hopi Clans* and *Hopi Kinship,* by Robert H. Lowie. *American Anthropologist* 33 (Apr.–June): 232–36.

Ed. "Ballads and Chanties Sung by May Hoisington." *Journal of American Folklore* 44 (Apr.–June): 296–301.

1932 *Isleta, New Mexico.* Bureau of American Ethnology, Annual Report 47, 193–466. Washington, D.C.

"The Canes." *Mexican Folkways* 7 (Apr.–June): 81–86.

"The Kinship Nomenclature of the Pueblo Indians." *American Anthropologist* 34 (July–Sept.): 377–89.

"Zapoteca and Spanish Tales of Mitla, Oaxaca." *Journal of American Folklore* 45 (July–Sept.): 277–317.

"Folklore from Santa Ana Xalmimilulco, Puebla, Mexico." *Journal of American Folklore* 45 (July–Sept.): 318–62.

"Getting Married at Mitla, Oaxaca." *Mexican Folkways* 7 (July–Sept.): 129–37.

1933 "Spring Days in Zuñi, New Mexico." *Scientific Monthly* 36 (Jan.): 49–54.

Hopi and Zuñi Ceremonialism. Memoirs of the American Anthropological Association 39. Menasha, Wis.

Folk-Lore of the Antilles, French and English. Pt. 1. Memoirs of the American Folklore Society 26. New York. Reprint, Periodicals Service.

"Some Aztec and Pueblo Parallels." *American Anthropologist* 35 (Oct.–Dec.): 611–31.

1934 "The Sacred Clowns of the Pueblo and Mayo-Yaqui Indians." With Ralph L. Beals. *American Anthropologist* 36 (Oct.–Dec.): 491–514.

"Folklore from Georgia." *Journal of American Folklore* 47 (Oct.–Dec.): 386–89.

"War Verses." *Journal of American Folklore* 47 (Oct.–Dec.): 395.

1936 "Riddles and Metaphors among Indian Peoples." *Journal of American Folklore* 49 (Jan.–Mar.): 171–74.

Taos Pueblo. General Series in Anthropology 2. Menasha, Wis.

Mitla, Town of the Souls and Other Zapoteco-Speaking Pueblos of Oaxaca, Mexico. Chicago: University of Chicago Press.

"Early Relations between Hopi and Keres." *American Anthropologist* 38 (Oct.–Dec.): 554–60.

Ed. *Hopi Journal of Alexander M. Stephen.* 2 vols. Columbia Contributions in Anthropology 23. New York: Columbia University Press. Reprint, New York: AMS Press.

Folk-Lore of the Antilles, French and English. Pt. 2. Memoirs of the American Folklore Society 26. New York. Reprint, Periodicals Service.

"The House-Clan Complex of the Pueblos." In *Essays in Anthropology Presented to A. L. Kroeber,* 229–31. Berkeley: University of California Press.

1937 Review of *Zuñi Mythology,* by Ruth Benedict, and *Zuñi Texts,* by Ruth Bunzel. *Journal of American Folklore* 50 (Jan.–Mar.): 107–9.

"Some Mexican Idolos in Folklore." *Scientific Monthly* 44 (May): 470–73.

"Naming Practices in Arizona." *American Anthropologist* 39 (July–Sept.): 561–62.

1938 "The Family." In *America Now: An Inquiry into Civilization in the United States by Thirty-Six Americans,* ed. Harold E. Stearns, 404–10. New York: Charles Scribner's Sons.

"The Humpbacked Flute Player of the Southwest." *American Anthropologist* 40 (Apr.–June): 337–38.

1939 *Pueblo Indian Religion.* 2 vols. Chicago: University of Chicago Press. Reprint, with introductions by Pauline Turner Strong and Ramón Gutiérrez, Lincoln: University of Nebraska Press, 1996.

"Picurís, New Mexico." *American Anthropologist* 41 (Apr.–June): 206–22.

"The Franciscans Return to Zuni." *American Anthropologist* 41 (Apr.–June): 337–38.

"The Last Zuni Transvestite." *American Anthropologist* 41 (Apr.–June): 338–40.

Review of *Singing for Power: The Song Magic of the Papago Indians of Southern Arizona,* by Ruth Murray Underhill. *American Anthropologist* 41 (July–Sept.): 482–83.

1939–41 "The World Changes: An Essay in Anthropologic Philosophy." Manuscript. American Philosophical Society Library.

1940 "Relations between Ethnology and Archeology in the Southwest." *American Antiquity* 5 (Jan.): 214–20.

Review of *The History of Ethnological Theory,* by Robert H. Lowie. *Journal of American Folklore* 53 (Jan.–Mar.): 78–80.

"A Pre-Spanish Record of Hopi Ceremonies." *American Anthropologist* 42 (July–Sept.): 541–42.

"Cosmography of Indians of Imbabura Province, Ecuador." *Journal of American Folklore* 53 (Oct.–Dec.): 219–24.

"Filipino Village Reminiscence." *Scientific Monthly* 51 (Nov.): 435–49.

Taos Tales. Memoirs of the American Folklore Society 34, no. 7. New York.

1941 *Notes on the Caddo.* Memoirs of the American Anthropological Association 57. Menasha, Wis.

Review of *The Hopi Child,* by Wayne Dennis. *Journal of American Folklore* 54 (July–Dec.): 220–23.

1942 "Anthropology and Prediction." *American Anthropologist* 44 (July–Sept.): 337–44.

1943 *Folk-Lore of the Antilles, French and English.* Pt. 3. Ed. Gladys Reichard. Memoirs of the American Folklore Society 26. New York. Reprint, Periodicals Service.

1945 *Peguche, Canton of Otavalo, Province of Imbabura, Ecuador: A Study of Andean Indians.* Chicago: University of Chicago Press.

1956 "A Note on Zuni Deer-Hunting." *Southwestern Journal of Anthropology* 12 (autumn): 325–26.

1962 *Isleta Paintings.* Ed. Esther S. Goldfrank. Bureau of American Ethnology Bulletin 181. Washington, D.C. Reprint, Saint Clair Shores, Mich.: Scholarly Press; Reprint Service, 1995. Revised edition, with a new foreword by Esther S. Goldfrank, 1970.

INDEX

Page references to illustrations are indicated in boldface type. Elsie Clews Parsons is referred to throughout as ECP.

Nusbaum, Jesse, 418n. 38
Nuttall, Zelia, 336

Oakman, Renée, 367
Oaxaca (Mexico), 319, 392
Ogburn, William, 260
Old-Fashioned Woman, The (Parsons),
83, 87, 123–24, 133, 147
Olivera, Victor, 345
Osborn, Henry Fairfield, 197, 245
Ostwald, Wilhelm, 101

Pach, Walter, 222
Papini, Giovanni, 75
parenthood: modernism as revolt against
parents, 14; mothers as conservers of
tradition, 54; parent's contract, 134,
136; separating sex from, 133–35. See
also children
Parsons, Mary Dumesnil McIlvaine
(mother-in-law), 40
Parsons, Edward, 43
Parsons, Elsie Clews
—as anthropologist: on acculturation,
147, 155–56, 172–76, 196, 201, 222,
241, 273, 305, 313, 319, 324, 337–
40, 344, 350, 356–62, 381, 383; as
American Anthropological Association
president, xiii, 373, 378; as American Anthropological Association president-elect, 365, 372; and American
Anthropologist, 149; in American Ethnological Society, 194; and American
Museum of Natural History group, 97,
110, 154, 194, 198, 233, 244; "Anthropology and Prediction," 381–82;
applied anthropology, 246; attempt to
close rift in anthropology, 248; avoidance and ceremony articles, 148;
"Avoidance in Melanesia," 431n. 9;
and Benedict, 275–78, 461n. 67; Boas
defended by, 178–79; and Boas group,
107–8; with Boas in Southwest, 248–
55; and Boas's women students,
255–58, 256; Bourne on, 169; and
Bunzel, 108, 268–69, 272; Bunzel's
fieldwork method adopted by, 324; on
ceremonialism, 148, 149, 154–56, 224,
226–30, 249–51, 337–40; on classification, 128–30; collaborative work
plan, 195, 198; on cultural anthropology's educational use, 146–48, 382; on
cultural data in their sensational nudity,
126; diversifying anthropology, 274;
on educational utility of, 129, 146–48,

156; on ethnographic observation, 46–
47; on evolutionary theory, 163, 248;
as fieldworker, 131, 161, 324, 330,
333–34, 464n. 24; and Goddard,
108–10, 151–52, 421n. 21; on gossip
as psychological data, 239, 343, 345,
383; "Home Study in Ethnology,"
431n. 9; and hybrid cultures, 201; influence of, 281, 361, 372–73; at International Congress of Americanists
(1928), 310–12; and Kidder, 261–62;
on Kroeber's superorganic conception
of culture, 162–63, 369; and life histories, 241–42, 347, 376–77, 383; of literate societies, 147, 155–56; "Making
Ethnology Popular," 148; male scholars supported by, 272–73; Mencken
on, 126, 233, 449n. 31; as native informant, 124–28; new way of speaking
about Native Americans provided by,
222; observing her own social milieu,
46, 110, 122–28, 133–34, 140,
146–52, 155–58, 233, 373, 426n. 26;
paper coauthored with Kroeber, 210,
213; plan for school of ethnology, 147;
posthumous presidential message,
381–82; on psychological aspects of
acculturation, 324, 339–40, 350; psychological orientation of, 148, 155–56,
160–63, 237–42; as reviewer for Current Anthropological Literature, 110;
Sapir on, 260, 277; and sexual barriers
to fieldwork, 258–65; on Steward's
Handbook, 372; and Strong, 370–72;
as a teacher, 274; "Teleological Delusion," 181; Waters influenced by,
230–31
—children: birth and death of infants, 66,
71, 77, 158, 412n. 39; children desired
by, 53–54; Herbert Jr.'s birth, 81, 380;
John's birth, 59; on John's engagement,
303–4; Lissa's birth, 57; on Lissa's
marriage to Patterson, 243, 451n. 2;
Lissa's new relationship with, 367;
McIlvaine's birth, 87, 380; photograph
with Lissa in 1902, 58; pregnancy terminated, 71, 76; pregnancy with Herbert Jr., 79, 82, 114; pregnancy with
Lissa, 56–57; responsibility for after
Herbert's death, 300–303, 352
—documentation of life of, xiii–xiv
—early life: birth of, xii, 1, 5; in Europe
with her mother in 1894, 27; family
claim on at Bobby's death, 18; on her
father, 6; and her mother, 11–12,

sexuality (continued)
67; women's hostility toward, 64; women's sexual behavior controlled, 13, 56; and women's work, 142; in the workplace, 137. See also birth control; contraception
shalako ceremony, 155, 176, 226, 228, 229, 250, 339
Shaw, Anna, 115
Shaw, George Bernard, 68
Silva, Gregorio Teixeira, 173
Simkhovitch, Mary Kingsbury: birth of Stephen, 58; death of, 365; on the East Side, 32; at Friendly Aid House, 34, 38–39, 404n.15; at Greenwich House, 58–59, 111, 365; friendship with ECP, 43, 47, 49; marriage, 46; on Herbert Parsons's election to Congress, 61; photograph in mid-1890s, 38; pregnancy with Helena, 58–59; pregnancy with Stephen, 57; social circle of, 168; wealthy women drawn to the settlements by, 111; writes ECP on Herbert Parsons's death, 300
Simkhovitch, Vladimir, 46, 168, 439n.33
Simmel, Georg, 126
Simonson, Lee, 439n.37
sincerity, 138
Slaughter, Frances Ann (great-grandmother), 397n.12
Slaughter, Gabriel (great-great-grandfather), 397n.12
Sloan, John, 220
Slosson, Edwin, 427n.32
Small, Albion, 148
Smith, Emily James, 30, 46, 49, 233, 234
Social Freedom (Parsons), 127–28; on classification, 128; Day on, 157; Ford's review of, 133; Lippmann on, 179; and ECP's dual nature, 160; publicity surrounding, 156, 157
socialism, 111
Socialist Party, 63
Social Organization of the Tewa of New Mexico, The (Parsons), 228, 291, 306
Social Rule (Parsons), 127, 128, 129
Social Science Research Council, 313, 349, 381
sociology: and acculturation studies, 349; American Journal of Sociology, 148, 153; American Sociological Society, 77–78; at Columbia, 29, 30; having its truths become commonplaces, 69; Mencken on, 232; ECP as fieldwork di-

rector in, 45; ECP as lecturer in at Barnard, 59; ECP breaks with, 153. See also Baldwin; Giddings; Tarde; Westermarck
Sorchan, Charlotte, 122, 141, 233, 234, 366, 430n.14
Sorokin, Pitirim, 456n.32
Southwest cultures. See Pueblos
Southwest Society, 216, 244–46, 272, 273
"Spanish Elements in the Kachina Cult of the Pueblos" (Parsons), 228, 307, 310
Spier, Erna Gunther, 256–57, 272, 455n.26
Spier, Leslie: on acculturation studies, 349–50; at American Museum of Natural History, 197; and Boas, 255; dining at Lounsberry, 202; as editor of American Anthropologist, 245, 272; with Kroeber at Zuni, 155; marriage to Gunther, 257; on ECP, 11; ECP's support for, 272; to Seattle, 256, 442n.9; tribute to ECP, 383, 384
Spinden, Herbert, 155, 244, 451n.6, 453n.9
Stanton, Elizabeth Cady, 15
Starr, Frederick, 98
Stead, Christina, 14
Stearns, Harold, 165, 292, 373, 439n.37
Steffens, Lincoln, 425n.22
Stein, Gertrude, 14, 17, 118, 121, 125–26, 427n.33
Stephen, Alexander M., 353–54, 478n.17
Stetson, Charlotte Perkins, 77, 78, 114, 121, 365
Stevenson, Matilda Coxe, 417n.21
Stevenson, Robert Louis, 20–21, 25, 28, 30, 52, 82, 125
Steward, Julian, 372, 476n.1
Stocking, George, 245, 247
Stonover Farm, 57, 144, 146, 353, 367, 379
Story, Joseph, 217
Stowe, Harriet Beecher, 17
Straight, Dorothy Whitney, 152, 180, 233
Straight, Willard, 180
Strong, Duncan, 370–72, 375, 481n.16
Strunsky, Simeon, 148
suffrage movement, 25, 114–16
Sumner, William, 78
"Supernatural Policing of Women" (Parsons), 145
Swadesh, Mary Haas, 268
Swadesh, Morris, 268
Swanton, John, 245